Professional Stage

Module E

Information for Control
and
Decision Making

ACCA Textbook

0238J99

British Library Cataloguing-in-Publication Data

A catalogue record for this book is available from the British Library.

Published by AT Foulks Lynch Ltd
Number 4
The Griffin Centre
Staines Road
Feltham
Middlesex
TW14 0HS

Printed in Great Britain by Ashford Colour Press, Gosport, Hants.

ISBN 0 7483 4023 8

© AT Foulks Lynch Ltd, 1999

Acknowledgements

We are grateful to the Association of Chartered Certified Accountants, the Chartered Institute of Management Accountants and the Institute of Chartered Accountants in England and Wales for permission to reproduce past examination questions. The answers have been prepared by AT Foulks Lynch Ltd.

CONTENTS

PREFACE

This Textbook is the ACCA's official text for paper 9, Information for Control and Decision Making, and is part of the ACCA's official series produced for students taking the ACCA examinations. It has been produced with direct guidance from the examiner specifically for paper 9, and covers the syllabus and teaching guide in great detail giving appropriate weighting to the various topics.

This Textbook is, however, very different from a reference book or a more traditional style textbook. It is targeted very closely on the examinations and is written in a way that will help you assimilate the information easily and give you plenty of practice at the various techniques involved. Particular attention has been paid to producing an interactive text that will maintain your interest with a series of carefully designed features.

- **Introduction with learning objectives**. We put the chapter into context and set out clearly the learning objectives that will be achieved by the reader.

- **Definitions**. The text clearly defines key words or concepts. The purpose of including these definitions is **not** that you should learn them - rote learning is not required and is positively harmful. The definitions are included to focus your attention on the point being covered.

- **Brick-building style**. We build up techniques slowly, with simpler ideas leading to exam standard questions. This is a key feature and it is the natural way to learn.

- **Activities**. The text involves you in the learning process with a series of activities designed to arrest your attention and make you concentrate and respond.

- **Conclusions**. Where helpful, the text includes conclusions that summarise important points as you read through the chapter rather than leaving the conclusion to the chapter end. The purpose of this is to summarise concisely the key material that has just been covered so that you can constantly monitor your understanding of the material as you read it.

- **Self test questions**. At the end of each chapter there is a series of self test questions. The purpose of these is to help you revise some of the key elements of the chapter. The answer to each is a paragraph reference, encouraging you to go back and re-read and revise that point.

- **End of chapter questions**. At the end of each chapter we include examination style questions. These will give you a very good idea of the sort of thing the examiner will ask and will test your understanding of what has been covered.

Complementary Revision Series, Lynchpins and Audio Tapes

Revision Series - The ACCA Revision Series contains all the relevant current syllabus exam questions from June 1994 to December 1998 with the examiner's own official answers, all updated in January 1999.

What better way to revise for your exams than to read and study the examiner's own answers!

Lynchpins - The ACCA Lynchpins, pocket-sized revision aids which can be used throughout your course, contain revision notes of all main syllabus topics, all fully indexed, plus numerous examples and diagrams. They provide invaluable focus and assistance in keeping key topics in the front of your mind.

Audio Tapes - Our new 'Tracks' audio tapes are fully integrated with our other publications. They provide clear explanations of key aspects of the syllabus, invaluable throughout your studies and at the revision stage.

FORMAT OF THE EXAMINATION

The examination will have the following format:

	Number of marks
Section A: 2 (out of 3) questions of 35 marks each	70
Section B: 2 (out of 3) questions of 15 marks each	30
	100

Time allowed: 3 hours

A present value table and an annuity table will be provided in the exam. Formulae will be provided in the exam where relevant.

The Section A questions may be scenario-type questions which may draw upon many areas. The questions in Section B will focus on particular management accounting issues.

Students are reminded that in Paper 9 you are expected to be able to prepare a structured analysis of the relevant information in the question and where appropriate, to make relevant comments as to the uses, strengths and weaknesses of management accounting.

SYLLABUS

Professional stage - Module E Paper 9: INFORMATION FOR CONTROL AND DECISION MAKING

Chapter reference

(1)   MANAGEMENT ACCOUNTING FRAMEWORK

Management accounting operates in a changing environment in which management accounting techniques must be continuously appraised and reviewed. The management accounting framework must be reviewed in relation to the following areas.

(a)   The evaluation of, and promotion of change in, management accounting techniques

(i)	budgetary planning and control	17-19
(ii)	standard costing and variance analysis	20-22
(iii)	decision making including quantitative aids.	7 -10

(b)   Trends and developments in management accounting methods and techniques, business organisation and structure such as

(i)	transfer pricing and divisionalised organisations	25, 26
(ii)	performance measurement and divisionalised organisations.	23, 24, 27

(c)   Evaluating the impact of changes in business structure, functions and performance measures on the applicability and appropriateness of management accounting techniques and methods eg

(i)	relevance of standard costing and variance analysis	5, 6, 22
(ii)	use of traditional absorption costing methods.	5, 6

(d)   Identifying and evaluating existing and new methods and techniques and measures for management planning and control provision eg

(i)	JIT (Just-in-time) procedures	5
(ii)	computer integrated manufacturing	5
(iii)	world class manufacturing	5
(iv)	total quality management	6
(v)	activity based budgeting.	5

(2)   DESIGN OF MANAGEMENT ACCOUNTING SYSTEMS

(a)   Developing/implementing an appropriate system including

(i)	identification of cost units, establishing cost/profit/responsibility centres	1 - 3
(ii)	determining methods for recording relevant information	1 - 3
(iii)	sources of information and recording/processing	1 - 3
(iv)	computer based information storage and processing	1 - 3
(v)	analysis of output information and its dissemination to relevant individuals/departments.	1 - 3

(b) Consideration and application of information requirements in relation to

   (i) the costing/pricing of products and services — 15, 16
   (ii) preparing plans — 17 - 19
   (iii) monitoring and controlling performance — 17 - 19
   (iv) decision making. — 7 - 10

(c) Negotiating/agreeing information requirements taking into account — 4

   (i) influence of size and type of entity
   (ii) nature of activities and output of each entity
   (iii) long or short term nature of decisions
   (iv) management structure and style
   (v) conditions of uncertainty and risk
   (vi) qualitative/quantitative nature
   (vii) frequency, timing, format, degree of accuracy.

(3) INFORMATION FOR PLANNING AND CONTROL

(a) Budgeting and budgetary control — 17 - 19

   (i) budgeting as a multi-purpose activity

   (ii) budgeting and behavioural influences

   (iii) quantitative aids in budgeting; learning curve theory and application; limiting factors and linear programming

   (iv) activity based budgeting

   (v) control theory and budgeting; feedback and feedforward control

   (vi) budgeting and new developments/good practice eg JIT procedures, added value activities, total quality management

   (vii) uncertainty and budgeting

   (viii) identification of relevance, strengths and weaknesses of budgeting and budgetary control.

(b) Standard costing — 20 - 22

   (i) use of planning and operational variances

   (ii) trend, materiality and controllability of variances

   (iii) uncertainty and variance analysis

   (iv) identification of relevance, strengths and weaknesses of standard costing and variance analysis. — 20 - 22

(c)   Performance measurement   23 - 27

(i)   measurement of activity, productivity, profitability, quality, service

(ii)   relationship of measure to type of entity eg manufacturing or service, profit or non-profit making, centralised or decentralised

(iii) range of measures: monetary and non-monetary: use of percentages, ratios, indices

(iv)   use of indices to allow for price and performance changes through time

(v)   identification of areas of concern from the information produced

(vi)   relationship between business performance and managerial performance

(vii) assessing management performance by reference to comparable internal and external information

(viii) performance measurement and developments in management accounting eg activity based budgeting, total quality management.

(4)   INFORMATION FOR DECISION MAKING

(a)   Pricing of goods and services   15, 16

(i)   target and minimum pricing
(ii)   price/demand relationships
(iii) pricing of special orders and short life products
(iv)   transfer pricing between divisions in a group.

(b)   Identification and application of   7 - 10

(i)   relevant costs (such as fixed/variable, direct/indirect, avoidable/ unavoidable, opportunity/sunk)

(ii)   appropriate techniques (CVP analysis, use of limiting factors, recognition of risk and uncertainty).

(c)   Selection of relevant information for decision making   7 - 12

(i)   application and interpretation of quantitative techniques in decision making

- decision criteria
- expected value and expected profit, maximin
- decision trees, rollback analysis
- expected value of perfect and imperfect information

- linear programming
  - graphical and computer solution analysis
  - assumptions and limitations
  - shadow prices
  - opportunity costs
  - sensitivity analysis

(ii)   use of indexing of costs and revenues

(iii)   use of discounted cash flow techniques in longer term decision making situations.

(d)   Use in a range of decision making situations: adoption of new products, product mix choice, discontinuance of products, make or buy, sell or further process, shutdown or temporary closure.   7 - 12

THE OFFICIAL ACCA TEACHING GUIDE

Paper 9 - Information for Control and Decision Making

		Syllabus Reference	*Chapter Reference*

Session 1   *Accounting Information Systems 1*

♦	define information with particular reference to accounting systems	2a,c	1
♦	explain ways in which accounting systems collect, process and disseminate information		
♦	identify ways in which accounting information is used for internal and external reporting to different groups of interested parties		
♦	contrast the roles of financial and non-financial information in management		
♦	describe the information available from the financial accounting records		
♦	name sources of monetary and non-monetary information available within and external to the organisation for use in the management accounting system		
♦	describe the systems involved in collection and recording monetary and non-monetary information		
♦	identify types of information which are relevant for different purposes		
♦	identify how the collection and analysis of information is influenced by the management accounting principles and techniques in use		
♦	describe how information requirements are influenced by trend, materiality and controllability considerations		

Session 2   *Accounting Information Systems 2*

♦	explain the use of information for planning, control and decision making	2a,c	2
♦	describe the impact of responsibility accounting on information requirements		
♦	describe and illustrate the use of cost, revenue, profit and investment centres		
♦	identify and discuss controllable and non-controllable costs as part of cost analysis		
♦	explain the nature and use of quantitative and qualitative information		
♦	relate the required accuracy of information as related to its intended use		
♦	explain and illustrate ways in which the measurement and processing of information may contribute to the degree of accuracy achieved		
♦	explain how the impact of volume change and time may affect the accuracy of information		
♦	explain and illustrate ways in which accuracy may be more controllable in some situations than in others		
♦	outline ways in which uncertainty as to the accuracy of information may be allowed for in the operation of a management accounting system		

Session 3   *Information Technology and The Management Information System*

♦	identify the stages in the information processing cycle in the context of accounting information	2a	3
♦	evaluate the transaction recording procedures in a computer based accounting system		
♦	describe the use of software packages in the analysis of management accounting information		

- identify the advantages and disadvantages of the use of spreadsheets databases in the provision and analysis of management accounting information
- list the procedures for the preparation and layout of a spreadsheet model
- evaluate the use of spreadsheet models in 'what-if' analysis of decision making information
- explain the use of spreadsheet data-tables in the provision of decision making information
- explain the use of spreadsheet modelling in the implementation of simulation techniques using random number generation

Session 4   *Impact of the Environment on the Accounting Information Systems*

- identify the accounting information requirements for strategic planning, management control and operational control for decisions   2c, 3a   4
- distinguish between hierarchical and democratic management styles
- describe, with reference to management accounting, ways in which the information requirements of a management structure are affected by the features of that structure
- identify how hierarchical and democratic management structures affect information requirements
- evaluate the objectives of management accounting and management accounting information
- list the attributes and principles of management accounting information
- itemise and comment on factors which must be considered when setting up a management accounting system
- explain the integration of management accounting information within an overall management information system
- define and discuss the merits of open and closed systems
- define and discuss the use of programmed and non-programmed information, feedback and feedforward control
- suggest ways in which contingent factors (internal and external) influence management accounting information and its use
- illustrate the impact of human behaviour on the operation of a management accounting system in an organisation

Session 5   *Modern Developments in Industry & Commerce and The Accounting Response 1*

- list and comment on the goals of world class manufacturing   1d, 2b, 3a   5
- name the main features of world class manufacturing and explain the principal benefits to be derived from them
- distinguish between value added and non-value added activities and carry out analysis which will identify and quantify each
- explain the principles of just-in-time procedures and discuss their implications for cost systems and cost control, including the use of backflush accounting
- identify benefits of production procedures (such as dedicated cell layout) for quality improvement, cost reduction and cost systems
- illustrate the use of activity based costing and discuss its impact on product costing and cost control

Session 17   *Accounting Control Systems 1*

♦ describe the internal and external sources of planning information for an organisation	3a	17
♦ list the information used in the preparation of the master budget and its functional components		
♦ contrast the information used in the operation of zero based budgeting and incremental budgeting		
♦ list the factors which distinguish long term from short term planning information requirements		
♦ classify costs relevant to long term planning information		
♦ discuss the significance of inflation and the time value of money in long term planning		
♦ evaluate the significance of uncertainty in long term planning		
♦ explain and illustrate the use of budgeting as a planning aid in the co-ordination of business activity		
♦ explain and illustrate the relevance of budgeting in the co-ordination of business activities		
♦ explain and quantify the application of positive and negative feedback in the operation of budgetary control		
♦ explain and quantify the application of feedforward control in the operation of budgeting		
♦ discuss the inter-relationship of planning, co-ordination and control in budgeting		

Session 18   *Accounting Control Systems 2*

♦ identify quantitative aids which may be used in budgetary planning and control	2a, 3a	18
♦ discuss and evaluate methods for the analysis of costs into fixed and variable components		
♦ give examples to demonstrate the use of forecasting techniques in the budgetary planning process		
♦ explain the use of forecasting techniques in the budgetary planning process		
♦ describe the use of learning curve theory in budgetary planning and control		
♦ implement learning curve theory		
♦ identify factors which may cause uncertainty in the setting of budgets and in the budgetary control process		
♦ identify the effect of flexible budgeting in reducing uncertainty in budgeting		
♦ illustrate the use of probabilities in budgetary planning and comment on the relevance of the information thus obtained		
♦ explain the use of computer based models in accommodating uncertainty in budgeting and in promoting 'what-if' analysis		

Session 19   *Accounting Control Systems 3*

♦ identify the factors which affect human behaviour in budgetary planning and control	1a, c, 3a	19
♦ contrast ways in which alternative management styles may affect the operation of budgetary planning and control systems		
♦ explain budgeting as a bargaining process between people		
♦ explain the conflict between personal and corporate aspiration and its impact on budgeting		

- explain the use of statistical control charts in monitoring variance trend and controllability
- describe and illustrate the use of the statistical decision theory approach to variance investigation decisions
- critically appraise the use of standard costing and variance analysis in management accounting
- compare and evaluate alternative approaches to variance analysis
- discuss the impact of staff and management attitudes on the operation of analysis
- discuss the applicability of standard costing and variance analysis in changing environmental and cultural situations eg, variances and quality costs.

Session 23   *Performance Measurement: The Principles*

- describe the essential features of responsibility accounting   1b, c, 3c   23
- identify the relevant factors in the design of a responsibility accounting system
- outline the essential features of an effective internal control system
- distinguish between quantitative and qualitative performance measures
- identify, explain and give examples of performance measures including monetary and non-monetary, percentages, ratios and indices
- analyse the application of financial performance measures including cost, profit, return on capital employed
- identify the areas in which performance measurement is required in a typical business
- assess and illustrate the measurement of profitability, activity and productivity
- discuss the measurement of quality and service
- discuss the conflict between profit and other objectives including reference to critical success factors
- describe management performance measures
- analyse the strengths and weaknesses of a range of management performance measures
- discuss the potential conflict in the use of a measure for both business and management performance

Session 24   *Performance Measurement: Applications 1*

- describe the qualitative and quantitative performance measures relevant   1b, c, 3c   24
for sales, material, labour and overhead in manufacturing industries
- analyse performance measures in job, batch, contract manufacturing environments
- analyse performance measures in process manufacturing environments
- describe quantitative and qualitative performance measures relevant in the service sector
- compute and discuss the implications of performance measures in the provision of a range of services such as accountancy and law, retail and distribution, transport
- discuss the behavioural implications of the performance measures used

Session 28   *Divisional Performance Evaluation*

♦ describe quantitative and qualitative performance measures relevant in a divisionalised organisation structure	1b, 3c	27

♦ describe quantitative and qualitative performance measures relevant in a divisionalised organisation structure

♦ compute and evaluate performance measures used in a divisionalised organisation structure

♦ discuss the conflict between performance measures and decision making in a divisionalised organisation structure

♦ discuss the behavioural implications of the performance measures used

♦ discuss the impact of the divisional autonomy versus corporate goal congruence debate on divisional performance and transfer pricing

♦ recommend suitable measures and discuss the relevance of a range of monetary and non-monetary measures for divisional performance measurement

♦ interpret and discuss the behavioural implications of performance measures and transfer pricing methods in divisional structures

♦ recommend for a given situation the appropriate transfer pricing method and discuss its implications for performance measurement and corporate profit maximisation

Present value table

Present value of £1 ie, $\dfrac{1}{(1+r)^n}$ or $(1+r)^{-n}$

where r = discount rate
       n = number of periods until payment

Discount rates (r)

Periods

(n)	1%	2%	3%	4%	5%	6%	7%	8%	9%	10%	
1	0.990	0.980	0.971	0.962	0.952	0.943	0.935	0.926	0.917	0.909	1
2	0.980	0.961	0.943	0.925	0.907	0.890	0.873	0.857	0.842	0.826	2
3	0.971	0.942	0.915	0.889	0.864	0.840	0.816	0.794	0.772	0.751	3
4	0.961	0.924	0.888	0.855	0.823	0.792	0.763	0.735	0.708	0.683	4
5	0.951	0.906	0.863	0.822	0.784	0.747	0.713	0.681	0.650	0.621	5
6	0.942	0.888	0.837	0.790	0.746	0.705	0.666	0.630	0.596	0.564	6
7	0.933	0.871	0.813	0.760	0.711	0.665	0.623	0.583	0.547	0.513	7
8	0.923	0.853	0.789	0.731	0.677	0.627	0.582	0.540	0.502	0.467	8
9	0.914	0.837	0.766	0.703	0.645	0.592	0.544	0.500	0.460	0.424	9
10	0.905	0.820	0.744	0.676	0.614	0.558	0.508	0.463	0.422	0.386	10
11	0.896	0.804	0.722	0.650	0.585	0.527	0.475	0.429	0.388	0.350	11
12	0.887	0.788	0.701	0.625	0.557	0.497	0.444	0.397	0.356	0.319	12
13	0.879	0.773	0.681	0.601	0.530	0.469	0.415	0.368	0.326	0.290	13
14	0.870	0.758	0.661	0.577	0.505	0.442	0.388	0.340	0.299	0.263	14
15	0.861	0.743	0.642	0.555	0.481	0.417	0.362	0.315	0.275	0.239	15

	11%	12%	13%	14%	15%	16%	17%	18%	19%	20%	
1	0.901	0.893	0.885	0.877	0.870	0.862	0.855	0.847	0.840	0.833	1
2	0.812	0.797	0.783	0.769	0.756	0.743	0.731	0.718	0.706	0.694	2
3	0.731	0.712	0.693	0.675	0.658	0.641	0.624	0.609	0.593	0.579	3
4	0.659	0.636	0.613	0.592	0.572	0.552	0.534	0.516	0.499	0.482	4
5	0.593	0.567	0.543	0.519	0.497	0.476	0.456	0.437	0.419	0.402	5
6	0.535	0.507	0.480	0.456	0.432	0.410	0.390	0.370	0.352	0.335	6
7	0.482	0.452	0.425	0.400	0.376	0.354	0.333	0.314	0.296	0.279	7
8	0.434	0.404	0.376	0.351	0.327	0.305	0.285	0.266	0.249	0.233	8
9	0.391	0.361	0.333	0.308	0.284	0.263	0.243	0.225	0.209	0.194	9
10	0.352	0.322	0.295	0.270	0.247	0.227	0.208	0.191	0.176	0.162	10
11	0.317	0.287	0.261	0.237	0.215	0.195	0.178	0.162	0.148	0.135	11
12	0.286	0.257	0.231	0.208	0.187	0.168	0.152	0.137	0.124	0.112	12
13	0.258	0.229	0.204	0.182	0.163	0.145	0.130	0.116	0.104	0.093	13
14	0.232	0.205	0.181	0.160	0.141	0.125	0.111	0.099	0.088	0.078	14
15	0.209	0.183	0.160	0.140	0.123	0.108	0.095	0.084	0.074	0.065	15

Annuity Table

Present value of an annuity of 1 ie, $\dfrac{1-(1+r)^{-n}}{r}$

where   r   =   discount rate

         n   =   number of periods

Discount rates (r)

Periods (n)	1%	2%	3%	4%	5%	6%	7%	8%	9%	10%	
1	0.990	0.980	0.971	0.962	0.952	0.943	0.935	0.926	0.917	0.909	1
2	1.970	1.942	1.913	1.886	1.859	1.833	1.808	1.783	1.759	1.736	2
3	2.941	2.884	2.829	2.775	2.723	2.673	2.624	2.577	2.531	2.487	3
4	3.902	3.808	3.717	3.630	3.546	3.465	3.387	3.312	3.240	3.170	4
5	4.853	4.713	4.580	4.452	4.329	4.212	4.100	3.993	3.890	3.791	5
6	5.795	5.601	5.417	5.242	5.076	4.917	4.767	4.623	4.486	4.355	6
7	6.728	6.472	6.230	6.002	5.786	5.582	5.389	5.206	5.033	4.868	7
8	7.652	7.325	7.020	6.733	6.463	6.210	5.971	5.747	5.535	5.335	8
9	8.566	8.162	7.786	7.435	7.108	6.802	6.515	6.247	5.995	5.759	9
10	9.471	8.983	8.530	8.111	7.722	7.360	7.024	6.710	6.418	6.145	10
11	10.37	9.787	9.253	8.760	8.306	7.887	7.499	7.139	6.805	6.495	11
12	11.26	10.58	9.954	9.385	8.863	8.384	7.943	7.536	7.161	6.814	12
13	12.13	11.35	10.63	9.986	9.394	8.853	8.358	7.904	7.487	7.103	13
14	13.00	12.11	11.30	10.56	9.899	9.295	8.745	8.244	7.786	7.367	14
15	13.87	12.85	11.94	11.12	10.38	9.712	9.108	8.559	8.061	7.606	15

	11%	12%	13%	14%	15%	16%	17%	18%	19%	20%	
1	0.901	0.893	0.885	0.877	0.870	0.862	0.855	0.847	0.840	0.833	1
2	1.713	1.690	1.668	1.647	1.626	1.605	1.585	1.566	1.547	1.528	2
3	2.444	2.402	2.361	2.322	2.283	2.246	2.210	2.174	2.140	2.106	3
4	3.102	3.037	2.974	2.914	2.855	2.798	2.743	2.690	2.639	2.589	4
5	3.696	3.605	3.517	3.433	3.352	3.274	3.199	3.127	3.058	2.991	5
6	4.231	4.111	3.998	3.889	3.784	3.685	3.589	3.498	3.410	3.326	6
7	4.712	4.564	4.423	4.288	4.160	4.039	3.922	3.812	3.706	3.605	7
8	5.146	4.968	4.799	4.639	4.487	4.344	4.207	4.078	3.954	3.837	8
9	5.537	5.328	5.132	4.946	4.772	4.607	4.451	4.303	4.163	4.031	9
10	5.889	5.650	5.426	5.216	5.019	4.833	4.659	4.494	4.339	4.192	10
11	6.207	5.938	5.687	5.453	5.234	5.029	4.836	4.656	4.486	4.327	11
12	6.492	6.194	5.918	5.660	5.421	5.197	4.988	4.793	4.611	4.439	12
13	6.750	6.424	6.122	5.842	5.583	5.342	5.118	4.910	4.715	4.533	13
14	6.982	6.628	6.302	6.002	5.724	5.468	5.229	5.008	4.802	4.611	14
15	7.191	6.811	6.462	6.142	5.847	5.575	5.324	5.092	4.876	4.675	15

1 ACCOUNTING INFORMATION SYSTEMS: DATA AND INFORMATION

INTRODUCTION & LEARNING OBJECTIVES

When you have studied this chapter you should be able to do the following:

- Explain the difference between data and information.
- Explain how data may be captured.
- Explain how information is communicated.
- Distinguish between internal and external reporting.

- Explain how accounting information systems provide the source data for internal and external reports.

1 DATA AND INFORMATION

1.1 Introduction

Information is different from data. Although the two terms are often used interchangeably in everyday language, it is important to make a clear distinction between them, as follows:

The word **data** means facts.

> **Definition** Data consists of numbers, letters, symbols, raw facts, events and transactions which have been recorded but not yet processed into a form which is suitable for making decisions.

> **Definition** Information is data which has been processed in such a way that it has a meaning to the person who receives it, who may then use it to improve the quality of decision-making.

Data on its own is not generally useful, whereas information is very useful. For example, in cost accounting the accounting system records a large number of facts (data) about materials, times, expenses and other transactions. These facts are then classified and summarised to produce accounts, which are organised into reports designed to help management to plan and control the organisation's activities.

1.2 Relationship between data and information

Data processing converts data into information:

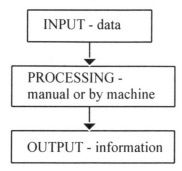

Data processing can be seen as a system, whose interfaces with the environment are data and information. Data is processed into information, perhaps by classifying it or summarising it and producing total figures. For example, a sales ledger system could be required to process data about goods dispatched to satisfy customer orders and:

- produce and send out invoices;
- record the invoices sent out in the customers' personal ledgers;
- produce a report of the total value of invoices sent out in the day/week etc;
- record the total value of invoices sent out in the debtors' control account.

1.3   Activity

A typical market research survey employs a number of researchers who interview a sample of the target market and ask them a number of questions relating to the product or service. Several hundred questionnaires may be completed and they will then be processed.

Why does the data need processing and what processing operations will be carried out?

1.4   Activity solution

Individually a completed questionnaire would not tell the organisation very much, only the views of one consumer. Once the individual questionnaires have been processed and analysed, the resulting report is information. The company will use the information to make decisions regarding its product.

The processing operations carried out to obtain the results for the reports will include:

- classifying
- calculating
- sorting
- analysing, and
- summarising.

2   DATA CAPTURE, REPORTING, AND COMMUNICATING

2.1   Reporting

The data that an organisation gathers and stores is determined by the information that management needs to control the operations of the organisation. Control will be exercised at several levels in the organisation: operational; tactical; and strategic. Each of these levels requires different information.

(a)   **Strategic information** is required by the business or entity in order to take a 'long-range' view of how that business is going to perform, over the next *n* years. The period of years depends upon the type of business and the ability of the management to scan the planning horizon. Strategic information could relate to the study of overseas markets, the development of new products or to the threats and opportunities in the business environment.

(b)   **Tactical information** is required for management planning and control. It is generally concerned with a shorter time period and is concerned with commitments to particular courses of action. For example, a sales budget for a twelve-month period dedicated to the achievement of an increased sales volume.

(c)   **Operational information** is information which is concerned with a much shorter time scale and relates to more immediate action. Collection of actual sales for comparison with budget or preparing a labour turnover report for a week are both examples of operational information.

This information is generally supplied in the form of reports. Reports may be produced in a number of forms ranging from periodic printed reports, through to a senior executive producing an individual report on an executive information system.

Typical reports produced in a medium-sized manufacturing company might include the following.

(a)   Production and material control

        (i)   forward loading plans for production cycles;
        (ii)   machine capacity forecast;
        (iii)   departmental operating statements;
        (iv)   stock and work-in-progress reports;
        (v)   wastage report;
        (vi)   labour utilisation report.

(b)   Marketing, including distribution

        (i)   market surveys;
        (ii)   order reports by product and geographical area;
        (iii)   discount trends;
        (iv)   transport and warehouse cost statements;
        (v)   salesperson performance;
        (vi)   product service and support costs.

(c)   Personnel

        (i)   numbers employed by category;
        (ii)   overtime hours;
        (iii)   sickness, absence, lateness;
        (iv)   training requirements;
        (v)   career development plans;
        (vi)   recruitment policy;
        (vii)   job descriptions.

(d)   Financial and management accounting

        (i)   annual statutory accounts;
        (ii)   budgets and forecasts;
        (iii)   sales and contribution analyses;

        (iv)   cash, management and working capital evaluation;
        (v)   capital project appraisal;
        (vi)   standard cost and variance analysis reports;
        (vii)   returns to government departments eg, VAT.

From the above list of reports, some assumptions can be drawn:

(a)   information is needed for many different purposes;

(b)   the information produced is a mixture of financial and statistical data;

(c)   information is needed by different groups of users who work at different levels within the firm;

(d)   the information is produced at different times and frequencies in the form of both *ad hoc* and regular reports;

(e)   information is required on internal and external factors;

(f)   there are likely to be common pieces of information that are required in different functions;

(g)   information is required for decision making, planning and control.

Managers demand a great deal of information to carry out their functions. This raises a question of costs, data capture being the major cost in reporting.

2.2   Methods of data capture

Design of the data collection methods is an important part of designing a computer system. The organisation needs to consider its strategic plans in order to assess the future uses of its systems. If it is thought likely that it will be networking with other systems then it will need to ensure that any new equipment purchased will be compatible with the network it wishes to join. When choosing input methods and media, most users are concerned with the following:

(a)   how to economise on the use of manpower;
(b)   how to prevent or detect errors in the source data;
(c)   how to achieve data capture at the lowest possible cost;
(d)   how to achieve input sufficiently quickly;
(e)   how data gets into the system.

Input devices can be divided into two main categories:

(a)   those using a keyboard;
(b)   those using direct input of the data.

2.3   Key aspects of communication

[Definition]   Communication in business can be defined as the transmission of information so that it is received, understood and leads to action.

This definition enables us to understand some of the key aspects of business communication:

(a)   Information, and not data, should be communicated. Information is active, relevant and prompts action; data, on the other hand, is passive, may be historical or irrelevant and does not necessarily lead to action.

Information can be classified as 'hard' or 'soft'. Hard information includes documents, reports and facts, whereas soft information covers less tangible information such as feelings, points of view, morale and body language.

(b)   Clearly, if information has not been received or is not understood by the receiver, then communication has not taken place.

(c)   The communication should lead to action. This action may take the form of a positive decision or may be a change in attitude. If the communication does not lead to any action then, probably, it ought not to have taken place.

Communication means transmitting messages to people in a manner which stimulates response. In some cases, the response will be direct to the sender, as when two people are engaged in debating the merits and demerits of some proposition. In other cases the response will be indirect as when transfer of the information gives rise to some independent action on the part of the recipient or when he or she merely stores it for future reference.

Communication in an organisation supports planning of the objectives of the firm, deciding upon courses of action and measuring performance of the actions taken. In the context of an organisation, communication may be considered as:

(i)   an individual's ability to express himself;
(ii)   the method of circulating information within the organisation.

2.4   How data and information are communicated

Modern communication technologies have changed the nature of how people communicate. Until the telephone became available people had to communicate with one another at the same place unless they used messengers or the mail. Now it is possible to communicate rapidly with anyone virtually anywhere in the world. This will become increasingly common as networks proliferate and mobile communications become more widespread, and as the cost of the communications falls due to advancing technology and competition.

Data and information may be circulated in a number of ways, for example:

(a)   verbally, as feedback of information such as lunch-time conversations;

(b)   as written reports and schedules, for example, monthly accounts;

(c)   as data on forms for processing such as goods inwards notes;

(d)   as data on graphs, charts and diagrams;

(e)   as visual presentations, for example, notices on boards and closed circuit TV.

The two main methods of communicating are still oral and written.

Oral communication can range from **speech without visual contact** – radio, tannoy, personal pager and telephone to **speech with visual contact** – television presentation, television link and face-to-face conversation.

The advantages of oral communication include the following.

(a)   Apart from broadcasting, it is a quick, direct and cheap medium with little time lapse between sending and receiving.

(b)   The meaning of an oral message can be underlined by using stress, timing and pitch.

(c)   It has the potential for informality and the sensitive handling of some communications eg, bad news, reprimand, sympathy, or encouragement.

(d)   Instant feedback is usually possible, so that misunderstandings can be cleared and messages can be received and acknowledged.

(e)   In speech with visual contact, the meaning can be reinforced by facial expression or gestures.

The disadvantages may include the following.

(a)   Noise can interfere with the message.

(b)   Little time may be allocated to the planning of the communication and this can lead to inferior decisions being made.

(c)   The communication may be distorted because the listener interprets the facial expression or body language wrongly.

(d)   Communications that require memory are better written down than spoken.

(e)   Clash of personalities may be a barrier to conversation.

Written communication can range from permanent hand-written, typed or printed documents, through semi-permanent output such as screen displays to transient outputs such as written information on television screens and electronic bill boards.

Permanent records have

(a)   **advantages** in avoiding personal contact, assisting with long and complex messages and being able to reach a large audience. They have the potential for formality and their permanence enables them to be used as records.

(b)   **disadvantages** in that their permanence can lead to rigidity. Moreover they demand considerable linguistic skills, are time-consuming to produce, slower to transmit and can be expensive.

2.5   Formal and informal communication systems

All organisations have formal, acknowledged, and often specified communication channels. There will be lists of people who are to attend briefings or meetings, and distribution lists for minutes of meetings or memos. There will be procedures for telling people of decisions or changes, and for circulating information received from outside the organisation.

In addition, an informal 'grapevine' exists in all organisations; people talk about their work, their colleagues, and about the state of their firm, whenever they meet: in corridors; over lunch; after work. They swap rumour, gossip, half-truths and wild speculation.

Communication flows exist within the company in three main directions:

(a)   downwards, or superior-subordinate communication;

(b)   upwards or subordinate-initiated communication;

(c)   horizontal or lateral.

2.6   Process of communication

Whilst communication flows through channels in organisations, the ultimate success lies in the ability of the individuals to communicate effectively. It is not simply a matter of transmitting the information, care must be taken to ensure that it is relevant and in a usable format for the recipient. Effective communication is a two-way process, or cycle, where signals or messages are sent by the communicator and received by the other party, who sends back some sort of confirmation that the message has been received and understood. This can be a very complicated process, especially in face-to-face communication where the workings of two or more minds and bodies, with nodding and gesturing, add to the difficulty. The diagram below is a model of interpersonal communication, showing the two important parties involved in this process, the sender and the receiver of the information, and each having an important part to play to ensure the effectiveness of the process.

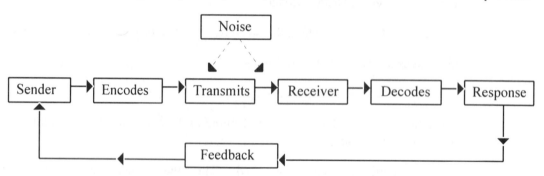

Explanation of stages:

(a)   There must be some idea or thought to be conveyed. The sender has to have a message that he or she wishes to transmit to another party. Effective communication depends on the clear identification of the subject of the message; this helps to ensure that the message does not include irrelevant information.

There are endless reasons for interpersonal communication eg, to inform, to persuade, to instruct and to gain information. It is vital that the sender formulates the communication in an effective way to meet the objective.

Attention should also be paid to the relationship between and the relative status of the sender and the receiver. This will influence both the willingness of the individuals involved to interact and the credence given to the information transmitted.

(b)   Next, the message must be encoded and put in a form suitable for transmission. At this point the sender must organise the material of the message into the most coherent and appropriate device. Matters such as: whether it should it be written or verbal; whether it needs illustrations or just text; and whether it should be translated into some foreign language; are the sort of issues to be considered at this stage.

(c)   The means of transmission has to be decided. Some messages should be conveyed orally because speed is essential and face-to-face feedback is desirable. Other messages will be best suited to the written form eg, formal announcements for the notice-board.

(d)   The message needs to be received by the other party. The receiver needs to be alert and attentive ('tuned-in'), aware that a message has been transmitted and of the need to receive it.

(e)   The transmission must be correctly decoded. Receivers have to reconstruct the signs, symbols and language in a form that makes sense to them and which is, hopefully, in line with the intentions of the sender.

Individuals do not passively receive information; rather they are involved in an active process of selection and interpretation known as 'perception'. This is a psychological process in which stimuli are organised into meaningful patterns. Each individual also uses a filtering process known as 'perceptual selectivity', which effectively acts as a barrier when either a large volume of information exceeds the capacity of the brain to deal with it or when the information is deemed irrelevant.

Having allowed the information through the perceptual filter, the receiver must then perceptually organise the information, fitting it into an existing framework known as the 'perceptual set'. This framework enables the receiver to interpret and see the information in the light of past experiences and current needs and interests.

(f)   Action should follow. Communication is carried out to bring about a response in the receiver. Sometimes this response involves direct action whilst in other cases it may be a matter of giving information which may or may not involve action at a later date. Even so, registering the new information is to be seen as a form of action resulting from effective communication.

(g)   The final element in the process is that of feedback. As illustrated in the diagram above, it is the feedback that makes communication a two-way process rather than a series of send and receive events. It is crucial, though it is sometimes overlooked, for the person sending the communication to get feedback from the receiver. Not only does this confirm that the message was received and understood, it also enables corrective action to be taken in the event of some breakdown of communication. Feedback can take different forms; it can be immediate, as in a conversation or delayed while waiting for the post. It can be simple, as in a yes/no answer or formal, as a reply to a wedding invitation, or computerised, such as the printed receipt that you can request when making a withdrawal from a bank account via the ATM. Ignoring feedback or failing to seek or offer it, is one of the major problems in communication.

From the diagram illustrating the communication process it is also important to note that communication takes place in a specific environment and that a characteristic of most environments is 'noise'. The good communicators will take into account the specific environment adjusting their communication to the demands of the situation. The problem of 'noise' ie, anything in the environment that impedes the transmission of the message, is significant. Noise can arise from many sources eg, factors as diverse as loud machinery, status differentials between sender and receiver, distractions of pressure at work or emotional upsets. The effective communicator must ensure that noise does not interfere with successful transmission of the message.

3   ACCOUNTING INFORMATION AND REPORTING

3.1   Internal reporting

Within an organisation there are many different levels of management. Some managers are responsible for the day-to-day activities whilst others are responsible for long-term planning and decision making. Each of these managers requires information to assist them in carrying out their duties.

It is the responsibilities of the manager which determine the type of information required. Those managers responsible for long-term planning and decisions will require summarised information, including performance reports which compare actual achievements with budgets and forecasts. Those managers responsible for medium term targets will usually have departmental or functional responsibilities. These managers will receive reports for their responsibility area which, although summarised, are quite detailed. These reports will often include a comparison between actual and target performance, but may also be specific information on a particular aspect of the business eg, the running cost and activity of a machine. Managers responsible for day-to-day activities are likely to receive information on a daily or even more frequent basis. Much of the information they receive may not be measured in financial terms; for example output units, number of labour hours worked, machine hours lost etc, would be important information for these managers.

3.2   External reporting

The Corporate Report identified a number of different external user groups:

(a)   suppliers;
(b)   customers;
(c)   shareholders;
(d)   loan creditors;
(e)   trade unions and employees; and
(f)   governmental agencies and departments.

Each of these external user groups will have different information needs, some will primarily be interested in profitability and stability, others will be more interested in liquidity.

Limited companies are required to prepare statutory accounts which summarise the activities of the business and are available at Companies House. However other types of organisation do not have any legal obligation to make their accounts available to the public. Nevertheless there is a flow of information to external user groups in the form of invoices, statements, delivery notes, payslips, newsletters, etc. These are in addition to any statutory accounts or formal accounts which may be prepared for government agencies, or loan creditors.

4   FINANCIAL AND NON-FINANCIAL INFORMATION

4.1   Financial information

> **Definition**   Financial information is information which measures the cost or revenue of an activity.

Financial information is that usually found to be the dominant feature of reports to middle and senior management, where it is often shown as a profit statement or balance sheet.

4.2   Non-financial information

> **Definition**   Non-financial information is information which measures activity or non-quantifiable information such as the views of people on a particular course of action.

Non-financial information is often found in reports used for lower levels of management ie, those responsible for day-to-day activities. The type of non-financial information which they would regularly receive would include:

(a)   activity achieved;
(b)   machine utilisation and efficiency;
(c)   material usage;
(d)   labour hours and efficiency.

At higher levels of management non-financial information is likely to be qualitative rather than quantitative. This has been referred to earlier as soft information. It represents opinions of individuals and user groups and should be considered when determining long-term plans.

5   USING FINANCIAL ACCOUNTING RECORDS

The financial accounting records of an organisation are a valuable source of data. Some of this data is automatically sorted to provide information by summarising income and costs in various analysis groups. Examples include sales values (possibly by product type), and costs, analysed by type eg, purchases, wages and salaries, fuel and power, stationery etc. Summaries will be found of assets and liabilities, analysed into groupings suitable for balance sheet presentation. In addition there will be other financial data which could be converted into information. For example invoices will contain details of items bought and sold. If these were analysed, information could be obtained regarding the quantities of each item bought and sold, the profitability of each item, and the percentage that an individual item contributes to the organisation in terms of sales and profits. However, the cost of converting such data into information may be unjustifiable.

In addition there is non-financial data within the accounting records, for example,

(a)   invoice numbers;

(b)   cheque numbers;

(c)   employee reference numbers and tax codes.

These may be used to produce statistical summaries, for example,

(i)   the percentage of cancelled invoices;

(ii)   the number and percentage of uncleared cheques;

(iii)   employees in each part of the business.

6   SOURCES OF INFORMATION FOR MANAGEMENT ACCOUNTING

6.1   Internal sources

There are many internal information sources for management accounting, not all of which may be considered to be part of the accounting system. The boundaries of an accounting system are not always clearly defined, particularly in management accounting. There is a grey area between the accounting system and the management information system. The following internal accounting sources may be used:

Source	*Information*
Sales ledger system	Number and value of invoices
	Volume of sales
	Value of sales, analysed by customer
	Value of sales, analysed by product
Purchase ledger system	Number and value of invoices
	Value of purchases, analysed by supplier
Payroll system	Number of employees
	Hours worked
	Output achieved
	Wages earned
	Tax deducted
Fixed asset system	Date of purchase
	Initial cost
	Location
	Depreciation method and rate
	Service history
	Production capacity

In addition the following internal, non-accounting sources may be used:

Source	*Information*
Production	Machine breakdown times
	Output achieved
	Number of rejected units
Sales and marketing	Types of customer
	Market research results
	Demand patterns, seasonal variations etc

6.2   External sources

In addition to the internal information sources referred to above, there is much information to be obtained from external sources as illustrated below:

Source	*Information*
Suppliers	Product prices
	Product specifications
Newspapers, journals	Share price
	Information on competitors
	Technological developments
Government	Industry statistics
	Taxation policy
	Inflation rates
Customers	Product requirements
	Price sensitivity
Employees	Wage demands
	Working conditions

7   COLLECTING AND RECORDING INFORMATION

7.1   Structured information systems

Some of the data referred to above is required to be collected and recorded in such a way as to provide information for inclusion in a structured report. This will apply to financial information which is used to prepare accounting reports. Such data must be collected. It may be collected by manual or electronic means, the objective being to minimise the cost of collecting the data whilst trying to ensure its accuracy.

Some organisations, particularly larger ones also have a structured system for some of their management information requirements. These systems are designed to collect non-financial information alongside the financial information to which it relates. Examples include: units of raw material purchased and used, number of labour hours worked. These are essential pieces of non-financial information if detailed variance reports are to be prepared.

However, management accounting is not a rigid framework, often ad-hoc reporting is required, and the information requirements for these reports are often unknown when the exercise begins. For these a different collection and recording method is required.

7.2   Non-structured information systems

The data and information to be collected and recorded for ad-hoc management reports is extremely varied, and a major problem lies in recognising whether a piece of data is likely to be useful or not in the future.

To collect and record such varied forms of data manually is almost impossible but fortunately electronic devices ease the task.

In the simplest scenario microfiche may be used to copy the entire contents of newspapers, magazines etc, onto viewing slides which may then be viewed using special equipment at a later date. The disadvantage is that each microfiche must be indexed if many hours are not to be used searching for a particular piece of information. Secondly this method does not allow for any classification or sorting of information.

A second approach is to use a computer database. This is more sophisticated and with the use of scanning devices allows original text and pictures to be stored alongside key descriptions of the information. These key descriptions may be used to manipulate the data stored, thereby allowing data to be sorted, classified into logical groups. The disadvantage of this technique is the time taken to store the data appropriately together with the storage space required on the computer system. The advantage however is the ease of accessibility to the data once it has been stored.

8   INFORMATION FOR DIFFERENT PURPOSES

8.1   Relevance of information

Data is collected and processed into information in many different ways for a variety of different users of information and purposes. For information to be useful it must be relevant to the needs of the recipient. For example a departmental manager would be interested in the results of his department and its effect on the organisation as a whole, but would not be interested in the results of every department.

Each transaction can provide information which is relevant to different people. Consider the purchase of a fixed asset:

-       the asset's cost and useful life is needed by the accounts clerk to calculate depreciation;

-       the operation of the machine is relevant information for the machine operator;

-       the machine shop supervisor needs details of the service contract and who to contact in the event of a breakdown;

-       the cashier needs details of the terms of payment for the machine together with details of the supplier, the machine cost, the payment authority and the manager responsible.

There are many transactions in a business, not all of them providing information to so many different people. Much of this depends on the size of an organisation and its structure.

8.2   Activity

Consider the purchase of raw materials. What information is available from such a transaction and to whom is it relevant?

8.3   Activity solution

Information	*User*
Quantity purchased	Storekeeper
Storage conditions	Storekeeper
Price per unit	Buyer
Invoice value	Accountant/Cashier
Payment terms	Cashier

9   MANAGEMENT ACCOUNTING AND INFORMATION ANALYSIS

9.1   Management accounting in organisations

Management accounting is intended for internal use within organisations and is thus designed to meet the requirements of internal management. As a consequence data is collected and analysed in such a way as to meet those requirements. Whilst every organisation is different there are two fundamental management accounting principles which may be identified:

(a)   Marginal costing; and
(b)   Absorption (or total) costing.

Most organisations will base their management accounting system on one of these fundamental principles, though some organisations will analyse data so as to operate both depending upon the use of the information.

9.2   Marginal costing

This is also known as variable costing because it emphasises the variable cost of the cost unit. If this method is to be used costs must be classified as being either variable or fixed.

> **Definition**   Variable cost - a cost which varies depending upon the level of activity.

> **Definition**   Fixed cost - a cost which remains unaffected by changes in the level of activity.

This analysis is required because only variable costs of production are attributed to the cost unit. Other costs are written off against profits in the period in which they are incurred.

9.3   Absorption (total) costing

This technique attributes all production costs to the cost unit. When using this technique costs are classified initially by function eg, production, selling, administration. The production costs are then classified into direct costs and indirect costs.

> **Definition**   Direct cost - a cost which can be economically identified with the cost unit.

> **Definition**   Indirect cost - A cost which cannot be economically identified with a single cost unit, otherwise known as an overhead cost.

The direct costs are identified with the cost units to which they relate, and the indirect costs are usually identified with the cost centre responsible for incurring them. These indirect costs are then attributed to cost units using absorption rates.

9.4   Activity based costing

This is similar in principle to absorption costing but requires that indirect costs be identified by the activity which caused them to be incurred. These activity cost pools are then attributed to cost units using cost drivers.

10   TREND, MATERIALITY AND CONTROLLABILITY

10.1   Introduction

One of the most important principles about information is that its value is derived from the benefits obtained from its use. There is however a cost associated with obtaining the information. A judgement must therefore be made, often based on trend, materiality and controllability.

10.2   Trend

Often information in respect of a single period is given greater meaning when it is combined with similar information for other periods. When this is done it is possible to identify patterns and trends.

This may be useful because a minor deviation from a plan may not of itself be significant, but if it reflects a continuing trend management may need to take action.

10.3   Materiality

Materiality is another word for significance. What is significant to one organisation may not be significant to another; it depends on the size of the organisation. To use the earlier example a deviation from a plan may or may not be significant enough to warrant an investigation into its cause. Such an investigation might be costly and if the value to be gained is small it may not be worthwhile.

10.4   Controllability

The term controllability is used in connection with costs and revenues **and** the organisation or individuals within it. Again using the earlier example if the cause of the deviation is not controllable by the organisation then no benefit can be gained by identifying the cause.

There is also relevance here to reporting and information. It was stated earlier that information should be relevant to its intended recipient. It is a widely held belief that only items controllable by the recipient should be reported to them.

11   CHAPTER SUMMARY

This chapter has distinguished between data and information and explained how data may be collected and information communicated to different user groups.

The sources of financial and non-financial information have been explained and the importance of analysis and classification of data and information discussed.

Finally the principles of such classifications have been applied to management accounting and the value of information has been considered.

12   SELF TEST QUESTIONS

12.1   Distinguish between data and information. (1.1)

12.2   Distinguish between strategic, tactical and operational information. (2.1)

12.3   What are the key aspects of communication? (2.3)

12.4   Distinguish between internal and external reporting. (3.1, 3.2)

12.5   Distinguish between financial information and non financial information. (4.1, 4.2)

12.6   Identify an internal source of information for management accounting **and** the information it provides. (6.1)

12.7   Distinguish between structured and non structured information systems. (7.1, 7.2)

12.8   Explain why information should be relevant. (8.1)

12.9   Distinguish between marginal and absorption costing. (9.2, 9.3)

12.10   Why are trend, materiality and controllability important? (10.2 - 10.4)

13   EXAMINATION TYPE QUESTION

13.1   Information for decision making

The over-riding feature of information for decision making is that it should be relevant for the decision being taken. However, decision making varies considerably, at different levels within an organisation, thus posing particular difficulties for the management accountant.

You are required

(a)   to describe the characteristics of decision making at different levels within an organisation;

(6 marks)

(b)   to explain how the management accountant must tailor the information provided for the various levels;   **(5 marks)**

(c)   to give an example of a typical management decision, state at what level this would normally be taken and what specific information should be supplied to the decision maker.   **(6 marks)**

(Total: 17 marks)

14   ANSWER TO EXAMINATION TYPE QUESTION

14.1   Information for decision making

(a)   The characteristics of decision making vary at different levels of the management hierarchy. The types of decisions taken by the junior managers are quite different to those taken by middle managers or senior managers. One way of classifying the different types of decisions is:

(i)   strategic decisions;
(ii)   tactical decisions; and
(iii)   operational decisions.

(i)   **Strategic decisions**

These are long-term decisions (usually over three years or longer), taken by senior managers at the top hierarchy of management. They include such decisions as the geographical markets in which the company should operate, new products the company should launch, the type of organisation structure the company should have and so on.

(ii)   **Tactical decisions**

These decisions relate to the shorter term (usually up to one year) and are taken by the middle managers of the organisation. Examples of tactical decisions are pricing policies the company should adopt, methods of promotion the company should use etc.

(iii)   **Operational decisions**

These are day to day decisions taken by junior level managers. These decisions include the quantity of raw materials to be purchased, the number of workers that are required, the level of discounts to be given etc.

Another classification for the different types of decisions was given by Herbert Simon. He classified decisions as programmed decisions and non-programmed decisions. Programmed decisions are those taken in repetitive situations, where clearly defined rules and procedures are in place. Non-programmed decisions are usually 'one-off decisions', where there are no set procedures to guide the decision maker.

Strategic decisions taken by the higher levels of management are regarded as non-programmed decisions, while the operational decisions taken by junior managers are regarded as programmed decisions. The tactical decisions taken by middle management could fall into either category, depending on the nature of the decisions.

(b)   The management accountant must tailor the information to the type of decision being taken. For example, in the case of strategic decisions, the information presented tends to be both quantitative and external in nature. Since these decisions relate to the long-term, the feedback tends to be quarterly or over longer periods.

The type of information provided for tactical decisions could be internal and/or external and could also be both quantitative and qualitative, depending on the nature of the decision. Since the time horizon for such decisions is up to a year, the feedback tends to be on a monthly basis.

The information provided for the day to day operational decisions is quite detailed and both quantitative and internal in nature. Since this information relates to day-to-day decisions, the feedback is very frequent, usually daily or weekly.

(c)   Take the situation of a multi-national company, considering the setting up of a new factory in a third world country. This would be an example of a strategic decision taken at the highest level of management. The type of information that should be supplied to the decision makers is listed below.

(1)   The economic conditions and political stability of the country.

(2)   The rate of exchange and details of exchange control restrictions.

(3)   The attitude of the host government to foreign multi-nationals.

(4)   The availability of labour, rates of pay, trade union restrictions.

(5)   Details of market surveys.

(6)   Full details of capital costs, detailed cashflow forecasts and budgeted profit and loss accounts.

(7)   An appraisal of the investment using DCF techniques.

(8)   A sensitivity analysis of the key variables that would affect the project.

(9)   Information on the methods of raising finance etc.

The above list is not exhaustive. As can be seen from above, a large amount of the information supplied would be external and qualitative in nature.

2 ACCOUNTING INFORMATION SYSTEMS: THE ANALYSIS OF INFORMATION

INTRODUCTION & LEARNING OBJECTIVES

In the previous chapter we considered how information may be provided from the accounting system. In this chapter we consider the use of such information.

When you have studied this chapter you should be able to do the following:

- Explain the processes of planning, control and decision making.
- Explain responsibility accounting and the importance of controllability.
- Explain the importance of accuracy of information.

1 INFORMATION FOR PLANNING, CONTROL AND DECISION MAKING

1.1 Past exam question

In June 1994, a question was set concerning required characteristics of information if the management accounting system is to realise its full potential, with particular reference to relevance and lack of bias. Examples were required to illustrate the points made. This emphasises the need for you to be able to relate general principles discussed to particular circumstances. Bear this in mind when reading this chapter.

1.2 Process overview

The processes of planning, control, and decision making may be inter-connected as is shown by the following diagram. Information is required during each part of the overall process.

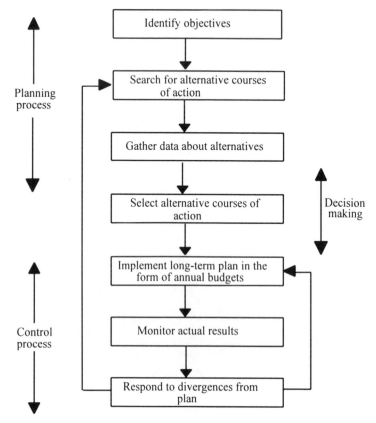

1.3   Identifying objectives

This is the first stage of the planning process. In order to identify objectives, information must be obtained concerning the present position of the organisation and of the feasibility of possible strategies.

The present position is likely to be known by referring to existing internal information, profit statements, marketing reports etc, but future strategies will require information from external sources. This may include governmental plans and the views of customers, employees etc.

1.4   Alternative action plans

This is a 3-stage process which commences when objectives have been determined. The first stage is to identify the means by which the objectives can be achieved. This is stated as 'Search for alternative courses of action'. Once these alternatives have been identified, then information can be gathered about them, and the course of action selected.

Since there are such a variety of objectives and plans to meet them, each with differing information, an example may be useful.

1.5   Example

Suppose the objective is to increase production by 50%.

The following alternative courses of action have been identified to achieve the 50% increase.

(a)   Increase the workforce by 50% and commence a night-shift. Premium wage rates will have to be paid, variable overheads will change proportionately with productive hours. The useful life of the machines will be reduced (on a time basis) from 6 years to 4 years. Machinery servicing and maintenance costs will double.

(b)   Replace the existing machines with higher capacity ones, re-train existing staff in the use of the new machine.

Information must be gathered for each of these alternatives. Some of the information will be financial, the effect on costs per unit of the proposals, the capital expenditure requirement (for (b)); whereas some will be non-financial, eg the attitude of the workforce to shift-working, or to using new machines.

All of this information must be gathered and evaluated before the choice can be made between (a) and (b). This choice is decision making, and clearly shows how decision making is implicit within the planning process.

1.6   Implement long-term plan

A long-term plan usually communicates an organisation's objectives and how they are to be achieved over a 5 – 10 year period. This plan is then broken down into annual targets which are known as budgets. These budgets communicate detailed plans to managers within the organisation.

Plans and budgets are therefore information which is communicated within an organisation.

1.7   Monitoring actual results

Before actual results can be monitored by comparing them with the budget (target), data must be collected relating to actual transactions and converted into information. To convert the data into information it must be classified into the same form of analysis used to prepare the budget.

The results obtained by the comparison of actual and budget performance are reported to management as part of the feedback process.

1.8 Responses to divergences

The reporting of divergences from the plan to the manager responsible provides information to enable the manager to investigate and take action as appropriate. Managerial involvement in the planning process will encourage a sense of responsibility which may be built upon using responsibility accounting.

2 RESPONSIBILITY ACCOUNTING AND RESPONSIBILITY CENTRES

2.1 Responsibility accounting

> **Definition** **Responsibility accounting - a** system of accounting based upon the identification of individual parts of a business which are the responsibility of a single manager.

2.2 Responsibility centre

> **Definition** **Responsibility centre** - an individual part of a business headed by a manager having responsibility for its performance.

2.3 Budgetary control and responsibility accounting

Budgetary control and responsibility accounting are inseparable. An organisation chart must be drawn up in order to implement a budgetary control system satisfactorily. It may even be necessary to revise the existing organisation structure before designing the system. The aim is to ensure that each manager has a well-defined area of responsibility and the authority to make decisions within that area, and that no parts of the organisation remain as 'grey' areas where it is uncertain who is responsible for them. This area of responsibility may be simply a **cost centre,** or it may be a **profit centre** (implying that the manager has control over sales revenues as well as costs) or an **investment centre** (implying that the manager is empowered to take decisions about capital investment for his department). Once senior management have set up such a structure, with the degree of delegation implied, some form of responsibility accounting system is needed. Each centre will have its own budget, and the manager will receive control information relevant to that budget centre. Costs (and possibly revenue, assets and liabilities) must be traced to the person primarily responsible for taking the related decisions, and identified with the appropriate department.

Some accountants would go as far as to advocate charging ie, actually debiting, departments with costs that arise strictly as a result of decisions made by the management of those departments. For example, if the marketing department insists on a special rush order which necessitates overtime working in production departments, then the marketing department and not the production departments should be charged with the overtime premiums incurred. However, there are practical problems with such an approach:

(a)   The rush order itself might actually be produced during normal time because, from a production scheduling angle, it might be more convenient to do it then (eg, because it would not involve a clean-down of the machines as it was compatible with some other orders currently in production) - normal orders thereby actually being produced during the period of 'overtime'.

(b)   Re-charging costs to other departments can become a common occurrence because managers see it as a way of passing on not only the costs but also the associated responsibility eg, if the rush order is produced inefficiently in overtime, should the costs of the inefficiency also be charged to the marketing department?

> **Conclusion** All managers work for the same organisation and, if the costs are shunted around, there is a nil effect on the overall profit of the organisation (except to the extent of any extra costs incurred in operating such a recharging system). Perhaps the effort expended on such a system could be more positively used to increase overall profit.

3 COST, REVENUE, PROFIT, AND INVESTMENT CENTRES

3.1 Cost centre

> **Definition** Cost centre - a production or service location, function, activity or item of equipment whose costs may be attributed to cost units.

The performance of a manager responsible for a cost centre will be judged on the extent to which cost targets have been achieved. In order to make an appropriate evaluation costs should be classified as being either fixed costs or variable costs. Fixed cost comparisons should be made on a total basis, whereas variable costs should be compared on a per unit basis. An appropriate cost coding and collection system is essential to ensure that the data collected and consequently the information produced from it, is reliable.

3.2 Revenue centre

> **Definition** Revenue centre - a centre devoted to raising revenue with no responsibility for the cost of doing so.

The performance of a manager responsible for a revenue centre is judged based on the revenue raised. Information would need to be collected from sales figures to establish both the total and per unit revenues.

3.3 Profit centre

> **Definition** Profit centre - a part of the business accountable for costs and revenues.

The performance of a manager responsible for a profit centre is measured on profits. The manager must therefore be responsible for both costs and revenues. Such managers therefore have significant authority.

Profit centres are often found in large organisations which have a divisionalised structure. In such structures trading between the divisions gives rise to transfer pricing which is dealt with later in this text.

To operate a profit centre data must be collected relating to both costs and revenues. This data is then used to measure profit trends and to compare actual and target costs and revenues.

3.4 Investment centre

> **Definition** Investment centre - a profit centre whose performance is measured by its return on capital employed.

Managers of investment centres are also responsible for investment decisions, so that their performance can be measured in terms of profit relative to the level of investment. In its simplest form Return on Capital Employed (ROCE) is measured by:

$$\frac{\text{Profit}}{\text{Capital Employed}}$$

To operate an investment centre it is necessary to collect data on costs, revenues and investments. Within this context the principle of controllability is highly important. Whilst controllability refers mainly to costs, it is important to remember that its principles can also apply to revenues and investments.

4   CONTROLLABLE COSTS

4.1   Introduction

> **Definition**   **Controllable costs** are costs incurred as a result of a decision or course of action of a manager; or which could be avoided by such a decision or course of action.

4.2   Identifying controllable costs

Performance reports should concentrate only on **controllable costs.** Controllable costs are those costs controllable by a particular manager in a given time period. Over a long enough time-span most costs are controllable by someone in the organisation eg, factory rental may be fixed for a number of years but there may eventually come an opportunity to move to other premises. Such a cost, therefore, is controllable in the long term by a manager fairly high in the organisation structure.

However, in the short term it is uncontrollable even by senior managers, and certainly uncontrollable by managers lower down the organisational hierarchy.

There is no clear-cut distinction between controllable and non-controllable costs for a given manager, who may in any case be exercising control jointly with another manager. The aim under a responsibility accounting system will be to assign and report on the cost to the person having **primary** responsibility. The most effective control is thereby achieved, since immediate action can be taken.

Some authorities would favour the alternative idea that reports should include all costs caused by a department, whether controllable or uncontrollable by the departmental manager. The idea here is that, even if he has no direct control, he might influence the manager who does have control. There is the danger of providing the manager with too much information and confusing him but, on the other hand, the uncontrollable element could be regarded as for 'information only', and in this way the manager obtains a fuller picture.

An illustration of the two different approaches is provided by raw materials. The production manager will have control over usage, but not over price, when buying is done by a separate department. For this reason the price and usage variances are separated and, under the first approach, the production manager would be told only about the usage variance, a separate report being made to the purchasing manager about the price variance. The alternative argument is that if the production manager is also told about the price variance, he may attempt to persuade the purchasing manager to try alternative sources of supply.

4.3   Activity

What are the potential dangers of including uncontrollable costs in a performance report?

4.4   Activity solution

The dangers of including uncontrollable costs in a performance report are:

(a)   Managers might be demotivated if their performance is apparently affected by costs over which they have no influence.

(b)   Uncontrollable cost information can divert managers' attention away from what they actually are responsible for.

(c)   The manager who **is** responsible for the costs in question might feel that they are not his or her responsibility as they are reported elsewhere.

4.5   The problem of dual responsibility

A common problem is that the responsibility for a particular cost or item is shared between two (or more) managers. For example, the responsibility for payroll costs may be shared between the personnel and production departments; material costs between purchasing and production departments; and so on. The reporting system should be designed so that the responsibility for performance achievements (ie, better or worse than budget) is identified as that of a single manager.

The following guidelines may be applied:

(a)   If manager controls quantity **and** price - responsible for all expenditure variances.

(b)   If manager controls quantity but **not** price - only responsible for variances due to usage.

(c)   If manager controls price but **not** quantity - only responsible for variances due to input prices.

(d)   If manager controls **neither** quantity **nor** price - variances uncontrollable from the point of view of that manager.

4.6   Guidelines for reporting

There are several specific problems in relation to reporting which must be identified and dealt with:

(a)   **Levels of reporting**

The problem is how far down the management structure should responsibility centres be identified for reporting purposes? On the one hand, lower reporting levels encourage delegation and identify responsibility closer to the production process. On the other hand, more responsibility centres increase the number of reports and hence the cost of their production. One solution may be to combine small responsibility centres into groups (eg, departments) for reporting purposes.

(b)   **Frequency of reports and information to be reported**

The frequency of reports should be linked to the purposes for which they are required. This may well mean a variety of reports being produced to different time-scales for different purposes eg, some control information will be required weekly, or even daily. However, comprehensive budget reports are only likely to be required monthly.

The related problem is the content of such reports. It has been suggested that in computerised information systems the problem is often too much, rather than too little information. Generally, as reporting proceeds up the management pyramid, the breadth of the report should increase, and the detail should decrease. The following series of reports illustrate this principle:

	\multicolumn{2}{c}{*Budget*}	\multicolumn{2}{c}{*Variance*}	
	Current month	*Year to date*	*Current month*	*Year to date*

Managing director

Factory A
Factory B
Administration costs
Selling costs
Distribution costs
R&D costs

Production director Factory A

Machining department
Casting department
Assembly department
Inspection and quality control
Factory manager's office

Head of machining department

Direct materials
Direct labour
Indirect labour
Power
Maintenance
Other

The above layout should only be regarded as illustrative, but it does indicate how detail increases as span decreases.

4.7 Degree of summarisation

Even where data is of the correct kind for a particular task, if it is presented in its raw form it will normally be too detailed to be described as information. This is why information usually consists of a large number of data items which have summarised into a smaller number of data items. The degree of summarisation is the comparison between the original number of data items and the number of data items finally presented. For example a report on the sales of 120 individual sales staff summarised into 4 regions is more summarised than a report of the same individuals summarised into 24 sales teams.

Summarisation has the benefit of allowing an individual to gain an overall picture of a situation. However in the process of stepping back to gain this overall view some detail is lost. Therefore the overall reporting procedures should include methods of highlighting individual data items which need management attention. In our sales team example this may include a report which identifies all staff whose total sales were more than 30% above or below the average for the organisation.

5   QUANTITATIVE AND QUALITATIVE INFORMATION

5.1 Introduction

Information can be classified as being either quantitative or qualitative.

5.2 Quantitative information

Quantitative information is information that can be expressed in numerical terms; it may therefore be measured in monetary or non-monetary units. Such information may be used to make comparisons between alternatives, for example when choosing between two machines the following quantitative information may be compared:

(a)   capital cost;
(b)   running cost per hour;
(c)   output per hour;
(d)   estimated useful life in hours.

5.3 Qualitative information

Qualitative information is information that cannot normally be expressed in numerical terms. It is often opinions which may affect decisions involving the environment and human reaction. For example a decision concerning the closure of a segment of a business may impact on the morale of the workforce which remains, as well as the infrastructure and environment in which the particular segment operates. These factors should be considered in addition to any quantitative information.

6   ACCURACY OF INFORMATION

6.1   Introduction

Information should always be sufficiently accurate for its intended purpose. Such accuracy of information depends on a number of factors, for example collection and processing techniques.

6.2   Accuracy and precision

In order to process data into information it must be appropriately accurate and precise. These two attributes are closely related yet they are distinct.

Precision refers to the detail included in data. This is sometimes referred to as granularity.

Accuracy refers to how close the data is to whatever is being measured.

For example if a decision has been taken that the monthly sales will be reported to the precision of the nearest £1,000 and the sales for a particular month were £24,501 then data which stated £25,000 would be accurate and £24,000 inaccurate. However, if the precision had been decided as the nearest £1 then £25,000 would be inaccurate.

If data is recorded and presented in great precision it can give the impression that the data is accurate, when in fact precision is no indicator of accuracy. Both precision and accuracy can be measured. Precision is relatively easy to measure. In the case of numerical data precision it is stated as the number of significant digits. One measure of accuracy is error rate, this can be expressed as the percentage of data which, after allowing for the specified precision, is not the same as the reality which the data is intended to represent. Inaccuracy can occur due to systematic bias and or error.

Systematic bias is inaccuracy due to a feature of the system used for the collection and processing of data. The raw data in a business system is not normally subject to bias. It is normally the system which collects and presents the data which is biased. Collection bias is in effect distorting reality by withholding certain information. In the case of an information system this would mean that the system had either deliberately or accidentally been designed in such a way that it failed to collect relevant data. Presentation bias occurs when data is presented in a way which only presents one point of view. The axis on graphs can be set in order to bias the presentation of data.

Sometimes collection and presentation bias are used together. An example is a newspaper headline which stated that 25% of chief executives of major companies did not have a university degree or professional qualification, indicating that many unqualified individuals become chief executives. An unbiased presentation would state that 10% of the workforce and 75% of chief executives had degrees or professional qualifications. This data could be further enhanced to state that qualified individuals are seven times more likely to become chief executives than unqualified individuals.

Error in data usually occurs as a result of the inherent variability in the system used to record the data. This should not be confused with random variation in what is being measured. For example measuring devices are normally manufactured to operate within certain limits, a micrometer may be capable of measuring to plus or minus 50 microns. If the device reported measurements larger than whatever is being measured on one occasion and smaller on another then this variation would introduce random error into the data. Conversely if the micrometer was exactly accurate but the parts being measured varied in size then the data would be accurate but would vary randomly (although probably within certain limitations).

Other sources of error are:

- Incorrect methods of data collection and measurement
- Loss of data
- Failure to process some of the data

6.3   Source

The source of data is the system, person, group or organisation which produced it. Knowing the source helps the user to compensate for systematic bias. If for example the managing director of an organisation receives a sales forecast from the sales director and another from the finance director he will use his knowledge of the two individuals involved to make adjustments to the data, In doing so he would probably consider their personal biases and those placed upon them by their positions within the firm.

Data may either be formal or informal depending upon its source:

(a)   Formal sources are all sources of data which have authority to make statements on behalf of the organisation. Formal data includes:

- statements from the organisation's officials;
- data from the formal systems of the organisation;
- published documents;
- company advertising.

(b)   Informal sources include all data which is not classified by the company as official:

- informal discussions with colleagues;
- rumours;
- meetings with suppliers or customers;
- reports compiled for personal use.

Another classification of source is whether the data is from within the organisation or from outside sources. Most information which is based upon verifiable data is from within the organisation. The vast majority of information produced and consumed in the organisation is from data collected in the organisation.

6.4   Completeness

Completeness refers to the extent to which the data is sufficient for the task. With the exception of a few totally controlled and structured tasks, it is impossible to have complete data. Examination of most decision making tasks no matter how trivial normally reveals a number of assumptions which have been adopted because of the incompleteness of data. Data which is produced to aid the process of planning will always be incomplete because the future cannot be predicted with certainty.

Data is normally considered complete if the users feel that they have all the data that they can justify for the task or decision. This means that tasks may be carried out with incomplete information yet the information is available but only at a cost either in money or time which the user feels is not worthwhile. A feature of many managers' jobs is that of making decisions which, due to time pressure, they have to make without data which exists and is available. This will be explored in greater detail shortly under the heading relevance and value.

6.5   Accessibility

Data and information have already been discussed in terms of its completeness. A user of data rarely has complete data. One of the factors creating this condition is the time required to gather complete data, which in turn is related to how accessible data is. The factors which affect accessibility are:

- the user's knowledge of what data is available;
- the user's skill in locating and retrieving data;
- where data is recorded;
- the media used to record the data;
- the access procedures.

Recording data in computer systems has made a major difference to accessibility of information. A skilled user can usually obtain the data required fairly quickly and cheaply. This contrasts with the situation where the user has physical access to manual records, but because of the quantity involved the cost of manually sifting through many records may effectively render the data inaccessible.

6.6   Relevance and value

In order to be of use data must be relevant. At the beginning of this section information was defined as data which amongst other things is meaningful. Relevance is the attribute of data which allows it to become meaningful in a particular organisational setting. Information systems are conceived to supply information to users of the system, in designing the system planners will define informational requirements and from this relevant data can be identified.

7   ACCURACY, VOLUME AND TIME

7.1   Introduction

The accuracy and reliability of information can be significantly affected by changes in operating conditions (ie, volume changes) and the passage of time.

7.2   Accuracy and volume

A significant use of information in management accounting is the prediction of future costs from past information. This is made more difficult when the future predicted level of activity differs from that of the past.

Some costs are affected by changes in activity (variable costs) whilst others are not affected (fixed costs). If these differences are not considered then the predictions made and the information communicated from them will be inaccurate and unreliable.

7.3   Age of data

The age of the data is the time that has elapsed since the data was collected. Establishing the age of the data which is part of a regular reporting system is easy. For example, if monthly accounts are produced in a particular organisation, then a user can assume the stock value included in the latest report is less than one month old. Other data can be much harder to age, this typically occurs where the data originated from an *ad hoc* report.

Associated with the age of the data is its timeliness or the degree to which its age is suitable for the decision or control process it is to be used in. Control processes and decisions differ in their timeliness requirements. For example, the mechanism which controls the stock held on the shelves of a busy supermarket will require data that is only a few hours old. This is because of two factors, the first is that management will have specified that the shelves should always have some stock on them, the second is that the situation changes very rapidly. An example of a data requirement where the data can be much older would be in long range company planning. The data used in this process would be part of the information on trends rather than short term fluctuations, therefore some of the data could refer to a number of years ago.

The duration of data is the period of time that the data spans. For example a set of monthly accounts will span one month and so the data on sales is the aggregation of all individual sales data for the month in question. Where systems produce forecasts the data may refer to some period in the future. The actual duration of the data in the report or forecast can range between hours and years.

8   CONTROLLING ACCURACY

8.1   Introduction

The accuracy of information depends on two factors:

(a)   source reliability; and
(b)   data capture techniques.

8.2   Source reliability

Data may be collected from sources internal and external to the organisation. Internal sources can in many instances be verified, for example a comparison can be made between sales data and finished goods stock records. Such a comparison would prove (or disprove) the accuracy of the data. However other internal sources (eg, an employee's time sheet) and most external sources do not cross-reference to a second source. Thus information derived from such single sources is dependent on the reliability of the source for its accuracy.

8.3   Data capture techniques

On the assumption that the source of the data is reliable and accurate, such data can cause inaccurate information to be provided if the data capture technique is not controlled.

Today, much data is processed by computer, and to facilitate this data must be entered into the computer system. This may be done manually using a keyboard or by electronic means using scanning devices. Where manual input techniques are used there is a much greater risk of error, due to human involvement. System controls are needed to verify and validate the input. Although this does not guarantee 100% accuracy such controls will minimise the production of inaccurate and meaningless information.

9   MANAGEMENT ACCOUNTING AND UNCERTAINTY

9.1   Introduction

Much of management accounting is concerned with the future and to this extent it relies on predictions based on past data. To produce a single set of values based on the past data may therefore give a misleading sense of accuracy. To overcome this sensitivity analysis and probabilities are used to give a more balanced view of the future.

9.2   Sensitivity analysis

This is a technique which is similar to the 'what-if' facility provided by computer spreadsheet packages. Initial predictions are produced based on past data. Then each of the variables is changed, usually by the same percentage, and the effect on the final result measured. By using this technique it is possible to establish which variables are more critical than others in achieving a given result. At the same time management may be made aware of the range of outcomes which may occur.

9.3   Using probability

Instead of predicting a single value from past data a common technique is to predict three values:

(a)   most likely;
(b)   optimistic; and
(c)   pessimistic

and predict the probability of each occurring. These predictions are made for each variable. It is then possible to combine each of the possible outcomes so as to produce a range of values together with their related probabilities. This again enables management to be made aware of possible outcomes, but the use of probabilities enables the likelihood of each outcome occurring to be shown.

10   CHAPTER SUMMARY

In this chapter we have considered the use of information for planning, control and decision making and seen how it impacts on responsibility accounting. We have considered cost controllability in terms of performance appraisal using cost centres, revenue centres, profit centres and investment centres. Finally we considered the accuracy of information and its importance in a management accounting context.

11 SELF TEST QUESTIONS

11.1 Outline the planning, control and decision making process. (1)

11.2 Explain responsibility accounting (2.1)

11.3 Distinguish between cost, revenue, profit and investment centres. (3.1 - 3.4)

11.4 What is a controllable cost? (4.2)

11.5 Distinguish between quantitative and qualitative information. (5.2, 5.3)

11.6 Distinguish between accuracy and precision. (6.2)

11.7 Explain the effects of volume on the accuracy of information. (7.2)

11.8 Explain the effect of time on the accuracy of information. (7.3)

11.9 Discuss difficulties of controlling the accuracy of information. (8.2, 8.3)

11.10 Explain two management accounting techniques which are used to deal with uncertainty. (9.2, 9.3)

12 EXAMINATION TYPE QUESTION

12.1 Management accounting criteria

Management accounting information should comply with a number of criteria including verifiability, objectivity, timeliness, comparability, reliability, understandability and relevance if it is to be useful in planning, control and decision-making.

(a) Explain the meaning of each of the criteria named above and give a specific example to illustrate each. **(14 marks)**

(b) Give a brief explanation of how the criteria detailed in (a) might be in conflict with each other giving examples to illustrate where such conflict might arise. **(3 marks)**

(Total: 17 marks)

(ACCA June 88)

13 ANSWER TO EXAMINATION TYPE QUESTION

13.1 Management accounting criteria

(Tutorial notes: part (a) is fairly easy. Note there are seven criteria each requiring an explanation and an illustration. Fourteen separate parts for 14 marks. Remember to attempt each of these parts.

Part (b) is only worth 3 marks. Therefore attempt to make three distinctive points in your answer.

Overall a question requiring little technical knowledge. A little common sense, plus a good command of the English language, is all that is required.)

(a) **Verifiability**

This means that managerial accounting information can be confirmed by reference to documentation and schedules maintained by the company. This is especially important when information is being used to aid decision making - the decision maker will want to be in a position to check the information being made available to him. It is also important that the calculations used in planning and forecasting can be checked and that the subsequent control information based on these plans (budgets) can be verified. Proper documentation is essential to verification. Verifiability can be illustrated by reference to the stock records that would be used in valuing material issues for cost control.

Objectivity

It is highly unlikely that management accounting information will contain no subjective bias. However, efforts should be made to ensure that such bias is kept within acceptable limits and is appreciated during the planning and decision-making process. An example of the need for objectivity would be the setting of standard costs for labour or materials.

Timeliness

It is essential that information is produced and communicated to the management in time for it to be used. Delays in data gathering, processing or communication can transform potentially vital information into worthless waste paper. An example would be material price variances which should be reported at the time of purchase not usage.

Comparability

Most information does not 'stand on its own'. It must be in a form which enables it to be compared with either data from previous periods or with some planned (budgeted) data. This is especially important for control purposes. A good example is the use of flexible budgets to ensure that the actual results are compared with the budgeted results for that level of activity. It is also very useful to use percentages instead of absolute values to enhance comparability.

Reliability

This means that the management accounting information should be processed and presented in such a way that the user can safely use the information while planning, controlling or making decisions. For example, analysis using a computerised system is likely to be more reliable than when using a manual system.

Understandability

Management must receive information in a style and format it finds readily comprehensible. This means that the management accountant must be aware of the recipient's knowledge of technical accounting terms, numeracy/literacy levels and his personal characteristics. An example would be the use of graphs and charts instead of tables of figures for (say) CVP analysis. Information which cannot be understood is at best useless and at worst 'dangerous', resulting in poor planning and decision-making and incorrect use of control devices.

Relevance

This is the primary criterion to be met by management accounting information. The information provided should be that which is required for the manager to plan, control or make decisions in the current environment. Information which is relevant in one environment, at a particular time, may not be relevant as the environment changes. An example would be information based on marginal costing principles, giving the contribution per unit, instead of total absorbed costs, for decisions relating to changes in activity level. This data may not be relevant to decisions on product pricing.

(b)   Several of the criteria could be in conflict eg, relevant data is not always verifiable or easily understood. The major conflict is likely to be, however, between timeliness and some (or all) of the other criteria. For example, it may be possible to improve the understandability of the information but not within the period when it is considered to be timely. Some objectivity may be lost in an effort to get the information out in time. The management accountant will have to balance the criteria to find the optimal practical position, which is not necessarily the optimal theoretical position for information.

3 INFORMATION TECHNOLOGY AND THE MANAGEMENT INFORMATION SYSTEM

INTRODUCTION & LEARNING OBJECTIVES

When you have studied this chapter you should be able to do the following:

- Explain the information processing cycle.
- Explain the processing procedures associated with using computerised packages.

1 THE INFORMATION PROCESSING CYCLE

1.1 The three stages of information processing

The processing of information can be divided into three stages: input, processing, and output. These are often illustrated by a simple diagram:

It is the process activity which converts input data into information which is output to users. All systems follow this principle whether they are computerised or manual systems.

1.2 Processing accounting information

The processing of accounting information adheres to the above principle of input, process, output. For example, if we consider a payroll system the three stages would involve:

INPUT		
	-	wage rates
	-	number of hours
	-	PAYE codes
	-	Tax and NI tables

for each employee

PROCESS		
	-	calculate gross pay
	-	calculate deductions
	-	calculate net pay

OUTPUT		
	-	wage slips (for each employee)
	-	bank/cash analysis
	-	nominal ledger analysis

1.3 Activity

Identify the components of each stage of processing a sales ledger.

1.4   Activity solution

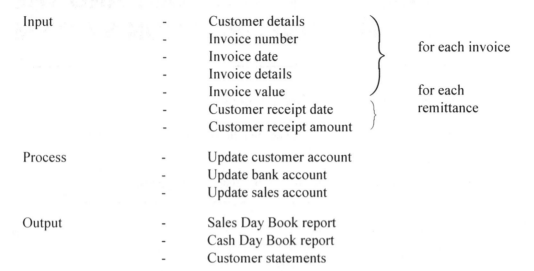

Input	-	Customer details
	-	Invoice number
	-	Invoice date
	-	Invoice details
	-	Invoice value
	-	Customer receipt date
	-	Customer receipt amount

for each invoice

for each remittance

Process	-	Update customer account
	-	Update bank account
	-	Update sales account

Output	-	Sales Day Book report
	-	Cash Day Book report
	-	Customer statements

2   TRANSACTION RECORDING IN A COMPUTER BASED SYSTEM

2.1   Information levels

Transaction processing is the information level below that of operational needs. It comprises the most fundamental, routine transactions. Every organisation perceives, documents, and controls such transactions in order to undertake necessary tasks or to assist management in their decision-making. Examples are: invoices and receipts, sales and purchase orders.

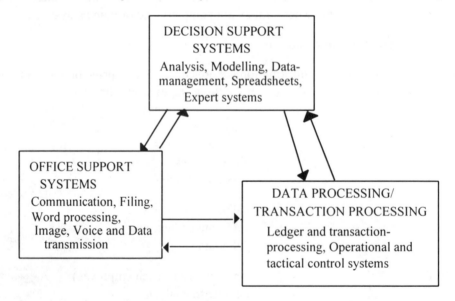

Data is input to the system during the transaction, for example, to amend existing records. In a supermarket, for instance, transaction processing would entail recording the sale and the sum involved, maintaining a continuing total of incoming payments and updating stock levels.

2.2   Systems options

A system may adopt different processing approaches. These include:

- Batch processing.
- Demand processing.
- Batch-demand processing mix.
- On-line.

The approach chosen depends firstly on management requirements. These may be:

(a)   Routine recording of accounts data eg, purchase ledger, sales ledger, payroll.

(b)   Preparation of regular 'packages' of management information eg, monthly reports.

(c)   Fact retrieval for decision-making eg, can customer Y exceed its credit limit? This will also include facts for strategy evolution.

The processing system must also take into account:

(a)   input volumes;

(b)   management priorities;

(c)   the purpose of the information processed;

(d)   response-time (ie, the time between the collection of the source data and the processing results).

2.3   Batch processing mode

A group of similar (routine) transactions are processed in the same processing-run. Input data could be entered into the system over a period of time, or at the same time. But the actual processing of the data commences only when the transactions data collection is complete and is held in a **transactions file**.

A classic example of batch processing is an organisation's payroll. Typically, the wages section segments transaction records into small batches (eg, one per department). In this way, most input data is in smaller collections.

The data may accumulate over a given time resulting in a delay before it is all processed at once; for example, when purchase invoices are processed and paid on a monthly basis.

This mode was formerly the major form of processing. It is still the most logical method of dealing with large transaction volumes at a specific time.

Advantages

- Error detection is simpler (facilitated by the nature of the single processing run).
- No special hardware/software is needed (all computer systems should be able to adopt this).
- It contributes to large-scale economies due to bulk processing.
- System design is simple.
- If necessary, part may be processed now and the remainder later.

Disadvantages

- The system is 'time-driven' and so is not geared to rapid action.
- The system provides bulk information and so is not selective.
- Preparing batches results in duplication of effort.

The method of input is usually by disk or tape for the encoding of transactions. This is also the transactions file input medium.

2.4   Demand processing mode

This is undertaken when a transaction must be processed straightaway, and delay through batch processing cannot be allowed. It is often referred to as **transaction-processing**. Here, the user literally processes 'on demand'.

This may arise due to:

(a)   a request for information from transaction files (eg, the amount owed by a customer);

(b)   the decision to pay a large account immediately (eg, if previously delayed because of an error);

(c)   recording of an infrequent or special activity.

2.5   Batch-demand processing 'mix'

Various combinations of batch and demand processing can occur. The 'mixes' are:

(a)   batch input/processing of all transactions (including such activities as file enquiries and updating activity);

(b)   batch input/processing of all transactions, plus file enquiries on-line;

(c)   remote job entry (RJE) plus batch processing and on-line file enquiry (RJE is the transmission of user data for processing from an on-line terminal);

(d)   on-line (including real-time (OLRT) updating) and on-line enquiry, allowing data input from remote terminals, the updating of the relevant master file on an immediate basis, and *ad hoc* file enquiries as necessary.

The next section will clarify the 'on-line' and 'OLRT' references.

2.6   On-line mode

A system is referred to as 'on-line' when the data is input directly to the computer from the point of origination, and where the output is transmitted to the user's location.   This involves **data communications**.

An on-line system may be **batch-based**. This permits input to be held in backing storage so that processing may be subsequently carried out during an off-peak period. An on-line system which processes the input immediately is said to be operating in **real time**.

The **response time** is the period within which the computer is able to carry out the input instruction transmitted from the terminal. This usually includes transmitting the result back to the terminal.

Good examples of such a system are ground-to-air missile control, or a bank's cashpoint dispenser.

Advantages of the real-time system

- A higher level of customer satisfaction is achieved (eg, the real-time banking system).

- Information needed is obtained by adopting very simple procedures.

- Prompt and early information assists in improving and maintaining the quality of management decisions.

Disadvantages

- The system is relatively high-cost (in terms of hardware and software required, installation, and essential storage).

- A high level of security is required (eg, the OLRT bank cash dispenser).

- To avoid loss should the system fail ('go down'), duplicate processors and files are needed.

- System failure could cause great organisational problems.

2.7   Activity

When deciding on the type of processing to use, what considerations would you take account of?

2.8   Activity solution

The following are some of the considerations:

- Regularity of processing - payroll is only monthly (for salaries).
- Response time required - output may be time critical.
- Volume of processing - batch may be more suitable for large volumes.
- Accuracy required - batch processing lends itself to accuracy checks more readily.
- Cost - alternatives should be compared.
- Efficiency and security of processing.
- Storage media used - sequential access or direct access storage.
- Is there a need to access up-to-date files regularly?
- The availability of hardware and trained operators to collect data.
- Availability of finance to purchase equipment.

3   MANAGEMENT ACCOUNTING INFORMATION AND SOFTWARE PACKAGES

3.1   Introduction

Software packages may be specially written or they may be purchased 'off the shelf.' The difference between these is that those purchased 'off the shelf' are designed so as to be useful to many different businesses and they have the advantage of being thoroughly tested before being sold. Specialist software packages are very expensive in comparison because they are written for a single user who will be heavily involved in the testing of the package.

3.2   Program suites

Most packages are written in modules which may be thought of as sub-systems within the overall package. These modules link together to produce a comprehensive accounting system from which management reports may be obtained. The modules which are most commonly found in such systems include:

(a)   sales accounting;
(b)   purchases;
(c)   cash/bank;
(d)   fixed assets;
(e)   nominal ledger.

The next two paragraphs consider the sales and purchases systems in more detail.

4   SALES ACCOUNTING SYSTEM

4.1   Scope

This system is designed to deal with:

(a)   order processing;
(b)   preparation of daily invoices and despatch notes;
(c)   cash-posting;
(d)   preparation of sales analysis reports;
(e)   monthly ledger balancing and statements preparation.

In addition the system will provide various error and exception reports. Some of these will be available by screen display only. Others will be in the form of printouts. For example, a system might be configured as follows:

- Three IBM-compatible PCs are used as intelligent workstations to the central computer.
- The central computer is based on a 32-bit processor offering 16 MB of RAM.
- Hard disk storage is available up to 1 GB.
- Two serial impact printers are connected to the system.

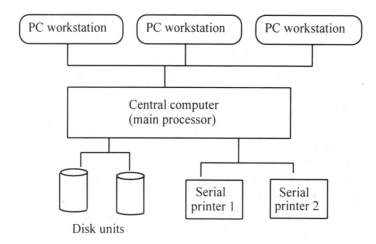

4.2   Files

The example system is based on two **master files** – a customer master file and a product master file. The files are designed to provide direct access, and the data items associated with each file are as follows:

Customer		Product	
Description	*Number of characters*	*Description*	*Number of characters*
Account no.	8	Part no.	8
Name	20	Description	12
Address	20	Made in/bought out indicator	2
Credit limit	6	Main supplier code	8
Agent no.	5	Standard cost per unit	8
Sales, year to date	10	Standard price per unit	8
Balance	10	Maximum quantity	8
Balance × 30 days	10	Minimum quantity	8
Balance × 60 days	10	Reorder quantity	8
Balance × 90 days	10	Balance in hand	10
Date last paid	8	Total receipts this period	15
Bad debt indicator	2	Total issues this period	15
Overdue a/c indicator	2	Date of last issue	8

4.3   Processes

(a)   **Order** – All orders whether for cash or credit are input and validated for:

- correct stock code;
- stock availability;
- account on order (credit items only).

The operator performs the relevant operation via a menu and appropriate screen dialogues (see Figure below). From the main sales ledger menu the user can key '1' in order to get to the Order Processing screen.

SALES LEDGER SYSTEM	ORDER PROCESSING
1 Order processing 2 Cash payments 3 Journals 4 New/amended account details 5 Account display 6 Month-end routines **Select option number 1 - 6**	Order number [ ] Date [ ] Cash/credit [ ] Customer number [ ] Stock number [ ] Quantity [ ] Correct Y/N 'Y' Press 9 to continue Q to end 'Q'
Screen menu	**Screen dialogue**

When the order details have been entered and stored, the fields are cleared to permit the operator to enter the next order.

Once the order is complete, the program evaluates it by multiplying quantities by prices and summing for all the products. VAT is computed as appropriate. If the resulting transaction value is greater than that permitted by the customer's credit limit then the order is rejected. A printout of rejected orders is generated for follow-up by sales staff.

If the order is accepted, an invoice/despatch note record is created on a file which is periodically printed out. This may be shown on a **systems overview chart**.

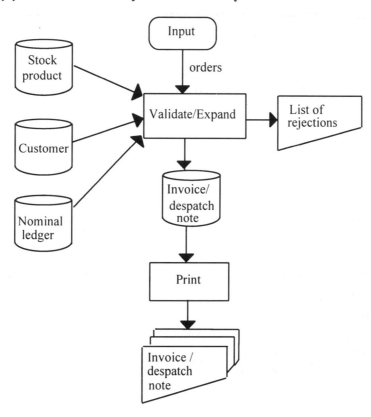

Each time an order is processed the stock file and debtor (customer) file are **updated**. The nominal ledger containing the sales account and the ledger control account is also updated. The invoice file can be used by various **report-writing** routines to generate:

(i)   a VAT extract for the VAT return;

(ii)   a sales analysis for month-end reporting;

(iii)   a cost of sales reconciliation for monthly stock control.

(b)   **Cash** – is identified with orders (if we are dealing with cash transactions) or with account numbers (if we are dealing with credit customers). Most commercial companies maintain their ledger files on an **open-item** system, in which sub-files are maintained of all open or uncleared items ie, there is no opening balance.

If an open-item system is kept, all cash transactions have also to be identified with individual transactions or the system 'throws them out' as unallocated. This affects the ability of the program logic to 'age' the ledger balances when producing a monthly statement.

(c)   **Journals** – The system has a facility for entering journal items. These are used for:

(i)   making transfers between accounts (in the event of mis-coding a cash payment);

(ii)   adjusting for discounts or write-offs.

4.4   Outputs

The typical outputs from the system are:

(a)   **Invoices** – These are produced on a printer to give near-letter quality (NLQ) results. The system provides continuous numbering (to avoid the problems of sequential control of pre-printed paper).

(b)   **Statements/remittance advice** – The statement/remittance advice is a turnaround document. The open-item ledger allows all debits and credits to be itemised on the remittance advice as well as on the statement. The remittance advice can then be utilised as a source document for cash-posting purposes when it is returned by the customer.

(c)   **Sales reports and audit trail reports** – The system produces:

(i)   daily listings and totals of invoices;

(ii)   daily cash-posting reports;

(iii)   monthly sales analysis reports;

(iv)   monthly reconciliation of the debtors' ledger comprising:

- opening balance;
- invoices;
- cash;
- journals;
- closing balance.

5   PURCHASES SYSTEM

5.1   Scope

This example system is not integrated with the stock system and essentially deals with:

(a)   purchase invoices;

(b)   cost analysis;

(c)   cheque payments/remittance advice;

(d)   ageing of creditors' balances;

(e)   journals and cash receipts;

(f)   updating of nominal ledger.

5.2   Files

The system is supported by a supplier master file. Each record is structured as follows:

Description	Number of characters
Supplier name and address	40
Account number	8
Credit limit	6

Purchases, year to date	8
Payment code (prompt/7 days/30 days/60 days)	1
Balance	9
Date of last payment	8
Amount of last payment	8

5.3   Processes

Invoices are received by the accounts department who attach a coding label which contains the following items:

(a)   serial number;
(b)   account code(s);
(c)   net amount(s);
(d)   VAT;
(e)   gross total.

Invoices are pre-listed and batch controlled. Each batch is controlled by a **batch control slip** and entered in a **batch control register**.

Invoices are entered into the system **prior to approval** for payment. This reduces the risk of lost invoices. Invoices are listed on a daily purchase journal which shows:

(a)   supplier name;
(b)   serial number;
(c)   expense analysis by cost code;
(d)   VAT analysis;
(e)   total invoice value.

This listing comprises both approved and non-approved items.

The invoices are then circulated to various staff members who have the responsibility for validating them. The validated invoices are passed back to the accounts department to be filed. Payments can be generated by creating a payments report which is a listing of:

(a)   supplier name;
(b)   invoice number(s);
(c)   amount(s);
(d)   total for supplier;
(e)   grand total.

Individual payments can be suppressed by marking the list and returning it to accounts to cancel the printing of cheques. Otherwise, cheques are printed out on two-part stationery; the second part is a proof listing which provides totals for the cash book.

Lists of balances can be printed out on demand.

The cost analyses and VAT analyses can also be used to update the nominal ledger if the system is integrated with a nominal ledger routine.

5.4   Outputs

To summarise, the outputs from the purchases system are:

(a)   purchases journal listing showing the invoices and their analysis between costs and VAT;
(b)   cheques and remittance advice;
(c)   aged list of balances;
(d)   cost analysis by expense type and cost centre.

The system can be depicted in an overview diagram.

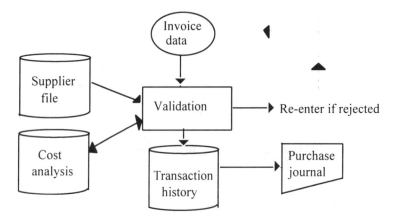

Processing invoices in batch mode and production of purchase journal

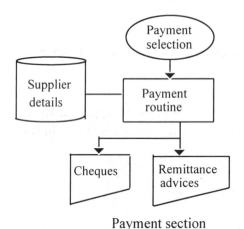

Payment section

Generation of cheque payments

6   **USING SPREADSHEETS AND DATABASES IN MANAGEMENT ACCOUNTING**

6.1   **Introduction**

Spreadsheets and databases are both forms of computer package which may be used to store and manipulate data.

6.2   **What is a spreadsheet?**

A spreadsheet is a computer package which stores data in a matrix format where the intersection of each row and column is referred to as a cell. Columns are referenced alphabetically and rows numerically with the result that a cell reference is a combination of these. This is illustrated below:

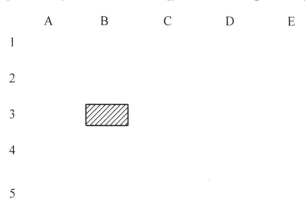

The reference of the shaded cell is B3 because it is the intersection of column B and row 3.

Each cell within a spreadsheet may be used to store:

(a)   a label (description) eg, the title of the spreadsheet;

(b)   a value; or

(c)   a formula.

The formula is used to carry out calculations on values entered in other parts of the spreadsheet.

The spreadsheet may be used to make numerous calculations based upon the data contained in other cells of the same or another spreadsheet, or using values incorporated within the formulae. As a consequence changes to any of the data within the spreadsheet will automatically revise the values contained in any formula related cells.

The simple example of a cash flow model which follows shows how this linking of cells is used. In this example the cash flow data has been reduced to balance brought forward, receipts and payments:

	A	B	C	D	E
1		Jan	Feb	Mar	April
2					
3	Opening balance	1,000	1,100	1,000	550
4	Add: Receipts	700	800	500	850
5	Less: Payments	600	900	950	400
6					
7	Closing balance	1,100	1,000	550	1,000
8					

This table could equally well have been prepared manually, but in fact the columns containing balances consist of relationships, rather than numeric values:

	A	B	C	D	E
1		Jan	Feb	Mar	April
2					
3	Opening balance	1,000	=B7	=C7	=D7
4	Add: Receipts	700	800	500	850
5	Less: Payments	600	900	950	400
6					
7	Closing balance	=B3+B4−B5	=C3+C4−C5	=D3+D4−D5	=E3+E4−E5
8					

Thus the opening balance for every month except January equals the previous month's closing balance. Similarly the closing balance is the Opening balance + Receipts − Payments.

The great advantage of this approach becomes apparent when applied to a large and complex problem:

(a)   this program can handle up to 8,192 rows and 234 columns, enough to accommodate a very complex model (though most micros would run out of memory if all the cells were used);

(b)   if any figure is amended, all the figures will be immediately recalculated;

(c)   the results can be printed out without going through an intermediate typing phase; and

(d)   most programs can also represent the results graphically eg, the above balances can be shown in a bar diagram:

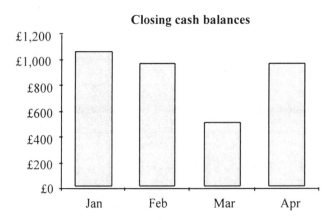

Closing cash balances

In total spreadsheet cash flow models represent a very powerful tool for use by the accountant.

6.3   Example of a cash budget

The following worksheet illustrates a screen showing part of a budgeting spreadsheet that has been set up for a cash budget.

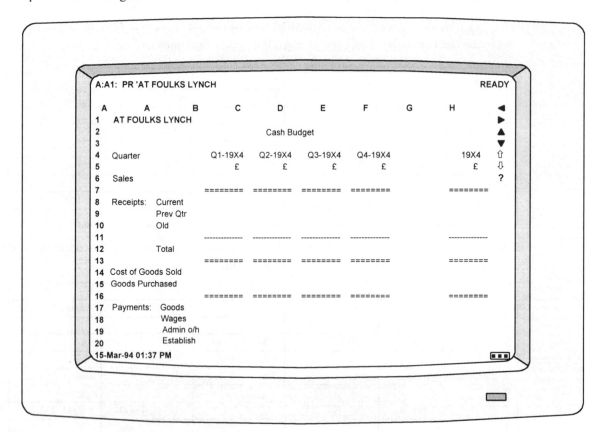

(a)   **Quarterly sales**

Sales are expected to be £60,000 in quarter 1, increasing in volume by 10% per quarter.

Thus insert £60,000 in C6. A formula can then be inserted into D6:

+C6*1.1

This can be copied into E6 to G6 using:

/ C(opy) D6 ↵ E6..G6 ↵

The figures for quarters 2-4 should be:

£66,000, £72,600, £79,860 (and £87,846 for the first quarter of 19X5 which will be needed to find purchases below. This 19X5 quarter is shown in column G.)

Total sales revenue (@SUM(C6..F6)) is £278,460.

(b)   **Receipts**

50% of sales are expected to be received in the quarter that the sale is made, 40% is received one quarter later and 10% received two quarters later.)

The formulae: for cell F8 will be   F6*0.5

                     for cell F9 will be   E6*0.4

                     for cell F10 will be   D6*0.1

These can be copied into rows C, D and E.

In cells H8..H10 an @SUM function is required to add the total of columns C to F. In row 12 the three elements of receipts can be totalled. The result is shown below.

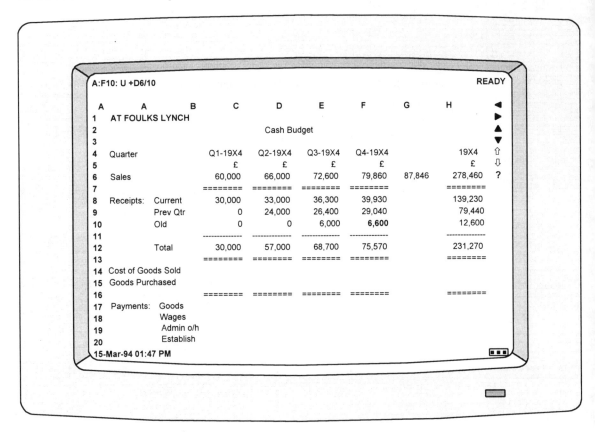

(c)   **Cost of sales and purchases**

The company will use a mark up on cost of 60%. 1½ months stock is to be held, therefore purchases in a quarter will correspond to 50% of the current quarter's cost of sales plus 50% of the next quarter's, the exception being quarter 1 of 19X4 when sufficient goods will be purchased to satisfy the next 4½ months.

The formula for cell C14 can be worked out by looking at the cost structure:

Cost of goods sold   +   profit   =   sales revenue

100   +   60   =   160

Cost of goods sold are $\dfrac{100}{160}$ times sales revenue.

The formula for cell C14 is:

+C6*100/160

When this is copied into rows D to G, the figures that appear are:

£37,500, £41,250, £45,375, £49,912.5 (and £54,903.75)

The cost of goods purchased shown in cell C15 must be:

+C14+D14/2

However in D15 (and copied into E and F) will be:

+D14/2 + E14/2

The totals can be shown in row H. The total of the Cost of Goods Sold is £174,037.50 (£278,460 $\times \dfrac{100}{160}$) and of Goods Purchased £201,489.4.

(d)   **Payments for goods**

Assume that 50% of purchases in each quarter are paid for in the quarter in which the purchases were made and 50% in the following quarter.

A similar approach can be adopted as for receipts by entering a formula in cell C17:

+C15/2 + B15/2

This can be copied into cells D17..F17 and the row summed to give the following worksheet.

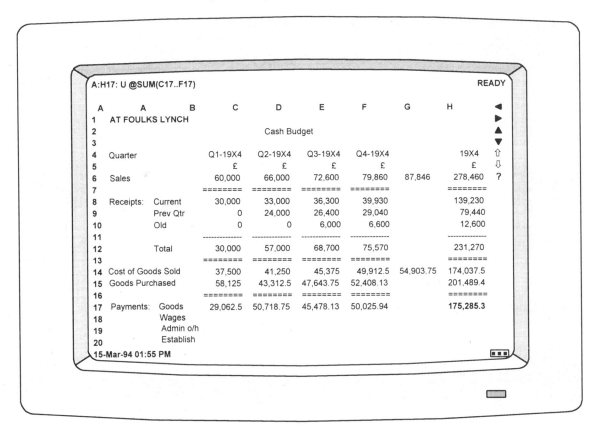

6.4   Advantages and disadvantages of spreadsheets

The above example illustrates many of the advantages of spreadsheets, namely:

(a)   data is easily manipulated, changes in one item of data being quickly recalculated throughout the spreadsheet;

(b)   the data can be formatted and printed to suit the needs of the user. This may be in the form of reports, tables of values, or graphs which may be linked together; and

(c)   the user may identify different outcome possibilities by using the 'what-if' facility. This would often be too time consuming to be done manually, thus the spreadsheet brings computer modelling to the data user.

However, there are some disadvantages to the use of spreadsheets. Spreadsheets take time to develop and it is important to ensure that this is to be time well spent. There is no benefit in taking many hours to develop a spreadsheet which is then only used occasionally to complete a task which could easily be done efficiently using a manual method. In addition, the following disadvantages can be identified:

(a)   data can be accidentally changed (or deleted) without the user being aware of this occurring;

(b)   errors in design, particularly in the use of formulae, can produce invalid output. Due to the complexity of the model, these design errors may be difficult to locate; and

(c)   the manipulation of the data using such a mathematical approach may lead to the loss of the original concepts, these being replaced with a seemingly accurate set of output reports. In the context of budgets and forecasts it must be remembered that such output is based on data which are estimates and which may therefore be incorrect.

6.5   What is a database?

A database consists of a number of files, each containing information on a similar topic. Each file comprises a number of records which individually contain fields which hold data relating to a specific item within the file. For example a vehicle maintenance/service organisation may use a database for the work it provides. There could be two files:

(i)   for jobs which are completed; and

(ii)   for jobs which are in progress.

There would be a record for each job which would be uniquely identified by a job number. The record would contain fields for:

(a)   vehicle registration number;

(b)   description of work;

(c)   date work started;

(d)   date job completed;

(e)   number of hours;

(f)   details of parts used;

(g)   cost incurred.

In practice this would be much more detailed than the outline example above but this should enable you to understand the relationship between files, records and fields within a database.

6.6   Activity

Consider your own organisation or your college. Describe how they might use a database to store data.

6.7   Advantages and disadvantages of databases

The advantage of databases is their ability to manipulate data; many people would suggest that they are more powerful than spreadsheets. Mathematical functions may be carried out on values contained within fields, and searching/sorting of data may be used to produce meaningful reports. For example, in the context of the vehicle maintenance/service organisation above, the files could be searched to produce a report showing the details of all work carried out on a particular vehicle between specified dates.

The disadvantages of databases are that they are often very complex, and there is a large amount of time required to structure them appropriately. Often once the structure has been defined, it is very difficult to modify it, without losing some of the data previously stored.

7   PREPARATION AND LAYOUT OF A SPREADSHEET MODEL

7.1   Introduction

Good spreadsheet models should always be designed by dividing the spreadsheet into two areas:

(i)   a data input area; and

(ii)   a reports area.

For a complex model where intermediate workings/calculations are required, these may be kept in a third area of the spreadsheet.

By using this approach data entry can be made on a small number of screen areas, facilitating ease of data entry and allowing the use of data input forms which look like the screen display, a useful device where large amounts of data are involved.

7.2   Using formulae

When using formulae within a spreadsheet it is better **not** to include values within the formulae themselves. For example, if a formula is to be used to adjust values for inflation of 5%, the inflation factor of 1.05 is best included in a cell which is referenced within the formula. This approach will allow the rate(s) of inflation to be changed easily by amending the contents of the cell(s).   The alternative would be to identify all of the relevant formulae and edit them individually.

There should be cross-referencing within the spreadsheet eg, notes could be used to explain the effects of each formula used.   The main purpose is to enable any user to follow through what the spreadsheet does.   Formulae should therefore be logical, and often two small formulae are easier to follow than one large complex formula.

8   WHAT-IF ANALYSIS

8.1   Introduction

'What if' analysis is a form of sensitivity analysis, which allows the effects of changing one or more data values to be quickly recalculated.

8.2   What-if analysis and decision making

Most decisions are made under conditions of uncertainty where the majority of input values are estimated.   These input values are combined to produce an output value which appears to be mathematically accurate, but such accuracy may be misleading.

Most decisions are quite complex, involving a range of different input values.   What-if analysis enables each of these to be changed both individually and in combination to see the effects on the final results.   An example may be useful to illustrate this.

8.3   Example

PH Ltd is considering a new product and has estimated the following details:

Selling price/unit	£5.00
Monthly sales volume	1,000 units
Variable cost/unit	£2.00
Monthly fixed cost	£2,000

Assuming that the production and sales volumes are always equal, the profit based upon this data is

$$[1,000 \times (£5.00 - £2.00)] - £2,000 = £1,000 \text{ PROFIT}$$

If the volume is reduced by 20% the effect on profit is:

$$[800 \times (£5.00 - £2.00)] - £2,000 = £400 \text{ PROFIT}$$

8.4   Activity

Design a spreadsheet using the above data to prove the original profit of £1,000.

Now change the sales volume to prove that a 20% reduction results in a revised profit of £400.

What is the effect of a reduction in sales volume of 20% and **at the same time** an increase in the variable cost/unit of 15%?

8.5   Activity solution

The new profit is £160.

9   SPREADSHEET DATA-TABLES

9.1   Past exam questions

The use of data-tables was examined in June and December 1995. The latter required you to briefly discuss their role in allowing for uncertainty in decision making; the former required an interpretation of the information shown in a specific data-table. You should therefore be familiar with both the mechanics and the uses of these spreadsheet tools.

9.2   What is a data-table?

A spreadsheet data-table is a separate area within a spreadsheet that is created by the data-table command. It tabulates the results of sensitivity analysis - ie the outcome values when one or two of the input values are altered in a 'what-if' exercise.

Spreadsheets that will be subject to sensitivity analysis may be organised in three sections:

- *Input* - variable data (eg, sales volume, prices, costs, expected increases etc)

- *Output* - the results of desired calculations on the input data (profits, cash flows etc) - obtained by applying appropriate formulae to input data cells

- *Data table* - analysing the effects of varying one or two of the input variables

9.3   Example - one-way data table

Division Q of XYZ Ltd manufactures and sells one product. A marginal costing system is used. It wishes to evaluate its expected gross profit (defined as contribution less fixed production costs) at its expected sales level for Month 1, and to determine the effect of varying this to other possible levels. There was no opening stock.

The input section of the spreadsheet shown below (rows 3 to 7) quantifies the current estimates of the values of the various input variables:

(a)   Sales are expected to be 10,000 units, at a selling price of £20

(b)   Closing stock required is 2,000 units

(c)   Variable production costs are expected to be £8 per unit

(d)   Fixed production costs are £90,000 per month up to production quantities of 20,000, with a 15% increase applicable to production quantities of 20,000 to 30,000 (maximum capacity).

The output (or calculation) section contains data that would either be derived from an input cell reference (eg B11 would be =C3 or +C3 and B14 would be =C4 or +C4), or from a calculation given by a formula, as in previous examples, eg:

- E11 formula =B11*E3
- B13 formula =B11 + B14 etc

The data table section would be created as follows:

- The table headings are input

- The data table itself occupies the rectangular array of cells B23 to E27. Cell B23 is left empty, and previously calculated gross profits, based upon a 10,000 unit sales level, are copied into E23 (using the formula =E18 or +E18)

- Underneath the empty cell are placed new values of the variable being changed (four alternative levels of sales)

- The cursor is placed on the empty cell and the data table command is used. The range of the data table is requested (B23:E27) and the source of the variable being changed (from the input section - in this case, sales quantity, C3)

- The program will then re-compute the gross profit values at the different sales levels (using the same set of formulae as in the output/calculation section) and display them in E24 to E27.

The table shows that breakeven is somewhere between 6,000 and 10,000 units; and shows the impact of the increased fixed costs as sales (and thus production) quantities are increased

	A	B	C	D	E	F	G
1		XYZ LTD - DIVISION Q - GROSS PROFIT FORECAST - MONTH 1					
2	**INPUT SECTION**						
3	Sales	Quantity	10,000	Price (£)	20		
4	Closing stock	Quantity	2,000				
5	Production costs:						
6	Variable:	Per unit (£)	8				
7	Fixed:	Per month (£)	90,000	Increase (%)	15	Trigger quantity	20,000
8							
9	**OUTPUT SECTION**						
10		Units		£	£		
11	Sales	10,000			200,000		
12							
13	Variable production cost	12,000		96,000			
14	Closing stock	2,000		16,000			
15	Cost of sales				80,000		
16	Contribution				120,000		
17	Fixed production cost				90,000		
18	Gross profit				30,000		
19							
20	**DATA TABLE FOR SENSITIVITY ANALYSIS ON SALES QUANTITY**						
21					Gross profit		
22					£		
23					30,000		
24	Sales (units)	6,000			-18,000		
25		15,000			90,000		
26		20,000			136,500		
27		30,000			256,500		

9.4   Example two-way data table

The data table in the above example showed the impact on gross profit of changing values of one variable - sales quantity. A two-way data table will show the impacts of changing the values of two variables.

For example, suppose that the management of Division Q wanted to assess the effects of variability in both sales quantity and variable cost per unit. The two-way table at the bottom of the spreadsheet would appear as follows:

	A	B	C	D	E
20	**Two-way data table monitoring changes in gross profit for a range of**				
21	**changes in sales quantity and unit variable cost**				
22					
23	Variable cost per unit				
24			£7.50	£8	£9
25	Sales quantity	6,000	-15,000	-18,000	-24,000
26		10,000	35,000	30,000	20,000
27		15,000	97,500	90,000	75,000
28		20,000	146,500	136,500	116,500
29		30,000	271,500	256,500	226,500

9.5   Activity

Construct a data-table within your spreadsheet from paragraph 8.4 to see the effects of changes in selling price to £4 and £5.50. Check that you obtain profits of £NIL and £1,500.

10   SIMULATION USING RANDOM NUMBERS

10.1   Introduction

Simulation is a modelling technique based on probability distributions for each input variable. Usually a three-point probability estimate is used together with random numbers to identify the combinations of input variables which may occur.

10.2   Using random numbers

Random numbers are used to generate a number of combinations of input variables. Each combination is then used to produce an output value, and based upon these results, a probability distribution of those output values may be made.

10.3   Example

If the earlier example of PH Ltd is used as a basis it can be assumed that the selling price is fixed at £5.00 per unit. Volume and unit variable cost may be considered uncertain with the following percentages being representative of their likely values:

Volume		Unit variable cost	
900	20%	£1.80	15%
1,000	70%	£2.00	60%
1,050	10%	£2.10	25%

Random numbers would be assigned as follows:

Volume		Unit variable cost	
900	00 - 19	£1.80	00 - 14
1,000	20 - 89	£2.00	15 - 74
1,050	90 - 99	£2.10	75 - 99

Pairs of random numbers are then selected to represent volumes and unit variable costs. An extract from a random number table is given below:

03 47 43 73 86	36 96 47 36 61	46 98 63 71 62	33 26 16 80 45	60 11 14 10 95
97 74 24 67 62	42 81 14 57 20	42 53 32 37 32	27 07 36 07 51	24 51 79 89 73
16 76 62 27 66	56 50 26 71 07	32 90 79 78 53	13 55 38 58 59	88 97 54 14 10
12 56 85 99 26	96 96 68 27 31	05 03 72 93 15	57 12 10 14 21	88 26 49 81 76
55 59 56 35 64	38 54 82 46 22	31 62 43 09 90	06 18 44 32 53	23 83 01 30 30

Using the first row:

03 = volume of 900 units
47 = variable cost £2.00/unit
} contribution = 900 × (£5.00 − £2.00) = £2,700

43 = volume of 1,000 units
73 = variable cost £2.00/unit
} contribution = 1,000 × (£5.00 − £2.00) = £3,000

86 = volume of 1,000 units
36 = variable cost £2.00/unit
} contribution = 1,000 × (£5.00 − £2.00) = £3,000

96 = volume of 1,050 units
47 = variable cost of £2.00/unit
} contribution = 1,050 × (£5.00 − £2.00) = £3,150

36 = volume of 1,000 units
61 = variable cost of £2.00/unit
} contribution = 1,000 × (£5.00 − £2.00) = £3,000

The results can now be summarised:

Contribution	*No. of times*	*Probability*
£2,700	1	20%
£3,000	3	60%
£3,150	1	20%
	5	100%

The above example illustrates the method of the approach but clearly five scenarios is insufficient, and the example was simplified to just two variables. A computer model could consider the interaction of all of the variables many times and would produce more reliable results.

11   CHAPTER SUMMARY

This chapter commenced by considering the information processing cycle and how it is related to accounting systems. These systems tend to be used to record transactions and the second half of this chapter explained how spreadsheets and databases may be used for management accounting information.

12   SELF TEST QUESTIONS

12.1   What are the three stages of information processing? (1.1)

12.2   Explain 'batch processing'. (2.3)

12.3   Explain 'demand processing'. (2.4)

12.4   Explain 'on-line mode'. (2.6)

12.5   Explain the meaning of 'modules' or 'program suites' within the context of software packages. (3.2)

12.6   What is a spreadsheet? (6.2)

12.7   What is a database? (6.5)

12.8   Explain 'What If' analysis. (8.2)

12.9   What is a data-table? (9.2)

12.10   Explain the use of random numbers in modelling and simulation. (10.2)

13   EXAMINATION TYPE QUESTION

13.1   Computerised financial packages/risk and uncertainty

(a)   'Computerised financial planning packages have revolutionised the process of budget preparation.'

Describe the main features of such packages and give your views on the quotation.

(7 marks)

(b)   Describe some of the approaches that have been suggested for incorporating risk and uncertainty into cost-volume-profit analysis. **(10 marks)**

(Total: 17 marks)

14   ANSWER TO EXAMINATION TYPE QUESTION

14.1   Computerised financial packages/risk and uncertainty

(Tutorial notes:

(1)   The two parts of the question should be attempted independently; remember that a majority of the marks are allocated to part (b).

(2)   Part (a) has two distinct requirements:

(i)   describing the main features of computerised financial planning packages;

(ii)   **your views** on the quotation given in the question.

Your views on the quotation should concentrate on the word 'revolutionised' in the context of budget preparation; this will make for a more interesting answer.

(3)   Part (b) of the question is quite straightforward. Ensure that your answer covers sensitivity analysis, probability distributions and simulation.)

(a)   Computerised financial planning packages are mathematical statements of the relationships among all operating and financial activities, as well as other major internal and external factors that may affect decisions. These packages come in varying degrees of sophistication. The most rudimentary merely produce standard financial statements and supporting schedules from specific company data input. They are packages applicable to companies in general. At the other end of the package spectrum are special purpose-built models designed for the specific company in question; such models would include interactive capabilities, integrate detailed activities of all sub-units of an organisation and permit probabilistic analysis.

The most obvious application for computerised financial planning packages is in the preparation of budgets. The quotation states that the packages have 'revolutionised the process of budget preparation'. Whether they have revolutionised or merely 'helped' is a subjective argument, but nobody can deny that they have made a difference. The packages can make computations, based on data input such as product selling prices, variable cost, type of expense, etc, very quickly and produce a number of different statements from the database. The packages will also greatly assist in budget revisions and assessment of the effects (financial) resulting from the various courses of action that may be open to management. Statistical techniques such as sensitivity analysis may also be easily incorporated into the budget preparation.

Any management accountant will confirm that these packages have helped in tasks which are time-consuming when undertaken manually, but to say 'revolutionised' may undermine the prior and current abilities of the professional accountant.

(b)   **Sensitivity analysis**

This is undertaken to discover how sensitive the CVP analysis is to errors (or changes) in the values attributed to the parameters. This technique involves the systematic adjustment of the value of a variable to determine the effect that this has on the profit reported in the CVP analysis. Sensitivity analysis, however, has a major defect in that normally it is used to deal with changes in one variable at a time, whilst all the other variables remain unchanged. It is more difficult to determine the effect of simultaneously changing the values of two or more variables.

Simulation

The idea of simulating actual conditions is basic to most, if not all, analytical techniques, but often situations are encountered which are too complex to be represented by a single expression or set of equations, usually because their factors are subject to random variations in value and size. In these circumstances, simulation (or the Monte Carlo method) can be used. In this procedure the behaviour of each element relevant to the problem is observed, measured and converted into some form of probability distribution. Random numbers are allotted pro rata to the relative probability of the occurrence of each value in the data and the interaction of the elements is developed by taking each number (or combination of numbers) in turn from a chosen series in a random number table, each number indicating the occurrence of a certain value. Variations in conditions can be introduced into the situation and, with the time-condensing power of a computer, it is possible to produce indications of the results likely to be obtained if the 'real life' situation were similarly altered. This technique is very useful in CVP analysis where there is variability in supply and demand.

Normal probability distributions

This method allows the management accountant to calculate the probability of achieving the break-even point (or level of margin of safety or level of targeted profit). If the probabilities are assumed to be normally distributed, then the expected results can be computed. However, if there is more than one probabilistic variable, there may be problems with the arithmetic: the multiplication of the various normal variants is no easy task.

Discrete probability distributions

It may be unreasonable to make the assumptions of normal distribution to allow for continuous probabilities; a discrete probability approach may be more realistic. It is usual to have three discrete probabilities - optimistic, most likely, pessimistic - for each of the probabilistic variables. From this analysis the management accountant can estimate the likelihood of achieving the profit targets required by the company.

4 IMPACT OF THE ENVIRONMENT ON THE ACCOUNTING INFORMATION SYSTEMS

INTRODUCTION & LEARNING OBJECTIVES

When you have studied this chapter you should be able to do the following:

- Identify accounting information requirements for planning, control, and decision making.
- Distinguish different management styles.
- Identify the role of management accounting.
- Explain how to design a management accounting system.
- Distinguish different types of system.
- Illustrate the effects of human behaviour on systems.

1 APPLICATION OF CONTROL SYSTEMS TO MANAGEMENT

1.1 Planning and control

The tasks of management are traditionally seen as planning and control. The stages in the planning and control cycle have already been shown in a previous chapter, as follows:

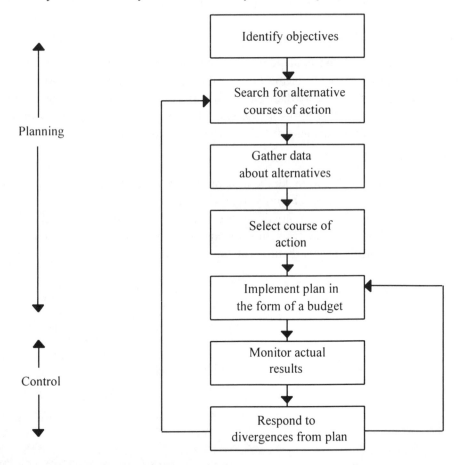

1.2 Criticisms of the planning and control model

The view of management planning and control put forward above has been criticised by several writers. For example, R N Anthony argues that, although it is possible to identify the different types of mental activity that are required for planning and control decisions, it is wrong to suggest that the activities are clearly separable in practice. All managers make both planning and control decisions; ie, a foreman who is unhappy with the production figures for his section may revise future forecasts (a planning decision) as well as taking action to motivate his team to perform better in future (a control decision). Where participation is used as a management style, planning and control decisions are bound to be inter-related.

Anthony identified three types of management activity:

(a)   strategic planning;

(b)   management control (or tactical planning);

(c)   operational control.

1.3   Strategic planning

Strategic planning involves making decisions about:

(a)   the objectives of the organisation;

(b)   changes in these objectives;

(c)   the resources used to attain the objectives;

(d)   policies governing:

    (i)   acquisition;

    (ii)   use;

    (iii)   disposition of these resources.

Strategic planning is usually, but not always, concerned with the long term. For example, a company specialising in production and sale of tobacco products may forecast a declining market for these products and may therefore decide to change its objectives to allow a progressive move into the leisure industry, which it considers to be expanding. Strategic decisions involve the formulation of the new objectives and deciding on the manner in which these new objectives will be achieved ie, by acquisition of companies which are already established in the industry, or by starting new businesses itself ('organic growth').

Although strategic planning is concerned with long term goals it often involves short term action. For example, the acquisition of a new company in the leisure industry is made in order to fulfil a long term objective but it requires short-term planning and control action, all of which is classified under the heading of strategic planning.

1.4   Management control and tactical planning

Definition   Management control is the process by which managers ensure that resources are obtained and used effectively and efficiently in the accomplishment of the organisation's objectives.

Effectively means that resources are used to achieve the desired ends. **Efficiently** means that the optimum (best possible) output is produced from the resources input to the system. Sometimes the word **effectual** is used. **Effectual** means both effective and efficient.

Decisions at the management control, or tactical, level are numerous. They include pricing decisions and other elements of the 'marketing mix', such as advertising, promotion and distribution decisions relating to purchases and suppliers, stock levels and other aspects of working capital management and fixed asset replacement decisions.

Decisions at this level are usually based on financial analysis, money being the common unit of measurement of resources. The control systems are performance reports relating to profit, cost or revenue centres. These reports are a summary of many different operations. The detailed control over each individual operation is exercised at the operational level, which is described below.

1.5   Operational control

Definition   Operational control is the process of ensuring that specific tasks are carried out effectively and efficiently.

As more tasks become automated, the human factor in operational control becomes less important. Many tasks are subject to **programmed control**, that is where the relationship between inputs and outputs is clearly specified. However, where processes are carried out by people, the human factor in operational control will always be important, as people need to be motivated to perform routine tasks to a high standard consistently.

1.6   The pyramid of management decision-making and control

The three levels of management activity described by Anthony can be illustrated by the following diagram:

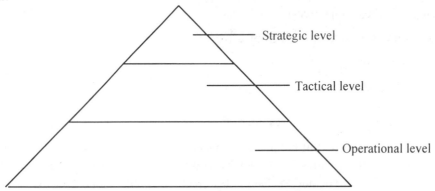

Note that the division into these three levels refers to **types of activity** and does not necessarily refer to divisions of duties between staff. For example, staff involved mainly in tactical level activities may also participate in strategic decisions and may also have certain routine operational level tasks of their own. All three levels involve both planning and control activities. However, at the strategic end, the emphasis is on planning whereas at the operational end it is on control. The diagram can thus be extended as follows:

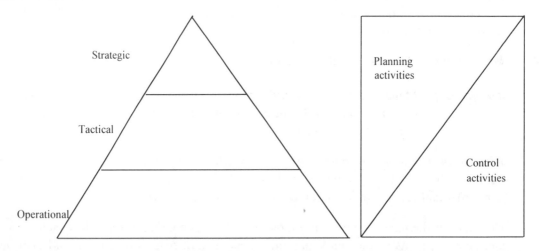

These concepts will be examined later to consider the information needs of management at each level.

1.7   Is management confined to planning and control?

The systems approach to management can sometimes overemphasise the activities of planning and control. In practice, as Mintzberg has shown, managers have many roles. Mintzberg summarises them under the headings of:

- Interpersonal (leadership, liaison, etc)
- Informational (receiving and giving information, formally and informally)
- Decisional (new projects, unusual situations, resource allocation, negotiation)

The working day for most managers is fragmented. Not all routine tasks can be delegated - in practice managers perform a great many of these themselves. Urgent tasks must be finished before time can be set aside for planning. Consequently planning is carried out on a day-to-day basis in the manager's free moments.

Further, most managers prefer to exchange information verbally. Lengthy reports produced by formal information systems may not be regarded as important as information gained from talking to colleagues.

Clearly most managers are far from the efficient processors of information which they are assumed to be by some designers of information systems. Whereas management training (eg, time management) can improve the effectiveness and efficiency of managers, designers of information systems have to allow for the reality of the manager's situation.

2   CONTROL AND ACCOUNTING INFORMATION SYSTEMS

2.1   The function of management

Beer (1959) described management as the profession of control. Certainly managerial work involves control and monitoring of junior employees to ensure some organisation purpose is achieved. Managers are responsible for all the aspects of control described earlier:

(a)   Setting objectives, and developing plans that are acceptable to other members of the organisation.

(b)   Monitoring activities to measure achievement against plan.

(c)   Taking corrective action where required.

It is also noteworthy that as a manager rises in the organisation, he becomes increasingly concerned with events external to the organisation, and with a longer time horizon. He also becomes increasingly dependent on formal information systems.

2.2   What managers actually do

A major study (Mintzberg, 1973) of the activity of senior managers indicates certain characteristics of their work:

(a)   A high level of activity.
(b)   Items for attention being processed quickly, usually in 5-10 minutes.
(c)   Oral communication dominates over written reports and letters.
(d)   Day structured around scheduled meetings.

The result of this hectic pace is a concentration on current urgent matters, rather than longer term issues. Formal information is only used when the manager needs to consider it for some current problem; rather, formal information is 'the backdrop against which action takes place' (Emmanuel and Otley, 1985). Mintzberg himself summarises his conclusion as follows:

'Managers prefer issues that are current, specific and ad hoc. As a result there is virtually no science in managerial work. The management scientist has done little to change this. He is unable to understand work that has never been adequately described and has poor access to a manager's information, most of which is never documented'.

This then is the environment in which the accounting information system must operate. It may well be, as Emmanuel and Otley suggest, that formal information is more relevant to long-term policy than day-to-day operating decisions.

2.3   Accounting information and management control

Anthony (1965) categorised managerial tasks into three groups:

(a)   Strategic planning - setting overall strategies and objectives ie, long-term.

(b)   Management control - monitoring activities and action to ensure effective use of resources ie, medium term.

(c)   Operational control - day-to-day execution of tasks ie, short-term.

These may be summarised as follows:

	Strategic planning	*Management control*	*Operational control*
Focus	One aspect at a time	Whole organisation	Single task
Persons involved	Top management, staff specialists	Top management, in-line managers	First line supervisors
Nature of information	Tailor made External Predictive	Integrated Mainly internal More historical	Tailor made Internal Real-time
Type of cost	Committed	Managed	Engineered
Time horizon	Years	Months	Days
Academic discipline	Economics	Social psychology	Physical science and technology

Thus management control serves an integrating function between long range strategic planning and day-to-day operational control. Accounting information becomes the major tool for achieving management control.

2.4   Use made of management accounting information

The management accounting information system is a structured formal information system, and concentrates its attention on the regular quantifiable parts of the management process. The analysis above indicates that these activities are only parts of the management process; informal information is at least as important. A study by Dew and Gee (1973) of 85 managers indicated the following use of budgets.

	No.
Full use	12
Limited use	35
No use	38
	—
Total	85

Thus the largest group made no use at all of the budgets, and only 12 made full use of the budgets.

A further study by Mintzberg (1975) revealed a significant difference in the perception of the purpose of cost information by senior and middle manager, respectively. Whilst senior managers saw its prime purpose as a control tool for managers, middle managers saw cost information as a measure of personal (ie, their) efficiency.

This led Mintzberg to the conclusion that four major factors reduced the effectiveness of formal information systems:

(a)   Too limited - weak on external information, ignores non-quantitative and non-economic information.

(b)   Too aggregated - data is summarised and aggregated to the point where essential detail is often missing.

(c)   Too late - often the information arrives too late to be useful.

(d)   Unreliable - often numbers are put in to represent information that is essentially qualitative.

Given these problems, Mintzberg makes certain recommendations about formal information:

(a)   Broad based - independent of the computer (remember this was written in 1975 when computer output used to be large quantities of badly designed output; this is hardly a realistic recommendation today).

(b)   Filtering systems - these should be more sophisticated than merely aggregating data, so as to leave in important detail and remove irrelevant detail.

(c)   Channels of information should be capable of in-depth searching, and should encourage alternative, conflicting sources of information.

These conclusions on the design of accounting information systems are best summarised by Emmanuel and Otley:

'(The designer) must be aware of the organisational and environmental situation in which he is designing the information system, and its inter-relationships with other mechanisms of integration and control. He must also be responsive to the political process in which accounting information plays a role, for the accounting system will inevitably be moulded by such pressures'.

3   INFORMATION AND ORGANISATIONS

3.1   Information for management

Information should be provided to managers at all levels in order to assist them with planning and controlling the activities for which they are responsible. Information will be gathered from all relevant sources (internal and external) in order to help managers make timely and effective decisions.

It is very difficult to generalise further on the principles of presenting information to managers. There are many influencing factors, including:

(a)   The objectives of the organisation.

(b)   The size and diversity of its operations.

(c)   Management structure.

(d)   Management style eg,

(i)   Centralised or decentralised
(ii)   Authoritarian or participative

(e)   The types of decisions which are made.

(f)   The degree to which the organisation is an open system and interacts with its environment.

It is useful to start by considering the information needs of managers at different levels: the strategic, tactical and operational levels assumed in the 'Anthony' triangle.

3.2   Management structure

This classification applies to information used internally (as opposed to that provided by the organisation for outside parties).

(a)   **Strategic information**
This is mainly used by directors and senior managers to plan the organisation's overall objectives and strategy and to measure whether these are being achieved. Examples of this information include:

(i)   profitability of main business segments
(ii)   prospects for present and potential markets

        (iii)   investment appraisal studies

        (iv)   cash requirements

        (v)   availability and prospects for raising long term funds, etc.

Strategic information is, in short, used for strategic planning and is prepared irregularly, when required. Decision making tends to be unstructured (non-programmable).

(b)   Tactical information

This is used by managers at all levels, but mainly at the middle level for tactical planning and management control activities, such as pricing, purchasing, distribution and stocking.

Examples of information of this type include:

        (i)   sales analysis

        (ii)   stock levels

        (iii)   productivity measures

        (iv)   current purchasing requirements

        (v)   budgetary control and variance reports

        (vi)   labour turnover statistics.

Tactical information is prepared regularly (eg, weekly or monthly). Decision making is semi-structured, relying quite heavily on the skills of managers.

(c)   Operational information

This is used mainly by managers on the operational level such as foremen and section heads who have to ensure that routine tasks are properly planned and controlled, although, as described earlier, all managers have some operational tasks.

Examples of this information include:

        (i)   listings of debtors and creditors

        (ii)   payroll details

        (iii)   raw materials requirements and usage

        (iv)   listings of customer complaints

        (v)   machine output statistics

        (vi)   delivery schedules.

Operational decisions are highly structured and usually repetitive (ie, 'programmable'). Information is presented very regularly: weekly, daily, hourly or even minute by minute.

3.3   Planning, control and operating information

This is an alternative way of classifying information, but it can be linked to the methods used in the last section.

(a)   Planning information

This is information needed to choose between alternative courses of action and to create plans. It is essentially forward looking, consisting of forecasts and estimates, including

        (i)   demand forecasts

        (ii)   economic forecasts (eg, inflation, interest rates)

        (iii)   cost predictions

        (iv)   estimates of competitor's behaviour.

All such predictions are characterised by uncertainty. A key element in choosing between alternatives and making plans is finding the right balance between the likely benefits of a course of action and the risk involved.

Planning information is not necessarily limited by the organisational structure. Because sub-systems interact, the plans of one department are bound to affect those of others.

(b)   **Control information**

This compares actual past results against targets. Examples are:

(i)   cost variance reports
(ii)   sales variance reports
(iii)   production efficiency reports
(iv)   working capital reports.

This information usually follows the organisation structure.

Planning and control information are usefully summarised in the following table:

	Planning information	*Control information*
Boundary	Not limited by organisation structure	Follows organisation structure
Direction	Estimates of the future	Shows past results compared with targets
Time scale	Varies from short to long	Generally short
Detail	No more than is reasonable for estimation	More accurate measurement
Uncertainty	Much	Little

(c)   **Operating information**

This is the information needed to carry out day-to-day operations. It includes:

(i)   cash listings
(ii)   purchase order listings
(iii)   daily delivery schedules
(iv)   job schedules, etc.

Operating information is eventually summarised and incorporated into reports which then become control information.

(d)   **Passive background information**

Information statistics produce regular summary reports which are put on file until they are needed. This is referred to as passive background information. Examples include:

(i)   total amounts paid to suppliers
(ii)   various types of customer analysis
(iii)   numbers of employees

and many other reports which are produced as a by-product of producing control information. This information is kept on file until it is needed, usually to assist in the planning process.

As stated earlier, the cost of holding this information on computer systems has fallen dramatically over the last twenty years, but it should only be held if it can be accessed easily.

3.4   The effect of computers on information systems

Computers have revolutionised information systems for the following reasons:

Speed - Computers are ideal for dealing with repetitive processes. The limiting factors, for example, in processing a payroll by computer are not the speed of calculation by the computer, but the speed with which data can be input and the speed of the printer at the output.

Accuracy - In general, computers do not suffer from errors, or lapses of concentration but process data perfectly. Any mistakes which computers make nowadays are not caused by electronic error, but by human error, for example at the input stage, or in designing and programming software.

Volume - Not only do computers work fast, but they do not need to rest. They can work twenty four hour days when required. They are therefore able to handle vast volumes of data.

Complexity - Once subsystems are computerised they can generally function more reliably than human beings. This makes it easier to integrate various subsystems. Computers are therefore able to handle complex information systems efficiently. However, one of the problems with this is that when the computer does fail, there is often a major breakdown in the system, with many personnel unable to perform their work functions.

Cost - All the above advantages mean that computers have become highly cost-effective providers of information. The process of substituting computers for human beings has revolutionised information-oriented industries such as accountancy, banking and insurance and this process is continuing.

Presentation - More recently, emphasis has been placed on displaying information in as 'user-friendly' a way as possible. Modern packages containing sophisticated word processors, spreadsheets and graphics combined with the development of the laser printer now enable accountants to present their most boring reports in new and exciting ways!

Judgement - It is necessary, however, to remember the advantages which human beings have as providers of information. Chief amongst these is judgement of reasonableness. Human beings can usually see when an item of information looks unreasonable. Although it is possible to program limited reasonableness tests into computer systems, it is still very difficult to program judgement. The computer remains a highly-trained idiot, which is particularly apparent when a programming error is made or it is subject to a computer virus.

3.5   Activity

Why does a computer system process information better than a manual system?

3.6   Activity solution

The advantages of computers in information processing include:

- processing information more quickly;
- handling bigger volumes of processing;
- undertaking complex operations;
- processing information more reliably ie, with less chance of errors and mistakes;
- processing information at less cost than a manual system;
- improving the scope and quality of management information.

3.7   Qualities of information

Just as raw materials can be turned into a good product or a sub-standard one, so raw data can be processed into good or bad information. Good information is useful to the recipient, can be relied upon and helps in the decision-making process.

Basically, information for control purposes must be:

(a)   the right information, in terms of it being complete, relevant, understandable, accurate and significant;

(b)   at the right time;

(c)   delivered to the right person via an appropriate channel;

(d)   for the right cost.

It is also worth noting that the greater the degree of accuracy required, the greater the cost in producing it - and the longer the delay in presenting it.

3.8   The right information

(a)   **Completeness of information**

The reliability of information increases with its completeness. However, the appropriate level of completeness varies enormously, according to the type of information. For example, it is a fundamental principle of financial accounting that all the transactions should be included in the books. The law would be broken if transactions were deliberately left out. In the same way personnel records should contain details of all employees.

However, suppose a buyer has to make a decision about purchasing commonly available raw materials. In order to obtain the best price he obtains quotes from suppliers. Does he have to ask for quotes from all the suppliers? Clearly not, because to do so might delay the purchase, and incur unnecessary costs. He would therefore obtain quotes from a representative sample. This is an example of the cost of information influencing completeness. Thus, rather than arguing that all information must be absolutely complete, we are left with the concept that information should be **complete enough for its purpose**.

(b)   **Relevance of information**

Information must be relevant to the problem under consideration. It is often the case that reports contain irrelevant sections which cloud the understanding and can irritate the user searching to find what is required. In the same way, financial analyses can sometimes confuse the reader by presenting a mixture of relevant and irrelevant information, or information with unnecessary detail. Care must be taken with management accounts to present the costs and revenues which are relevant to a particular decision or course of action. For example, 'sunk costs' are irrelevant when making decisions about the future and apportioning cost between departments is irrelevant when seeking to assign responsibility for the control of those costs.

(c)   **Understandability of information**

Information which is easy to understand is more likely to produce action. Because managers are busy they will resent having to spend unnecessary time interpreting badly presented reports. Managers can, however, often assist their own cause by specifying the format, layout and style of presentation of the information they need. Modern computer packages contain tables, graphics and charts all of which can assist in speeding up and improving the understanding process. Information must be understandable by the person receiving it. It is pointless presenting it in a way that assumes knowledge and abilities that the recipient could not be expected to have.

(d)   **Accuracy**

Information should be sufficiently accurate for its intended purpose and the decision-maker should be able to rely on the information. However, there is often some trade-off in terms of cost and it is possible to supply information in a much more accurate form than is required. The key question is whether increased accuracy will improve the quality of the user's decision making. For example, in deciding whether to make a component in-house or buy the equivalent part from an outside supplier, we need an estimate of the internal production cost of making the component, which we may estimate by examining the costs of producing test samples. The required accuracy of these estimates depends on how close the internal production cost appears to be to the external buying cost. If the two costs are very similar, a higher level of accuracy in the measurement of the internal production cost is warranted, but if the internal cost is clearly much cheaper, the accuracy of the estimate is less important.

In addition to accuracy with which information is measured, there is the further question of the accuracy to which it is reported. For example, data in the accounting system is collected with accuracy to the nearest penny. For some purposes this is necessary: for example, paying suppliers and employees and receiving cash from debtors. However, in reports given to cost centre managers, the figures are usually rounded to an acceptable level of accuracy (say to the nearest £100 or £1,000), which makes the information easier to assimilate. In the same way top management, who are examining summary financial reports of the whole organisation, may be satisfied with results reported correct to the nearest £100,000 or million pounds.

(e)   **Significance**

Part of the art of keeping information simple and understandable is to highlight the significant factors, screening out any facts which are not important enough to affect the decision-making process. Information has no value if it is already known by the user: we say that information must have a 'surprise' value. This significant information is both new and important for the decision making process.

For example, when reporting production or financial figures to managers it is often useful to operate a system of exception reporting. Facts which simply tell the manager that things are going according to plan need not be reported at all. The system concentrates on significant deviations from plan, in other words variances. This principle is even more important when a computer report summarises the work it is processing. The information that two invoices have been rejected is of more importance than the fact that 1,000 invoices have been processed without problem.

3.9   Timeliness

Information can only be of use if it is received in time to influence the decision-making process. Occasionally this means a compromise in terms of completeness. Routine information should be processed at time intervals which are relevant to the process involved. For example, information on the temperature of a chemical process may be reported every day, while routine production statistics and management accounts are produced monthly. Financial accounting reports to shareholders are produced quarterly or less frequently. It is pointless producing information more frequently than it is used. On the other hand, once information is available, there should be the minimum possible delay in reporting it.

3.10   Communication to the right person

Information must be communicated to the person who has to take action. In most cases, this causes no problems. For example, monthly reports on the production efficiency of a department should be reported to the manager responsible for the operations of the department. In doing this care must be taken to distinguish between those elements of production which are directly controllable by the manager and those which are not.

In some cases, however, the person who is best able to understand the information is not always the person who has authority for actioning change. For example, inefficient production may be caused by a machine which has outlived its usefulness and breaks down frequently. If the departmental manager has no authority for replacing the machine, the information may be 'sat on' because it refers to a situation which is outside the manager's control. If the information is not passed on to the superior in a way which is readily understandable, it may be that appropriate action is not taken.

In the same way, if a report on the failings of the machine is given only to the superior and not to the departmental manager, the superior may not understand the seriousness of the situation and may simply file the report without consulting the subordinate. An improvement on this situation would be to give a detailed report to the department manager and a summary report to the superior.

However, this situation, which is caused by organisation structure and division of responsibilities, can never be fully rectified by a formal information system. A necessary pre-requisite for prompt action is good communication between the superior and the subordinate using a combination of formal and informal channels.

4   MANAGEMENT ACCOUNTING SYSTEMS

4.1   Introduction

Management accounting systems are part of the management information system which assist managers in decision making and control.

4.2   Designing the system

When designing a management accounting system there are a number of principles which should be followed:

(a)   there should be a set of formalised procedures;

(b)   designed to provide appropriate information to managers at all levels;

(c)   the information should be obtained from both internal and external sources; and

(d)   should enable managers to make timely and effective decisions for planning and controlling the organisation.

The system should collect routine information and compare it with targets in the form of budgets and standard costs. Non-routine information should also be processed so as to provide information for decision making.

When the requirements have been identified the system designer should consider the environment in which the business operates and the technology which is available to collect and process the data.

4.3   Management accounting and control

An important aspect of management accounting is in providing control information for managers. This is achieved by comparing actual and target performance, as shown by the following diagram:

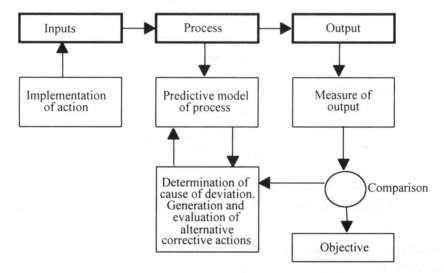

4.4   Management accounting and contingent factors

A contingent factor is any factor which may affect the management accounting system, it may be internal or external. Examples include the style of management, the business environment and the availability of technology.

4.5   Management accounting and human behaviour

People have their own objectives and where they are part of the process of providing information they may manipulate it or withhold it to increase their own power. To overcome this there must be a culture which avoids the need for individuals to hold power, thus encouraging behaviour which is consistent with organisational objectives.

5   CONTROL SYSTEMS

In order to understand this section it is useful to start with an example of a control system which is in everyday use. General concepts can then be abstracted from this example, developed and applied to business situations.

5.1   Thermostat example

All central heating systems contain thermostats to regulate the temperature of the rooms they are heating. The user sets the thermostat to the required temperature on the dial. There is a thermometer in the system which measures the temperature of the rooms. The room temperature is continually compared with the preset temperature on the thermostat dial. If room temperature is above the dial temperature, the power (eg, gas) is switched off. When room temperature falls below the dial temperature, the power is switched on. This system can be represented diagrammatically as follows:

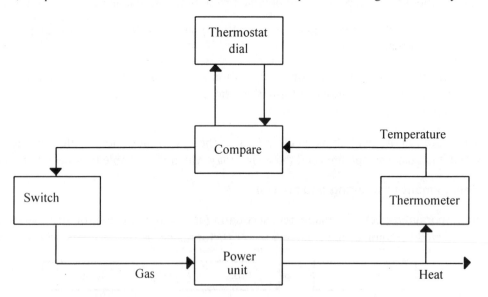

5.2   General terms for elements of a control system

The basic gas-burning system is:

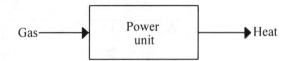

The thermostat system introduces a **controller** which is made up of four elements, a pre-set temperature on the dial, a thermostat, a comparison unit and a switch. The general terms for the elements of a controller are:

(a)   **Standard:** This is what the system is aiming for. In the thermostat system it is the pre-set temperature.

(b)   **Sensor:** (or detector). This measures the output of the system. In the thermostat system it is the thermometer.

(c)   **Comparator:** This compares the information from the standard and the sensor.

(d)   **Effector:** (or activator). This initiates the control action. In the thermostat system it is the switch.

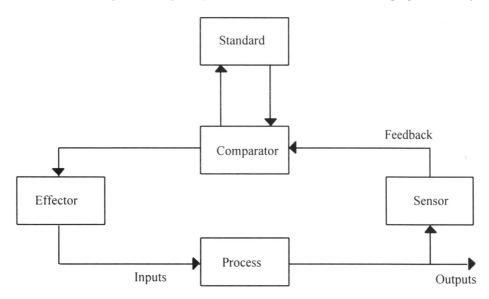

The general term for the information which is taken from the system output and used to adjust the system is **feedback.** In the thermostat example the feedback is the actual room temperature

5.3   Application to an accounting system - budgetary control

In a budgetary control system the financial performance of a department is compared with the budget. Action is then taken to improve the department's performance if possible. The elements of the control system are:

(a)   **standard:** the budget (eg, standard costs);

(b)   **sensor:** the costing system, which records actual costs;

(c)   **feedback:** the actual results for the period, collected by the costing system;

(d)   **comparator:** the 'performance report' for the department, comparing actual with budget (eg, variance analysis);

(e)   **effector:** the manager of the department, in consultation with others, takes action to minimise future adverse variances and to exploit opportunities resulting from favourable variances.

The opportunity may also be taken to adjust the standard (ie, the budget) if it is seen to be too easy or too difficult to achieve.

A number of complications make this budgetary control system more difficult than it appears at first sight:

(a)   the impact of the environment on the system has not been shown ie, prices of raw materials may rise uncontrollably or interest rates may increase;

(b)   differences between actual and budgeted results may not be controllable directly by the departmental manager ie, rises in certain input costs may be caused by another department;

(c)   the accounting system cannot measure all the output of the department, hence feedback may be incomplete ie, an investment for longer term profits may have been made at the expense of short-term cost control.

A more complete diagram of the control system would be as follows:

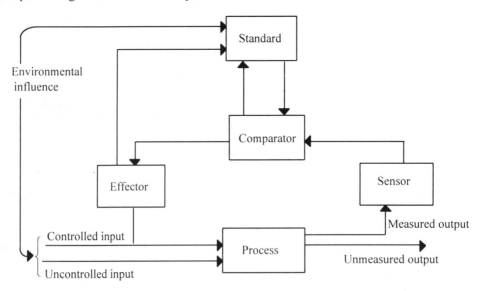

5.4   Open and closed loop systems

The systems described above, and any systems involving feedback are called **closed loop** systems. Associated terms are **feedback loop** and **control cycle**.

Control systems which do not involve feeding back output information are called **open loop** systems. Control is exercised regardless of output.

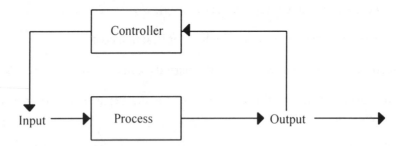

Closed loop system

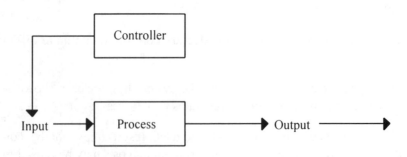

Open loop system

The term **open loop** implies there is a break in the feedback loop. This may arise either because feedback is not produced or because it is not used. For example, in some accounting systems useful cost information is collected but it is 'not reported' to the right people. In other systems the report is given to the right person but it is not read. Both would be examples of open loop systems.

5.5   Feedback

[Definition]   Feedback makes the difference between open and closed loop systems. Feedback can be defined as:

"modification or control of a process or system by its results or effects, by measuring differences between desired and actual results. Feedback is an element in a feedback system and forms the link between planning and control."

5.6   Double loop feedback

Double loop feedback, or higher level feedback, is when information is transmitted to a higher level in the system. It indicates differences between actual and planned results allowing for control adjustments to be made to the plan itself. Double loop feedback gathers information from both the system output and the environment.

The production system of a firm seen as a double loop feedback control system

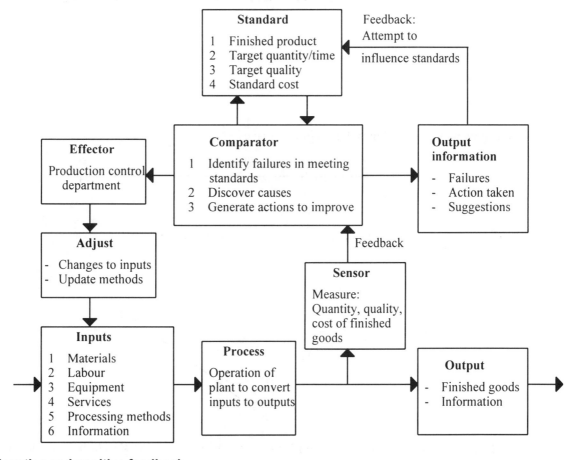

5.7   Negative and positive feedback

Negative feedback is information which shows that the system is deviating from its planned course in a way which is detrimental to its operation. Action is needed to return the system to its original course.

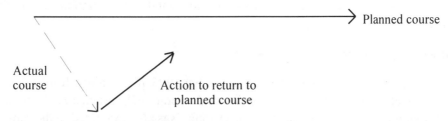

The crash barriers on a motorway provide a graphic example of the action of negative feedback. Most routine management accounting information is used to create negative feedback.

Positive feedback results in deviations from the plan being continued or increased. Sometimes this can be detrimental, leading to a 'vicious circle'. For instance, if sales prices are increased to make up for a shortfall in the sales budget, the result may be a lower sales volume, resulting in a lower sales value and a further attempt to increase sales prices. More often, however, positive feedback results from favourable variances. If sales beat budget, for example, action may be taken to continue this trend.

5.8   Control delay

For feedback to be effective, it is necessary for the information to be reported quickly and for corrective action to be taken promptly. For example, if an inspection shows that faulty products are being made by a particular machine, the information needs to be reported to the maintenance department immediately and action needs to be swift.

The diagram below shows the proper receipt, and action upon, the feedback in a system at the correct time (X):

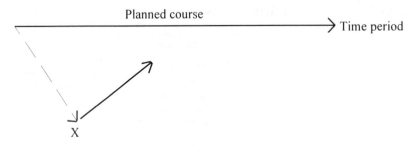

The following diagram shows delays in two places:

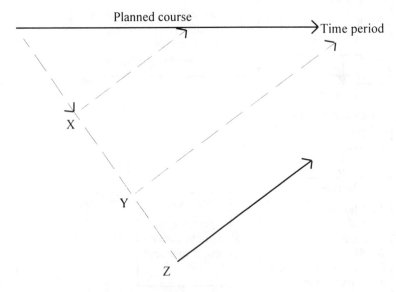

X is the point at which feedback should have been given, and action should have been taken. Y is the point at which feedback was actually given and Z the point at which action was taken. XY represents the reporting delay and YZ the action delay.

It is a general principle of management accounting reports that they should be produced promptly and in a form which is easy for the user to understand. Information which does not satisfy these requirements is of limited use.

5.9   Past exam questions

Questions in June 1994, June 1995 and December 1995 all examined feedback control in the context of variance analysis - in particular, planning and operational variance analysis, covered in Chapter 21. Feedforward control, covered next in this chapter, was also examined in the same context.

Once you have studied the mechanics of this topic, you should refer back to this section to see how such an analysis will help in both types of control.

5.10   Feedforward control

Feedback control measures deviation of **actual (historic) data** from control (expected/desired) data. These deviations are analysed as to their cause and action taken where possible to put the system back on course (if deviations are detrimental).

Feedforward control is anticipatory - it measures the deviation of **predicted future results** from the desired future results ie checking where we are likely to be versus where we want to be. Causes of deviations are analysed and action taken where possible to minimise their impact.

For example, in a target costing exercise, a particular required rate of return will be required over the life of a proposed product initiative. If the selling price and demand are assumed to be held constant, a feedforward control exercise may be to ascertain by how much and in what way the product unit cost would have to be reduced from current estimates if the target return is to be achieved.

The information used to predict future results may to some extent arise as a result of the analysis carried out in the feedback control system.

For example, the planning and operational variance analysis (covered in Chapter 21) involves the use of "ex-post" standards - standards that have been revised in hindsight, once the actual operating and external environment of the period under review are known. Their identification allows traditional variances to be split between amounts caused by inappropriate standard setting (planning variances) and amounts that can fairly be attributed to operations.

The feedback control will then focus on the operational variances, identifying the extent to which these are controllable and thus can be eliminated in future by taking suitable action.

Feedforward control can be aided by the use of the "ex-post" standards as a basis for predicting future results.

6   CHAPTER SUMMARY

This chapter has explained the information requirements for planning, control and decision making. These requirements were then considered in the context of management accounting systems.

7   SELF TEST QUESTIONS

7.1   Identify the stages of the planning and control cycle. (1.1)

7.2   What is strategic planning? (1.3)

7.3   Define operational control. (1.5)

7.4   What are the factors which influence the presentation of information to managers? (3.1)

7.5   Distinguish between strategic, tactical and operational information. (3.2)

7.6   Distinguish between planning and control information. (3.3)

7.7   Identify the features of the 'right information'. (3.8)

7.8   What principles should be followed when designing a management accounting system? (4.2)

7.9   Distinguish between open and closed loop systems. (5.4)

7.10   Distinguish between negative and positive feedback. (5.7)

7.11   Explain feedforward control. (5.10)

5 MODERN DEVELOPMENTS IN INDUSTRY AND COMMERCE AND THE ACCOUNTING RESPONSE

INTRODUCTION & LEARNING OBJECTIVES

When you have studied this chapter you should be able to do the following:

- Explain the various techniques which collectively are referred to as world class manufacturing.
- Explain how accounting systems have been modernised to reflect the changes in the working environment.

1 WORLD CLASS MANUFACTURING

There is no official definition of 'world class manufacturing'. The first allusions appear in Johnson and Kaplan's 'Relevance Lost' under the heading 'The New Global Competition'. The first characteristic they identify is a multi-national (or at the very least a multi million pound/dollar organisation) that has adopted total quality control. It is in this context they allude to companies like Toyota but also Asea-Brown Boveri (Sweden/Switzerland) and a number of leading German companies with multinational markets such as BMW. These companies strive to eliminate defects with its resultant impact upon reduced inventory, rejects, rework, waste, scrap, and warranty expense. To achieve such targets, greater consideration had to be given to the manufacture and operation of the product, not just its performance.

World class companies regard the world as their market. In the West, many firms had either tied markets, or operated in a virtual closed system oligopoly. Such a system pervaded in the US automobile market. The classic American gas-guzzler was a model of inefficient manufacturing. However, the faults in Ford were repeated in GM and Chrysler, so there was no real problem. However, when the Japanese began to make inroads into the American market, the quality of the product was a prime selling point. Whatever the jokes about Friday afternoon cars and the inherent poor quality, this did not happen in a Japanese car.

Other features of world class manufacturing companies are alluded to in Bromwich and Bhimani. World class companies invest in R&D where appropriate, they are highly capital intensive and hence highly productive, and have delayered their corporate bureaucracies. Such companies also have a diversity of products, albeit from standard parts and a flexible manufacturing system, high quality, better delivery and aim to satisfy customers at a global level.

This is well seen in the German "Mittelsand" (medium sized) companies. All satisfy their customers through a combination of customer-contact, customer training and extensive rapid response customer service. They are highly capital intensive, highly reliant on CAD/CAM technology and sell over half their production outside Germany. There is also an obsession for staying ahead of the competition through continual improvement.

Total quality management

Definition TQM is defined as "the continuous improvement in quality, productivity and effectiveness obtained by establishing management responsibility for processes as well as outputs. In this every process has an identified process owner and every person in an entity operates within a process and contributes to its improvement."

It is apparent from this rather lengthy definition that it goes beyond the isolated notions of statistical quality control into the whole operating process. This means designing in quality manufacturing procedures possibly through the use of CAD/CAM, training all personnel involved with the product/service, continually maintaining equipment to ensure that standards remain up to specification and working with suppliers to eliminate defects. The latter may well involve the use of JIT. It is worth adding that TQM is expected to cross all the company's functional activities, even the accounting function.

2   THE MODERN BUSINESS ENVIRONMENT

2.1   The development of the modern factory

The historical trend in manufacturing progress in the western industrial world was for greater automation and greater economies of scale. The great emphasis in a world of full employment and militant workers was to increase output through more mechanisation. Now, however, faced with intense competition, the emphasis has changed. The successful manufacturer will have to compete by responding rapidly to changing market conditions, tailoring products to meet different tastes and quickly introduce new and innovative products. All this has to be accomplished at much reduced costs in a very much more competitive market place.

One possible solution to the problem is the use of **computer integrated manufacturing (CIM)**. This is defined in Bromwich and Bhimani as "the use of computers and other advanced manufacturing techniques to monitor and perform manufacturing tasks." It enables a firm to link all its functions (both offices and shopfloor) to a system of total automation using computers. As a result, firms will be able to manufacture one-of-a-kind products in small batches for specific customers at short notice. This will replace the much criticised mass production of often defective, unsaleable standard items with a job-shop production of high quality unique items. This approach will reduce processing time, cut finished goods inventory, reduce direct labour costs and speed up response times.

2.2   CAD, CAE and CAM

The automated factory has to be capable of performing various functions with the aid of computers including product design, engineering and manufacturing.

(a)   **Computer Aided Design (CAD)** is defined as "computer based technology allowing interactive design and testing of a manufacturing component on a visual display terminal."

Designers can move pieces of a design around their drawings and manipulate them to see how the shapes change from various angles on their CAD terminals. Such systems are more convenient and economical, especially now that they are run on microcomputer networks. Although there is an initial high cost, the benefits are quickly realised. At Chrysler, a network of over 500 design workstations has reduced the time taken to generate engineering drawings from three months in the 1950s to 15 minutes today.

(b)   **Computer Aided Engineering (CAE)** enables designers to test whether their design can be manufactured on the available machines and ascertain the cost. This has eliminated much of the effort hitherto carried out by production engineers.

Once the CAE system has verified the feasibility of a new design, the necessary information for manufacture can be transmitted to a computer aided manufacturing system (CAM).

(c)   A **CAM system** uses "computer-based technology to permit the programming and control of production equipment in the manufacturing task." Such a system cuts the time lag between design and manufacturing, and the time taken setting and retooling machines for a new product.

2.3   Flexible manufacturing system (FMS)

This is "an integrated production system which is computer controlled to produce a family of parts in a flexible manner." (Bromwich & Bhimani)

Lee (**Managerial Accounting Changes for the 1990s**) describes FMS as "a bundle of machines that can be reprogrammed to switch from one production run to another". It consists of a cluster of machine tools and a system of conveyor belts that shuttle the work piece from tool to tool in a similar fashion to the traditional transfer line used in mass (large batch) production. Thus the benefits lie in being able to switch quickly from making one product to another.

As the Bromwich & Bhimani definition suggested, the major strength of an FMS system is its ability to manufacture not just a family of parts, but a family of products. By using this system, General Electric has been able to produce a range of diesel engines that are of substantially different sizes on the same automated production line, without substantially retooling and time consuming start ups.

Dilts and Russell (**Accounting for the Factory of the Future 1985**) have identified the following benefits:

• More variety of products as compared to conventional automation without the low rate of capacity utilisation of a typical job shop system.

• Better product quality thanks to accuracy and repeatability of the production process.

• Shorter machine setup times for new production runs which results in reduced lead times to meet customer demands. This, in turn, decreases work-in-progress inventories and plant space.

• Reduced labour costs and the capital costs of human environmental protection. This offers a stability in production even with machine breakdown, because of computer scheduling, which also allows instant responses to changes in demand.

There are risks with implementation. These are:

• FMS may lead to resistance from the labour force who may fear for their jobs.

• There must be an innovative approach to justifying the capital investment since it is likely that conventional appraisal techniques may not yield positive results.

• There may be a lack of qualified engineers and other management systems to support FMS.

3   MATERIALS REQUIREMENTS PLANNING (MRP)

3.1   Introduction

Definition   MRP is a system which maximises the efficiency in the timing of raw material orders through to the manufacture and assembly of the final product. (Bromwich & Bhimani).

MRP was first introduced by IBM in 1970 and essentially substitutes excessive inventories for better information systems. MRP schedules the production of jobs through the factory and eliminates the excessive WIP inventory levels required to compensate for job-scheduling problems that arise in decoupled cost or operation centres. MRP releases works orders for parts based upon a master production schedule and the current number and location of parts within the plant.

If there is an order for 100 units of a product, it may be that the economic lot size indicates that 500 should be produced. A Bill of Materials (a specification of the materials and parts required to make the product) is programmed into the computer. The computer will record the number of inventory components required along with time standards for moving, any waiting, setting up and running. This information allows production to be time phased so that the final assembly can begin with all the required components at the ready. The key factor in MRP is that it is demand dependent. Finished products are assembled to order from families of standard components. This is in contrast to traditional systems where components are ordered on the EOQ basis remote from the pattern of final product demand.

3.2   MRPII

MRPII (also written MRP 2) adds the MRP schedule into a capacity planning system and then builds the information into a production schedule. It is also seen as a link between strategic planning and manufacturing control. The sequence of events is as follows:

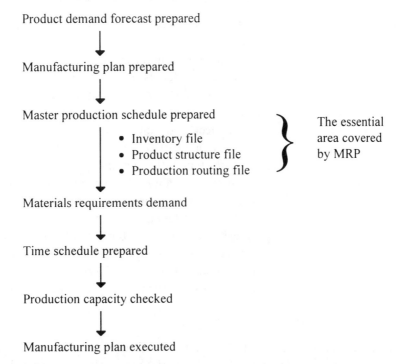

The student will readily see that MRPII forms a sequence of events that start with the product demand forecast that is prepared by marketing and approved by management. From that document, a manufacturing, plan is developed based upon inputs from purchasing and production. Adjustments may be necessary to allow for production rates, possible inventory levels in seasonal trades and the size of the workforce. The manufacturing plan leads into a detailed master production schedule which is akin to the original philosophy of MRP already outlined.

If correctly applied, MRPII provides a common data base for the different functional units such as manufacturing, purchasing and finance within a firm.

The student should be aware that MRP has not been an unbridled success over the years. While it is beyond the scope of the syllabus to academically discuss the problems encountered, you should be aware that reports of MRP failures were presented by Harrison (1990), Archer 1991 and Maskell (1993), and advice on how to make it work effectively and painlessly was given by both Barekat (1991) and Barrat (1990).

4   SYNCHRONOUS MANAGEMENT/MANUFACTURING

4.1   Introduction

The profitability of the modern organisation is dependent on a number of factors, not least of which is the rate at which sales are made. Other factors include the reduction of costs and maximisation of efficiency.

Management must identify what is referred to as 'the bottleneck factor'. This is the factor of production which limits the organisation's ability to increase the rate at which sales are achieved. You should recall that this is similar in principle to the limiting factor used in contribution analysis as part of short-term decision making.

The combination of management policies and practices to improve efficiency and identify and alleviate the bottleneck factor are collectively referred to as synchronous management and manufacturing practices.

4.2 Optimised production technology and synchronous manufacturing

Optimised Production Technology (OPT) has developed out of MRP systems. It is both a technique, and in its diminutive form of OPT, a computer software package. Although the initials are used interchangeably, the emphasis in this section is upon the technique. Like its precursor, MRP, OPT requires detailed information about inventory levels, product structures, routings and the set-up and operation timing for each and every procedure within each product. However, in stark contrast to MRP, the technique actively seeks to identify what prevents output and hence productivity from being higher by distinguishing between bottleneck and non-bottleneck resources. A bottleneck might be a machine whose capacity limits the throughput of the whole production process. It might be a key department with highly specialist skills that holds up the process. To avoid large build-ups of inventory, the non-bottleneck areas should be balanced to produce what the bottleneck can absorb in the short term. Thus, if the bottleneck can only absorb 60% of the output of the non-bottleneck areas, then the output should be scaled down to that level, since any excess over that level is only going to increase the piles of work-in-progress inventory standing about. It has also been suggested that overhead should be absorbed on the basis of throughput based upon the duration of production from the initial input of raw materials and components to the delivery of the finished products. By adopting this approach, management can see how costs can be reduced by cutting the throughput time.

4.3 Synchronous manufacturing

This is a combination of MRP and OPT and JIT and quality. The term was coined in 1984, as an attempt to widen the perceived limited scope of OPT. The pioneer behind both techniques is a mathematician, Eli Goldratt, famed for his book 'Goal'. He also prefers the term 'theory of constraints'.

[Definition]   Umble and Srikanth (1990) have defined synchronous manufacturing as:

> "... an all-encompassing manufacturing management philosophy that includes a consistent set of principles, procedures and techniques where every action is evaluated in terms of the common goal of the organisation."

The use of the term 'philosophy' is deliberate. OPT is perceived as narrow and very technique based. The use of the term 'Optimised' implied that a theoretical optimum existed and could be achieved. While such a goal might be possible, it implies that a level can be achieved where one can be satisfied, content or even complacent. Such a theoretical level is conceptually contrary to the notions of continuous improvement. Equally, the terms 'Production' and 'Technology' were perceived as failing to encompass the total range of constraints and challenges faced by the firm in trying to achieve its objectives. Markets, logistics, managerial ability, cultural and behavioural problems can all place constraints upon production capacity.

In widening the understanding of terms, it is worth adding that resource is not just confined to materials. Resource means materials, components, the direct labour force and machinery and equipment.

Seven principles are associated with synchronous manufacturing:

(a)   Management should not focus on balancing capacities, but focus on synchronising the flow.

(b)   The marginal value of time at a bottleneck resource is equal to the throughput rate of the products processed by the bottleneck. That is the area of potential savings and improvements.

(c)   The marginal value of time at a non-bottleneck resource is negligible. As we have already seen, lack of synchronisation in these areas merely builds up inventory.

(d)   The level of utilisation of a non-bottleneck resource is controlled by other constraints within the system. (If you cannot get it painted, why build it?)

(e)   Resources must be utilised, not simply activated.

(f)   A transfer batch may not, and many times should not, be equal to a process batch.

A point of clarification is appropriate here. The transfer batch can only relate to what can be accommodated in the next batch. Thus, it must be lined up with what can be handled. Anything above this will pile up inventory.

(g)   A process batch should be variable both along its route and over time. Thus, batches of work along the line must reflect what can be taken by the next area.

Synchronous manufacturing purports to be an improvement on JIT based techniques by advocating a more focused approach. JIT works upon the principle of continuous improvement. Such an approach is prone to overlook the capacity constraints upon resources in advance. Rather it waits until the problems occur and disrupt the system. Synchronous manufacturing, by balancing throughput so that there is an even flow and no inventory build up, has to anticipate where the log jams are, accommodate them in the short term, and then plan for their eventual removal. In addition, JIT works on the approach of improvement right across the business. While this is commendable, the potential for savings at the point of a bottleneck is enormous. Thus it is a better use of resources to focus on the bottlenecks and clear them and thus gain the global improvements.

A further characteristic is that JIT is limited to the final assembly process, and as such, takes no account of the resulting loads at bottleneck work stations. It can also create bottleneck conditions at the final assembly, where tasks have to be done in less than ideal conditions. Thus if throughput is to be improved, and hence output and hence profit, consideration must be given to identifying the bottlenecks and how they may be avoided.

Synchronous manufacturing also employs a drum-buffer-rope system. The drum is a systematic approach to the problem by developing a master production schedule that is consistent with the constraints of the system. It uses a thorough analysis of a plant's capabilities, the manufacturing and hence marketing environment, and identifies these constraints. The 'buffers' are time buffers, designed to protect overall plant performance from any disruption. This is not the universal application of inventory piles such as recently dispensed with by Borg-Warner, but the strategic placing of protective inventory at key locations throughout the plant. The 'rope' is the control process. However, it only controls the schedule release points at the key bottleneck locations to maintain a smooth and timely flow.

5   VALUE ADDED AND NON VALUE ADDED ACTIVITIES

5.1   Value added activities

Definition   A value added activity is an activity which adds value to the customer's perception of the product. Examples include quality and price.

5.2   Non value added activities

Definition   A non value added activity is an activity which does not add value to a product in the eyes of its customers. Examples include the activities of setting up a production run, purchasing and planning.

5.3   Identifying value added

The student should be familiar with the definition of value added: "sales value less the cost of purchased materials and services. This represents the worth of an alteration in form, location or availability of a product or service." However, not all costs incurred add value to the basic bought in good or service. Thus **value analysis** has been developed. This is "a systematic inter-disciplinary examination of factors affecting the cost of a product or service, in order to devise means of achieving the specified purpose most economically at the required standard of quality and reliability."

The table below illustrates some of the cost categories that could be scrutinised under this form of analysis.

Value added versus non-value added activities

Activity	Value added	Non-value added
Purchasing		
Vetting suppliers	X	
Producing orders	X	
Returning goods		X
Correcting orders		X
Customer order processing		
Assessing credit rating		X
Liaising with customer	X	
Expediting delivery		X
Dealing with returns inwards		X

Activity	Value added	Non-value added
Quality control		
Supplies received		X
In process		X
On completion		X
Material scheduling		
Identifying line needs	X	
Storage		X
Movement from store to line		X

In theory, all costs that do not add value to the product should be targets for elimination. However, some, such as quality control, are essential to the running of the business in the short term. Quality control ensures that the product is up to customer expectation. It does not add value, but its removal could further add costs. Some judgement may be seen to be needed in the classification. Expediting delivery could mean ensuring that orders do not fall behind (non-value adding) or saying we can deliver to your schedule but at a premium cost.

A further development in this form of analysis breaks activities into three components - core, support and discretionary. In the case of sales costs, time spent with customers and potential customers would be core work. That is the essential business of winning orders for the firm. Travelling time would be a support activity while dealing with sales order processing errors would be pure discretionary. Thus effective cost management is about reducing the amount of resources that are being expended on non-core activities. This may mean changing territories to reduce travel time or travel costs, or changing the order process system to minimise errors.

5.4   The mechanics of value analysis

A team approach is the most appropriate and successful. This team should be drawn from:-

Design

Purchasing   (Maximum cost savings are often associated with the bought in goods and services.)

Marketing   (Important in the context of the esteem value of the product. Also marketing costs are now often 30% of the sales price.)

Production

Maintenance   (Could make the product more user friendly.)

Accounts

Such an approach is essential since value can be determined at any or all the stages between initial conception, through production to final delivery and after sales care. This also means that everybody gets together to talk about what is being done. Not to do this, argues Tom Peters, (**Liberation Management**) alienates the essential creative workers and induces misunderstandings and dysfunctional competitiveness. The following steps are recommended.

Step 1   Determine the function of the product

Step 2   Develop alternative designs

The relative importance placed by the customer upon the following will determine design or redesign objectives.

(a) Function
(b) Appearance
(c) Esteem associated with possession
(d) Intrinsic cost of materials and/or labour
(e) Replacement, exchange or disposal value

Step 3   Ascertain the costs

Step 4   Evaluate the alternatives

For existing products, the following questions will help to identify areas of potential value improvements:

(a) Which areas appear to offer the largest savings?

(b) What percentage of total cost is associated with bought out items?

(c) What percentage of total cost is associated with labour?

A consideration of labour cost may be relevant here. With the low content of traditional direct labour, scope for savings is limited. However, by identifying "people cost" the value analysis exercise embraces indirect hourly paid workers such as store-keepers, conversion indirect salaried staff and the whole gamut of non-conversion salaried staff, many of whom add little value to the product or service.

(d) What percentage of total cost is associated with materials?

Often the maximum cost saving associated with existing products relates to bought-in parts, materials and services. The value of such purchased parts and materials can be investigated with a view to material or design changes by asking the following questions:

- How does it contribute to the value of the product?

- How much does it contribute to the total cost of the product?

- Are all its features and its specification necessary?

- Is it similar to any other part?

- Can a standard part be used?

- Will an alternative design provide the same function?

A simple example might be the fender on a car. Traditionally, these were made of steel, and coated with chrome to give that bright silver finish. No true all-American gas-guzzler was complete without such a fender to match its whitewall tyres. However, steel was heavy and expensive, so was chrome. Also, the cost of maintenance was high, and there was a tendency for such fenders to become very shabby if used as buffers. Chrome also wore off causing the steel underneath to rust.

The idea to replace chrome on cheaper models with black plastic was tried. The effect did not look cheap, but rather sporting. The black contrasted well with the body colours and did not suffer from the drawbacks of chrome and steel. In these days of economy, it was cheaper and also lighter. It also rode collisions better, and was easier and cheaper to replace. Additionally, it did not detract from the value of the car. The result was that most cars now have plastic fenders.

(e) What marketing savings can be made?

Another example from marketing might be useful. A substantial cost of marketing cars is in the dealer network. In the United States, there are still too many of them, poorly managed, with high costs and dubious reputations. With the GM-Saturn range, GM have given dealers territories, made all the dealers look the same, insisted on the same standard of service, and encouraged many of the small family ("mom and pop") outfits to merge. By the year 2000, GM will have reduced its dealer network to 7,000 from the 14,000 in the 1970s. Those that remain will give a better service, enhance the image of the product and be cheaper to operate. (**Fortune** April 4 1994)

5.5   Implementing value analysis in practice

We have seen that there are four steps in the value analysis process (determine the function, develop alternative designs, ascertain costs and evaluate alternatives).

Developing alternative designs and techniques is a vital part of the process eg, alternative methods of achieving the required function as illustrated by the fender and dealership examples above. This is the creative aspect of value analysis, and may require "brainstorming" sessions. No reasonable or even ostensibly unreasonable alternative or suggestion should be rejected during this stage. The literature suggests that the session should be frenzied, chaotic, energetic, playful, intuitive and structured. It should be possible to come in at any time and at any level. The possibility of a back-to-back brainstormer, whereby employees meet either suppliers or customers should not be eliminated.

Among the objects to be considered at this stage might be:

(a)   eliminate parts or operations;

(b)   simplify parts or operations;

(c)   substitute alternative materials like plastic for chrome steel;

(d)   use standard parts or materials;

(e)   relax manufacturing tolerances; (Is the product being over-engineered for its place in the market?)

(f)   use standard manufacturing methods;

(g)   eliminate unnecessary design features;

(h)   change design to facilitate easier manufacture or maintenance; (Do we have to remove the dashboard to change a light bulb in the instrument panel?)

(i)   buy in rather than manufacture if it is cheaper;

(j)   use prefinished materials;

(k)   use prefabricated parts from cheaper specialists;

(l)   rationalise product ranges; (Or explore the possibility of putting different products on the same line. The Lexus is made on a standard Toyota production line.)

(m)   introduce low cost manufacturing processes;

(n)   rationalise the purchase of parts - single sourcing?

(o)   identify and eliminate material waste.

The above check list emphasises materials. However, what about procedures? Tom Peters illustrates how TIteflex, a US subsidiary of the British TI Group streamlined its procedures and facilitated faster order turnrounds.

6   JUST IN TIME (JIT)

6.1   Introduction

JIT has been defined as a "workflow organisation technique to allow rapid, high quality, flexible production whilst minimising stock levels and manufacturing waste." (Bromwich & Bhimani).

This system has gained considerable popularity in both the United States and Europe. It has a wide ranging impact upon many of the traditional organisational functions.

In practice, this means producing components only when they are needed and in the quantity that is needed. This shortens lead times and virtually eliminates work in progress and finished goods inventories. The resultant differences in production are:-

- Conventional production

    Provides monthly production schedules to every process including the final assembly line. The preceding process supplies the parts to the subsequent process (push through system) which is unable to respond quickly. Each process must adjust their schedule simultaneously requiring back up inventory between processes.

- JIT

    Does not provide simultaneous schedules to every process, only for the final assembly line. Goods are built for the customer, not for stock. The system works on a pull through basis, drawing components through the system. It can respond quickly drawing parts as required. As soon as items are completed in one process, so the next process produces to replace.

6.2   Impact on purchasing and production

(a)   Under JIT, a buyer can reduce their the number of suppliers. GM reduced their suppliers by 50%. Westinghouse has reduced inventories by 45% and plant stockouts by 95%. Warner-Lambert has replaced its costly batch production by a JIT based controlled process. Suppliers are also chosen because of close proximity to the plant. Long term contracts and single sourcing is advocated to strengthen buyer-supplier relationships and tends to result in a higher quality product. Inventory problems are shifted back onto suppliers, with deliveries being made as required.

(b)   **JIT delivery and transportation**

    The spread of JIT in the production process inevitably impinges upon those in delivery and transportation. This emphasises to the student who may feel that JIT is too production orientated that it can turn up in the service sector. Ryder has established centres close to its manufacturing plants. These are not warehouses, but rather extensions of the production process. As soon as an order to move material or to call off material is received, the truck moves and delivers. This means smaller more productive loads, more frequently. The use of freight cars and railways fits less well into the JIT pattern, although Union Pacific has developed a system whereby freight can be moved on a JIT basis.

The use of JIT puts new demands on the schedules of the hauliers. Tighter schedules are required, with penalties for non-delivery. The haulier is regarded as almost a partner to the manufacturer.

Does the haulier benefit from JIT? Tom Peters describes Union Pacific, a JIT haulier. As a result of moving to the JIT philosophy, traffic volume is up 18%, revenue 25%, productivity per employee nearly doubled, failure costs reduced to 15% of gross revenue, a saving of $750 million, and locomotive downtime reduced from 13% to 8% a further saving of $150 million. More important, Union Pacific is now regarded by its parent company as an "invest and grow" division.

(c)   **Impact on cost systems**

Accounting in an advanced manufacturing environment is dealt with in detail below. Suffice it to say that the traditional short term approach of the cost accountant is seen as an obstacle to the implementation of JIT. Costing systems need to be simpler and more flexible. However, before making any changes, a thorough review of the costing systems is required.

(d)   **Inventory valuation**

The inevitable reduction in inventory levels will reduce the time taken to count inventory and the clerical cost. As for valuing inventory, Hewlett-Packard no longer add conversion costs to inventory, but treat them as period costs.

As a final point on JIT, the system also renders the elegant EOQ model virtually useless. The student will recall that the optimal EOQ equals:

$$q^* = \sqrt{\frac{2C(1)D}{C(2)}} \qquad \text{where}$$

C(1)	=	variable costs of placing a production/purchase order
D	=	annual demand for inventory item,
C(2)	=	annual holding costs of one inventory item.

JIT causes the ordering cost to decline towards zero and since the model is optimal when holding costs equal ordering costs, the optimum becomes a virtually zero inventory level.

6.3   The concept of JIT

JIT is a series of manufacturing and supply chain techniques that aim to slash inventory levels and improve customer service by manufacturing not only at the exact time customers require, but also in the exact quantities they need and at competitive prices.

JIT is said to have originated from Toyota's *'Kanban'* system which is named after a card which is passed from workstation to workstation to control the production flow. The card ties production to actual orders effectively pulling orders through the factory. (Compare this with traditional production which is based on maintaining finished goods inventory.)

JIT extends much further than a concentration on inventory levels and also centres around the elimination of **waste**. Waste is defined as any **activity** performed within a manufacturing company which **does not add** value to the product. Example of waste are:

- raw materials inventories;
- work-in-progress inventories;
- finished goods inventories;
- materials handling;
- quality problems (rejects and reworks etc);

- queues and delays on the shop-floor;
- long raw material lead times;
- long customer lead times;
- unnecessary clerical and accounting procedures.

JIT attempts to eliminate waste at every stage of the manufacturing process notably by the:

- elimination of WIP by reducing batch sizes (often to one);

- elimination of raw materials inventories by the suppliers delivering direct to the shop-floor just in time for use;

- elimination of scrap and rework by an emphasis on total quality control of design, of the process, and of the materials;

- elimination of finished goods inventories by reducing lead times so that all products are made to order;

- elimination of material handling costs by re-design of the shop-floor so that goods move directly between adjacent work centres.

The combination of these concepts brings about JIT, which provides a smooth flow of work through the manufacturing plant, a flexible production process which is responsive to the customer's requirements and massive reductions in capital tied up in inventories. The end result of JIT is radical improvements in true productivities; more products of higher quality getting to the customers more quickly at a lower cost.

6.4   The characteristics of an 'ideal' factory layout

Far from 'batching up', JIT manufacturers aim for smaller and smaller batch size (and hence shorter and shorter lead times) in order to become even more reactive to customer demands.

To the traditional manufacturing manager, this sounds like a recipe for disaster, as it removes the slack in the systems that allows things to go wrong without causing immediate disruption. The lengthy customer lead times and large batch sizes tend to cushion the manufacturing if things don't work out the way they were planned.

Only now are such managers beginning to realise that it is often because of these lead times and batch sizes that things go wrong in the first place. JIT works so well precisely because all the conflicts, confusions and soft options that these various safety nets raise have been removed, leaving lean and hungry factories that outperform traditionally managed shop-floors.

Briefly the characteristics of an *ideal* system would seem to be the following:

- It should have a short manufacturing cycle time, to minimise work-in-progress inventory and maximise customer service.

- It should have manufacturing batch sizes identical to customer order quantities (even if this is one), to minimise finished goods inventory and maximise customer responsiveness.

- It should be flexible enough to make products in the same order as the customer wants them, again in order to minimise finished goods inventory and maximise responsiveness.

- It should be able to rapidly trap and cure deviations from quality standards in order to maximise customer service and minimise scrap and rework.

- It should call in raw materials as late as possible in order to minimise raw material inventory.

6.5   JIT purchase contracts

Obtaining the co-operation of suppliers is a vital first step when implementing a JIT system. A company is a long way towards JIT if its suppliers will give it shorter lead-times, deliver smaller quantities more often, guarantee a low reject rate and perform quality-assurance inspection at source.

If a company's suppliers make more frequent deliveries of small quantities of material, then it can ensure that each delivery is just enough to meet its immediate production schedule. This will keep its inventory as low as possible.

If suppliers will guarantee the quality of the material they deliver and will inspect it at source, then a company can make enormous savings on both time and labour. Materials handling time will be saved because as there is no need to move the stock into a store, the goods can be delivered directly to a workstation on the shop-floor. Inspection time and costs can be eliminated and the labour required for reworking defective material or returning goods to the supplier can be saved.

In return for this improved service from the supplier, the company can guarantee to give more business to fewer suppliers, place long-term purchase orders and give the suppliers a long-range forecast of its requirements.

The successful JIT manufacturer deliberately sets out to cultivate good relationships with a small number of suppliers and these suppliers will often be situated close to the manufacturing plant. It is usual for a large manufacturer which does not use the JIT approach to have multiple suppliers. When a new part is to be produced, various suppliers will bid for the contract and the business will be given to the two or three most attractive bids. A JIT manufacturer is looking for a single supplier which can provide high quality and reliable deliveries, rather than the lowest price. This supplier will often be located in close proximity to the manufacturing plant.

There is much to be gained by both the company and its suppliers from this mutual dependence. The traditional approach where companies and suppliers regard each other as adversaries has to change because with JIT, the company and the supplier need to work together co-operatively. In the longer term this can lead to some very fruitful partnerships. For example, co-operation between the company and the supplier can go right back to the design stage.

6.6   Example

Jaguar, when it analysed the causes of customer complaints, compiled a list of 150 areas of faults. Some 60 per cent of them turned out to be faulty components from suppliers. One month the company returned 22,000 components to different suppliers. Suppliers were brought on to the multi-disciplinary task forces the company established to tackle each of the common faults. The task force had the simple objective of finding the fault, establishing and testing a cure, and implementing it as fast as possible. Jaguar directors chaired the task forces of the twelve most serious faults, but in one case the task force was chaired by the supplier's representative.
(Source: Goldsmith, W, and Clutterbuck, D, 'The winning streak', Penguin, 1985)

Establishment of long-term purchase orders is commonplace among JIT manufacturers. The purpose is to give the supplier an assurance of long-term sales which enables the supplier to plan for the purchase of raw material, specialised machines etc. These long-term purchase orders also create the right environment for the setting up of SMART contracts. A SMART contract (systematic material acquisition and review technique) allows for a short lead-time *'call off'* of material from the supplier within the framework of a longer term contract. Each time material is called off, the company provides the supplier with a detailed schedule of future requirements. This schedule is not a firm commitment but it enables the suppliers to do their own planning well ahead of time and minimise the company's forward commitment of inventory investment.

These SMART or blanket orders are not a new idea but what is different about a JIT manufacturer is the degree to which this type of purchase order is used. The majority of the raw material piece parts and bought-in subassemblies are procured in this way.

There are significant savings to be made within the purchasing department of the company by use of these techniques. It is not necessary for the buyer to negotiate contracts and raise a purchase order on the supplier each time an order is placed. The SMART contract call-off can be done by the material planner, eliminating that additional administrative step and the paperwork associated with it. It is also possible for the MRP computer-run automatically to generate these SMART releases (within certain constraints) and pass them on to the supplier without even the material planner becoming involved. This allows the material planner to concentrate his or her efforts on resolving the problem areas, rather than spending a great deal of time handling the run-of-the-mill requirements.

6.7   Multi-functional workers

A key element of just-in-time manufacturing is the flexibility of the workforce. Demarcation of functions must be eliminated and replaced by a team approach where each person is trained in multiple functions and can move quickly within the plant to meet the changing requirements of the customers. The same kind of flexible team approach must also be taken by non-direct personnel such as management accountants. Management accountants must be willing to see their role change significantly as the needs of the business change and, in fact, initiate change as part of the continuous improvement concept of just-in-time manufacturing.

There must be a clear and shared understanding of what the critical success factors of the business are. There must be recognition throughout all levels of the organisation of what the overall business objectives are, and how each unit or department can contribute to satisfying these objectives. The management process itself must be integrated in the sense of sharing a common purpose and approach.

In order for the business objectives to be understood and accepted by personnel at all levels, communications and training become increasingly important. Organisations must be slimmer, with fewer levels of management and a removal of traditional barriers. Only by doing this is there a possibility that the top management philosophy and objectives will filter down through the organisation. Equally important, it is the only way that the degree of adherence to these objectives at lower levels will become visible to senior management.

6.8   Dedicated cell layouts

A dedicated cell layout is a team-based approach where flows of material occur around a 'U' shaped production unit as shown by the following diagram

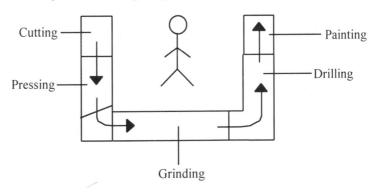

Each operative undertakes several different tasks working with the material around the 'U'. The result is often an increase in quality as operators are responsible for activities within the production process.

7   ACCOUNTING IN AN ADVANCED MANAGEMENT TECHNIQUES ENVIRONMENT

7.1   Cost behaviour patterns

Investment in advanced management techniques and technologies (AMT) dramatically changes cost behaviour patterns. The introduction of computer technicians, software engineers, and programmers replaces traditional direct labour. Most variable costs, other than direct material and energy also disappear. Overheads, both conversion and non-conversion become an even bigger part of the total cost.

To demonstrate how the accounting may be undertaken, we will illustrate from a real example. Borg-Warner at Ithaca (NY) operates a JIT system producing automotive chain systems in a process system. The operation is completely integrated, the old system of moving piles of work-in-progress having been removed.

Standard transactions

1	Dr	Raw material
	Cr	Account payable

Record material purchases

2	Dr	WIP components/material
	Cr	Raw materials

Issue to production

3	Dr	Conversion costs
	Cr	Conversion costs payable
	Cr	Conversion cost variances

This entry is made after the components have been inspected and passed for assembly.

4		Treatment of scrap for both material and rejected completed items.
5		Finished goods

Charged with conversion costs when the products are finished.

6		Cost of sales

From this outline, the student should observe:

- costs are only allowed to accumulate when the product is finished. This directs effort and attention towards output rather than production;

- JIT emphasises the elimination of waste. Thus allowances for waste, scrap and rework are removed from the standard costs and detailed reports produced on these items. This means a move to the ideal standard, rather than an achievable standard;

- Output is credited at standard. Thus any difference in input and output is a variance, which can be analysed as either a cost or efficiency variance.

7.2   Cost classification

In a JIT and hence advanced manufacturing environment, cost classifications will change:

	Traditional	*JIT*
Material handling	Indirect	Direct
Repair & maintenance	Largely direct	Direct
Energy	Indirect	Direct
Operating supplies	Indirect	Direct
Supervision	Indirect	Direct
Production support	Indirect	Largely direct
Depreciation	Indirect	Direct

Inevitably many of these costs will be allocated to products on the basis of the cost drivers, hence using activity based costing (see later).

7.3   Overhead absorption

Where it is necessary to absorb conversion overhead into the cost then the machine hour rate must be favoured. Despite the technical advances, especially in the defence industry, the Howell Report of 1987 found most advanced manufacturers still using a labour hours based system. The predilection for retaining labour hours has resulted in overhead rates in both the UK and the USA well in excess of 1,500% (Innes & Mitchell **Overhead Cost** 1993).

7.4   Revised performance measures

The introduction of JIT related manufacturing will also change the performance measures.

Traditional	JIT
Direct labour (efficiency, utilisation, productivity)	Total Head Count productivity (Note the emphasis on 'people' rather than labour)
Chalos is critical of the excessive focus on a relatively small cost.	
	Days of inventory
Machine utilisation	Group or cell incentives
Stock turnover	
	Knowledge & capability based promotion
Cost variances	Ideas generated and implemented
Individual incentives	Customer complaints
Seniority	

In addition, Chalos (**Managing cost in today's manufacturing environment** 1992) stresses that raw material variances give rise to excess inventories in order to gain discounts, cost centres do not effectively control overhead spends, overhead costs ought to be based upon theoretical capacity rather than the financial accountant's normal capacity to gain an accurate measure of idle facilities and time, and most variances detract from other vital measures of productivity.

8   BACKFLUSH ACCOUNTING

8.1   Introduction

> **Definition**   Backflush accounting is a cost accounting system which focuses on the output of an organisation and then works backwards to attribute costs to stock and cost of sales.

This system records the transactions only at the termination of the production and sales cycle. The emphasis is to measure costs at the beginning and at the end with greater emphasis on the end or outputs. Since backflushing is usually employed in parallel with JIT, there is no work-in-progress to consider, nor does work-in-progress materially fluctuate. What is essential, however, is an accurate bill of materials, good measures of yield, generally effective production control and accurate engineering change notices when yields do change.

The principle of a just-in-time system is that production is pulled by customer demand and this in turn pulls the purchasing procedures. Thus, theoretically there are zero stocks of raw materials, work-in-progress and finished goods. For such a situation to exist there needs to be an excellent system of production planning and communications with material suppliers.

8.2   The philosophy of traditional cost accounting methods

Traditional cost accounting methods are based upon the principle that value is obtained by the creation of the asset known as stock. As a consequence this value must be measured and cost accumulation systems are used for this purpose. In modern JIT based production, stock does not exist and therefore such cost accumulation techniques are unnecessary. Instead costs are recognised at the point of sale rather than at the point of production.

8.3   The variants of backflush accounting

There are a number of variants of the backflush system, each differing as to the "trigger points" at which costs are recognised within the cost accounts and thus associated with products. All variants, however, have the following common features:

- *the focus is on output* - costs are first associated with output (measured as either sales or completed production) and then allocated between stocks and cost of goods sold by working back.

- *conversion costs (labour and overheads) are never attached to products until they are completed (or even sold)* - thus the traditional WIP account doesn't exist. Materials are recognised at different points according to the variant used, but only to the extent of being either stock of raw materials or part of the cost of stock of finished goods. Again, materials are not attached to WIP.

Two variants of the backflush system are summarised below. Note that in each case, as conversion costs (labour and overheads) are incurred they will be recorded in a conversion cost (CC) account.

Variant 1

This has two trigger points (TP):

TP1   -   *purchase of raw materials/components*. A 'raw and in process (RIP)' account will be debited with the actual cost of materials purchased, and a creditor credited.

TP2   -   *completion of good units*. The finished goods (FG) account will be debited with the standard cost of units produced, and the RIP and CC accounts will be credited with the standard costs

Under this variant, then, there will be two stock accounts:

- raw materials (which may, in fact, be incorporated into WIP)
- finished goods.

Variant 2

This has only one trigger point - *the completion of good units*. The FG account is debited with the standard cost of units produced, with corresponding credits to the CC account and the creditor account.

Thus the cost records exclude:

- raw materials purchased but not yet used for complete production
- the creditor for these materials (and any price variance)

and there is only one stock account, carrying the standard cost of finished goods stock.

Other variants include those using the *sale of complete good units* as a trigger point for the attachment of conversion costs to units - thus there is no finished goods account, just a raw materials stock account, carrying the materials cost of raw materials, WIP and finished goods.

It should be seen that as stocks of raw materials, WIP and finished goods are decreased to minimal levels, as in a "pure" JIT system, these three variants will give the same basic results.

8.4   Backflush accounting - example

The following example will be used to illustrate the first two variants outlined above.

The manufacturing cost information for March for a division of XYZ plc is as follows:

Costs incurred in March	£'000
Purchase of raw materials	4,250
Labour	2,800
Overheads	1,640

Activity in March	Units('000)
Finished goods manufactured during the period	180 u.
Sales	145

Standard cost per unit	(£)
Materials	20
Labour	15
Overheads	9
S C /u.	44

There were no opening stocks of raw materials, WIP or finished goods. It should be assumed that there are no direct materials variances for the period.

Variant 1

			DR £'000	CR £'000
1.	RIP account		4,250	
	Creditor			4,250
2.	CC account		4,440	
	Cash			2,800
	Cash/creditor			1,640
3.	FG account	(180 × 44)	7,920	
	RIP account	(180 × 20)		3,600
	CC account	(180 × 24)		4,320
4.	COGS	(145 × 44)	6,380	
	FG account			6,380

The double entry would be as follows:

The ledger accounts would appear as follows:

Raw and in process materials

	£'000		£'000
Creditor	4,250	FG	3,600
		Bal c/d	650
	4,250		4,250
Bal b/d	650		

Conversion costs

	£'000		£'000
Cash/creditor	4,440	FG	4,320
		Bal c/d	120
	4,440		4,440
Bal b/d	120		

Finished goods

	£'000		£'000
RIP	3,600	COGS	6,380
CC	4,320	Bal c/d	1,540
	7,920		7,920
Bal b/d	1,540		

Cost of goods sold

	£'000		£'000
FG	6,380		

The stock balances at the end of March would be

	£'000
Raw and in process materials	650
Finished goods	1,540
	2,190

The balance on the conversion costs account would be carried forward and written off at the end of the year.

Variant 2

The accounting entries where there is only one trigger point (on completion of units) would be simpler:

			DR £'000	CR £'000
1.	CC account		4,440	
	Cash			2,800
	Cash/creditor			1,640
2.	FG account	(180 × 44)	7,920	
	Creditors	(180 × 20)		3,600
	CC account	(180 × 24)		4,320
3.	COGS	(145 × 44)	6,380	
	FG account			6,380

There would just be one stock balance at the end of March, on the finished goods account, of £1,540,000. The raw materials purchased but not yet attributed to complete production (£650,000) will not have been recorded in the costing system.

This variant is thus only suitable for JIT systems with minimal raw material stocks.

8.5   Suitability of backflush accounting

Both variants illustrated above eliminate the WIP account. If stocks are low in general, a large proportion of manufacturing costs will be attributable to cost of goods sold. The principle of backflush costing is that in these circumstances, the work involved in tracking costs through WIP, COGS and FG is unlikely to be of benefit. As noted above, the stock and cost of goods sold values will be close to those derived from a conventional costing system, with a considerably reduced volume of recorded transactions.

9   THROUGHPUT ACCOUNTING

9.1   Definition

[Definition]   Throughput Accounting (TA) is a method of performance measurement which relates production and other costs to throughput. Throughput accounting product costs relate to usage of key resources by various products.

TA is seen as very much in sympathy with the JIT philosophy. It assumes that a manager has a given set of resources available. These comprise the existing buildings, capital equipment and labour force. Using these resources, purchased materials and components must be processed to generate sales revenue. To achieve this, the maximum amount of throughput is required with the financial definition of:

> Sales revenue – Direct material cost

The cost of all other factors is deemed at least time related rather than fixed.

9.2   Influences on throughput

Throughput is influenced by:

- selling price,
- direct purchase price,
- usage of direct material,
- volume of throughput.

Students should understand that throughput is not production at any price. Rather, throughput is only concerned about output that will effect sales. Stocks are only considered desirable when they can enhance and increase throughput. Such a situation might be maximising output in a seasonal market.

Constraints on throughput might include:

- the existence of an uncompetitive selling price;
- the need to deliver on time to particular customers;
- the lack of product quality and reliability;
- the lack of reliable material supplies;
- the existence of shortages of production resources.

It becomes management's task to eliminate these constraints. Shortages of resources are usually termed bottlenecks, and their elimination often only moves a problem from one location to another. Thus the careful planning to minimise and eliminate all bottlenecks becomes very important.

9.3   Throughput reporting

Progress analysed over a range of products can be monitored using a report similar to the one illustrated below.

Product	A	B	C	D	E	F
	£	£	£	£	£	£
Sales						
Direct materials						
Throughput						
Labour						
Other prod overhead						
Administration						
Selling						
Operating profit						

Costing of any stocks is based upon direct material costs. No conversion costs are added to the inventory valuation whatsoever. The student will recognise that where only materials and components are variable, such a schedule relates very closely to a contribution analysis statement as used for short term volume decisions.

The principle is that there is no profit and therefore no value in manufacturing for stock unless there is a clear link between increasing stock and future sales (as may occur in seasonal businesses).

9.4   Cost classification

In a throughput accounting system the only costs which are considered to be variable are material costs. Conversion costs (labour and indirect costs) are classified as being fixed and therefore may be grouped together as 'Total factory costs'. A calculation may be made of the cost per factory hour by relating this cost to the number of hours available on the bottleneck resource.

9.5   Return per factory hour

Throughput is defined as sales less material costs. Other costs are considered to be fixed so this is similar in principle to the concept of contribution. The efficiency with which a particular product makes use of the bottleneck resource is calculated by:

$$\frac{\text{Sales} - \text{material costs}}{\text{Usage (in hours) of the bottleneck resource}}$$

You should notice the similarity of this calculation to the contribution per unit of a limiting factor used in short-term decision making.

9.6   The throughput accounting ratio

This is the relationship between the return per factory hour and the cost of each factory hour. This is found by:

$$\frac{\text{Return per factory hour}}{\text{Cost per factory hour}}$$

9.7   Example

A Ltd manufactures a single product which it sells for £10 per unit. The direct material cost of the product is £3 per unit. Other factory costs amount to £50,000 per month. The bottleneck factor is the assembly of the unit which is a labour intensive process. There are 20,000 assembly hours available each month, with each unit taking two hours to assemble.

Calculate the throughput accounting ratio for the product.

9.8   Solution

Return per factory hour $=$ $\dfrac{\text{Sales} - \text{material costs}}{\text{Usage of bottleneck resource}}$

$=$ $\dfrac{£10 - £3}{2}$

$=$ **£3.50**

Cost per factory hour $=$ $\dfrac{\text{Total factory costs}}{\text{Bottleneck resource hours available}}$

$=$ $\dfrac{£50,000}{20,000}$

$=$ **£2.50**

$$\text{Throughput accounting ratio} = \frac{\text{Return per factory hour}}{\text{Cost per factory hour}}$$

$$= \frac{£3.50}{£2.50}$$

$$= \mathbf{1.4 : 1}$$

9.9   Activity

X Ltd manufactures a product which requires 1.5 hours machining. Due to a lack of machines this has been determined as the bottleneck resource. There are ten machines each of which may be operated for up to 40 hours per week.

The product is sold for £8.50 and has direct material costs of £4.25. Total factory costs are £800 per week.

Calculate the product's:

(i)   return per factory hour;

(ii)   throughput accounting ratio.

9.10   Activity solution

(i) $\dfrac{£8.50 - £4.25}{1.5 \text{ hours}} = £2.83$

(ii) $\dfrac{£2.83}{£2} = 1.42 : 1$

TF Cost = 800 = £2 = cost/fact hr.
(10 × 40)

9.11   Treatment of bottlenecks

Bottlenecks can be identified by profiling capacity usage through the system. Usually they will be areas of most heavy usage. Thus monitoring build ups of inventory and traditional idle time and waiting time will indicate actual or impending bottlenecks.

Traditional efficiency measures will be important in managing bottlenecks. Changes in efficiency will indicate the presence of bottlenecks and the need for a response. This may take the form of creating short term build ups of stock to alleviate the problem. Another possible solution might be to prioritise the work at bottlenecks to ensure that throughput is achieved. Measures that highlight throughput per bottleneck capacity measures will need to be developed.

In view of the fact that the JIT philosophy sees all non-value adding activities as potential waste, TA looks for anything that will enhance saleable output. Thus, anything that will reduce costly lead times, set-up times and waiting times will enhance the throughput. Again, these need to be identified and reported on and monitored to see if they are being reduced.

9.12   Other factors

All constraints should be considered in the reporting process. If quality is a throughput constraint, then detailed quality cost reports on rework, scrap levels and returns need to be added to the performance measuring process. Equally, if delivery times are crucial, then failure to meet delivery times needs to be reported. The student should begin to see that the essence of throughput accounting is contingent on what is needed and the circumstances that prevail.

9.13   Assessment

TA will appear to the student to be going against the trend of emulating Japanese style methods as described by H Thomas Johnson. It is a highly short term perspective on costs, regarding only material as variable or directly activity related. It neglects the costs of overhead and people. As a result, there will always be the risk of sub-optimal profit performance. TA will really only work effectively where material remains a high proportion of the cost or selling price. Also, there must be a situation where demand is constant enough or high enough to always put pressure on output and production resources.

It is suggested that TA with its emphasis on direct material is an ideal complement to ABC which can draw attention to the overheads. In that way, a comprehensive cover of costs can be achieved.

10   ACTIVITY BASED APPROACHES TO COST ANALYSIS

10.1   Introduction

Definition   Activity Based Costing is the process of cost attribution to cost units on the basis of benefit received from indirect activities eg, ordering, setting up, assuring quality.

Bromwich & Bhimani give a somewhat wider definition using the term "Activity Based Accounting."

"Examination of activities across the entire chain of value adding organisational processes underlying causes (drivers) of cost and profit."

The wider definition introduces the important aspect that costs are incurred in selling and distributing a product and the costs of servicing customers are possibly now more important than production.

Another important definition is the cost driver:

Definition   A cost driver is an activity or factor which generates cost.

10.2   The origins of activity based costing

ABC first appeared in the 1950s when some US firms made attempts to accurately allocate their selling and distribution overheads. There was a plea in the literature in 1968 when Solomons (**Studies in Cost Analysis**) explored the need to obtain a reasonably accurate and objective indication of the differing factors driving overhead as a basis for more reliable variance computations. In the 1970s, when Zero-based budgeting came into vogue, some of the analysis was based upon activity. However, it was the work of Robin Cooper and R S Kaplan that eventually codified ABC into a coherent framework and disseminated it among academics, consultants and practitioners.

ABC is most appropriate where overhead is a relatively important cost element and there is a diversity of product lines and possibly markets. Essentially, it requires pooling the overhead spend and allocating it out over activities. Note the use of the term "allocate" indicating an objective cost driven charge rather than a subjective apportionment.

10.3   Past exam questions

The use of ABC was examined in December 1994 and December 1995. Both questions required the candidate to compute product unit costs under both a traditional overhead absorption basis and using ABC techniques. Discussion of the relevance of such costs in decision making and target costing was also required. You must therefore be able to carry out the required calculations and appreciate the usefulness or otherwise of the information thus obtained.

10.4   The mechanics of ABC

Three stages can be identified.

Step 1   The collection of overhead costs in the same way as traditional overhead control accounts would operate.

Step 2 The pooling of costs based upon the activities which have consumed resources rather than on the basis of production departments or centres. The activities selected are based upon four classes of transaction:-

- Logistical transactions - the moving and tracking of materials in and through the production process.

- Balancing transactions - matching resources with the demands of the production operation. This will include ensuring that resources are available when required.

- Quality transactions - ensuring output conforms with established specifications which will meet all market expectations.

- Change transactions - the need to respond to changes in customer demand, design changes, scheduling, supply and production methods.

Such transactions will frequently cross the traditional functional boundaries of an organisation.

Step 3 The various overhead transactions are then allocated to the products based upon a series of cost drivers which indicate how the product has made demands upon the various activities. The rates for charging out are based upon dividing the activity cost for a period by the cost driver volume. Thus the cost of the purchasing function will be divided by the number of purchase orders raised by each department.

10.5   Illustrative example

Oceanides has four departments who make use of the procurement function. The total cost of the function is £10,000,000 per annum. The four departments use the function in the following way:-

Department	No of orders	Cost allocation £
A	200,000	6,666,667
B	50,000	1,666,667
C	40,000	1,333,333
D	10,000	333,333
	300,000	10,000,000

Simply dividing the total cost by the cost driver we get:

$$\frac{£10,000,000}{300,000} = £33.33 \text{ per order}$$

10.6   Activity

Pelleas has the following indirect costs:

	£	No. of cost drivers
Quality control	90,000	450 inspections
Process set-up	135,000	450 set-ups
Purchasing	105,000	1,000 purchase orders
Customer order processing	120,000	2,000 customers
Occupancy costs	150,000	75,000 machine hours
	600,000	

Calculate the charge out rates for each of the activities.

10.7   Activity solution

Quality control	90,000	÷	450	=	£200 per inspection
Process set-up	135,000	÷	450	=	£300 per set-up
Purchasing	105,000	÷	1,000	=	£105 per order
Customer order processing	120,000	÷	2,000	=	£60 per customer
Occupancy costs	150,000	÷	75,000	=	£2 per machine hour

Note that occupancy cost has been allocated on traditional machine hours. The cost driver there is time, and as such, a conventional ABC method is not applicable. The student should remember that ABC will never cater 100% for all overheads.

10.8   Example

Pelleas, (the company in the above activity), makes a standard product called the Melisande.

The cost details are as follows:

Unit material cost	£0.50
Unit labour cost	£0.40
Total production for the coming year	1,000,000 units
Number of production runs	50
No. of purchase orders required	50
Number of customer orders	10
Unit machine time	3 minutes

The product run is inspected once at the end of each production run.

You are required to calculate the standard cost of a Melisande.

10.9   Solution

We need to draw up a grid for the overheads.

Function	Rate × Usage		£
Quality control	£200 × 50	=	10,000
Process set-up	£300 × 50	=	15,000
Purchasing	£105 × 50	=	5,250
Customer orders	£60 × 10	=	600
Occupancy	£2 × 50,000	=	100,000
			———
			130,850
			———

Dividing the total overhead cost by the number of units produced we get:

$$\frac{130,850}{1,000,000} = £0.1385 \text{ (say £0.14)}$$

Thus the standard unit cost for a Melisande is:

	£
Material	0.50
Labour	0.40
Overhead	0.14
	——
	1.04
	——

The typical examination question that has appeared thus far has required the student to compute overhead rates in the traditional manner and using the ABC method and compare the results over two or more products, one like the Melisande, (standard and with long runs), and others which are likely to be non-standard with short runs.

10.10   Selecting the cost drivers

In the main, the cost driver will be measured in terms of volume of transactions. However, ABC also tries to identify costs that are not contributing to the value of the product/service so the following questions are relevant:

- What services does this activity provide?
- Who receives the services?
- Why do you require so many people?
- What might cause you to require more/less staff?
- Why does over/idle time exist?

Three types of cost driver have emerged.

(a)   **Pure activity output volume** - where the basic transactions of the activity are identical in terms of their resource demands such as the purchasing of raw materials or a similar range of items.

(b)   **Activity/output volume/complexity** - where the basic transactions differ in terms of their resource demands as when purchases are made from different overseas suppliers.

(c)   **Situation** - where an underlying factor can be identified as driving the workload of an activity such as the number of suppliers when supplier vetting and liaison were vital components of the cost pool.

10.11   Examples of cost drivers

The following are examples of cost drivers.

Activity	*Cost driver*
Material procurement	No. of purchase orders
Material handling	No. of movements
Quality control	No. of inspections
Engineering services	No. of change orders
Maintenance	No. of break-downs
Line set-up	No. of set-ups

For the service sector the following taken from the field of Health Care may serve as an example. The cost drivers form the basis of costs charged to patients.

Activity	*Cost driver*
Patient movement	No. of in-patients
Booking appointments	No. of patients
Patient reception	No. of patients
X-ray:	
Equipment preparation	Time taken
Patient preparation	Time taken
Patient aftercare	Time taken
Film processing	No. of images
Film reporting	No. of images

From Kirton "ABC at Luton & Dunstable Hospital" 1992

10.12   The merits of ABC

An improved more accurate product cost may enable a company to concentrate on a more profitable mix of products or customers. ABC has been effectively used in identifying customers who are unprofitable to service.

It is argued that traditional overhead apportionment leads to incorrect commitment of resources to products.

ABC extends the variable cost rationale to both short and long term costs by quantitatively addressing the cost behaviour patterns in terms of both short run volume changes as well as long term cost trends.

It helps identify value added and non-value added costs so that the non-value added items can be appraised effectively with a view to elimination. As such it forces managers and supervisors to consider the drivers that effect costs and what these drivers contribute to the final product.

Thus the managers will have a better understanding of the economics of production and the economics of the activities performed by the company.

10.13   A warning

Ahmed and Scapens (**Cost allocation: theory and practice 1991**) warned that ABC was unlikely to relate all overheads to specific activities. It also ignores the potential for conflict, especially where there are more than one potential cost driver.

More recently, the warning has been reiterated by emphasising that there is no such thing as a 100% accurate cost. At best, ABC will only improve the quality of cost information. The student should perhaps note Brimson's 1991 definition of product cost - "a summation of the cost of all traceable activities to design, procure material, manufacture and distribute a product."

Perhaps the key word in that definition is traceable, whether or not a cost can be traced objectively to the production/delivery of a good/service.

11   ACTIVITY BASED MANAGEMENT (ABM)

11.1   Definition

There is no formal definition of ABM in Bromwich & Bhimani. Effective management is about ensuring a product/service meets the demands of the market. To ensure this, managers have to understand their organisation's ability to deliver at the required time, of a standard of quality that is expected, and at a competitive price. To achieve this requires a knowledge of the organisation's cost structure, an appreciation of how costs are determined, and how costs may be influenced.

11.2   Cost visibility

The activity based approach brings costs out into the open and helps management see what they get for the commitment of resources. For example, the buying department ties up people, equipment (office space, desks, filing cabinets) and uses stationery, telephones etc, and produces purchase orders. Ignoring the classic cynical view of R C Townsend, the effectiveness of the department can be monitored in terms of delays, reductions in lead times and errors. This would enable the purchasing function to be monitored effectively and improved upon. A purchasing department is not just concerned with buying. It will have input from the design area, perhaps being told to find standard parts for specialist products, it will obviously buy and track prices, it may be responsible for receiving and it will pass invoices to accounting. The speed and effective way it performs these tasks can all be used to monitor performance and control costs.

It is suggested that ABC is perhaps most useful in monitoring how effectively the traditional overhead departments operate. Since a factory needs material, it follows that it needs buyers. It is tempting to say that they are indispensable and not track the cost. What ABC does do is enable management to really ask whether or not any department is as cost effective as it could be. One way of doing this is to create cost profiles to measure resource consumption.

11.3 Activity cost profile

This is not a new idea. Students should already be familiar with traditional overhead reporting statements which show last year's figures as a comparison. The profile is merely a different approach.

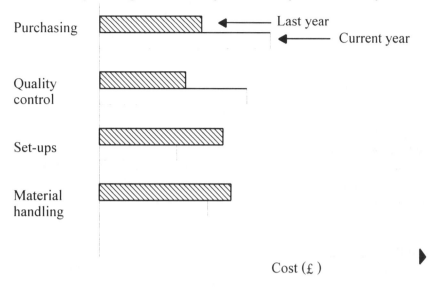

The activity cost profile

From the profile, it can be asked, "Why has purchasing gone up?" This could be because of increased volume, diversity of products, change in mix of production runs, etc.

The dramatic increase in quality control may be offset by fewer external failures, fewer warranty claims and fewer recalls. It may be due to the changing expectation of the customer, demanding a higher quality product. Similar analyses can be performed on set-up and material handling costs.

11.4 Cost behaviour patterns

The student should be familiar with the traditional narrow view of cost behaviour patterns. In essence a linear assumption is made that is based upon one variable, production or possibly sales volume. Common sense indicates that not all costs vary in a direct linear relationship with activity. One obvious example is the telephone. It may actually be used far more if activity is slack in order to drum up more business.

Fixed costs have increased in proportion to the total but have also not remained unchanged. More resources are being committed to elements of the fixed cost structure. What is required is an analysis of what is driving these increases. One approach to investigating and exploring ways of reducing these costs is to establish a hierarchy which classifies types of activity and identifies how costs are driven.

ABC based cost hierarchy

Level 1	Unit basis	Costs depend on the volume of production eg, machine power.
Level 2	Batch basis	Costs depend upon the number of batches eg, set-up and monitoring.
Level 3	Process level	Costs depend upon the existence of the process eg, quality control and supervision.
Level 4	Product level	Costs depend upon the existence of a group or line eg, product management and parts administration.
Level 5	Facility level	Costs depend on the existence of a facility of plant eg, rent, rates, general management.

This approach highlights the pattern of costs as one moves further away from the product. It also highlights the position in the hierarchy of decision making. The fixed set-up cost can be reduced by longer runs, but at the expense of increased storage if there is no immediate demand. Further up the hierarchy, consideration can be given to reducing the number of processes, merging lines and changing facility capacity. Such an approach requires a different view of costs which traditional analysis does not give. Traditional analysis with its subjective apportionments assumes that the product drives all the costs. By definition, fixed costs cannot be product driven and what is required is to find out how they are driven and if they add value to the product. It also provides an attention directing signal that highlights the cost of resources consumed by a product in order to gain a particular market price. Such a signal enables consideration of future strategies towards volumes and product development.

11.5   Customer driven costs

This is an area that has been traditionally neglected. All the emphasis has been upon manufacturing costs with over emphasis on direct labour. It may come as a salutary shock to the student that the labour cost content of a $18,000 (£12,000) car is about $840 (£560) while the selling and distribution cost is about 30% of the showroom price ie, $5,400 (£3,600) (**Fortune** April 4 1994). Major potential cost savings can be achieved in this hitherto almost sacred area. The following customer driven costs have been identified.

- **Supply and delivery patterns**

  Influenced by the frequency of delivery - a JIT system will need more but smaller deliveries compared with a customer who maintains high buffer inventories.

- **Customer location**

  Distribution, communication and contact costs are all influenced by distance.

- **Quality provided**

  Different customers may require different standards, both of supply and product. A JIT customer will demand a higher quality of service.

- **Provision of after sales service**

  This will have been negotiated with the individual customer. Obviously, the customer who wants 24 hours support for his PCs is going to pay a premium over the customer who is happy to buy the cheapest "box" from a specialist supermarket.

- **Required documentation**

  This may be determined by the needs of the customer.

- **Sales and promotion effort**

  This again may be geared to different types of customers, who may be attracted to different attributes of the product on offer.

- **Discounts given**

  Repeat business, special relationships, offers or promptness of paying can all differ among customers.

11.6   Illustrative example

Diomed manufactures a single product with a production cost of £40 per unit which is sold to three customers. The details are:

Sales pattern:	Customer	X	10,000 units per annum
		Y	10,000 units per annum
		Z	10,000 units per annum

All sales are made at £75 per unit.

Non-production overhead is:

	£
Delivery	220,000
Quality inspection	200,000
Salesmen	80,000
After sales service	100,000
	600,000

This is currently apportioned on the basis of a rate on the production cost. The MD is unhappy about this and asks for an analysis based upon ABC methods.

The following period activity volumes have been identified.

Customer	X	Y	Z
No. of deliveries	2,500	50	12
No. of inspections	10,000	500	0
No. of salesmen visits	200	24	6
After sales visits	200	100	50

11.7   Solution

Cost driver rates:

$$\text{Delivery} \quad \frac{£220,000}{2,562} \quad = \quad £85.87 \text{ per delivery}$$

$$\text{Inspection} \quad \frac{£200,000}{10,500} \quad = \quad £19.05 \text{ per inspection}$$

$$\text{Salesmen} \quad \frac{£80,000}{230} \quad = \quad £347.83 \text{ per visit}$$

$$\text{After sales} \quad \frac{£100,000}{350} \quad = \quad £285.71 \text{ per after sales visit}$$

Analysing these costs:

Customer			X	Y	Z
			£	£	£
No. of deliveries	2,500 @	85.87	214,675		
	50 @	85.87		4,294	
	12 @	85.87			1,030
Inspection	10,000 @	19.05	190,500		
	500 @	19.05		9,525	
Salesmen visits	200 @	347.83	69,566		
	24 @	347.83		8,348	
	6 @	347.83			2,087
After sales visits	200 @	285.71	57,142		
	100 @	285.71		28,571	
	50 @	285.71			14,286
			531,883	50,738	17,403

Final unit cost analysis:

	Production cost £	Non-production cost £	Total cost £	Selling price £	Profit (loss) £
Customer X	40	53.19	93.19	75.00	(18.19)
Customer Y	40	5.07	45.07	75.00	29.93
Customer Z	40	1.74	41.74	75.00	33.26

Thus the MD's misgivings were justified. The high cost of serving customer X effectively wipes out the profit being made on producing and selling the product and some consideration has to be given to the quality of service offered for the price charged.

11.8   Activity based budgeting (ABB)

Activity based budgeting extends the use of ABC from individual product costing, for pricing and output decisions, to the overall planning and control system of the business.

The basic principle of ABB is that the work of each department for which a budget is to be prepared is analysed by its major activities, for which cost drivers may be identified. The budgeted cost of resources used by each activity is determined (from recent historical data) and, where appropriate, cost per unit of activity calculated.

Future costs can then be budgeted by deciding on future activity levels and working back to the required resource input.

11.9   ABB - example

The following "activity matrix" shows the resources used (rows) and major functions/activities (columns) of the stores department of a manufacturing business.

The total current annual costs of each resource consumed by the department are shown in the final column; they have then been spread back over the various activities to establish the cost pools. The allocation of resource costs between activities will, to some extent, be subjective.

Each of the first four activities has an identifiable cost driver, and the total resource cost driver rates can be determined (cost per unit of activity).

The last two activities that occur within the department are non-volume related, and are sometimes referred to as "sustaining costs". They are necessary functions and should not be ignored in the budgeting process; however, they should not be attributed to particular cost drivers, as this would not reflect their true cost behaviour and would result in inappropriate budgets being set.

Activity cost matrix for stores department

Activity:	Goods inwards	Goods out	Stock orders	Monthly stock counting	Records maintenance	Supervision	Total
Cost driver:	Deliveries	Stores requisitions	Orders	Counts	-	-	
Resource	£'000	£'000	£'000	£'000	£'000	£'000	£'000
Management salary	-	-	-	1.5	3.5	25	30
Storekeepers' wages	50	30	10	4	20	-	114
Overtime	15	-	-	5	5	-	25
Stationery, etc	1	2	2	1	3	-	9
Other	6	4	2	1	2	4	19
Total	72	36	14	12.5	33.5	29	197

Volume of activity 450	375	100	12	-	-
Cost per activity unit £160	£96	£140	£1,042	£33,500	£29,000

The budget for the stores department for next year will be set by deciding upon the expected number of deliveries, stores requisitions, orders etc and costing these up accordingly. Sustaining costs will effectively be treated as fixed costs.

11.10   Advantages of ABB

- The costs of activities are identified. Each delivery of goods costs £160 to process. This should be taken into account when determining optimum order sizes etc. Is it necessary to have monthly stock counts at a cost of £1,042 each? To what extent can the stock records be relied upon if counts are reduced?

- It takes into account the impact of activity levels on resource costs, of assistance in cost reduction programmes and in setting realistic cost targets

- Activity unit costs allow easier analysis of cost trends over time and intra-departmental comparisons

- Resource allocation decisions are assisted by the activity related cost information

- ABB links directly to a TQM programme by relating the cost of an activity to the level of service provided (eg stores requisitions processed) - do the user departments feel they are getting a cost-effective service?

12   SELF TEST QUESTIONS

12.1   Explain the role of computers in an automated factory. (2.2)

12.2   What is a flexible manufacturing system? (2.3)

12.3   Explain Materials Requirements Planning (MRP). (3.1, 3.2)

12.4   Explain Just In Time. (6.1 - 6.3)

12.5   Explain the key features of a backflush accounting system. (8.3)

12.6   What is Activity Based Costing? (10.1)

12.7   What is a cost driver? (10.1)

12.8   State the advantages of Activity Based Costing as identified by its supporters. (10.12)

12.9   Explain Activity Based Management. (11.1)

12.10   What is an activity cost profile? (11.3)

13   EXAMINATION TYPE QUESTIONS

13.1   Limitation of traditional management accounting

The new manufacturing environment is characterised by more flexibility, a readiness to meet customers' requirements, smaller batches, continuous improvements and an emphasis on quality. In such circumstances, traditional management accounting performance measures are, at best, irrelevant and, at worst, misleading.

You are required

(a)   to discuss the above statement, citing specific examples to support or refute the views expressed;   **(10 marks)**

(b)   to explain in what ways management accountants can adapt the services they provide to the new environment.   **(7 marks)**

(Total: 17 marks)

13.2   ABC terms

(a)   In the context of activity based costing (ABC), it was stated in **Management Accounting - Evolution not Revolution** by Bromwich and Bhimani, that

"Cost drivers attempt to link costs to the scope of output rather than the scale of output thereby generating less arbitrary product costs for decision making."

You are required to explain the terms 'activity based costing' and 'cost drivers'.   **(8 marks)**

(b)   XYZ plc manufactures four products, namely A, B, C and D, using the same plant and processes.

The following information relates to a production period:

Product	Volume	Material cost per unit	Direct labour per unit	Machine time per unit	Labour cost per unit
A	500	£5	½ hour	¼ hour	£3
B	5,000	£5	½ hour	¼ hour	£3
C	600	£16	2 hours	1 hour	£12
D	7,000	£17	1½ hours	1½ hours	£9

Total production overhead recorded by the cost accounting system is analysed under the following headings:

Factory overhead applicable to machine-oriented activity is £37,424.

Set-up costs are £4,355.

The cost of ordering materials is £1,920.

Handling materials - £7,580.

Administration for spare parts - £8,600.

These overhead costs are absorbed by products on a machine hour rate of £4.80 per hour, giving an overhead cost per product of:

A = £1.20   B = £1.20   C = £4.80   D = £7.20

However, investigation into the production overhead activities for the period reveals the following totals:

Product	Number of set-ups	Number of material orders	Number of times material was handled	Number of spare parts
A	1	1	2	2
B	6	4	10	5
C	2	1	3	1
D	8	4	12	4

You are required

(i)   to compute an overhead cost per product using activity based costing, tracing overheads to production units by means of cost drivers;   **(6 marks)**

(ii) to comment briefly on the differences disclosed between overheads traced by the present system and those traced by activity based costing. **(3 marks)**

(Total: 17 marks)

14 ANSWERS TO EXAMINATION TYPE QUESTIONS

14.1 Limitation of traditional management accounting

(a) The traditional management accounting techniques for performance measurement are based around budgetary control and standard costing and the associated variances. The budgets are normally prepared annually and the standards are applied to all products of a particular type.

The move towards more flexibility, a readiness to meet customer requirements, smaller batches and continuous improvements results in a wider range of products or 'jobs' geared to customers' specifications with an associated variation in cost, making it difficult to apply a single standard cost. If a single standard were used in this context to calculate variances, these variances would be partly attributable to changes in product specification.

The effect of advanced manufacturing technology is that a greater emphasis is placed on machines and much less emphasis on direct labour. This has two major implications. Firstly the traditional direct labour efficiency variance is of limited use and secondly the method for calculation of unit cost needs to be amended.

The increased emphasis on quality contradicts assumptions made by traditional management accounting, which assumes that products should be made as reliable as is 'cost-effective'. This has been shown to be a short-sighted approach. In the long run, an emphasis on total quality, not only of products but of services to customers and services within the organisation not only increases sales but enormously reduces many costs associated with re-working and correcting errors.

Overall the traditional performance measures may, therefore, be misleading in the new manufacturing environment.

(b) Activity based costing is being introduced in order to identify more accurately the activities or 'cost drivers' which are causing costs to be incurred. The advantage of this technique is that not only can standard costs be adapted more quickly to custom-made products or batches made to customers' specifications, but also they can be quickly updated for changes in methods of manufacture.

If management accountants are to produce meaningful performance reports in the future, they should be concerned not only with comparing results against budgets but also against alternative methods of working. For example, they should be comparing the costs of traditional stock-holding policies against new techniques such as 'just-in-time'.

They should also be concerned with non-financial measures of performance, particularly those associated with quality, such as statistical control charts and reject rates.

Ultimately, management accountants are judged by the usefulness of the information which is given to management. They should be aiming to 'own' the information system of a company so that they can present integrated reports involving financial and non-financial factors. In order to do this, they must become very familiar with their firm's technical operations.

14.2 ABC terms

(a) Activity based costing is a method of costing which is based on the principle that activities cause costs to be incurred not products. Costs are attributed to activities and the performance of those activities is then linked to products.

A cost driver is the factor which causes costs to be incurred (eg, placing an order, setting up a machine).

(b)   (i)   Cost per set-up

$$\frac{£4,355}{1+6+2+8} = \frac{£4,355}{17} = \mathbf{£256}$$

Cost per order

$$\frac{£1,920}{1+4+1+4} = \frac{£1,920}{10} = \mathbf{£192}$$

Cost per handling of materials

$$\frac{£7,580}{2+10+3+12} = \frac{£7,580}{27} = \mathbf{£281}$$

Cost per spare part

$$\frac{£8,600}{2+5+1+4} = \frac{£8,600}{12} = \mathbf{£717}$$

Cost per machine hour (No. of m/c hours = 125 + 1,250 + 600 + 10,500)

$$= \frac{£37,424}{12,475} = \mathbf{£3.00/hr}$$

Costs are then attributed to products using the cost driver rates calculated above, for example:

Product A requires one machine set-up, therefore 1 × £256 = £256;
Product B requires six machine set-ups, therefore 6 × £256 = £1,536;
and so on.

Product	A	B	C	D
	£	£	£	£
Activities:				
Set-ups	256	1,536	512	2,048
Orders	192	768	192	768
Handling	562	2,810	843	3,372
Spare parts	1,434	3,585	717	2,868
Machine time	375	3,750	1,800	31,500
	2,819	12,449	4,064	40,556
No. of units	500	5,000	600	7,000
Cost per unit	£5.64	£2.49	£6.77	£5.79

The costs are then totalled and divided by the number of units to give the cost per unit for each product.

(ii)   The activity based costing approach attributes more costs to products A, B and C and less to product D than the traditional method of accounting for overhead costs. The activity based costing method gives a more accurate cost by relating it to the resources used to manufacture each product, consequently these costs are more useful for decision making than those provided by the traditional method.

6 QUALITY

INTRODUCTION & LEARNING OBJECTIVES

In the previous chapter we considered specific techniques of world class manufacturing and the development of accounting systems to reflect these changes. In this chapter you will learn about the importance of quality.

When you have studied this chapter you should be able to do the following:

- Explain the importance of quality and its meaning within a Total Quality Management environment.
- Explain how quality may be measured.
- Explain how quality costs may be collected, anlaysed, and reported to management.

1 QUALITY AS A STRATEGIC VARIABLE

1.1 The concept of quality

In recent times a great deal of attention has been devoted to quality issues. Although there has always been a general awareness of the need to ensure the satisfaction of the customer, it is the worldwide nature of competition that has focused attention on the need to act. Competitor pressure has often come from the Japanese, whose basic premise is that poor quality is unacceptable.

The term 'quality' is difficult to define because it has a wide range of meanings, covering a large and complex area of businesses and processes. Quality is also a matter of perception and relative measure. For example, if you asked a group of people to each nominate a 'quality sound system', it could be that you would get a different suggestion from each of them.

The Japanese have shown, with their highly competitive products, that high quality does not always mean high cost. The response in the West to improve quality is still really in its infancy.

1.2 Quality equals profit

The evidence of the value that customers place on quality is all around us. For many years, both in the UK and the US, every survey of car quality showed Japanese producers way ahead. For ten years after establishing the PIMS database, the researchers argued that market share was the best way to achieve profits. But a re-analysis of the data showed that, while high market share does bring profit, sustainable market share comes from leadership in perceived product or service quality. The PIMS researchers now call relative quality ie, vis-à-vis competitors, the most important single factor affecting a business unit's long term performance.

2 QUALITY MANAGEMENT

2.1 Management role

Quality management suggests a concern that the organisation's products or services meet their planned level of quality and perform to specifications. Management has a duty to ensure that all tasks are completed consistently to a standard which meets the needs of the business. To achieve this they need to:

(a)   set clear standards;
(b)   plan how to meet those standards
(c)   track the quality achieved;
(d)   take action to improve quality where necessary.

(a)   **Setting standards**

To manage quality everyone in the organisation needs to have a clear and shared understanding of the standards required. These standards will be set after taking account of:

(i)   the quality expected by the customers;

(ii)   the costs and benefits of delivering different degrees of quality;

(iii)   the impact of different degrees of quality on:

- the customers and their needs;
- contribution to departmental objectives;
- employee attitude and motivation.

Having decided on the standards these must be communicated to everyone concerned to ensure that the right standards are achieved. Documentation of the standards must be clear, specific, measurable and comprehensive.

(b)   **Meeting the standards**

Having decided on appropriate quality standards management should then:

(i)   agree and document procedures and methods to meet the standards;

(ii)   agree and document controls to ensure that the standards will be met;

(iii)   agree and document responsibilities via job descriptions and terms of reference; and

(iv)   prepare and implement training plans for employees to ensure they are familiar with the standards, procedures, controls and their responsibilities.

(c)   **Tracking the quality**

After the process to achieve quality has been set up, an information system to monitor the quality should be set up. This is called quality control.

When a good system to track the quality has been achieved, it can be used constructively to improve quality and work on problem areas.

Employees within the organisation have a huge influence on the quality of their work and to gain their commitment and support the management should:

(i)   publish the quality being achieved;

(ii)   meet regularly with the staff involved to discuss the quality being achieved as well as the vulnerabilities and priorities as they see them and also agree specific issues and action points for them to work on to improve quality;

(iii)   encourage ideas from the staff about improvements and consider introducing short-term suggestion schemes.

2.2   Quality revolution

Tom Peters in his book *Thriving on Chaos*, concentrates on the twelve attributes of a quality revolution.

(i)   Management obsessed with quality.

(ii)   A guiding system or ideology.

(iii)   Quality is measured.

(iv)   Reward for quality.

(v)   Training in technologies for assessing qualities.

(vi)   Teams involving multiple functions or systems are used.

(vii)   Concentration on small improvements.

(viii)   Constant stimulation.

(ix)   Creation of a shadow or parallel organisation structure devoted to quality improvement.

(x)   Everyone is involved. Suppliers especially, but distributors and customers too, must be a part of the organisation's quality process.

(xi)   Quality improvement is the primary source of cost reduction.

(xii)   Quality improvement is a never-ending journey.

These are traits which companies like IBM, Ford and Federal Express share in their quality improvement programs.

Peters argues that most quality programs fail for one of two reasons: they have a system without passion, or passion without a system. The type of system to follow, and the results obtained, causes some controversy. There are many ideologies used in quality processes. Should one follow Deming via statistical process control or Phil Crosby, author of *Quality is free* or Armand Feigenbaum's Total Quality Control or Joseph Juran's 'fitness for purpose'?

2.3   W Edwards Deming

In the 1920s and 1930s in America, statistical quality control methods were used to monitor and control the quality of output in flow line production processes. These methods, the origins of modern quality management, were introduced into Japan by American consultants like Deming, who were involved in the aid program to rejuvenate the industry in Japan after the war.

Some companies (and governments) blame unions for having a negative impact on worker productivity. Deming insists that management is 90% of the problem. Organisations need to address the problems of the quality of direction being given to the workforce, the resources available to get the job done efficiently and the opportunities for workers to contribute ideas about how to do the job better.

Deming, in his book *Quality, Productivity and Competitive Position*, suggests that improving quality leads to improved productivity, reduced costs, more satisfied customers and increased profitability. His system for management to improve quality and competitiveness covers the following main areas.

*   The organisation should have a constant purpose of improving their product or service.

*   Quality objectives should be agreed and action taken to accomplish them.

*   Systems for production and service delivery should be improved, eliminating all waste.

*   Consideration of quality and reliability should be just as important as price when choosing a supplier.

*   Attention must be paid to training people so they are better at their jobs and understand how to optimise production.

*   Mass inspection of goods ties up resources and does not improve quality.

*   Education and self improvement should be encouraged in all members of the organisation. Management should enable staff to take a pride in their work.

*   Barriers between staff areas should be broken down.

2.4   Phil B Crosby

Crosby is another theorist on quality. He is so prominent in America that General Motors bought a 10% stake in his firm. His thinking is based on his background working on the Pershing missile programme, where the main objectives were zero defects. The zero defects concept and his assertion that a product should not have to be corrected once it is built (right first time) are embodied in his four standards.

(i)   Quality is conformance to standards.
(ii)   Prevention is the system for advancing quality, not appraisal.
(iii)   The goal should be zero defects.
(iv)   The importance of quality is measured by the cost of not having quality.

The problem for Crosby's standards is that quality must be judged as the customer perceives it, as we discussed earlier. He asserts that his process is customer-oriented but companies, such as Milliken and IBM in the USA, after pounding away at quality for many years, have found that a second revolution is required - to become more responsive to customers. Crosby firmly believes that quality is not comparative, it either conforms to customer requirements or it is unacceptable. It is the role of management to make sure that the customer's needs are reflected in the specifications set within the organisation. Quality is, therefore, an attribute and not a variable.

2.5   Joseph Juran

Juran defines quality as 'fitness for purpose'. This can be described loosely as 'that which relates to the evaluation of a product or service for its ability to satisfy a given need'. The elements of this theory are:

*   **quality of design**, which can include customer satisfaction which is built into the product;
*   **quality of conformance**, or a lack of defects;
*   **abilities**; and
*   **field service**.

Because customers incorporate such things as 'value for money' in their 'fitness for purpose' equation, Juran's theory is looking at quality from the point of view of the customer and is a more practical concept.

2.6   Armand Feigenbaum

Feigenbaum emphasises the relevance of quality issues in all areas of the operation of a business. He believes that 'prevention is better than cure', stressing the importance of identifying the costs of quality in economic and accounting terms.

Organisations adopting his ideas are encouraged to change the role of the quality control function from inspecting and rejecting output to one in which quality is given a planning role, involving the design of systems and procedures to reduce the likelihood of sub-optimal production.

2.7   Kauro Ishikawa

Although modern quality management practices have their roots in the USA, some of the best Japanese principles offer significant lessons to Western organisations. Studies have shown that the success of some Japanese companies has been due to progress in design quality, especially in miniaturisation, rather than conformance quality.

The late Ishikawa is noted for his proposals on quality circles and quality control. The Ishikawa cause and effect diagram, known as the 'fishbone diagram' because of its shape, illustrates the relationship between possible causes and effect and helps to discover the source of the problem.

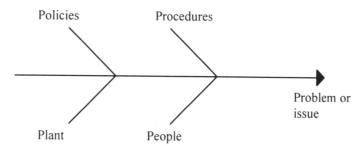

The diagram above follows the 4P pattern of policies, procedures, people and plant of non-manufacturing areas. The 5M pattern has branches comprising machinery, method, material, manpower and maintenance.

After the initial diagram has been drawn, the major causes of problems can be further expanded and treated as separate branches.

2.8   Genichi Taguchi

Taguchi developed a mathematical model of loss, measuring costs incurred or profits forgone relative to some baseline of performance. In his terms loss is more than cost. Quality is 'the loss imparted to society from the time the product is shipped'. Because goods use up time and resources in production, a measure of quality is the fact that this 'loss' is minimised.

Taguchi identifies two aspects of quality control; off-line and on-line.

(a)   Off-line quality control incorporates systems design, parameter design and tolerance design. Systems design should reflect appropriate technology.

(b)   On-line quality control aims to minimise the loss due to variations between goods produced, weighing the cost of the variation against the cost of correcting the variation. Examples of these variations could include slight differences in weight between identical parts or slight differences in time to produce something.

3   QUALITY CONTROL AND QUALITY ASSURANCE

3.1   The difference between quality control and quality assurance

Quality control is the title given to the more traditional view of quality. It may be defined as the process of:

(a)   establishing standards of quality for a product or service;

(b)   establishing procedures or production methods which ought to ensure that these required standards of quality are met in a suitably high proportion of cases;

(c)   monitoring actual quality;

(d)   taking control action when actual quality falls below standard.

Quality assurance, however, is the term used where a supplier guarantees the quality of goods supplied and allows the customer access while the goods are being manufactured. This is usually done through supplier quality assurance (SQA) officers, who control the specification of the goods supplied.

Some companies follow Japanese practice and use supervisors, work people or quality circles to control suppliers' quality. These representatives or the SQA officer may enter the supplier's plant, to verify that production is to the correct specification, working tolerances, material and labour standards. For example, the Ministry of Defence would reserve the right to ensure that defence contractors produce to specification, since defective work could mean the failure of a multi-million pound aircraft, loss of trained pilots and possibly ground crew as well as damage to civilian life and property. Likewise, a weapons system failure could have disastrous consequences.

One great advantage of SQA is that it may render possible reduction of the in-house quality control headcount, since there will be no need to check incoming materials or sub-assemblies or components.

3.2   Quality control

Quality control is concerned with maintaining quality standards. There are usually procedures to check quality of bought-in materials, work-in-progress and finished goods. Sometimes one or all of these functions is the responsibility of the research and development department on the premise that production should not self-regulate its own quality.

Statistical quality control through sampling techniques is commonly used to reduce costs and production interruptions. On some occasions, where quality assurance has been given, customers have the contractual right to visit a manufacturer unannounced and carry out quality checks. This is normal practice with Sainsbury's and Tesco's contracts with manufacturers producing 'own label' goods (eg, Tesco Baked Beans).

In the past, failure to screen quality successfully has resulted in rejections, re-work and scrap, all of which add to manufacturing costs. Modern trends in industry of competition, mass production and increasing standards of quality requirements have resulted in a thorough reappraisal of the problem and two important points have emerged:

(a)   It is necessary to single out and remove the causes for poor quality goods before production instead of waiting for the end result. Many companies have instigated 'zero defects' programmes following the Japanese practice of eradicating poor quality as early in the chain as possible and insisting on strict quality adherence at every stage – as Crosby points out in his book *Quality is Free*, this is cost effective since customer complaints etc. reduce dramatically.

(b)   The co-ordination of all activities from the preparation of the specification, through to the purchasing and inspection functions and right up to the function of delivery of the finished product, is essential.

It is accepted that it is not possible to achieve perfection in products because of the variations in raw material quality, operating skills, different types of machines used, wear and tear, etc. but quality control attempts to ascertain the amount of variation from perfect that can be expected in any operation. If this variation is acceptable according to engineering requirements, then production must be established within controlled limits and if the variation is too great then corrective action must be taken to bring it within acceptable limits.

3.3   The role of standards

The British Standards Institution, through its Certification and Assessment Services, provides industry with first class product certification and company quality assessment schemes. When an organisation operates to the quality standard BS5750 it is a way of demonstrating that the organisation is committed to quality and has been assessed accordingly.

There are three parts to the BS5750 standard:

(a)   specification for design;

(b)   specification for manufacture and installation;

(c)   specification for final inspection and test.

In 1987 the ISO 9000 series of international standards on quality systems were published by the International Organisation for Standardisation.

This series consists of five individual standards, ISO 9000-9004. Two of them are guideline standards and the others are reference standards.

•   ISO 9000 is the *Guide to Selection and Use,* which is the guide to other standards in the series.

- ISO 9001 is the *Specification for Design/Development, Production, Installation and Servicing,* covering organisations concerned with all activities from conceptual design to after-sales service.

- ISO 9002, the *Specification for Production and Installation,* concerning organisations with product and service quality in production and installation only.

- ISO 9003 is the *Specification for Final Inspection and Test.* This is for activities which can only be quality assured at final inspection and test.

- ISO 9004 is the *Guide to Quality Management and Quality System Elements.* This is a guide to good quality management practice.

4   TOTAL QUALITY MANAGEMENT (TQM)

4.1   Approaches

Total quality management (TQM) is the name given to programmes which seek to ensure that goods are produced and services are supplied of the highest quality. Its origin lies primarily in Japanese organisations and it is argued that TQM has been a significant factor in Japanese global business success. The basic principle of TQM is that costs of prevention (getting things right first time) are less than the costs of correction.

This contrasts with the 'traditional' UK approach that less than 100% quality is acceptable as the costs of improvement from say 90% to 100% outweigh the benefits. Thus in the analysis of quality related costs there may be a trade-off between a lowering of failure (internal and external) at the expense of increased prevention and appraisal costs.

Which view is correct is a matter of debate but the advocates of TQM would argue that in addition to the cost analysis above the impact of less than 100% quality in terms of lost potential for future sales also has to be taken into account.

4.2   Past exam questions

Exam questions on quality management will generally be of a discursive nature, although they may be related to specific situations. In June 1995, information was given about energy cost items in a manufacturing business, and candidates were asked to explain, with examples, how a TQM programme might help in energy cost reduction. In December 1995, a more general question required a discussion of the role of TQM in the provision of effective information for cost control and reduction.

The implication, therefore, is that quality is not an end in itself - the ultimate aim in improving quality is the reduction of costs, by getting things 'right first time'.

Computational questions are also possible in this area - see the example in paragraph 11.4, based upon a question set in December 1994.

4.3   Features of TQM

The philosophy of TQM is based on the idea of a series of quality chains which may be broken at any point by one person or service not meeting the requirements of the customer. The key to TQM is for everyone in the organisation to have well-defined customers - an extension of the word, beyond the customers of the company, to anyone to whom an individual provides a service. Thus the 'Paint shop' staff would be customers of the 'Assembly shop' staff who would themselves be the customers of the 'Machine shop' staff. The idea is that the supplier-customer relationships would form a chain extending from the company's original suppliers through to its ultimate consumers. Areas of responsibility would need to be identified and a manager allocated to each, and then the customer/supplier chain established. True to the principle outlined above the quality requirements of each 'customer' within the chain would be assessed, and meeting these would then become the responsibility of the 'suppliers' who form the preceding link in the chain.

Quality has to be managed - it will not just happen. To meet the requirements of TQM a company will probably need to recruit more staff and may also need to change the level of services on offer to its customers, which includes 'internal' customers. This would probably entail costs in terms of the redesign of systems, recruitment and training of staff, and the purchase of appropriate equipment.

Thackray indicated the following features of companies which follow TQM:

(a)   There is absolute commitment by the chief executive and all senior managers to doing what is needed to change the culture.

(b)   People are not afraid to try new things.

(c)   Communication is excellent and multi-way.

(d)   There is a real commitment to continuous improvement in all processes.

(e)   Attention is focused first on the process and second on the results.

(f)   There is an absence of strict control systems.

The last two points appear to go against the central thrust of UK management accounting. The point being made is that concentrating on getting a process right will result in an improved result. A process is a detailed step in the overall system of producing and delivering goods to a customer. Improving a process without worrying about the short-term effects will encourage the search for improvement to take place, the improvement will more likely be permanent, and will lead to further improvements. A concentration on results and control generally means attaching blame to someone if things go wrong. Therefore employees would not have an incentive to pick up and correct errors but rather would be encouraged to try and conceal them.

4.4   Analysis and restructuring of resources

In many businesses, employees' time is used up in **discretionary activities**. Discretionary activities are activities such as checking, chasing and other tasks related to product failures. Some/most of this time may be capable of being redeployed into the two other categories of work:

(a)   Core activities, and
(b)   Support activities.

Core activities add direct value to the business. They use the specific skills of the particular employees being examined and are the reason for their employment. Support activities are those activities which clearly support core activities and are thus necessary to allow core activities to add value. The importance of this analysis can be seen in a quote from a US Chief Executive some years ago: 'The only things you really need to run a business are materials, machines, workers and salesmen. Nobody else is justified unless he's helping the worker produce more product or the salesman sell more product.'

Analysis of employees' time will provide a clearer view of the costs of poor quality and whether efforts in other departments could reduce the amount of time spent by a department further down the product chain on discretionary activities. For example, suppose there are seven processes from purchasing of raw materials through various stages of production to delivery of the product to the customer. If each process is 90% effective then there will be only a 48% success rate at the end of the seventh stage (90% × 90% × 90% etc). What happens in practice however may be that personnel employed in stage 4 of the process spend a lot of their time on discretionary activities trying to remedy the effect of defects at earlier stages. It is suggested that it would be more sensible for departments in the earlier stages to get things right the first time.

An example has been quoted of an office equipment supplier which analysed employees' time into core, support and discretionary activities. It was found that half of the salesmen's face-to-face selling time with customers consisted of listening to their complaints about poor customer service.

4.5 Quality circles

Quality circles consist of about ten employees possessing relevant levels of skill, ranging from the shop-floor through to management. They meet regularly to discuss the major aspect of quality, but other areas such as safety and productivity will also be dealt with.

The main aim is to be able to offer management:

(a)   ideas connected with improvement and recommendation;

(b)   possible solutions and suggestions;

(c)   organising the implementation of (a) and (b).

The development of Quality circles allows the process of decision making to start at shop floor level, with the ordinary worker encouraged to comment and make suggestions, as well as being allowed to put them into practice. Circle members experience the responsibility for ensuring quality, and have the power to exercise verbal complaint. Quality circles may be applied at any level of organisational activity, being used to cover all aspects and could conceivably involve all employees.

Jaguar, the established motor company, has effectively used this system resulting in the involvement of ten percent of the workforce. A notable point here is that in one decade the number of quality inspectors required has been roughly halved. Clearly, quality circles are a practical means of gaining employee participation, they are not mainly for reducing costs although this aspect will be a major topic for discussion. Other benefits are increased awareness of shop-floor problems, members gain confidence over problem solving etc, greater output, improved quality and shop-floor participation.

Equally, putting this system into practice can prove difficult. The well established system of hierarchical management is difficult to penetrate, and to some organisations it would present extreme changes. Some systems may not be able to accommodate such change eg, the armed forces or Police Force where a powerful hierarchy has developed.

5 THE PURSUIT OF EXCELLENCE: CHARACTERISTICS OF A SUCCESSFUL ORGANISATION

5.1 Peters and Waterman

Tom Peters and Robert Waterman, in their book *In Search of Excellence*, identified certain core values that were associated with 'excellent' organisations:

(a)   **A bias for action:** the excellent companies get on with it. They are analytical in their decision making but this does not paralyse them as it does some companies.

(b)   **Close to the customer:** they get to know their customers and provide them with quality, reliability and service.

(c)   **Autonomy and entrepreneurship:** leaders and innovators are fostered and given scope.

(d)   **Productivity through people:** they really believe that the basis for quality and productivity is the employee. They do not just pay lip service to the notion 'people are our most important asset'. They do something about it by encouraging commitment and getting everyone involved.

(e)   **Hands-on, value driven:** the people who run the organisation get close to those who work for them and ensure that the organisation's values are understood and acted upon.

(f)   **Stick to the knitting:** the successful organisations stay reasonably close to the businesses they know.

(g)   **Simple form, lean staff:** the organisation structure is simple and corporate staff are kept to the minimum.

(h)   **Simultaneous loose-tight properties:** they are both centralised and decentralised. They push decisions and autonomy as far down the organisation as they can get, into individual units and profit centres. But, as Peters and Waterman state, 'they are fanatic centralists around the few core values they hold dear'.

Though Peters and Waterman stress the positive benefits of having a strong organisational culture there are also potential drawbacks.

(a)   Strong cultures are difficult to change.

(b)   Strong cultures may stress inappropriate values.

(c)   Where two strong cultures come into contact eg, in a merger, then conflicts can arise.

(d)   A strong culture may not be attuned to the environment eg, a strong innovative culture is only appropriate in a dynamic, shifting environment.

Despite these problems it is still possible to agree with Alan Sugar, Chairman of Amstrad, who said in 1987 'It is essential to retain a strong corporate culture and philosophy, otherwise the business can drift and become confused and lost in direction'.

5.2   Goldsmith and Clutterbuck

Other studies on excellence have followed Peters and Waterman. Goldsmith and Clutterbuck in *The Winning Streak,* made some observations on the characteristics of top British companies. They showed a similarity to those quoted for American corporations.

The factors in the British companies were:

(a)   **leadership**, with visible top management and clear objectives;

(b)   **autonomy,** with encouragement to take 'controlled initiative';

(c)   **control**, with detailed planning but an ability to deal with the unexpected;

(d)   **involvement**, which is a commitment and a positive attitude at all levels;

(e)   **market orientation**;

(f)   **zero basing**, or keeping in touch with the fundamentals;

(g)   **innovation**, a recognition that innovation and change is the norm;

(h)   **integrity**, with everyone knowing where they stand.

5.3   The end of sustainable excellence?

Because the performance of some of the excellent organisations of the 1980s has deteriorated, the issue of sustainable excellence has been raised. The problems that they face is that their markets are changing faster than before and as companies grow larger it becomes more difficult to maintain the flexibility needed to match the changes.

Excellence may be difficult to sustain for other reasons, such as:

- the successful company leader may retire or run out of steam;
- the leaders may grow away from their customers and staff as the business grows;
- 'Empire building' can limit flexibility and creativity;
- loss of customer focus can be the outcome if companies assume that they dominate the market.

The key to maintaining excellence seems to be continuous improvement and the ability to recognise complacency throughout the organisation.

6   MONITORING AND MAINTAINING QUALITY

6.1   Quality and reliability

Quality itself must be regarded as relative to other factors such as price, consistency and utility. The market for a product or service will accommodate itself to various degrees of quality.

A concept met today is that of a quality and reliability system, including the following elements:

(a)   A study of customer requirements, particularly as they relate to performance and price.

(b)   The design of the product or service.

(c)   Full specification of the requirements of the design, clearly understood by everybody concerned with production.

(d)   Assurance that operational processes can meet the requirements of the design.

(e)   Acceptance by everybody of responsibility for meeting standards. Many people share in this responsibility. The manager plays a part by declaring what quality standards are to be. Design engineers must work within the parameters which give satisfaction to the customer. Production controllers make sure that output of the right quality is produced on time. Purchasing officers must find reliable suppliers. Operatives must be trained to achieve standards.

(f)   Checking that the product or service conforms to the specification.

(g)   Instructions on the use, application and limitation of the product or service.

(h)   Study of consumer experience of the product, feedback to the departments concerned and immediate remedial action if necessary, otherwise praise all round.

6.2   Barriers to quality and excellence

It has been shown that it is much easier to achieve quality and excellence in a new business, where the principles are built in from the start. It is much harder to develop and improve quality and excellence in an existing company because it may be necessary to overcome a series of barriers. These barriers may be human, technical or financial.

(a)   Human barriers exist because people are naturally resistant to change. Some kind of revolutionary process is usually necessary to provide the momentum and incentive for change. This transformation of attitudes needs total commitment from the top and requires one or more champions as well as involvement at all levels.

(b)   Technical barriers concern the knowledge and skills that are required to plan, implement and control the best performance practices.

(c)   The finance required to sustain excellence and improve quality may be yet another barrier for the company to surmount.

It takes commitment to quality and excellence. Tom Peters's advice to managers is: 'Starting this afternoon, don't walk past a shoddy product or service without comment and action - ever again!'

In his seminars on quality he poses a situation where a brochure is going out to customers. The deadline is missed; five thousand have been printed, inserted into envelopes, addressed and sealed. They are packed and ready to take to the post office. The unit you are in charge of has a not-too-healthy cash flow. You then discover a single typo on page two, in the small print. Should you walk past it or act?

He argues that you should act and throw it out. If you knowingly ignore a tiny act of poor service or quality, you have destroyed your credibility and any possibility of moral leadership on this issue.

6.3   A total quality programme

The characteristics of a total quality programme should include the following:

(a)   Everyone in the organisation is involved in continually improving the processes and systems under their control and each person is responsible for his or her own quality assurance.

(b)   A commitment to the satisfaction of every customer.

(c)   Employee involvement is practised and the active participation of everyone in the organisation is encouraged.

(d)   There is an investment in training and education to realise individual potential.

(e)   Teamwork is used in a number of forms eg, quality circles.

(f)   Suppliers and customers form an integrated part of the process of improvement.

(g)   Process re-design is used to simplify processes, systems, procedures and the organisation itself.

7   PERFORMANCE MEASUREMENT IN A TQM ENVIRONMENT

7.1   Quality of inputs

Inputs may be in the form of materials from suppliers and skills and efficiency from the employees of the organisation.

Targets or benchmarks must be set against which the performance of suppliers can be measured. These may include delivery times, rejection rates, the percentage of incorrect/short deliveries and similar measures.

The achievement of BS5750 is a sign of quality in suppliers.

7.2   Quality of outputs

Outputs too must be measured for quality against pre-determined targets. Such targets may be based on the number of rejects as a result of internal inspection procedures, but customer reaction is also important. Customer reaction may be measured by number of customer complaints, the percentage of returned goods and similar factors.

7.3   Use of control charts

An example of a control chart is shown below:

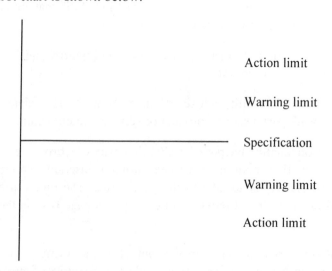

The specification or target shows what is expected in respect of the particular performance measure which is measured along the vertical (y) axis. The horizontal (x) axis is normally used to represent time. Individual values are plotted on the control chart and provided the points lie within the upper and lower warning limits, the performance is acceptable. Outside these tolerances it is not acceptable but the cost of action is likely to exceed its rewards; only when the individual values exceed the upper or lower action limits is management action required.

8   TRAINING FOR QUALITY

8.1   Introduction

As mentioned above, one of the inputs to a product is the skills and efficiency of the employees; training can improve these employee skills and efficiencies provided the employee also perceives the benefits of such training.

8.2   Commitment to training

Training can occur both inside and outside the workplace. Internal training could be in the ideas of team working and quality discussion groups which are known as quality circules (see earlier in this chapter). Quality attitudes are important, for no amount of discussion or training are likely to have the desired effect unless employees understand and accept the benefits of quality.

8.3   Costs and benefits of training for quality

The benefits of training can include:

(a)   improved productivity;
(b)   improved quality through less wastage;
(c)   improved employee commitment.

The costs of training include:

(a)   cost of external courses;
(b)   lost output caused by training.

9   DESIGNING FOR QUALITY

9.1   Introduction

When a product is designed, its specification should consider factors which will minimise future rectification costs. Production methods should be as simple as possible and use the skills and resources existing within the sphere of knowledge of the organisation and its employees.

9.2   Costs and benefits of design quality

The costs of design quality include:

(a)   the costs of design staff;
(b)   the costs of quality control staff; and
(c)   the cost of the equipment to monitor and control performance.

The benefits to be derived from a quality design include:

(a)   lower rectification costs;
(b)   lower rejection rates;
(c)   fewer customer complaints;
(d)   improved sales.

10   QUALITY INFORMATION SYSTEMS

10.1   Introduction

An information system is needed to provide feedback on the success or otherwise of quality procedures. Such systems should attempt to measure both monetary and non-monetary factors.

10.2   Monetary and non-monetary measures

Quality can be measured in terms of its effect on profit via costs and revenues, and also in non monetary terms. An example of a monetary measure would be the costs of rectification whereas non-monetary measures may include the percentage of wastage or the number of customer complaints.

Care must be taken with regard to traditional performance reports such as variance analysis, which can operate in opposition to quality. For example favourable price variances can arise because of using poorer quality resources. These poorer quality inputs may lead to a reduction in the quality of outputs.

11   MEASURING THE COST OF QUALITY

11.1   Introduction

There are costs associated with quality which may be divided into costs of ensuring quality and costs of quality failure.

11.2   Quality related costs

A report *'The effectiveness of the corporate overhead in British business'* Develin & Partners 1989, estimates that the average cost of waste and mistakes in the UK represents 20% of controllable corporate overhead.

(a)   **Quality related costs**

> **Definition**   Cost of ensuring and assuring quality, as well as loss incurred when quality is not achieved. Quality costs are classified as prevention cost, appraisal cost, internal failure cost and external failure cost.

(b)   **Prevention costs**

> **Definition**   The cost incurred to reduce appraisal cost to a minimum.

(c)   **Appraisal costs**

> **Definition**   The cost incurred, such as for inspection and testing, in initially ascertaining and ensuring conformance of the product to quality requirements.

(d)   **Internal failure costs**

> **Definition**   The cost arising from inadequate quality before the transfer of ownership from supplier to purchaser.

(e)   **External failure costs**

> **Definition**   The cost arising from inadequate quality discovered after the transfer of ownership from supplier to purchaser such as complaints, warranty claims and recall cost.

11.3   Calculating quality costs

Quality costs may be measured both in terms of costs incurred in assuring quality and rectifying units, and also in the opportunity cost of lost sales. Each item must be analysed and individually considered and where possible a cost benefit approach applied to a quality control programme.

11.4   Quality cost evaluation - example

The following question is based upon a past exam question:

Boatbits Ltd moulds fibre glass sheets into body parts for leisure cruise boat manufacturers. Its main products are parts X215 and Y54. The company is planning a TQM programme at a cost of £320,000. The following information relates to the costs incurred by Boatbits Ltd both before and after the implementation of the programme.

Fibre glass sheets

The sheets cost £25 each. On average 5% of the sheets received are returned to the supplier as scrap because of deterioration in stores. The supplier allows a credit of £5 per sheet for such returns. In addition, specification conformity checks carried out in stores on receipt of a delivery cost a total of £24,000 per annum.

A move to a just-in-time purchasing system will eliminate the holding of stocks of fibre glass sheets. This has been negotiated with the supplier who will deliver sheets of guaranteed quality specification for £28 each, eliminating all stockholding costs.

Moulding process

Upon receipt of a stores requisition, the sheets are issued to the moulding process which has variable conversion costs of £15 per sheet. Losses of 8% of process input arise through poor process temperature control, which can be sold as scrap at £8 per unit.

The TQM programme will improve the temperature control and reduce losses to 1% of input.

Each sheet input into the process produces two basic parts, X2 and Y5, each with the same cost structure.

Finishing process

The finishing process has a bank of machines which perform additional operations on basic parts X2 and Y5 in order to convert them to the finished parts X215 and Y54 respectively. The variable conversion costs for this process are £10 and £18 per unit of X215 and Y54 respectively. At the end of the finishing process, 10% of the units are found to be defective, and can be sold as scrap for £12 per unit (for either part).

The TQM programme will convert the finishing process into two dedicated cells, one for each part, with variable costs per unit of £7 and £16 for X215 and Y54 respectively. Defective units are expected to fall to 1% of input to each cell, and will be sold as scrap as at present.

Finished goods

A finished goods buffer stock of parts X215 and Y54 of 400 and 600 units respectively is held throughout the year in order to allow for variability in customer demand and replacement of faulty parts returned by customers. Customer returns are currently 4% of sales. Variable stock holding costs are £3 per part per annum for both products.

The revised "cell" format of the finishing process will reduce the stockholding requirement to that required for one month's replacement of faulty parts, estimated at 15 and 20 units for parts X215 and Y54 respectively. Variable stockholding costs will be unaffected.

Quantitative data

Some calculations have already been made of the number of units of fibre glass sheets, basic parts X2 and Y5 and finished parts X215 and Y54 required before and after the implementation of the TQM programme, based upon the projected sales and information given above. The figures are summarised below:

| | Current position | | Post TQM position | |
| | *Part X2/215* | *Part Y5/54* | *Part X2/215* | *Part Y5/54* |
	(units)	*(units)*	*(units)*	*(units)*
Sales	20,000	24,000	20,000	24,000
Customer returns	800	960	180	240
Parts delivered	20,800	24,960	20,180	24,240
Finishing proc. losses	2,311	2,773	204	245
Input to fin. proc.	23,111	27,733	20,384	24,485
		50,844		44,869
Moulding losses	4,421		453	
Input to moulding	55,265		45,322	
Returns to supplier	2,909		-	
Purchases of fibre glass sheets	58,174		45,322	

Requirement

Evaluate and present a statement showing the net financial benefit or loss per annum of implementing the TQM programme.

Solution

It is important to lay out your answer clearly, including any necessary workings. The logical approach would be to work through the manufacturing stages in order. But don't forget one of the biggest savings - the reduced volume of purchases necessary under the TQM system (reduced by the increased purchase price for guaranteed quality).

Financial (costs)/savings of proposed TQM programme

	£
Purchase cost savings	
$58,174 \times £25 - 45,322 \times £28$	185,334
Move to JIT system - purchasing	
Deteriorated stock savings $(2,909 \times £(25-5))$	58,180
Specification check savings	24,000
Improved temperature control - moulding	
Conversion cost savings $(55,265 - 45,322) \times £15$	149,145
Reduced scrap proceeds $(4,421 - 453) \times £8$	(31,744)
Cell format production - finishing	
Conversion cost savings	
$(23,111 \times £10 + 27,733 \times £18 - (20,384 \times £7 + 24,485 \times £16))$	195,856
Reduced scrap proceeds $((2,311 + 2,773) - (204 + 245)) \times £12$	(55,620)
Reduction of stockholding requirements - finished goods	
Holding cost savings $((400 + 600) - (15 + 20)) \times £3$	2,895
	528,046
Less: cost of TQM programme	(320,000)
Net financial benefit of implementation of TQM programme	208,046

Note: it would appear that the cost of implementation of the TQM programme (£320,000) is a one-off cost, whereas the net savings before this cost are per annum. Thus the overall benefit will be much greater than shown above.

12   SELF TEST QUESTIONS

12.1   Explain quality assurance. (3.1)

12.2   Explain the main aims of quality circles. (4.5)

12.3   Explain what is meant by quality of inputs. (7.1)

12.4   Explain the use of control charts. (7.3)

12.5   Explain training for quality. (8.1 - 8.3)

12.6   Explain designing for quality. (9.1, 9.2)

12.7   Explain quality information systems (10.1, 10.2).

12.8   How are quality costs classified? (11.2)

12.9   Explain prevention costs. (11.2)

12.10   Explain appraisal costs. (11.2)

12.11   Explain internal failure costs. (11.2)

12.12   Explain external failure costs. (11.2)

13   EXAMINATION TYPE QUESTION

13.1   Quality assurance

You have just been informed by the MD that 'something drastic has to be done about quality'. In his view, quality is the responsibility of your department and he has suggested that you take a tougher line with those responsible for quality problems, raise quality standards, increase inspection rates, and give greater authority to quality control inspectors.

You are required:

(a)	to evaluate the suggestions made by the MD.	**(10 marks)**
(b)	to state what additional or alternative proposals you would offer.	**(15 marks)**
		(Total: 25 marks)

14   ANSWER TO EXAMINATION TYPE QUESTION

14.1   Quality assurance

In general terms, the suggestions made by the MD reflect a mistaken view of quality and how it is assured. His emphasis is 'reactive' rather than 'pro-active', is 'feedback' based rather than 'feedforward', and is concerned with quality control rather than quality assurance.

(a)   Specifically:

   (i)   His initial statement that 'something drastic has to be done about quality' does not seem to be based on any kind of systematic analysis or measurement. Nor does it suggest that the MD understands the meaning of quality, which according to Crosby is 'conformity to requirements'.

   (ii)   His statement that 'quality is the responsibility of your department' ignores the fact that quality is the responsibility of all staff at all stages, in all departments and at all levels.

   (iii)   The 'tougher line' suggests a punishment-oriented approach which contradicts the advice of Deming 'to drive out fear', and to seek co-operation.

(iv)   'Raising quality standards' without targeting particular areas, and without understanding why such quality improvement is necessary, is likely to be a costly and unproductive exercise.

(v)   'Increasing inspection rates' and 'giving greater authority to quality control inspectors' reinforces the 'control' approach, and the 'specialist' emphasis discussed earlier.

(b)   An alternative approach involves viewing quality control as part of a more strategic approach to quality - quality assurance. This requires:

(i)   An analysis of existing quality performance and problems. Such an analysis should involve all levels and all departments, and should concern itself with the customers, with the competition, and with suppliers as well as the activities of the firm itself. Crosby advocates the creation of 'quality committees' composed of members drawn from different departments.

(ii)   Calculating the 'cost of quality', which involves measuring the costs of not 'getting it right first time', and includes 'prevention costs', 'appraisal costs', and 'failure costs'. Such an analysis should identify a sizeable potential cost saving (or to quote Crosby 'quality is free').

(iii)   The careful selection and monitoring of suppliers, perhaps involving an 'active' rather than a passive relationship.

(iv)   The design of the product, to ensure an appropriate level of quality.

(v)   The installation of quality information systems which measure and feedback quality performance to those involved, and which can serve as the basis for targets.

(vi)   Quality improvement, perhaps involving the creation of quality circles.

(vii)   Quality staff, which involves investment in recruitment, selection, training, development, appraisal and reward.

In conclusion, such an approach is essentially long term, and requires a shift in thinking about quality at all levels. The essential ingredient in this cultural shift is a 'right first time' mentality which encompasses all activities that impinge on quality. In short, the MD and other staff need to be educated in 'total quality management'.

7 DECISION MAKING AND SHORT RUN DECISIONS: THEORETICAL ASPECTS

INTRODUCTION & LEARNING OBJECTIVES

When you have studied this chapter you should be able to do the following:

* Distinguish between relevant and irrelevant information.
* Identify cost classifications used in decision making.
* Distinguish between quantitative and qualitative information and explain how they are used in decision making.
* Explain the importance of the timing, format and accuracy of information for decision making.
* Explain the decision making cycle.
* Distinguish between different types of problem.
* List typical decision-making situations.

1 RELEVANT AND IRRELEVANT INFORMATION

1.1 Introduction

Decision making requires both quantitative and qualitative information. Such quantitative information comprises costs and revenues which to be of use to the decision maker must be relevant.

1.2 What are relevant costs and revenues?

Relevant costs and revenues are those which are different as a consequence of the decision made or its recommended course of action being taken. Since relevant costs and revenues are those which are different it effectively means costs and revenues which **change** as a result of the decision. Since it is not possible to change the past (because it has already happened), then relevant costs and revenues must be future costs and revenues. Past costs are usually referred to as sunk costs.

1.3 Relevant costs and opportunity costs

Definition Opportunity cost is the value of a benefit sacrificed in favour of an alternative course of action.

An opportunity cost may also be described as the cost of a particular course of action compared to the next best alternative course of action.

Relevant costs may involve incurring a cost or losing a revenue which could be obtained from an alternative course of action. The incurrence of costs is sometimes referred to as cashflow costs whereas the loss of revenue is an opportunity cost. Both are relevant for the purposes of decision making.

1.4 Cashflow costs

Cashflow costs are those arising in cash terms as a consequence of the decision. Such costs can never include past costs or costs arising from past transactions. Costs such as depreciation based on the cost of an asset already acquired can never be relevant, nor can committed costs eg, lease payments in respect of an asset already leased, nor will re-allocations of total costs ever be relevant to the decision. Only costs which change in total because of the decision are relevant costs.

2   COST CLASSIFICATION AND DECISION MAKING

2.1   Introduction

You should recall from your earlier studies that many different classifications of cost may be used depending upon the purpose of the information. For decision making purposes one of the most useful forms of classification is by behaviour.

2.2   Cost behaviour

Production cost comprises three elements - materials, wages and expenses; it can also be noted that production cost includes both fixed and variable segment elements. It is useful to look at the way costs behave in response to changes in production volume.

(Definition)   Cost behaviour is the way in which costs of output are affected by fluctuations in the level of activity.

2.3   Example

	Production	
	500 units	*1,000 units*
	£	£
Sales (@ £3 per unit)	1,500	3,000
Total costs	1,000	1,500
Profit	500	1,500
Average unit cost	£2.00	£1.50
Average unit profit	£1.00	£1.50

Total costs have increased by only 50% although production has doubled. This is because some costs will not rise in relation to the increase in volume.

Suppose the product is widgets and the only costs are:

(a)   rental of a fully equipped factory, £500 pa;
(b)   raw materials, £1 per widget.

2.4   Solution

Then the way these two costs react to producing varying numbers of widgets is as follows:

(a)   **Factory rental - a fixed cost**

Although production rises, the same rent is payable.

Graph showing relationship between rent and output

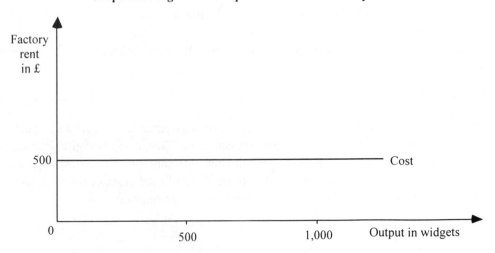

Conclusion   Fixed costs, within certain output and turnover limits, tend to be unaffected by fluctuations in the levels of activity.

This may be also shown by plotting the average fixed cost per unit on a graph.

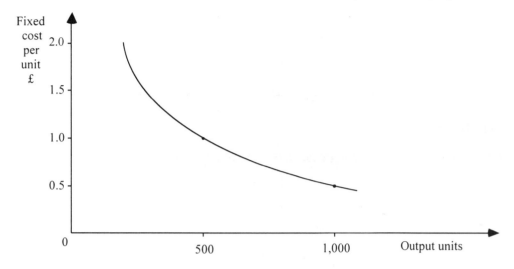

Conclusion   As output increases, unit fixed costs decline.

This only changes if a new or larger factory is rented.

(b)   **Raw materials - a variable cost**

Every widget has a raw material cost of £1; therefore, the cost varies directly with the level of production.

Definition   Variable costs are costs which tend to vary with the level of activity.

Graph showing relationship between raw materials, costs and output

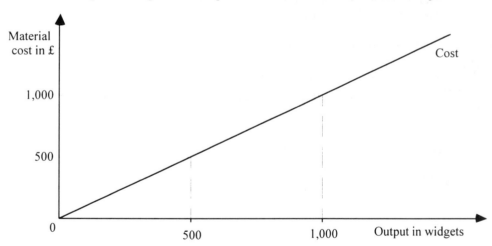

Conclusion   In the case of variable costs unit cost remains constant irrespective of the level of output (provided that there are no discounts for bulk purchase).

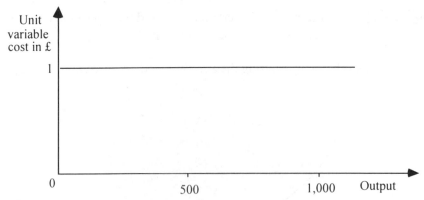

2.5   Contribution

If the two types of cost are segregated, the operating statement can be presented in a different way:

| | *Production of widgets* | | |
	1 unit £	*500 units* £	*1,000 units* £
Sales	3	1,500	3,000
Variable costs - Raw materials	1	500	1,000
Contribution	2	1,000	2,000
Fixed costs - Factory rent	500	500	500
Profit/(loss)	(498)	500	1,500

The revised presentation is based on the concept that each unit sold **contributes** a selling price less the variable cost per unit. Total contribution provides a fund to cover fixed costs and net profit.

Definition   Contribution is the sales value less variable cost of sales.

Thus: Sales – Variable cost of sales =   Contribution
        Contribution – Fixed costs   =   Net profit

Note that unit contribution is a constant number unless prices or the specification for variable costs change.

Conclusion   As output increases total unit costs gravitate towards the unit variable cost:

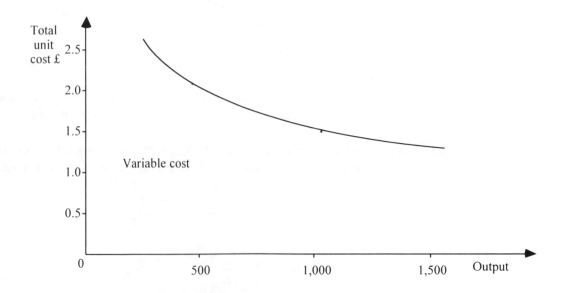

2.6   Relevant range of activity

The analysis of cost behaviour is only appropriate when considering the kind of movement in activity which could reasonably be expected, ie, within the relevant range of volume (output) levels. A number of simplifying assumptions are, therefore, usually made.

2.7   Costs which change per unit

When buying items such as tyres, it is normal to obtain special prices for larger orders. Thus, the more tyres ordered, the lower the price paid for each tyre.

Graph showing relationship between the total cost of tyres and the output of cars

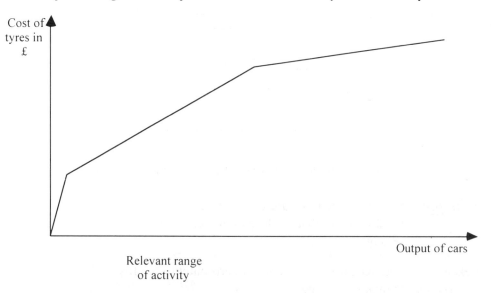

However, in practice it is likely that only relatively limited changes in the level of production will be considered. This is described as the **relevant range of activity**, and within that range unit prices are likely to be constant.

2.8   Step costs

Some costs rise in a series of steps. Large steps (renting a second factory) or small steps (renting a typewriter) may occur.

(a)   If the steps are large, the concept of the relevant range of activity usually applies ie, only occasionally is a new factory considered and therefore one can assume the cost to be fixed for the relevant range.

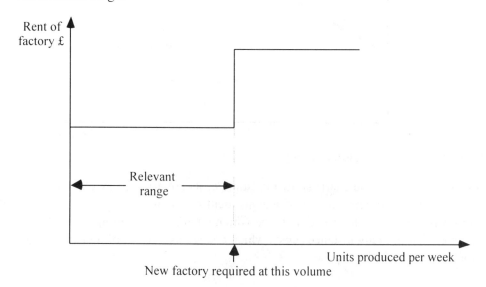

(b)   If the steps are small they may be ignored, ie, the cost may be treated as a variable cost.

Graph showing relationship between total rent of typewriters and output

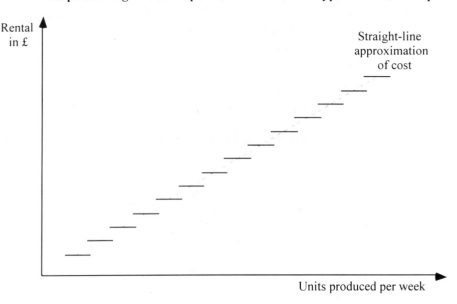

2.9   Semi-variable costs (unfortunately also referred to as semi-fixed costs)

Definition   Semi-variable costs are costs which exhibit the characteristics of both variable and fixed costs, in that while they increase with output they never fall to zero, even at zero output.

An example is maintenance costs: even at zero output **standby** maintenance costs are incurred. As output rises so do maintenance costs.

Graph showing relationship between machine maintenance costs and output

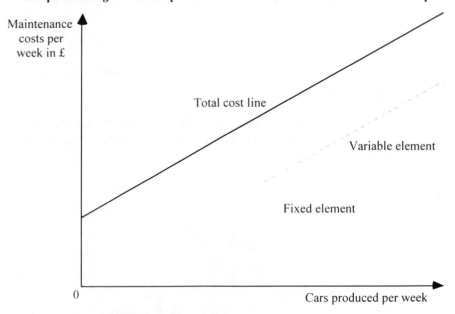

2.10   Cost behaviour and decision making

The above illustrations and charts show that some costs are affected by changes in activity to a greater or lesser extent than others. Much of management decision making is concerned with activity, and relevant costs have been described as those which change as a consequence of the decision. Thus it can be stated that in many instances costs which change as a result of a change in activity are relevant costs for decision making purposes.

2.11   The relevance of variable costs

Variable costs are those costs which change in proportion to changes in the level of activity. Thus whenever the decision involves increases or decreases in activity it is almost certain that variable costs will be affected and therefore will be relevant to the decision.

2.12   The relevance of fixed costs

Fixed costs are generally regarded as those costs which are **not** affected by changes in the level of activity. However a variation on the basic fixed cost, known as a stepped fixed cost was depicted above as follows:

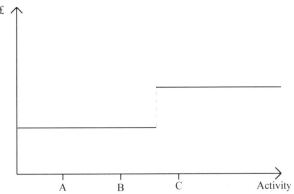

A change in activity from point A to point B does not affect the level of **total** fixed costs because both activity levels lie on the same fixed cost step. For such a decision the fixed cost is irrelevant because it is not changing. However a change in activity from point B to point C does affect the level of total fixed costs. Thus such a decision causes the total fixed costs to change and in such circumstances they are relevant. When fixed costs become relevant to a decision by changing in this way the extra fixed cost is usually referred to as the INCREMENTAL FIXED COST.

2.13   The relevance of semi-variable costs

Semi-variable costs are those costs which comprise both a fixed and variable element. The variable element is relevant to decision making using the same reasoning as was applied to variable costs. The fixed element is irrelevant unless it is a step fixed cost element as described above. It is therefore necessary to separate the fixed and variable components of semi-variable costs to isolate the relevant and non-relevant parts of the cost.

2.14   Separating elements of semi-variable costs

The following paragraphs explain the different methods which may be used to separate the fixed and variable elements of semi-variable costs. Each of these methods assumes that the fixed cost element is constant in total (ie, not a step fixed cost).

2.15   High low (or range) method

This and the next two methods that follow are based on an analysis of historic information on costs at different activity levels. To illustrate the methods the data below will be used as an example.

Example

The data for the inspection costs for six months to 31 December 19X8 is as follows:

Month	Units produced	Cost
		£
July	340	2,260
August	300	2,160
September	380	2,320
October	420	2,400
November	400	2,300
December	360	2,266

The variable element of a cost item may be estimated by calculating the unit cost between high and low volumes during a period.

Six months to 31/12/X8	Units produced	Inspection costs
		£
Highest month	420	2,400
Lowest month	300	2,160
	——	——
Range	120	240
	——	——

The additional cost per unit between high and low is $\dfrac{£240}{120 \text{ units}} = £2$ per unit

which may be estimated as the variable content of inspection costs. Fixed inspection costs are, therefore:

$$£2,400 - (420 \times £2) = £1,560 \text{ per month}$$
$$\text{or} \quad £2,160 - (300 \times £2) = £1,560 \text{ per month.}$$

ie, the relationship is of the form $y = £(1,560 + 2x)$.

The limitations of the high low method are:

(a)   Its reliance on historic data, assuming that (i) activity is the only factor affecting costs and (ii) historic costs reliably predict future costs.

(b)   The use of only two values, the highest and the lowest, means that the results may be distorted due to random variations in these values.

2.16   Activity

Use the high-low points method to calculate the fixed and variable elements of the following cost:

	Activity	*£*
January	400	1,050
February	600	1,700
March	550	1,600
April	800	2,100
May	750	2,000
June	900	2,300

2.17   Activity solution

	Activity level	*£*
High	900	2,300
Low	(400)	(1,050)
	500	1,250

Variable cost = £1,250/500 = £2.50/unit

Fixed cost = £1,050 − (400 × £2.50) = £50.

2.18   Scatter charts

If the data from the example was plotted on a graph, the result would be a scatter-chart of inspection costs.

Scatter chart showing the relationship between total inspection costs and output

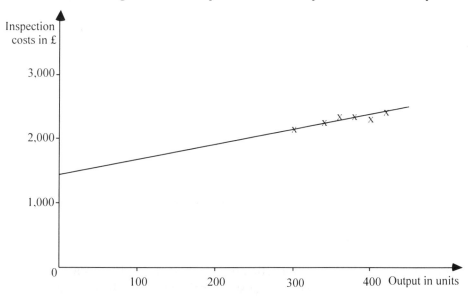

The **line of best fit** (a line which passes through the plotted points to equalise the number of points on each side and the aggregate distance from the line) may be drawn as accurately as possible by inspection. The point at which that line cuts the vertical axis indicates the fixed cost (about £1,460 in the illustration).

Scatter charts suffer from the general limitations of using historic data referred to above. In addition, their problem is that the estimate of the best linear relationship between the data is subjective. Finally, it should be noted that this can only be converted into a mathematical relationship by actual measurement.

2.19   Activity

Plot the data points from the previous activity on a scatter graph and draw a line of best fit to find the fixed cost. Measure the gradient of the line to determine the variable cost.

2.20   Activity solution

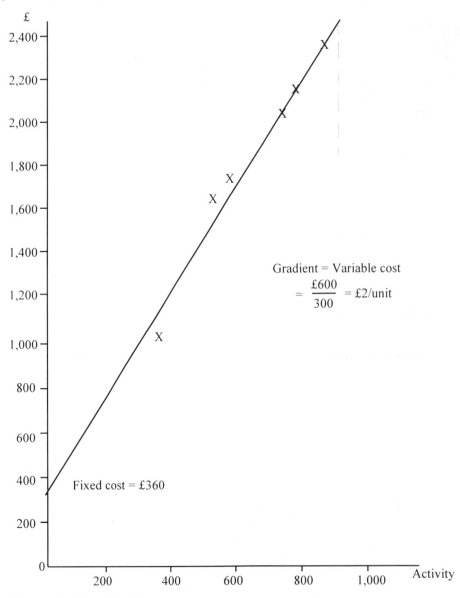

Gradient = Variable cost

$$= \frac{£600}{300} = £2/\text{unit}$$

Fixed cost = £360

2.21   Regression analysis method

Regression analysis is a technique for estimating the line of best fit, given a series of data of the type in the example above. It is essentially a statistical technique, and the description that follows is only a working guide for application of the technique to cost prediction.

Regression analysis is based on the concept of drawing the line that minimises the sum of the squares of the deviations of the line from the observed data (hence it is sometimes referred to as the least squares method). Therefore, it is possible to calculate two different regression lines for a set of data. This is because the horizontal deviations and the vertical deviations of the points from the line are considered separately. It is the sum of the **squares** of these deviations that is minimised; this overcomes problems that might arise because some deviations would be positive and some negative depending on whether the point was above or below the line. It is not necessary to go into the theory of this method any more deeply at this level.

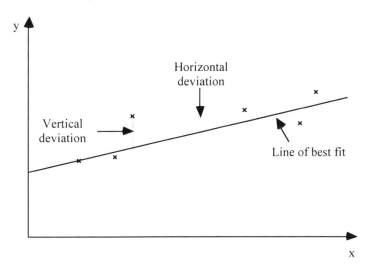

The two regression lines that result from applying this method are:

(a)   The regression line of y on x - this must be used when an estimate of y is required for a given value of x.

This line minimises the sum of the squares of the vertical distances of the points from the line.

(b)   The regression line of x on y - this must be used when an estimate of x is required for a known value of y.

This line minimises the sum of the squares of the horizontal distances of the points from the line.

The scatter diagram has the following appearance when the regression lines are graphed:

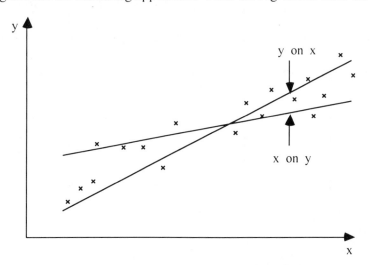

In most cost accounting circumstances it is the cost (y) which is being predicted from a given output value (x). Thus the regression of line of y on x is the one to be calculated.

2.22   Calculating the regression line

The objective is to state the regression line in the form $y = a + bx$.

There are various formulae available which may be used to calculate the values of a and b; all are equally valid. Those used below are regarded as the simplest to operate.

The simplest approach is to think in terms of column headings:

Column 1 lists the values of x (production); from this the mean production ($\overline{x}$) is calculated;

Column 2 calculates the deviation of each observed production level from the mean (dx).

Column 3 shows the costs (y), and from this the mean ($\overline{y}$) is calculated;

Column 4 calculates the deviation of each observed cost from the mean cost (dy).

Column 5 multiplies each value in column 2 by the corresponding value in column 4 (dydx), and then sums the result;

Column 6 is the square of the values in column 2 (dx^2), and then sums the results (Σdx^2).

The value of b is then given by:

$$b = \frac{\Sigma dxdy}{\Sigma dx^2}$$

and a is given by

$$a = \overline{y} - b\overline{x}$$

2.23   Example

Column 1 Production units (x)	Column 2 Deviation from mean (dx)	Column 3 Inspection costs (y)	Column 4 Deviation from mean (dy)	Column 5 dxdy	Column 6 dx^2
340	−27	2,260	−33	891	729
300	−67	2,160	−133	8,911	4,489
380	+13	2,320	+27	351	169
420	+53	2,400	+107	5,671	2,809
400	+33	2,300	+7	231	1,089
360	−7	2,320	+27	−189	49
2,200		13,760		15,866	9,334

Mean = $\overline{x}$ = 367 $\overline{y}$ = 2,293

$$b = \frac{\Sigma dxdy}{\Sigma dx^2} = \frac{15,866}{9,334}$$

b   =   £1.70 per unit.

a   = $\overline{y} - b\overline{x}$

    =   2,293 - (1.70 × 367)

    =   1,669

Cost   y = 1,669 + 1.70x

2.24   Activity

Using the data from the previous activity, calculate the fixed variable costs using regression analysis and basic algebra

2.25   Activity solution

Production activity (x)	(dx)	Costs (y)	(dy)	dxdy	dx^2
400	−266.66	1,050	−741.66	197,771	71,108
600	−66.66	1,700	−91.66	6,110	4,444
550	−116.66	1,600	−191.66	22,359	13,610
800	+133.33	2,100	+308.33	41,110	17,777
750	+83.33	2,000	+208.33	17,360	6,944
900	+233.33	2,300	+508.33	118,609	54,443
4,000		10,750		403,319	168,326

$\overline{x} = 666.66$ $\overline{y} = 1,791.66$

$$\text{Variable cost} = \frac{403,319}{168,326} = 2.40$$

Fixed cost   = $1,791.66 - (666.66 \times £2.40)$

=   £192.

3   INFORMATION REQUIREMENTS AND THE ENTITY

3.1   Introduction

Entities vary both in size, and in their type (manufacturer, service). Each of these differences affects the decision making information required by the entity.

3.2   The effect of size

The size of an organisation will affect its management structure, and the number and responsibilities of people in decision making positions.

In small organisations many of the decisions will be made by the owners of the business who do not require a formalised information system to tell them what is happening within the entity. They work full time in the business and are therefore aware of what is happening on a day-to-day basis.

As organisations grow managers are employed and charged with certain responsibilities. As part of this process, these managers are given authority to make decisions within their own area of responsibility. A more formalised information system is required as organisations grow so as to ensure that the effects of decisions on all areas of the business are considered.

In addition, it is unlikely that the owners would delegate responsibility for strategic decisions and so they would require information to assist them in co-ordinating the various aspects of the decision.

3.3   The type of entity and its effect

Different types of entity will have different information requirements. Manufacturers and wholesalers/retailers deal with tangible products to which costs and revenues can be attributed. In these organisations some direct costs will be identifiable to individual product lines, thus enabling the profitability of each to be measured.

In service industries it is more difficult to identify the 'product' and therefore even more difficult to identify direct costs. Instead costs are collected and a measure of activity made, from which an average cost is then calculated.

In service organisations non-monetary quantitative information may be more useful, for example professional practices such as solicitors and accountants record time spent on services for their clients which are used to assess fees.

4   USING QUANTITATIVE AND QUALITATIVE INFORMATION IN DECISION MAKING

4.1   Introduction

Quantitative information is information expressed in numerical terms. Although in the context of decision making this is often costs and revenues, quantitative information for decision making can also be non-financial information.

Qualitative information is information which cannot be expressed in numerical terms. It is often opinions connected with the effects of a decision.

4.2   Quantitative information

Although often measured in financial terms using costs and revenues measured in monetary units, other forms of quantitative information may be used in a decision making situation. For example the quantity of resources required (materials, labour, machines); or the effects of the decision on percentage market shares could be useful quantitative information.

4.3   Qualitative information

Qualitative information is often in the form of opinions which show the effects of decisions on people and the community within which the entity operates. Interested groups include:

(a)   **Employees** will be affected by certain decisions which may threaten their continued employment, or cause them to need re-training.

(b)   **Customers** will be interested to know about new products, but will want to be assured that service arrangements etc, will continue for existing products;

(c)   **Suppliers** will want to be aware of the entity's plans, especially if smart orders are used within a JIT environment;

(d)   **Competitors** will want to assess their market position following the entity's decision. They may have to make their own decisions as a consequence.

In addition the following other qualitative factors need to be considered when making a decision:

(i)   the effects of inflation

-     inflation can seriously affect the validity of cost/revenue estimates.

(ii)   the effects on the environment

-     certain decisions may affect emissions and pollution of the environment. The green issue and the entity's responsibility towards the environment may seriously affect its public image.

(iii)   legal effects

-     there may be legal implications of a course of action, or a change in law may have been the cause of the decision requirement.

(iv)   political effects

-    government policies, both in taxation and other matters may impinge on the decision.

(v)   timing of decision

-    the timing of a new product launch may be crucial to its success.

Each of these factors must be considered before making a final decision. Each of these factors is likely to be measured by opinion. Such opinions must be collected and co-ordinated into meaningful information.

5   ATTRIBUTES OF DECISION MAKING INFORMATION

5.1   Introduction

There are four attributes of decision making information:

(a)   Frequency;
(b)   Timing;
(c)   Format; and
(d)   Accuracy.

5.2   Frequency

Decisions are made daily, weekly, monthly and annually so information is needed to assist managers to make these decisions. Many organisations provide management information on a regular basis, so this may be a source of decision making information. However, more decision specific information is likely to be required, and this should be provided whenever a decision is to be made.

5.3   Timing

Timeliness is a valuable attribute of any good information system. Information should be provided as soon as possible after the event to which it relates. In this context information is part of the feedback system which is used by management to make decisions to control activities. This is often concerned with tactical decisions. Timeliness of reporting is very important in such situations as the following illustration shows.

It is quite usual for actual outcomes to oscillate about a norm, with management action being used to minimise the fluctuations. Thus the following pattern of outcomes would be quite normal:

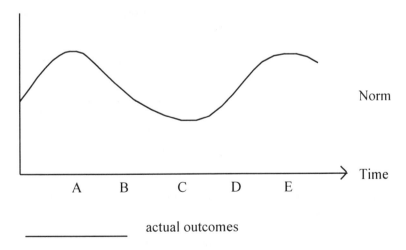

The above diagram shows the oscillating effect where there is no management decision/action being used.

If information is provided to managers earlier than time point A and appropriate action taken the positive and negative oscillations can be reduced:

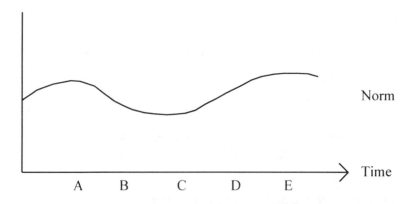

This is known as negative feedback. Managers take decisions and actions to reduce the extent of the oscillation so that when there is positive oscillation there is negative management influences and vice-versa.

However, if the information is delayed so that the initial oscillation effects are not reported until between time points A and B, negative management influences are applied when negative oscillation has already commenced with the following results:

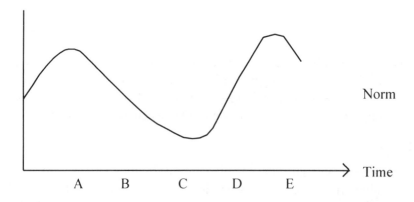

As can be seen, instead of reducing the size of the fluctuations they have been increased. This is caused by the lateness of the information, and as a consequence negative feedback information has been converted into positive feedback information.

5.4   Format

The format of the information depends upon the complexity of the decision and the recipient decision taker.

The information could be presented in the form of a written report, or a presentation which may be supplemented by graphic displays.

Many managers are more comfortable with pictorial representations of information rather than tabulated data. Sometimes the use of charts and diagrams makes it easier to understand the information being presented.

5.5   Accuracy

Accuracy and precision have been discussed earlier in this text. In the context of information for decision making, information should be:

'sufficiently accurate for the purpose for which it is intended.'

It is not always possible or even necessary for information to be 100% accurate. Provided the extent of an error is not sufficient to alter the decision made it does not matter. There is often a conflict between accuracy of information, timeliness of reporting, and the cost of producing the information. Accuracy of 100% is costly in time as well as money: such accuracy is often unnecessary. Provided the information is sufficiently accurate timeliness is more important.

6   THE DECISION MAKING CYCLE

6.1   Introduction

The following diagram illustrates the decision making cycle:

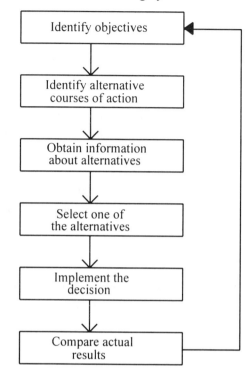

You should note the similarities between this diagram and that of the planning, control and decision making process earlier in this text. The component parts of the decision making cycle are considered in the following paragraphs.

6.2   Identify objectives

The objectives within a decision making context are likely to be to solve a problem although they may be more of a planning nature to improve profitability. You should appreciate that decision making is an integral part of the planning process.

6.3   Alternative courses of action

Once the objectives have been identified the next stage is to determine the courses of action which may be used to meet those objectives and gather information about them. Such information may be quantitative (both monetary and non-monetary) and qualitative. Once the information has been gathered it must be considered and the best course of action chosen.

6.4   Implement the decision

Once the course of action has been chosen the next step is to implement the decision. This may require management to place orders for plant or equipment or other assets, or it may be simply a decision to work overtime or change the product mix. Clearly the timescale in which the decision is implemented will differ depending upon the original objective and the chosen course of action.

6.5   Comparing actual results

This part of the cycle might be described as a post implementation review or audit. Before results can be compared they must be collected using both quantitative and qualitative measures. These results are then compared with the original objectives and where necessary a further decision is made to modify the action being taken.

7   CLASSIFYING PROBLEMS FOR MODELLING

7.1   Introduction

Problems may be classified as being either

(a)   simple;
(b)   complex; or
(c)   dynamic.

7.2   Simple problems

Simple problems are those which have just one or two variables, for example the effects on profit of a single product being sold at differing prices (with the related demand effects).

7.3   Complex problems

These problems are more complicated because they involve a number of variables, for example a multi-product situation where the selling price of a product affects the demand for that product and for other products with the consequential effects on production of all products.

7.4   Dynamic problems

These are complex problems where the variables of the problem are constantly changing due to other influences eg, government policies, etc.

8   ASPECTS OF MODEL BUILDING

8.1   Introduction

A model is a representation of a real system which is used to test the likely results of a particular course of action before a decision is made to implement those actions. A model comprises:

(a)   Endogenous variables;
(b)   Exogenous variables;
(c)   Policies and controls;
(d)   Performance measures; and
(e)   Intermediate variables.

8.2   Past exam question

Understanding of the meaning and relevance of these terms to short term decision making was examined in December 1994.

8.3   Endogenous variables

Endogenous variables are those which originate from within a model and are therefore in the control of the decision maker. Management can examine the outputs from the model for different values of the endogenous variables and may then reconsider their plans and decisions.

8.4   Exogenous variables

These are variables which originate outside the model and are therefore not in the control of the decision maker. For a particular model the input variables may have a known constant value, such as the cost of placing an order; these are also known as parameters. The value of other input variables may be uncertain.

8.5   Policies and controls

Policies are created by decisions, eg in the context of an inventory model a policy might be to always order the economic order quantity. Such a policy may be controlled by reviewing stock levels and related cost data to ensure that the EOQ model is valid.

8.6   Performance measures

The measurement of performance may be by comparing the outputs of the model with the original objectives to see if the proposed plans and decisions will achieve the objective set. This is a feedforward control system. Alternatively, performance measures may be applied after the plans and decisions have been implemented by comparing the actual results achieved with the model outputs (and indirectly therefore with the original objectives). This is a feedback control system.

8.7   Intermediate variables

An intermediate variable is one which has relevance to the model at certain times. For example if a model is used to predict sales which follow a seasonal pattern, the seasonal adjustment factor would be an intermediate variable. These are also known as status variables.

9   DECISIONS AND QUANTITATIVE TECHNIQUES

9.1   Introduction

Decisions made by management can be divided into different types, which can affect the quantitative techniques used to assist in those decisions. The following chapters explain these decision types in more detail, but the following table identifies the types of decision and the quantitative techniques which may be used.

9.2   Typical decision situations

Type of decision	*Quantitative technique*
(1) ACCEPT/REJECT eg, opening a new factory, buying an asset	CONTRIBUTION ANALYSIS using marginal costing
(2) RANKING eg, product mix	CONTRIBUTION PER UNIT OF RESOURCE using marginal costing
(3) CONTROL	VARIANCE ANALYSIS comparisons between actual and target
(4) INVESTMENT	INVESTMENT APPRAISAL using discounted cashflow techniques

Each of these decision types may include variables, the value of which is uncertain. Uncertainty may be dealt with using probability, expected values and decision trees.

10   CHAPTER SUMMARY

In this chapter we have considered the principles of decision making, starting with the distinction between relevant and irrelevant information.

We then noted that both quantitative and qualitative information may be relevant to a decision and explained how each of these types of information may be used.

The decision making cycle was then compared to the planning process, and the principles of modelling discussed.

Finally different types of decision were identified and the appropriate quantitative techniques for their solution matched with each decision type.

11   SELF TEST QUESTIONS

11.1   Define a relevant cost. (1.2)

11.2   Define an opportunity cost. (1.3)

11.3   Distinguish between fixed and variable costs. (2.2 - 2.4)

11.4   Explain the relevance of variable costs. (2.11)

11.5   Explain the relevance of fixed costs. (2.12)

11.6   Explain how an entity's size affects the information required for decision making. (3.2)

11.7   Distinguish between quantitative and qualitative information. (4.2, 4.3)

11.8   Describe the attributes of decision making information. (5)

11.9   Explain the decision making cycle. (6)

11.10   Distinguish between simple, complex and dynamic problems. (7)

11.11   Distinguish between endogenous and exogenous variables. (8.3, 8.4)

12   EXAMINATION TYPE QUESTION

12.1   Relevant costs in decision making

For decision making it is claimed that the relevant cost to use is *opportunity cost*. In practice, management accountants frequently consider costs such as *marginal costs*, *imputed costs* and *differential costs* as the relevant costs.

You are required

(a)   to explain the terms in italics and to give an example of each;   **(6 marks)**

(b)   to reconcile the apparent contradiction in the statement;   **(6 marks)**

(c)   to explain in what circumstances, if any, fixed costs may be relevant for decision making.

(5 marks)

(Total: 17 marks)

13   ANSWER TO EXAMINATION TYPE QUESTION

13.1   Relevant costs in decision making

(a)   **Opportunity cost**

Opportunity cost is 'the value of a benefit sacrificed in favour of an alternative course of action'. It is a measure of the sacrifice made in addition to the price paid for a resource. If, for example, skilled labour is in short supply, then the opportunity cost of using some of that labour for a contract would be the contribution that could otherwise be earned with that labour.

Marginal cost

Marginal cost is 'the cost of one unit of product or service which would be avoided if that unit were not produced or provided'. It is usually the variable cost per unit but could include fixed costs if these are increased as a result of producing one more unit (if 'stepped') and can also include the opportunity cost of scarce resources used to make the product.

Imputed costs

Imputed costs are 'costs recognised in particular situations that are not regularly recognised by usual accounting procedures' (*Horngren*). Imputed costs are not usually recognised because they do not represent actual expenditure incurred by the company. Opportunity cost is an imputed cost. An example is notional rent charged to a division which occupies a factory owned by the company to enable comparison with divisions with rented premises.

Differential cost

Differential cost or incremental cost is 'the difference in total cost between alternatives, calculated to assist decision-making'. For example, if alternative 1 involves a rental of £2,000 and alternative 2 involves a rental of £2,500, then choosing alternative 2 instead of alternative 1 will involve a differential cost of £500.

(b)   The apparent contradiction is partly caused by the overlap between the terms used. As mentioned above opportunity cost is an imputed cost. Opportunity cost is also a differential cost, ie, if selecting one course of action results in use of scarce resources, then the marginal cost plus the lost contribution is the differential cost of consuming the scarce resource.

(c)   Fixed costs may be relevant when they increase as a result of undertaking a particular course of action. For example, if it is necessary to rent an additional piece of equipment for £6,000 in order to increase production volumes from the current maximum capacity of 5,000 units to a capacity of 9,000 units of a product, then that rent is a relevant cost of increasing production even though it is fixed for the range from 5,001 to 9,000 units. For decisions regarding current capacity (up to 5,000 units) the existing fixed costs are not relevant. Fixed costs of this type are often referred to as 'stepped costs'. In the medium to long-term, fixed costs can be affected by a decision and therefore become relevant.

The marginal cost of using a scarce resource is the opportunity cost of an additional unit of that resource. If there are no alternative uses for a resource which has not yet been acquired, the 'value of the benefit sacrificed' is simply the cash spent in acquiring it.

Marginal, imputed and differential costs can be seen to be different examples of opportunity costs. The original statement in this question is therefore seen to be correct. The main difficulty in terminology arises when 'marginal cost' is taken to be the same as 'variable cost'. Variable cost will only be equal to marginal cost under certain circumstances.

8 DECISION MAKING AND SHORT RUN DECISIONS: CVP ANALYSIS

INTRODUCTION & LEARNING OBJECTIVES

In the previous chapter the principles of decision-making information were explained. We will now apply those principles to the decision making technique known as CVP analysis.

When you have studied this chapter you should be able to do the following:

- Explain and calculate the breakeven point from data using graphical or mathematical methods.
- Distinguish between the accountant's and economist's breakeven charts.
- Justify the assumptions concerning linearity.
- Comment on the limitations of CVP analysis.
- Explain avoidable, incremental and opportunity costs.

Note: This chapter builds on Paper 3 studies. In Paper 9 CVP will tend to be integrated into questions, rather than be the sole focus of a question. In December 1995, for example, a minimum CS (P/V) ratio was set as the basis for proceeding with a product and candidates were required to analyse and discuss the situation provided.

Relevant and opportunity costs are more likely to be a significant element in a question - see section 8.

1 WHAT IS CVP ANALYSIS?

1.1 Introduction

Cost-volume-profit (CVP) analysis is a technique which uses cost behaviour theory to identify the activity level at which there is neither a profit nor a loss (the breakeven activity level).

It may also be used to predict profit levels at different volumes of activity based upon the assumptions of cost and revenue linearity.

1.2 Cost and revenue assumptions

CVP analysis assumes that selling prices and variable costs are constant per unit and that fixed costs are constant in total.

1.3 What is contribution?

Contribution is the term used to describe the difference between sales revenues and variable costs. This may be calculated in total, or on a per unit basis using selling prices and variable costs per unit.

The difference between contribution and fixed costs is profit (or loss); thus when contribution equals fixed costs, breakeven occurs. In this way a target profit may be converted into a target contribution which may be used to calculate the number of units required to achieve the desired target profit.

1.4 Contribution target

It has been seen that unit contribution can be assumed to be constant for all levels of output in the relevant range. Similarly, fixed costs can be assumed to be a constant amount in total.

The relationships may be depicted thus:

(a)   Unit contribution   = Selling price per unit – variable costs per unit.

(b)   Total contribution   = Volume × (Selling price per unit – variable costs per unit).

(c)   Contribution target   = Fixed costs + Profit target.

(d)   Volume target $= \dfrac{\text{Contribution target}}{\text{Unit contribution}}$

Bearing in mind the concept of **relevant range**, the formulae can be useful in simplifying predictions for planning and decision making.

1.5   Applications of break-even analysis

To illustrate the application, an example is used.

1.6   Example

Company   :   Widgets Ltd
Product   :   Widgets
Selling price   :   £3 per unit
Variable costs :   Raw materials, £1 per unit
Fixed costs   :   Factory rent, £500 pa.

(a)   How many widgets must be sold per annum to break-even?

$$\text{Volume target} \quad = \quad \frac{\text{Contribution target}}{\text{Selling price - variable costs per unit}}$$

$$= \quad \frac{£500 + £0}{£3 - £1} = 250 \text{ widgets.}$$

At sales volume of 250 units per annum, Widgets Ltd will make nil profit or loss:

		£
Sales	250 × £3	750
Variable costs	250 × £1	250
		500
Fixed costs		500
Profit/(loss)		Nil

(b)   If rent goes up by 10% and Widgets Ltd aims to make £200 pa profit, what annual output is needed?

$$\text{Volume target} = \frac{\text{Contribution target}}{\text{Unit contribution}} = \frac{£500 + £50 + £200}{£3 - £1} = 375 \text{ widgets}$$

(c)   Assuming the maximum possible output of Widgets Ltd is 250 widgets pa, what selling price would achieve the required profit target of £200 (assuming the increased rent)?

Contribution target   =   Fixed costs + Profit target
                      =   £550 + £200 = £750

and

Total contribution   =   Volume × (Selling price per unit – Variable costs per unit)

$\therefore$ 750   =   250 × (SP – 1)
         750   =   250 SP – 250
       1,000   =   250 SP

The required selling price (SP) is therefore, £4 per unit, giving:

			£
Sales	:	250 widgets × £4 =	1,000
Variable costs	:	250 × £1	250
Contribution			750
Fixed costs:			550
Profit			200

The simple example above illustrates that, given the cost/selling price structure, a range of alternative predictions can be easily calculated. Any change in selling price or variable costs will alter unit contribution; changes in fixed costs or profit required will affect the contribution target.

1.7   Contribution to sales ratio

In the above illustration, it was assumed that Widgets Ltd had sold only one product. If it had produced three products, say widgets, gidgets and shmidgets and the unit contribution of each product was different, then it would be uninformative to assess total volume in terms of units.

If, however, the relative proportion of each product sold could be assumed to remain similar or if each product has the same ratio of contribution to sales value, then similar calculations could be made for the business as a whole. Output would be expressed in terms of sales revenue rather than numbers of units, ie:

$$\text{Contribution to sales ratio (C/S ratio)} = \frac{\text{Contribution in £}}{\text{Sales in £}}$$

Note: students may encounter the term profit to volume (or P/V) ratio, which is synonymous with the contribution to sales ratio. Profit to volume is an inaccurate description, however, and should not be used. The C/S ratio is conveniently written as a percentage.

1.8   Example

Widgets Ltd operating statement for year 3 shows:

	Widgets	Gidgets	Schmidgets	Total
Sales units	100	40	60	200
	£	£	£	£
Sales value	400	240	300	940
Variable costs	220	130	170	520
Contribution	180	110	130	420
Fixed costs				350
Profit				70
C/S ratio	45%	46%	43%	44½%

$$\text{Break-even volume in sales value} = \frac{\text{Fixed costs}}{\text{C / S ratio}}$$

$$= \frac{£350}{44\frac{1}{2}\%} = £786.50$$

Thus, the business must sell about £790 of a mixture of widgets, gidgets and shmidgets before it starts to make a profit. The calculation in this instance would be acceptably accurate because the three products have almost identical C/S ratios. If the ratios were significantly different, however, use of the total C/S ratio would imply that the proportions of widgets, gidgets and schmidgets to total sales remained the same over the range of output considered.

1.9   Margin of safety

The difference between budgeted sales volume and break-even sales volume is known as the **margin of safety**. It indicates the vulnerability of a business to a fall in demand. It is often expressed as a percentage of budgeted sales.

1.10   Example

Budgeted sales	:	80,000 units
Selling price	:	£8
Variable costs	:	£4 per unit
Fixed costs	:	£200,000 pa

$$\text{Break even volume} = \frac{200,000}{8-4}$$

$$= 50,000 \text{ units}$$

$$\therefore \text{ Margin of safety} = 80,000 - 50,000$$

$$= 30,000 \text{ units or } 37\tfrac{1}{2}\% \text{ of budget.}$$

The margin of safety may also be expressed as a percentage of actual sales or of maximum capacity.

Students should note the relationship between the margin of safety when expressed as a percentage of actual sales and the C/S and profit to sales (P/S) ratio.

P/S ratio   =   Margin of safety × C/S ratio.

1.11   Example

	£
Sales	10,000
Variable costs	6,000
	4,000
Fixed costs	2,500
	1,500

(a)   P/S ratio $= \dfrac{1,500}{10,000}$

$= 15\%$

(b)   C/S ratio $= \dfrac{4,000}{10,000}$

$= 40\%$

(c)   Break-even sales $= \dfrac{2,500}{0.4}$

$= £6,250$

Excess sales	=	3,750	
Margin of safety	=	$\dfrac{3,750}{10,000}$	
	=	37.5%	
∴ P/S ratio	=	37.5% × 40%	
	=	15%	

2   THE ACCOUNTANT'S AND ECONOMIST'S BREAKEVEN CHARTS

2.1   The accountant's breakeven chart

The accountant's breakeven chart makes certain assumptions concerning the linearity of costs and revenues:

(i)   that selling price is constant per unit irrespective of the number of units to be sold;

(ii)   that fixed costs are constant in total; and

(iii)   that variable costs are constant per unit irrespective of the number of units produced.

There is also an assumption that if there is any difference between sales and production volumes such stocks are valued at their variable cost.

The accountant's breakeven chart is thus depicted with costs and revenues as straight lines as shown below.

Accountant's break-even chart

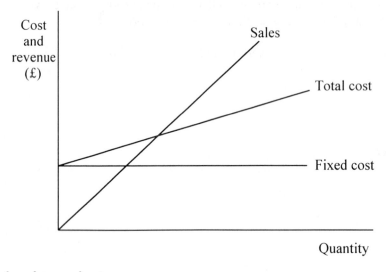

2.2   The economist's breakeven chart

However, most firms would ultimately encounter the conditions generally postulated by the economist:

(a)   it is unlikely the last unit could be sold for the same price as the first; and

(b)   material costs and labour costs rise as output tends upward. The effect of quantity discounts is offset by less efficient production and overtime rates or less skilled labour force.

The break-even chart then becomes nearer to the economist's concept having two break-even points thus:

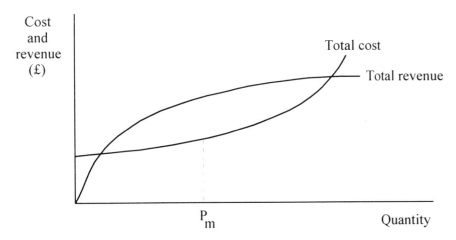

Profit is maximised at the level of output P_m where there is the greatest vertical difference between the total cost and total revenue curves.

3   LINEARITY ASSUMPTIONS AND RELEVANT RANGE

3.1   Introduction

As shown above the economist's model uses curves to represent costs and revenues. This is based on the theory that values are not constant per unit.

3.2   Revenue curves

The economist's model is based on the principle that in order to sell more units demand must be increased, and to do this the price must be reduced. On this basis sales revenue may be depicted thus:

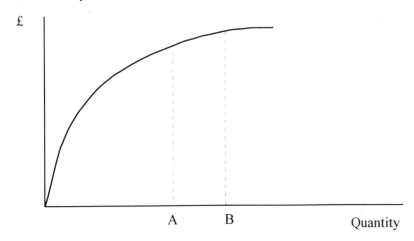

However, such a chart assumes that the range of activity levels depicted is from zero to maximum and this is unlikely to occur in reality. It is more likely that the range of activity will lie between points A and B. It can be seen that between these points the revenue curve is virtually a straight line.

3.3   Curvi-linear variable costs

A similar principle applies to variable costs where it could be argued that the effects of quantity discounts on materials, and overtime/inefficiencies on labour costs cause these to be depicted as curves:

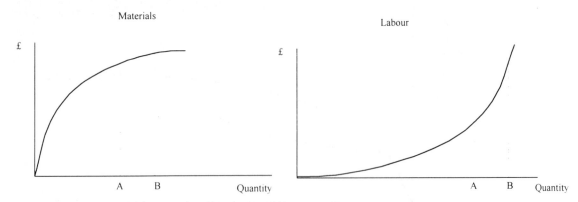

However, two arguments exist to support the accountant's linear model in respect of these costs:

(i)   that if each of these types of cost are added together, their total will approximate to a straight-line; and

(ii)   that within a likely range of activity the curves themselves are virtually linear.

4 BREAK-EVEN CHARTS

4.1 The conventional break-even chart

The conventional break-even chart plots total costs and total revenues at different output levels:

Conventional break-even chart

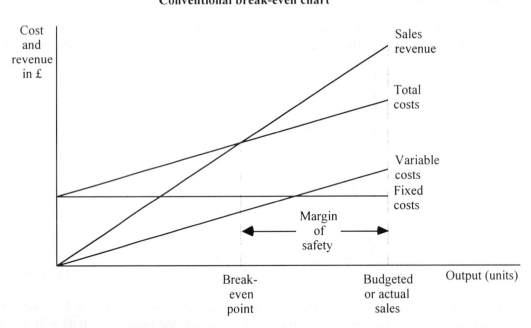

The chart or graph is constructed by:

(a)   plotting fixed costs as a straight line parallel to the horizontal axis;
(b)   plotting sales revenue and variable costs from the origin;
(c)   total costs represent fixed plus variable costs.

The point at which the sales revenue and total cost lines intersect indicates the break-even level of output. The amount of profit or loss at any given output can be read off the chart.

The chart is normally drawn up to the budgeted sales volume.

The difference between the budgeted sales volume and break-even sales volume is referred to as the margin of safety.

4.2   Usefulness of charts

The conventional form of break-even charts was described above. Many variations of such charts exist to illustrate the main relationships of costs, volume and profit. Unclear or complex charts should, however, be avoided as a chart which is not easily understood defeats its own object.

Generally, break-even charts are most useful to:

(a)   Compare products, time periods or actual versus plan.
(b)   Show the effect of changes in circumstances or to plans.
(c)   Give a broad picture of events.

4.3   Contribution break-even charts

A contribution break-even chart may be constructed with the variable costs at the foot of the diagram and the fixed costs shown above the variable cost line.

The total cost line will be in the same position as in the break-even chart illustrated above; but by using the revised layout it is possible to read off the figures of contribution at various volume levels, as shown in the following diagram:

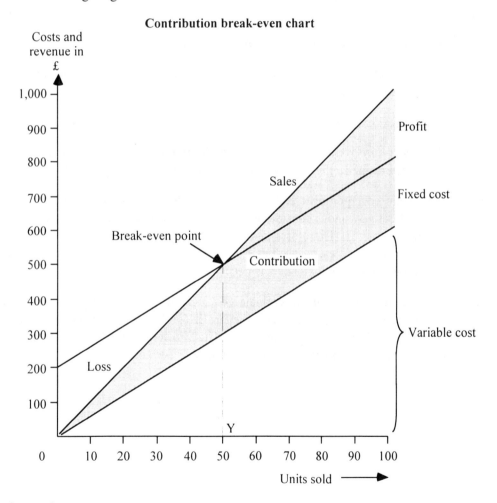

Contribution break-even chart

4.4   Profit-volume chart

Break-even charts usually show both costs and revenues over a given range of activity and they do not highlight directly the amounts of profits or losses at the various levels. A chart which does simply depict the net profit and loss at any given level of activity is called a **profit-volume chart (or graph)**.

Profit-volume chart (1)

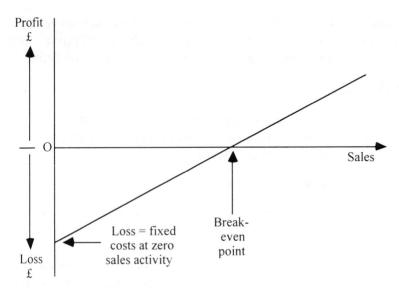

From the above chart the amount of net profit or loss can be read off for any given level of sales activity.

The points to note in the construction of a profit-volume chart are:

(a)   The horizontal axis represents sales (in units or sales value, as appropriate). This is the same as for a break-even chart.

(b)   The vertical axis shows net profit above the horizontal sales axis and net loss below.

(c)   When sales are zero, the net loss equals the fixed costs and one extreme of the 'profit volume' line is determined - therefore this is one point on the graph or chart.

(d)   If variable cost **per unit** and fixed costs **in total** are both constant throughout the relevant range of activity under consideration, the profit-volume chart is depicted by a straight line (as illustrated above). Therefore, to draw that line it is only necessary to know the profit (or loss) at one level of sales. The 'profit-volume' line is then drawn between this point and that determined in (c) and extended as necessary.

(e)   If there are changes in the variable cost per unit or total fixed costs at various activities, it would be necessary to calculate the profit (or loss) at each point where the cost structure changes and to plot these on the chart. The 'profit-volume' line will then be a series of straight lines joining these points together, as simply illustrated as follows:

Profit-volume chart (2)

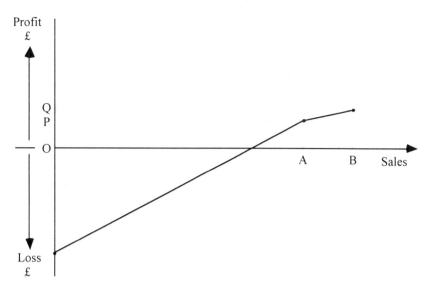

This illustration depicts the situation where the variable cost per unit increases after a certain level of activity (OA) eg, because of overtime premiums that are incurred when production (and sales) exceed a particular level.

Points to note:

(a)   the profit (OP) at sales level OA would be determined and plotted;

(b)   similarly the profit (OQ) at sales level of OB would be determined and plotted;

(c)   the loss at zero sales activity (= fixed costs) can be plotted;

(d)   the 'profit-volume' line is then drawn by joining these points, as illustrated.

4.5   Multi-product profit-volume chart

A further complication that could be encountered is in situations where there is more than one product.

4.6   Example

Budgeted data:

	Sales £	Contribution £
Product A	10,000	2,000
Product B	14,000	7,000
Product C	8,000	2,400

Total fixed costs £8,000 pa.

There are two approaches which may be adopted:

(a)   assume constant sales mix;

(b)   assume, somewhat unrealistically, that products are sold in descending order of contribution sales ratios.

It is recommended that the profit-volume chart drawn in this context should incorporate both (a) and (b).

Data needed for graph:

$$\text{Contribution sales ratios } (\frac{\text{Contribution}}{\text{Sales}} \times 100)$$

Product A $\frac{2,000}{10,000} \times 100 = 20\%$ 3rd

Product B $\frac{7,000}{14,000} \times 100 = 50\%$ 1st

Product C $\frac{2,400}{8,000} \times 100 = 30\%$ 2nd

The order of sale and cumulative profit figures will be assumed to be as follows:

		Total sales £	Total contribution £	Fixed costs £	Profit/(loss) £
1st	Product B	14,000	7,000	8,000	(1,000)
2nd	Product C	8,000	2,400		
		22,000	9,400	8,000	1,400
3rd	Product A	10,000	2,000		
		32,000	11,400	8,000	3,400

The multi-product profit-volume chart would appear as follows:

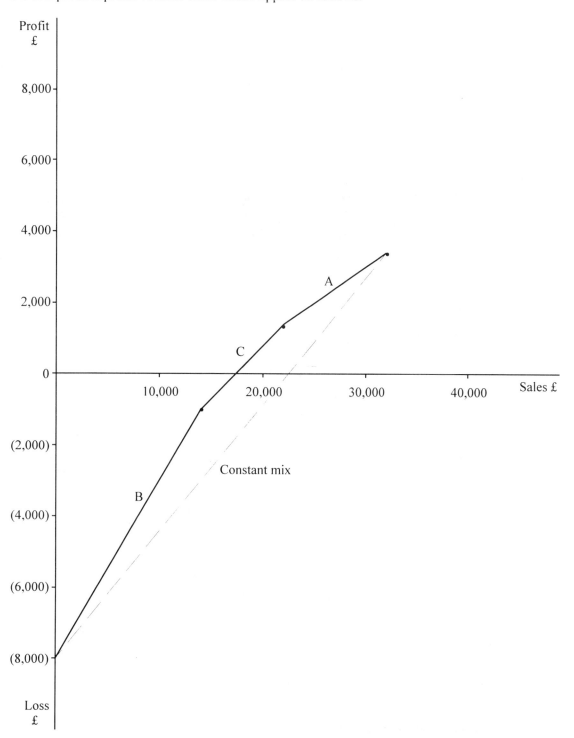

Data for the month of April was as follows:

Product	Sales volume in units	Selling price each, £	Contribution/ sales ratio %
Budget:			
W	8,000	30	25
X	12,000	20	15
Y	6,000	10	30
Z	4,000	25	10

Fixed overhead for month, £40,000

Product	Sales volume in units	Selling price each, £	Contribution/ sales ratio %
Actuals:			
W	6,000	34	3
X	14,000	15	Negative 10
Y	8,000	15	40
Z	3,000	24	8

Fixed overhead for month, £35,000.

4.8 Activity solution

(a) Profit-volume chart

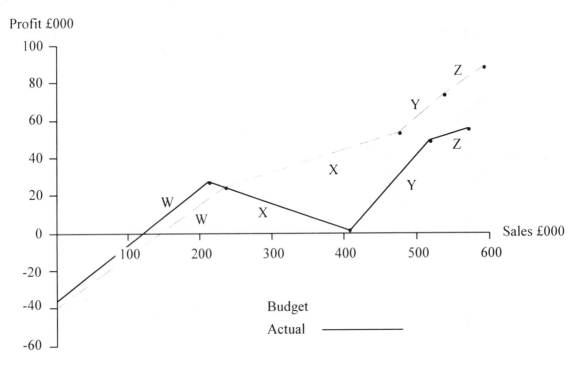

(b) Useful management points

- Expectations of profitability were mainly centred on products W and X;

- overall profit fell appreciably short of expectation, mainly due to the bad result shown by product X;

- the position was retrieved to some extent by an excellent result on product Y;

- a saving was effected on fixed overhead;

- actual profit was well below budgeted profit;

- overall sales were less than the budgeted level;

- the steeper climbing lines of products W and Y indicate that their actual contributions to sales ratios were better than expected.

WORKINGS

Budget:

Product		Sales value £'000	Cumulative £'000	Contribution ratio %	Contribution £'000	Cumulative £'000
W	8×30	240	240	25	60	60
X	12×20	240	480	15	36	96
Y	6×10	60	540	30	18	114
Z	4×25	100	640	10	10	124

Similarly for 'Actual'.

4.9   Requirements of break-even analysis model

Break-even analysis is useful insofar as it either meets or approximates to the requirements of the model. These requirements are:

(a)   Cost can be classified as either fixed or variable.

(b)   Over the time scale and activity range under review, unit variable costs remain constant and total fixed costs remain constant.

(c)   Unit sales price remains constant.

(d)   The costs and relationships are known.

Despite the obvious limitations these requirements impose, break-even analysis is of great practical importance. This is not just for itself, but because of the understanding it gives of cost behaviour patterns for decision purposes, considered further below.

5   LIMITATIONS OF CVP ANALYSIS

5.1   Introduction

The requirements of the breakeven model referred to above, limit the usefulness of CVP analysis for planning and decision making. In particular its usefulness is limited in multi-product situations and where uncertainty of input values exists.

5.2   Multi-product situations

When an organisation sells more than one product there is always difficulty in identifying the fixed costs relating to a specific product, and inevitably there will be some fixed costs which are not product specific. Consequently a particular sales mix has to be assumed in order to use the model, and then the breakeven point can only be quantified in terms of sales values.

5.3   Uncertainty

The model is over-simplistic by assuming that variable costs are constant per unit and fixed costs are constant in total. In reality there will be economies and diseconomies of scale which occur, although it is uncertain as to the level of activity which causes them, and the extent to which the costs will be affected. The CVP model cannot be manipulated to deal with these and other forms of uncertainty.

6   AVOIDABLE AND INCREMENTAL COSTS

6.1   Avoidable cost

> **Definition**   An avoidable cost is a cost which will not be incurred if a particular decision is made. It is usually used in the context of a fixed cost. For example if a fixed cost can be identified to the production of a single product, and the production of that product is stopped, then the fixed cost would not be incurred: it is therefore avoided because of the decision.

6.2   Incremental cost

> **Definition**   An incremental cost is the extra cost incurred as a result of a decision. Thus if a decision is made to increase production and to do so an additional machine is to be leased, then the lease cost of the additional machine is an incremental cost.

7   FIXED COSTS AND TIME

7.1   Introduction

A fixed cost is a cost which is assumed in CVP analysis to remain constant irrespective of the level of activity. Such costs are often considered to be uncontrollable, but this is not usually true within the longer term.

7.2   Controllability and time

The controllability of costs must be considered in connection with the powers of the managers concerned. In the context of fixed costs it is common for costs to be uncontrollable because of a contractual agreement or similar long-term arrangement. Thus the cost is uncontrollable within the short-term but outside this timescale the agreement will eventually lapse, or significant changes can be made to production methods. When this occurs costs which were uncontrollable become controllable because of a decision opportunity. However, once the decision has been made, the cost becomes uncontrollable at its new level and therefore fixed once again.

8   RELEVANT COSTS FOR SPECIFIC DECISION SITUATIONS

8.1   Past exam questions

This topic was examined in June 1994 and December 1995. Both questions required the identification of relevant costs for a decision from information given. Work through the illustration below to ensure you fully understand the principles involved.

8.2   Accept or reject decision analysis: an illustration

Spartan plc manufactures a wide range of soft toys. The managers of the business are considering whether to add a new type of toy animal, the Wimble, to the product range. A recent market research survey, undertaken at a cost of £2,000, has indicated that demand for the Wimble would last for only one year, during which time 100,000 of these could be sold at £6 each.

It is assumed that production and sales of the Wimble would take place evenly throughout the year. Manufacturing cost data is available as below.

Raw materials

Each Wimble would require three types of raw material, A, B and C. Material A is used regularly in the business and stocks are replaced as necessary. Material B is currently being held as surplus stock as a result of over-ordering on an earlier contract. This material is not used regularly by Spartan plc and would be sold if not required for the manufacture of the Wimble. Material C would have to be bought in specially for the Wimble, since stocks of this item are not normally held.

Current stock levels and costs of each raw material are shown below:

Raw material	Amount required per Wimble (m)	Current stock level (m)	Original cost (£/m)	Replacement cost (£/m)	Realisable value (£/m)
A	0.8	200,000	1.05	1.25	0.90
B	0.4	30,000	1.65	1.20	0.55
C	0.1	0	-	2.75	2.50

Labour

In producing one Wimble, half an hour of skilled labour and a quarter of an hour of unskilled labour would be required, at wage rates of £3 per hour and £2 per hour respectively. One supervisor would be required full-time at an annual salary of £7,000.

Skilled labour for the production of Wimbles would have to be recruited specially, whilst 25,000 surplus unskilled labour hours are expected to be available during the coming year if Wimbles are not manufactured. However, company policy dictates that no unskilled worker will be made redundant in the foreseeable future.

The supervisor has agreed to delay immediate retirement for one year, and to waive his annual pension of £4,000 in return for his annual salary during this period.

Machinery

Two machines, X and Y, would be required to manufacture Wimbles, details of which are as below:

	X	Y
Original cost	£35,000	£25,000
Accumulated depreciation	£24,000	£18,000
Written down value	£11,000	£7,000
Age	4 years	6 years
Estimated remaining useful life	1 year	2 years
Estimated value at end of useful life	£5,000	£1,000

Details are also available of cash values relating to the two machines at the start and end of the year during which Wimbles would be produced.

		Start of the year £	End of year £
Machine X:	Replacement cost	40,000	45,000
	Resale value	7,000	5,000
Machine Y:	Replacement cost	30,000	33,000
	Resale value	4,000	3,000

If machine X is not used for the manufacture of Wimbles then it would be used to manufacture existing products, the sale of which would result in an estimated £50,000 net receipts.

Machine X is one of a number of identical machine types used regularly on various products by Spartan plc. Each of this type of machine is replaced as soon as it reaches the end of its useful life.

Machine Y is the only one of its type within the firm and if not used in the manufacture of Wimbles would be sold immediately.

Overheads

Variable overhead costs attributable to Wimbles are estimated at £1.50 per item produced. Production fixed overheads are allocated by Spartan plc to products on the basis of labour hours, and the rate for the coming year has been established at £2.50 per labour hour. The manufacture of Wimbles will not result in any additional fixed costs being incurred.

We can now turn our attention to assessing whether, on the basis of the information given the manufacture and sale of Wimbles represents a profitable opportunity to Spartan plc. In doing so, the relevant cost of using each resource required to produce Wimbles must be identified. For each resource, a comparison is required showing the cash flows associated with manufacture and those associated with non-manufacture. The difference between the two represents the incremental cost of applying each resource to the production of Wimbles.

Cash flows (explanations follow)

	Manufacture	*Non-manufacture*	*Incremental cost of manufacture*
	£	*£*	*£*
Raw materials			
A	(100,000)	0	(100,000)
B	(12,000)	16,500	(28,500)
C	(27,500)	0	(27,500)
			(156,000)
Labour			
Skilled	(150,000)	0	(150,000)
Unskilled	(50,000)	(50,000)	0
Supervisor	(7,000)	(4,000)	(3,000)
			(153,000)
Machinery			
X	(35,000)	(40,000)	5,000
Y	3,000	4,000	(1,000)
			4,000
Overheads			
Variable	(150,000)	0	(150,000)
Fixed	-	-	-
			(150,000)
Total incremental cost			(455,000)
Total sales revenue			600,000
Net cash inflow (contribution)			145,000

Thus, £455,000 is the relevant cost to Spartan plc for producing 100,000 Wimbles during the forthcoming year. Taking the cash generated from sales into consideration a net cash inflow of £145,000 would result from this trading opportunity. At this stage you are advised to review critically the build-up of incremental cost shown above before reading further, in order to establish whether or not the principle of relevance has been fully understood. The basis for establishing the relevant cost of each resource is examined below.

Raw materials

A: since this material is used regularly within the business and stocks are replaced as used, the 80,000 metres required would be replaced for subsequent use on other jobs at the current replacement cost of £1.25 per metre.

B: if Wimbles are manufactured a further 10,000 metres would have to be purchased at £1.20 per metre. The historic cost of the 30,000 metres already in stock is a sunk cost and is therefore not relevant. If Wimbles are not manufactured, the existing stock would be sold off at the realisable value of £0.55 per metre.

C: the only cash flow arising here is that relating to the special purchase of 10,000 metres at £2.75 per metre if Wimbles are produced.

To summarise, the relevant cost of raw materials is identified as being their current replacement cost, unless the material in question is not to be replaced, in which case the relevant cost becomes the higher of current resale value or the value if applied to another product (economic value).

Labour

Skilled: in manufacturing Wimbles additional wage payments of £150,000 would be made ie, 50,000 hours @ £3 per hour. These payments relate to specifically recruited labour.

Unskilled: the cost of 25,000 hours of unskilled labour will be incurred by Spartan plc regardless of whether Wimbles are produced. Company policy has effectively turned this unskilled labour wages element into a fixed cost which cannot be adjusted in the short term and is therefore not relevant to the decision at hand.

Supervisor: the relevant cost of the supervisor is the difference between the wages paid if Wimbles are produced, and the pension cost that would be avoided in this situation.

In assessing the relevant cost of labour the avoidable costs of production have been identified ie, those which will not be incurred unless Wimbles are produced. If any element of the labour resource could be used for some other profitable purpose, then the opportunity cost representing the income forgone would have to be included in the analysis.

Machine X

Using the machine to manufacture Wimbles.

Start of year	cash outflow from purchasing another machine X	(£40,000)
End of year	cash inflow from selling machine X at the end of its useful life	£5,000

Decision not to manufacture Wimbles.

Start of year	no cash movement	
End of year	cash outflow from buying new machine X	(£45,000)
	cash inflow from selling machine X	£5,000

This is summarised as:

	Manufacture £	Non-manufacture £	Increment £
Start of year	(40,000)	0	(40,000)
End of year	5,000	(45,000)	45,000
		5,000	
	(35,000)	(40,000)	5,000

Thus the net effect of manufacturing the Wimble is to accelerate the purchase of a machine X by 1 year to the start of the year, thereby saving £5,000 due to the lower cost of machine X at the start of the year.

Y: the manufacture of Wimbles would delay the sale of machine Y by one year, during which time the resale value of the machine would have been reduced by £1,000 as shown in the table of machine values above.

In determining the relevant costs associated with the use of plant and machinery, similar considerations apply as to those identified in respect of raw materials. If plant and equipment is to be replaced at the end of its useful life, or would be immediately replaced should the business be deprived of the use of an asset, then current replacement cost is the relevant cost. If the asset is not to be replaced, then the relevant cost becomes the higher of resale value or associated net receipts arising from use of the asset (economic value).

In this analysis of relevant cost, the assumption is made that the use of machine X is profitable for the company. If a situation arises in which an asset is not generating sufficient net receipts to meet a target rate of return the replacement of the asset would presumably not be encouraged since its use is uneconomic, and thus replacement cost is not relevant since it would not represent a viable option.

You should note however, that correctly identifying the true cost of using a particular asset may be difficult in practice, since economic values are not easily identified.

Overheads

Variable costs of £1.50 per Wimble are avoidable, being incurred only if Wimbles are produced. In contrast, fixed overhead may be assumed to be fixed regardless of the product being produced and the level of activity over a given range. Since fixed overhead is unaffected by the opportunity being considered, any apportionment of fixed cost is meaningless and would serve only to distort the profitability of the project.

For decision purposes, only those costs that will vary as a result of the decision taken are relevant.

A form of statement similar to that shown above for the analysis of differential cash flows could be used for presentation to management. In addition, supplementary information should be provided in order to disclose the principles adopted in evaluating the cost of use of each resource. Attention should be drawn to the fact that the surplus cash figure of £100,000 is the anticipated increase in Spartan plc's cash reserves arising from the manufacture of Wimbles rather than applying the required resources to their best alternative use.

Thus from a purely financial viewpoint the production and sale of Wimbles appears to be worthwhile. However, as was noted earlier, there may be other factors of interest to the decision-maker. Non-quantifiable qualitative factors such as the effect on longer term marketing strategy, customer reaction, competitor reaction etc, should be identified and incorporated into the analysis so that a balanced judgement may be made.

| Conclusion | In the above analysis the principle of relevance was applied in the evaluation of the financial factors surrounding the manufacture of Wimbles. At no time was historic cost suggested as being an appropriate measure of the relevant cost of a resource.

This presents a practical problem since conventional cost accounting records deal with costs already incurred ie, historic cost. It may therefore be difficult to extract replacement costs or opportunity costs from the organisation's information system. Moreover, if the relevant cost approach is to be adopted, the accountant is faced with the task of educating managers, if the correct interpretation is to be placed on the figures presented.

However, despite these obstacles to adopting the correct approach to decision-making, the alternative route of applying conventional cost accounting principles is likely to lead to sub optimal decisions.

The dangers inherent in the historic cost accounting approach are discussed below.

Generally, the conventional cost accounting approach involves the identification of the historical or estimated costs of the resources actually used on a project, and these are then related to the revenues arising. The costs as identified often include fixed costs which are assigned on a subjective basis and do not therefore directly relate to the project under consideration. As a result, the worthiness of the particular opportunity may well be under or over-estimated.

Consider the conventional profitability statement set out below in relation to the manufacture of Wimbles:

Trading statement: Wimbles

	£	£	£
Sales			600,000
Less: Costs:			
Raw materials			
A (80,000m @ £1.05)	84,000		
B (30,000m @ £1.65 + 10,000m			
@ £1.20)	61,500		
C (10,000m @ £2.75)	27,500		
	———	173,000	
Labour			
Skilled (50,000 hours @ £3)	150,000		
Unskilled (25,000 hours @ £2)	50,000		
Supervisor	7,000		
	———	207,000	
Depreciation of machinery			
X [(11,000 - 5,000) ÷ 1]	6,000		
Y [(7,000 - 1,000) ÷ 2]	3,000		
	———	9,000	
Overheads			
Market research survey	2,000		
Variable (100,000 @ £1.50)	150,000		
Fixed (75,000 @ £2.50)	187,500		
	———	339,500	
Total costs			728,500
Trading loss			(128,500)

In applying conventional cost accounting practice, some specific resources are charged to a project at their original cost. Consider, for example, the costs of raw materials applied to the trading statement above. However, the inclusion of historic cost is incorrect for decision analysis. The crucial question to be answered in evaluating a course of action is: how will the cash flows of the business be affected? Thus, in the case of raw materials in our example, only the costs of the extra 10,000 metres of B and the 10,000 metres of additional material C are relevant costs; the historic costs are not, since they do not have any impact on future cash flows.

A second major difference of approach lies in the treatment of depreciation of assets. The traditional accounting methods of depreciation, such as those on a straight line or reducing balance basis, are an extension of the practice of matching or recovering past costs. Yet for decision purposes what is required is an evaluation of the sacrifice involved in using the asset on the project under consideration.

The third area of difference concerns fixed costs. In the example above, there are unskilled labour wages and fixed overhead costs in respect of the decision to manufacture Wimbles since they cannot be affected by it. Nevertheless, fixed costs such as these are often assigned to available project opportunities under conventional accounting practice.

It has been shown that the differences between conventional accounting practice and differential cash flow analysis may give rise to alarming discrepancies. In our example a conventional trading 'loss' of £128,500 is in fact an incremental cash flow surplus of £100,000. It is therefore not difficult to envisage sub-optimal decisions being taken as a result of advice which is based on conventional accounting practice. The notion of 'different costs for different purposes' should be borne in mind when providing financial information for managers.

9   CHAPTER SUMMARY

This chapter has considered the application of cost behaviour to CVP analysis and the calculation of output levels to achieve target profits using breakeven theory.

We have then seen how the accountant's and economist's breakeven charts differ and explained the concept of the relevant range.

Finally the limitations of CVP analysis were considered and related to avoidable, incremental and controllable costs within the short and long term time horizon.

10   SELF TEST QUESTIONS

10.1   What is CVP analysis? (1.1)

10.2   What is contribution? (1.3)

10.3   What is the contribution to sales ratio? (1.7)

10.4   Explain the term 'Margin of Safety'. (1.9)

10.5   Distinguish between the accountant's and economist's breakeven chart. (2.1, 2.2)

10.6   Explain the concept of the 'relevant range' in the context of CVP analysis. (3)

10.7   Explain the limitations of CVP analysis. (5)

10.8   Explain the term 'avoidable cost'. (6.1)

10.9   Explain the term 'incremental cost'. (6.2)

10.10   Explain the importance of the time horizon in respect of fixed cost classification. (7)

11   EXAMINATION TYPE QUESTION

11.1   JK Ltd

JK Ltd has prepared a budget for the next 12 months when it intends to make and sell four products, details of which are shown below:

Product	Sales in units (thousands)	Selling price per unit £	Variable cost per unit £
J	10	20	14.00
K	10	40	8.00
L	50	4	4.20
M	20	10	7.00

Budgeted fixed costs are £240,000 per annum and total assets employed are £570,000.

You are required

(a)   to calculate the total contribution earned by each product and their combined total contributions;   **(2 marks)**

(b)   to plot the data of your answer to (a) above in the form of a contribution to sales graph (sometimes referred to as a profit-volume graph) on the graph paper provided;   **(6 marks)**

(c)   to explain your graph to management, to comment on the results shown and to state the break-even point;   **(4 marks)**

(d)   to describe briefly three ways in which the overall contribution to sales ratio could be improved.   **(3 marks)**

(Total: 15 marks)

12   ANSWER TO EXAMINATION TYPE QUESTION

12.1   JK Ltd

(a)

	Product				
	J	*K*	*L*	*M*	*Total*
	£'000	£'000	£'000	£'000	£'000
Sales	200	400	200	200	1,000
Variable costs	140	80	210	140	570
Contribution	60	320	(10)	60	430

(b)   Calculate the contribution/sales ratios and plot each product starting with the product having the greatest C/S ratio.

J	*K*	*L*	*M*
30%	80%	(5%)	30%

Contribution - Sales Graph

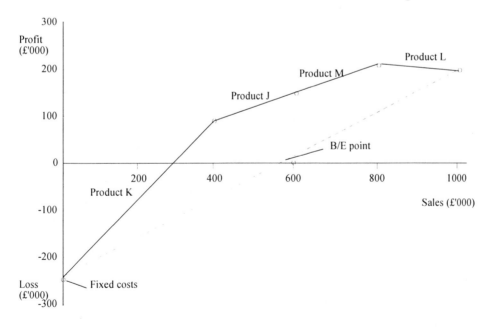

(c)   The products are plotted in the order of their c/s ratios. The steeper the line for an individual product the greater the c/s ratio for that product. Thus it can be seen that product K provides the greatest contribution with respect to sales value.

It can be seen from the graph that product L should be dropped as it provides negative contribution.

The breakeven point can be calculated using the c/s ratio of the mix. This can also be approximately seen from the graph.

$$B/E \quad = \quad \frac{\text{Fixed costs}}{\text{c / s ratio of the mix}}$$

$$= \quad \frac{240,000}{430 / 1,000}$$

$$= \quad £558,140$$

(d)   The overall ratio could be improved by:

(i)   increasing the selling prices

(ii)   decreasing the sales of products J, L or M

(iii)   automating the process. This would increase fixed costs but would reduce variable costs thus increasing contribution.

9 DECISION MAKING AND SHORT RUN DECISIONS: TECHNIQUES

INTRODUCTION & LEARNING OBJECTIVES

In this chapter a number of decision making situations are illustrated with examples.

When you have studied this chapter you should be able to do the following:

- Identify different types of decision making situation.
- Explain the technique to be used in different decision making situations.
- Select and use relevant data to solve decision making problems.

1 DECISION MAKING AND TIME HORIZONS

1.1 Introduction

Decision making may be applied to solve short-term operating problems or be part of the longer term planning process. In this way decision making may be stated to be short-term or long-term.

1.2 Short term decision making

Short term decision making assumes that decisions previously made concerning fixed plant and equipment cannot be altered. Thus such decisions often involve making the best use of existing resources.

1.3 Long term decision making

In the longer term earlier decisions may be altered, new investment in plant and equipment may be considered, and so such decisions have more variables and are more complex.

Long term decisions require more assumptions about the future and must consider the opportunity cost of investing for a future reward. These aspects of uncertainty and the time value of money are considered later in this text.

2 QUALITATIVE FACTORS IN SOURCING AND PRODUCT LINE DECISIONS

2.1 Introduction

In any decision making situation, the decision made will impact on a number of interested groups, such as employees, customers, suppliers and competitors and may also affect the scarce resource management. Each of these factors is considered below.

2.2 Qualitative factors

The following factors (interested groups) may be affected by a decision:

- employees. Any decision which affects working practices will have a morale effect on employees. Some decisions, such as to close a department, will have a greater effect than others, for example an increase in production, but both will affect employees.

- customers. Customers will be affected by any decision which changes the finished product or its availability. For example, the deletion of a product will force customers to choose an alternative item.

- suppliers. Suppliers will be affected by changes to production which require different raw materials or delivery schedules. For example an increase in production may cause the supplier to increase their production of the raw material.

- competitors. Any decision to change product specification or pricing will affect competitors who will then choose whether or not to respond.

- scarce resource management. A change in production as a result of the decision may alter the demand for individual resources thus changing the resource availability.

3   QUANTITATIVE AND QUALITATIVE FACTORS AND THE DECISION MAKING CYCLE

3.1   The decision making cycle

The decision making cycle was explained earlier in this text; you should remember that it contains three fundamental phases:

- identify objectives and courses of action available;
- select alternative and implement the decision;
- compare actual results.

3.2   Quantitative factors

In each of the three phases identified above numerical data will be collected to establish the objective, to identify the best course of action, and to compare the actual results with the target. Examples of such quantitative factors include:

- percentage market share
- likely demand patterns
- cost of investment
- actual sales volume (units)
- actual sales value
- market sales volume (units).

3.3   Qualitative factors

In each phase there are also qualitative factors to be considered, which may include:

- social and environmental effects of a particular objective;
- the opinions of customers and employees.

4   LIMITING FACTORS

4.1   Introduction

In most business situations only a limited number of business opportunities may be undertaken. Some factor will limit the ability to undertake all the alternatives. This factor is referred to as the **limiting factor**.

4.2   Production scheduling with one limiting factor

Consider the situation where there is one factor limiting operations and two or more possible products. The management accountant must advise management on how to schedule production so as to maximise profits subject to the constraint.

The essential elements of the problem are as follows:

(a)   The object is to maximise profits. Therefore only costs and revenues that vary according to the decision are considered; since fixed costs do not, they are irrelevant and may be ignored.

(b)   This leaves revenue and variable costs, which together specify the contribution of each product line. The aim is to maximise the total contribution.

(c)   The real cost of producing Product 1 rather than Product 2 is the contribution of Product 2 forgone - the opportunity cost. It must be ensured that the total contribution of Product 1 gained exceeds that of Product 2 lost.

(d)   Total contribution is given by units multiplied by contribution per unit. The number of units is limited by the limiting factor. In the evaluation of alternative products consideration must be given not only to contribution per unit, but also to the number of units that can be produced, subject to the limiting factor.

(e)   To take both of these factors together, total contribution is maximised by concentrating on that product which yields the highest contribution per unit of limiting factor.

4.3   Example

A company makes and sells two products - X and Y. It has a shortage of labour, which is limited to 200,000 hours pa. This is insufficient to satisfy the full demand for both products. The unit costs, contributions and labour hours used are as follows:

	Product X	*Product Y*
Labour hours per unit of output	5	10
	£	£
Selling price	80	100
Variable cost	50	50
Contribution per unit	30	50

There are two ways in which the production scheduling problem can be solved.

(a)   Calculate total contribution if each is produced in turn:

Total contribution

$$\text{Product X units} = \frac{200,000}{5} = 40,000$$

Contribution × units = £30 × 40,000   £1,200,000

$$\text{Product Y units} = \frac{200,000}{10} = 20,000$$

Contribution × units = £50 × 20,000   £1,000,000

Thus, Product X would be produced since it maximises total contribution.

(b)   The quicker alternative is to find which product has the higher contribution per unit of limiting factor ie, per labour hour:

Contribution per labour hour

$$\text{Product X} = \frac{£30}{5} = \qquad £6$$

$$\text{Product Y} = \frac{£50}{10} = \qquad £5$$

This is of course merely a way of short-cutting the calculations in (a) above, and exactly the same conclusion is reached: production should concentrate on Product X.

4.4   Other considerations in the limiting factor situation

(a)   In the long run management must seek to remove the limiting factor. In the above example management should be recruiting and training additional labour. Thus, any one limiting factor should only be a short-term problem. However, as soon as it is removed it will be replaced by another limiting factor.

(b)   Even in the short run management may be able to find ways round the bottleneck eg, overtime working, temporary staff and sub-contracting might all be solutions to the situation described.

(c)   Nor may it always be easy to identify the limiting factor. In practice several limiting factors may operate simultaneously. However, even in examination questions, where there is only one limiting factor, it may be necessary to identify between several possible limiting factors.

(d)   It is also possible that there may be other parameters setting minimum production levels eg, there may be a contract to supply Y so that certain minimum quantities must be produced.

4.5   Example

X Ltd makes three products, A, B and C, of which unit costs, machine hours and selling prices are as follows:

	Product A	Product B	Product C
Machine hours	10	12	14
	£	£	£
Direct materials @ 50p per lb	7 (14 lbs)	6 (12 lbs)	5 (10 lbs)
Direct wages @ 75p per hour	9 (12 hours)	6 (8 hours)	3 (4 hours)
Variable overheads	3	3	3
Marginal cost	19	15	11
Selling price	25	20	15
Contribution	6	5	4

Sales demand for the period is limited as follows:

Product A	4,000
Product B	6,000
Product C	6,000

As a matter of company policy it is decided to produce a minimum of 1,000 units of Product A. The supply of materials in the period is unlimited, but machine hours are limited to 200,000 and direct labour hours to 50,000.

Indicate the production levels that should be adopted for the three products in order to maximise profitability, and state the maximum contribution.

4.6   Solution

First determine which is the limiting factor. At potential sales level:

	Sales potential units	Total machine hours	Total labour hours
Product A	4,000	40,000	48,000
Product B	6,000	72,000	48,000
Product C	6,000	84,000	24,000
		196,000	120,000

Thus, labour hours is the limiting factor. The next stage is to calculate contribution per labour hour:

Product A $\qquad \dfrac{£6}{12} = £0.500$

Product B $\qquad \dfrac{£5}{8} = £0.625$

Product C $\qquad \dfrac{£4}{4} = £1.000$

Thus, production should be concentrated on C, up to the maximum available sales, then B, and finally A.

However, a minimum of 1,000 units of A must be produced. Taking these factors into account, the production schedule becomes:

	Units produced	*Labour hours*	*Cumulative labour hours*	*Limiting factor*
Product A	1,000	12,000	12,000	Policy to produce 1,000 units
Product C	6,000	24,000	36,000	Sales
Product B	1,750	14,000	50,000	Labour hours

5 PROBLEMS INVOLVING PRODUCT MIX AND DISCONTINUANCE

5.1 Introduction

It is considered more informative to present comparison statements on a contribution basis. The term **contribution** describes the amount which a product provides or contributes towards a fund out of which fixed overhead may be paid, the balance being net profit. Where two or more products are manufactured in a factory and share all production facilities, the fixed overhead can only be apportioned on an arbitrary basis.

5.2 Example

A factory manufactures three components – X, Y and Z – and the budgeted production for the year is 1,000 units, 1,500 units and 2,000 units respectively. Fixed overhead amounts to £6,750 and has been apportioned on the basis of budgeted units: £1,500 to X, £2,250 to Y and £3,000 to Z. Sales and variable costs are as follows:

	Component X	*Component Y*	*Component Z*
Selling price	£4	£6	£5
Variable cost	£1	£4	£4

The budgeted profit and loss account based on the above is as follows:

	Component X	*Component Y*	*Component Z*	*Total*
Sales units	1,000	1,500	2,000	4,500

	£	£	£	£	£	£	£	£
Sales value		4,000		9,000		10,000		23,000
Variable cost	1,000		6,000		8,000		15,000	
Fixed overhead	1,500		2,250		3,000		6,750	
		2,500		8,250		11,000		21,750
Net profit/(loss)		1,500		750		(1,000)		1,250

Clearly there is little value in comparing products in this way. If the fixed overhead is common to all three products, there is no point in apportioning it. A better presentation is as follows:

	Component X	Component Y	Component Z	Total
Sales units	1,000	1,500	2,000	4,500
	£	£	£	£
Sales value	4,000	9,000	10,000	23,000
Variable cost	1,000	6,000	8,000	15,000
Contribution	3,000	3,000	2,000	8,000
Fixed cost				6,750
Net profit				1,250

Analysis may show, however, that certain fixed costs may be associated with a specific product and the statement can be amended to differentiate specific fixed costs (under products) from general fixed costs (under total).

5.3   Closure of a business segment

Part of a business may appear to be unprofitable. The segment may, for example, be a product, a department or a channel of distribution. In evaluating closure the cost accountant should identify:

(a)   loss of contribution from the segment;

(b)   savings in specific fixed costs from closure;

(c)   penalties eg, redundancy, compensation to customers etc;

(d)   alternative use for resources released;

(e)   non-quantifiable effects.

5.4   Example

Harolds department store comprises three departments - Menswear, Ladies' Wear and Unisex. The store budget is as follows:

	Mens £	Ladies £	Unisex £	Total £
Sales	40,000	60,000	20,000	120,000
Direct cost of sales	20,000	36,000	15,000	71,000
Department costs	5,000	10,000	3,000	18,000
Apportioned store costs	5,000	5,000	5,000	15,000
Profit/(loss)	10,000	9,000	(3,000)	16,000

It is suggested that Unisex be closed to increase the size of Mens and Ladies.

What information is relevant or required?

5.5   Solution

Possible answers are:

(a)   Unisex earns £2,000 net contribution (store costs will be re-apportioned to Mens/Ladies).

(b)   Possible increase in Mens/Ladies sales volume.

(c)   Will Unisex staff be dismissed or transferred to Mens/Ladies?

(d)   Reorganisation costs eg, repartitioning, stock disposal.

(e)   Loss of custom because Unisex attracts certain types of customer who will not buy in Mens/Ladies.

5.6   Comparing segment profitability

When presenting information for comparing results or plans for different products, departments etc, it is useful to show gross and net contribution for each segment. The information in the example above would be presented in the following form.

	Menswear	*Ladies Wear*	*Unisex*	*Total*
	£'000	£'000	£'000	£'000
Sales	40	60	20	120
Direct cost of sales	20	36	15	71
Gross contribution	20	24	5	49
Department costs	5	10	3	18
Net contribution	15	14	2	31

Note that the store costs if shown would only appear in the total column. In addition, the statement should include performance indicators relevant to the type of operation. For a department store, such indicators would include:

(a)   C/S ratios (based on **gross** contribution);
(b)   gross and net contribution per unit of floor space;
(c)   gross and net contribution per employee.

For a manufacturing company, more relevant indicators would include:

(a)   contribution per labour/machine hour;
(b)   added value/conversion cost per hour;
(c)   added/value conversion cost per employee.

5.7   Temporary shut-down

When a business has experienced trading difficulties which do not appear likely to improve in the immediate future, consideration may be given to closing down operations temporarily. Factors other than cost which will influence the decision are:

(a)   suspending production and sales of products will result in their **leaving the public eye;**

(b)   dismissal of the labour force will entail bad feeling and possible difficulty in recruitment when operations are restarted;

(c)   danger of plant obsolescence;

(d)   difficulty and cost of closing down and restarting operations in certain industries eg, a blast furnace.

The temporary closure of a business will result in additional expenditure eg, plant will require protective coverings, services will be disconnected. In the same way, additional expenditure will be incurred when the business restarts.

On the other hand, a temporary closure may enable the business to reorganise efficiently to take full advantage of improved trading conditions when they return.

In the short term a business can continue to operate while marginal contribution equals fixed expenses. In periods of trading difficulty, as long as some contribution is made towards fixed expenses, it will generally be worthwhile continuing operations.

5.8   Example

A company is operating at 40% capacity and is considering closing down its factory for one year, after which time the demand for its product is expected to increase substantially. The following data applies:

	£
Sales value at 40% capacity	60,000
Marginal costs of sales at 40% capacity	40,000
Fixed costs	50,000

Fixed costs which will remain if the factory is closed amount to £20,000. The cost of closing down operations will amount to £4,000.

Prepare a statement to show the best course of action.

5.9   Solution

Statement of profit or loss

Continuing operation	£	Temporary closure	£
Sales	60,000	Fixed expenses	20,000
Marginal cost of sales	40,000	Closing down costs	4,000
	———		
Contribution to fixed costs	20,000		
Fixed costs	50,000		
	———		———
Net loss	(30,000)		(24,000)

Ignoring non-cost considerations, the company will minimise its losses by closing down for one year.

Students should note that the marginal contribution of £20,000 does not cover the difference between existing fixed costs and those that remain on closure (ie, £(50,000 – 24,000) = £26,000 compared to £20,000).

6   DIVESTMENT

6.1   Introduction

A company may have to drop existing product-market areas as well as develop new ones. For instance, a product might be nearing the end of its life cycle and it might be better to 'kill it off' once sales have fallen below a certain level rather than let it decline to zero. Advertising expenditure to boost the sale of a declining product is often not worthwhile in terms of the return achieved.

The precise timing of a decision to drop a certain line (or cease selling it in a particular market) is admittedly difficult, but most companies probably tend to leave it too late. Some of the reasons for the reluctance to drop products are:

(a)   The company might have invested large sums of money in the project and does not want to abandon it. Management accountants will recognise that this is a quite erroneous standpoint – the money already spent is a sunk cost and it is the future not the past which is important. Companies should be prepared to 'cut their losses' – it is no good throwing good money after bad.

(b)   Perhaps the person who designed the product is still with the firm. He and probably many others are 'attached' to the product and want to keep it going. In addition, the marketing director might be an optimist who thinks that sales of the product will suddenly turn up again. This can happen, but is unlikely unless the cause of the fall in demand is the general economic climate – but we are really talking about products which have a history of continuously falling demand.

(c)   Attention is directed towards new products and no-one thinks what should happen to the old ones (until resources are scarce and there is a search for economies).

(d)   There is a feeling that customers should be kept happy and a fear that they will be lost to the firm if the particular product is withdrawn. This fear need have no foundation if a new product is launched as the old one is withdrawn. Anyway, does it matter if some old customers are lost, as long as more new ones are gained?

(e)   A very real problem exists of what to do with the work force who have been running an existing production line if it is suddenly shut down. It may be easier to absorb the work force into other areas if production is run down gradually. There are, however, arguments against this:

    (i)   Morale among those remaining on the product may fall if they know that their job is eventually going to go and they do not know when, or where they will be moved. If this loss of morale is reflected in their work the product may become even more uneconomic.

    (ii)   A sensible programme of retraining can ensure that workers released from an old line will be available for a new process.

    (iii)   It may prove more costly to keep the workers employed on the old process than to pay them for doing nothing until their services are again required elsewhere.

The detailed programming of divestment is of course a matter for the administrative and operating plans, but at the strategic level it is important to emphasise that this is one area for examination.

7   MAKE OR BUY DECISIONS

7.1   Types of make or buy decisions

Occasionally a business may have the opportunity to purchase, from another company, a component part or assembly which it currently produces from its own resources.

In examining the choice, management must first consider the following questions:

(a)   Is the alternative source of supply available only temporarily or for the foreseeable future?

(b)   Is there spare production capacity available now and/or in the future?

7.2   Spare capacity

If the business is operating below maximum capacity, production resources will be idle if the component is purchased from outside. The fixed costs of those resources are irrelevant to the decision in the short term as they will be incurred whether the component is made or purchased. Purchase would be recommended, therefore, only if the buying price were less than the variable costs of internal manufacture.

In the long term, however, the business may dispense with or transfer some of its resources and may purchase from outside if it thereby saves more than the extra cost of purchasing.

7.3   Example

A company manufactures an assembly used in the production of one of its product lines. The department in which the assembly is produced incurs fixed costs of £24,000 pa. The variable costs of production are £2.55 per unit. The assembly could be bought outside at a cost of £2.65 per unit.

The current annual requirement is for 80,000 assemblies per year. Should the company continue to manufacture the assembly, or should it be purchased from the outside suppliers?

7.4   Solution

A decision to purchase outside would cost the company £(2.65 - 2.55) = 10p per unit, which for 80,000 assemblies would amount to £8,000 pa. Thus, the fixed costs of £24,000 will require analysis to determine if more than £8,000 would actually be saved if production of the assembly were discontinued.

7.5   Other considerations affecting the decision

Management would need to consider other factors before reaching a decision. Some would be quantifiable and some not:

(a)   **Continuity and control of supply.** Can the outside company be relied upon to meet the requirements in terms of quantity, quality, delivery dates and price stability?

(b)   **Alternative use of resources.** Can the resources used to make this article be transferred to another activity which will save cost or increase revenue?

(c)   **Social/legal.** Will the decision affect contractual or ethical obligations to employees or business connections?

7.6   Capacity exhausted

If a business cannot fulfil orders because it has used up all available capacity, it may be forced to purchase from outside in the short term (unless it is cheaper to refuse sales). In the longer term management may look to other alternatives, such as capital expenditure.

It may be, however, that a variety of components is produced from common resources and management would try to arrange manufacture or purchase to use its available capacity most profitably. In such a situation the limiting factor concept makes it easier to formulate the optimum plans; priority for purchase would be indicated by ranking components in relation to the excess purchasing cost per unit of limiting factor.

7.7   Example

Fidgets Ltd manufactures three components used in its finished product. The component workshop is currently unable to meet the demand for components and the possibility of sub-contracting part of the requirement is being investigated on the basis of the following data:

	Component A £	Component B £	Component C £
Variable costs of production	3.00	4.00	7.00
Outside purchase price	2.50	6.00	13.00
Excess cost per unit	(0.50)	2.00	6.00
Machine hours per unit	1	0.5	2
Labour hours per unit	2	2	4

You are required:

(a)   to decide which component should be bought out if the company is operating at full capacity

(b)   to decide which component should be bought out if production is limited to 4,000 machine hours per week

(c)   to decide which component should be bought out if production is limited to 4,000 labour hours per week

7.8   Solution

(a)   Component A should always be bought out regardless of any limiting factors, as its variable cost of production is higher than the outside purchase price.

(b)   If machine hours are limited to 4,000 hours:

	Component B	Component C
Excess cost	£2	£6
Machine hours per unit	0.5	2
Excess cost per machine hour	£4	£3

Component C has the lowest excess cost per limiting factor and should, therefore, be bought out.

Proof:

	Component B	Component C
Units produced in 4,000 hours	8,000	2,000
	£	£
Production costs	32,000	14,000
Purchase costs	48,000	26,000
Excess cost of purchase	16,000	12,000

(c)   If labour hours are limited to 4,000 hours:

	Component B	Component C
Excess cost	£2	£6
Labour hours	2	4
Excess cost per labour hour	£1	£1.50

Therefore, component B has the lowest excess cost per limiting factor and should be bought out.

Proof:

	Component B	Component C
Units produced in 4,000 hours	2,000	1,000
	£	£
Production costs	8,000	7,000
Purchase costs	12,000	13,000
Excess cost of purchase	4,000	6,000

8   EVALUATING PROPOSALS

8.1   Volume and cost structure changes

Management will require information to evaluate proposals aimed to increase profit by changing operating strategy. The cost accountant will need to show clearly the effect of the proposals on profit by pin-pointing the changes in costs and revenues and by quantifying the margin of error which will cause the proposal to be unviable.

8.2   Example

A company produces and sells one product and its forecast for the next financial year is as follows:

	£'000	£'000
Sales 100,000 units @ £8		800
Variable costs:		
Material	300	
Labour	200	
		500
Contribution (£3 per unit)		300
Fixed costs		150
Net profit		150

As an attempt to increase net profit, two proposals have been put forward:

(a)   to launch an advertising campaign costing £14,000. This will increase the sales to 150,000 units, although the price will have to be reduced to £7;

(b)   to produce some components at present purchased from suppliers. This will reduce material costs by 20% but will increase fixed costs by £72,000.

Proposal (a) will increase the sales revenue but the increase in costs will be greater:

	£'000
Sales 150,000 × £7	1,050
Variable costs	750
	300
Fixed costs plus advertising	164
Net profit	136

8.3   Solution

Proposal (a) is therefore of no value and sales must be increased by a further 7,000 units to maintain net profit:

Advertising cost	=	£14,000
Contribution per unit	=	£2
∴ Additional volume required	=	7,000 units

Proposal (b) reduces variable costs by £60,000 but increases fixed costs by £72,000 and is therefore not to be recommended unless the total volume increases as a result of the policy (eg, if the supply of the components were previously a limiting factor). The increase in sales needed to maintain profit at £150,000 (assuming the price remains at £8) would be:

Reduced profits at 100,000 units	=	£12,000
Revised contribution per unit	=	£3.60
∴ Additional volume required	=	3,333 units

8.4   Utilisation of spare capacity

Where production is below capacity, opportunities may arise for sales at a specially reduced price, for example, export orders or manufacturing under another brand name (eg, 'St Michael').   Such opportunities are worthwhile if the answer to two key questions is 'Yes':

(a)   Is spare capacity available?

(b)   Does additional revenue (Units × Price) exceed additional costs (Units × Variable cost)?

However, the evaluation should also consider:

(i)   Is there an alternative more profitable way of utilising spare capacity (eg, sales promotion, making an alternative product)?

(ii)   Will fixed costs be unchanged if the order is accepted?

(iii)   Will accepting one order at below normal selling price lead other customers to ask for price cuts?

The longer the time period in question, the more important are these other factors.

8.5   Example

At a production level of 8,000 units per month, which is 80% of capacity, the budget of Export Ltd is:

	Per unit £	8,000 units £
Sales	5.00	40,000
Variable costs:		
Direct labour	1.00	8,000
Raw materials	1.50	12,000
Variable overheads	0.50	4,000
	3.00	24,000
Fixed costs	1.50	12,000
Total	4.50	36,000
Budgeted profit	0.50	4,000

An opportunity arises to export 1,000 units per month at a price of £4 per unit.

Should the contract be accepted?

8.6   Solution

(a)   Is spare capacity available?   Yes

			£
(b)	Additional revenue	1,000 × £4	4,000
	Additional costs	1,000 × £3	3,000
			1,000

Increased profitability

Therefore, the contract should be accepted.

Note that fixed costs are not relevant to the decision and are therefore ignored.

8.7   Calculation of basic selling price

When a business manufactures a limited range of repetitive products, initial estimation of economic selling prices is most useful.

8.8   Example

The Dainty Dolly Co manufactures a single product, the Dainty, which is a life-size doll selling in the high-price toy market through approved dealers.

The standard cost of the doll is as follows:

	£
Direct material	9
Direct labour	7
Variable factory overhead	4
Variable selling overhead	2

Production capacity is 60,000 pa and market research suggests that with an aggressive sales effort this quantity could be sold.

The company expects a return on capital employed of 20% before tax.

Calculate the list selling price for the Dainty which will cover a dealership discount of 20% on list price and enable the company to achieve its profit objective.

8.9   Solution

	£	£ per unit
Variable costs:		
Direct materials £9 + 2%		9.18
Direct labour £7 + 5%		7.35
Factory overhead £4 + 2%		4.08
Selling overhead		2.00
		22.61
Fixed costs:		
Production	80,100	
Selling and administration	63,300	
	143,400	
Units of production	60,000	
Fixed cost per unit		2.39
Total cost		25.00
Profit required (see workings)		3.00
Sales price to dealer		28.00
20% dealer discount $\frac{20}{80} \times £28.00$		7.00
List price		35.00

WORKINGS

The company requires 20% return on capital employed.

		£
Capital employed:		
	Land and buildings	135,000
	Plant and equipment	125,000
	Fixtures and fittings	40,000
	Current assets 60,000 units × £10	600,000
		900,000
	20% return	180,000
	Return per unit of production	£3.00

8.10   Special contract pricing

A business which produces to customer's order may be working to full capacity. Any additional orders must be considered on the basis of the following questions:

(a)   What price must be quoted to make the contract profitable?

(b)   Can other orders be fulfilled if this contract is accepted?

In such a situation the limiting factor needs to be recognised so that the contract price quoted will at least maintain the existing rate of contribution per unit of limiting factor.

8.11   Example

Oddjobs Ltd manufactures special purpose gauges to customers' specifications. The highly skilled labour force is always working to full capacity and the budget for the next year shows:

	£	£
Sales		40,000
Direct materials	4,000	
Direct wages 3,200 hours @ £5	16,000	
Fixed overhead	10,000	
		30,000
Profit		10,000

An enquiry is received from XY Ltd for a gauge which would use £60 of direct materials and 40 labour hours.

(a)   What is the minimum price to quote to XY Ltd?

(b)   Would the minimum price be different if spare capacity were available but materials were subject to a quota of £4,000 per year?

8.12   Solution

(a)   The limiting factor is 3,200 labour hours and the budgeted contribution per hour is £20,000 ÷ 3,200 hours = £6.25 per hour. Minimum price is therefore:

	£
Materials	60
Wages 40 hours @ £5	200
	260
Add: Contribution 40 hours @ £6.25	250
Contract price	510

At the above price the contract will maintain the budgeted contribution (check by calculating the effect of devoting the whole 3,200 hours to XY Ltd.)

Note, however, that the budget probably represents a mixture of orders, some of which earn more than £6.25 per hour and some less. Acceptance of the XY order must displace other contracts, so the contribution rate of contracts displaced should be checked.

(b)   If the limiting factor is materials, budgeted contribution per £ of materials is £20,000 ÷ 4,000 = £5 per £1.

Minimum price is therefore:

	£
Materials/wages (as above)	260
Contribution £60 × 5	300
Contract price	560

Because materials are scarce, Oddjobs must aim to earn the maximum profit from its limited supply.

9   FURTHER PROCESSING DECISIONS

9.1   Introduction

In processing operations, particularly those involving more than one product, there is often a choice to be made between selling a product in an unfinished state (to another manufacturer) or to further process it into a finished product for sale to the consumer.

9.2   Relevant costs and revenues of further processing decisions

Relevant costs are those which are incurred as a consequence of the decision to further process the item. Thus common costs incurred already, for example pre-separation costs, should always be ignored.

Relevant revenues are the extra revenues earned from selling the product in its further processed state instead of selling it in its semi-processed state.

9.3   Example

PST Ltd produces three products from a common process which costs £104,000 per month to operate. Typical monthly outputs are:

Product	Output (litres)
P	10,000
S	5,000
T	8,000

Each of the products may be further processed. Selling prices and further processing costs per litre are as follows:

	Product		
Cost/Revenues/litre	*P*	*S*	*T*
	£	£	£
Further processing	5.00	3.00	9.00
Selling price:			
Before further processing	11.00	14.00	13.00
After further processing	15.00	19.00	20.00

Advise PST Ltd whether it should further process any of its products.

9.4   Solution

The common cost is irrelevant, only the incremental costs and revenues should be considered:

	Product		
	P	S	T
	£	£	£
Selling price:			
Before further processing	11.00	14.00	13.00
After further processing	15.00	19.00	20.00
Incremental revenue	4.00	5.00	7.00
Further processing cost	(5.00)	(3.00)	(9.00)
Incremental contribution	(1.00)	2.00	(2.00)

The above table, based on values per litre, shows that the further processing of product S is the only further processing activity which leads to an increase in contribution.

Therefore, PST Ltd should further process product S, but should sell products P and T without further processing them.

9.5   Activity

Z Ltd operates a process which produces three products: X, Y, and Z. Each of these may be sold without further processing or refined and sold as higher quality products. The following costs/revenues have been determined:

	Product		
	X	Y	Z
Refining cost/litre (£)	3.00	2.50	3.50
Selling prices/litre (£):			
Refined	6.00	5.50	7.00
Unrefined	2.50	2.75	4.00

On the basis of the above, which products, if any, should Z Ltd refine?

9.6   Activity solution

	Product		
	X	Y	Z
	£	£	£
Incremental revenue/litre (£)	3.50	2.75	3.00
Incremental cost/litre (£)	(3.00)	(2.50)	(3.50)
	0.50	0.25	(0.50)

Products X and Y should be refined.

10   THE CHOICE BETWEEN INTERNAL SERVICE DEPARTMENTS AND EXTERNAL SERVICES

10.1   Introduction

Typically these decision choices are concerned with the administration function of a business, though it is possible to make these choices in other areas, for example in selling a choice may be made between using selling agents or company employees.

10.2   Relevant costs

The decision is very similar to that described earlier as make or buy, the difference being that it is likely that if internal service departments are to be used there will be a significant amount of fixed costs incurred whereas if external services are used the cost may be significantly variable.

10.3   Example

KRS Ltd is considering whether to administer its own purchase ledger or to use an external accounting service. It has obtained the following cost estimates for each option:

Internal service department:

Purchase computer cost	£1,000
Purchase computer software	£600
Hardware/software maintenance	£750 per annum
Accounting stationery	£500 per annum
Part-time accounts clerk	£6,000 per annum

External services:

Processing of invoices/credit notes	£0.50 per document
Processing of cheque payments	£0.50 per cheque
Reconciling supplier accounts	£2.00 per supplier per month

KRS Ltd would have to assess the forecast volumes of transactions involved before making its decision.

10.4   Qualitative factors

Such decisions will also involve qualitative factors, such as:

- the reliability of supply;
- the quality of supply; and
- security of information.

11   CHAPTER SUMMARY

This chapter has considered a number of specific decision making situations, and illustrated which costs and revenues are relevant to their solution.

12   SELF TEST QUESTIONS

12.1   Distinguish between short and long term decision making. (1.2, 1.3)

12.2   List the qualitative factors in product line decisions. (2.2)

12.3   What is a limiting factor? (4.1)

12.4   What information is relevant in the decision to close down a segment of a business? (5.3)

13   EXAMINATION TYPE QUESTION

13.1   A company

The annual flexible budget of a company is as follows:

Production capacity	40%	60%	80%	100%
Costs:	£	£	£	£
Direct labour	16,000	24,000	32,000	40,000
Direct material	12,000	18,000	24,000	30,000
Production overhead	11,400	12,600	13,800	15,000
Administration overhead	5,800	6,200	6,600	7,000
Selling and distribution overhead	6,200	6,800	7,400	8,000
	51,400	67,600	83,800	100,000

Owing to trading difficulties the company is operating at 50% capacity. Selling prices have had to be lowered to what the directors maintain is an uneconomic level and they are considering whether or not their single factory should be closed down until the trade recession has passed.

A market research consultant has advised that in about twelve months' time there is every indication that sales will increase to about 75% of normal capacity and that the revenue to be produced in the second year will amount to £90,000. The present revenue from sales at 50% capacity would amount to only £49,500 for a complete year.

If the directors decide to close down the factory for a year it is estimated that:

(a)   the present fixed costs would be reduced to £11,000 per annum;

(b)   closing down costs (redundancy payments, etc) would amount to £7,500;

(c)   necessary maintenance of plant would cost £1,000 per annum; and

(d)   on re-opening the factory, the cost of overhauling plant, training and engagement of new personnel would amount to £4,000.

Prepare a statement for the directors, presenting the information in such a way as to indicate whether or not it is desirable to close the factory.

14   ANSWER TO EXAMINATION TYPE QUESTION

14.1   A company

To: the board of directors

From: the management accountant

Date: X-X-19XX

Subject: desirability of closing the factory for a year

In the forthcoming year (19X1) our alternatives are:

(1)   Continue operating

	£
Sales	49,500
Total cost	59,500
Loss	10,000

(2)   Close down for 19X1 and re-open in 19X2.

		£
(a)	Unavoidable fixed cost	11,000
(b)	Redundancy payment	7,500
(c)	Necessary maintenance	1,000
(d)	Re-opening cost	4,000
		23,500

This is more than twice the loss incurred if we continue at 50% capacity and I would suggest continuing production.

(3)   The anticipated result for 19X2 would be

	£
Sales	90,000
Total cost	79,750
Profit	10,250

Finally assuming the consultant's forecast is correct and we carry on producing, the cumulative position at the end of year 19X2 would be a small profit of £250 without the trauma of closing down.

WORKINGS

(W1)   Since direct labour and direct material increase from zero by equal increments of cost for each 20% change in volume they must be entirely variable. The increments for activity changes on production, administration and selling overhead do not account for all the cost and these must therefore include a fixed proportion.

Production capacity	40%	60%	Increment for 20%	Fixed
	£	£	£	£
Direct material	16,000	24,000	8,000	-
Direct wages	12,000	18,000	6,000	-
Production overhead	11,400	12,600	1,200	9,000
Administration	5,800	6,200	400	5,000
Selling and distribution	6,200	6,800	600	5,000
Total			16,200	19,000

$$\text{Allowance for 50\%} = \frac{50}{20} \times 16,200 + 19,000 = £59,500$$

or

				£
Direct material	$=$	$\dfrac{50}{20} \times 8{,}000$	$=$	20,000
Direct wage	$=$	$\dfrac{50}{20} \times 6{,}000$	$=$	15,000
Production overhead	$=$	$\left(\dfrac{50}{20} \times 1{,}200\right) + 9{,}000$	$=$	12,000
Administration	$=$	$\left(\dfrac{50}{20} \times 400\right) + 5{,}000$	$=$	6,000
Selling	$=$	$\left(\dfrac{50}{20} \times 600\right) + 5{,}000$	$=$	6,500

	£
Total cost	59,500
Revenue at 50%	49,500
Loss at 50% activity	(10,000)

(W2)   Second year

				£
Total cost	$=$	$\left(\dfrac{75}{20} \times 16{,}200\right) + 19{,}000$	$=$	79,750
Revenue at 75% activity				90,000
Profit at 75% activity				10,250

10 DECISION MAKING AND SHORT RUN DECISIONS: LINEAR PROGRAMMING

INTRODUCTION & LEARNING OBJECTIVES

When you have studied this chapter you should be able to do the following:

- Identify scarce resources within a decision problem.
- Recognise when linear programming is required to solve the problem.
- Formulate a two-variable problem.
- Solve a two variable problem using graphical linear programming.
- Formulate and interpret a problem with more than two variables.

1 SCARCE RESOURCES

1.1 What is a scarce resource?

Definition Economics defines a scarce resource as a good or service which is in short supply. This definition is modified in the context of decision-making to a resource which is in short supply and which, because of this shortage, limits the ability of an organisation to provide greater numbers of products or service facilities.

1.2 Decision-making objectives

These are really organisational objectives which are many and varied; however, in order to evaluate a decision mathematically one single objective is assumed, that of profit maximisation.

Other factors may then be considered before a final decision is taken, but this is part of the management process after the profit maximising solution has been found.

2 SINGLE SCARCE RESOURCE PROBLEMS

2.1 Identifying the scarce resource

In any situation it can be argued that all of the resources required are scarce. What is important is to identify the key resource(s) which limit the ability of the organisation to produce an infinite quantity of goods or services.

2.2 Example

X Ltd makes a single product which requires £5 of materials and 2 hours labour. There are only 80 hours labour available each week and the maximum amount of material available each week is £500.

2.3 Solution

It can be said that the supply of both labour hours and materials are limited and that therefore they are both scarce resources. However, there is more to this problem than meets the eye. The maximum production within these constraints can be shown to be:

Materials:	£500/£5	=	100 units
Labour hours:	80 hours/2 hours	=	40 units

Thus the shortage of labour hours is the significant factor - the scarcity of the materials does not limit production.

In the context of the decision in this example the materials are not a scarce resource.

2.4   Multiple product situations

When more than one product or service is provided from the same pool of resources, profit is maximised by making the best use of the resources available.

2.5   Example

Z Ltd makes two products which both use the same type of materials and grades of labour, but in different quantities as shown by the table below:

	Product A	Product B
Labour hours/unit	3	4
Material/unit	£20	£15

During each week the maximum number of labour hours available is limited to 600; and the value of material available is limited to £6,000.

Each unit of product A made and sold earns Z Ltd £5 and product B earns £6 per unit. The demand for these products is unlimited.

Advise Z Ltd which product they should make.

2.6   Solution

Step 1   Determine the scarce resource.

Step 2   Calculate each product's benefit per unit of the scarce resource consumed by its manufacture.

Each resource restricts production as follows:

Labour hours	600/3	=	200 units of A; or
	600/4	=	150 units of B
Materials	£6,000/£20	=	300 units of A; or
	£6,000/£15	=	400 units of B

It can be seen that whichever product is chosen the production is limited by the shortage of labour hours, thus this is the limiting factor or scarce resource. (Again this is not an easy point to notice and the method used later will overcome the problem of identifying resources that are not limiting.)

Benefit per hour

Product A benefit per labour hour

$$= \quad £5/3 \text{ hours} \quad = \quad £1.66 \text{ per hour}$$

Product B benefit per labour hour

$$= \quad £6/4 \text{ hours} \quad = \quad £1.50 \text{ per hour}$$

Thus Z Ltd maximises its earnings by making and selling product A.

2.7   Conclusion

Where there is only one 'real' scarce resource the method above can be used to solve the problem, however where there are two or more resources in short supply which limit the organisation's activities, (for example if materials had been limited to £3,000 per week in the example above), then **linear programming** is required to find the solution.

2.8 Activity

A Ltd makes two products, X and Y. Both products use the same machine and the same raw material which are limited to 200 hours and £500 per week respectively. Individual product details are as follows:

	Product X	*Product Y*
Machine hours/unit	5	2.5
Materials/unit	£10	£5
Benefit/unit	£20	£15

Identify the limiting factor

2.9 Activity solution

Production is restricted as follows:

Machine hours	200/5	=	40 units of X; or
	200/2.5	=	80 units of Y

Materials	£500/£10	=	50 units of X; or
	£500/£5	=	100 units of Y

Therefore machine hours is the limiting factor since X's and Y's production are most severely limited by machine hours.

2.10 Activity

Using the data of the activity above recommend which product A Ltd should make and sell (assuming that demand is unlimited).

2.11 Activity solution

Benefit per machine hour:

Product X	£20/5 hours	=	£4/hour
Product Y	£15/2.5 hours	=	£6/hour

Product Y should be made.

3 FORMULATION OF A LINEAR PROGRAMMING MODEL

3.1 Introduction

Linear programming is one of the most important post-war developments in **operations research**. It is in fact the most widely used of a group of mathematical programming techniques.

Linear programming can be thought of as a method of balancing many factors (eg, distance, time, production capacity) to obtain a predetermined objective (eg, minimum cost). Some of the factors are variable, while others are fixed.

In order to apply linear programming there must be, as its title suggests, a linear relationship between the factors. For example, the cost of shipping 5 extra units should be 5 times the cost of shipping one extra unit.

3.2   Field of application of linear programming

(a)   Mixing problems

A product is composed of several ingredients, and what is required is the least costly mix of the ingredients that will give a product of predetermined specification.

(b)   Job assignment problems

A number of jobs or products must be handled by various people and/or machines, and the least costly arrangement of assignments is required.

(c)   Capacity allocation problems

Limited capacity is allocated to products so as to yield maximum profits.

(d)   Production scheduling

An uneven sales demand is met by a production schedule over a period of time, with given penalties for storage, overtime, and short-time working.

(e)   Transportation problems

Various suppliers (or one company with several plants) throughout the country make the same products, which must be shipped to many outlets that are also widely distributed. This may involve different transportation costs and varying manufacturing costs. Linear programming can determine the best way to ship; it denotes which plant shall service any particular outlet. It can also evaluate whether it pays to open a new plant.

(f)   Purchasing

Multiple and complex bids can be evaluated, in order to ensure that the orders placed with suppliers comply with the lowest cost arrangement.

(g)   Investment problems

The results of alternative capital investments can be evaluated when finance is in short supply.

(h)   Location problems

Linear programming can help to select an optimum plant or warehouse location where a wide choice is possible.

3.3   Past exam question

Linear programming was examined in June 1995. The discursive question required an explanation of its use in the budgetary planning process.

3.4   Method of linear programming

Linear programming reduces the kind of problems outlined above to a series of linear expressions and then uses those expressions to discover the best solution to achieve a given objective. The student should appreciate that not all situations can be reduced to a linear form. Nevertheless, a surprising number of problems can be solved using this relatively straightforward technique.

3.5   Stages in linear programming – graphical method

Step 1   Define the unknowns ie, the variables (that need to be determined).

Step 2   Formulate the constraints ie, the limitations that must be placed on the variables.

Step 3   Graph the constraints.

Step 4   Define the objective function (that needs to be maximised or minimised).

Step 5   Manipulate the objective function to find the optimal feasible solution.

We will now look at each of these steps in more detail by working through a comprehensive example

3.6   Step 1 - defining the unknowns

Hebrus Ltd manufactures summer-houses and garden sheds. Each product passes through a cutting process and an assembly process. One summer-house, which makes a contribution of £50, takes six hours cutting time and four hours assembly time; while one shed makes a contribution of £40, takes three hours cutting time and eight hours assembly time. There is a maximum of thirty-six cutting hours available each week and forty-eight assembly hours.

The variables that need to be determined in this example are the number of summer-houses and garden sheds to be produced each week.

Let x =   number of summer-houses produced each week;

and y =   number of garden sheds produced each week.

3.7   Further example

Alfred Ltd is preparing its plan for the coming month. It manufactures two products, the flaktrap and the saptrap. Details are as follows.

| | Product | | Price/wage rate |
	Flaktrap	Saptrap	
Amount/unit:			
Selling price (£)	125	165	
Raw material (kg)	6	4	£5/kg
Labour hours:			
Skilled	10	10	£3/hour
Semi-skilled	5	25	£3/hour

The company's variable overhead rate is £1/labour hour (for both skilled and semi-skilled labour). The supply of skilled labour is limited to 2,000 hours/month and the supply of semi-skilled labour is limited to 2,500 hours/month. At the selling prices indicated, maximum demand for flaktraps is expected to be 150 units/month and the maximum demand for saptraps is expected to be 80 units/month. The directors of Alfred believe that demand for each product could be increased by advertising.

You are required to define the decision variables.

3.8   Example solution

The variables are:

(1)   The quantity of Flaktraps to produce per month.

(2)   The quantity of Saptraps to produce per month.

Let x   =   number of Flaktraps produced per month.
Let y   =   number of Saptraps produced per month.

3.9   Step 2 - define the constraints

As we saw earlier in the chapter most resources are limited to a certain degree which usually puts some limitation on what can be achieved. When formulating a linear programming problem those limitations are included as a set of conditions which any solution to the problem must satisfy and they are referred to as **constraints**.

The constraints (limitations) in our Hebrus example are the amounts of cutting and assembly time available.

If   1 summer-house requires 6 hours cutting time,
     x summer-houses require 6*x* hours cutting time.

If   1 shed requires 3 hours cutting time,
     y sheds require 3*y* hours cutting time.

Hence total cutting time required = 6x + 3y hours

Similarly, if 1 summer-house and 1 shed require 4 and 8 hours assembly time respectively, the total assembly time for *x* summer-houses and *y* sheds will be 4*x* + 8*y*.

The conventional way of setting out the constraints is to place the units utilised on the left, and those available on the right; the inequality sign is the link.

Constraint		Utilised		Available
cutting time	(i)	6x + 3y	≤	36
assembly time	(ii)	4x + 8y	≤	48

In addition, two other logical constraints must be stated ie,

$$x \geq 0$$
$$y \geq 0$$

These simply state that negative amounts of garden sheds or summer-houses cannot be made.

3.10   Activity

Using the information in the previous example (Alfred Ltd), formulate the constraints.

3.11   Activity solution

Skilled labour	10x	+ 10y	≤	2,000
Semi-skilled labour	5x	+ 25y	≤	2,500
Flaktrap demand	x		≤	150
Saptrap demand		y	≤	80
Non-negative constraints {	x		≥	0
		y	≥	0

3.12   Step 3 - define the objective function

Definition   The objective function is a quantified statement of what is trying to be achieved, for instance the minimisation of costs or maximisation of profit. The objective function is always expressed in terms of the unknown variables (defined in Step 1). In the Hebrus example, these are x and y. Hence, continuing this example:

The objective is to maximise contribution C, given by:

C = 50x + 40y

The company undoubtedly wishes to maximise profit, however, given the usual assumptions of linear programming (stated later), this is achieved by maximising contribution. Take care that the coefficients of *x* and *y* (ie, 50 and 40 respectively) represent the amount by which contribution (and hence profit) increases per unit of each item produced and sold.

3.13   Graphing a straight line

This section is for those students who have not done any basic mathematics for a while. This is a revision section on graphing a straight line, a technique which is required for evaluating linear programming problems.

Step 1   We must have a linear relationship between two measurements, in other words if we know the value for x we can work out the value for y.

Examples

$$y = 3x + 1$$
$$y = 2x + 42 \text{ etc.}$$

Note:

(1)   To recognise a **linear** relationship the equation must have only 'x' not 'x' to the power of anything eg, x^2.

(2)   A straight line has two characteristics.

(i)   A slope or gradient - which measures the 'steepness' of the line.

(ii)   A point at which it cuts the y axis - called the intercept.

$$y = \text{slope} \times x + \text{intercept}$$

eg, $$y = 2x + 3$$

∴ the gradient is 2 and the point at which the line cuts the y axis is 3.

Step 2   To draw a straight line graph we only need to know two points which can then be joined.

Consider the following two equations.

(i) $y = 2x + 3$

(ii) $y = 2x - 2$

In order to draw the graphs of these equations it is necessary to decide on two values for x and then to calculate the corresponding values for y. Let us use x = 0 and 3. These calculations are best displayed in tabular form.

	x	0	3
(1) y = 2x + 3		3	9
(2) y = 2x − 2		−2	4

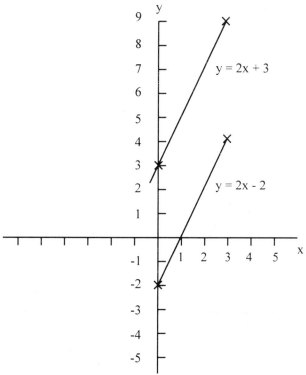

Note: the lines are parallel because the equations have the same gradient of 2.

3.14   Step 4 - graph the constraints

Having revised how to plot a straight line on a graph, we can now move on to graphing the constraints which are simply linear equations of the type we have just looked at.

In order to plot the constraints it is normally best to compute the intercepts of the equalities on the horizontal and vertical axes. Thus, x and y are each set equal to zero in turn and the value of y and x computed in these circumstances.

Returning to the Hebrus example.

For the equation $6x + 3y = 36$ - cutting time constraint

when x = 0, $y = \dfrac{36}{3} = 12$

when y = 0, $x = \dfrac{36}{6} = 6$

For the equation $4x + 8y = 48$ - assembly time constraint

when x = 0, $y = \dfrac{48}{8} = 6$

when y = 0, $x = \dfrac{48}{4} = 12$

The constraints can now be represented graphically:

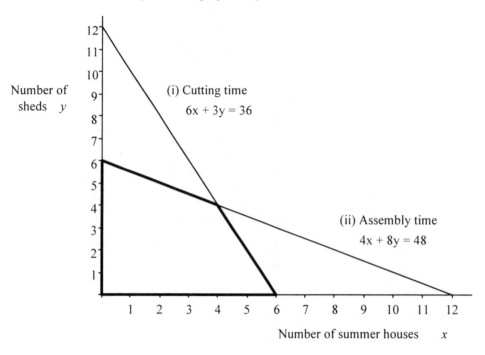

3.15   The feasible region

Having inserted the straight lines in the graph, we are then ready to work out what is called the **feasible region**.

If you recall each line inserted on the graph represents a constraint. In the Hebrus example, there can only be 36 hours of cutting time and no more and only 48 hours of assembly time and no more. Therefore the area on the graph **above** these lines is 'out of bounds' or more technically 'not feasible'. The area below these lines is therefore called the feasible region; it is possible for total cutting time and total assembly time to be any of these values up to and on the constraint line **but not above**.

Hence, the feasible region for Hebrus is as shown below.

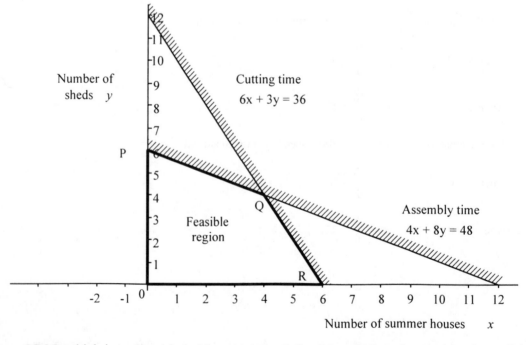

The area OPQR which is outlined in bold represents all feasible solutions ie, combinations of the two products which are achievable given the constraints. It is therefore called the **feasible region**.

To recognise that feasible solutions are, as in this case all **below** the constraint lines, it is normal practice to hatch **above** the line indicating that anything above is outside the feasible region. Some questions can be minimising problems eg, the objective function will be to minimise costs subject to minimum output levels. The constraints will be minimum output levels, therefore the feasible region will be on or above the line and will be hatched under the line ~~\\\\\\\\\\\\\\~~.

3.16   Example

Using the Alfred Ltd example again **you are required** to define the constraints, plot them on a graph and indicate on the graph the feasible region.

Alfred Ltd is preparing its plan for the coming month. It manufactures two products, the flaktrap and the saptrap. Details are as follows.

	Product		Price/wage rate
	Flaktrap	Saptrap	
Amount/unit:			
Selling price (£)	125	165	
Raw material (kg)	6	4	£5/kg
Labour hours:			
Skilled	10	10	£3/hour
Semi-skilled	5	25	£3/hour

The company's variable overhead rate is £1/labour hour (for both skilled and semi-skilled labour). The supply of skilled labour is limited to 2,000 hours/month and the supply of semi-skilled labour is limited to 2,500 hours/month. At the selling prices indicated, maximum demand for flaktraps is expected to be 150 units/month and the maximum demand for saptraps is expected to be 80 units/month. The directors of Alfred believe that demand for each product could be increased by advertising.

3.17   Example solution

Let x be the number of flaktraps to be produced each month and y be the number of saptraps to be produced each month.

Skilled labour	:	$10x + 10y$	$\leq$	2,000
Semi-skilled labour	:	$5x + 25y$	$\leq$	2,500
Flaktrap demand	:	x	$\leq$	150
Saptrap demand	:	y	$\leq$	80
Non-negative constraints $\{$	:	x	$\geq$	0
	:	y	$\geq$	0

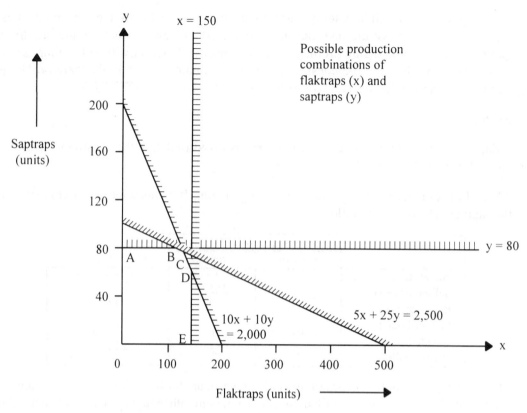

This give a feasibility region of OABCDE.

3.18   Step 5 - manipulate the objective function

Having found the feasible region the problem now is to find the optimal solution within this feasible region.

There are two approaches to this final stage:

(a)   by inspection it is clear that the maximum contribution will lie on one of the corners of the feasible region. In the Hebrus example the corners are P, Q, R (it could lie on the line PQ or the line QR) – the optimal solution can be reached simply by calculating the contributions at each; or

(b)   by drawing an **iso-contribution** line (an objective function for a particular value of C), which is a line where all points represent an equal contribution. This is the recommended approach, particularly for more complex problems.

Using the Hebrus example, consider a contribution of £200. This would give the contribution line $50x + 40y = 200$ and could be achieved by producing four summer-houses, or five sheds, or any combination on a straight line between the two.

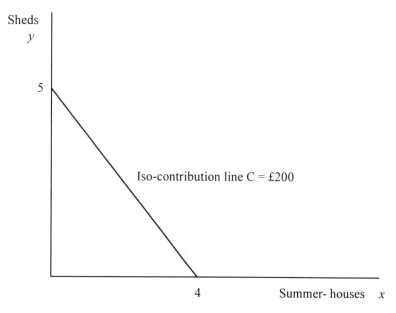

Another iso-contribution line could be drawn at £240 ie, $50x + 40y = 240$:

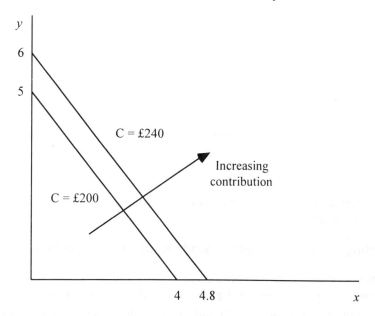

Clearly, iso-contribution lines move to and from the origin in parallel; the arrow indicates increasing contribution. The object is to get on the highest contribution line within (just touching) the binding constraints.

The point is found by drawing an example of an iso-contribution line on the diagram (any convenient value of C will do), and then placing a ruler against it. Then, by moving the ruler away from the origin (in the case of a maximisation problem) or towards the origin (in the case of a minimising problem) but keeping it parallel to the iso-contribution line, the last corner of the feasible solution space which is met represents the optimum solution.

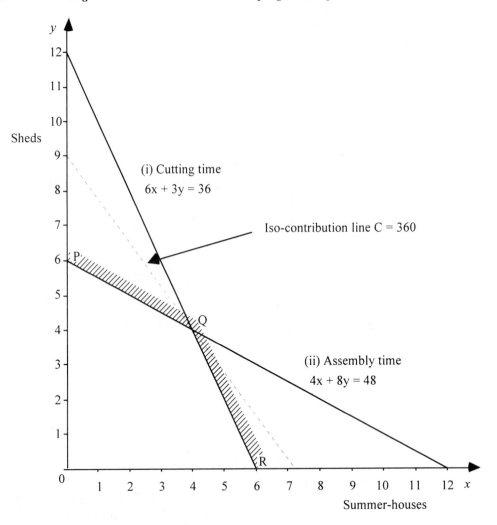

The highest available iso-contribution line occurs at $C = 360$, at point Q, where, reading from the graph, $x = 4$ and $y = 4$.

3.19   Evaluating the optimal solution using simultaneous equations

You may consider that the whole process would be easier by solving the constraints as sets of simultaneous equations and not bothering with a graph. This is possible and you may get the right answer, but such a technique should be used with caution and is not recommended until you have determined graphically which constraints are effective in determining the optimal solution. Furthermore if the question asks for a graphical solution, then a graph **must** be used.

The technique can however, be used as a check. For example using the Hebrus example the optimal solution can be checked by solving the two simultaneous equations for the two constraint boundaries.

Point Q is the intersection of the lines:

Constraint

$6x + 3y = 36$ (i)
$4x + 8y = 48$ (ii)

$3 \times$ (ii) $- 2 \times$ (i) gives

$18y = 72$
$y = 4$

Substituting into (i)

$x = 4$

Thus, the maximum contribution is obtained when four summer-houses and four sheds per week are produced, and the maximum contribution is $4 \times £50 + 4 \times £40 = £360$.

3.20   Limitations to linear programming

There are a number of limitations to this technique.

- Single value estimates are used for the uncertain variables.

- Linear relationships must exist.

- Only suitable when there is one clearly defined objective function.

- When there are a number of variables, it becomes too complex to solve manually and a computer is required.

- It is assumed that the variables are completely divisible.

- It is assumed that the situation remains static in all other respects.

4   INTERPRETING THE SOLUTION

4.1   Shadow (or dual) prices

Definition   Shadow prices (also known as opportunity costs or dual prices) are one of the most important aspects of linear programming. The shadow price of a resource is the increase in contribution obtained when one extra unit of the constraint is made available.

4.2   Example

Refer back to the earlier example concerning Hebrus Ltd.

Suppose one extra hour was available for the cutting process each week.

By how much would contribution (and profit) be increased?

The extra hour would alter the constraints to:

Cutting   (i) $6x + 3y \le 37$; and

Assembly   (ii) $4x + 8y \le 48$;

To solve simultaneously multiply (ii) by 1.5.

(iii) $6x + 12y \le 72$

Solving as before:

Subtracting (i) from (iii) gives

$$9y = 35$$

and thus $y = 3\tfrac{8}{9}$

Inserting this value in (i) gives

$$6x + (3 \times 3\tfrac{8}{9}) = 37$$

$$6x + 11\tfrac{6}{9} = 37$$

$$6x = 25\tfrac{3}{9}$$

$$x \qquad\qquad = \quad 4\tfrac{2}{9}$$

$$\begin{array}{llll}
 & & & \text{£} \\
C & = & (£50 \times 4\tfrac{2}{9}) + (£40 \times 3\tfrac{8}{9}) & = \quad 366\tfrac{2}{3} \\
\text{Original contribution} & & & \qquad 360 \\
\hline
\text{Increase} & & & \qquad 6\tfrac{2}{3} \\
\hline
\end{array}$$

Thus, £6$\tfrac{2}{3}$ is the shadow price of one hour in the cutting process.

Note: there is a great potential for rounding errors when finding dual prices. The problem has been avoided here by working in fractions. If decimals are used retain several decimal places.

Similarly the shadow price of assembly time may be found by keeping the cutting time constraint unchanged, but relaxing the assembly constraint by one unit so that it becomes:

Assembly $4x + 8y \le 49$ (ii)

Whilst (i) remains as:

Cutting $6x + 3y \le 36$ (i)

Solving as before:

$$3 \times \text{(ii)} - 2 \times \text{(i)} \quad \Rightarrow \quad 18y \quad = \quad 75$$

$$y \quad = \quad 4.16667 \qquad \text{(Keep this value in the memory}$$
$$\text{of your calculator.)}$$

Substituting into (i) gives x = 3.91667

$$\begin{array}{lll}
 & & \text{£} \\
\text{Contribution C} = (£50 \times 3.91667) + (£40 \times 4.16667) & = & 362.5 \\
\text{Original contribution} & = & 360.0 \\
\hline
\text{Increase} & & 2.5 \\
\hline
\end{array}$$

Thus, the shadow price of assembly time = £2.5.

(Note: in view of these calculations it is important that no attempt is made to simplify the original constraints by cancelling, otherwise you will not be able to calculate correct values for the shadow prices.)

4.3   Tabular approach

An alternative method of arriving at the shadow price is to set out the two critical constraints (cutting and assembly) as a table:

Column		(1)		(2)		
Cutting	Cu	6x	+	3y	= 36	(i)
Assembly	As	4x	+	8y	= 48	(ii)
Contribution	=	50x	+	40y		

The shadow prices are found by solving the **columns** (1) and (2), replacing *x* and *y* with the constraint symbols Cu and As.

Column	(1)	(2)
replace *x* and *y* with Cu	6 Cu	3 Cu
replace *x* and *y* with As	4 As	8 . As
Contribution	50	40

Turning these into equations:

$$6Cu + 4As = 50 \quad (1)$$
$$3Cu + 8As = 40 \quad (2)$$

Solve simultaneously

Multiply (1) by 2:

$$12Cu + 8As = 100 \quad (3)$$

Subtract (2) from (3):

$$9Cu = 60$$

$$Cu = \frac{60}{9} = £6\tfrac{2}{3} \quad \text{(the same solution as above for shadow price)}$$

Substituting in (2) gives: As = £2.5.

These shadow prices represent the amount of contribution forgone by **not** having one extra hour available in each department.

4.4   Activity

Using the following data, calculate the shadow prices of respectively one hour of machine time and one hour of finishing time.

(i) $20x + 25y \le 500$ (machining time)

(ii) $40x + 25y \le 800$ (finishing time)

$C = 80x + 75y$ (contribution)

Solution: x = 15, y = 8

Use the constraint alteration (incremental) method for machining time and the table method for finishing time.

4.5   Activity solution

Machining time - the constraints become:

(i) $20x + 25y \le 501$

(ii) $40x + 25y \le 800$

Subtracting (i) from (ii) gives

$$20x = 299$$

and thus x   =   14.95

Inserting into (i) gives

$$(20 \times 14.95) + 25y = 501$$
$$25y = 202$$
$$y = 8.08$$

Original contribution:

$$\begin{array}{lr} & \pounds \\ (15 \times \pounds 80) + (8 \times \pounds 75) & = \quad 1{,}800 \end{array}$$

Amended contribution

$$(14.95 \times \pounds 80) + (8.08 \times \pounds 75) \quad = \quad 1{,}802$$

Increased contribution   2

The shadow price per machine hour is £2.

Finishing time:

Machining	M	$20x + 25y$	=	500
Finishing	F	$40x + 25y$	=	800

Contribution $80x + 75y$

becomes:

(i) $20M + 40F \quad = \quad 80$

(ii) $25M + 25F \quad = \quad 75$

Multiply (i) by 1.25 gives

(iii) $25M + 50F \quad = \quad 100$

Subtracting (ii) from (iii) gives

$$25F \quad = \quad 25$$

$$F \quad = \quad 1$$

Thus the dual price of finishing time is £1.

4.6   Usefulness of shadow prices - conclusion

Shadow prices have the following relevance:

(a)   The shadow price is the extra profit that may be earned by relaxing by one unit each of the constraints.

(b)   It therefore represents the maximum **premium** which the firm should be willing to pay for one extra unit of each constraint.

(c)   Since shadow prices indicate the effect of a one unit change in each of the constraints, they provide a measure of the sensitivity of the result (but see later).

The shadow price for any constraint which is not binding at the optimum solution is zero. In the above example suppose production of summer-houses and sheds was also limited by the amount of painting time available – each product took 4 hours to paint and only 40 hours a week were available.

Since the optimum plan involved production of 4 sheds and 4 summer-houses the painting time would only be 32 hours a week – consequently it would make no difference to the optimum solution if painting time availability either increased to 41 hours or decreased to 39. Under these circumstances the dual price of painting time is zero.

However, if the painting time was reduced to only 32 hours this too would become a binding constraint, and a reduction by one further hour, to 31 may affect the optimum solution. It should be noted that shadow prices are valid for only a small range of changes before, eventually, they become non-binding or make different resources critical. The shadow price of a non-binding resource is zero.

5   SENSITIVITY ANALYSIS

5.1   Introduction

Having calculated the shadow prices of each of the constraints these can then be used to ascertain how sensitive the results are. For instance, what would happen to the optimal solution if the following questions were asked?

(1)   What if the contribution from product X were £1 higher than expected?

(2)   What if the sales price of produce Y was reduced by 15%?

(3)   What would happen if we had ten or more quantities of a scarce resource?

This type of 'what if' questioning is known as sensitivity analysis.

5.2   Example

Returning once again to the Hebrus example.

Suppose the contributions from summer-houses and sheds turned out to be slightly different from £50 and £40 respectively, perhaps due to an error in estimating costs.

Would the optimal solution change?

This question is best answered by looking again at the graphical solution:

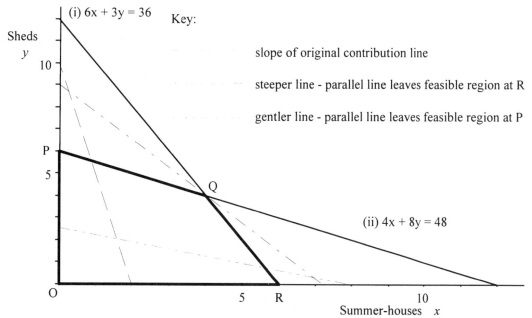

As the contribution line is moved further from the origin, point Q will be the last point of the feasible region which it touches, unless the slope of the contribution line alters considerably. If the slope was steeper than that of the line $6x + 3y = 36$, point R would be the last point to be touched and so would represent the revised optimum solution. Conversely, if the slope was gentler than that of the line $4x + 8y = 48$, point P would be the last point to be touched.

These slopes (or gradients) may be expressed mathematically.

(a)   Cutting constraint line

$6x + 3y = 36$

This may be rewritten, in standard form, $3y = 36 - 6x$ or $y = 12 - 2x$

This is of the form y = a + bx where a represents the intercept of the line with the y axis and b represents the gradient.

Thus, in the case of the cutting constraint line, the gradient is –2.

(b)   **Assembly constraint line**

$4x + 8y = 48$

$8y = 48 - 4x$

$y = 6 - \frac{1}{2}x$

The gradient is therefore $-\frac{1}{2}$

(c)   **Contribution line**

In general terms   C = px + qy, where   p = contribution from a summer-house
                                and   q = contribution from a shed

Re-arranging: $qy = C - px$

$$y = \frac{C}{q} - \frac{px}{q}$$

The gradient is ∴ $\frac{-p}{q}$ (The coefficient of x ÷ the coefficient of y.)

It was stated above that the optimal solution would not alter provided that the gradient of the contribution line lay between the gradients of the constraint lines.

∴   Optimal solution will not alter provided that:

$\frac{-p}{q}$ lies between -2 and $-\frac{1}{2}$

In other words, $\frac{p}{q}$ must lie between 2 and $\frac{1}{2}$

Initially *p* was £50. If this does not alter, *q* may vary so that $50/q$ lies between 2 and $\frac{1}{2}$. Therefore, *q* can vary between 25 and 100.

Similarly, *q* was initially £40 and if this does not alter, *p* may vary so that $p/40$ lies between 2 and $\frac{1}{2}$. Therefore *p* can vary between 80 and 20.

The optimal product mix is, therefore, remarkably insensitive to changes in the original data. Note, however, that the above contribution ranges are valid only if the contributions of the two products are varied independently. For instance, if contribution from a summer-house falls to the extreme value of £20, the optimal solution will change if contribution from a shed simultaneously rises above £40, since p/q will then be less than $\frac{1}{2}$.

Note: also that if the unit contribution alters, so will the shadow prices calculated earlier. This will also be the case if the optimal solution lies at the intersection of different lines of constraint.

5.3   Activity

Given the following machine time constraint calculate the gradient of the line.

$$20x + 25y = 500$$

5.4   Activity solution

Rearranging gives: $\qquad 25y \quad = \quad 500 - 20x$

Dividing by 25 gives: $\qquad y \quad = \quad 20 - 0.8x$

The gradient is therefore -0.8.

5.5   Activity

Given the answer to the previous activity and the following finishing time constraint calculate the range of contribution gradients which will not cause the optimal solution to alter.

$$40x + 25y = 800$$

5.6   Activity solution

Re-arranging gives: $\qquad 25y \quad = \quad 800 - 40x$

Dividing by 25 gives: $\qquad y \quad = \quad 32 - 1.6x$

The gradient is therefore -1.6.

The gradient of the objective function $= \dfrac{p}{q} = \dfrac{-\text{ contribution from X}}{\text{contribution from Y}}$

which must lie between -0.8 and -1.6

Thus $\dfrac{p}{q}$ must lie between 0.8 and 1.6 for the optimal solution not to alter.

6   PROBLEMS INVOLVING MORE THAN TWO VARIABLES

6.1   Introduction

The above examples involved only two variables. When three or more variables are involved, it is usually impossible to solve the problem graphically and the best method of solution is the simplex method. Although simplex is outside the syllabus, the **formulation** of problems involving more than two variables and interpretation of the results is within the syllabus.

6.2   Simplex method - introduction

The simplex method is an algorithm developed in the 1960s for solving linear programming problems.

In the two-variable problem considered in the last section, it was seen that the optimum solution was to be found at a corner of the feasible region. This is still true in the multi-variable problem, even though one cannot draw a region with corners in more than two dimensions. The technique of the simplex method is to move from corner to corner of the feasible region, calculating the value of the objective function at each successive corner, and ensuring that each move is to a corner which gives a higher profit than the one before.

The simplex method, which readily lends itself to computer solution, is invaluable in problems with three or more variables which cannot be solved graphically and which would be inordinately time-consuming to solve by any clerical method other than simplex. For simplicity, however, it will be demonstrated on a two-variable problem, even though in such a case it offers little or no advantage over the methods already discussed and indeed may be thought to be somewhat more complicated. One advantage, however, is that shadow prices emerge automatically as part of the solution.

It is not necessary from an examination point of view to know how to **find** the solution using simplex. However, to aid your understanding of how to interpret a simplex tableau, the method is explained below. The method will be demonstrated on the problem solved in the last section. This is repeated here for ease of reference.

Example

Hebrus Ltd manufactures summer houses and garden sheds. Each product passes through a cutting process and an assembly process. One summer house, which makes a contribution of £50, takes 6 hours cutting time and 4 hours assembly time, while one shed, which makes a contribution of £40, takes 3 hours cutting time and 8 hours assembly time. There is a maximum of 36 cutting hours available each week and 48 assembly hours.

Solution

Let x =   number of summer houses produced per week
and y =   number of sheds produced per week,

the objective is to maximise contribution, £C, where

$$C = 50x + 40y$$

subject to:

$$6x + 3y \leq 36$$
$$4x + 8y \leq 48$$
$$(x \geq 0) \quad \text{non-negative constraint}$$
$$(y \geq 0) \quad \text{non-negative constraint}$$

6.3   Slack variables

Inequalities are difficult to deal with algebraically and for the simplex method must be converted into equations. If an unknown quantity z say, is less than 36, then another quantity can be added to z to make it equal to 36. Similarly, if $z \geq 36$, then another quantity can be subtracted from z to make it equal to 36. The variable which is added or subtracted is called a *slack variable*.

As both inequalities in the Hebrus model are '$\leq$', the slack variables are added. Denoting these by S_1 and S_2, we get:

$$6x + 3y + S_1 = 36$$
$$4x + 8y + S_2 = 48$$

S_1 represents the amount by which the utilised cutting time $(6x + 3y)$ falls short of the available cutting time (36) and therefore is the amount of unused cutting time. Similarly, S_2 is the amount of unused assembly time.

6.4   The initial simplex tableau

The constraint equations and objective function are first set out so that the variables are aligned in columns. This necessitates re-arranging the objective function to bring the x and y terms to the left-hand side, giving:

$$6x + 3y + S_1 = 36$$
$$4x + 8y + S_2 = 48$$
$$C - 50x - 40y = 0$$

The coefficients of each term are then tabulated, putting zeros in the blank spaces.

C is placed in a separate column called the basic variable or basis column. The other entries in this column are the slack variables associated with each constraint, S_1 for the first constraint and S_2 for the second constraint.

Basic variable	x	y	S_1	S_2	Solution
S_1	6	3	1	0	36
S_2	4	8	0	1	48
C	-50	-40	0	0	0

Note that the non-negativity constraints are not included. The simplex method implicitly assumes that all variables are greater than or equal to zero.

6.5   Interpretation of initial tableau

The basic variable column is not essential, but it makes the interpretation of the simplex tableau much easier. It contains those variables whose values are listed in the solution column. Reading across the rows from the basic variable column to the solution column,

$$S_1 = 36$$
$$S_2 = 48$$
$$C = 0$$

This means that if all the variable time is slack ie, no work is being done, then the contribution will be zero. If no work is being done, x and y both $= 0$. This is readily inferred from the tableau; any variables not listed in the basic variable column always have a value of zero.

The initial tableau therefore represents the feasible but trivial solution, that if no items are produced, there will be no contribution.

(Note: the basic variables can be identified from those columns having one cell, and one only, equal to 1, and all the other cells in that column equal to zero. The position of the 1 gives the row to which the basic variable relates. Thus, in the above tableau, the S_1 column has a 1 in the first row and all other values in this column are zero. Hence S_1 is the basic variable for the row in which the 1 occurs ie, row 1.)

6.6   The simplex process

The simplex process is an iterative one, that is, the optimum solution is approached in a series of repetitive stages called *iterations*, each iteration giving a solution nearer to the optimum. For an iterative process, it is necessary to start with a feasible solution, however trivial it may be, and work to improve it.

The process can be summarised as follows:

- The initial tableau (like the one shown in 6.4) would be the starting point for the process

- A set of rules (the "simplex algorithm") would then be applied to this tableau, and a second tableau would be derived. This will represent the effects of moving from the origin (x,y = 0), as depicted by the initial tableau, to the next corner of the feasible region.

- This tableau would then be tested for optimality (all values in the objective function row (basic variable C) need to be positive or zero)

- If the tableau is not optimal, the rules would be applied to the new tableau to arrive at a third, which would be tested for optimality.

- The process would be repeated until the optimum tableau is reached (the final tableau).

As you are not required to be familiar with the technique itself, the simplex process has been omitted, and we shall move straight to the final tableau for the Hebrus Ltd example.

6.7   The final tableau and its interpretation

The final tableau for the Hebrus problem is in fact reached after two iterations of the above process:

Basic variable	x	y	S1	S2	Solution
x	1	0	$\dfrac{2}{9}$	$-\dfrac{1}{12}$	4
y	0	1	$-\dfrac{1}{9}$	$\dfrac{1}{6}$	4
C	0	0	$6\dfrac{2}{3}$	$\dfrac{15}{6}$	360

Reading from the basic variable column to the solution column, maximum value of $C = 360$, achieved when:

$$x = 4$$
$$y = 4$$
$$S_1 = 0$$
$$S_2 = 0$$

The last two variables are zero because they do not appear in the basic variable column. Zero solutions are often as important as non-zero solutions and should be stated.

The final conclusions must always be stated in terms of the original problem ie:

Produce 4 summer-houses and 4 sheds per week. This uses all the cutting and assembly time, and gives the maximum contribution of £360 per week.

6.8   Shadow prices in the final tableau

The values in the objective function row of the final tableau are the shadow prices for cutting and assembly times which were derived earlier (any discrepancy is due to rounding errors). The other values in these columns show how the shadow costs are made up. Taking for example, the S_1 column, S_1 is the slack variable for cutting time. Hence if one extra hour of cutting time could be made available, it would increase the contribution by £ $6\frac{2}{3}$. This would be made up of additional production of x of $\frac{2}{9}$ units and reduced production of y of $\frac{1}{9}$ units. Substituting these values into the contribution equation, the extra contribution would be:

$$£\left(50\left(\frac{2}{9}\right)+40\left(-\frac{1}{9}\right)\right) = \frac{100}{9} - \frac{40}{9} = \frac{60}{9} = £6\frac{2}{3}$$

This assumes that x and y can have fractional values, which is not true in this particular example. This is one of the limitations of the simplex method.

There is a limit to the extra contribution that could be achieved by extra cutting hours being made available, because y cannot be reduced below zero. The present optimum has 4 units of y. If each extra hour of cutting time reduces this by $\frac{1}{9}$, then the number of extra cutting hours to reduce y to zero would be   4 /(1/9) = 36 hours. Any increase in cutting hours above 36 would not increase the contribution, but result in slack or idle time in the cutting department unless available assembly hours were also increased.

6.9   Example

Three products, X, Y and Z are processed in three departments, 1, 2 and 3. The number of hours required in each department per unit of product is given in the table below, together with the maximum number of hours available in each department, and the contribution per unit of product.

The simplex method has been used to produce the final tableau also given below. Set up the linear programming model to maximise the total contribution and fully interpret the final tableau.

Dept.	Hours/unit of product			Maximum hours available
	X	Y	Z	
1	2	5	1	40
2	1	1	1	10
3	3	1	1	20
Unit contribution (£)	9	12	4	

Third tableau

Basic variable	x	y	z	S_1	S_2	S_3	Solution
y	0	1	−0.33	0.33	−0.67	0	6.67
x	1	0	1.33	−0.33	1.67	0	3.33
S_3	0	0	− 2.67	0.67	−4.33	1	3.33
C	0	0	4	1	7	0	110

As all the values in the bottom row are now ≥ 0, this is the final tableau.

6.10   Example solution

The algebraic model is:

Let x =   no. of units of product X produced
  y =   no. of units of product Y produced
  z =   no. of units of product Z produced
  C =   total contribution in £

Objective function, to be maximised:
  $C = 9x + 12y + 4z$

Constraints:

Dept 1:	2x	+	5y	+	z	$\leq$ 40
Dept 2:	x	+	y	+	z	$\leq$ 10
Dept 3:	3x	+	y	+	z	$\leq$ 20

Rearranging and adding slack variables S_1, S_2, S_3:

$$2x + 5y + z + S_1 = 40$$
$$x + y + z + S_2 = 10$$
$$3x + y + z + S_3 = 20$$
$$C - 9x - 12y - 4z = 0$$

Interpretation of final tableau

Variables

The maximum value of $C = 110$, obtained when $y = 6.67$, $x = 3.33$, $S_3 = 3.33$ and all other variables $(z, S_1, S_2) = 0$.

This means that the maximum contribution is £110, obtained when production is 3.33 units of X, 6.67 units of Y and no units of Z. This uses all available time in departments 1 and 2, but leaves 3.33 hours spare time in department 3.

Shadow prices

Department 1:

The shadow price is £1. Each additional hour in this department will increase the contribution by £1. This would be effected by an increase in y of 0.33, a decrease in x of 0.33 and an increase in S_3 of 0.67.

$$\text{The extra amount of time to reduce } x \text{ to zero} \quad = \quad \frac{3.33}{0.33}$$

$$= \quad 10 \text{ hours}$$

Hence time in department 1 should not be increased by more than 10 hours.

Department 2:

The shadow price is £7. Each additional hour in this department will increase the contribution by £7. This would be effected by a decrease in y of 0.67, an increase in x of 1.67 and a decrease in S_3 of 4.33.

$$\text{The extra time to reduce } S_3 \text{ to zero} \quad = \quad \frac{3.33}{4.33}$$

$$= \quad 0.77 \text{ hours}$$

$$\text{The extra time to reduce } y \text{ to zero} \quad = \quad \frac{6.67}{0.67}$$

$$= \quad 10 \text{ hours}$$

Taking the lower of these two values, the time in department 2 should not be increased by more than 0.77 hours.

Product Z

The shadow price is £4. This means that if management ignores the recommendation to make no product Z, each unit of Z produced will decrease the contribution by £4.

It should be noted that whereas increasing resources increases contribution, increasing a non-profitable product will decrease contribution. The effect is opposite to that of increasing resources. Hence the values in column z show that for each unit of Z produced, y will *increase* by 0.33, x will *decrease* by 1.33 and S_3 *increase* by 2.67. As x is at present 3.33, and cannot be reduced below zero, the maximum amount by which z could be increased is 3.33/1.33 = 2.5 units. This would reduce the total contribution by 2.5 × 4 = £10.

7   COMPUTER GENERATED SIMPLEX OUTPUT

7.1   Introduction

A computer package is likely to be used for solving simplex linear programming problems. Examination questions on this topic are likely to give data in the form of a computer print-out and it is important that you can interpret the final tableau when given in this format.

7.2   The Hebrus example - computer print-out of final tableau

The output from a computer package designed to solve linear programming problems for the Hebrus problem may look something like this:

HEBRUS LTD

Optimal solution - detailed report

	Variable	Value
1	Sum Hse	4.000
2	Shed	4.000
3	Slack 1	0.000
4	Slack 2	0.000

	Constraint	Type	RHS	Slack	Shadow price
1	Cutting	<=	36	0.000	6.667
2	Assembly	<=	48	0.000	2.500

Objective function value = 360.000

Sensitivity analysis of objective function coefficients

	Variable	Current coefficient	Allowable minimum	Allowable maximum
1	Sum Hse	50.000	20.000	80.000
2	Shed	40.000	25.000	100.000

Sensitivity analysis of right hand side (RHS) variables

	Constraint	Type	Current value	Allowable minimum	Allowable maximum
1	Cutting	<=	36	18	72
2	Assembly	<=	48	24	96

7.3   Interpretation of computer print-out

Optimal solution section

This gives the values of the variables at the optimum solution and shadow prices of the constraints. Any constraint with a zero shadow price will correspond to a slack variable with non-zero value (not applicable here).

Sensitivity of objective function coefficients section

This corresponds to the calculations in section 5.2. It shows that the coefficient of the summer house variable in the objective function (ie the unit contribution) is currently £50, and can vary between a minimum of £20 and a maximum of £80 before the optimal solution changes. A similar interpretation applies to the data in the shed row.

Note that an alternative presentation of this information identifies the allowable *decrease* and *increase* in the value of the coefficient - in this example, these would be 30.000 for both for the summer house, and 15.000 and 60.000 respectively for the shed.

Sensitivity of RHS values section

This refers to the relevant ranges of the shadow prices, as briefly discussed in section 6.8. It was demonstrated there that any increase in cutting hours available above 36 hours would change the value of the shadow price of cutting hours (in this case it would actually become zero). As the current hours available are 36, this takes the maximum hours available, over which the current shadow price applies, to 72.

Similar reasoning, using information from the final tableau in its original form (in section 6.7), can be used to show that the number of cutting hours may be *decreased* by up to 18 hours before changing the shadow price (one less hour would result in 1/9 *extra* unit of y and 2/9 unit *less* of x. As x is currently 4 units, the maximum decrease will be 4/(2/9) = 18 hours). Thus the allowable minimum is 36 - 18 = 18.

Again, this data may be presented in the form of the allowable *decrease/increase*.

8   CHAPTER SUMMARY

This chapter has considered decision problems where activity is limited by the existence of one or more scarce resources.

The distinction between one or more scarce resource problems has been illustrated and solved, two and more than two variable problems have also been shown and the former solved using graphical linear programming techniques.

9   SELF TEST QUESTIONS

9.1   What is a scarce resource? (1.1)

9.2   What is linear programming? (3.1)

9.3   List some common applications of linear programming. (3.2)

9.4   What is the feasible region? (3.15)

9.5   What is an iso-contribution line? (3.18)

9.6   What are the limitations of linear programming? (3.20)

9.7   What is a shadow price? (4.1)

9.8   What is the importance of sensitivity analysis in the context of linear programming? (5.1)

9.9   What method can be used for solving problems with more than two variables? (6.2)

9.10   What is a slack variable in the context of linear programming? (6.3)

10   EXAMINATION TYPE QUESTION

10.1   Flintstones

The Flintstones are involved in the manufacture of two products, Chip and Dale. Due to an industrial dispute, which is expected to go on for some time, material B, which is required in the production of Dale, is expected to be limited to 300 units per week. Material A, required for both products, is freely available.

Flintstones are experiencing labour shortages and it is expected that only 800 hours of unskilled labour and 1,000 hours of skilled labour will be available in any week, in the short run.

Due to a transport problem, the Flintstones will be able to import only 400 Dinos into the country each week. This item is required in the manufacture of both Chip and Dale.

It is the company's policy to limit the production of Dale to not more than three times the production of Chip.

The following information is available:

	Chip £	*Dale* £
Material B (2 units for Dale only)	–	10
Material A	15	10
Labour – unskilled £3 per hour	12	15
– skilled £5 per hour	50	20
Dinos (£10 each)	20	20
Total cost	97	75

Selling price   127   100
                                                                               ___   ___

Fixed costs each week amount to £3,000.

You are required to calculate the optimal plan for Flintstones together with the weekly profit which may be earned.

11   ANSWER TO EXAMINATION TYPE QUESTION

11.1   Flintstones

From the tabulated information given, per week:

No. of hours unskilled labour per Chip $= \dfrac{12}{3} =$ 4 hours

No. of hours unskilled labour per Dale $= \dfrac{15}{3} =$ 5 hours

No. of hours skilled labour per Chip $= \dfrac{50}{5} =$ 10 hours

No. of hours skilled labour per Dale $= \dfrac{20}{5} =$ 4 hours

No. of Dinos per Chip $= \dfrac{20}{10} =$ 2

No. of Dinos per Dale $= \dfrac{20}{10} =$ 2

Contribution per Chip $=$ £(127 – 97) $=$ £30
Contribution per Dale $=$ £(100 – 75) $=$ £25

As each Dale requires 2 units of B, and only 300 units of B are available, this limits the number of Dales to 150.

There is no constraint on the amount of material A.

Fixed costs will be the same, whatever mix of Chip and Dale is produced, hence they can be ignored for the purpose of obtaining the optimum product mix, but must be included in the calculation of profit.

Let C =   number of Chips produced per week.
Let D =   number of Dales produced per week.
Let Z =   total contribution per week.

The objective function then is to maximise contribution to fixed overheads ie,

Maximise: Z = $30C + 25D$

						Constraint Number	
Subject to:	4C	+	5D	≤	800	(1)	Unskilled labour
	10C	+	4D	≤	1,000	(2)	Skilled labour
	2C	+	2D	≤	400	(3)	Dinos
			D	≤	3C	(4)	Production policy
			2D	≤	300	(5)	Material B
			C, D	≥	0		

Note: that there is a constraint which appears confusing at first, that of company policy with regard to the production of Chips and Dales. However, it can be dealt with simply by taking the expression of the policy, as expressed in words, and turning it into symbols, thus:

The production of Dales is to be not more than (ie, less than or equal to) three times the production of Chips.

$$D \leq 3C$$

or $$-3C + D \leq 0$$

For graph see below. The feasibility region is CBAO (outlined in bold).

The solution is at the intersection of constraints (1) and (2), the two labour constraints. The solution can be found by solving (1) and (2) simultaneously.

$$4C + 5D = 800 \quad (1)$$
$$10C + 4D = 1,000 \quad (2)$$

$5 \times (2) - 4 \times (1)$ gives $$34C = 1,800$$

$$C = 52.94 \approx 53$$

$$D = 117.65 \approx 118$$

Contribution $= 30C + 25D = £30 \times 53 + £25 \times 118 = £4,540$

Thus, profit $= £4,540 - £3,000 = £1,540$ per week

Note: the non-integer solutions have been rounded up. Strictly speaking this puts the optimal solution outside the feasible region (52 and 117 might be more appropriate). The values of C and D have been rounded since, in any one week it is difficult to sell 117.65 Dales. However the Flintstones might consider making on average 117.65 Dales per week.

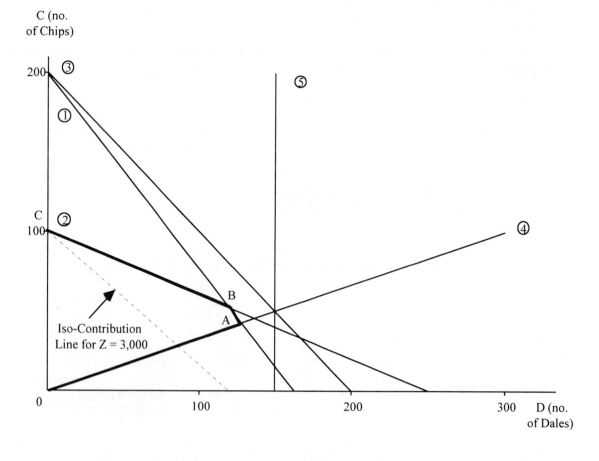

11 THE TIME VALUE OF MONEY

INTRODUCTION & LEARNING OBJECTIVES

When you have studied this chapter you should be able to do the following:

- Calculate an Accounting Rate of Return (ARR) and a payback period.
- Understand the principle behind Discounted Cash Flow methods.
- Calculate a Net Present Value (NPV) and Internal Rate of Return (IRR).
- Discuss the relative merits of ARR, payback period and DCF methods.
- Use the NPV and IRR methods to assess investment projects and compare the use of these methods.

1 INTRODUCTION TO INVESTMENT APPRAISAL

1.1 The capital budgeting cycle

A common feature of industrial activity is the need to commit funds by purchasing land, buildings, machinery, etc, in anticipation of being able to earn, in the future, an income greater than the funds committed. This indicates the need for an assessment of the size of the outflows and inflows of funds, the life of the investment, the degree of risk attached (greater risk being justified perhaps by greater returns) and the cost of obtaining funds.

Basic stages in the capital budgeting cycle may be identified as:

Step 1 Needs for expenditure are forecast.

Step 2 Projects to meet those needs are distinguished.

Step 3 Alternatives are appraised.

Step 4 Best alternatives are selected and approved.

Step 5 Expenditure is made and monitored.

Step 6 Deviations from estimates are examined.

Step 3 occupies a major place in the theory and practice of management decision making, and it will be examined later in considerable depth. The rest of this section will concentrate on summarising the main stages in capital budgeting.

1.2 Types of capital project

Reasons for capital expenditure vary widely. Projects may be classified into the following categories:

(a) **Maintenance** – replacement of worn-out or obsolete assets, safety and security, etc.
(b) **Profitability** – cost savings, quality improvement, productivity, relocation, etc.
(c) **Expansion** – new products, new outlets, research and development, etc.
(d) **Indirect** – office buildings, welfare facilities, etc.

A particular investment project, of course, could combine any number or all of the above classifications.

1.3   Working capital

In most industrial projects, investment is required, both in fixed assets and in working capital, although the risk attached to working capital is less than that for fixed assets. Values of land and buildings may appreciate and so present less risk, but money invested in machinery is a sunk cost, which is unlikely to be recovered, save for perhaps minimal scrap values.

In project appraisal, accurate estimates of working capital requirements are desirable, not only for assessment of project profitability, but also to facilitate forecasting of capital requirements.

1.4   Capital expenditure forecast

In preparing budgets, it is necessary to consider how much money can or must be allocated to capital expenditure. Capital development schemes may be started because a surplus of cash resources is revealed by the long-term plan, but usually management decide on a capital development scheme and then seek the means to finance it.

Initially, the budget will be an expression of management's intention to allocate funds for certain broad purposes. In the budget period, money will be required:

(a)   for previously authorised existing projects; and

(b)   for new projects, full details of which may not yet be available.

The forecasts will indicate whether sufficient funds are available, and perhaps when additional funds will need to be obtained. It is advisable, therefore, for managers to submit long-term capital expenditure forecasts, say for two to five years ahead; consequently, the possibility of obsolescence (and the direction of the future development of the firm) must be borne in mind.

The capital budget is the outcome of a dual process:

(a)   higher management allocating funds to various areas in relation to the corporate plan ie, according to the long-term objectives of the company; and

(b)   individual managers seeking to utilise the funds for specific projects.

The importance of this aspect of planning cannot be over-emphasised, because present capital investment will determine the structure and profitability of the company in the near future. Errors made in forecasting and planning will, therefore, have serious results, and may prove difficult to rectify.

1.5   Methods of appraising capital investment projects

The most important step in the capital budgeting cycle is determining whether the benefits from investing large capital sums outweigh the large initial costs of those investments. There are a range of methods that are used in reaching these investment decisions; broadly speaking they fall into two categories; traditional (non-discounting) methods and discounted cash flow (DCF) methods. DCF methods should be familiar from previous studies.

2   NET PRESENT VALUE

2.1   Introduction

There are two basic discounted cash flow (DCF) methods:

* net present values (NPV)
* internal rate of return (IRR).

The first is theoretically more sound (as will be shown later), but the second is more popular (almost three times as common in a recent survey). Both have the advantage over the traditional methods in that they recognise the 'time value of money'.

2.2   The time value of money

A simple method of comparing two investment projects would be to compare the amount of cash generated from each – presumably, the project which generates the greater net cash inflow (taking into account all revenues and expenses) is to be preferred. However, such a simple method would fail to take into account the **time value of money**, the effect of which may be stated as the general rule below:

> 'There is a time preference for receiving the same sum of money sooner rather than later. Conversely, there is a time preference for paying the same sum of money later rather than sooner.'

2.3   Reasons for time preference

The reasons for time preference are threefold:

(a)   **Consumption preference** – money received now can be spent on consumption.

(b)   **Risk preference** – risk disappears once money is received.

(c)   **Investment preference** – money received can be invested in the business, or invested externally.

If consideration is given to these factors it can be seen that inflation affects time preference but is not its only determinant. Higher inflation for instance, will produce greater consumption preference and thus greater time preference, all else being equal. It is best to ignore inflation initially when considering DCF techniques.

The discounting analysis is based on (c), and in particular the ability to invest or borrow and receive or pay interest. The reason for this approach is that even where funds are not actually used and borrowed in this way, interest rates do provide the market measure of time preference.

The analysis, therefore, proceeds in terms of the way interest payments and receipts behave.

2.4   Compound interest

In previous studies it would have been noted that the discounting process that is fundamental to DCF calculations is analogous to compound interest in reverse. A short compound interest calculation is included here as revision.

Simple interest arises when interest accruing on an investment is paid to the investor as it becomes due, and is **not** added to the capital balance on which subsequent interest will be calculated.

Compound interest arises when the accrued interest is added to the capital outstanding and it is this revised balance on which interest is subsequently earned.

Example

Barlow places £2,000 on deposit in a bank earning 5% compound interest per annum.

You are required

(a)   to find the amount that would have accumulated:

   (i)   after one year;
   (ii)   after two years; and
   (iii)   after three years.

(b)   to find the amount that would have to be deposited if an amount of £2,500 has to be accumulated:

(i)   after one year;

(ii)   after two years; and

(iii)   after three years.

Solution

(a)   **Terminal values**

Although compound interest calculations can be produced using common sense, some may prefer to use a formula:

$$S \quad = \quad P(1 + r)^n$$

where S =   Final amount accumulated (terminal value)
P =   Principal (initial amount deposited)
r =   interest rate per annum (as a decimal)
n =   number of years principal is left on deposit

(i)   After 1 year, S =   £2,000 × (1.05)   =   £2,100

(ii)   After 2 years, S =   £2,000 × 1.05 × 1.05

=   £2,000 × 1.05^2 =   £2,205

(iii)   After 3 years, S =   £2,000 × 1.05^3 =   £2,315.25

(b)   **Present values**

In this case the final amount, S, is known and the principal, P, is to be found. Again the formula could be used, rearranging it to become:

$$\text{Principal, } P \quad = \quad \frac{S}{(1 + r)^n}$$

(i)   If £2,500 is required in 1 year's time, a principal, P, has to be invested such that:

$$P \times 1.05 \quad = \quad £2,500$$

$$P \quad = \quad £2,500 \times \frac{1}{1.05} \quad = \quad £2,380.95$$

(If £2,381 is invested for a year at 5% interest, 5% of £2,380.95 or £119.05 is earned making the total amount £2,500 as required.)

(ii)   If £2,500 is required in 2 years time:

$$P \times 1.05^2 \quad = \quad £2,500$$

$$P \quad = \quad £2,500 \times \frac{1}{1.05^2} \quad = \quad £2,267.57$$

(It can be checked that £2,267.57 will accumulate to £2,500 after 2 years.)

(iii)   If £2,500 is required in 3 years time:

$$P \quad = \quad £2,500 \times \frac{1}{1.05^3} \quad = \quad £2,159.59$$

This second group of calculations is the mechanics behind discounted cash flow calculations, the calculation of a present value. For example in (b) (i) one would be equally happy with receiving £2,500 in one year's time or £2,380.95 now. Although the immediate receipt is less than £2,500, if invested for a year at 5% it would amount to £2,500 hence the indifference between the two sums. £2,380.95 is called the **present value** (at 5%) of a sum of £2,500 payable or receivable in one year's time.

2.5 Discounting

Having said that people have a time preference for money and would prefer to receive money sooner rather than later, it is inappropriate to give the same value to similar sums receivable at different times over the life of a project. This is what traditional methods of investment appraisal do as illustrated in the context of the payback period. Because of investors' rates of time preference for money, a more suitable method of investment appraisal reduces the value of later cash flows (discounts them) to find that sum with which one would be equally happy now as a given receipt due in several years' time. This calculation (of a present value) is what was illustrated with the compound interest calculations.

2.6 Formula

The present value (PV) of a single sum, S receivable in n years' time, given an interest rate (a discount rate) r is given by:

$$PV = S \times \frac{1}{(1 + r)^n}$$

Illustrations

Find the present values of:

(a)   £1,000 receivable in 1 year's time given a discount rate of 10%;
(b)   £4,000 receivable in 2 years time given a discount rate of 5%; and
(c)   £10,000 receivable in 5 years time given a discount rate of 8%.

In each case the process of reducing the cash flows to find that sum with which one would be equally happy now follows a procedure similar to compound interest backwards.

(a)   PV   = $£1,000 \times \dfrac{1}{1.10}$ =   £909.09

(One would be equally happy with £909.09 now as £1,000 in one year's time. With £909.09 available now to invest for one year at 10%, £90.91 interest is earned and the whole sum accumulates to £1,000 in one year's time.)

(b)   PV   = $£4,000 \times \dfrac{1}{(1.05)^2}$ =   £3,628.12

(Check for yourself that £3,628.12 will accumulate to £4,000 in two years if interest is earned at 5% pa.)

(c)   PV   = $£10,000 \times \dfrac{1}{(1.08)^5}$ =   £6,806

(It is conventional to state present values to the nearest £ and, with the present value table available to help you, inappropriate to assume too great a level of accuracy.)

2.7   Annuities

It may be the case that certain types of cash flow (since cash flows rather than accounting profits are discounted) are expected to occur in equal amounts at regular periods over the life of a project. Calculating the present value of annuities can be made more simple by use of a second formula.

Illustration

Find the present value of £500 payable for each of three years given a discount rate of 10% if each sum is due to be paid annually in arrears.

The PV can be found from three separate calculations of the present value of a single sum.

$$PV = \left[£500 \times \frac{1}{(1.10)} \right] + \left[£500 \times \frac{1}{(1.10)^2} \right] + \left[£500 \times \frac{1}{(1.10)^3} \right]$$

Although this can be evaluated

$$= \qquad £455 \qquad + \qquad £413 \qquad + \qquad £376 \qquad = \qquad £1,244$$

it might be worth looking again at the expression for the present value and restating it as:

$$PV = £500 \times \left[\frac{1}{(1.10)} + \frac{1}{(1.10)^2} + \frac{1}{(1.10)^3} \right]$$

This can be evaluated

$$= \qquad £500 \times 2.48685 \qquad = \quad £1,243$$

(The difference is attributable to rounding.)

The last expression for the present value might be recognised as a geometric progression and a formula can be produced (which could be proved although there is no need to do so) for the present value of an annuity:

$$PV = A \times \frac{1}{r} \left(1 - \frac{1}{(1 + r)^n} \right)$$

where now A is the annual cash flow receivable in **arrears**.

In this case

$$PV \quad = \qquad £500 \times \frac{1}{0.10} \left(1 - \frac{1}{(1.10)^3} \right)$$

$$= \qquad £500 \times \frac{1}{0.10} (1 - 0.7513148)$$

$$= \qquad £500 \times 2.48685 \quad = \quad £1,243$$

(Tables exist for the value of this formula given different figures for r and n; for the next activity note that tables will not be used.)

2.8   Activity

Lindsay Ltd wishes to make a capital investment of £1.5m but is unsure whether to invest in one of two machines each costing that amount. The net cash inflows from the two projects are shown below.

Time	1	2	3
Denis plc Machine (£'000)	900	600	500
Thomson plc Machine (£'000)	700	700	700

> **You are required** to find the present value of the two patterns of cash flows at the company's required rate of return of 10% and thus decide which of the two identically priced machines (if any) should be acquired. (Assume all cash flows occur annually in arrears on the anniversary of the initial investment.)

2.9   Activity solution

Cash inflows from Denis machine:

$$PV = \frac{£900,000}{1.10} + \frac{£600,000}{1.10^2} + \frac{£500,000}{1.10^3}$$

$$= £818,182 + £495,868 + £375,657 = £1,689,707$$

Cash inflows from Thomson machine:

$$PV = \frac{£700,000}{1.10} + \frac{£700,000}{1.10^2} + \frac{£700,000}{1.10^3}$$

$$= £700,000 \times \frac{1}{0.10} \times \left(1 - \frac{1}{(1.10)^3}\right)$$

$$= £700,000 \times 2.48685 = £1,740,796$$

Despite the earlier receipts from the Denis machine, the extra £100,000 in total receipts gives the Thomson machine the advantage.

Since the present value of the inflows exceeds the (present value of) the initial cost, the Thomson machine project is worthwhile. (It has a net present value of £1,740,796 – £1,500,000 = £240,796.)

The required rate of return (10%) might well be referred to as a **cost of capital** in the case of a company making an investment decision. The cost of capital is considered further in a later paper.

Simple projects such as these two can be analysed by calculations taking a single line; but slightly more complex projects merit a tabular layout as follows.

Denis machine

Time		Cash flow £'000	10% Discount Factor	Present Value £'000
0	Capital cost	(1,500)	1	(1,500)
1	Inflow	900	$\frac{1}{1.10}$	818
2	Inflow	600	$\frac{1}{1.10^2}$	496
3	Inflow	500	$\frac{1}{1.10^3}$	376
	Net present value (£'000)			190

Thomson machine

Time		Cash flow £'000	10% Discount Factor	Present Value £'000
0	Capital cost	(1,500)	1	(1,500)
1 - 3	Inflow	700	2.48685	1,741
	Net present value (£'000)			241

The Thomson machine project has the higher NPV and would be preferred.

Note:

- A narrative column has been included which here is not of great use, but in larger projects makes workings much clearer.

- PV's have been rounded to the nearest £'000; it is not worth stating them to the nearest penny and, when using tables, round to the nearest three significant figures (perhaps to the nearest £'000 or £m if that is not too different from 3 significant figures) although only the first 2 significant figures are really accurate.

- Again brackets are used for outflows.

- The first column has been headed 'Time' rather than year, since the calendar year in which expenditure falls is not as important (yet) as whether it falls one or two years, say after the initial outlay - which is usually taken to occur at time 0. The stated assumption of cash flows at annual intervals is common in DCF calculations.

- For larger calculations with many cash flow estimates changing from year to year another layout will be recommended.

2.10 Present value factor tables

To make investment appraisal calculations simpler, tables are produced (and are available for use in exams) of discount factors. A copy of the tables issued in the exam appears at the front of this Examination Text. These provide values of:

$$\text{Individual discount factors} = \frac{1}{(1+r)^n} \text{ (or } (1+r)^{-n})$$

$$\text{Cumulative discount factors for annuities, } A_{\overline{n}|}r = \frac{1}{r}\left(1 - \frac{1}{(1+r)^n}\right)$$

The two NPV calculations for Lindsay, using the present value tables might look as follows.

Denis machine

$$\text{NPV (£'000)} = -1,500 + [900 \times 0.909] + [600 \times 0.826] + [500 \times 0.751]$$

$$= 189.2$$

Thomson machine

$$\text{NPV (£'000)} = -1,500 + [700 \times 2.487]$$

$$= 240.9$$

2.11 Perpetuities

Sometimes it is necessary to calculate the present values of annuities which are expected to continue for an indefinitely long period of time, 'perpetuities'. The cumulative present value factor tables only go up to 15 years and so a formula is required. The present value of £A receivable for n years given a discount rate r is:

$$A \times \frac{1}{r}\left(1 - \frac{1}{(1+r)^n}\right)$$

What happens to this formula as n becomes large? As n tends to infinity, $(1+r)^n$ also tends to infinity and $\frac{1}{(1+r)^n}$ tends to zero. The cumulative discount factor tends to $\frac{1}{r}(1-0)$ or $\frac{1}{r}$.

Conclusion   The present value of an annuity, A receivable in arrears in perpetuity given a discount rate r is given by

$$PV \text{ perpetuity} = \frac{A}{r} \left(= \frac{\text{Annual cash flow}}{\text{discount rate (as a decimal)}} \right)$$

Example

The present value of £5,000 receivable annually in arrears at a discount rate of 8% is:

$$= \frac{£5,000}{0.08} = £62,500$$

2.12   Past exam question

The DCF method of investment appraisal was examined in December 1995, as part of a business decision question. The main aspect of this question was the identification of the relevant cash flows to use in the DCF calculation, as covered in Chapter 8.

In the same paper, there was also a discursive question involving the application of various investment appraisal methods in divisional performance measurement.

3   INTERNAL RATE OF RETURN (IRR)

3.1   Definition

For so-called conventional projects, that is those where a single cash outflow is followed by subsequent cash inflows, it is often useful to compute the internal rate of return (IRR) of the project.

Definition   The internal rate of return is that discount rate which gives a net present value of zero.

It is sometimes known as the yield, or DCF yield, or internal yield, but these terms are confusing and their use is not recommended.

In general, it is necessary to compute the IRR by trial and error, that is to compute NPVs at various discount rates until the discount rate is found which gives an NPV of zero.

The IRR can be thought of as the maximum rate of interest that can be paid on the finance for a project without making a loss.

Example

Find the IRR of the Denis machine that Lindsay decided not to acquire.

Solution

The net present value at 10% was £190,000.

The aim is to find the discount rate that gives an NPV of zero. Since the project has a positive NPV at 10%, the later cash flows haven't been reduced, discounted enough, and a higher discount rate must be chosen; try 15%.

$$\text{NPV at 15\% (£'000)} = -1,500 + \frac{900}{1.15} + \frac{600}{(1.15)^2} + \frac{500}{(1.15)^3} = 65$$

This is clearly closer to the IRR than 10%, but not that close. However, rather than continue to try ever increasing discount rates an approximate short cut can be taken. If the two discount rates and NPV's are plotted on a graph, the following is seen.

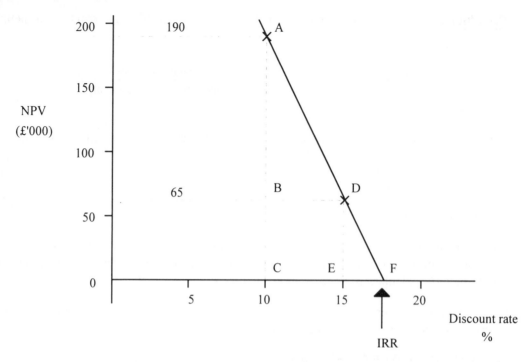

From the graph the IRR appears to be about 17½%. An estimate of the IRR could be found logically:

- NPV has fallen from 190 to 65 (by 125) as the discount rate has increased by 5% (from 10% to 15%) - this is a fall of 25 per %age point increase.

- To find the IRR the NPV needs to fall another 65.

- To achieve this, the discount rate must be increased by $65 \times \dfrac{5\%}{125} = 2.6\%$ to 17.6%.

A formula could be produced (based on similar triangles)

$$\frac{AC}{CF} = \frac{AB}{BD} \quad \text{or} \quad \frac{190}{IRR - 10\%} = \frac{190 - 65}{5\%}$$

Rearranging this one gets:

$$190 \times 5\% \quad = \quad (IRR - 10\%)(190 - 65)$$

$$\text{or} \quad IRR \quad \approx \quad 10\% + \left(\frac{190}{190 - 65}\right) \times 5\% \quad = \quad 17.6\%$$

3.2   Formula

Although, for projects such as this with uneven cash flows, one of the above approaches is perfectly satisfactory (even estimating the IRR from a graph would do), it may be quicker for exam purposes to remember the form of the expression used to find the IRR.

$$IRR \approx A + \frac{N_A}{N_A - N_B}(B - A)$$

where A = lower discount rate   (10%)
       B = higher discount rate   (15%)
       N_A = NPV at rate A   (190)
       N_B = NPV at rate B   (65)

Note:

- The formula applies whether the discount rates chosen both give positive NPV's, both give negative NPV's, or give one of each.

- If negative NPV's appear, be careful with signs.

- The formula is only approximate since it assumes that the relationship between NPV and discount rate is linear; as the graph below shows, it is not; it is not worth quoting an IRR found in this way to more than one decimal place (and even that might be too much).

- The closer the two rates (A and B) are to the true IRR the more accurate will be the result. (It is sometimes suggested that the IRR can only be found if one NPV is positive and one negative; this is not so and may lead to inaccuracy or wasting time as attempts are made to produce these types of result.)

Graph of NPV v discount rate
(showing non-linearity)

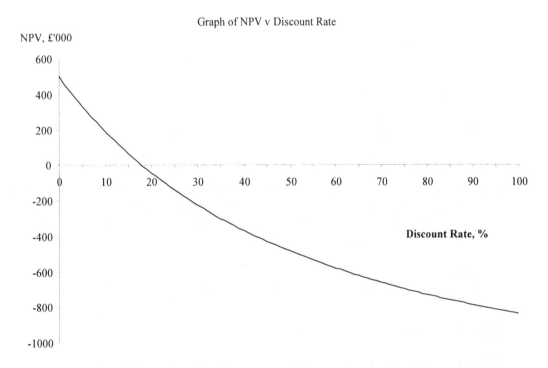

Graph of NPV v Discount Rate

3.3   Activity

The Thomson machine required an outlay of £1.5m to produce three inflows of £0.7m. At 10% the NPV of this project was £241,000. Find the IRR using the method above and taking 20% as the next discount rate.

3.4   Activity solution

NPV at 20% (£'000)   = $-1,500 + \dfrac{700}{1.20} + \dfrac{700}{(1.20)^2} + \dfrac{700}{(1.20)^3} = -25.$

In using 20% a discount rate has been found that is slightly higher than the IRR. The IRR can be estimated using:

IRR $\approx$ $A + \left(\dfrac{N_A}{N_A - N_B}\right)(B - A)$

$$\approx \quad 10 + \left(\frac{241}{241 - (-25)}\right)(20 - 10)$$

$$\approx \quad 10 + \left(\frac{241}{241 + 25}\right)10 \qquad = \qquad \mathbf{19\%}$$

(Note a cumulative discount factor, 2.10648 or 2.11 to two decimal places, could have been used to find the NPV at 20% and would have given the same IRR.)

3.5   Even annual cash flows

A simpler approach can be used to find the IRR of simple projects in which the annual cash inflows are equal (as with the previous example). The IRR can be found via a cumulative discount factor as the following exercise with the Thomson machine project shows.

NPV calculation

Time		Cash flow £'000	(c)% Discount Factor	Present Value £'000
0	Investment	(1,500)	1	(1,500)
1 - 3	Inflow	700	(b)	(a)
	Net present value (£'000)			NIL

The aim is to find the discount rate that produces an NPV of nil; therefore the PV of inflows (a) must equal the PV of outflows, £1,500,000. If the PV of inflows (a) is to be £1,500,000 and the size of each inflow is £700,000, the discount factor required must be $1,500,000 \div 700,000 = 2.14$. The discount rate (c) for which this is the 3 year factor can be found by looking along the 3 year row of the cumulative discount factors shown in the annuity table. The figure of 2.14 appears under the 19% column suggesting an IRR of 19% (you may have to settle for the nearest figure to 2.14 on another occasion). The necessary procedure for exam purposes can be summarised as follows.

Step 1   Find the cumulative discount factor, $A\,\overline{n}|r = \dfrac{\text{Initial investment}}{\text{Annual inflow}}$.

Step 2   Find the life of the project, n.

Step 3   Look along the n year row of the cumulative discount factors till the closest value to $A\,\overline{n}|r$ is found.

Step 4   The column in which this figure appears is the IRR.

3.6   Perpetuities

Just as it is possible to calculate the present value of a perpetuity so it is a simple matter to find the internal rate of return of a project with equal annual inflows that are expected to be received for an indefinitely long period.

Formula

The IRR of a perpetuity $= \dfrac{\text{Annual inflow}}{\text{Initial investment}} \times 100$

This can be seen by looking at the formula for the PV of a perpetuity and considering the definition of internal rate of return.

Illustration

Find the IRR of an investment that costs £20,000 and generates £1,600 for an indefinitely long period.

$$IRR = \frac{\text{Annual inflow}}{\text{Initial investment}} \times 100 = \frac{£1,600}{£20,000} \times 100 = \mathbf{8\%}$$

4   NPV v IRR

4.1   Different types of investment decision

Two different basic DCF methods have been seen, NPV and IRR. When used to analyse a project, the decision is easily made:

- if a project has a positive NPV it should be accepted;
- if a project has an IRR greater than the required rate of return, accept it.

Since the two basic DCF methods are based on the same underlying principle, the time value of money, one would expect them to give identical investment decisions. This is not always so.

Four types of investment decision can be identified.

- Single investment decision.
- Mutually exclusive investments.
- Projects with multiple yields.
- Capital rationing decisions.

The two DCF methods may not always give the same conclusion. The four types of decision are considered in turn.

4.2   Single investment decision

When deciding whether or not to accept a single capital project if neither of the other conditions apply, no ambiguity arises. A project will be accepted if it has a positive NPV at the required rate of return; if it has a positive NPV then it will have an IRR that is greater than the required rate of return. The previous graph of NPV v Discount Rate should illustrate the point.

4.3   Mutually exclusive investments

Organisations may often face decisions in which only one of two or more investments can be undertaken; these are called mutually exclusive investment decisions. In these circumstances NPV and IRR may give conflicting recommendations.

Example

Barlow Ltd is considering two short-term investment opportunities which they have called project A and project B which have the following cash flows.

Time	0	1
Project A (£'000)	(200)	240
Project B (£'000)	(100)	125

Barlow has a cost of capital of 10%. Find the NPV's and IRR's of the two projects.

Solution

		NPV £'000	IRR %
Project A:	240 ÷ 1.10 – 200	18.18	20
Project B:	125 ÷ 1.10 – 100	13.64	25

The IRR's could be found either by trial and error or by using a formula. It would be easier to notice that project A, over 1 year, earns £40,000 on an investment of £200,000 (a 20% return) whilst project B earns £25,000 on £100,000 (25%).

It is worth noticing that A has the higher NPV whilst B has the higher IRR - a conflict.

Graphical explanation

If the NPV's of the two projects were calculated for a range of discount rates and two graphs of NPV against rate plotted on the same axes it would look as shown below. (This is worth trying yourself.)

NPV v Discount rate for mutually exclusive projects

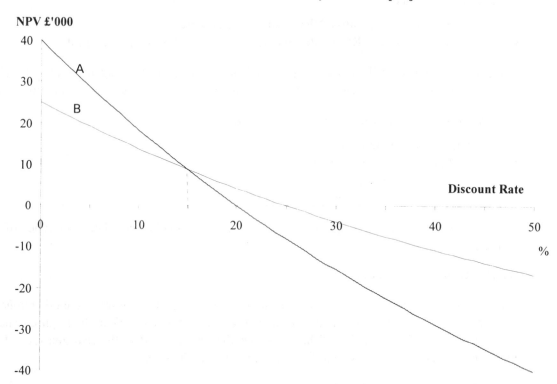

As in the previous section (when describing IRR) each graph slopes downwards (NPV decreases as r increases for a 'conventional' project) and shows a slight curve. Line A starts at (£240,000 – £200,000) £40,000; line B starts at (£125,000 – £100,000) £25,000. The lines cut the horizontal axis at their IRR's of 20% and 25% and intersect at (what seems to be) 15%. Project B has the higher IRR, whereas at the cost of capital of 10% (in fact at any rate below 15%) project A has the higher NPV.

4.4   Mutually exclusive projects - rationale and resolution

Although NPV and IRR are based on the same principle of the time value of money they are calculated in very different ways and there is no reason why they should give the same ranking for mutually exclusive projects. However if firm reasons for the different ranking are required one would cite:

- **Absolute and relative measures** - the NPV is an absolute measure but the IRR is a relative measure of a project's viability.

- **Reinvestment assumption** - the two methods are sometimes said to be based on different assumptions about the rate at which funds generated by the projects are reinvested - NPV assumes reinvestment at a firm's cost of capital, IRR assumes reinvestment at the IRR. The author Carsberg has said that this reinvestment argument "... has no relevance ...".

When deciding between the two projects it must be realised that it is only their nature that causes us to choose between them, not shortage of funds (see capital rationing later). These might represent two alternative uses of the same building which can't be carried out together. Going for B or, more particularly A, does not restrict our ability to accept other profitable projects that become available. In view of this the decision should be:

Accept the project with the larger NPV

The reasons for this are:

- **Better reinvestment assumption** - if the relevance of reinvestment is accepted, the NPV's assumption is more realistic than that of the IRR.

- **Achieving corporate objectives** - use of the NPV method is consistent with achieving a firm's corporate objective of maximising share price (maximising shareholder wealth).

In addition to these two reasons in favour of using the NPV, the futility of the IRR could be seen if the firm, Barlow Ltd, surrendered their chance to accept either of these two projects in exchange for the possibility of a third project:

	Time	Cash flow £
Project C:	0	(10)
	1	14

This project has a much higher IRR (40%) than either of the first two, but its NPV at 10% ([£14 ÷ 1.10] – £10) of £2.73 will not have much effect on any company's market value.

Several authors, particularly advocates of the use of the IRR, propose a means of reconciling the two conflicting conclusions, to use an IRR method to choose project A, using 'incremental projects'. Such exercises achieve little and simply distract from the main principle that the NPV is theoretically superior to the IRR.

4.5   Projects with multiple yields

If mutually exclusive investments provide one reason why the IRR should not be used as a principal investment appraisal method, multiple yields serve to reduce IRR's importance still further.

A weakness of the IRR method is that projects may either have no IRR or several IRR's.

4.6   Activity

Consider the following projects with cash flows over a three year period.

Time	Project A £	Project B £	Project C £
0	(5,000)	(10,000)	(100,000)
1	2,000	23,000	360,000
2	2,000	(13,200)	(431,000)
3	2,000	(1,000)	171,600

You are required to calculate the NPV of these projects over the range 0 - 40% at 5% intervals and plot the results on three separate graphs. (Hint: it may be safer to use a formula rather than tables.)

4.7   Activity solution

The NPV at 0% is found by adding up the (undiscounted) cash flows.

Rate	0	5	10	15	20	25	30	35	40
NPV$_A$	1,000	447	(26)	(434)	(787)	(1,096)	(1,368)	(1,608)	(1,822)
NPV$_B$	(1,200)	(932)	(751)	(639)	(579)	(560)	(574)	(612)	(671)
NPV$_C$	600	162	0	(25)	0	19	0	(76)	(219)

The three graphs are shown below.

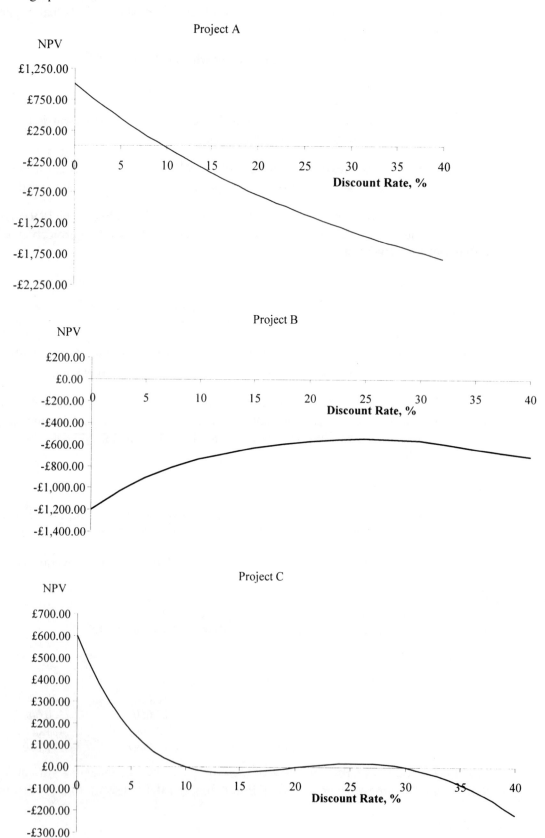

Comment

•   Project A is a 'conventional' project, with one outflow followed by several net inflows and shows the expected pattern of NPV decreasing as discount rate increases.

•   Project A has one IRR at 10%.

- Project B has no IRR.

- Project B's cash flows could be described as unconventional with outflows **of a significant size** appearing at the beginning and end of the 'project' (which is always unprofitable but is least unprofitable at 25%).

- Project C's cash flows alternate between being outflows and inflows and the graph of NPV v discount rate alternately falls and rises.

- Project C has three IRR's at 10%, 20% and 30%.

4.8 The problem of non-conventional cash flows

The feature of projects which causes the graph of NPV v discount rate to change from the standard shape as shown by project A is more than one 'change in sign'. Project A had an outflow followed by inflows (one change in sign), whereas project B had outflows then inflows (a first change in sign), but then further outflows (two changes in sign).

Rule: There **may** be as many IRR's as there are changes in sign in the patterns of cash flows. Clearly project C has three changes in sign and has three IRR's; although project B has two changes in sign but no IRR's. Project B's cash flows could be adjusted to produce a project with two IRR's simply by ignoring the last outflow. In that case a new project, D, would show the following.

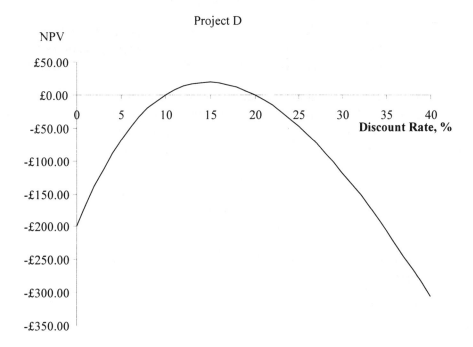

This type of cash flow pattern might occur with projects such as mining or oil exploration. An initial investment is followed by receipts from sales for a few years but, at the end of the project, the sizeable cost of reparations have a major effect on the project. The authors Lorie and Savage discussed this type of project at length.

Clearly it is difficult to use the IRR method in these circumstances. Attempts can be made to modify the cash flows in such a way as to be able to find a single IRR without invalidating the analysis. However, multiple yields merely provide further evidence that the NPV method is superior to IRR. Despite having several IRR's projects will have only one NPV at the required rate of return which will be either positive or negative (or zero).

4.9   Capital rationing

If a firm has several investment opportunities available, but insufficient funds to accept all projects with a positive NPV, it is said to be facing capital rationing and some means has to be found to select those projects that will provide the firm with the greatest benefit. Projects could be ranked according to NPV or by IRR; the rankings may not be the same. In this case neither approach need be correct.

The problem is analogous to the capacity decisions seen earlier when a production plan had to be formulated when a single resource was in limited supply or when several capacity constraints existed. The approach is similar and depends upon the number of constraints. Previously key factor analysis was used if a single resource was in short supply and linear programming if several constraints affected production. So for capital rationing:

Cash short in a single year   -   Rank products by NPV/£ invested

Cash short in several years   -   Apply linear programming approach

Details of the methods used are not required here but will be studied in detail in a later paper.

5   PAYBACK PERIOD

5.1   Introduction

Definition   The period, usually expressed in years, which it takes the cash inflows from a capital investment project to equal the cash outflows.

When deciding between two or more competing projects the usual decision is to accept the one with the shortest payback. Payback is commonly used as a first screening method. It is a rough measure of liquidity and not of profitability.

The term payback period is almost self-explanatory and the rider to the definition that it is a useful screening process that assesses liquidity is worth noting. In practice it is slightly more popular than the accounting rate of return; but, as will be shown later, it has weaknesses and should not be used as the main decision criterion (and certainly not for choosing between alternative investment opportunities).

In the simplified case of a project with equal annual cash inflows, it is easy to find the payback period.

$$\text{Payback period} \quad = \quad \frac{\text{Initial payment}}{\text{Annual Cash Inflow}}$$

Eg, if £2m is invested to earn £500,000 per annum for 7 years (these being net cash earnings) the payback period (P) is given by:

$$P \quad = \quad \frac{£2,000,000}{£500,000} \quad = \quad \textbf{4 years}$$

However, if cash inflows are uneven (a more likely state of affairs), the payback has to be calculated by working out the cumulative cash flow over the life of a project.

5.2   Payback period with uneven cash flows

At this stage a convention needs to be introduced, cash outflows will be shown as negative figures (in brackets) and cash inflows or receipts shown as positive figures.

Illustration

A project has the following cash flows.

You are required to calculate the project payback period.

Year	Cash flow	Cumulative cash flow
	£'000	£'000
0	(2,000)	(2,000)
1	500	(1,500)
2	500	(1,000)
3	400	(600)
4	600	Nil
5	300	300
6	200	500

The payback period is exactly 4 years.

For such a project it is possible that the payback period does give a realistic measure of its 'worthwhileness' – the point being that no account is taken of the time value of money (explained later). As far as payback is concerned, the shorter the payback period the better the project. However, the limitations of the technique can be seen when it is used to appraise several projects together and hence compare them.

Further illustration

Year				Cash flow			
Project		A	B	C	D	E	F
0		(100)	(100)	(100)	(100)	(80)	(80)
1		10	10	40	40	40	40
2		20	20	30	30	(20)	40
3		30	30	20	20	30	30
4		40	40	10	10	10	20
5		-	10	10	40	20	20
6		-	40	40	10	40	(40)
Payback period (years)		4	4	4	4	4 or 5	2?

The payback period for all of projects A, B, C and D is four years – and thus in terms of this measure the four projects are equivalent. However, since there is a time value to money (as explained later) the projects are not equivalent. In particular:

B is preferred to A because of the extra receipts in years 4 and 5.

C is preferred to B because the cash receipts in years 1, 2, 3 and 4 are received more rapidly.

D is preferred to C because the post payback period receipts are greater in the earlier years.

Additional problems arise when determining the payback for projects E and F. For project E, the payback may be deemed to be four years – the length of time taken for the cash receipts to cover the initial outlay, or five years, the length of time before cumulative cash flows are zero. For project F the initial outlay is recovered by the end of the second year but it seems very imprudent to totally ignore the cash flow arising at the end of year 6 (of course in line with the nature of conservative accountants positive cash flows arising after the payback period have been ignored in projects B to E also.)

5.3   Merits of payback period as an investment appraisal technique

(a)   **Simplicity**

As a concept, it is easily understood and is easily calculated.

(b)   **Rapidly changing technology**

If new plant is likely to be scrapped in a short period because of obsolescence, a quick payback is essential.

(c)   **Improving investment conditions**

When investment conditions are expected to improve in the near future, attention is directed to those projects which will release funds soonest, to take advantage of the improving climate.

(d)   **Payback favours projects with a quick return**

It is often argued that these are to be preferred for three reasons:

(i)   Rapid project payback leads to rapid company growth – but in fact such a policy will lead to many profitable investment opportunities being overlooked because their payback period does not happen to be particularly swift.

(ii)   Rapid payback minimises risk (the logic being that the shorter the payback period, the less there is that can go wrong). Not all risks are related to time, but payback is able to provide a useful means of assessing time risks (and only time risk). It is likely that earlier cash flows can be estimated with greater certainty.

(iii)   Rapid payback maximises liquidity – but liquidity problems are best dealt with separately, through cash forecasting.

(e)   **Cash flows**

Unlike the other traditional methods it uses cash flows, rather than profits, and so is less likely to produce an unduly optimistic figure distorted by assorted accounting conventions which might permit certain costs to be carried forward and not affect profit initially.

5.4   Weaknesses of payback period

(a)   **Project returns may be ignored**

In particular, cash flows arising after the payback period are totally ignored.

(b)   **Timing ignored**

Cash flows are effectively categorised as pre-payback or post-payback – but no more accurate measure is made. In particular, the time value of money is ignored.

(c)   **Lack of objectivity**

There is no objective measure as to what length of time should be set as the minimum payback period. Investment decisions are therefore subjective.

(d)   **Project profitability is ignored**

Payback takes no account of the effects on business profits and periodic performance of the project, as evidenced in the financial statements. This is critical if the business is to be reasonably viewed by users of the accounts.

5.5   Conclusions on payback

Payback is best seen as an initial screening tool – eg, no project with a payback of more than ten years is to be considered.

It is an appropriate measure for relatively straightforward projects eg, those which involve an initial outlay followed by constant long term receipts.

However in spite of its weaknesses and limitations the payback period is one of the most common initial methods of investment appraisal in use in the UK. It is not, however, often used exclusively - rather in conjunction with other methods.

Various variations on the basic payback calculation are occasionally seen:

Discounted payback - determining how long it takes to recoup the initial capital investment from the present value of the cash inflows.

Payback reciprocal - the reciprocal of the payback period (often expressed as a percentage); in certain circumstances it approximates to the DCF method, the internal rate of return.

Multiple payback - the time taken to recover the initial outlay not once but several times.

6 ACCOUNTING RATE OF RETURN

6.1 Definition

The accounting rate of return (ARR) which may also be called the return on capital employed (ROCE) expresses the profits from a project as a percentage of capital cost. However, what profits are used and what figure for capital cost may vary. The most common approach produces the following definition.

$$\text{ARR} = \frac{\text{Average annual (post depreciation) profits}}{\text{Initial capital costs}} \times 100$$

In the absence of any instructions to the contrary, this is the method that should be used (profits before interest and tax, but after depreciation). Other methods discovered by the Carsberg and Hope survey were:

- using average book value of the assets over their life;
- using first year's profits;
- using total profits over the whole of the project's life.

Example

A project involves the immediate purchase of an item of plant costing £110,000. It would generate annual cash flows of £24,400 for five years, starting in year 1. The plant purchased would have a scrap value of £10,000 in five years, when the project terminates. Depreciation is on a straight line basis.

You are required to calculate the ARR.

Solution

Annual cash flows are taken to be profit before depreciation.

Average annual depreciation	=	(£110,000 – £10,000) ÷ 5
	=	£20,000
Average annual profit	=	£24,400 – £20,000
	=	£4,400

$$\text{ARR} = \frac{\text{Average annual profit}}{\text{Initial capital cost}} \times 100$$

$$= \frac{£4,400}{£110,000} \times 100 = 4\%$$

6.2 Using average book values of investments

This variation on the calculation of an ARR produces a figure which is, under certain circumstances, closer to the conventional financial accounting view of return on capital employed. However, students have been known to suffer amazing mental aberrations when calculating a simple average in these circumstances.

Example

Using the figures in the previous example produce revised calculations based on the average book value of the investment.

Solution

Average annual profits (as before) =   £4,400

Average book value of assets $=\dfrac{\text{Initial capital cost} + \text{* Final scrap value}}{2}$

$$=\dfrac{£110,000 + £10,000}{2} = £60,000$$

ARR $=\dfrac{£4,400}{£60,000} \times 100 = 7\tfrac{1}{3}\%$

*   Note that the scrap value **increases** the average book value.

6.3   Merits of accounting rate of return for investment appraisal

(a)   **Simplicity**

As with the payback period, it is easily understood and easily calculated.

(b)   **Link with other accounting measures**

Return on capital employed, calculated annually to assess a business or sector of a business (and therefore the investment decisions made by that business), is widely used and its use for investment appraisal is consistent with that. The ARR is expressed in percentage terms with which managers and accountants are familiar. However, neither this nor the preceding point necessarily justify the use of ARR.

6.4   Criticisms of ARR

There are a number of specific criticisms of the ARR:

(a)   It fails to take account of either the project life or the timing of cash flows (and time value of money) within that life.

(b)   It will vary with specific accounting policies, and the extent to which project costs are capitalised. Profit measurement is thus 'subjective', and ARR figures for identical projects would vary from business to business.

(c)   It might ignore working capital requirements.

(d)   Like all rate of return measures, it is not a measurement of absolute gain in wealth for the business owners.

(e)   There is no definite investment signal. The decision to invest or not remains subjective in view of the lack of an objectively set target ARR.

Conclusion   To summarise, it is concluded that the accounting rate of return does not provide a reliable basis for project evaluation.

6.5   Activity

A project requires an initial investment of £800,000 and then earns net cash inflows of:

Year	1	2	3	4	5	6	7
Cash inflows (£'000)	100	200	400	400	300	200	150

In addition, at the end of the seven-year project the assets initially purchased will be sold for £100,000.

You are required

(a)   to calculate the project's payback period;

(b)   to determine its accounting rate of return.

6.6   Activity solution

(a)   **Payback period**

Cumulative cash flows are tabulated below.

Year	0	1	2	3	4	5	6	7
Cumulative (£'000)	(800)	(700)	(500)	(100)	300	600	800	950

The payback period appears during the fourth year in which £400,000 arises. Since £100,000 still has to be paid off at the start of the fourth year, the payback period is **3¼ years**.

(b)   **Accounting rate of return**

This uses **profits** rather than cash flows.

Average annual inflows	=	£1,750,000 ÷ 7	=	£250,000
Average annual depreciation	=	(£800,000 – £100,000) ÷ 7	=	£100,000

(A net £700,000 is being written off as depreciation over 7 years.)

Average annual profit	=	£250,000 – £100,000	=	£150,000

$$\text{ARR} = \frac{\text{Average annual profit}}{\text{Initial investment}} \times 100 = \frac{£150,000}{£800,000} \times 100$$

$$= \textbf{18.75\%}$$

(Note: If ARR had been based on the average book value of assets, £150,000 would have been divided by the average of initial capital cost, £800,000, and final scrap value, £100,000 ie, £450,000, to give an accounting rate of return of 33⅓%.*)*

7   NET PRESENT VALUE AND RESIDUAL INCOME USING ANNUITY DEPRECIATION

7.1   What is residual income?

Residual income is a performance measure based on charging notional interest on the capital investment; if the resulting net benefit from the investment is positive, this means that the investment is worthwhile.

7.2   Calculating the notional interest charge

This can be based on discounted cashflow techniques which results in the annual repayment on a sum borrowed to make the investment. If an annuity depreciation method is used, the annual repayment can be separated into its capital (depreciation) and interest elements.

7.3   The effects of annuity depreciation

If profits are constant then the use of annuity depreciation will result in a constant measure of residual income.   The total present value of the residual income will equal the net present value of the investment project.

8   CHAPTER SUMMARY

- Capital investment appraisal attempts to determine whether the benefits from investing large capital sums compensate for the initial outlay.

- The traditionally used methods are the payback period and the accounting rate of return:

  Payback =   Number of years taken to recoup the initial investment
  from the cash flows of the project

  $$ARR = \frac{\text{Average annual profits}}{\text{Initial investment}} \times 100$$

  There are variations of each method.

- The main drawback of ARR over all other methods is its use of accounting profits, while both ARR and payback suffer from ignoring the timings of the benefits and therefore the time value of money.

- The two discounted cash flow (DCF) methods (NPV and IRR) take into account the rate of time preference for money of an investor - that most people would prefer to receive money sooner rather than later.

- The present value of a single sum, £S, receivable in n years time given a discount rate r (as a decimal) is given by:

  $$PV = £S \times \frac{1}{(1+r)^n}$$

- The present value of an annuity of £A per annum received for each of n years (in arrears) given a discount rate r is given by:

  $$PV = £A \times A_{\overline{n}|r} = £A \times \frac{1}{r}\left(1 - \frac{1}{(1+r)^n}\right)$$

  Tables of present value and annuity factors exist and are supplied in the exam.

- NPV and IRR may not produce the same conclusion for mutually exclusive investments for which the NPV method should be used.

- The IRR also suffers since some projects may have zero or more than one IRR; projects may have as many IRR's as changes in sign in their patterns of cash flow.

- The NPV method is superior to IRR since its use is consistent with a company's objective of maximising shareholder wealth.

9   SELF TEST QUESTIONS

9.1   What are the two DCF methods of investment appraisal? (2.1)

9.2   Explain what is meant by the time value of money. (2.2)

9.3   What is an internal rate of return? (3.1)

9.4   How can an IRR be calculated? (3.2, 3.5)

9.5   Why might NPV and IRR give conflicting conclusions and how should this be resolved? (4.4)

9.6 Under what circumstances may a project have more than one IRR? (4.8)

9.7 Despite its limitations, why is the payback period a popular means of investment appraisal? (5.3)

9.8 What variations of the payback method exist? (5.5)

9.9 What are the limitations of the use of the accounting rate of return? (6.4)

10 EXAMINATION TYPE QUESTION

10.1 Paradis plc

Stadler is an ambitious young executive who has recently been appointed to the position of financial director of Paradis plc, a small listed company. Stadler regards this appointment as a temporary one, enabling him to gain experience before moving to a larger organisation. His intention is to leave Paradis plc in three years time, with its share price standing high. As a consequence, he is particularly concerned that the reported profits of Paradis plc should be as high as possible in this third and final year with the company.

Paradis plc has recently raised £350,000 from a rights issue, and the directors are considering three ways of using these funds. Three projects (A, B and C) are being considered, each involving the immediate purchase of equipment costing £350,000. One project only can be undertaken and the equipment for each project will have a useful life equal to that of the project, with no scrap value. Stadler favours project C because it is expected to show the highest accounting profit in the third year. However, he does not wish to reveal his real reasons for favouring project C and so, in his report to the chairman, he recommends project C because it shows the highest internal rate of return. The following summary is taken from his report:

Years				*Net cash flows (£'000)*						*Internal rate of return*
Project	0	1	2	3	4	5	6	7	8	%
A	(350)	100	110	104	112	138	160	180	-	27.5
B	(350)	40	100	210	260	160	-	-	-	26.4
C	(350)	200	150	240	40	-	-	-	-	33.0

The chairman of the company is accustomed to projects being appraised in terms of payback and accounting rate of return, and he is consequently suspicious of the use of the internal rate of return as a method of project selection. Accordingly, the chairman has asked for an independent report on the choice of project. The company's cost of capital is 20% and a policy of straight-line depreciation is used to write off the cost of equipment in the financial statements.

You are required

(a) to calculate the payback period for each project; **(3 marks)**

(b) to calculate the accounting rate of return for each project; **(5 marks)**

(c) to prepare a report for the chairman with supporting calculations indicating which project should be preferred by the ordinary shareholders of Paradis plc. **(12 marks)**

(Total: 20 marks)

Note: ignore taxation.

11 ANSWER TO EXAMINATION TYPE QUESTION

11.1 Paradis plc

Note: this question requires fairly standard calculation and discussion.

(a)   **Payback period for each project**
(Time taken to repay original outlay of £350,000.)

Project A: £'000

Cash in first 3 years	314
Balance required	36
Initial investment	350
Cash in 4th year	112

Payback = 3 years + $\dfrac{36}{112}$ years =   3.32 years

(assuming cash flows accrue evenly - otherwise 4 years)

Project B:

Cash in first 3 years	350,000
Payback	3 years

Project C:

Cash in first 2 years	£350,000
Payback	2 years

(b)   **Accounting rate of return for each project**

	Project A £'000	Project B £'000	Project C £'000
Total cash flow	904	770	630
Less: Total depreciation (no scrap value)	350	350	350
Total accounting profit	554	420	280
Project life (years)	7	5	4
Average profit per year (£'000)	79.14	84	70[1]
Initial capital employed	350	350	350[2]
Accounting rate of return (1) ÷ (2)	22.6%	24%	20%
(Alternatively, ARR could be computed as average profit ÷ average capital employed, giving)	45.2%	48%	40%

(c)

REPORT

To: Chairman, Paradis plc

From: An Analyst

Date: XX-X-19XX

**Report on the choice of capital investment project to
be financed by proceeds of recent rights issue**

Terms of reference

To provide an independent report on which of three projects, A, B and C, should be preferred by the ordinary shareholders of Paradis plc.

Introduction

This report looks at the strengths and weaknesses of various project appraisal techniques which are in common use, examines how the three projects stand up in the light of each method, and reaches a conclusion as to the best choice of project.

Conclusion

It is recommended that the net present value method of project appraisal be used. On this basis, project A appears to be the best, being marginally better than B. However, it is suggested that further investigations into the uncertainty of cash flow estimates of projects A and C are undertaken.

Traditional appraisal methods

Since you are familiar with both the payback and the accounting rate of return methods, this report deals immediately with their advantages and limitations.

(1)   Payback

The payback method is easy both to calculate and to understand. Its use is that it shows how long investors have to wait before their investment starts to repay the initial outlay. Because no future results are known with certainty, it gives investors an idea of 'how long their money will be at risk', and since uncertainty usually tends to increase the further into the future we look, a short payback period is taken to mean low risk as well as quick returns.

The weakness of using the payback method in isolation is that it does not measure profitability or increase in investor wealth.

For example, refer to the payback period of projects A, B and C. Project C has the shortest payback period and A has the longest. However, the cash flows of A last much longer than those of C, which may make A more profitable in the long run.

(2)   Accounting rate of return

This method gives a measure of relative project profitability by comparing the average accounting profit per annum to come from the project with the average capital employed in it. Its advantages are that it is relatively easy to understand, it does measure profitability of returns compared with outlay, and it gives an indication as to whether the firm's target return on capital employed is exceeded.

Its main weaknesses are:

(i)   it pays no attention to the **timing** of project returns. Cash received at an early stage is more valuable than the same cash received in a few years time because it can be reinvested to earn interest. For example, project C returns cash very quickly compared with project B, but this effect is lost in the process of averaging profits. Thus B has a higher ARR than C even though its IRR (see later) is lower;

(ii)   it is a relative rate of return, rather than an absolute measure of gain in wealth. All rate of return methods ignore the **size** of the project;

(iii)   because it is a percentage measure, there is a tendency to compare the ARR with interest rates, which is totally invalid;

(iv)   it uses accounting profits where cash flows may be more appropriate;

(v)   there is no objective means of finding a target ARR for a project.

Discounted cash flow methods

Both of the traditional methods are surpassed by discounted cash flow methods. The basic arguments are:

(i)   it is better to consider cash rather than profits because cash is how investors will eventually see their rewards (ie, dividends, sale of shares, interest);

(ii)   the timing of the cash flows is important because early cash can be reinvested to earn interest.

The technique of discounting reduces all future cash flows to equivalent values now (present values) by allowing for the interest which could have been earned if the cash had been received immediately.

There are two possible techniques, net present value and internal rate of return.

Net present value

This is simply the net of the present values of the project cash flows after allowing for reinvestment at the company's 'cost of capital' (ie, the average required return which is set by the market for the company's operations considering the risk of those operations).

Provided that the project is of average risk for the firm and that there is no shortage of capital, the NPV gives a best estimate of the total increase in wealth which accrues to the shareholders if the project is accepted. This should be reflected in an increased market value of the shares.

NPV computations are attached at Appendix A. On this basis, project A gives the greatest increase in shareholder wealth.

Internal rate of return

This is defined as the discount rate which gives the project a net present value of zero. When looking at a single project, the IRR will give the same decision as the NPV (ie, if the project NPV is greater than zero, its IRR is higher than the cost of capital).

However, the IRR can give an incorrect signal when it is necessary to rank projects in order. Like all rate of return methods, it ignores the size of the project and hence the absolute gain in wealth to come from it. For example, project C has the highest IRR, but although the original outlay is as high as the other two projects, it returns most of that outlay after one year, and thereafter effectively becomes a smaller project with a high rate of return.

The IRR also makes an incorrect assumption about the rate at which cash surpluses can be reinvested: it assumes they are reinvested at the internal rate of return. For example, it assumes that cash from project C can be reinvested at 33%, but cash from A is reinvested at 27.5%. Both of these are wrong: the 20% cost of capital figure is more appropriate. The IRR is therefore unsuitable for comparing projects.

The best appraisal method

Following the arguments above, the best appraisal method is the net present value approach because it takes into account the time value of money in a way which indicates the absolute gain which will be made by shareholders as a result of accepting the project.

On this basis, project A should be accepted, with C just second. However, it should be noted that there are many other factors which affect the decision which have been left out of this report. The most obvious of these is an assessment of project risk. For example, it may be that A is regarded as riskier than C simply because it takes longer to pay back. It can then be argued that A should be discounted at a higher rate than C. This may give it a lower NPV than C.

We must therefore recommend that further analysis is made of the uncertainty attached to the cash flows of projects A and C.

Appendix A: Project net present values

Time	20% factor	Project A	PV £'000	Project B	PV £'000	Project C	PV £'000
0	1.000	(350)	(350.0)	(350)	(350.0)	(350)	(350.0)
1	0.833	100	83.3	40	33.3	200	166.6
2	0.694	110	76.3	100	69.4	150	104.1
3	0.579	104	60.2	210	121.6	240	139.0
·4	0.482	112	54.0	260	125.3	40	19.3
5	0.402	138	55.5	160	64.3		
6	0.335	160	53.6				
7	0.279	180	50.2				
Net present values			83.1		63.9		79.0

(This assumes that cash flows arise at annual intervals.)

12 STRATEGIC MANAGEMENT ACCOUNTING

INTRODUCTION & LEARNING OBJECTIVES

When you have studied this chapter you should be able to do the following:

- Distinguish strategic management accounting from traditional management accounting.
- Explain the characteristics of strategic decisions.
- Distinguish between long run and short run decisions.
- Identify and evaluate the information required for long run decisions.

This subject area was examined in a discursive question in June 1995, where the characteristics of, and co-ordination between, strategic planning and operational planning were discussed.

---

1 WHAT IS STRATEGIC MANAGEMENT ACCOUNTING?

1.1 Definition

Strategic management accounting provides information to executives to assist them in making strategic decisions.

Such information is often provided from external sources whereas traditional management accounting provides information based on data collected from internal sources.

Bromwich and Bhimani (Management Accounting: Evolution not Revolution) describe strategic management accounting as:

> "accounting procedures which stress extra-organisational variables as well as value added results on internal activities and non-financial data evaluation."

David Allen agrees with this view. He criticises accounting systems because they are inward and backward looking, and he argues that managers make decisions and must therefore be forward and outward looking.

1.2 Characteristics of strategic decisions

Drucker, in his book **Managing for Results,** discusses business strategies and states that whatever a company's programme it must decide:

(a)   what opportunities it wants to pursue and what risks it is willing and able to accept;

(b)   its scope and structure, and especially the right balance between specialisation, diversification and integration;

(c)   between time and money, between building its own or buying, ie using sale of a business, merger, acquisition and joint venture to attain its goals;

(d)   on an organisation structure appropriate to its economic realities, its opportunities and its programme for performance.

There are three kinds of opportunities

(a)   **Additive** – exploitation of existing resources.

(b)   **Complementary** – involving structural changes in the company.

(c)   **Breakthrough** – changing the fundamental economic characteristics of the business.

Risks can be placed in four categories

(a)   those that must be accepted;

(b)   those that can be afforded;

(c)   those that cannot be afforded; and

(d)   those the company cannot afford to miss.

The right opportunities will not be selected unless the company attempts to maximise opportunities rather than to minimise risk. Quantitative techniques can be used to evaluate the likely outcomes of different decisions.

1.3   Characteristics

In their book, **Exploring Corporate Strategy**, Johnson and Scholes outline the characteristics of strategic decisions. They discuss the following areas:

(i)   Strategic decisions are likely to be affected by the **scope of an organisation's activities**, because the scope concerns the way the management conceive the organisation's boundaries. It is to do with what they want the organisation to be like and be about.

(ii)   Strategy involves the **matching of the activities of an organisation to its environment**.

(iii)   Strategy must also **match the activities of an organisation to its resource capability.** It is not just about being aware of the environmental threats and opportunities but about matching the organisational resources to these threats and opportunities.

(iv)   Strategies need to be considered in terms of **the extent to which resources can be obtained, allocated and controlled** to develop a strategy for the future.

(v)   **Operational decisions will be affected** by strategic decisions because they will set off waves of lesser decisions.

(vi)   As well as the environmental forces and the resource availability, the strategy of an organisation will be **affected by the expectations and values of those who have power** within and around the organisation.

(vii)   Strategic decisions are apt to affect the long-term direction of the organisation.

Johnson and Scholes argue that what distinguishes strategic management from other aspects of management in an organisation is the complexity. There are three reasons for this:

- it involves a high degree of uncertainty;
- it is likely to require an integrated approach to management; and
- it may involve major change in the organisation.

2   MANAGEMENT ACCOUNTING INFORMATION AND STRATEGIC MANAGEMENT

2.1   Introduction

Most of the information required will be external information, but a good starting point is the position audit.

2.2   The position audit

A Position Audit is an important (some would say essential) part of the strategic planning process. The carrying out of a Position Audit focuses the attention of those responsible for the formulation of strategic plans upon the question of 'where are we now?' In other words it is an examination of the organisation's **current** situation.

[Definition]   A Position Audit is part of the planning process which examines the current state of the entity in respect of:

(a)   resources of tangible and intangible assets and finance;
(b)   products, brands and markets;
(c)   operating systems such as production and distribution;
(d)   internal organisation;
(e)   current results;
(f)   returns to stockholders.

The primary purpose of the Position Audit is to identify, through systematic analysis and review, the entity's current state and to isolate its strengths and weaknesses. Drucker provides us with a good explanation of the purpose of this analytical approach in his book 'Managing for Results': 'The basic business analysis starts with an examination of the business as it is now, the business as it has been bequeathed to us by the decisions, actions and results of the past. We need to see the hard skeleton, the basic stuff that is the economic structure. We need to see the relationship, and inter-relationship of resources and results, of efforts and achievements, of revenues and costs'.

A company's operational environment is composed of those dimensions which directly or indirectly influence corporate success or failure. Most external factors are beyond the control of the company, whereas **internal** dimensions are generally within its management ambit. The essential purpose of a strategic Position Audit is to collect and analyse all the relevant and available information about the company and its **current** operations which will provide strategic planners with information on:

(a)   The competitive strengths and weaknesses of the company's current strategic position;

(b)   The consequences of the company continuing its present strategy;

(c)   The internal resources which are available for implementing any strategic change that may be required.

2.3   The detailed audit

It is not possible to provide a definitive list of the aspects that should be analysed in a strategic position audit. This must depend on the particular situation, circumstances and forces at work in the operational environment of a given organisation. However, the analytical audit approach should utilise a systematic set of questions that takes the auditor into the main areas of a company's structure and operations. A typical position audit questionnaire form might therefore contain questions in the following business areas:

POSITION EVALUATION QUESTIONNAIRE FORM (extract)

A   Corporate dimension

1.   Is the rate of corporate profits and profitability acceptable?

2.   Are corporate resources used to their optimum effectiveness?

3.   What is the nature and significance of the key factors which:

-    have shaped past corporate performances?
-    will determine the shape of the corporate future?

4.   What are the actual and potential problem situations?

---

5. Is optimal allocation of resources between business units and products currently achieved?

6. Are acceptable operational standards and targets in use for monitoring and control purposes?

7. How does the company's operational efficiency compare with that of its major competitors?

8. How adaptable is the organisation to change?

9. Are contingency strategies available?

10. Is the company securing an adequate return on its investment in research and development?

B **Market dimension**

For each market the company operates in:

11. What is the speed of technological change affecting the market?

12. Is the market susceptible to the trade cycle?

13. What are the prospects of government intervention in the market?

14. What are the prospects for market growth?

15. Is the market susceptible to substitutes:

    - that the company can introduce?

    - that competitors can introduce?

16. What is the size and nature of barriers to market entry?

17. What are the prospects of new competitors entering the market?

18. What is the product life cycle position for each of the company's main products in the market?

19. What is the company's image in the market?

20. What is the company's absolute, and relative market share?

C **Marketing dimension**

21. Are distribution methods and channels adequate?

22. Is the market information and intelligence system adequate?

23. Is the balance between market segments optimum?

24. What are the competitive strengths or weaknesses of the company's products in terms of:

    - after-sales service?

    - quality?

    - specification?

    - packaging?

    - price?

- standardisation?

- guarantees?

25.   What is the rate of new product development? How does this compare against main competitors?

26.   Are the advertising and sales promotions effective, in terms of:

- campaigns?

- size of budget?

- quality of advertising agency?

27.   How adaptable is the company to customers' special requirements?

28.   Does the company have adequate patent protection?

29.   Is the company's sales force effective, in terms of:

- technical expertise?

- structure?

- geographical location?

- size of budget?

30.   Does the company maximise the advantages of its brand names and other goodwill?

D   Manufacturing dimensions

31.   Is the geographical location of plant and equipment optimum?

32.   Is the capacity of production facilities optimum?

33.   Is the correct balance obtained between various items of plant with different optimum operational levels?

34.   What is the age of plant, and the associated threat of obsolescence?

35.   Are production methods, plant layout, and organisation efficient and effective?

36.   Is the workforce skill and balance adequate?

37.   Are quality assurance systems adequate?

38.   Are inventory levels optimum?

39.   What is the capacity for expansion?

40.   Are the costs of manufacture competitive?

The above extract indicates the comprehensive nature of the audit. The audit would cover all aspects of the company and would not just concentrate on one or two activities that seem to be problematic. Activities are interrelated and a problem in one may be caused by troubles in another.

3   COMPETITION IN THE MARKET

3.1   The competitive perspective

Competition is the existence of rival products or services within the same market, and in addition to analysing all the company's critical competence and resources, strategic planners need to survey competition in its totality, including such critical strategic elements as the company's competitors' R&D capabilities, sales, services, costs, manufacturing and procurement (including all the other businesses in which competitors may be engaged). Strategists need to put themselves mentally in the place of planners in rival companies and to persistently search out the key perceptions and assumptions on which the competitors' strategies are formulated.

Example

Suppose you were a management accountant involved in helping to formulate a two-year strategy for a maturing product. Here's what your competitive analysis might turn up:

- an existing UK competitor has drastically reduced overhead and input costs by a policy of rapid decentralisation and global sourcing;

- another existing UK competitor has just fended-off a hostile take-over bid by selling off the division that competes with you to another strong competitor who will use technological synergy to reduce costs, and who has a distribution system better than yours;

- a competitor has just installed a computerised customer on-line system hooking-up to each of its 1,800 distributors, reducing order-to-delivery time by 75%;

- another competitor has recently introduced a just-in-time assembly system at the centre of which is a computerised manufacturing resources planning (MRP) system, enabling the company to tailor-make the product to the specifications of its customers;

- an existing Japanese competitor continues to add product features, improve quality and reduce prices;

- a new Korean competitor has just entered the UK market;

- a new company, led by a team of breakaway managers from a large competitor, has claimed a technological breakthrough.

It is because this scenario is now commonplace - for every industry and every segment of industry - that your company is not alone in requiring major strategic surgery.

3.2   Identifying the competitor(s)

The first problem in analysing competitors is to establish who exactly is the competition? This is a simple-to-understand but difficult-to-answer question. Too often companies have focused on the wrong adversary, by being obsessed with old rivalries.

Examples

By concentrating its attention on its cross-town rival Kodak, and its new, and good, high-price copiers, Xerox effectively ignored the *'small timers'* Savin and Canon who were operating in unimportant market segments. Then suddenly, or so it seemed, these mice turned into lions, and Xerox lost more than half its market share before it stemmed the tide.

While the two Detroit giants of General Motors and Ford were looking over their shoulders at each other, Toyota stormed into both their markets.

So seeking an answer to the *'who'* is no easy task. Strategists will need to check out:

- obvious majors in the market;
- the next best competitors, region by region;
- new, big companies, with troubles of their own likely to intrude into their market;
- small domestic companies perhaps operating in small premium market niches;

- foreign companies, with special emphasis on the first unobtrusive move into small domestic niches;
- oddball forays from unexpected competitors.

3.3   Need to focus beyond brand

Kotler suggests that companies are myopic if they focus attention only on their brand competitors, and gives the example of confectionery companies whose real challenge, he says, is to expand their primary market, namely the sweet market, and not simply to battle for a larger share in a reducing market. Sweet manufacturers have to be concerned about mega trends in the environment, such as people eating less in general, and eating less sweets in particular, and switching to substitutes, other forms of confectionery; and dietetic confectionery, and so on. Indirect competitors are often overlooked because they are not apparent. Cadbury's and Rowntree's presentation boxes of chocolates were once the main personal gifts in a variety of social situations; now they have been replaced by flowers, plants, wine and gift-vouchers. There is a danger for companies only concentrating on their brand competitors and neglecting the opportunities to build the whole market or failing to make moves to prevent it from declining. Kotler supports this view by distinguishing four types of competition:

(a)   **Desire** competitors: other needs and wants that a consumer may desire to satisfy.

(b)   **Generic** competitors: alternative ways in which the consumer can satisfy a particular desire.

(c)   **Form** competitors: other forms of product (or service) that can satisfy the consumer's particular desire.

(d)   **Brand** (or **enterprise**) competitors: other brands (or enterprises) offering the same product (or service) that can satisfy the consumer's particular desire.

The consumer decision process follows the path shown in the diagram below:

Figure 1   Kotler's classification of four types of competition*

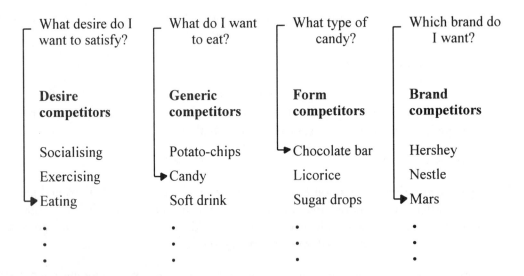

(* Kotler, P. 'Marketing Management: Analysis, Planning and Control', Prentice-Hall, 1984.)

3.4   Example

The competition facing a private college offering education for the qualifying examinations of professional accountancy institutions provides another example. A student, say female, after graduation from university could decide to travel the world, get a job, carry on with full time education, or study for an accountancy qualification (**desire competitors**). Suppose she favours getting a job and studying for the ACCA qualification. She then considers how best do this (**generic competitors**), choices are to purchase a correspondence course, read books, enrol on an college evening course, or enrol on a college weekend course. She decides in favour of joining a weekend course. Next she needs to consider what type of college (**form competitors**): private college or state college. She favours a private college. This leads her to compare the offerings of the private colleges and to consider which one to use: Accountancy Tutors, and so on. Thus the planners in the private college face at least four types of competitors in attempting to enrol this student on a course of study. Managers planning competitive strategy for a college would therefore need to be involved in trying to build their market as well as attempting to build their brand share in that market.

3.5 The fallacy of 'perfect competition'

There is also the problem of the competitive state of the market. Economists refer to the state of perfect competition which is the only market form which can be considered as a comprehensive self-contained system.

However one of the objectives of the marketer is to distort perfect competition in the interests of the company by differentiating its product, and deterring potential competition from entering the market, thus making the company's product a quasi-monopoly in the market. (In other words aiming to make the product become *a big fish in a small pond*, rather than *a small fish in a big pond*.) Marketing techniques for this include: adding product features, advertising, sale promotion, pricing, merchandising and personal selling.

Example

The colour-generating system behind Sony's Trinitron television tube, with its single electronic-beam gun, challenged the industry which had always used three electronic guns for the three primary colours: red, blue and green. It gave Sony virtually a two-year monopoly in the market.

3.6 Activity

You will perhaps remember from your studies of economics the main characteristics of a perfectly competitive market. Try to list these characteristics now.

3.7 Activity solution

The main characteristics of a perfectly competitive market are listed below.

(a)   A large number of buyers and sellers, none of whom is large enough to affect the total supply or demand, nor powerful enough to dictate or influence market price.

(b)   The market price is determined by the equilibrium point resulting from the combined pressures of the aggregate demands and supplies of all buyers and sellers in the market and will change when the forces of demand and supply change.

(c)   Barriers to entry are low and potential entrants find no difficulty in competing if they so choose. Ease of entry and exit of the market in response to movements of market prices ensures that over the long term companies produce up to the point where marginal cost is equal to market price. Although in the short term, the market price may be pushed up above the marginal cost, this will not persist over the long term, as potential entrants would be attracted by the higher profit and their additional capacity would soon bring prices and profits down. By contrast, if market prices fell below marginal costs, the less efficient companies would be forced to leave the industry until the price level increased.

(d)   The product is standardised so that buyers are indifferent from whom they purchase. Promotional activity such as advertising is pointless, because price is the sole purchasing determinant.

(e)   Buyers and sellers are fully informed of the market conditions, so that no one can buy or sell at an advantageous price.

(f)   As the demand curve forced on an individual supplier is perfectly elastic and the market price is known, the theoretically optimum for the supplier is to produce at that volume where marginal cost equals marginal revenue.

4   COMPETITIVE FORCES

4.1   The five forces model

The key text dealing with competitive analysis is Professor Michael Porter's work 'Competitive Strategy: Techniques for Analysing Industries and Competitors' and this provides a useful guide. Porter states that 'competition in an industry is rooted in its underlying economics, and competitive forces exist that go well beyond the established combatants in a particular industry'. The problem for the strategist is to determine which of these forces are relevant, and to what extent. The approach to industry analysis discussed in this section is relatively new, having been developed by Porter in 1980. It is based on the concept of an industry being shaped by five forces. These are illustrated below, and explained in the following subsections:

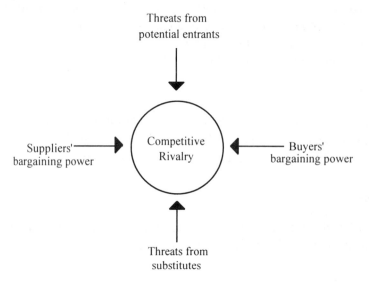

4.2   Threats from potential entrants

(a)   By increasing the extent of competition.

New competitors to an industry may make it more competitive in three ways.

- Expanding capacity without necessarily increasing market demand.
- Their need to penetrate the market to achieve **critical mass** and then build market share, which may include product and marketing innovations.
- Increasing costs as they bid for factors of production.

(b)   Barriers to entry.

It is in the interests of existing competitors to deter new entrants. There are seven main barriers to entry.

- Economies of scale.
- Brand (or product) differentiation
- Capital requirements.
- Switching costs.
- Access to distribution channels.
- Cost disadvantages independent of scale.
- Government regulation (including legal barriers).

Economies of scale

Many industries, such as cement and chemicals, offer increasing returns in manufacture, and companies benefit by being able to lower unit costs by increasing output volume. Thus potential entrants would be at a considerable cost disadvantage, unless they can immediately set up their operations on a scale large enough to reap similar economies. (This scale is termed the 'critical mass'.) In any case, it might take several years and a heavy investment programme to construct and equip the necessary factories to put them on a competitive footing.

For example, Avon, the cosmetics company, sells part of its line direct to housewives, so any company intending to compete on a similar footing would have to:

- recruit and train an efficient sales force skilled in 'party-selling';
- establish warehouses to maintain buffer stocks;
- hire a design team to develop a competitive product range;
- manufacture and distribute the volume and quality of products required.

Brand (or product) differentiation

Some brands generate a greater consumer loyalty than others and consumers will not be easily lured away by competing products even though they are similar or close substitutes. The cost for a new entrant attempting to penetrate the market in such a situation is likely to be high. The task will involve persuading entrenched consumers to trial their products, perhaps by offering special inducements, such as free samples or gifts. Although the exercise is costly, there is no guarantee of success, particularly as the defending company will combat entry tactics.

Products can be differentiated in terms of: price, quality, brand image, features, distribution, exclusivity, packaging, value.

For example, Procter & Gamble in the US uses its enormous $500 million media advertising budget to buy and maintain its high market share and deter other companies entering or trying to increase their shares in the markets dominated by P&G products.

Capital requirements

This also relates to economies of scale. For example the long-lead, high-cost, high-risk business cycle of the pharmaceutical industry, where the number of successful products reaching the market is relatively small, but development costs are between £25m to £50m per product has deterred all but the largest new companies from entering the market. (In fact with the exception of Janssen and Syntex no totally new company to this market has succeeded, from start up, in becoming medium-sized in the last forty years.)

Switching costs

These are one-off costs facing a company which switches from one supplier's product to another's. Switching costs may include costs of certification, product redesign, costs and time in assessing a new source, or even the cultural problems of severing a relationship.

For example, In the mid-1970s, FFW-Fokker indicated to British Aerospace (BAe) that it would not tolerate their planned HS-146 aircraft in direct competition against their own existing F28 short-haul jet airliner. Fokker had over 40% of the total cost of both their F-17 and F-28 aircraft supplied by British companies, and indicated that this would be at risk if the HS-146 project continued. BAe correctly considered the threat was not credible since cost-shifting (re-design, re-tooling and re-certification for both aircraft using non-British equipment) would be prohibitive to Fokker.

Access to distribution channels

One of the biggest dilemmas facing the producer is obtaining shelf or floor space in retail outlets. In order to sell brands the producer must not only persuade the retailer to stock them, but to give them a fair share of shelf/floor space and to feature them periodically. Shelf and floor space is limited (consider here how much 'High street' space an electric dish-washing machine takes to display), and already faced with a bewildering array and assortment of similar products (for example a large Sainsbury store carries some 7,000 products) retail management are not anxious to accept new products, particularly from new entrants lacking a proven track record in the market.

Although BIC, by using its competence in plastics technology, took the initiative by creating the volume market for disposable razors and lighters in the US, it was new to the market and needed to divide its resources between promotion and establishing a national distribution network. BIC did not have the resources to win a battle on two-fronts and leadership went to Gillette.

Cost disadvantages independent of scale

Established companies may have costs advantages not available to potential entrants, no matter what their size and cost levels. Critical factors include: proprietary product technology, favourable locations, learning or experience curve, favourable access to sources of raw materials and government subsidies.

Government regulation (including legal barriers)

Legal restrictions still prevent companies from entering into direct competition with most nationalised industries, while many governments have permitted the establishment of quasi-nationalised bodies controlling marketing operations in milk, eggs, agriculture, etc. Patents and copyright offer inventors some protection against new entrants. Governments also licence the right to produce certain categories of products.

Japanese companies use the complexity of the distribution and legal system in Japan to deter potential entrants in the domestic market. Disney spent five years negotiating the licensing agreement for its Tokyo theme Park. Coca-Cola, which now has a 60 percent share of the Japanese soft-drink market suffered a full decade of red tape, and ROLM, as a small firm, succeeded in Japan but only after senior officers made twenty odd trips, just to conclude the first, tiny sale.

4.3 Threats from substitutes

These are alternative products that serve the same purpose, eg, gas central heating systems in competition with solid fuel systems. (One of the starkest examples of substitution, and a rapid one at that, was the way in which gas-fired central heating overtook electrical central-heating after the OPEC oil crisis of 1973/74, one result of which was the insolvency of at least one major British company.) The main threat posed by substitutes, though, is that they limit the price that a company can charge for its products. There is also a danger that the threat of a substitute may not be realised until it is too late to arrest their entry. Substitute products that warrant most attention are those that are:

(a)   subject to an environment improving their price-performance trade-off with the industry's product, or

(b)   produced by industries earning high profits and who have the resources available to bring them rapidly into play.

For example, in 1978 the producers of fibreglass insulation enjoyed unprecedented demand as the result of high energy costs and severe winter weather in US. But the industry's ability to raise prices was impeded by the plethora of insulation substitutes, including cellulose, rock wool, and styrofoam.

4.4   Threats from the bargaining power of buyers

The power used by buyers in an industry may make it more competitive in three ways.

(a)   Forcing down prices.

(b)   Bargaining for higher quality or improved services.

(c)   Playing competitors against each other.

All three of these are at the expense of industry profitability.

Porter claims that the power of the industry's buyer groups depends on the characteristics of its market situation and of the relative importance of its purchases from the industry compared with its overall business. He suggests that buyers are particularly powerful in seven situations.

- Purchasers are large relative to sellers.
- Purchases represents a significant proportion of the buyers' costs.
- Purchases are undifferentiated.
- Buyers earn low profits.
- Buyers have the potential for backward integration.
- The buyer's product is not strongly affected by the quality of the suppliers' product.
- The buyer has full information.

4.5   Threats from the power of suppliers

Suppliers can exert bargaining power over companies within an industry in two main ways.

(a)   Threatening to raise their prices.

(b)   Threatening to reduce the quality of their goods and services.

The effect of this power will be to squeeze profitability out of an industry unable to recover cost increases by raising its own prices.

Porter suggests that suppliers are particularly powerful in six situations.

- There are few suppliers.
- There are few substitutes for their products.
- The industry supplied is not an important customer.
- The supplier's product is an important component to the buyer's business.
- The supplier's product is differentiated.
- Suppliers can integrate forward.

4.6   Rivalry and competition among competitors

Conflict among existing competitors takes some form of offensive strategy, which we discuss later in this chapter. Tactics commonly used to implement such strategy include product innovations and improvements, price competitions, advertising battles and increased customer services. Rivalry occurs because one or more companies feels threatened or sees a market opportunity to improve its position, although competitive moves by the initiator company usually results in counter-defensive strategies from its competitors. This interactive pattern of offensive and defensive strategies may not leave the initiating company and the industry better off, and on the contrary may leave all the companies in the industry worse off than before.

Porter suggests that there are seven main determinants relating to the strength of internal competition and rivalry within an industry.

- Many equally balanced competitors.
- Slow rate of industrial growth.
- Lack of differentiation.
- Capacity can only be increased by large amounts.
- High fixed costs in the industry.

- There are many diverse competitors.
- There are high exit barriers.

5 COMPETITIVE ANALYSIS

5.1 The build up of a detailed picture

A detailed profile should be built up on each major competitor. Some competitors span many industries whereas others are part of multi-national organisations, some are concerned almost exclusively with the domestic market while others depend on exports for a high proportion of their sales.

Although it is tempting to evaluate a company's position solely on the basis of whether its products and services are superior to those offered by its competitors, there are a wide range of additional factors that determine competitive success. The objective features of a company's products and services, although important, often form a relatively small part of the competitive picture. In fact, all the elements making up consumer preference, such as product quality, service, price and location are only part of the competitive analysis. The other part involves examining the internal strengths and weaknesses of each major competitor. In the long run a company possessing strong operational assets, with an organisation structure and industrial culture conducive for motivation and innovation, and having ownership of significant financial resources will prove to be a tough, enduring competitor.

The competitive analysis portion of an *'environmental analysis'* for a company will need to focus on four areas of concern.

- Identifying the company's major competitors.
- Establishing on what basis competitive strengths are to be assessed.
- Comparing the company with its major competitors.
- Identifying potential new competitors.

5.2 Some general rules worth remembering about competitive analysis

It would be useful, although not always practicable, if every person in the company had ready, visible access to the numbers on market share updated monthly (weekly if possible).

Competitive analysis should be everyone's business - design engineers, manufacturing managers, service staff, sales force, MIS people. The fact is that everyone will hear things - from service and salespeople, from a customer, from a former employee and friend now working with a competitor, from a bank clerk, from a braggart at a professional institute meeting, from tit-bits here and there. Also of course, the benefit of getting every employee to think about competition is the positive effect it has on general readiness to accept change.

The company should be positive rather than negative about competitors' products and should not hesitate to copy if this is legal. ('The best leaders are the best note-takers, the best 'askers', the best learners.')

6 THE STRUCTURE OF COMPETITION

Companies operating in a market pursue different competitive strategies and hold different competitive positions. The competitive positions of companies, (or the market structure), can be described in different ways. For example, Arthur D. Little, in the book 'A System for Managing Diversity', sees companies occupying one of six competitive positions in their market, as *dominant, strong, favourable, tenable, weak* or *non-viable*. Each company will be able to place itself in one of these competitive positions, which along with an analysis of its product life cycle and resource balance between its product-markets, will help it decide whether to build, hold, harvest, or withdraw from the market. We will look at these four product-market strategies later.

Philip Kotler in his book, 'Marketing Management: Analysis, Planning and Control', develops a different classification of competitive positions. He bases this on the behaviour, or market strategy, of different companies and suggests that ideas for strategies can be generated by classifying a company's situation in one of four positions:

(a)   market leader,

(b)   market challenger,

(c)   market follower, or

(d)   market nicher.

We will consider this classification next.

7   MARKET LEADER

7.1   Characteristics of the market leader

It is usual for an industry to contain a company which is recognised as market leader. The company has the largest share in the market (and *'leads'* in terms of size) and may spearhead product innovation, distribution, strategy, pricing strategy and promotional emphasis and intensity. This is not always the case and it may be that a particular brand is so strong and differentiated in its market that planners do not want to *'tinker'* and limit the number of changes. There is a danger, however, in restricting innovation even if the existing strategy is clear, strong and well executed, although the fear of strategists of too much interference with a proven formula is also well based.

UK Brand Leaders

Category	*No 1 position*
Chocolate bars	Cadbury
Cornflakes	Kellogg's
Custard	Bird's
Digestive biscuits	McVities'
Film	Kodak
Floor polish	Johnson's
Margarine	Stork
Razor blades	Gillette
Soup	Heinz
Tea	Brooke Bond

7.2   Brand strength

Some leading companies use their brand name as a broad platform to introduce new products, sometimes by streaming products within their brands, ie, by removing one product and introducing another. IBM has demonstrated the power of a brand image. The company has over time extended its product range across large, medium and smaller computers using the strong IBM name to retain its vanguard position. The same applies to: Kodak (photography), General Motors (motor vehicles), Coca-Cola (soft-drink), McDonalds (fast food) and Procter & Gamble (selected packaged goods), and others too numerous to list here.

7.3   Position not secured

Unless a dominant company enjoys a legal monopoly its position is not secured. It must maintain a constant vigilance. Other companies will keep probing for its weaknesses and challenging its strengths.

Example

In 1986 IBM suffered a 27% fall in net profits while increasing its sales by only 2.5%. In fact IBM was under direct attack from the innovators - Hypres, using Josephson Junction technology, Cray *et al* in super computers, Convex *et al* in super minicomputers, Apollo *et al* in engineering work stations, Digital *et al* in minicomputers and networks, and Apple *et al* in personal computers.

The market leader can easily take a wrong turn, and within a short time, one or two years at most, plunge into second or third place. Many of the traditional blue-chip companies of UK industry, for example Courtaulds, ICI and Tube Investments have either previously adopted, or are now adopting, turnaround strategies.

A product innovation by a competitor offering distinctive better value is a constant threat. Also the dominant company might become seen as staid and old-fashioned compared with up-and-coming rivals. The business then becomes stagnant resulting in under-utilised assets and a reduction in profits. (Playboy magazines now take second place in circulation to Penthouse on news-stands.)

Some examples of successful past challenges in the UK are:

Market	*Brand pioneer*	*Overtaker*
Crisps	Smiths	Walkers
Hairsprays	Supersoft	Sunsilk
TV 'soap-opera'	Coronation Street	East Enders
Stainless steel razor blades	Wilkinson	Gillette
Cat food	Kitekat	Whiskas

7.4 Activity

You can see from the above example that during the mid-1980s the ITV 'soap-opera' **'Coronation Street'** temporarily lost market share to BBC's **'East Enders'**. Taking into account changing environmental factors consider the reasons for this.

7.5 Activity solution

Different reasons can be given for the market take-over.

(a) Coronation Street is a programme set in the North of England. The majority of TV viewers live in the South East. East Enders was 'positioned' in the east-end of London.

(b) Coronation Street was then a story of middle-aged people. Young people do not relate easily to such dialogue. East Enders included life-stories of young people.

(c) Coronation Street predominantly dealt with the life-style of the 'working-class'. This did not 'fit' the emerging 'yuppie' life-style of the mid-1980s.

8 THE MARKET CHALLENGER

A market challenger is a company that attacks the leader or other competitors in an aggressive attempt to increase its market share. Porter suggests that offensive strategy is most intense in industries with:

(a) high fixed costs,

(b) high exit penalties, and

(c) stagnant primary demand.

Basically, an aggressor can choose to attack on four fronts.

(a) Attack the market in general, without identifying specific enemy targets.
(b) Attack the market leader.
(c) Attack companies of its own size who are vulnerable in one or more ways.
(d) Attack small local companies who are vulnerable in one or more ways.

Critical to choosing the game-plan is the need for a systematic competitive analysis.

9   THE MARKET FOLLOWER

The market follower is a company that adopts a strategy of *'not rocking the boat'* being content to maintain its position in the market. Market followers, although having a lower share position than the leader, may be as profitable, or even more profitable. The company will still require strategy - it needs to hold its current customers, to win a fair share of growth in the overall market and to stay at a predetermined distance from the leader. Each follower attempts to bring distinctive competitive advantages to its target market - product quality, features, distribution location, and services. The follower is a prime target for the challenger and must be responsive and competitive.

10   LONG RUN AND SHORT RUN DECISIONS

10.1   Introduction

The planning and decision making cycle have been shown to be closely interlinked; this is even more true in the long run, than in short-run decisions which may solve problems not envisaged at the planning stage.

10.2   Long run decisions

Long run decisions are otherwise known as strategic decisions. They form part of the organisation's policies and corporate plans. Such decisions are often made over a long time horizon which is measured in years. This means that there is much uncertainty surrounding both the input and output values. As a consequence probability and simulation modelling may be used.

10.3   Short-termism

Although there is no specific definition of short-termism, it generally means the following.

> [Definition]   The tendency to place pressure and emphasis upon the achievement of results in the near future rather than in the medium or long-term future

This pressure for 'jam today' could come from within the organisation or it could be external eg, where the financial markets expect results from strategies to have a quick pay off.

Short termism is often used in relation to complaints about such things as: the difficulties of raising capital for investment; the government's attitude to public transport; the UK's record in R&D expenditure compared to Japan; and the volatility of profits.

As we have shown already, objectives, targets and plans are all aspects of the planning process. Long and medium range plans provide a framework for short-range plans, which refer primarily to current operations.

The designation 'long term' or 'long range' varies by organisation. For a mail order company, long range may be the next season's catalogue. For an organisation engaged in growing timber as a crop, the outlook may approximate 100 years. On this relative basis, long range may vary from a few months to a matter of centuries. Most authors writing about long term planning emphasise that it involves decision-making that commits resources over the long run future and that planning is necessary in dealing with the uncertainty of the future. On the one hand, there is rapidly advancing technology, changing market and competitive environments, increasingly active governments and many other forces that make forecasting the future environment extremely difficult. Yet organisations must plan their activities over a long run period and must commit resources in spite of future uncertainties. This causes the dilemma - the need for long range commitments of resources and organisational endeavour in the face of an increasingly dynamic environment and future uncertainties.

There may have to be a trade-off between long and short term objectives, with organisations sacrificing longer term plans to address current threats or opportunities. For example, an organisation might have a long term objective of achieving steady growth in earnings or profits, but in the short term may be faced with a severe price war and have to reduce its prices in order to survive. Newspapers in the UK have recently suffered from this type of short-termism. Individual performance is often measured by achievements in the short term. This is not conducive to long range objectives when progress is measured by targets.

Fortunately, there is a recognition that long range planning must provide for organisational flexibility in meeting changes. E Kirby Warren suggests that 'the major purpose of planning is the development of processes, mechanisms, and managerial attitudes which will do two things. First, they will make it possible to make commitment decisions today with a greater awareness of future implications, and second, they will make it possible to make future decisions more rapidly, more economically and with less disruptions to the ongoing business'. His second point emphasises that long-run planning must provide for future flexibility in decision-making.

11   DISCOUNTED CASH FLOW

11.1   Introduction

It is an accepted principle that there is an opportunity cost of money which should be considered when there is a significant time difference between the respective outflows and inflows of cash for a decision. This cost is measured by using discounted cashflow techniques.

11.2   DCF and strategic decisions

Strategic decisions have been stated to be long-term decisions which may include a large amount of uncertainty. DCF, in contrast, appears to be a technique which provides clear, accurate answers as to whether or not a particular course of action is worthwhile.

In order to use DCF techniques for strategic decisions it will be necessary to make assumptions; these assumptions must be clearly stated to managers and where possible the effects of errors in these assumptions on the final results should be quantified.

12   COSTS AND REVENUES

12.1   Strategic decisions

Strategic decisions are concerned with long-term profitability and survival which may be obtained at the expense of competitors. It is thus argued that absolute costs and revenues are not as important as relative values.

12.2   Relative costs and revenues

By measuring costs and revenues relative to those of competitors it is possible to judge the profitability and efficiency of the organisation relative to others. It is relative superiority which will ensure survival and long-term profitability.

13   SELF TEST QUESTIONS

13.1   What is strategic management accounting? (1.1)

13.2   What are the characteristics of strategic decisions? (1.2, 1.3)

13.3   What is a position audit? (2.2)

13.4   Explain the five forces model. (4)

13.5   Distinguish between the market challenger and the market follower. (8.9)

13.6   Distinguish between long run and short run decisions. (10)

13.7   Explain short-termism. (10.3)

13 RISK AND UNCERTAINTY: SINGLE DECISIONS

INTRODUCTION & LEARNING OBJECTIVES

This chapter analyses decisions made under conditions of risk and uncertainty.

Most decisions which a company's management has to make can be described as *decisions made under uncertainty*. The essential features of making a decision under uncertain conditions are:

(a)   The decision-maker is faced with a choice between several alternative courses of action.

(b)   Each course of action may have several possible outcomes, dependent on a number of uncertain factors ie, even when a decision has been made the outcome is by no means certain.

(c)   Which choice is made will depend upon the criteria used by the decision-maker in judging between the outcomes of the possible courses of action.

This chapter is concerned with techniques available for evaluating and deciding which decision alternative to adopt.

When you have studied this chapter you should be able to do the following:

●   Produce a pay-off matrix.
●   Understand the minimax and maximin rule.

1   UNCERTAINTY AND RISK PREFERENCE

1.1   Introduction

Uncertainty exists in virtually all decision making situations, however in some scenarios the extent of the uncertainty is less significant than others. It is the uncertainty of the outcome which creates risk for the investor. If the outcome is certain, there is no risk.

1.2   Risk preference

Risk preference is the term used to describe an investor/decision maker's attitude to risk. There is a relationship between risk and required reward, though individuals have different risk/reward profiles.

Decision makers are often classified into one of three groups:

(a)   Risk seekers

-     people who will take risks to achieve the best outcome no matter how small is the chance of it occurring.

(b)   Risk neutral

-     people who only consider the most likely outcome

(c)   Risk averse

-     people who make decisions based on the worst possible outcome.

1.3   Techniques to appraise uncertainty

The most commonly used techniques to appraise uncertainty and provide information to the decision maker are

(i)   the pay-off matrix; and

(ii)   decision trees.

The pay-off matrix is often used for single decisions, whereas decision trees are used for more complex situations where there are a number of interconnected decisions required.

2   SINGLE DECISIONS

2.1   Past exam questions

This subject area was examined in June 1994 and June 1995. Both questions required the construction of a pay-off table from given information. The table was then used to support a decision, based upon either "maximin" type criteria, or expected values. It is important that you are able to handle these techniques as explained in the following text.

The use of expected values in the context of investigation of variances was examined in December 1994. This specific application is covered in Chapter 22, but employs the basic probability laws set out in this chapter.

2.2   The pay-off matrix

The pay-off matrix is a tabular layout specifying the result (pay-off) of each combination of decision and the 'state of the world', over which the decision-maker has no control.

Example

A company has three new products A, B and C of which it can introduce only one. The level of demand for *each* course of action might be low, medium or high. If the company decides to introduce product A, the net income that would result from the levels of demand possible are estimated at £20, £40 and £50 respectively. Similarly, if product B is chosen, net income is estimated at £80, £70 and – £10, and for product C, £10, £100 and £40 respectively.

Construct a pay-off matrix to present this information concisely.

Solution

Level of demand	Decision (action to introduce)		
	A £	B £	C £
Low	20	80	10
Medium	40	70	100
High	50	(10)	40

(Tutorial note: a realistic assumption might be that the company is obliged to meet whatever level of demand arises (for fear of incurring customer *bad will* and thus fewer sales of its other products).

This would justify the fall in net income at higher levels of demand in the case of product B in particular, where it appears that there are considerable diseconomies of scale.)

2.3   Activity

The Zeta company has estimated that the demand for one of its products is either 100, 200 or 300 units in a month. The product is sold for £15/item and total variable costs amount to £7/item. If demand is less than supply the product may be sold off cheaply for £5 per item. There is no penalty cost for not meeting demand.

Considering only production levels of 100, 200 and 300, draw up a payoff table for this situation.

2.4   Activity solution

		Production level		
		100	200	300
Possible	100	800	600	400
demands	200	800	1,600	1,400
	300	800	1,600	2,400

Note on workings.

When supply equals demand the contribution = £15 – 7 = £8. So, in the first cell, demand = supply = 100 and total contribution = 100 × £8 = £800. Similarly if demand exceeds supply, the same contribution applies.

eg, Supply = 100, demand = 300, still only 100 sold giving £800.

If supply exceeds demand then the surplus will be sold off at a loss of £(7–5) = £2/item
eg, Supply = 300, demand = 100
Contribution for the 100 supplied   = £800
Less loss on 200 @ £2   = £400
                                                              ———
                                                              £400
                                                              ———

2.5   Decision-making criteria

In the example 2.2 above it is by no means clear which decision is going to produce the most satisfactory result, since each product gives the most desirable outcome at one level of demand.

Three techniques for choosing between A, B and C in this situation are:

(a)   maximin rule;
(b)   minimax regret rule:
(c)   maximisation of expected values.

2.6   Maximin rule

Select the alternative which maximises the minimum pay-off achievable.

Note that this pessimistic approach seeks to achieve the best results if the worst happens.

2.7   Example

Apply the *maximin rule* to the example in 2.2 above to select a course of action.

Demand	Action		
	A £	B £	C £
Low	20	80	10
Medium	40	70	100
High	50	(10)	40
Minimum pay-off	20	(10)	10

Thus, introducing product A will ensure the maximum pay-off if the worst result were to happen in each case.

If the worst result in each strategy is a loss, then this criterion amounts to choosing the strategy which has the lowest loss ie, which *mini*mises the *max*imum loss. Hence, it is also called the *minimax* rule. This should not be confused with the *minimax regret* criterion described below.

2.8   Minimax regret rule

'Regret' in this context is defined as the opportunity loss through having made the wrong decision.

In the pay-off matrix above, if the market state had been low, the correct decision would have been B (net income £80). If A had been chosen instead, the company would have been out of pocket by £60 (ie, 80-20) and if C had been chosen, it would have been out of pocket by £70 (ie, 80-10). The opportunity loss associated with each product is A = 60, B = 0, C = 70.

It will be seen that the opportunity losses for a given market state are obtained by subtracting each value in the row from the highest value in that row.

The opportunity loss table is therefore:

State	Decision		
	A	B	C
Low	60	0	70
Medium	60	30	0
High	0	60	10
Maximum regret	60	60	70

The minimax regret strategy is the one which minimises the maximum regret.

The maximum regret value for:

A	=	60
B	=	60
C	=	70

The minimum value of these is 60, hence the minimax regret strategy would be either A or B.

3   EXPECTED VALUES

3.1   Introduction

The fundamental weakness of the above rules is that they take no account of the relative likelihood of each of the possible outcomes occurring.

For instance, in the example above if there was a 98% chance that demand would be medium and only a 2% chance of it being low or high, there would be a very strong temptation to choose product C (pay off £100 when outcome is medium demand).

In order to have a *rational* basis for decision making it is therefore necessary to have some estimate of the probabilities of the various outcomes and then to use them in the decision criterion. Thus, the third possible criterion is the *maximisation of expected value.*

The expected value of a particular action is defined as the *sum of the values of the possible outcomes, each multiplied by their respective probabilities.*

3.2   Example

Using the same data as above which we reproduce here, apply the criteria of *maximisation of expected value* to decide the best course of action for the company, assuming the following probabilities:

P (Low demand)	0.1
P (Medium demand)	0.6
P (High demand)	0.3
	———
	1.0
	———

A company has three new products A, B and C of which it can introduce only one. The level of demand for *each* course of action might be low, medium or high. If the company decides to introduce product A, the net income that would result from the levels of demand possible are estimated at £20, £40 and £50 respectively. Similarly, if product B is chosen, net income is estimated at £80, £70 and – £10, and for product C, £10, £100 and £40 respectively.

3.3 Solution

The expected value of the decision to introduce product A is given by the following summation:

$$0.1 \times 20 + 0.6 \times 40 + 0.3 \times 50 = \quad\quad £41$$

(ie, on 10% of all occasions demand will be low and net income £20, on 60% of all occasions will be medium and net income £40 and on 30% of all occasions demand will be high and net income £50. Thus on average, net income will be the weighted average of all three net incomes, weighted by their respective probabilities.)

The expected value of all the products may be calculated by a table:

Table of expected values

				Product			
		A		*B*		*C*	
Level of demand	*Prob of demand*	*Income* £	*Income × Prob.* £	*Income* £	*Income × Prob.* £	*Income* £	*Income × Prob.* £
Low	0.1	20	2	80	8	10	1
Medium	0.6	40	24	70	42	100	60
High	0.3	50	15	(10)	(3)	40	12
Total	1.0		41		47		73

Thus, if the criterion is to maximise the expected value, it means that the product with the highest expected value will be chosen, in this case product C, unless, of course, all products have negative expected value, in which case none should be chosen.

3.4 Activity

(a) Determine the Maximin and Minimax regret solutions to the payoff table determined in the activity in 2.3.

(b) If the probabilities of demands are as follows:

Demand	100	200	300
Probability	0.3	0.6	0.1

determine the optimal solution using expected values.

3.5   Activity solution

(a)   **Maximin solution**

		Production level		
		100	200	300
Possible	100	800	600	400
demands	200	800	1,600	1,400
	300	800	1,600	2,400
	Min	800	600	400

The maximum of the minimums is 800 from the 100 column, therefore produce only 100 items.

Minimax regret solution

MINIMAX REGRET TABLE

		Production level		
		100	200	300
Possible	100	0	200	400
Demands	200	800	0	200
	300	1,600	800	0
	Max	1,600	800	400

Note on calculations of regrets:

For each row subtract the values in the row from the maximum value in the row. The minimum of the maximum regrets is 400 in the 300 column. Hence produce 300 items.

(b)   **Expected value**

			100	200	300
Possible	100	0.3	800	600	400
Demands	200	0.6	800	1,600	1,400
	300	0.1	800	1,600	2,400
Expected values:			800	1,300	1,200

Working: eg, Expected value for last column:

$$400 \times 0.3 + 1,400 \times 0.6 + 2,400 \times 0.1 = 1,200$$

Maximum expected value is 1,300 in the 200 column, hence produce 200 items only.

3.6   Applicability of expected values

The criterion of expected value is only valid where the decision being made is either:

(a)   one that is repeated regularly over a period of time; or

(b)   a one-off decision, but where its size is fairly small in relation to the total assets of the firm and it is one of many, in terms of the sums of money involved, that face the firm over a period of time.

In other words, the *law of averages* will apply in the long run, but clearly the result of any single action must, by definition, be one of the specified outcomes. Thus, while the expected value of introducing product C is £73, each actual outcome will result in either £10, £100 or £40 net income, and it is only if a whole series of product introductions were involved that the *average* over a period of time would approach £73, so long as the expected value criterion was applied consistently to all the decisions.

Therefore, it is quite acceptable to adopt the expected value as the decision-making criterion for the company, so long as it has several other products and the same sort of marketing decision arises fairly regularly.

To illustrate the distinction being made, consider a man insuring his house against fire damage for a year. Suppose the house is worth £50,000 and the probability of the house being burnt down is 0.0001 (the only other outcome being that the house is not burnt down with a probability of 0.9999). The man would be quite prepared to pay, say, £15 pa to insure his house even though the expected value (or expected cost in this case) is only $0.0001 \times £50,000 + 0.9999 \times 0 = £5$. The man cannot afford to pay £50,000 out more than once in his lifetime and therefore cannot afford to *play the averages* by using expected value as his decision criterion (if so he would refuse to pay a premium greater than £5). However, to the insurance company, £50,000 is not a large sum, most of their transactions being for similar or greater amounts and therefore expected value would be appropriate as a decision criterion for them. In fact, the expected value of the insurance company's decision to insure the house at £15 pa is:

$$0.0001 \times (- £49,985) + 0.9999 \times £15$$
or $\quad - £4.9985 + £14.9985 = £10$

and any positive expected value would, in theory, have made it worth their while to insure.

4   LAWS OF PROBABILITY

4.1   Addition law

Mutually exclusive events: two or more events are said to be mutually exclusive if the occurrence of any one of them precludes the occurrences of all the others ie, only one can happen. For example, when a die is thrown once, it can only show one score. If that score is 6 (say), then all the other possible outcomes (1, 2, 3, 4 or 5) will not have occurred. Hence the six possible outcomes are all mutually exclusive. On the other hand, the outcomes 'score 6', and 'score an even number' are not mutually exclusive because both outcomes could result form one throw.

Mutually exclusive events may be written in symbols as:

$$P \text{ (A and B)} = 0$$

The probability of a 6 and a 1 in a single throw of one dice is clearly zero. In terms of set theory, this statement corresponds to ' the intersection of A and B is the empty set'.

If A and B are two mutually exclusive events, then the probability that either A or B occurs in a given experiment is equal to the sum of the separate probabilities of A and B occurring ie,

$$P \text{ (A or B)} = P \text{ (A)} + P \text{ (B)}$$

This law can cover any number of events, as long as they are mutually exclusive:

$$P \text{ (A or B or C or D or ...)} = P \text{ (A)} + P \text{ (B)} + P \text{ (C)} + P \text{ (D)} + ...$$

4.2   Example

A bag contains 4 red, 6 blue and 10 black balls; the probability of selecting either a red or a black ball when one ball is drawn from the bag is calculated as follows:

Clearly, the events are mutually exclusive, since if the ball is red, it cannot be black, and vice versa.

$\therefore$ P(red) = 4/20 $\qquad$ P(black) = 10/20

$\therefore$ P(red or black) $\quad = \quad$ P(red) + P(black)

$\qquad\qquad\qquad\quad = \quad$ 4/20 + 10/20

$\qquad\qquad\qquad\quad = \quad$ 14/20 (or 0.7)

4.3   Addition law for non-mutually exclusive events

Non-mutually exclusive events: two events are not mutually exclusive if they can occur at the same time. This is sometimes regarded as an 'overlap situation'.

If A and B are two non-mutually exclusive events, then the probability that either A or B occurs in a given experiment is equal to the sum of the separate probabilities minus the probability that they both occur.

ie, $P (A\ or\ B) = P (A) + P (B) - P (A\ and\ B)$

The term P(A and B) must be subtracted to avoid double counting. This is best illustrated by an example.

4.4   Example

The probability of selecting a heart or a queen, when one card is drawn at random from a pack of playing cards, is calculated as follows

The probability of selecting a heart or a queen is an overlap situation, as the Queen of Hearts would be included in both events. To avoid including this probability twice, it must be subtracted once.

P(any heart) = 13/52   P(any queen) = 4/52   P(queen of hearts) = 1/52

∴ P(heart or queen)   =   P(heart) + P(queen) – P(queen of hearts)

=   13/52 + 4/52 – 1/52

=   16/52 (or 0.31)

This situation may also be illustrated by reference to set theory

Drawing the Venn diagram of this situation, we have:

Universal set (= cards in the pack)

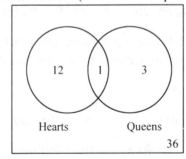

From this diagram it can be seen that, using the symbol n(A) to denote the number of occurrences of A:

n(hearts)	=	13
n(queens)	=	4
n(hearts and queens)	=	1
n(heart or queen)	=	16

4.5   Multiplication law

(a)   **Independent events:** two or more events are said to be independent if the occurrence or non-occurrence of one event does not affect the occurrence or non-occurrence of the other.

For example, consider the events:

A   =   'I will be successful in the examination.'
B   =   'I will undergo a course of study for the examination.'
C   =   'I have blue eyes.'

Clearly A will have a higher probability if B occurs than if it does not occur. A is therefore dependent on B. But the colour of ones eyes has no known effect on the ability to pass examinations or vice versa, hence A and C are independent.

If any two events, A and B, are independent, then the probability of both A and B occurring is the product of the separate probabilities.

$$P (A \text{ and } B) = P (A) \times P (B)$$

Example

The probability of drawing an ace from a pack of cards and throwing a six with an unbiased dice is calculated as follows:

P(ace) = 4/52   P(6) = 1/6

∴ P(ace and 6)   =   P(ace) × P(6)

                       =   1/13 × 1/6

                       =   1/78 (or 0.013)

The two events are independent because which card is drawn from the pack will have no influence on which score will be given by the die and vice versa.

(b)   **Dependent events:** two or more events are said to be dependent when the probability of the second event occurring is conditional on the first event having taken place.

If A and B are two events such that B is conditional on A, then the probability of A and B occurring is the product of the probability of A and the conditional probability of B occurring.

Thus, P(A and B) = P(A) × P(B given that A has occurred)

The probability that event B occurs given that A occurs is denoted by the symbol $P(B \mid A)$. The ' | ' is read as 'given' or 'if'.

Example

Two cards are drawn from a pack, the first card is not replaced before the second is drawn. The probability that they are both aces is calculated as follows:

P(first card is an ace) = 4/52

This is not replaced, therefore three aces remain, out of fifty-one cards.

P(second card is an ace, given that the first card is an ace) = 3/51.

∴ P(both aces)   =   P(first card is an ace) × P(second card is an ace, given that first card is an ace)

                   =   4/52 × 3/51

                   =   1/221 (or 0.0045)

4.6   Complementary probabilities

There are two situations to be considered:

When a single event has only two possible outcomes, usually denoted as success and failure, then, if p and q are the probabilities of success and failure respectively, it follows that:

$$p = 1 - q$$

This is because $p + q = 1$, since they are the only possible outcomes of the event.

4.7   Example

When an unbiased die is thrown, a six is regarded as success and any other number as failure.

$\therefore$ p $=$ P(success) $=$ $1/6$

and q $=$ P(failure) $=$ $1 - 1/6$ $=$ $5/6$

4.8   Example

The probability that a job will be finished on time is 0.8, therefore the probability that it will not be finished on time is 0.2 because:

p $=$ P(success) $=$ 0.8

q $=$ P(failure) $=$ $1 - 0.8$ $=$ 0.2

The event 'A does not occur' is called the **negation** of A and is denoted by $\overline{A}$ or A'. Hence:

$$P(\overline{A}) = 1 - P(A)$$

$P(\overline{A})$ is called the **complement** of P(A).

When several events are being considered then the probability that at least one of them occurs is given by:

$$P \text{ (at least one)} = 1 - P \text{ (none of them)}$$

This is because either none of the events occurs or at least one of them does therefore:

$$P(\text{none of them}) + P(\text{at least one})   =   1$$

4.9   Example

If three dice are thrown together, then the probability of obtaining at least one six is calculated as follows:

P(at least one six) $= 1 - $ P(no sixes)

Assuming independence then:

P(no sixes) $=$ P(not six on first die and not six on second die and not six on third die)

$=$ $5/6 \times 5/6 \times 5/6$

$= \dfrac{125}{216}$

P(at least one six) $=$ $1 - 125/216$

$= \dfrac{91}{216}$ (or 0.42)

5   CONDITIONAL PROBABILITY

5.1   Introduction

This is a topic which has been implicitly considered earlier in the chapter when discussing dependent events, and the calculation of the probability of them both occurring. However, the methods will now be formalised further.

The symbol P(A|B) is read as 'the probability of A occurring given that B has already occurred' and we can say that:

$$P (A \text{ and } B) = P (A|B) \times P (B)$$

ie, the probability of both A and B occurring is equal to the probability of A occurring, given that B has occurred multiplied by the probability of B occurring in the first place.

Using Venn diagrams where the universal set is a pack of playing cards:

A	=	queens	$\Rightarrow$	n(A)	=	4	(Number of queens in a pack)
B	=	hearts	$\Rightarrow$	n(B)	=	13	(Number of hearts in a pack)

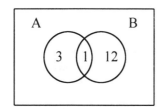

$$P(A|B) \quad = \quad \frac{1}{1+12} \quad = \quad \frac{1}{13} \qquad \text{(Probability of picking a queen, given that the card selected was a heart.)}$$

$$P(B) \quad = \quad \frac{1+12}{1+12+36+3} \quad = \quad \frac{13}{52} \qquad \text{(Probability of picking a heart)}$$

$$P(A|B) \times P(B) \quad = \quad \frac{1}{13} \times \frac{13}{52} \quad = \quad \frac{1}{52} \qquad \text{(Probability of picking the queen of hearts)}$$

and from the diagram:

$$P(A \text{ and } B) \quad = \quad \frac{1}{52}$$

Thus, the result is confirmed.

The formula is often turned around in order to enable the conditional probability to be computed, and becomes:

$$P (A|B) = \frac{P(A \text{ and } B)}{P(B)}$$

The use of this formula is demonstrated below.

5.2   Example

When a die is thrown, what is the probability that the number is greater than 1, given that it is odd?

5.3   Solution

$$P(>1|\text{odd}) = \frac{P(>1 \text{ and odd})}{P(\text{odd})}$$

$$= \frac{2/6}{3/6} \text{ (The odd numbers} > 1 \text{ are 3 and 5)}$$

$$= \frac{2}{3}$$

We know that $P(A \text{ and } B)$ = $P(A|B) \times P(B)$

and by symmetry $P(A \text{ and } B)$ = $P(B|A) \times P(A)$

This is so because if, after the event, we consider a situation and find that both A and B have occurred, it is irrelevant to ask 'which occurred first, A or B?'.

Hence:

$$P(A|B) \times P(B) = P(B|A) \times P(A)$$

5.4   Contingency tables

Another method for dealing with conditional probabilities is by use of contingency tables. These are created by taking the given probabilities and then by multiplying by some convenient number, typically 100 or 1,000, drawing a table to show the various combinations of factors which may exist. This technique will be demonstrated by means of the following example.

5.5   Example

40% of the output of a factory is produced in workshop A and 60% in workshop B. Fourteen out of every 1,000 components from B are defective and six out of every 1,000 components from B are defective. After the outputs from A and B have been thoroughly mixed, a component drawn at random is found to be defective.

Calculate the probability that it came from workshop B.

5.6   Solution

The problem will be solved by drawing a contingency table, showing defective and non-defective components and output from workshops A and B.

A suitable multiple will be 10,000 (because the probabilities of components being faulty are quite small and yet we wish to end up working with whole numbers, the multiple must be high).

Consider 10,000 components, we know that of these 4,000 are from workshop A and 6,000 from workshop B. Of the 4,000 from workshop A, 1.4%, that is 56 will be defective, and from workshop B 0.6%, that is 36 will be defective. Hence the table can be completed so far:

	A	*Workshop B*	*Total*
Defective	56	36	
Non-defective	3,944	5,964	
Total	4,000	6,000	10,000

Finally, the total number of defective items can be inserted into the table, and the final contingency table becomes:

	A	Workshop *B*	*Total*
Defective	56	36	92
Non-defective	3,944	5,964	9,908
Total	4,000	6,000	10,000

Hence, the problem may now be solved, which, to remind you, was what is the probability that a component came from workshop B, given that it is defective?

Given that it is defective, we know that we are dealing with one of the ninety two components in the top row of the table. We can see that of these ninety-two components, thirty-six come from workshop B.

Hence P(came from workshop B given that it is defective) $= \dfrac{36}{92}$

$= 0.39$

The above problem could have been dealt with using conditional probabilities.

Thus, let

A   =   item came from workshop A
B   =   item came from workshop B
D   =   item is defective
N   =   item is non-defective

We require $P(B \mid D)$

$$P(B \mid D) = \frac{P(B \text{ and } D)}{P(D)}$$

We are told that $P(B) = 0.6$

$P(D)$ must be computed as:

$P(D) = (P(D \mid A) \times P(A)) + (P(D \mid B) \times P(B))$

$= (0.014 \times 0.4) + (0.006 \times 0.6)$

$= 0.0056 + 0.0036$

$= 0.0092$ (This is out of 92 out of 10,000 defectives)

$P(B \text{ and } D) = P(D \mid B) \times P(B) = 0.006 \times 0.6 = 0.0036.$

Hence $P(B|D) = \dfrac{0.0036}{0.0092}$

$= 0.39$

It is expected that most students will find the method using the contingency table easier to follow and therefore, this is the recommended method.

5.7 Activity

30% of the new cars of a particular model are supplied from a factory X, the other 70% from factory Y. 10% of factory X's production has a major fault, 12% of factory Y's production has such a fault.

A purchaser's new car has a major fault: what is the probability that it was made at factory Y?

5.8 Activity solution

Using 1,000 as a suitable multiple ie, considering 1,000 cars are manufactured, the contingency table is:

| | Made at factory | | |
	X	Y	Total
Has major fault	30	84	114
No major fault	270	616	886
Total	300	700	1,000

Hence P(made at factory Y/major fault exists) $= \dfrac{84}{114}$

$= 0.737$

6 CHAPTER SUMMARY

In this chapter we have distinguished between uncertainty and risk preference and illustrated how single decisions may be evaluated using a pay-off matrix.

The chapter then revised the basic rules of probability which you should remember from your earlier studies.

7 SELF TEST QUESTIONS

7.1 When making decisions under uncertainty, which decision rule uses a criterion based on opportunity cost? (2.8)

7.2 What are mutually exclusive events? (4.1)

7.3 Explain the Addition Law for non-mutually exclusive events. (4.3)

7.4 Define a dependent event. (4.5)

7.5 What is a contingency table used for? (5.4)

8 EXAMINATION TYPE QUESTION

8.1 Homeworker Ltd

Homeworker Ltd is a small company that manufactures a lathe attachment for the DIY market called the 'Homelathe'.

The data for manufacturing the attachment are as follows:

| | For each batch of 10 Homelathes | | | | | |
| | | Components | | | | Total |
	A	B	C	D	E	
Machine hours	10	14	12			36
Labour hours				2	1	3

	£	£	£	£	£	£
Variable cost	32	54	58	12	4	160
Fixed cost (apportioned)	48	102	116	24	26	316
Total component costs	80	156	174	36	30	476

Assembly costs (all variable)   £40 per 10
Selling price   £600 per 10

General purpose machinery is used to make components A, B and C and is already working to the maximum capability of 4,752 hours and there is no possibility of increasing the machine capacity in the next period. There is labour available for making components D and E and for assembling the product.

The marketing department advises that there will be a 50% increase in demand next period so the company has decided to buy *one* of the machine-made components from an outside supplier in order to release production capacity and thus help to satisfy demand.

A quotation has been received from General Machines Ltd for the components but, because this company has not made the components before, it has not been able to give single figure prices. Its quotation is as follows:

	Pessimistic		Most likely		Optimistic	
	Price	Probability	Price	Probability	Price	Probability
	£		£		£	
Component A	96	0.25	85	0.5	54	0.25
Component B	176	0.25	158	0.5	148	0.25
Component C	149	0.25	127	0.5	97	0.25

It has been agreed between the two companies that audited figures would be used to determine which one of the three prices would be charged for whatever component is bought out.

As management accountant of Homeworker Ltd, it is your responsibility to analyse the financial and production capacity effects of the proposed component purchase and **you are required** to:

(a)   show in percentage form the maximum increased production availability from the three alternatives ie, buying A or B or C;   **(4 marks)**

(b)   analyse the financial implications of the purchase and, assuming a risk neutral attitude, recommend which component to buy out, noting that the production availability will be limited to a 50% increase;   **(6 marks)**

(c)   prepare a profit statement for the period assuming that the component chosen in (b) is bought out and that the extra production is made and sold (show your workings);   **(6 marks)**

(d)   state **three** other factors you would consider if you were advised that management had decided to avoid risk as much as possible when buying out a component. (Calculations are not required for this section.)   **(4 marks)**

(Total: 20 marks)

9   ANSWER TO EXAMINATION TYPE QUESTION

9.1   Homeworker Ltd

(a)   Increased production availability

Present production	4,752 hours ÷ 36 machine hours	= 132 batches
Buying out A		
Production capacity	4,752 hours ÷ 26 machine hours	= 182.77 batches
	INCREASE	= 38.46%
Buying out B		
Production capacity	4,752 hours ÷ 22 machine hours	= 216 batches
	INCREASE	= 63.64%
Buying out C		
Production capacity	4,752 hours ÷ 24 machine hours	= 198 batches
	INCREASE	= 50%

(b)   Financial implications

(Tutorial note: assuming a risk neutral attitude, the appropriate cost price for the bought out components is the 'expected' purchase price.)

Expected purchase price:

Component A	96 (0.25) + 85 (0.5) + 54 (0.25) = £80
Component B	176 (0.25) + 158 (0.5) + 148 (0.25) = £160
Component C	149 (0.25) + 127 (0.5) + 97 (0.25) = £125

Contribution possibilities:

	Present position	*Buy out Component A*	*Buy out Component B*	*Buy out Component C*
Number of batches	132	182.8	198*	198
	£	£	£	£
Per batch:				
Variable cost A	32	80	32	32
Variable cost B	54	54	160	54
Variable cost C	58	58	58	125
Variable cost D + E	16	16	16	16
Assembly costs	40	40	40	40
	200	248	306	267
Selling price	600	600	600	600
Contribution	400	352	294	333
Total contribution	52,800	64,346	58,212	65,934

* Only a 50% increase in demand next period.

Decision: Buy out C to maximise contribution.

(Tutorial note: an incremental approach would have been equally satisfactory.)

(c)   **Revised profit statement**

	Per batch £	Total (198 batches) £
Sales	600	118,800
Variable cost (as per part (b))	267	52,866
Contribution	333	65,934
Fixed costs (316 × 132 batches)		41,712
Profit		24,222

(d)   **Other factors to consider to avoid risk**

(i)   **Component prices**. The expected price for Component C is £125. It could be as high as £149. There appears to be no incentive for General Machines Ltd to keep down costs.

(ii)   **Dealing with risk**. The use of expected values is only one way of dealing with risk. A calculation of the worst possible outcome may have suggested a different choice.

(iii)   **Uncertainty of sales estimate**. The sales estimate was assumed to be certain. A range of probabilities should have been used.

(iv)   Would fixed costs remain constant with a 50% increase in output?

(v)   There will be an added risk in obtaining an essential component from only one outside supplier.

(Tutorial note: only three factors are required. You should choose the three considered most pertinent to the question.*)*

14 RISK AND UNCERTAINTY: DECISION TREES

INTRODUCTION & LEARNING OBJECTIVES

This chapter builds on the knowledge gained from the previous chapter and considers more complex decisions.

When you have studied this chapter you should be able to do the following:

- Calculate expected values.
- Construct decision trees.
- Calculate the sensitivity of a decision.
- Calculate the value of information.

1 DECISION TREES

1.1 Introduction

So far only a single decision has had to be made. However, many managerial problems consist of a rather long, drawn-out structure involving a whole sequence of actions and outcomes. Where a number of decisions have to be made sequentially the complexity of the decision-making process increases considerably. By using *decision trees,* however, highly complex problems can be broken down into a series of simpler ones while providing, at the same time, opportunity for the decision-maker to obtain specialist advice in relation to each stage of his problem.

A *decision tree* is a way of applying the expected value criterion to situations where a number of decisions are made sequentially.

It is so called because the decision alternatives are represented as *branches* in a *tree* diagram.

1.2 Example

A retailer must decide whether to sell a product loose or packaged. In either case, the product may sell, or not sell.

The decision facing the retailer can be represented by a tree diagram:

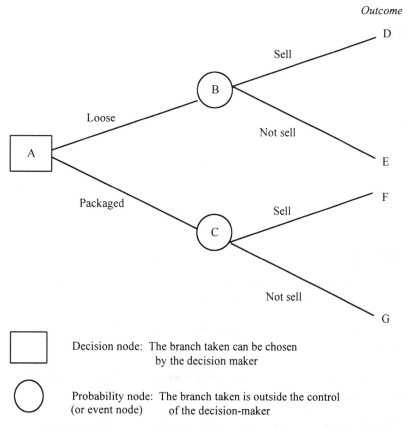

In this example, say the profitability of selling packaged products is £10, loose products £15. The loss through not selling is £5 in either case. The probability of the product being sold is 0.7 for packaged products, 0.5 for loose products.

You are required to evaluate the expected values of each decision alternative.

The decision tree is evaluated working back from right to left. At each probability node the expected value of the possible outcomes is computed. At each decision node it is assumed, initially, that the decision-maker will choose the route with the highest EV. All other branches from such a node are therefore eliminated.

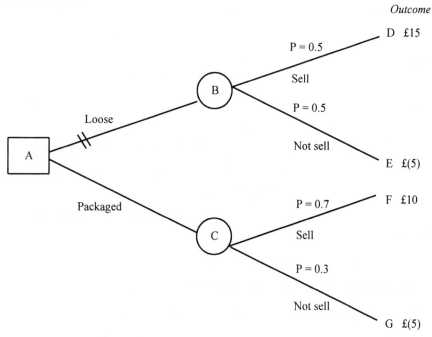

The diagram is then evaluated as follows (using obvious notation):

$$EV_B = (0.5 \times EV_D) + (0.5 \times EV_E)$$
$$= (0.5 \times 15) + (0.5 \times (-5))$$
$$= 5$$

$$EV_C = (0.7 \times EV_F) + (0.3 \times EV_G)$$
$$= (0.7 \times 10) + (0.3 \times (-5))$$
$$= 5.5$$

∴ at node A the retailer will choose to go towards node C as this has the higher EV. The discarded routes are sometimes indicated by drawing two short parallel lines across that particular path.

Therefore the decision to sell a packaged product has the higher expected value.

1.3   Activity

The Janus company is considering expanding its activities either in the UK, or in Europe or in Asia. It can at this time only expand in one region.

If it expands in the UK, there is a probability of 0.3 that contribution will increase by £200,000 or 0.7 that it will increase by £800,000.

If it expands in Europe, there is a probability of 0.4 that contribution will increase by £100,000 or 0.6 that it will increase by £1,000,000.

If it expands in Asia, there is a probability of 0.6 that contribution will decrease by £1,000,000 or 0.4 that it will increase by £2,500,000.

(a)   Draw a decision tree and determine whether the company should expand and if so where?

(b)   What important aspect does this analysis ignore?

1.4   Activity solution

(a)

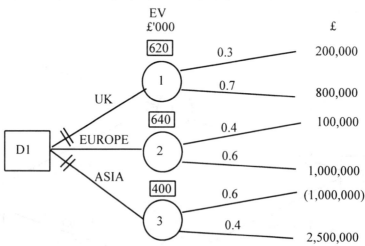

EV = Expected value

EV (Node 1) = 0.3 × 200,000 + 0.7 × 800,000 = £620,000

EV (Node 2) = 0.4 × 100,000 + 0.6 × 1,000,000 = £640,000 maximum

EV (Node 3) = 0.6 × (1,000,000) + 0.4 × 2,500,000 = £400,000

Maximum expected value is the Europe option at £640,000. Therefore reject UK and Asia (shown by scissor cuts on tree after D1) and accept expansion in Europe.

(b)   The expected value approach ignores risk. If the Asia option had worked out to give the highest expected value, and the Asia option had been adopted there would be a risk that a loss of £1,000,000 of contribution could occur.

1.5   Decision trees - a comprehensive example

The last problem could have been solved without a tree diagram, but the technique comes into its own in a more complex situation, as illustrated by the next example.

Plant Example

The manager of a newly formed specialist machinery manufacturing subsidiary has to decide whether to build a small plant or a large plant for manufacturing a new piece of machinery with an expected market life of ten years. One of the major factors influencing his decision is the size of the market that the company can obtain for its product.

Demand may be high during the first two years, but if initial users are unhappy with the product, demand may then fall to a low level for the remaining eight years. If users are happy then demand will be maintained at its high level. Conversely, caution by prospective buyers may mean only a low level of demand for the first two years but again, depending on how satisfied these few buyers are, demand may then either remain low or rise to a high level.

If the company initially builds a large plant, it must live with it for the whole ten years, regardless of the market demand. If it builds a small plant, it also has the option after two years of expanding the plant but this expansion would cost more overall, when taken with the initial cost of building small, than starting by building a large plant.

Various pieces of information have been collected, or estimated by the marketing manager, the production manager and the finance department.

(a)   **Marketing information**

The probabilities of the outcomes have been assessed as follows:

| | *First* | *Next eight years given first two years were:* | |
Outcome	*two years*	*High*	*Low*
High	0.8	0.75	0.25
Low	0.2	0.25	0.75

(b)   **Annual income estimate**

(i)   A large plant with high market demand would yield £1m pa, for each of ten years.

(ii)   A large plant with low market demand would yield only £0.1m pa because of high fixed costs and inefficiencies.

(iii)   A small plant with low demand would yield £0.4m pa.

(iv)   If demand was high, a small plant during an initial period of high demand would yield £0.45m pa for the first two years but this would drop to £0.25m pa for the next eight years, because of increasing competition from other manufacturers.

(v)   If the initially small plant were expanded after two years and demand was high in the last eight years, it would yield £0.7m pa ie, being less efficient than one that was initially large.

(vi)   If the small plant were expanded after two years but demand was low for the eight year period, then it would yield £0.05m pa.

(c)   **Capital costs**

    (i)   Initial cost of building a large plant   £3m
    (ii)   Initial cost of building a small plant   £1.3m
    (iii)   Additional cost of expanding a small plant £2.2m

Using expected value as the decision criterion, advise the manager on what choice of plant to make.

Ignore the time value of money and taxation.

1.6   Solution

The first stage in solving a problem of this nature, which involves more than one decision being made over a period of time, is to construct a decision tree to demonstrate the structure of the decisions which have to be made.

Diagram 1

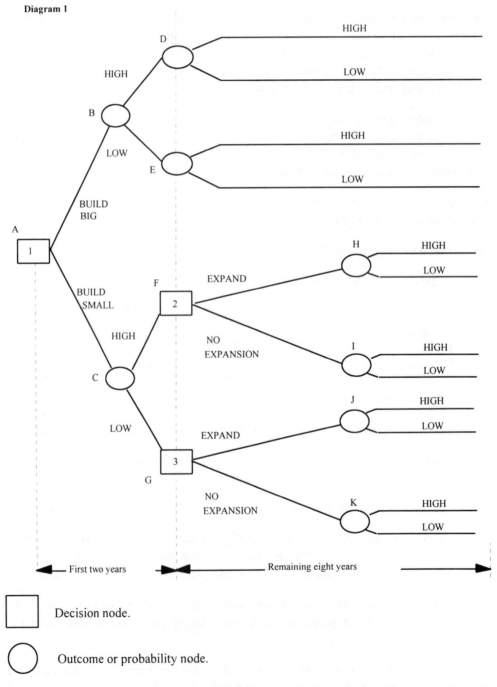

    ◻   Decision node.

    ◯   Outcome or probability node.

Each path represents a different series of events and outcomes; for example path A.C.F.H. Low represents an initial decision to build a small plant, demand for the first two years turns out be high, whereupon a further decision is taken to expand the plant, but unfortunately demand for the next eight years falls to a low level.

Each of the twelve possible monetary outcomes has a certain chance of occurring, depending on which decisions are made, and since expected value is the criterion to be used in making the decisions, the expected value of building the large plant must be compared with the expected value of building the small plant (whichever gives the higher value being chosen). This is done by a process known as *roll-back*.

Method

Insert relevant cash flows and probabilities on each branch. Starting from the right-hand side, work back towards the left-hand side. At each probability (outcome) node, calculate the expected monetary value (EMV) for events leading out from the node, and insert this value in the circle. At each decision node, after subtracting any decision costs from the EMVs, accept the decision with the highest net EMV and reject the others at that point by placing a barrier (a double line) across them. Insert this maximum net EMV in the square and use this value in subsequent EMV calculations. Continue working back in this way to the initial decision node. The calculations are shown in diagram 2, where cash flows are in £m.

Calculations

The cash inflows are the yields per annum multiplied by the number of years. These are inserted on each line. The cash outflows are put in brackets and treated as negative inflows. The probabilities are also inserted on each line where appropriate.

At node D,   EMV   = $(8.0 \times 0.75) + (0.8 \times 0.25)$ =   6.2

At node E,   EMV   = $(8.0 \times 0.25) + (0.8 \times 0.75)$ =   2.6

The total cash inflows from B are: 6.2 + 2.0 = 8.2   (high) and
2.6 + 0.2 = 2.8 (low)

At node B,   EMV   = $(8.2 \times 0.8) + (2.8 \times 0.2)$ =   7.12

At node H,   EMV   = $(5.6 \times 0.75) + (0.4 \times 0.25)$ =   4.3

At node I,   EMV   = $(2.0 \times 0.75) + (3.2 \times 0.25)$ =   2.3

From F,   expanding will yield an EMV of 4.3 – 2.2   =   2.1
not expanding will yield an EMV of 2.3

It is better not to expand, so a barrier is put across the expansion line and the EMV at F is then 2.3.

At node J,   EMV   = $(5.6 \times 0.25) + (0.4 \times 0.75)$ =   1.7

At node K,   EMV   = $(2.0 \times 0.25) + (3.2 \times 0.75)$ =   2.9

From G,   expanding will yield an EMV of 1.7 – 2.2   =   0.5 (a loss)
not expanding will yield an EMV of 2.9

It is better not to expand, so a barrier is put across the expansion line from G and the EMV at G is then 2.9.

The total cash inflows from C are: 2.3 + 0.9 = 3.2 (high) and
2.9 + 0.8 = 3.7 (low)

At node C,   EMV   = $(3.2 \times 0.8) + (3.7 \times 0.2)$ =   3.3

At node A,   building big has a net EMV of 7.12 – 3.0   =   4.12
building small has a net EMV of 3.3 – 1.3   =   2.0

Hence, it is better to build big, so a barrier is put across the build small line and the EMV of the optimum policy of building big is inserted in the square.

Diagram 2

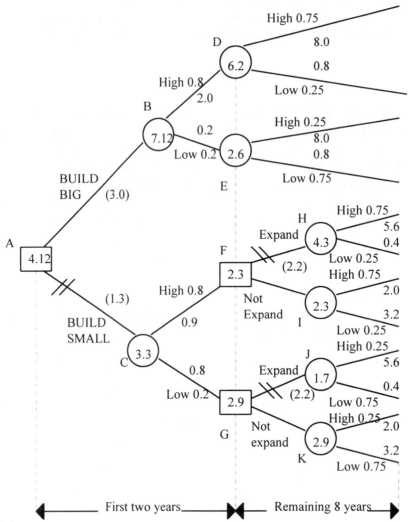

(Tutorial notes:

(1)   For the purpose of clarity, cash flows and probabilities have been inserted in a separate diagram (diagram 2). In practice, only one diagram is used and all data and results are inserted on the one tree.

(2)   Do *not* eliminate branches from a probability node. The decision-maker has no control over which of these branches will be taken and all outcomes must therefore be considered.

(3)   When stating the optimum policy, the route to be taken at each decision node must be specified. For example, if building small had been the best initial policy, the decision whether or not to expand at F and G should also have been stated.

(4)   No account has been taken in this example of the timing of cash flows ie, discounting has not taken place. This was omitted deliberately to keep the example simple. In practice, however, cash flows must not be added or subtracted unless they have been discounted to the same point in time. The simplest method of doing this is to discount all cash flows to their present values.

However, it should be borne in mind that decisions are often based on the cash flow occurring at the time when the decision is made. If, for example, an investor is considering aborting an investment after one year if it yields less than a specified amount of £x in the first year, then his decision would depend on the value of the cash flow at the end of the first year, not on its present value. In such cases, cash flows should be discounted to the point in time when the decision is to be made.*)*

2   SENSITIVITY ANALYSIS

2.1   Introduction

It is possible to assess how sensitive a decision is to changes in the various probabilities that have been used. If probabilities have been estimated, they may not be entirely accurate and it is important to check what the decision would have been if the probabilities had been different. If only a very slight change in the probability of one of the outcomes causes a different decision to be made, the situation is very sensitive, but where it requires a very large change in probability to alter the decision made, then the decision-maker can feel far more confident that he has made the correct choice.

2.2   Example

Using the data of the decision tree example above, the manager has doubts as to the probability forecasts and on closer questioning of the marketing director he ascertains that:

(a)   If demand in the first two years is low, there is very little chance at all of the product catching on. Thus, a more accurate probability of 'high demand in the last eight years given low demand in the first two years' is zero.

(b)   If demand is high in the first two years, there is almost as much chance of customers disliking as liking the product. He therefore estimates the following probabilities:

P (High last eight years/first two years high)   =   0.55

P (Low last eight years/first two years high)   =   0.45

(c)   The probability of high demand in the first two years may have been optimistic and a more cautious estimate would be 0.7.

You are required:

(a)   to state what the manager's decision will be if these new probabilities are used.

(b)   to discuss whether the original decision is sensitive.

2.3   Solution

The optimal decision is ascertained under these conditions by the means just explained.

Diagram 3

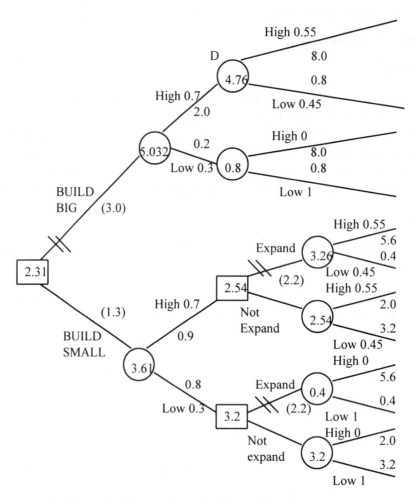

(a)   The manager's decision should now be to build small and not to expand even if initial demand is high, since this policy has a net expected value of (3.61 − 1.3) = 2.31 (£m) compared with (5.032 − 3.0) = 2.032 (£m).

(b)   The original decision is at least a little sensitive to a change in the various probabilities. By varying each probability in turn and continuing to vary it until the decision alters, the *degree* of sensitivity can be ascertained for each unknown outcome.

(It is advisable to check the extremes of probability at first to ascertain whether a decision is at all sensitive.)

3   MARKET SURVEYS

3.1   Introduction

Before a decision can be made to launch a new product, there must be some grounds for believing that there will be sufficient demand for the product, usually based on subjective probability. A more accurate assessment of demand may be obtainable by carrying out a market survey. This introduces a further decision as to whether such a survey is worthwhile, which depends on the reliability of the result from the survey as well as its cost.

3.2   Example

The probabilities of a good and bad market for a new product are initially assessed at 0.6 and 0.4 respectively. A survey can be carried out to improve the accuracy of these probability estimates. In previous launches of other products, when the market was good, market surveys had predicted that it would be good in eight cases out of every ten, and when the market was poor, surveys had predicted a poor market in seven cases out of every ten. The net present value of the yield will be £5m if the market is good, and –£3m (ie, a loss of £3m) if the market is poor. Should market research be undertaken, and if so, what is the maximum that should be paid for it?

3.3   Solution

Decision tree

Symbols used:

MS	=	Carry out market survey
MSIG	=	Market survey indicates a good market
MSIB	=	Market survey indicates a bad market
G	=	Market is good
B	=	Market is bad
L	=	Launch product
NL	=	Do not launch product

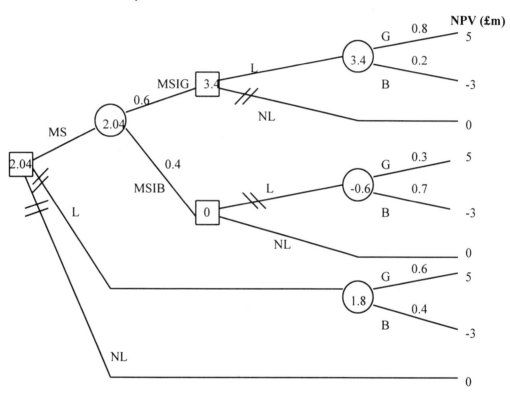

Tutorial note: the third branch (NL or Do Nothing) should always be included in decision trees as if the other branches prove to have negative EMVs, this would be the preferred option.

3.4   Calculation of probabilities

The branches from the top right-hand probability node represent the events 'Good market' and 'Bad market' respectively, given that the market survey indicated a good market; the probabilities are therefore P(G | MSIG) and P(B | MSIG) respectively.

The probabilities given in the question, however, are the probabilities of a given survey result conditional on a given state of the market ie, P(MSIG | G) and P (MSIB | B).

From Bayes' formula:

$$P(G \mid MSIG) \quad = \quad \frac{P(MSIG \mid G)\, P\,(G)}{P(MSIG \mid G)\, P\,(G) \; + \; P(MSIG \mid B)\, P\,(B)}$$

The given probabilities are:

P(G)	=	0.6	(initial assessment)
P(B)	=	0.4	(initial assessment)

$$P(MSIG \mid G) \quad = \quad \frac{8}{10} \qquad \text{(eight out of ten indicated good when market was good)}$$

$$= \quad 0.8$$

$$P(MSIB \mid G) \quad = \quad 1 - 0.8$$

$$= \quad 0.2$$

$$P(MSIB \mid B) \quad = \quad \frac{7}{10} \qquad \text{(seven out of ten indicated bad when market}$$

$$\text{was bad)}$$

$$= \quad 0.7$$

$$P(MSIG \mid B) \quad = \quad 1 - 0.7$$

$$= \quad 0.3$$

Substituting in the above formula:

$$P(G \mid MSIG) \quad = \quad \frac{0.8 \times 0.6}{(0.8 \times 0.6) + (0.3 \times 0.4)} = 0.8$$

$$P(B \mid MSIG) \quad = \quad 1 - 0.8$$

$$= \quad 0.2$$

Using the corresponding formula for P(G | MSIB):

$$P(G \mid MSIB) \quad = \quad \frac{P(MSIB \mid G)\, P(G)}{P(MSIB \mid G)\, P(G) \, + \, P(MSIB \mid B)\, P\,(B)}$$

$$= \quad \frac{0.2 \times 0.6}{(0.2 \times 0.6) + (0.7 \times 0.4)} = 0.3$$

$$P(B \mid MSIB) \quad = \quad 1 - 0.3$$

$$= \quad 0.7$$

From the probability relationship that $P(X) = P(X \mid A)\, P(A) + P(X \mid B)\, P(B) + ...$

P(MSIG)	=	P(MSIG | G) P(G) + P(MSIG | B) P(B)
	=	$(0.8 \times 0.6) + (0.3 \times 0.4) = 0.6$
P(MSIB)	=	1 – P (MSIG)
	=	1 – 0.6
	=	0.4

The probabilities are now inserted in the tree, and the tree evaluated by the *roll-back* method.

The optimum strategy without taking into account the cost of the survey is to carry out the survey and if it indicates a good market, launch the product, but if it indicates a poor market, do not launch. This strategy has an EMV of £2.04m.

---

4 EXPECTED VALUE OF INFORMATION (EVI)

4.1 Introduction

Definition This is defined as:

EVI = EMV of best strategy when the information is possessed *minus* EMV of best strategy when the information is not possessed.

Thus in the above example:

If the survey is not carried out, the best strategy would be to launch without survey, which has an EMV of £1.8m.

The expected value of the information from the survey is therefore:

EVI = £(2.04 – 1.8)m
= £0.24m

cost of the survey.

This is the maximum that management should be prepared to pay for the information from the survey.

4.2 Past exam question

This topic was examined in June 1994. The requirements included the quantification of the value of perfect information in a specific context, as illustrated below, and a discussion of the steps involved in the evaluation of the purchase of imperfect information, as illustrated by the above market survey example.

Both employ the same basic principle (as per the definition above); imperfect information situations may require more involved conditional probability calculations before being able to reach the required expected values.

4.3 Example - optimisation of stock levels

This is a problem that occurs in stock control when dealing with goods that are perishable or rapidly become obsolete. One example is the decision of the newspaper seller as to how many newspapers should be stocked at the start of each day. Too few will result in stock-out with lost sales and goodwill, while too many will result in surplus stock that becomes valueless once the day is out.

A confectioner has the following daily demand for cakes:

Demand (number of cakes)	Probability
100	0.1
200	0.2
300	0.3
400	0.3
500	0.1
	1.0

Each cake costs £0.10 to make and sells for £0.20. Any left over at the end of the day are sold off cheaply for £0.05 each.

(a) What is the optimum number of cakes to produce each day?

(b) How much would advance information as to the demand be worth? (This could be achieved, perhaps, by instituting a daily telephone survey among customers).

4.4   Solution

(a)   The pay-off matrix is (£):

Market state / Strategy		Demand per day				
		100	*200*	*300*	*400*	*500*
	100	10	10	10	10	10
	200	5	20	20	20	20
Production per day	300	0	15	30	30	30
	400	(5)	10	25	40	40
	500	(10)	5	20	35	50

Calculations

Taking production of 400 as an example:

Demand	*100*	*200*	*300*	*400*	*500*
Revenue @ £0.20	£20	£40	£60	£80	£80*
Surplus cakes	300	200	100	0	0
Revenue from surplus @ £0.05	£15	£10	£5	0	0
Total revenue	£35	£50	£65	£80	£80
Less: Production cost @ £0.10	£40	£40	£40	£40	£40
Net gain (£)	(5)	10	25	40	40

* If only 400 are produced, only 400 can be sold.

To find the expected value of each strategy, multiply each outcome by its probability.

Strategy	EMV (£)
100	$(10 \times 0.1) + (10 \times 0.2) + (10 \times 0.3) + (10 \times 0.3) + (10 \times 0.1) = 10.0$
200	$(5 \times 0.1) + (20 \times 0.2) + (20 \times 0.3) + (20 \times 0.3) + (20 \times 0.1) = 18.5$
300	$(0 \times 0.1) + (15 \times 0.2) + (30 \times 0.3) + (30 \times 0.3) + (30 \times 0.1) = 24.0$
400	$(-5 \times 0.1) + (10 \times 0.2) + (25 \times 0.3) + (40 \times 0.3) + (40 \times 0.1) = 25.0$
500	$(-10 \times 0.1) + (5 \times 0.2) + (20 \times 0.3) + (35 \times 0.3) + (50 \times 0.1) = 21.5$

The optimum strategy is to produce 400 per day as this has the highest EMV of £25.

*(**Tutorial notes:** students with a knowledge of matrices will recognise this as a matrix multiplication thus:*

$$\begin{bmatrix} 10 & 10 & 10 & 10 & 10 \\ 5 & 20 & 20 & 20 & 20 \\ 0 & 15 & 30 & 30 & 30 \\ -5 & 10 & 25 & 40 & 40 \\ -10 & 5 & 20 & 35 & 50 \end{bmatrix} \times \begin{bmatrix} 0.1 \\ 0.2 \\ 0.3 \\ 0.3 \\ 0.1 \end{bmatrix} = \begin{bmatrix} 10.0 \\ 18.5 \\ 24.0 \\ 25.0 \\ 21.5 \end{bmatrix})$$

(b)   With advance knowledge of the demand each day, the best strategy would be to make just sufficient to meet that demand.

Hence

Demand	Number produced	Pay-off*	Prob.	Expectation = Pay-off × Prob.
100	100	10	0.1	1.0
200	200	20	0.2	4.0
300	300	30	0.3	9.0
400	400	40	0.3	12.0
500	500	50	0.1	5.0
				31.0

* Obtained as the maximum value of each row of the pay-off table.

The expected value of this strategy is £31.0, and the expected value of the best strategy without the information is £25.0.

Hence, the expected value of the information is   £(31.0 – 25.0)

=   £6 per day

Thus, a daily survey amongst customers would only be worthwhile if it cost no more than £6 per day.

5   CHAPTER SUMMARY

Pay-off tables and decision trees are very useful tools for analysing decision problems, as they readily incorporate the laws of probability, making their application relatively easy. Any difficulties with probabilities on a decision tree are best dealt with by initially determining the joint probability table. From the table any decision tree probability can be obtained.

6   SELF TEST QUESTIONS

6.1   Do the probabilities on a decision tree occur after a decision node or after an event node? (1.2)

6.2   What is sensitivity analysis? (2)

6.3   What is the expected value of information? (4.1)

7   EXAMINATION TYPE QUESTION

7.1   Test marketing

A company has the opportunity of marketing a new package of computer games. It has two possible courses of action: to test market on a limited scale or to give up the project completely. A test market would cost £160,000 and current evidence suggests that consumer reaction is equally likely to be 'positive' or 'negative'. If the reaction to the test marketing were to be 'positive' the company could either market the computer games nationally or still give up the project completely. Research suggests that a national launch might result in the following sales:

Sales	Contribution £m	Probability
High	1.20	0.25
Average	0.30	0.50
Low	–0.24	0.25

If the test marketing were to yield 'negative' results the company would give up the project. Giving up the project at any point would result in a contribution of £60,000 from the sale of copyright etc to another manufacturer. All contributions have been discounted to present values.

You are required

(a)   to draw a decision tree to represent this situation, including all relevant probabilities and financial values;   **(8 marks)**

(b)   to recommend a course of action for the company on the basis of expected values;   **(8 marks)**

(c)   to explain any limitations of this method of analysis.   **(4 marks)**
                                                                                  (Total: 20 marks)

8   ANSWER TO EXAMINATION TYPE QUESTION

8.1   Test marketing

(a)

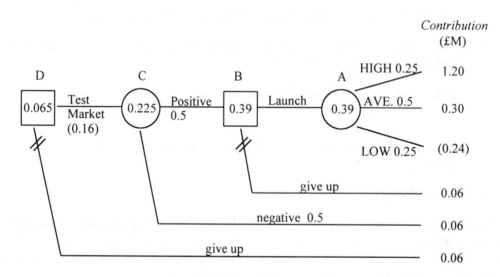

Notes:

(i)   The values by the events and the double bars should be ignored at this stage as they belong to the answer to part (b).

(ii)   Monetary amounts have been shown 'gross' and the cost inserted at that point in the tree where it becomes payable.

(b)   The tree is evaluated as follows, in £m

At A,   EMV = $(0.25 \times 1.2) + (0.5 \times 0.3) - (0.25 \times 0.24)$

                    =   0.39

At B,   EMV for 'launch'   =   0.39
               EMV for 'give up'   =   0.06
               ∴ choose 'launch' and insert its EMV by the decision point and block off the other branch.

At C   EMV = $(0.5 \times 0.39) + (0.5 \times 0.06)$

                    =   0.225

At D,   EMV of 'test market'   =   0.225 – 0.16

                                      =   0.065

               EMV of 'give up'   =   0.06
               ∴ choose 'test market' and block off the other branch.

The optimum strategy is to test the market and if it proves positive, to carry out the national launch. The net EMV of this policy is £0.065m or £65,000.

Notes:

(i)   In the evaluation, do **not** eliminate probability branches as the decision maker has no control over which branch is taken.

(ii)   The optimum strategy must state which branch is to be taken at **each** decision point.

(c)   Possible limitations of the method are:

(i)   There is difficulty in estimating the relevant cash flows and their probabilities.

(ii)   In practice there are likely to be a whole range of possible outcomes at each stage, rather than the two or three shown in this example.

(iii)   The EMV may not be the best criterion. A possible reason for this is that being an average, the EMV assumes that losses are permissible as well as gains, provided they have a relatively low probability. In practice, management may not be prepared to gamble on making a loss which might ruin the firm.

15 PRICING POLICY

INTRODUCTION & LEARNING OBJECTIVES

When you have studied this chapter you should be able to do the following:

- Explain the effects of market situations on pricing policy.
- Explain price elasticity of demand and use it to determine an optimum price/output level.
- Explain and comment on the use of cost based pricing policies.

1 MARKET SITUATIONS AND PRICING

1.1 Factors in pricing decisions

Several factors underlie all pricing decisions and effective decisions will be based on a careful consideration of the following:

(a) **Organisational goals**. If a goal of cash maximisation is assumed, then the setting of selling prices must be seen as a means of achieving this end.

(b) **Product mix**. If the organisation produces a range of different products, it is faced with the problem of setting selling prices for each individual product in such a manner as to obtain the optimum product mix ie, that mix which will maximise cash inflows generated from the sale of all products.

(c) **Price/demand relationships** (demand curves). For most products, there exists a relationship between selling price and the quantity demanded at that price. Customers will usually have an alternative source of supply and will be driven away by a selling price that is set too high, or, for instance in the case of certain luxury goods such as perfumes, jewellery and wines, by a selling price that is set too low. Product quality will also tend to influence the price and demand relationship.

A knowledge of the price elasticity of demand (ie, the responsiveness of changes in demand to changes in price) is therefore vital in the selling price decision.

(d) **Competitors and markets**. An organisation's competitors will usually react in some way to changes made to the selling price structure. In practice, therefore, price adjustments may be heavily influenced by expectations of competitor reaction.

(e) **Product life cycle**. During the life of an individual product, several stages are apparent: introduction, growth, maturity, saturation and decline. The duration of each stage of the life cycle varies according to the type of product, but the concept is nevertheless important as each stage is likely to influence the firm's pricing policy. The sales pricing mechanism is sometimes used to 'control' the life cycle of a product.

(f) **Marketing strategy**. Selling prices should be set with reference to overall marketing strategy. Product design and quality, advertising and promotion, distribution methods etc, are likely to influence the sales pricing decision. For example, by concentrating on advertising or packaging, a firm may be able to set higher prices for its product or, conversely, lower prices might be necessary in order to distribute the product through a supermarket chain.

(g) **Cost**. In the long run, all operating costs must be fully covered by sales revenue. However, as will be seen later, over-emphasis on cost in the short-run may result in sub-optimal decisions.

2 DEMAND AND ITS DETERMINANTS

2.1 Introduction

[Definition] Demand is the quantity of a good which consumers want, and are willing and able to pay for.

If you think about how you decide which goods to buy, you will realise that there are many factors entering into the decision.

2.2 Group demand

It is sometimes argued that the choices made by people are too unpredictable to form the basis of any realistic measurement of demand. This may be true of the actions of individuals, but it is a remarkable fact that if a sufficiently large group is examined, there is a sufficient degree of constancy for measurements and predictions to be made with a reasonable degree of accuracy. For example, you may be offered a choice of several breakfast cereals each morning and it would be difficult to predict which particular one to choose on any specific day. However, when a thousand people are observed over a period of time it may be possible to predict that, on average, a quarter will choose one brand, a fifth another and so on. If information of this type is available you can then estimate the size of weekly or monthly demand for the various types of breakfast cereal. In the same way, you can estimate the number of heart attacks likely to be suffered by people living in an area during a year, or the likely number of young people taking A-level examinations who will pass and qualify for higher education. This consistency of large numbers over a given period of time allows sufficient information to be gathered to provide the foundation for the study of economics.

People, of course, change and demand changes. The main influences bringing about changes in the demand for goods and services can be classified as follows:

2.3 Price

This is probably the most significant factor. For each of the goods, the higher the price, the less likely people are to buy it. Price is one of the most important elements of micro-economics and it will be discussed in considerable detail in the following sections.

2.4 Income

In general, the more people earn, the more they will buy. If someone is quite well-off, they are more likely to buy a certain pair of shoes (*ceteris paribus*), whereas if they are poor, they will not. Note the use of *ceteris paribus* here. We must say that 'all other things being equal' they will buy the shoes. An example of all other things **not** being equal would be if the weather suddenly changes; if it starts snowing heavily and they are wearing sandals, they may buy the shoes irrespective of how rich or poor they are.

The demand for most goods increases as income rises, and these goods are known as normal goods.

Do note, however, that people will not necessarily buy more of **all** goods as their incomes rise. Some goods are known as inferior goods, such as black and white televisions. They are cheap goods which people might buy when on a low income, but as their incomes rise, they switch to more attractive alternatives (in this case, colour televisions).

[Conclusion] For normal goods, demand rises as consumers' income rises, and vice versa. For inferior goods, demand **falls** as income rises, and vice versa.

2.5   The price of substitute goods

Definition   Two or more goods are defined as substitutes if they are interchangeable in giving consumers utility. Substitution is a matter of degree ie, all goods are substitutes, but some are closer than others.

For example, margarine is a substitute for butter. Other goods, such as milk, have few, if any, substitutes. If something has a substitute, you will probably compare the price of the substitute with the price of the good you are thinking of buying. Butter is more expensive than margarine, so, apart from the health considerations, you may decide to buy margarine. On the other hand, milk has very few substitutes, so your decision to buy it will not depend heavily on the price of other products.

If the price of a substitute rises, then demand for the good in question will also rise.

Suppose the price of margarine rose. Even if it is still cheaper than butter, some people will decide that the difference in price is so small that they would rather buy butter. Demand for margarine will fall, while that for butter will rise.

Conversely, if the price of a substitute falls, then demand for the good in question will also fall, as people switch to the substitute.

Conclusion   If good A and good B are **substitutes**, a **rise** in the price of one will cause a **rise** in demand for the other, and vice versa.

2.6   The price of complements

Definition   Complements are goods which must be used together.

For example, a compact disc player is no good without any compact discs. The price of a good's complements is very important when considering whether or not to buy it. You may be able to afford the player, but if you will not be able to buy any compact discs, there is little point in the purchase. A common marketing ploy is to price a product fairly low, but to set the prices of its complements very high; the low price attracts the customers, who are not aware of the amount they will ultimately have to pay to use the product.

If the price of a **complement** rises, then demand for the good in question will **fall**.

Suppose the price of compact discs rose. Fewer people would be able to afford them, so fewer people would find it worth their while to buy the compact disc players. Demand for the compact discs will fall, as will demand for the players.

Conversely, if the price of a complement falls, demand for the good will rise.

Conclusion   If good A and good B are **complements**, a **rise** in the price of one will cause a **fall** in demand for the other, and vice versa.

2.7   Taste

This is an all-embracing term. Taste is influenced by many different things. Advertising may make something popular or unpopular. You may decide not to buy butter purely on health grounds, having been made aware of its high cholesterol levels. Or fashion may induce you to buy a new pair of shoes even if you don't really need them and cannot afford them. The weather is a major factor. People will buy more umbrellas when it is raining and more ice creams when it is hot.

Of all the factors influencing demand, taste is the most difficult one to quantify.

2.8   Market size

Clearly, the size of total demand depends on the number of people who are aware of the good's existence, who are able to obtain it and who are likely to want it. Market size can, therefore, be altered by changes in the size and structures of the population. If the birth rate falls in an area, this will have a long-term effect on the total population size and will have a more immediate effect in reducing the number of babies hence influencing the demand for prams, equipment and clothing designed for babies. It will, of course, also affect the demand for school places, for schoolteachers and for people to train teachers.

2.9   Advertising

This may be regarded as a subsidiary influence affecting market size, but it can also be seen as a factor important in itself. In general, it is not only the volume and quality of advertising that can influence demand for a product but also the amount of advertising in comparison with that for competing products. Advertisers cannot often increase total consumption; more often they transfer it from one good to another. Some research indicates that there may be a direct relationship between the proportion of advertising carried out for a product within a market and the proportion of total market sales going to that product.

3   CALCULATING PRICE ELASTICITY OF DEMAND

3.1   The formulae for price elasticity of demand

> **Definition**   **Price elasticity of demand** is the degree of sensitivity of demand for a good to changes in price of that good.

We have already discussed the different influences on demand; one of the most important was price. It is useful to be able to analyse in numerical terms the effect on demand of a change in price. We do this using price elasticity of demand (often shortened to 'elasticity of demand' or PED).

Price elasticity can be defined in a number of ways. One possible formula is:

$$PED = \frac{\text{Percentage change in quantity demanded}}{\text{Percentage change in price}}$$

3.2   Activity

If PED for a certain good currently equals -2, how will sales be affected if price rises by 10%?

3.3   Activity solution

Use the formula, PED = (percentage change in quantity demanded) / (percentage change in price).

Here, -2 = (percentage change in quantity demanded) / +10%

So -2 × 10% = -20% = percentage change in quantity demanded.

In other words, quantity will **fall** by 20%. Note the minus sign, which is important. The PED given in the question was negative and this fed through to give a negative change in quantity demanded; in other words, a **fall.** This accords with all the previous work: price rose, so demand fell.

3.4   An alternative formula

An alternative presentation of the formula is suitable for calculations involving a straight-line demand curve, and is illustrated below:

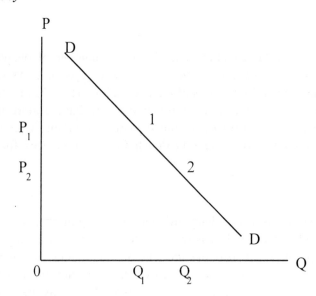

$$PED = \frac{\dfrac{(Q_2 - Q_1)}{Q_1} \times 100}{\dfrac{(P_2 - P_1)}{P_1} \times 100}$$

This equation calculates the elasticity at point 1 on the demand curve. The changes in quantity and price are expressed as a percentage of the quantity and price at point 1.

We will use an example to demonstrate how the equation works and how it relates to the first equation.

3.5 Example

A firm faces the following demand curve:

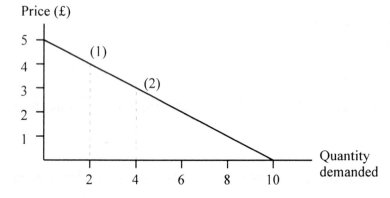

Figure 1

We want to work out the price elasticity of demand at point 1. The first step is to select any other point on the line to act as a reference point, point 2. Here we have chosen a point one step down the line from point 1, but on a straight-line demand curve any other point would give the same result.

The price and quantity at point 1 are P_1 and Q_1 respectively. So $P_1 = 4$ and $Q_1 = 2$. Similarly, price and quantity at point 2 are P_2 and Q_2 respectively. So $P_2 = 3$ and $Q_2 = 4$.

Applying the equation above:

$$PED = \frac{\dfrac{(4 - 2)}{2} \times 100}{\dfrac{(3 - 4)}{4} \times 100}$$

$$= \quad \frac{\frac{2}{2} \times 100}{\frac{-1}{4} \times 100} = \frac{100}{-25} = -4.$$

So price elasticity of demand at point 1 is -4.

We can relate this to the formula which was given in terms of percentages. Consider quantity first. The move from point 1 to point 2 on the demand curve represents an increase in quantity of 2 units, from 2 to 4. In fact, quantity has gone up by 100%. This is reflected in the above calculation by the fraction $\frac{2}{2} = 1$ or 100%.

Moving on to the price, a similar reasoning applies. The move from point 1 to point 2 represents a **decrease** in price of £1, from £4 to £3. Price has fallen by 25%. This is reflected by the fraction $\frac{-1}{4} = -25\%$.

Again, note the minus sign, which is there because price has **fallen**. Quantity demanded **rose**, so its change is **positive**. When we bring the two together in the fraction, the result is a negative number. The same would happen if price rose, giving a positive change, but quantity demanded fell, giving a negative change. Since for most goods price and quantity demanded move in opposite directions, most goods will have a negative price elasticity of demand.

So the second equation is simply a different form of the first equation. They are both measuring the response of quantity demanded to a price change; and they both measure the changes in the variables in terms of percentages.

3.6   Activity

Explain in layman's terms what a price elasticity of –4 means.

3.7   Activity solution

Return to the previous activity if you are unsure. There, an elasticity of -2 meant that when price rose by 10%, demand fell by 20% ie, by twice as much as the price rise. So an elasticity of -4 means that if price changes by a certain percentage, quantity demanded will change by four times as much. The minus sign indicates that if price goes up (has a positive change) quantity will fall (have a negative change), and vice versa. For example, if price rises by 10%, quantity demanded will fall by 40%.

3.8   Notes on PED

(a)   As mentioned above, PED for most goods is negative, so we often ignore the minus sign when talking about PED. For example, we could say that the price elasticity of demand at point 1 is 4, when strictly speaking it is -4.

(b)   PED is different at different points of a demand curve, even if that 'curve' is a straight line. The next section will go into this more deeply.

3.9   The meaning of elasticity and inelasticity

It is important to understand what 'elastic' and 'inelastic' mean, rather than simply assign numbers to price elasticity.

If you return to the formulae, you should be able to see that when PED is greater than 1, a certain (percentage) change in price will give rise to a **greater** (percentage) change in quantity demanded. For example, the first activity in this chapter showed that a PED of 2 means that a 10% rise in price will induce a 20% fall in quantity demanded. In other words, demand is very responsive to price changes.

Conversely, when PED is less than 1, a given percentage change in price will result in a **smaller** percentage change in demand, so demand is **not** responsive to price changes; and when PED equals 1, the percentage change in quantity demanded equals the percentage change in price.

> **Conclusion**   When PED>1, demand is relatively elastic and the quantity demanded is very responsive to price changes; when PED<1, demand is relatively inelastic and the quantity demanded is not very responsive to price changes.

Note that if demand is said to be inelastic, this does not mean that there will be no change in quantity demanded when the price changes, it means that the consequent demand change will be proportionately smaller than the price change. If demand does not change at all after a price change, demand is said to be perfectly inelastic, and this is a special case as will be seen below.

3.10   PED and revenue

When demand is elastic, total revenue rises as price falls. This is because the quantity demanded is very responsive to price changes. A fall in the price gives rise to a **more** than proportionate rise in the quantity demanded. The net effect is that revenue (= price × quantity) rises.

Conversely, when demand is inelastic, total revenue falls as price falls. Here a fall in price causes a **less** than proportionate rise in quantity demanded, the result being a net fall in total revenue.

Equally, when demand is elastic, total revenue falls when price rises; and when demand is inelastic, total revenue rises when price rises.

It would therefore be very useful to a producer to know whether he is at an elastic or inelastic part of his demand curve. This will enable him to predict the effect on revenue of raising or lowering his price.

4   PROFIT AND PROFIT MAXIMISATION

4.1   What is profit?

The simplest definition of **profit** is that it is the **difference between the total costs of an enterprise and the total revenue received by that enterprise.** If costs are greater than revenue, then there is a negative profit ie, a loss.

Consider the data in the table below.

Output units per week	Total revenues £	Total variable cost £	Fixed cost £	Total cost £	Marginal cost per 100 units £
100	1,000	600	1,000	1,600	
200	1,900	1,000	1,000	2,000	400
300	2,700	1,200	1,000	2,200	200
400	3,400	1,400	1,000	2,400	200
500	4,000	1,500	1,000	2,500	100
600	4,500	1,800	1,000	2,800	300
700	4,900	2,100	1,000	3,100	300
800	5,200	2,800	1,000	3,800	700
900	5,400	3,600	1,000	4,600	800
1,000	5,500	4,500	1,000	5,500	900
1,100	5,500	5,500	1,000	6,500	1,000

A graph can be drawn of costs and revenues:

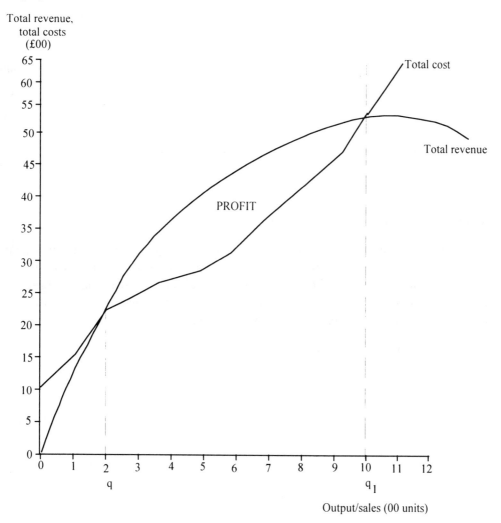

Notes:

(a)   The firm makes a loss on output levels below Oq (a little over 200 units per week).

(b)   It continues to make a profit at output levels above Oq until output reaches Oq_1 units per week (1,000 units).

(c)   Above output level Oq_1 the firm again makes a loss which rapidly increases as diminishing returns affect variable and marginal costs. This is the level where additional fixed costs and productive capacity are evidently needed.

The profit area can be indicated in another way by using average costs and revenue. Below is a table of average costs and revenues, and marginal costs and revenues based on the same set of figures.

Quantity per week units	Total cost £	Total revenue £	Average cost £	Average revenue £	Marginal cost £	Marginal revenue per 100 units £
100	1,600	1,000	16	10		
					4	900
200	2,000	1,900	10	9.50		
					2	800
300	2,200	2,700	7.3	9		
					2	700
400	2,400	3,400	6	8.50		
					1	600
500	2,500	4,000	5	8		
					3	500
600	2,800	4,500	4.7	7.50		
					3	400
700	3,100	4,900	4.43	7		
					7	300
800	3,800	5,200	4.75	6.50		
					8	200
900	4,600	5,400	5.1	6		
					9	100
1,000	5,500	5,500	5.5	5.50		
					10	0
1,100	6,500	5,500	5.9	5		

4.2   Profit maximising conditions

To find the best profit-making level from the above figure, the marginal revenue and marginal cost can be related. Now, assuming that the firm is operating in the area where marginal cost is rising and marginal revenue falling, then, if the firm finds that marginal cost is lower than marginal revenue it will pay it to increase output. To do so will bring in more revenue than it will pay in cost. This is because the change in revenue is more than the change in cost.

This relationship can be shown on a graph.

Cost/revenue (£)

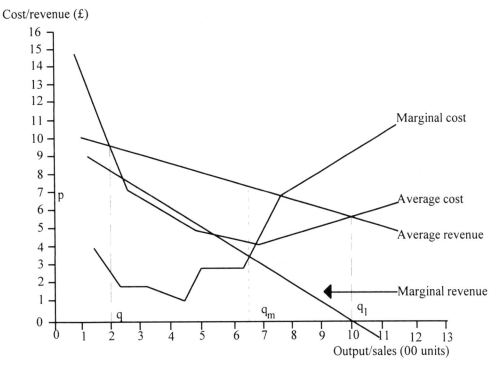

Here the marginal cost curve cuts the marginal revenue curve at an output level just below 700 units and a price (average revenue) just above £7. If fractions are avoided, it can be suggested that the profit maximising output is 700 units per week sold at a price of £7 per unit. In general terms, this is Oq_m units at a price of Op. To produce more would bring in less revenue than the additional cost; to produce less would lose more revenue than would be saved in cost.

This solution can be checked by referring back to the table of total cost and revenue. Adding a column to show total profit, being the difference between the total cost and total revenue, will reveal that, given the stages of the table, the highest profit figure (£1,800) appears at output level 700. The same answer is found by calculating total profit from the average figures. Given average revenue of £7 per unit and average cost per unit of £4.43 the profit per unit is £2.57 which, multiplied by the weekly output of 700, gives a weekly profit of roughly £1,800.

The best profit **(profit maximising)** output position is not altered if the firm faces a constant price for its goods at all possible ranges of output. Once again, the profit maximising output will be where marginal revenue is equal to the rising marginal cost.

5   APPLICATION OF DIFFERENTIATION - MAXIMISING PROFITS

5.1   Introduction

A typical problem concerns maximising profits when given functions for total revenue and total costs. There are two ways of doing this:

(a)   Equating marginal revenue and marginal cost; and

(b)   Maximising the function (total revenue - total cost)

Marginal cost can be defined as the gradient of the total cost curve and marginal revenue can be defined as the gradient of the total revenue curve when both are expressed in terms of the quantity of goods. Thus:

Marginal cost $= \dfrac{dC_T}{dq}$ where C_T is total cost of producing a quantity q.

Marginal revenue $= \dfrac{dR_T}{dq}$ where R_T is total revenue from selling a quantity q.

It is usually the case that where the quantity produced is the same as that sold (ie, there is no stock piling), then the maximum profit is obtained when marginal cost = marginal revenue.

5.2   Example

For one type of product it has been established that:

Total cost in £s	(C_T)	=	$120q + 5,000$	(£)
Total revenue in £s	(R_T)	=	$400q - 2q^2$	(£)

where q = quantity produced and sold.

Find the quantity that will maximise profit and the maximum profit.

5.3   Solution

(a)   Using marginal revenue = marginal cost.

   (i)   Find quantity that will maximise profit.

   Marginal cost $= \dfrac{dC_T}{dq} = 120$

   Marginal revenue $= \dfrac{dR_T}{dq} = 400 - 4q$

   For maximum profit, marginal cost = marginal revenue ie,

   $120 = 400 - 4q$

   $\therefore q = 70$

   (ii)   Find maximum profit

   Profit   = Revenue – cost

   $= (400q - 2q^2) - (120q + 5,000)$

   Substituting q   = 70,

   Maximum profit $= (400 \times 70 - 2 \times 70^2) - (120 \times 70 + 5,000)$

   $= (28,000 - 9,800) - (8,400 + 5,000)$

   $= £4,800$

(b)   Using: profit = total revenue – total cost

   Profit (π) $= (400q - 2q^2) \quad - \quad (120q + 5,000)$

   Differentiating $\dfrac{d\pi}{dq}$ $= 400 - 4q - 120$

   $= 280 - 4q$

   Find stationary points $280 - 4q = 0$

   $4q = 280$

   $q = 70$

This is as before and the profit can then be found in the same way.

5.4   Activity

Each week a company has fixed costs of £1,800 and variable costs of £$(100x + x^2)$, where x is the quantity of units of Brand Z made and sold. The company's weekly revenue equation is approximately £$(300x - x^2)$. The company has a maximum capacity of just less than 300 units per week and has a monopoly on Brand Z.

You are required to calculate the output level which will maximise profits and the value of profits at that level.

5.5   Activity solution

Method 1 - using the function

$$\text{Profit = total revenue - total cost}$$

Step 1   Determine the total revenue function.

$$\text{TR} = \text{P} \times \text{Q}$$

$$= £(300x - x^2) \qquad \text{given}$$

Step 2   Determine the total cost function.

$$\text{Total cost} = \text{Total fixed cost + Total variable cost}$$

$$= £1,800 + £(100x + x^2)$$

Step 3   Determine the profit function.

$$\Pi = \text{TR} - \text{TC}$$

$$= (300x - x^2) - (1,800 + 100x + x^2)$$

$$= 300x - x^2 - 1,800 - 100x - x^2$$

$$= 200x - 2x^2 - 1,800$$

Step 4   Differentiate the profit function with respect to x.

$$\Pi = 200x - 2x^2 - 1,800$$

$$\frac{d\Pi}{dx} = 200 - 4x$$

Maximum profit is attained when $200 - 4x = 0$ ie, when $x = 50$ units of output of Brand Z.

$$\left(\begin{array}{l} \text{Check to ensure a maximum:} \\[2mm] \frac{d^2\Pi}{dx^2} = -4 \quad \text{negative} \therefore \text{ a maximum point} \end{array} \right)$$

Step 5   Substitute the value of x calculated above into the profit function.

$$\text{When} \quad x = 50$$

$$\Pi = 200x - 2x^2 - 1,800$$

$$= 10,000 - 5,000 - 1,800$$

$$\text{Profit} = \textbf{£3,200}$$

Method 2 - using marginal cost = marginal revenue

Step 1 Establish the marginal cost function by differentiating the total cost function.

$$TC = \text{Total fixed cost} + \text{Total variable cost}$$

$$= 1{,}800 + 100x + x^2$$

$$\frac{dTC}{dx} = 100 + 2x$$

Step 2 Establish the marginal revenue function by differentiating the total revenue function.

$$TR = 300x - x^2$$

$$\frac{dTR}{dx} = 300 - 2x$$

Step 3 Equate the marginal revenue with marginal cost to find the profit maximising level of output.

$$300 - 2x = 100 + 2x$$

$$\Rightarrow \quad 4x = 200$$

$$\therefore \quad x = 50$$

Step 4 Substitute the value of x into the profit function. This obviously is the same as the previous step 5.

Thus the two methods give the same result and should be used according to what information is given in the question.

6   THE SALES MAXIMISATION MODEL

6.1   The revised objective

Perhaps the most widely quoted alternative theory of the firm is one based on the objective of revenue maximisation subject to a profit constraint. This idea was originally put forward by WJ Baumol (1958).

6.2   The rationale for the objective

The reasoning behind the sales objective is directly linked to the idea that managers see their own goals in relation to power and rewards more likely to be reflected in terms of sales than profit. However, because managers are never truly free of all constraints, the inclusion of a minimum profit requirement recognises the satisficing objective in relation to profit. The profit would be required in order to meet dividend expectations and maintain the market value of the company's shares.

6.3   The model

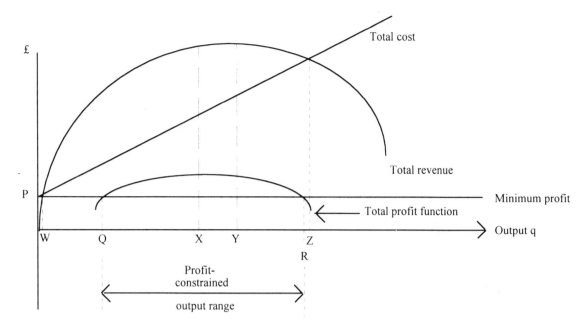

The diagram is based on the conventional curvilinear functions, and the total profit curve measures the distance between total revenue and total cost at all output levels. Profits are therefore maximised at output level X. No profits will be earned at output levels in excess of Z and less than W. Sales revenue is maximised where the total revenue curve is at its highest point ie, at output level Y.

Profits of P must be produced in order to satisfy shareholders' requirements. In order to meet this goal the output level must be greater than Q but less than R. The revenue maximising output level is therefore within the constraint region and the two objectives would be compatible. However the associated output level Y is greater than the profit-maximising output level, indicating that the unit price will have to be less than its optimal value in order to achieve the objective.

Example

Galbraith Ltd has estimated that its linear demand curve is $p = 2,000 - 0.02q$, where p is the price per unit and q is the demand and output level in units. The total cost function is budgeted at $300,000 + 400q$.

Managerial objectives are to maximise sales revenues subject to a minimum profit requirement of £30 million. You are required to compute the output range over which the profit objectives can be satisfied and to calculate total revenues and total profit if the sales maximisation objective is pursued. Also compute, for comparison purposes, the profit maximising output level, unit price and profit value.

Solution

(i)   The profit constraint is £30,000,000

Profit = Revenue – costs = $(2,000q - 0.02q^2) - (300,000 + 400q)$

Profit is equal to £30,000,000 when
$$[(2,000q - 0.02q^2) - (300,000 + 400q)] = 30,000,000$$

Rearranging
$$0.02q^2 - 1,600q + 30,300,000 = 0$$

Using the normal formula for the solution of a quadratic equation

$$q = \frac{-b \pm \sqrt{b^2 - 4ac}}{2a}$$

$$q = \frac{-(-1,600) \pm \sqrt{(-1,600)^2 - 4 \times 0.02 \times 30,300,000}}{2 \times 0.02}$$

$$= \frac{-(-1,600) \pm \sqrt{2,560,000 - 2,424,000}}{0.04}$$

$$\therefore \quad q = \frac{1,600 \pm 368.78}{0.04}$$

$$= 30,780 \text{ or } 49,219$$

(ii)   Total revenues will be maximised where MR = 0

If   p   =   2,000   –   0.02q

then   R   =   2,000q –   0.02q²

and   MR   =   2,000   –   0.04q

Therefore if MR =   0

   2,000 –   0.04q   =   0

                 q   =   50,000

This does not fall within the required range; therefore Galbraith should produce 49,219 units, selling them at £1,015.62 making a profit of £30,000,000.

(iii)   If the revenue maximising output level is 50,000 the price to be charged will be found from

           p   =   2,000   –   0.02q

                =   2,000   –   0.02 × 50,000

                =   £1,000

Revenue   =   £1,000 ×   50,000

                =   £50m

Costs   =   £300,000   +   50,000 × £400

                =   £20.3m

Profit   =   £29,700,000

confirming that the minimum profit of £30,000,000 would not be achieved.

(iv)   The maximum profit would be where MC = MR

Therefore: 400   =   2,000   –   0.04q

               q   =   40,000

and   p   =   2,000   –   0.02q

                      =   2,000   –   0.02 × 40,000

                      =   £1,200

and profit	=	Revenue – Costs
	=	$(40,000 \times £1,200) - [£300,000 + (40,000 \times £400)]$
	=	£48,000,000 – £16,300,000
	=	£31,700,000

6.4 The model and satisficing objects

This model is one within the category of 'satisficing' theories. In other words, once a satisfactory level of profits has been earned, the management are free to pursue alternative objectives. The major problem is the quantification of satisfactory profits. Baumol viewed it as a level of profits which would make the firm an attractive prospect to potential shareholders. However, this is a much vaguer goal than the precise profit maximising objective.

6.5 Maximisation of sales and maximisation of longer-term profits

As can be seen from the above diagram and calculations, the sales-revenue maximiser will charge a lower unit price in the short run than the profit maximiser. This could have implications for future profits.

(a) It may help to provide a barrier to entry and thus prevent new entrants into the market taking a share of the industry's profits.

(b) It will attract more consumers who may tend to remain loyal to the product despite future changes in pricing and advertising policy.

(c) It could provide a larger short-run base for the development of complementary products in the future.

Therefore, in the long run, a sales revenue maximisation policy could lead to a position which approximated to profit maximisation.

Sales maximisation and growth

In 1962 Baumol modified the theory in two ways

(a) maximising the rate of sales growth was substituted for the original objective

(b) the profit constraint is assumed not to be the result of external pressures, but reflects the 'means for obtaining capital needed to finance expansion'.

One implication might be that a growth-maximising firm would reach a higher level of investment than a profit maximiser and thus grow at a faster rate but sacrifice some of its market value.

7 COST PLUS PRICING

7.1 Introduction

Despite the theoretical superiority of the approach to pricing dealt with so far, it suffers from one major weakness. It is unlikely that perfect information of cost and revenue functions can be obtained; to get information of this nature is likely to be a costly and unreliable process, and therefore such calculations become virtually impossible. Commercial firms have to turn to other methods to determine selling prices. Whilst one might consider three main influences on the setting of a selling price, *costs, customers and competitors,* it is usually the first of these that represents the starting point for pricing decisions. A common method of pricing in practice is *'cost plus' pricing* and quite often prices are not calculated by reference to marginal costs, but rather *full absorption cost plus pricing* is adopted.

7.2 The principles behind full-cost plus pricing

The main principles which are used to explain its use are as follows

(a) The absorption of indirect costs over the firm's products will ensure that the indirect costs are all recouped in the sales of the products: this will be valid where all products can be sold at a price which covers their direct and absorbed costs and at the quantities assumed in the absorption base computations. This 'break-even' emphasis is consistent with risk aversion and satisficing objectives, rather than profit maximisation.

(b) The firm cannot afford to sell at less than full cost: the firm cannot survive in the long-term replacing its capital and incurring further amounts of fixed costs unless prices cover both variable and fixed elements. However, in the short term the contribution to be gained from selling at less than full cost may exceed that from a full cost policy, particularly where sales volumes are price sensitive eg, contribution from 1,000 units at 50p above direct variable cost will yield £500 which was unobtainable at the full cost price and is preferred to zero sales.

(c) The firm will be able to earn a reasonable rate of return: this is valid if the market will bear the price. It may be sensible pricing strategy to avoid new entrants to the market.

(d) The pricing system is simple and cheap to operate: whilst this is valid it is important to consider the loss of profit from failure to maximise contribution by recognising market factors.

(e) The system ensures that control is exercised over the firm's pricing so that no products are under or over priced: this is consistent with the needs of decentralised control in a large organisation, and standardisation as a mechanism for ensuring a satisfactory level of profit.

(f) Many contracts (particularly government) are full cost plus based.

The general structure

	£
Direct product/job cost	X
Absorption of overheads	
Variable overheads	X
Fixed production overheads	X
Non-production overheads	X
	—
Total cost	X
Profit margin (%)	X
	—
Selling price	X
	—

7.3 Example

Highwater Ltd has developed a new product, the grendle, and wishes to determine an appropriate selling price. Two possible levels of production/sales are being considered, 500 units and 800 units per month.

Each grendle requires 4 metres of material X at a basic price of £5 per metre; a bulk discount of 7.5% can be obtained for orders over 2,500 metres. Highwater will order each month's requirements at the beginning of the month.

The work is to be done in two departments:

Department A - employs skilled operators paid at £6.50 per hour. Each unit of output requires 4 direct labour hours in this department.

Department B - employs semi-skilled operators paid at £5 per hour. Each unit of output requires 1.5 hours in this department.

Overtime in each department is paid at time and a half. No premium for overtime is included in standard manufacturing overhead.

Standard manufacturing overhead per direct labour hour is as follows:

	Department A £	Department B £
Variable	2.50	3
Fixed	8	6

Fixed overhead absorption rates are based on budgeted labour capacities of 12,000 hours (dept A) and 8,000 hours (dept B). The departments are currently working at 80% and 60% capacities for Departments A and B respectively.There is no prospect of employing additional labour in the near future.

Current pricing practice of Highwater is to add the following margins on full costs in arriving at selling price:

Department A - 20%   Department B - 15%   Direct materials - 5%

Calculate the price per grendle under the normal pricing practices of Highwater

(i)   for each activity level, using the information above

(ii)   if the production was to be for a one-off order of 800 units only, and an 80% learning curve is expected to operate in department A. The first 100 units are expected to take a total of 650 hours.

(Note: if you don't feel confident on learning curves, wait until you have studied Chapter 18 before working through this part).

Solution

(i)

	Activity level	
	500 units £	800 units £
Direct material @ £20/unit	10,000	16,000
Less: Discount (7.5%)		(1,200)
	10,000	14,800
Add: Margin mark-up (5%)	500	740
	10,500	15,540

Conversion costs:

Department A (@£(6.50 + 2.50 + 8) = £17 per hr)

2,000 hours	34,000	
3,200 hours		54,400
Overtime pm (800 hrs (W) @ £3.25)		2,600
Add: Margin mark up (20%)	6,800	11,400

Department B (@£(5 + 3 + 6) = £14 per hr)

750 hours	10,500	
1,200 hours		16,800
Add: Margin mark up (15%)	1,575	2,520
	£63,375	£103,260
Price per grendle	£126.75	£129.08

WORKING

Dept A is currently working at 80% capacity = 80% × 12,000 = 9,600 hrs. Of the 3,200 hours required for the grendle, 2,400 will be worked within normal capacity and 800 hours in overtime.

(ii) The revised labour time in Department A is calculated using the learning curve percentage, and can be done using a formula or by tabulation. The latter is demonstrated here:

Tabulation

Cumulative production	Cumulative average time per unit	Cumulative total time	
100	6.50	650	(given in question)
200	× 0.8 = 5.20		
400	× 0.8 = 4.16		
800	× 0.8 = 3.328	2,662.4	say 2,662 hrs

The revised price per grendle is thus:

	£	£
Total price per (i)		103,260
Less: Basic Dept A cost savings (3,200 - 2,662) × £17	9,146	
Overtime savings (800 - 262) × £3.25	1,748.50	
	10,894.50 × 1.2	(13,073)
		90,187

Price per grendle = £112.73

7.4 Modification to cost plus price

The firm's master budget has a special role in cost plus pricing. This budget will be a primary source of absorption rates for overheads. Profit margin data from the master budget could take several forms

(a) target profit % of sales from master budget profit and loss account

(b) target return on capital employed taken from master budget and applied to the capital employed by the product.

Historical data based on the firm's previous experience in operating in various markets may provide an indication of the rate of return/mark-up which could be earned. An analysis of the profitability of other firms operating in a market into which the firm was about to enter would give an indication of the likely return to be earned.

7.5   Possible determinants of the 'plus element'

Market factors may affect the size of the 'plus element' and it would probably be more accurate to use the term 'modified cost plus' to describe the way in which cost plus pricing is used in practice. Although the 'plus element' is apparently derived from the cost base of the formula, the following are examples of situations which could influence the margins selected.

(a)   **The size of mark-up may be altered to take into account the stage of the product life**

The capacity of a product to withstand a large mark-up may need to be reviewed during the early introductory stages to enable it to become established and during its later stages as it attracts competition or enters a period of decline through obsolescence.

(b)   **The type of customer**

The size of the mark-up may be affected in situations where prices relate to individual customers. Examples would relate to the preparation of a quotation for a contract for an individual customer where the mark-up could depend more on knowledge of the competition and longer term considerations such as repeat orders.

(c)   **The reduction of unit profit mark-up for bulk customers**

This latter practice can be incorporated into a standard cost-plus procedure, whilst still retaining its apparent integrity, by the use of discounts whose purpose is to discriminate between different groups of purchasers with different capacities to pay.

(d)   **The nature of the market**

Differing mark-ups may be used for differing product groups or business segments to reflect differing degrees of competition facing different products or product groups. Thus, rather than using one target mark-up determined from a master budget, a variety of mark-up rates could be pre-determined and applied within the firm.

7.6   Limitations of full cost plus pricing

The general limitations of the full cost plus approach are as follows

(a)   The firm may either over-price or under-price its products in relation to the optimal price which maximises profit, if it fails to recognise formally the impact of price elasticity of demand in its pricing policy.

(b)   In both multi-product and single-product firms, the arbitrary nature of absorption costing can generate differing rates of overhead absorption according to the bases of cost allocation used between cost centres, and activity measures used for determining absorption rates. Levels of activity used in the absorption rates and profit mark-up are based on budgeted volumes of activity. However, the volume of activity may itself depend on product prices and the final price is thus indeterminable unless one presupposes a volume.

(c)   Absorption costing fails to distinguish between incremental fixed costs, relevant to pricing and output decisions, and committed fixed costs irrelevant to those decisions.

(d)   Being based on budgeted data, the cost information including the recovery rates may soon be out-of-date. Also, the use of fixed percentages in the formula gives an impression of accuracy which may mislead the decision marker. For many pricing situations the use of the full cost formula is too inflexible and too restrictive in its total cost recovery goal.

7.7 Marginal cost plus pricing

The principle behind marginal cost plus pricing is that the marginal cost can be clearly identified with the unit, thus justifying the price being charged.

However, marginal cost pricing must be considered either as a short-term or incremental pricing policy because it does not consider the impact of fixed costs (other than as part of the 'plus' factor).

7.8 Benefits and problems of marginal cost plus pricing

Marginal cost plus pricing is useful because, subject to a deliberate pricing policy, it shows the minimum price to be charged without incurring a loss. In some circumstances it may be necessary and advisable to sell at a price which is only a little above marginal cost, for example to enter a market or to make use of idle capacity. In these circumstances a price which yields a positive contribution is better than no sale.

The use of marginal cost plus pricing however, as a long-term policy may lead to a failure to recover fixed costs. Effectively fixed costs are part of the 'plus' factor but managers may view the 'plus' as being profit. If the fixed costs are high they will represent a significant proportion of the 'plus' and in the long run this cannot be ignored.

8 COST BASED PRICING AND PROFIT MAXIMISATION

Both full cost and marginal cost based pricing methods ignore the relationship between sales price and demand, however it is argued that marginal cost based pricing is more sensitive to demand than full cost based pricing.

The reason for this is that marginal costs can be traced to the unit and therefore must be related to its value and consequently its selling price. The inclusion of fixed costs on a per unit basis is arbitrary. It is based on budgeted expenditure and activity levels and a chosen basis of overhead absorption. This does not necessarily reflect the value of the resources used and therefore may have no relationship to the selling price/demand function.

9 CHAPTER SUMMARY

In this chapter the two basic techniques of pricing have been considered. Market based pricing uses supply and demand analysis whereas cost based pricing may use either full or marginal cost as its starting point.

10 SELF TEST QUESTIONS

10.1 Define price elasticity of demand and state its simple formula. (3.1)

10.2 Is price elasticity of demand usually positive or negative? (3.3)

10.3 If price elasticity of demand is –2 and price rises by 10%, by how much will quantity demanded fall? (3.3)

10.4 If demand for a product is relatively elastic and the price of that product rises, what will happen to the firm's total revenue? (3.10)

10.5 At what point of output will a firm maximise its profits? (4.2)

10.6 How far should a firm expand output? (4.2)

10.7 Distinguish between full cost and marginal cost plus pricing (7)

11   EXAMINATION TYPE QUESTIONS

11.1   Widgets

A manufacturing company producing widgets has weekly fixed costs of £900 and variable costs of £$(10x + x^2)$ where x is the quantity produced. The manufacturing company's capacity is about 70 units.

The demand function for this product is given by P = £$(120 - x)$ where £P = unit price and x = quantity sold.

You are required

(a)   to find the level of production at which **revenue** is maximised;   **(4 marks)**

(b)   to find any break-even points;   **(6 marks)**

(c)   to **sketch** a graph of revenue and profit for the range of values $0 < x < 70$;   **(4 marks)**

(d)   to recommend how many widgets the manufacturing company should produce, justifying your answer.   **(6 marks)**
                                                                                                                            (Total: 20 marks)

11.2   Nantderyn Products

(a)   Nantderyn Products has two main products, Exco and Wyeco, which have unit costs of £12 and £24 respectively. The company uses a mark-up of $33\frac{1}{3}$% in establishing its selling prices and the current prices are thus £16 and £32. With these prices, in the year which is just ending, the company expects to make a profit of £300,000 from having produced and sold 15,000 units of Exco and 30,000 units of Wyeco. This programme will have used all the available processing time in the finishing department. Each unit of Exco requires an hour of processing time in this department and every unit of Wyeco correspondingly requires half an hour.

Fixed overhead was £360,000 for the year and this has been charged to the products on the basis of the total processing hours used. All other costs may be assumed variable in relation to processing hours. In the current year it is estimated that £60,000 of the fixed overhead will be absorbed by Exco and £300,000 by Wyeco. With the existing selling prices it is considered that the potential annual demand for Exco is 20,000 units and that for Wyeco, 40,000 units.

You are required to comment critically on the product mix adopted by Nantderyn Products. Calculate what would have been the optimal plan given that there was no intention of changing the selling prices.   **(8 marks)**

(b)   For the forthcoming year increased capacity has been installed in the finishing department so that this will no longer be a constraint for any feasible sales programme. Annual fixed overhead will be increased to £400,000 as a consequence of this expansion of facilities, but variable costs per unit are unchanged.

A study commissioned by the sales director estimates the effect that alterations to the selling prices would have on the sales that could be achieved. The following table has been prepared:

	Exco		*Wyeco*	
Price	£13.50	£18.50	£29.00	£35.00
Demand	30,000	10,000	60,000	20,000

It is thought reasonable to assume that the price/demand relationship is linear.

Assuming that the company is now willing to abandon its cost plus pricing practices, if these can be shown to be deficient, **you are required** to calculate the optimal selling price for each product and the optimal output levels for these prices. State clearly any assumptions that you find it necessary to make.   **(8 marks)**

(c)   'The paradox is that, while cost plus pricing is devoid of any theoretical justification, it is widely used in practice.'

Discuss possible justifications for this use.   **(6 marks)**

(Total: 22 marks)

12   ANSWERS TO EXAMINATION TYPE QUESTIONS

12.1   Widgets

(a)   Revenue   =   price × quantity

= $(120 - x)x = 120x - x^2$

Differentiating with respect to x:

$$\frac{dR}{dx} = 120 - 2x = 0 \text{ at a turning point}$$

$$\therefore 120 = 2x$$

$$x = \frac{120}{2} = 60 \text{ widgets}$$

To check it's a maximum

$$\frac{d^2R}{dx^2} = -2 \text{ negative} \therefore \text{ maximum}$$

Revenue will be maximised when 60 widgets are sold.

(b)   The company will break-even when:

revenue = costs

ie, profit = 0

Profit   =   revenue - costs

P = $120x - x^2 - (10x + x^2 + 900)$

P = $-2x^2 + 110x - 900 = 0$ at break-even points

This is a quadratic with:

$$a = -2, \ b = 110, \ c = -900$$

$$x = \frac{-b \pm \sqrt{b^2 - 4ac}}{2a}$$

$$= \frac{-110 \pm \sqrt{110^2 - 4(-2)(-900)}}{2(-2)}$$

$$= \frac{-110 \pm \sqrt{4,900}}{-4} = \frac{-110 \pm 70}{-4}$$

$$\therefore x = \textbf{10 or 45}$$

(c)   **Graph showing profit (*P*) and revenue (*R*) functions: 0 < *x* < 70**

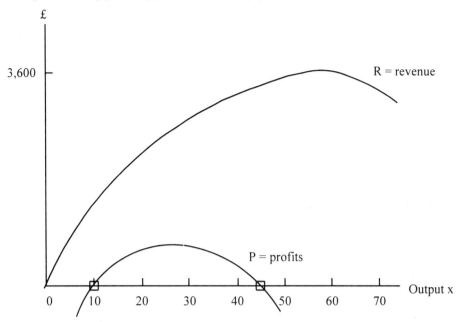

$R = 120x - x^2$. This passes through (0, 0)

and has a maximum at (60, £3,600)

$P = -2x^2 + 110x - 900$. This equals 0 when $x = 10$ and 45

(d)   To find the profit maximisation point:

$$\frac{dP}{dx} = -4x + 110 = 0$$

$$\therefore \quad 4x = 110$$

$$x = \frac{110}{4} = 27.5 \text{ widgets}$$

$$\frac{d^2P}{dx^2} = -4 \text{ negative} \therefore \text{ maximum}$$

Profit at this point $= -2(27.5)^2 + 110(27.5) - 900$
                          $= £612.50$

The manufacturing company would be advised to produce 28 widgets a week, as this production level maximises profits.

12.2   Nantderyn Products

(Tutorial notes:

(1)   Overall it is not difficult to achieve more than half marks on this question.

(2)   Part (a) is a straightforward 'limiting factor' question with no special problems.

(3)   Part (b) is not difficult if and only if you appreciate the need for differential calculus and the matching of marginal revenues and marginal costs.

(4)   Part (c) is quite easy, but you should ensure that you give a full answer.)

(a)   **Cost-plus pricing**

	Exco £		Wyeco £	
Total costs per unit	12		24	
Fixed costs per unit	4	$\left(\dfrac{£60,000}{15,000}\right)$	10	$\left(\dfrac{£300,000}{30,000}\right)$
Variable costs per unit	8		14	
Selling price per unit	16		32	
Contribution per unit	£8		£18	

	Exco	Wyeco
Processing time per unit	1 hour	0.5 hour
Contribution per processing hour	£8	£36
Ranking	2	1
Maximum demand	20,000 units	40,000 units
Use of processing hours	10,000 hours	20,000 hours
(Total available = (15,000 × 1 hour + 30,000 × 0.5 hour))		
Units produced	10,000 units	40,000 units
Contribution achieved	£80,000	£720,000

Total contribution of £800,000 is £140,000 in excess of current contribution of £660,000 (15,000 × £8 + 30,000 × £18).

The fixed costs are assumed to be unchanged and are therefore irrelevant.

(b)   **Optimal pricing policy**

(i)   **Exco**

The table provided indicates that an increase of 25p in selling price results in a fall in demand of 1,000 units. Therefore, an increase of 10 × 25p on top of the £18.50 selling price would eliminate demand. This would be at £21.00 per unit. The selling price can therefore be represented by:

$$SP = 21.00 - 0.25x \quad \text{where } x = \text{demand in 000 units}$$

and   Total sales revenue $R = 21.00x - 0.25x^2$

The marginal revenue (MR) can be calculated by using differential calculus:

$$MR = 21.00 - 0.50x$$

Optimal sales level is where MR = marginal cost.

$$8 = 21.00 - 0.50x$$

$$x = 26$$

Therefore, a price resulting in demand for 26,000 units is achieved with a selling price of £(21.00 − 0.25 × 26) = £14.50.

(ii)   **Wyeco**

Applying the same concepts as for Exco:

Increase in SP of 15p results in fall in demand of 1,000 units.

Selling price, P	=	$38.00 - 0.15x$
Total sales revenue, R	=	$38.00x - 0.15x^2$

MR	=	$38.00 - 0.30x$
Marginal cost	=	14
14	=	$38.00 - 0.30x$
x	=	80,000 units
∴ Selling price	=	£(38.00 − 0.15 × 80) = £26.00

*(**Tutorial note:** the recommended selling price for Wyeco is outside the range of the sales director's estimates and must therefore be reviewed to ensure that it is feasible. Moreover, many students may have thought that they had the wrong answer because the recommendation is not between £29.00 and £35.00.)*

(c)   **Why cost-plus pricing is used**

Several reasons can be advanced in favour of computing target selling prices by means of cost-plus formulae, even if the prices are later modified.

Firstly, the decision-maker is faced with a host of uncertainties. The use of cost-plus formulae enables the decision-maker to absorb some of these uncertainties and come up with a price that will be acceptable given the constraints at hand.

Secondly, cost may be viewed as a base from which the price setter moves, guarding against the possibility of setting the price too low and incurring losses. Cost-plus pricing will not guarantee against loss-making: for instance, there are problems of volume estimating. However, these will point the price setter in the right direction.

A third explanation of the popularity of cost-based pricing is that estimates of the company's own costs may help the decision-maker to predict either competitors' costs or a competitive price. For example, if a company is operating in an industry where a 30% mark-up is the norm, then the company may be able to assume that this pattern will hold for new products and thereby either to predict competitors' prices or to price in such a way as to gain quick acceptance of a new product line.

The main reason is that the information is rarely (if ever) available to allow an approach based on marginal cost and marginal revenue.

16 FURTHER ASPECTS OF PRICING POLICY

INTRODUCTION & LEARNING OBJECTIVES

In this chapter we will consider specific pricing situations and their impact on accounting information systems.

When you have studied this chapter you should be able to do the following:

- Calculate Activity Based Costing based prices, and comment on the use of ABC as a basis of cost plus pricing.
- Explain how pricing decisions are made in special order and new product situations.
- Explain target pricing.

1 ACTIVITY BASED APPROACHES TO COST BASED PRICING

1.1 Introduction

The technique of activity based costing (ABC) was examined in an earlier chapter, where overhead costs are allocated between products on the basis of the cost drivers identified as generating the overheads.

Here we examine the use of ABC as a basis for pricing, by use of an example which will start by revising the technique.

1.2 Example

Trimake Ltd makes three main products, using broadly the same production methods and equipment for each. A conventional product costing system is used at present, although an activity based costing (ABC) system is being considered. Details of the three products for a typical period are:

| | Hours per unit | | Materials per unit | Volumes |
	Labour hours	Machine hours	£	Units
Product X	½	1 ½	20	750
Product Y	1 ½	1	12	1,250
Product Z	1	3	25	7,000

Direct labour costs £6 per hour and production overheads are absorbed on a machine hour basis. The rate for the period is £28 per machine hour.

(a) **You are required** to calculate the cost per unit for each product using conventional methods.

Further analysis shows that the total of production overheads can be divided as follows:

	%
Costs relating to set-ups	35
Costs relating to machinery	20
Costs relating to materials handling	15
Costs relating to inspection	30
Total production overhead	100

The following total activity volumes are associated with the product line for the period as a whole.

Total activities for the period

	Number of set-ups	Number of movements of materials	Number of inspections
Product X	75	12	150
Product Y	115	21	180
Product Z	480	87	670
	670	120	1,000

You are required

(b)   to calculate the cost per unit for each product using ABC principles;

1.3   Solution to example

(a)   **Conventional cost per unit**

(*Tutorial note:* There is less to this than meets the eye; two hourly rates are given, for labour and for overheads, standard times are supplied and thus unit costs can be found. A sub-total of direct costs may speed up (b) a little.)

	X £	Y £	Z £
Materials	20	12	25
Labour (£6/hour)	3	9	6
Direct cost	23	21	31
Production overheads (£28/hour)	42	28	84
Total production cost/unit	65	49	115

(b)   **ABC cost per unit**

(Tutorial note: Each step required has been given its own sub-heading to make the procedure clear. The basic principle is to find an overhead cost per unit of activity for each element of overhead cost. In some cases it might then be possible to find an overhead cost per unit directly; here it is probably easier to split overheads between each product type first and then find a cost per unit as shown.)

(i)   **Total overheads**

Using the production and unit overhead cost information from (a):

Total overheads for a period

$$= (750 \times £42) + (1,250 \times £28) + (7,000 \times £84) = £654,500.$$

(ii)   **Total machine hours**

Product	Hours/unit	Production	Total hours
X	1½	750	1,125
Y	1	1,250	1,250
Z	3	7,000	21,000
Total machine hours			23,375

Both the total and the split by product will be used subsequently.

(iii)   **Analysis of total overheads and cost per unit of activity**

Type of overhead	%	Total overhead £	Level of activity	Cost/unit of activity £
Set-ups	35	229,075	670	341.903
Machining	20	130,900	23,375	5.60
Materials handling	15	98,175	120	818.125
Inspection	30	196,350	1,000	196.35
	100	654,500		

(*Note:* It is worth retaining the cost per set-up figure in the memory of your calculator; the memory can be used for the other unit costs in turn.)

(iv)   **Total overheads by product and per unit**

(*Note:* This makes use of the table of total activities for the period, where it is important not to confuse rows and columns and costs per unit of activity just found.)

Overhead	Product X Activity	Cost £	Product Y Activity	Cost £	Product Z Activity	Cost £	Total
Set-ups	75	25,643	115	39,319	480	164,113	229,075
Machining	1,125	6,300	1,250	7,000	21,000	117,600	130,900
M Handling	12	9,817	21	17,181	87	71,177	98,175
Inspection	150	29,453	180	35,343	670	131,554	196,350
Total o/h cost		71,213		98,843		484,444	654,500
Units		750		1,250		7,000	
Cost per unit		£94.95		£79.07		£69.21	

(*Note:* A little rounding has been done here.

- The unit costs could be rounded to £95, £79 and £69.

- Total costs could be split in the ratios of activities rather than finding cost per unit of activity.)

(v)   **Cost per unit**

	X £	Y £	Z £
Direct costs (from (a))	23.00	21.00	31.00
Overheads (from (iv))	94.95	79.07	69.21
	117.95	100.07	100.21

1.4   Activity based and volume based costs compared

A comparison of the results from the above example shows the following costs per unit:

Product	Volume	Activity based approach £/unit	Volume based approach £/unit
X	750	118	65
Y	1250	100	49
Z	7000	100	115

It can be seen that the costs per unit are not the same for each method. It is argued that the activity based approach should be used because it reflects the cost of the activities involved in the production of the product.

This is illustrated here with product Z being a major product line which may take longer to make than X or Y, but once production has started the process is simple to administer. Products X and Y are relatively minor products but still require a fair amount of administrative time by the production department; ie, involve a fair amount of 'hassle'. This is explained by the following table of 'activities per 1,000 units produced'.

	Set-ups	Materials movements	Inspections
X	100	16	200
Y	92	17	144
Z	69	12	96

This table highlights the problem.

- Product Z has fewer set-ups, material movements and inspections per 1,000 units than X or Y.

- As a consequence product Z's overhead cost per unit for these three elements has fallen.

- The machining overhead cost per unit for Z is still two or three times greater than for products X or Y.

- The machining overhead is only 20% of the total overhead.

- The overall result is Z's fall in production overhead cost per unit and the rise in those figures for X and Y.

1.5 Cost based pricing and activity based costing

For the purposes of illustration a pricing policy of 25% on cost will be applied to the above example. If this 25% mark-up is applied to the volume based costs the resulting selling prices are as follows:

	£/unit
X	81.25
Y	61.25
Z	143.75

In the case of products X and Y, these prices compared to unit costs on a activity cost basis yield losses of £36.75 and £38.75 per unit respectivley. On an activity cost basis the selling prices would be £147.50 and £125 respectively.

With regard to product Z the selling price calculated yields greater than 25% mark up on activity based cost. The danger with this is that the price may be uncompetitive as it does not accurately reflect the resources used.

2   SPECIAL ORDERS AND NEW PRODUCTS

2.1   Introduction

Special orders are often accepted to utilise spare capacity and new products are often priced differently to establish them in the market place. The following illustration identifies some of the key aspects of short-term pricing decisions.

2.2   Illustration of costs relevant to short-term pricing decisions

Earlier in this text examples were given of pricing decisions where the relevant costs of various resources were considered. The following illustration uses the same principles but in a slightly different context.

The Snipe Company is an electronics company having eight product lines. Income data for one of the products for the year just ended is as follows:

	£m	£m
Sales – 200,000 units @ average price of £100		20
Variable costs:		
Direct materials @ £35	7	
Direct labour @ £10	2	
Variable factory overhead @ £5	1	
Sales commission = 15% of selling price (£15)	3	
Other variable costs @ £5	1	
Total variable costs @ £70		14
Contribution		6
Fixed costs:		
Discretionary	3	
Committed	2	
		5
Operating income		1

Consider the following situations:

(a)   The electronics industry had severe price competition throughout the year. Near the end of the year, Albacone Co, which was experimenting with various components in its regular product line, offered £80 each for 3,000 units. The latter would have been in addition to the 200,000 units actually sold. Acceptance of the special order by Snipe would not affect regular sales. The salesman hoped that the order might provide entrance into a new application so he told John Hooper, the product manager, that he would accept half his regular commission rate if the order were accepted. Hooper pondered for a day, but he was afraid of the precedent that might be set by cutting the price. He said 'the price is below our full costs of £95 per unit. I think we should quote a full price, or Albacone Co will expect favoured treatment again and again if we continue to do business with them'. If Hooper had accepted the offer, what would operating income have been?

(b)   The Gall Company had offered to supply a key part (MIA) for £20 each. One MIA is used in every finished unit. The Snipe Company had made these parts for variable costs of £18 plus some additional fixed costs of £200,000 for supervision and other items. What would operating income have been if Snipe purchased rather than made the parts? Assume that discretionary costs for supervision and other items would have been avoided if the parts were purchased.

(c)   The company could have purchased the MIA parts for £20 each and used the vacated space for the manufacture of a different electronics component on a sub-contracting basis for Hewlett-Packard, a much larger company. Assume that 40,000 special components could have been made for Hewlett-Packard (and sold in addition to the 200,000 units sold through regular channels) at a unit variable cost of £150, exclusive of parts. MIA parts would be needed for these components as well as for the regular production. No sales commission would have to be paid. All the fixed costs pertaining to the MIA parts would have continued, including the supervisory costs, because they related mainly to the facilities used. What would operating income have been if Snipe had made and sold the components to Hewlett-Packard for £170 per unit and bought the MIA parts?

Solution to illustration

(a)   Analysis of special order:

	Per unit £	3,000 units £'000	3,000 units £'000
Additional sales	80		240
Variable costs (excluding commission)	55	165	
Commission ($15\% \times \frac{1}{2} \times 240$)		18	
		——	183
Contribution			57

Note that variable costs, except for commission, are affected by physical units of volume, not pounds revenue.

Operating income would have been £1,000,000 plus £57,000, or £1,057,000, if the order had been accepted. In a sense, the decision to reject the offer means that Snipe is willing to invest £57,000 in immediate gains forgone (an opportunity cost) to preserve the long run selling price structure.

(b)

	Make £'000	Purchase £'000
Purchase cost @ £20		4,000
Variable costs @ £18	3,600	
Avoidable discretionary costs	200	
Total relevant costs	3,800	4,000

Operating income would have fallen by £200,000, or from £1,000,000 to £800,000, if Snipe had purchased the parts.

(c)

	£'000	£'000	£'000
Sales would increase by 40,000 units @ £170			6,800
Additional costs to the company as a whole:			
Variable costs exclusive of MIA parts would increase by 40,000 units @ £150		6,000	
Effects on overall costs of MIA parts:			
Cost of 240,000 parts purchased @ £20	4,800		
Less: Savings from not making 20,000 parts @ £18 (only the variable costs are relevant because fixed costs continue)	3,600		
Additional cost of parts		1,200	7,200
Disadvantage of making components for Hewlett-Packard			(400)

Operating income would decline by £400,000 from £1,000,000 to £600,000.

2.3   Pricing in limiting factor situations

When there is a factor limiting production, opportunity cost (contribution per key factor) may be taken into account in price fixing.

Consider the following example.

Example

A company has the following budget based on orders from the home market:

	£	£
Sales (2,000 units)		10,000
Cost of sales:		
Direct material	1,000	
Direct labour	4,000	
Variable overhead	1,000	
Fixed overhead	3,000	
		9,000
		1,000

At this level of output, the company has spare capacity and it is therefore planning to develop export markets. It believes that it will be able to sell an additional 750 units – the limit of its production due to a shortage of raw materials. No additional fixed costs would be incurred and selling prices and variable costs per unit would be the same as for the home market.

Before launching its export campaign, however, the company is approached by a home buyer who wishes to purchase 200 de luxe models which use twice as much material as the standard model. What is the minimum price which should be charged if this order is accepted?

Solution

If the company accepts the de luxe order, it will lose export sales due to the shortage of materials. On export sales the contribution per unit would be:

	£	£
Selling price		5
Direct material	0.50	
Direct labour	2.00	
Variable overhead	0.50	
		3
Contribution		2
Contribution per £1 of raw material (£2.00 ÷ £0.50)		£4

Each de luxe model uses £1-worth of raw material. In order to be no worse off by accepting this order, therefore, the company must obtain a contribution of at least £4 per unit – the opportunity cost of the raw material. The minimum price to be charged is therefore:

	£
Direct material	1.00
Direct labour	2.00
Variable overhead	0.50
	3.50
Required contribution	4.00
Selling price per unit	7.50

If 200 de luxe models are made sales in the export market will fall by 400 to 350.

	De luxe order rejected		De luxe order accepted			
	Export sales		Export sales		De luxe sales	
	£	£	£	£	£	£
Sales						
(750 @ £5)	3,750					
(200 @ £7.50)					1,500	
(350 @ £5)			1,750			
Direct material (£0.50/£1)	375		175		200	
Direct labour (£2)	1,500		700		400	
Variable overhead (£0.50)	375		175		100	
		2,250		1,050		700
Contribution		1,500		700		800

Therefore, if it charges the minimum price recommended for the de luxe model, the company will obtain the same contribution as if it rejected the order and concentrated on the export market.

In practice, of course, the company will take other considerations into account eg, the de luxe order is definite, export sales are speculative; more labour is required if the company concentrates on exports; there may be additional selling costs or other fixed costs associated with exporting.

3   PRICING POLICIES

3.1   Introduction

It must be remembered that pricing decisions are not made in a vacuum and there are very few completely new products. Most new products are simply developments of older ones or substitutes for something that already exists.

There is, therefore, a background, or an expected price range, within which a new product will fit. This can sometimes give a completely new product development an enormous opportunity for profit. For example, when the ball-point pen first appeared, it was offered to the public as a competitor to good quality fountain pens, which were then selling for around £1.50. The ballpoint pen sold at around this price until competitors discovered that it cost only a few pence to make, whereupon the price tumbled. For some time, however, the ball-point continued with its fountain pen image being sold as a long lasting holder for which re-fills were supplied. Later the cheap throw-away ball-point became more general.

Occasionally, there are completely new products which create new markets. In this case price tends to follow supply costs. These costs can be expected to fall as mass markets develop, as production becomes more reliable and as initial research, development and fixed equipment costs are recovered. One such product has been the small electronic calculator. Until the development of microprocessors, a calculator was a piece of office equipment outside the price range of most individuals. Early electric calculators were unreliable and prone to breakdown; initially they were expensive.

The microprocessor made possible a cheap, efficient and reliable piece of equipment of value to any individual. There was no price background for such an item because nothing like this had previously existed. Prices were established by a combination of competition and falling supply costs – a good example of the working of a free market economy.

For more normal products the supplier is operating in a known market with a price history. Decisions may be taken with some knowledge of the likely demand within a given possible price range.

3.2 Charging the 'going rate'

There are situations where the producer is satisfied that he can sell a satisfactory quantity at a satisfactory profit at a price which is in line with prices of similar goods or services. The existence of such a situation depends on the nature and strength of competition, especially price competition in the market. The Hall & Hitch survey produced strong evidence for people charging what they felt was 'the fair price'.

Firms are more likely to charge the 'going rate' under the following conditions:

(a)   When the quality or some other feature of a product or a service is more important than price and the price elasticity of demand at the ruling price is largely inelastic. Examples include local hairdressing services, daily and local newspapers, beer and cigarettes.

(b)   When it is believed that a fixed price has become established for a particular product and identified with that product in the market. Inflation, metrication and the economic upheavals of the 1970s and 1980s have upset most of these identities, of which one of the best known examples was probably that of the 6d (2½p) bar of chocolate which lasted for a long period in the 1950s and early 1960s. Fixed prices of this type tend to be associated with 'oligopolies'.

(c)   When price competition will simply reduce revenue for all suppliers without giving additional profits or any other significant market advantage to any individual supplier. This position is associated with oligopolies and with what may be called, perhaps, local oligopolies where local supply is dominated by a small number of traders who are content to retain their local market share. Formal market sharing agreements or collusive behaviour are not necessary under these conditions. Self-interest builds up a form of custom and practice which all established suppliers observe as long as there is no internal or external threat to market stability. It is also likely that all suppliers will share similar cost conditions and will act together to avoid competing for factors and to preserve stable factor costs – including wages.

3.3 The price strategy

The price strategy to be adopted for any particular product is part of the total marketing strategy for the product. This, in turn, is part of the firm's total production strategy. Firms will adopt very different behaviour patterns for different products and markets.

For example, breaking into a market requires different tactics from those needed when defending an established market position from new entrants or possible new entrants to the market.

Similarly, the approach to a new market area in which there has been substantial recent investment and which, it is hoped, will expand, will be very different from one to an old area expected to be in decline and where a decision has already been made not to renew investment.

Failure to recognise a change in market demand and in supply conditions such as the arrival of new and more attractive substitutes can lead to expensive errors involving more than just mistakes in pricing.

It is desirable for the business manager to keep an open mind in his approach to the place of prices in the total marketing strategy, but at the same time to recognise clearly the economic forces operating in the market area.

3.4 Market penetration

This relates to the attempt to break into a market and to establish that market share which, it has been calculated, will enable the firm to achieve its revenue and profit targets.

Whether the market is an established one which the firm hopes to break open or a new and developing one, the most likely price strategy is to set price as low as possible and substantially below the ruling price of competitors without being so low that the product is thought to be inferior. To achieve this in an established market the firm is likely to need the benefit of a production or marketing innovation thought to give a special advantage.

Once the target market share has been achieved the next stage in the total strategy is likely to be to build up distributor and customer loyalty ie, to reduce the product's price elasticity of demand (make the demand curve steeper). By reducing the relative attraction of substitutes it will also influence the cross elasticity of demand with rival products. This is unlikely to be achieved solely through price changes. There will also have to be changes in advertising, in policies over distribution margins and services and possibly over the availability of services and even of packaging. At this stage there may be a greater emphasis on price stability and stress on quality and availability. This, of course, assumes that successful penetration is now leading to consolidation of the market share and probably an improvement in profitability.

3.5   Market skimming

This is also associated with the launching of a new product but represents a rather different approach – perhaps where the extent of market appeal is uncertain and the firm has not yet committed itself to a major investment programme in the project and its production. The supplier may also be the main or an important supplier of substitutes so that a successful launch will involve a major switch in production investment. Failure will not be too expensive if care is taken.

The skimming approach involves setting a relatively high price stressing the attractions of new features likely to appeal to those with a genuine interest in the product or its associated attractions. Reaction and support is thus solicited from the 'top end' of the particular market. If the launch is successful in this 'cream skimming' exercise, and when the decision has been taken to invest in the necessary new production resources so that larger scale production becomes possible, then the appeal of the new product can be enlarged through a shift in advertising and a reduction in price. The price reduction can be made in stages to coincide with supply side increases as new resources come into use.

One of the conditions necessary for market skimming is the existence of technical barriers to entry into the market; it must be difficult for competitors to come up with a similar product quickly with which they can undercut the price. Such policies are common in 'high-tec' fields which is why one saw calculators, personal computers, domestic stereo sets and videos initially sold at a high price but now those same products are sold for a fraction of their launch price. The same can be said of computer software, although in all of these cases the product life cycle has an influence on longer-term pricing policy.

3.6   Differential pricing

Differential pricing may be used whenever it is possible to differentiate the product or its market. There are many ways of differentiating sales; common techniques are to differentiate:

(i)   by product version;

(ii)   by time;

(iii)   by place; or

(iv)   by market segment.

One organisation which uses many of these techniques is British Rail. They differentiate their product by separating First Class and Economy Class travel accommodation. Further differentiation is then applied by time with higher prices being charged to travel at busy periods. Off-peak time travel is then further differentiated by market segment with special prices for students, family tickets, etc.

4   PRICING OF SHORT LIFE PRODUCTS

4.1   Introduction

Short-life products require special pricing considerations. Any costs which are product specific (fixed and variable) must be recovered within the short life of the product.

4.2   Short life pricing policies

When there is likely to be a high level of demand eg, annual diaries, then prices can be relatively low, but where demand is limited prices will have to be set at a high level so as to ensure cost recovery. This is a form of skimming policy but perhaps without the subsequent price reduction.

5   TARGET PRICING

5.1   Introduction

Target pricing is a term which implies that the firm has a sufficient knowledge of the conditions of the market for its product and for the production factors which it uses to be able to set a price which it calculates will achieve a desired target.

Possible targets might include the following:

(a)   **Short or long run profit maximisation**

In practice these are not normally considered to be specific targets and are not usually regarded as being within the scope of target pricing.

(b)   **Sales maximisation**

This may be regarded in a similar light to that of profit maximisation. Strictly it does not represent a specific target.

(c)   **A desired rate of return on capital invested in a product**

This is, perhaps, the most common target, chiefly because investment decisions are based on comparisons of future returns and on estimates of attainable returns. Managers will, therefore, seek to achieve the projections made when the decision was being reached. The techniques and knowledge required to achieve a target rate of return are not too far distant from those required for profit maximisation but greater attention is likely to be paid to the time dimension. Thus, achievement of an overall target may envisage successive sub-targets and successive price changes in the pursuit of a total strategy. For example, a low price may be set initially to break into a market and to secure distribution channels; a higher price may then be charged as the product gains acceptance and demand becomes less price elastic – and shelf space and retailer support is gained. The manager is operating in a dynamic environment and must adapt his tactics as the strategy develops. The setting of an initial low price to achieve a desired level of market acceptance is known as **penetration pricing.**

The important point is that there is a constant awareness of the price/quantity/cost set of relationships and the greater the knowledge of these the more precise the price calculation can become. The manager is seeking that combination of marginal cost, marginal revenue, price and cross elasticity of demand that will achieve the desired target rate of return on the amount invested.

(d)   **Market share**

This is rarely an end in itself; more often it is the necessary pre-condition for the firm to achieve the price and cost combination it desires.

The position, say, of being an acknowledged brand leader may ensure a given amount of shelf-space and selling attention from distribution channels and may give a degree of control over price and perhaps allow the firm to be the price leader in a period of changing costs.

(e)   **Achieve a given rate of growth**

Growth may be an important objective of the firm but because of the costs and risks of obtaining capital, a steady growth rate is desired because this can be obtained from available capital funds. An objective of growth at a particular rate is also likely to require the achievement of a profit rate considered acceptable to the finance markets. The firm cannot go to the capital market for additional finance unless it can prove to that market that it has achieved a satisfactory rate of profit on its existing capital. What is 'satisfactory' depends on a range of influences and conditions at any particular time.

(f)   **Keep out competitors**

This involves the use of price as a barrier to the entry of market competitors. This may mean that some degree of monopoly profit may be sacrificed in the desire to keep price below the level at which it would become profitable for a new firm to enter the market. An example of this policy is seen in the market for UK air passengers (in which less orthodox marketing strategies are also alleged to take place).

5.2   Target costing and value analysis

Target costing combines the twin disciplines of cost estimation and value analysis and this is discussed as an introduction to target costing. The essential idea is that where the price of a product is determined by the market place, costs have to be reduced to enable the product to be sold at that price. That gives the target cost and value analysis is used to help the business achieve that target cost.

5.3   Past exam questions

(p To 5.6.

Target costing was examined in December 1994 and December 1995, both in the context of an activity based costing environment. Both part questions were discursive, requiring an explanation of how target costing could be used to meet specified target criteria (based on the C/S ratio and net profit margin respectively). It is essentially a cost reduction exercise, which will be based upon value analysis. This was discussed in detail in Chapter 5 and is summarised below.

5.4   Value analysis   *Value Engineering –*

Value analysis is basically a form of *cost reduction* ie, a method of improving profitability by reducing costs without necessarily increasing prices; it is thus particularly useful to manufacturers or suppliers who are unable to fix their own price because of, for example, a competitive market. However, the use of value analysis in all circumstances should be considered as it should be obvious that any failure to reduce costs will result in sub-optimisation of profitability.

Value analysis resulted from a realisation by manufacturers that they were incorporating features into their product which the user of the product did not require and was not prepared to pay for. For instance, few manufacturers of bath taps are prepared to produce taps in solid gold, as the demand for such expensive taps is very limited – most people are quite satisfied with brass. In the same way, other not so obvious but equally *useless*, features can be incorporated into products. Value analysis takes a critical look at each feature of a product, questioning its need and its use, and eliminating any unjustifiable features.

It is useful to distinguish two types of value – utility value and esteem value.

Utility value is the value an item has because of the uses to which it can be put. *Esteem value* is the value put on an item because of its beauty, craftsmanship, etc. The difference may be illustrated by reference to furniture. An individual who requires something to sit on may be satisfied with a crudely-made three-legged stool, or even a tree stump. He will be prepared to pay a very low sum of money for this. He may be prepared, however, to pay a great deal more money for a well-made fashionable reclining leather chair. Both serve the same basic purposes – a seat – but while a tree stump only has utility value, the leather reclining chair has esteem value as well. Value analysis is basically concerned with those products for which no esteem value is paid. In these circumstances there is little need for craftsmanship and beauty, and it may be possible to reduce costs by excluding such unnecessary features.

5.5   The value analysis method

Value analysis is concerned with five basic areas:

Step 1   Establish the precise requirements of the customer. By a process of judicious enquiry it should be possible to discover precisely why customers want an item, whether the item has any esteem value, etc. Only in this way can the manufacturer be certain that each function incorporated into the product contributes some value to it.

Step 2   Establish and evaluate alternative ways of achieving the requirements of the customers. There may be methods of producing the item which have not been considered eg, replacing metal panels with plastic. Each alternative method must be costed out in units of:

(i)   **Materials** – amount required, acceptable level of wastage (can it be improved?), alternative, cheaper materials.

(ii)   **Labour** – can the cost be reduced by eliminating operations or changing production methods?

(iii)   **Other factors** – can new, cheaper processes be found? Would a cheaper finish be acceptable?

Step 3   Authorise any proposals put forward as a result of (b). The assessment in (b) may be carried out by middle management and, if so, it will require ratification by top management before implementation.

Step 4   Implementation of proposals.

Step 5   Evaluate feedback from new proposals to establish the benefits from the change.

Several benefits will result from value analysis. In the first place, many customers will be impressed by the interest shown in their requirements and this will lead to increased sales. In addition, a firm which adopts this approach is likely to attract better staff, due both to the prospects for an outlet for their ideas and the higher morale resulting from the team approach. Of course, there are the economic and financial benefits arising from the elimination of unnecessary complexity and the better use of resources.

5.6   Target costing

Target costing, as with several other effective new developments in management accounting, has come from Japan where manufacturers such as Sony and Toyota feel that it is responsible for those firms improving their market share. The main theme behind target costing is not finding what a new product does cost but what it should cost.

The starting point for target costing is an estimate of a selling price for a new product that will enable a firm to capture a required share of the market. The next step is to reduce this figure by the firm's required level of profit. This will take into account the return required on any new investment and on working capital requirements. This will produce a target cost figure for product designers to meet. The cost reduction process usually described as value analysis then tries to provide a product which meets that target cost. The only evidence of its use at the moment comes from Japan, but in time the idea will doubtless spread in the same way that JIT systems became popular.

5.7   Illustration

The following illustration of the application of target costing is based upon the two part exam questions referred to in 5.3:

ABC Ltd makes and sells two products, X and Y. Both products are manufactured through two consecutive processes - assembly and finishing. Raw material is input at the commencement of the assembly process. An activity based costing approach is used in the absorption of product specific conversion costs.

The following estimated information is available for the period ending 31 December 19X5:

	Product X	*Product Y*
Production/sales (units)	12,000	7,200
Selling price per unit	£75	£90
Direct material cost per unit	£20	£20
ABC variable conversion cost per unit		
- assembly	£20	£28
- finishing	£12	£24
Product specific fixed costs	£170,000	£90,000

Company fixed costs   £50,000

ABC Ltd uses a minimum C/S ratio target of 25% when assessing the viability of a product; in addition, management wish to achieve an overall net profit margin of 12% on sales in this period in order to meet return on capital targets.

Explain how target costing may be used in achieving the required returns and suggest specific areas of investigation.

Solution

The information given will give the following estimated product and company results:

	Product X		*Product Y*		*Company*	
Per unit	£	£	£	£		£
Selling price		75		90		
Less: variable costs						
materials	20		20			
conversion costs	32	(52)	52	(72)		
Contribution		23		18		
Contribution:sales ratio		*30.7%*		*20%*		
Total for period						
Sales		900,000		648,000	1,548,000	
Contribution (sales × cont/unit)		276,000		129,600		
Product specific fixed costs		(170,000)		(90,000)		
		106,000		39,600	145,600	
Company fixed costs					(50,000)	
Net profit					95,600	
Net profit margin on sales					6.2%	

The company is falling considerably short of its 12% net profit margin target. If sales quantities and prices are to remain unchanged, costs must be reduced if the required return is to be reached.

Product Y is falling short of the C/S ratio target. Cost reduction exercises must be concentrated particularly on this product if its production is to continue to be seen to be worthwhile.

The design specification for each product and the production methods should be examined for potential areas of cost reduction that will not compromise the quality of the products. For example:

- can any materials be eliminated, eg cut down on packing materials?

- can a cheaper material be substituted without affecting quality?

- can part-assembled components be bought in to save on assembly time?

- can the incidence of the cost drivers be reduced, in particular for product Y?

- is there some degree of overlap between the product-related fixed costs that could be eliminated by combining service departments or resources?

6 CHAPTER SUMMARY

In this chapter we have considered the application of activity based costing to pricing and some of the practical issues surrounding pricing policies.

7 SELF TEST QUESTIONS

7.1   Explain the principle of activity based costing. (1.1)

7.2   Explain activity based cost plus pricing. (1.5)

7.3   Explain market penetration. (3.4)

7.4   Explain market skimming. (3.5)

7.5   Explain differential pricing. (3.6)

7.6   Explain the problems of pricing short-life products. (4)

7.7   Explain target pricing. (5.1)

7.8   Explain value analysis. (5.5)

7.9   Explain target costing. (5.6)

8 EXAMINATION TYPE QUESTION

8.1 Distortions

"It is now fairly widely accepted that conventional cost accounting distorts management's view of business through unrepresentative overhead allocation and inappropriate product costing.

This is because the traditional approach usually absorbs overhead costs across products and orders solely on the basis of the direct labour involved in their manufacture. And as direct labour as a proportion of total manufacturing cost continues to fall, this leads to more and more distortion and misrepresentation of the impact of particular products on total overhead costs."

(From an article in the Financial Times, 2 March 1990)

You are required to discuss the above and to suggest what approaches are being adopted by management accountants to overcome such criticism.   **(15 marks)**

9   ANSWER TO EXAMINATION TYPE QUESTION

9.1   Distortions

Overhead absorption is the technique of attributing departmental overhead costs to a cost unit.

Traditionally the basis of overhead absorption was the number of labour hours expected within the budget period and this was then used to calculate an absorption rate per labour hour. This was then used to attribute costs to the cost unit on the basis of the number of labour hours used to produce the cost unit.

Alternative bases of apportionment exist such as the number of machine hours or a percentage of particular elements of prime cost incurred in respect of the cost unit. If the method of manufacture is machine intensive for example, it is more realistic to absorb the overhead cost on the basis of the number of machine hours instead of the number of labour hours.

A further development is to divide the overhead cost into those costs which are labour related and those which are machine hour related and apply a separate absorption rate to each part of the overhead cost. This use of multiple rates is similar to the principles of activity based costing.

Activity based costing is based on the principle that activities cause costs and therefore the use of activities should be the basis of attributing costs to cost units. Costs are identified with particular activities and the performance of those activities is linked with products. The activity is known as the cost driver and the costs associated with that activity are then attributed to cost units using a cost driver rate. This then more accurately reflects the usage of the activity by the product.

17 ACCOUNTING CONTROL SYSTEMS: THE PLANNING PROCESS

INTRODUCTION & LEARNING OBJECTIVES

When you have studied this chapter you should be able to do the following:

- Describe the information sources used in the planning process.
- List the information used when preparing a master budget.
- Compare budgeting methods.
- Distinguish between short term and long term planning.
- Explain the effects of inflation on long term planning.

Issues covered by this chapter were examined in June 1994 (two questions) and June 1995. Two questions were discursive, discussing the benefits of zero-based and activity based budgeting methods; the third was computational, requiring a profit forecast using cost and price indices and other information.

You should refer back to Chapter 5 for a discussion and illustration of activity based budgeting.

1 PLANNING INFORMATION

1.1 Position audit

A company's operational environment is composed of those dimensions which directly or indirectly influence corporate success or failure. Most external factors are beyond the control of the company, whereas **internal** dimensions are generally within its management ambit. The carrying out of a position audit was explained in an earlier chapter. The essential purpose of a strategic position audit is to collect and analyse all the relevant and available information about the company and its **current** operations which will provide strategic planners with information on:

(a)   The competitive strengths and weaknesses of the company's current strategic position;

(b)   The consequences of the company continuing its present strategy;

(c)   The internal resources which are available for implementing any strategic change that may be required.

1.2 The detailed audit

It is not possible to provide a definitive list of the aspects that should be analysed in a strategic position audit. This must depend on the particular situation, circumstances and forces at work in the operational environment of a given organisation. However, the analytical audit approach should utilise a systematic set of questions that takes the auditor into the main areas of a company's structure and operations.

1.3 Macro-economic statistics

Statistics are produced for all macro-economic variables such as:

- inflation
- balance of payments
- terms of trade
- exchange rates
- interest rates - domestic and international

- money supply
- growth of GDP.

Again, these are useful indicators of the country's overall economic position, but are of limited value to an individual company that is trying to assess its performance.

The figures will tell the company if the economy is pulling out of recession, or if factory gate prices or unit labour costs across the whole economy are increasing. But they will not tell the company anything of detail about its own performance compared to those of its immediate competitors in the same industry.

1.4 Interfirm comparison schemes

There are a number of schemes set up by agencies such as the Centre for Interfirm Comparisons, or by various trade associations.

These attempt to produce information about the relative performance of companies that contribute to the scheme.

The difficulties of such schemes are:

(a) Information supplied by different companies may not be based on the same accounting policies and will have to be adjusted.

(b) Companies may be reluctant to divulge information that will be used by the competition for reasons of confidentiality.

The problems are not insurmountable and the data provided does have benefit for participating companies.

2   PREPARING THE MASTER BUDGET

2.1   How to budget - the seven steps

Preparation of the budget involves seven steps. These are illustrated diagrammatically below:

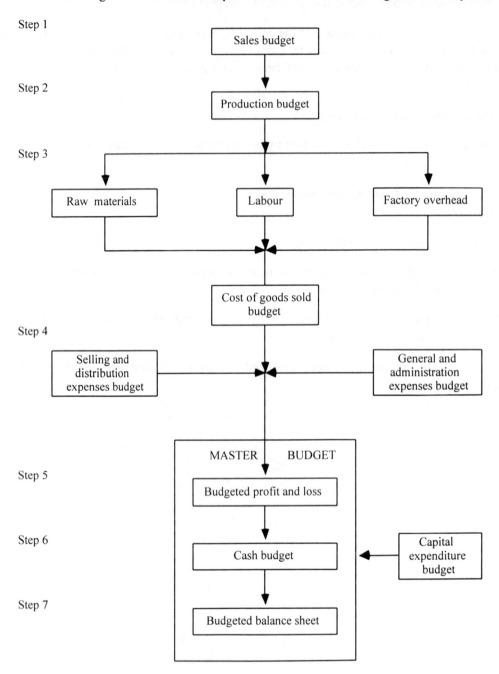

2.2   Principal budget factor

The sales budget is shown in the diagram because this is the pattern in most businesses, where it is the volume of the demand for the product which limits the scale of operation. It is possible, however, for there to be some other limiting factor eg, labour, material, cash or machinery. The limiting factor must be identified at the first stage of the budgeting process, since it will determine all the other budgets. In this context the limiting factor is referred to as the **principal budget factor.**

3   ZERO BASED BUDGETING

3.1   Introduction

[Definition]   A method of budgeting whereby all activities are re-evaluated each time a budget is set. Discrete levels of each activity are valued and a combination chosen to match funds available.

ZBB requires the budgeting of every part of an organisation from 'scratch' or 'base'. The technique forces managers to consider all the costs of an operation, consider the level of service provided and the costs of providing that service. Often the 'zero-option' is not feasible, nor desired, but different levels of operation are considered.

The costs of providing each level of service will be assessed against the level of service provided and the most appropriate chosen.

3.2   The technique of zero-based budgeting

The first requirement in a ZBB process which is most effective in controlling service department budgets is the development of a *decision package*.

This has been defined by its first proponent Peter A Pyhrr of Texas Instruments as:

'A document that identifies and describes a specific activity in such a manner that senior management can:

(a)   evaluate it and rank it against other activities competing for limited resources; and

(b)   decide whether to approve or disapprove it.'

Decision packages are developed by managers for their particular areas of responsibility.

Decision packages will contain information such as:

- the function of the department;
- a performance measure for the department;
- costs and benefits of operating a department at a range of different levels of funding;
- consequences of not operating at those levels.

The second requirement is the actual ranking of the decision packages, using cost/benefit analysis.

The result is a list of ranked projects or activities which senior management can use to evaluate needs and priorities in making budget approvals. The resources available to the organisation for the forthcoming budget period are thus allocated accordingly.

This in practice may be a formidable task, particularly with the interrelationships that exist within an organisation, and probably no organisation can afford to take the time to examine every activity in the necessary depth every year. A review cycle covering each activity once every three or four years may be more practical. ZBB is said to be particularly useful in local government. It may be easier to apply in that situation because it is possible to segregate and assess the benefits of each activity (eg, refuse collection, schools, road maintenance) and the complicated links often found in industry are minimal. In the private sector its most productive use would seem to be in the area of non-manufacturing costs. In this area efficiency standards are difficult to develop and costs often tend to mushroom.

3.3   Benefits of zero-based budgeting

Despite considerable practical problems associated with applying ZBB throughout the organisation, some important benefits are envisaged in its rationale:

(a)   it helps to create an organisational environment where change is accepted;

(b)   it helps management to focus on company objectives and goals;

(c)   it concentrates the attention of management on the future rather than on the past;

(d)   it helps to identify inefficient and obsolete operations within the organisation;

(e)   it provides a framework to ensure the optimum utilisation of resources by establishing priorities in relation to operational activity;

(f)   it should lead to a more logical and beneficial allocation of resources available to an organisation; and

(g)   it can assist motivation of management at all levels;

(h)   it provides a plan to follow when more financial resources become available;

(i)   it establishes minimum requirements from departments;

(j)   it can be done piecemeal.

It does have some disadvantages namely:

(a)   it takes more management time than conventional systems, in part because managers need to learn what is required of them;

(b)   there is a temptation to concentrate on short-term cost savings at the expense of longer-term benefits;

(c)   it takes time to show the real benefits of implementing such a system.

3.4   Example

ZBB Ltd has two service departments - material handling and maintenance, which are in competition for budget funds which must not exceed £925,000 in the coming year. A zero base budgeting approach will be used whereby each department is to be treated as a decision package and will submit a number of levels of operation showing the minimum level at which its service could be offered and two additional levels which would improve the quality of the service from the minimum level.

The following data have been prepared for each department showing the three possible operating levels for each:

Material handling department

Level 1. A squad of 30 labourers would work 40 hours per week for 48 weeks of the year. Each labourer would be paid a basic rate of £4 per hour for a 35 hour week. Overtime hours would attract a premium of 50% on the basic rate per hour. In addition, the company anticipates payments of 20% of gross wages in respect of employee benefits. Directly attributable variable overheads would be incurred at the rate of 12p per man hour. The squad would move 600,000 kilos per week to a warehouse at the end of the production process.

Level 2. In addition to the level 1 operation, the company would lease 10 fork lift trucks at a cost of £2,000 per truck per annum. This would provide a better service by enabling the same volume of output as for level 1 to be moved to a customer collection point which would be 400 metres closer to the main factory gate. Each truck would be manned by a driver working a 48 week year. Each driver would receive a fixed weekly wage of £155.

Directly attributable overheads of £150 per truck per week would be incurred.

Level 3. A computer could be leased to plan the work of the squad of labourers in order to reduce their total work hours. The main benefit would be improvement in safety through reduction in the time that work-in-progress would lie unattended. The computer leasing costs would be £20,000 for the first quarter (3 months), reducing by 10% per quarter cumulatively thereafter.

The computer data would result in a 10% reduction in labourer hours, half of this reduction being a saving in overtime hours.

Maintenance department

Level 1. Two engineers would each be paid a salary of £18,000 per annum and would arrange for repairs to be carried out by outside contractors at an annual cost of £250,000.

Level 2. The company would employ a squad of 10 fitters who would carry out breakdown repairs and routine maintenance as required by the engineers. The fitters would each be paid a salary of £11,000 per annum.

Maintenance materials would cost £48,000 per annum and would be used at a constant rate throughout the year. The purchases could be made in batches of £4,000, £8,000, £12,000 or £16,000. Ordering costs would be £100 per order irrespective of order size and stock holding costs would be 15% per annum. **The minimum cost order size would be implemented**.

Overheads directly related to the maintenance operation would be a fixed amount of £50,000 per annum.

In addition to the maintenance squad it is estimated that £160,000 of outside contractor work would still have to be paid for.

Level 3. The company could increase its maintenance squad to 16 fitters which would enable the service to be extended to include a series of major overhauls of machinery. The additional fitters would be paid at the same salary as the existing squad members.

Maintenance materials would now cost £96,000 per annum and would be used at a constant rate throughout the year. Purchases could be made in batches of £8,000, £12,000 or £16,000. Ordering costs would be £100 per order (irrespective of order size) and stock holding costs would now be 13.33% per annum. In addition, suppliers would now offer discounts of 2% of purchase price for orders of £16,000. The minimum cost order size would be implemented.

Overheads directly related to the maintenance operation would increase by £20,000 from the level 2 figure.

It is estimated that £90,000 of outside contractor work would still have to be paid for.

You are required

(a)   to determine the incremental cost for each of levels 1, 2 and 3 in each department. **(16 marks)**

(b)   In order to choose which of the incremental levels of operation should be allocated the limited budgeted funds available, management have estimated a 'desirability factor' which should be applied to each increment. The ranking of the increments is then based on the 'incremental cost × desirability factor' score, whereby a high score is deemed more desirable than a low score. The desirability factors are estimated as:

	Material handling	Maintenance
Level 1	1.00	1.00
Level 2 (incremental)	0.60	0.80
Level 3 (incremental)	0.50	0.20

Use the above ranking process to calculate which of the levels of operation should be implemented in order that the budget of £925,000 is not exceeded.   **(3 marks)**
(Total: 19 marks)

3.5   **Solution**

(a)   **Material handling department**

Level 1:

		£	£
Wages cost:	30 × 40 hours × 48 weeks × £4		230,400
	30 × 5 hours × 48 weeks × £2		14,400
			244,800
Employee benefits	20% × £244,800		48,960
Variable overhead	30 × 40 hours × 48 weeks × 12p		6,912
Incremental cost			**300,672**

Level 2:

		£
Leasing:	10 trucks @ £2,000	20,000
Drivers' wages	10 drivers × 48 weeks × £155	74,400
Overhead	10 trucks × 48 weeks × £150	72,000
Incremental cost		**166,400**

Level 3:

		£	£
Leasing:	(£20,000 + £18,000 + £16,200 + £14,580)		68,780
Savings:			
(30 men × 40 hours × 48 weeks × 10% = 5,760 hours)			
Wages cost:	5,760 hours × £4	23,040	
	2,880 hours × £2	5,760	
		28,800	
Employee benefits	20% × 28,800	5,760	
Variable overhead	5,760 hours × 12p	691	
			(35,251)
Incremental cost			**33,529**

Maintenance department

Level 1:

		£
Engineers' salaries	2 × £18,000	36,000
Outside contractors		250,000
Incremental cost		**286,000**

Level 2:

		£
Engineers' salaries	2 × £18,000	36,000
Fitters' salaries	10 × £11,000	110,000
Materials		48,000
Ordering costs (W1)		600
Stockholding costs (W1)		600
Overheads		50,000
Outside contractors		160,000
		405,200
Less level one costs		(286,000)
Incremental cost		**119,200**

Level 3:

Engineers' salaries	2 × £18,000	36,000
Fitters' salaries	16 × £11,000	176,000
Materials		96,000
Ordering costs (W2)		600
Stockholding costs (W2)		1,045
Discount		(1,920)
Overheads		70,000
Outside contractors		90,000
		467,725
Less level two costs		(405,200)
Incremental cost		**62,525**

(b)   **Factor scores:**

		Material handling		Maintenance
Level 1:	(£300,672 × 1.00)	300,672	(£286,000 × 1.00)	286,000
Level 2:	(£166,400 × 0.60)	99,840	(£119,200 × 0.80)	95,360
Level 3:	(£33,529 × 0.50)	16,765	(£62,525 × 0.20)	12,505

The budget will be spent as follows:

			£
Material handling	-	Level 3	
		(£300,672 + £166,400 + £33,529)	500,601
Maintenance	-	Level 2	
		(£286,000 + £119,200)	405,200
			905,801

WORKINGS

(W1)

Order size	No. of orders	Average stock	Ordering cost	Holding cost	Total cost
£4,000	12	£2,000	£1,200	£300	£1,500
£8,000	6	£4,000	£600	£600	£1,200
£12,000	4	£6,000	£400	£900	£1,300
£16,000	3	£8,000	£300	£1,200	£1,500

(W2)

Order size	No. of orders	Average stock	Ordering cost	Holding cost	Total cost
£8,000	12	£4,000	£1,200	£533.2	£1,733.2
£12,000	8	£6,000	£800	£799.8	£1,599.8
£16,000	6	£8,000	£600	£1,066.4	£1,666.4

The discount of 2% is worth (2% × £96,000) = £1,920 per annum; therefore net cost if orders are placed for £16,000 each time is negative, orders will be placed at this level.

At stock is thereby reduced by 2% the stock-holding cost is also reduced by 2% to £1,045.07.

4   INCREMENTAL BUDGETING

4.1   Introduction

[Definition]   A system of budgeting based on previous budgets and actual results. Data from past years is adjusted by adding or subtracting a percentage so as to adjust the values for known changes in activity and price effects.

4.2   Benefits of incremental budgeting

Incremental budgeting is a simple process which can easily be automated using spreadsheet models. Very little management intervention is required and as a consequence the method is not costly to operate.

4.3   Disadvantages of incremental budgeting

The incremental approach does not identify obsolete techniques or inefficiencies. In effect they are continued into the future and become built in to the target so that they may not be identified in the future.

4.4   Example

Narud plc is nearing the end of year 7 and has prepared summary profit and loss account data for year 6 (actual) and year 7 (projected actual) as shown in **Table 1. Table 1** also shows the bank overdraft at the end of year 6 and the projected bank overdraft at the end of year 7. Sales and production mix may be taken as constant from year 6 to year 9, with all production being sold in the year of production.

Budgeted direct material cost is variable with output volume but budgeted direct labour cost contains a fixed element of £50,000 in year 6 with the remainder varying with production volume and used in the calculation of the labour efficiency index in **Table 2.**

Production overhead contains a fixed element of £150,000 (at year 6 price levels). Included within this fixed element is a depreciation provision of £30,000 which will remain unaltered irrespective of price level changes.

Variable production overhead varies in proportion to units produced.

Budgeted administration/selling overhead is wholly fixed, whilst distribution expense should vary with sales volume.

The financial charges figure for each year is calculated as the average borrowing for the year times the borrowing rate (taken as 20%).

ie, Financial charges per year $= ((2x - y) \times 0.20)/2$

$$\text{where}\quad x \;=\; \text{previous year end overdraft and}$$
$$y \;=\; \text{net profit for current year before financial charges and depreciation.}$$

Narud plc are concerned about the level of borrowing and high financial charges. A number of changes are planned in order to attempt to eliminate the overdraft by the end of year 9 eg:

(i)   change the type of material used from year 8 onwards as a means of reducing scrap and hence improving efficiency.

(ii)   it is anticipated that the material change per (i) above together with extra training of operatives in each of years 8 and 9 will improve labour efficiency.

(iii)   selling prices will be cut in years 8 and 9 in order to stimulate demand.

Tables 2 and 3 show cost indices for performance and price respectively which show the projected changes from a year 6 base of 100. The performance indices show the cost effect of performance changes eg, material usage in year 8 indicates a 5% cost reduction from the base year level because of the reduced scrap level of material per product unit referred to in (i) above.

Table 4 shows the sales volume and price movements from a year 6 base of 100.

Required:

(a)   Give detailed working calculations which show how the year 7 projected figures (per Table 1) have been arrived at for (i) labour cost (ii) production overhead and (iii) financial charges, using the year 6 data per Table 1 as the starting point and using indices from Tables 2, 3 and 4 as necessary.

(b)   Prepare forecast profit and loss accounts for years 8 and 9 and calculate the forecast bank balance or overdraft at the end of years 8 and 9, assuming that the overdraft is affected only by net profit adjusted for the non-cash effect of the depreciation charge.

Table 1

Narud plc - Summary Profit and Loss Account

	Year 6 £	Year 7 £
Sales revenue	2,000,000	2,310,000
Less: Cost of sales:		
Direct material cost	1,000,000	1,201,200
Direct labour cost	150,000	163,300
Production overhead	310,000	350,124
Admin/selling overhead	100,000	115,500
Distribution overhead	140,000	158,466
Financial charges	130,000	124,859
	1,830,000	2,113,449
Net profit	170,000	196,551
Bank overdraft	800,000	573,449

Table 2

Indices reflecting the cost effect of changes in performance level from year 6

Year	Material usage	Labour efficiency	Production overhead utilisation (fixed and variable)	Admin/ selling verhead utilisation	Distribution overhead utilisation
6	100	100	100	100	100
7	104	103	103	110	98
8	95	99	99	105	95
9	85	97	97	100	95

Note: utilisation indices monitor the cost effect of a change in the quantity of a cost item used (a) other than changes due to a change in the number of units produced and (b) even where the cost is defined as fixed by the company.

Table 3

Indices reflecting the cost effect of price level changes from year 6

Year	Material price	Labour rate	All overheads expenditure
6	100	100	100
7	105	100	105
8	120	110	112
9	125	115	118

Table 4

Indices for sales/production volume changes and sales price changes from year 6

Year	Sales volume	Sales price
6	100	100
7	110	105
8	120	103
9	130	101

4.5   Solution

(a)

(i)   **Labour cost**

	Fixed £	Variable £
Yr 6 = £150,000	50,000	100,000
Volume + 10%	-	10,000
	50,000	110,000
Efficiency + 3%	-	3,300
Yr 7 = £163,300	50,000	113,300

(ii)   **Production overhead**

	Dep'n £	Fixed £	Variable £
Yr 6 = £310,000	30,000	120,000	160,000
Volume + 10%	-	-	16,000
	30,000	120,000	176,000
Eff'y + 3%	-	3,600	5,280
	30,000	123,600	181,280
Price + 5%	-	6,180	9,064
Yr 7 £350,124	30,000	129,780	190,344

(iii)   **Finance charges**

$$\frac{(((2 \times 800,000) - 351,410) \times 0.2)}{2} = £124,859$$

(b)   **Year 8**

		£	£
Sales (2m × 1.2 × 1.03)			2,472,000
Mat'ls (1m × 1.2 × 0.95 × 1.2)			1,368,000
Labour - F (50,000 × 1.1)		55,000	
- V (100,000 × 1.2 × 0.99 × 1.1)		130,680	185,680
Prod Ohd - D		30,000	
- F (120,000 × 0.99 × 1.12)		133,056	
- V (160,000 × 1.2 × 0.99 × 1.12)		212,890	375,946
Admin/Selling (100,000 × 1.05 × 1.12)			117,600
Dist (140,000 × 1.2 × 0.95 × 1.12)			178,752

Finance chgs (W1):

$$\frac{(((2 \times 573,449) - 276,022) \times 0.2)}{2} \qquad 87,088$$

PROFIT			158,934

Overdraft (573,449) + 158,934 + 30,000			(384,515)

Year 9

		£	£
Sales (2m × 1.3 × 1.01)			2,626,000
Materials (1m × 1.3 × 0.85 × 1.25)			1,381,250
Labour - F (50,000 × 1.15)		57,500	
- V (100,000 × 1.3 × 0.97 × 1.15)		145,015	202,515
Prod Ohd - D		30,000	
- F (120,000 × 0.97 × 1.18)		137,352	
- V (160,000 × 1.3 × 0.97 × 1.18)		238,077	405,429
Admin/Selling (100,000 × 1.00 × 1.18)			118,000
Distribution (140,000 × 1.3 × 0.95 × 1.18)			204,022

Finance charges (W2):

$$\frac{((2 \times 384,515) - 344,784) \times 0.2}{2} \qquad 42,425$$

PROFIT			272,359

Overdraft (384,515) + 272,359 + 30,000			(82,156)

WORKINGS

(W1)   The value of £276,022 is the profit before depreciation and finance charges

(W2)   The value of £344,784 is the profit before depreciation and finance charges.

5   INFORMATION FOR ZERO BASED BUDGETING AND INCREMENTAL BUDGETING

5.1   Zero based budgeting

ZBB requires that each activity be justified and be considered on a cost/benefit basis.   Thus information is required as to the nature of the organisation and its products and their alternative methods of provision. For each of the alternatives costs/revenues and other technical estimates are required so that relevant cost/benefit analysis may be carried out.

5.2   Incremental budgeting

Managers require details of the previous period, and must be aware of any activity changes which are expected during the budget period. Forecasts of changing price levels are then applied to previous prices to value the resources expected to be consumed. Basic cost behaviour analysis will be useful when adjusting for changes in the level of activity.

6   THE NATURE AND PURPOSE OF PLANNING

6.1   Corporate planning

Corporate planning should be the starting point for business planning. It is essentially a long run activity which seeks to determine the direction in which the firm should be moving in the future. A frequently asked question in formulating the corporate plan is 'Where do we see ourselves in ten years time?' To answer this successfully the firm must consider:

(a)   what it wants to achieve (its objectives);
(b)   how it intends to get there (its strategy);
(c)   what resources will be required (its operating plans);
(d)   how well it is doing in comparison to the plan (control).

These areas are discussed in the following sections.

6.2   Objectives

Objectives are simply statements of what the firm wishes to achieve. Traditionally it was assumed that all firms were only interested in the maximisation of profit (or the wealth of their shareholders). Nowadays it is recognised that for many firms profit is but one of the many objectives pursued. Examples include:

(a)   maximisation of sales (whilst earning a 'reasonable' level of profit);
(b)   growth (in sales, asset value, number of employees, etc);
(c)   survival;
(d)   research and development leadership;
(e)   quality of service;
(f)   contented workforce;
(g)   respect for the environment.

Many of these non-profit goals can in fact be categorised as:

(a)   surrogates for profit (eg, quality of service);

(b)   necessary constraints on profit (eg, quality of service);

(c)   'sub-optimal' objectives that benefit individual parties in the firm rather than the firm as a whole (eg, managers might try to maximise sales as this would bring them greater personal rewards than maximising profit).

A variety of objectives can therefore be suggested for the firm and it is up to the individual company to make its own decisions. For corporate planning purposes it is essential that the objectives chosen are quantified and have a timescale attached to them. A statement such as to maximise profits and increase sales would be of little use in corporate planning terms. The following would be far more helpful:

(i)   achieve a growth in EPS of 5% per annum over the coming ten year period;

(ii)   obtain a turnover of £x million within six years;

(iii)   launch at least two new products per year, etc.

Some objectives may be difficult to quantify (eg, contented workforce) but if no attempt is made there will be no yardstick against which to compare actual performance.

6.3   Strategy

Strategy is the overall approach that the company will adopt to meet its chosen objectives.

Strategy formulation usually involves:

(a)   an analysis of the environment in which the firm operates, a review of the strengths and weaknesses of the company and a consideration of the threats and opportunities facing it;

(b)   the results of the firm's existing operations are then projected forward and compared with stated objectives;

(c)   any differences between projected performance and objectives are referred to as 'gaps'.

To bridge these gaps the firm will either change its objectives (because they are too optimistic) or attempt to change the firm's direction to improve performance. This change of direction is strategy formulation.

Formulation of strategy is largely a creative process, whereby the firm will consider the products it makes and the markets it serves. Policies are usually developed to represent the firm's strategy and cover basic areas such as:

(i)   product development policy (eg, new products, discontinuation of old products);

(ii)   market development (continue in existing markets, develop new ones);

(iii)   technology;

(iv)   growth (ie, internally generated growth, or growth by acquisition).

These policies are sometimes known as 'missions', set out in 'mission statements'.

6.4   Operating plans

Strategic plans are essentially long term. Operating plans are the short-term tactics of the organisation. A strategic plan might call for expansion in a particular market, whereas the operating plan will detail how the extra products are to be made and how much is to be spent on advertising. A military analogy is useful here – strategy is how to organise to win the war, operating plans (or tactics) are how to fight individual battles.

Basically budgets are operating plans expressed in financial terms.

6.5   Control

It is not enough merely to make plans and implement them. The results of the plans have to be compared against stated objectives to assess the firm's performance. Action can then be taken to remedy any shortfalls in performance.

This is an essential activity as it highlights any weakness in the firm's corporate plan or its execution. Plans must be continually reviewed because as the environment changes so plans and objectives will need revision. Corporate planning is not a **once-in-every-ten-years activity,** but an **on-going process** which must react quickly to the changing circumstances of the firm.

6.6   Diagram of planning activities

The following diagram shows the relationships between planning and budgeting.

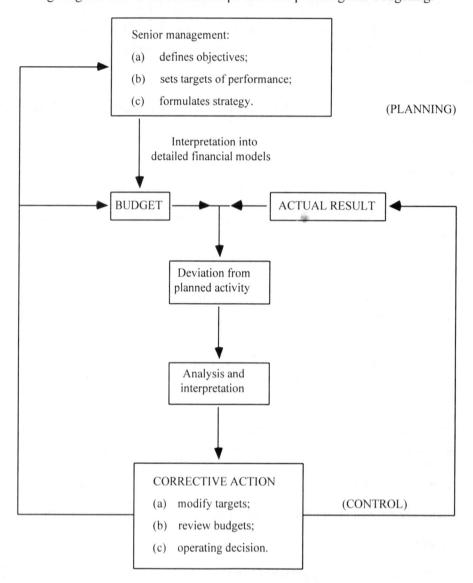

6.7   Importance of long-range planning for successful budgeting

No doubt some managers would argue that because long-range forecasting can never be completely accurate, it is pointless. However, a system of budgetary control introduced in isolation without any form of corporate or long-range planning is unlikely to yield its full potential benefit, and it is important to understand the reasons for this.

Firstly, a budget is not (or should not be) the same as a forecast. A forecast is a statement of what is expected to happen; a budget is a statement of what it is reasonable to believe can be made to happen. An organisation without a long-range plan probably starts with the sales forecast and perhaps tries to improve the expected results slightly by increasing the advertising budget. This modified sales forecast then becomes the budget on which the other budgets are based. However, this approach has several limitations, some of which are listed below:

(a)   In the absence of specified long-term objectives, there are no criteria against which to evaluate possible courses of action. Managers do not know what they should be trying to achieve.

(b)   Performance evaluation can only be on a superficial 'better/worse than last year' basis: no one has assessed the *potential* of the business.

(c)   Many decisions eg, capital expenditure decisions or the decision to introduce a new product, can only be taken on a long-term basis. Long-term forecasts may be inaccurate, but they are better than no forecast at all. A company with no long-range forecasting would be in dire straits when, sooner or later, sales of its existing products decline.

(d)   There is a limit to the influence a company can exert over events in the short term (eg, by increased advertising). If it wishes to improve its position markedly, it must think long term.

(e)   Eventually some factor other than sales may become the limiting factor eg, shortage of materials or labour. If the company has not anticipated the situation, it may simply have to live with the problem. With adequate long-range planning it might be able to avoid or overcome it.

6.8   What does management hope to get out of budgeting?

The principal advantages relate to:

(a)   planning and co-ordination;
(b)   authorising and delegating;
(c)   evaluating performance;
(d)   discerning trends;
(e)   communicating and motivating;
(f)   control.

6.9   Planning and co-ordination

Success in business is closely related to success in planning for the future. In this context the budget serves three functions:

(a)   It provides a formal planning framework that ensures planning does take place.

(b)   It co-ordinates the various separate aspects of the business by providing a master plan (the *master budget)* for the business as a whole (this is particularly important in a large organisation engaged in making several different products, where otherwise it is too easy for individual managers to concentrate on their own aspects of the business).

(c)   Though not all decisions can be anticipated, the budget provides a framework of reference within which later operating decisions can be taken.

6.10   Authorising and delegating

Adoption of a budget by management explicitly authorises the decisions made within it. This serves two functions:

(a)   the need continuously to ask for top management decisions is reduced;
(b)   the responsibility for carrying out the decisions is delegated to individual managers.

6.11   Evaluating performance

One of the functions of accounting information is that it provides a basis for the measurement of managerial performance. By setting targets for each manager to achieve, the budget provides a benchmark, against which his actual performance can be assessed objectively.

Note, however, that before a budget can successfully be used for this purpose, it must be accepted as reasonable by the individual manager whose area of responsibility it covers and whose performance is to be evaluated.

The effect of budgeting and performance appraisal on people is discussed in detail later.

6.12   Discerning trends

It is important that management should be made aware as soon as possible of any new trends, whether in relation to production or marketing. The budget, by providing specific expectations with which actual performance is continuously compared, supplies a mechanism for the early detection of any unexpected trend.

6.13   Communicating and motivating

The application of budgeting within an organisation should lead to a good communications structure. Managers involved in the setting of budgets for their own responsibility need to have agreed strategies and policies communicated down to them. A good system of downwards communication should itself encourage good upwards and sideways communication in the organisation. Budgets that have been agreed by managers should provide some motivation towards their achievement.

6.14   Control

When the goals have been set for the organisation, the management uses the budgetary system to control the running of the business to evaluate the extent to which those goals are achieved. By a continuous comparison of actual performance with planned results, deviations or variances are quickly identified and appropriate action initiated. This is a fundamental aspect of the whole process: if targets were set but little or no attempt were made to measure the extent to which they were achieved, then the advantages of budgeting would be severely curtailed.

There is, however, a danger in adhering to the budget too inflexibly. Circumstances may change, and the budget should change accordingly or the control system should identify separately the variances arising due to the changed conditions. Organisations operate within a dynamic environment, and the control systems need to be appropriately flexible.

6.15   Activity

List the four key components of corporate planning.

6.16   Activity solution

Components:	Objectives
	Strategy
	Operating plans
	Control

6.17   Distinguishing long-term and short-term planning

Long and short-term plans are both a means of communicating targets but they differ in terms of their style and sources of information.

These may be tabulated as below:

	Long term	*Short term*
Depth of information	Broad	Detailed
Source of information	External and internal	Internal
Style of information	Quantitative and descriptive	Quantitative

Long-term planning is usually concerned with a 5 year time horizon, whereas short-term plans (or budgets) are often constructed for a 1 year time horizon.

7 RELEVANT COSTS FOR LONG-TERM PLANNING

7.1 Introduction

The basic principles of relevant costs are no different to those you have learned earlier in this text, but the longer time horizon may make some costs relevant for long-term planning which would not be relevant in a shorter time period.

7.2 Future cash flows

Any costs which give rise to future cash flows within the planning period are relevant costs. These may include costs which are fixed in the short-term but which become controllable within the horizon of the long-term plan. Examples would include rents payable under lease agreements which terminate in the planning period.

7.3 Opportunity costs

Again the length of the time horizon may introduce a greater number of opportunities which do not exist within a shorter time-scale. Where such opportunities arise this could change or introduce opportunity costs which do not exist in the short-term. An example would be new products becoming possible because of technological developments and staff training.

8 COPING WITH INFLATION

8.1 Inflation

> **Definition** Inflation may be defined alternatively as:
>
> (a)   a general increase in prices; or
> (b)   a fall in the value of money.
>
> The effect is that money will buy less goods or, to put it another way, the same quantity of goods will cost more money.

8.2 Effect on budgets

In inflationary conditions budgeting is made more difficult because a prediction has to be made not only of future income and expenditure in real terms, but also an estimate of the level of inflation in order to arrive at a satisfactory value of the money which must be spent.

8.3 Example

LFC bought 500 tons of material for its production process last year at a cost of £2 per ton. It expects production levels to increase by 20% next year and inflation of 5% is expected to prevail. How much should LFC budget in respect of material?

Current situation	Increase due to production	Budget in real terms	Inflation	Budget in money terms
500 tons @ £2/ton = £1,000	20% × £1,000 = £200	£1,200	5% × £1,200 = £60	£1,260

Thus, if the price level remained constant LFC could expect to spend £1,200 on material. Because of inflation, however, an additional £60 must be budgeted, resulting in a total of £1,260.

8.4 Effect on control

Inflation will lead to changes in prices, as illustrated above. Because inflation is so difficult to predict, however, it is unlikely that estimates will in fact be met. Thus there is, almost inevitably, certain to be a price variance which is due to inflation - a situation outside the control of the company. It would be possible to isolate the effects of this inflation variance, but the cost of doing so may be prohibitive. Nevertheless, without such isolation the control function becomes much more difficult.

8.5   Effect on decisions

Decisions may become clouded in inflationary conditions for two reasons:

(a)   the problem of estimating: costs associated with different options may be wrongly adjusted for inflation;

(b)   different factors may have different rates of inflation associated with them.

For example, consider the following two options:

		Option (i) £	Option (ii) £
Costs:			
	Materials	8,000	3,500
	Labour	2,000	6,000
	Overheads	2,000	2,000
	Total	12,000	11,500

As option (ii) is cheaper, it would be selected.

Assume, however, that in the following year rates of inflation will be as follows:

	%
Material	Nil
Labour	25
Overheads	10

Forecasts for the next year would become:

	Option (i) £	Option (ii) £
Materials	8,000	3,500
Labour	2,500	7,500
Overheads	2,200	2,200
	12,700	13,200

Option (ii), as a result of the differing rates of inflation, is now the less attractive of the two options.

Other problem areas include:

(a)   Valuation of stock - inflation will erode the value of stock and a system such as FIFO will result in higher profit figures being recorded than may be applicable. Conversely, LIFO will result in an understatement of stock values.

(b)   Plant and machinery will be recorded at a value lower than their money value.

(c)   Prices will be difficult to set if a sufficient provision for inflation is to be allowed for.

8.6   The time value of money

The time value of money is really an opportunity cost, the value of which is partly derived (but not wholly caused) by inflation.

Money is a resource which can be invested in a number of alternatives in order to provide a reward for the investor. When considering short term plans and decisions the time that elapses between investing and being rewarded is short and consequently the opportunity cost of the money invested is small and insignificant. In such situations this opportunity cost is ignored.

However as the time horizon lengthens the value of the opportunity cost increases and begins to become significant and therefore relevant. The opportunity cost is the reward forgone and as any investor will expect a real return on their investment the cost will exceed the rate of inflation.

Thus the opportunity cost comprises an inflation cost plus the reward forgone from an alternative investment.

9 UNCERTAINTY AND LONG-TERM PLANNING

9.1 Introduction

Uncertainty is the risk element of long-term planning; if there were no uncertainty the control systems used to compare actual and planned performance would not be required.

9.2 Coping with uncertainty

It is an accepted fact that the further into the future one tries to predict the more uncertain is the outcome. The reason for this is the variety of non-controllable events that could occur and thus impinge on the plans of the organisation.

Earlier in this text probabilities have been explained in the context of decision making. Since planning also involves making choices it can be seen that it is not too different from decision making in principle. Thus the same techniques of probability estimates, random numbers and simulation modelling may be used in long-term planning.

10 CHAPTER SUMMARY

In this chapter we have considered the relationship between long-term and short-term planning and the detailed preparation techniques of budgets.

The effects of uncertainty, inflation and the time value of money were then considered in the context of long-term planning.

11 SELF TEST QUESTIONS

11.1   What is a principal budget factor? (2.2)

11.2   Define zero-based budgeting. (3.1)

11.3   What are the benefits of zero based budgeting. (3.3)

11.4   Define incremental budgeting. (4.1)

11.5   Distinguish the information required for zero-based budgeting and incremental budgeting. (5)

11.6   Explain corporate planning. (6.1)

11.7   Why is long-range planning important for successful budgeting? (6.7)

11.8   Explain the time value of money in the context of long-term planning. (8.6)

18 ACCOUNTING CONTROL SYSTEMS: QUANTITATIVE TECHNIQUES

INTRODUCTION & LEARNING OBJECTIVES

This chapter builds on the budgeting principles explained in the previous chapter and explains the quantitative aspects of budgeting.

When you have studied this chapter you should be able to do the following:

- Identify quantitative aids which may be used in budgeting.
- Analyse costs into fixed and variable components.
- Apply learning curve theory to budgeting.
- Explain the problems of uncertainty in budgeting.
- Explain the use of probability and what-if analysis in budgeting.

Some of the techniques covered in this chapter were the subject of a discursive question in June 1995, where candidates were asked to explain how a business might improve the budgetary planning process.

Any of the techniques could well be built into a budgeting, costing or pricing question in future examinations; you should ensure that you are familiar with their application.

1 COST PREDICTION

1.1 Introduction

The use of cost behaviour described in the previous sections rests on being able to predict costs associated with a given level of activity. Such data is not available from traditional cost analysis, and alternative approaches must be used. In this process historical information provides valuable guidance, but it must be recognised that the environment is not static, and what was relevant in the past may not be relevant in the future.

Five main approaches may be identified:

(a)   the engineering approach;
(b)   the account analysis approach;
(c)   the high-low method;
(d)   scatter charts; and
(e)   regression analysis.

(c), (d) and (e) are covered in detail in Chapter 7. Decision making and short run decisions: theoretical aspects. You should refer back to that chapter now before attempting the example that follows in this chapter.

In all of these approaches the assumption is made that the linear model of cost behaviour is valid, and therefore the relation between costs, y, and activity, x, is the form:

$y = a + bx$

where   y   =   total costs
          x   =   activity level
          a   =   fixed costs
          b   =   unit variable (or marginal) cost

These five approaches are considered below, followed by the possibility of making less restrictive assumptions about cost behaviour.

1.2   The engineering approach

This approach is based on building up a complete specification of all inputs (eg, materials, labour, overheads) required to produce given levels of output. This approach is therefore based on technical specification, which is then costed out using expected input prices.

This approach works reasonably well in a single product or start-up situation - indeed in the latter it may be the only feasible approach. However, it is difficult to apply in a multi-product situation, especially where there are joint costs, or the exact output mix is not known.

1.3   The account analysis approach

Rather than using the technical information, this approach uses the information contained in the ledger accounts. These are analysed and categorised as either fixed or variable (or semi-variable). Thus, for example, material purchase accounts would represent variable costs, office salaries a fixed cost. Since the ledger accounts are not designed for use in this way, some reorganisation and reclassification of accounts may be required.

Students should note that this is the approach implicit in many examination questions.

The problems with this approach are several:

(a)   Inspection does not always indicate the true nature of costs. For example, today factory wages would normally be a fixed cost, with only overtime and/or bonuses as the variable element.

(b)   Accounts are by their nature summaries, and often contain transactions of different categories.

(c)   It rests on historic information with the problems noted above.

2   REGRESSION

2.1   Linear correlation

When the points on a scatter diagram tend to lie in a narrow band, there is a strong correlation between the variables. This band may be curved or straight. For example:

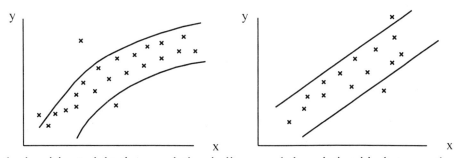

When the band is straight the correlation is linear and the relationship between the variables can be expressed in terms of the equation of a straight line. It is this type of correlation that will be studied throughout this chapter.

2.2   Regression analysis example

The following table shows the amount of fertiliser applied to identical fields, and their resulting yields:

Fertiliser (kg/hectare)	Yield (tonnes/hectare)
100	40
200	45
300	50
400	65
500	70
600	70
700	80

Calculate the regression line for y on x.

2.3   Solution

The calculation is set out as follows, where x is the amount of fertiliser in units of **hundreds** of kg/hectare and y is the yield in tonnes/hectare.

x	y	xy	x^2	
1	40	40	1	
2	45	90	4	
3	50	150	9	
4	65	260	16	
5	70	350	25	
6	70	420	36	
7	80	560	49	
28	420	1,870	140	n = 7

$$b = \frac{n\sum xy - \sum x \sum y}{n\sum x^2 - (\sum x)^2}$$

(Try to avoid rounding at this stage since, although n∑xy and ∑x∑y are large, their difference is much smaller.)

$$= \frac{(7 \times 1,870) - (28 \times 420)}{(7 \times 140) - (28 \times 28)}$$

$$= \frac{13,090 - 11,760}{980 - 784} = \frac{1,330}{196}$$

$$= 6.79$$

(Ensure you make a note of this fraction in your workings. It may help later.)

$$a = \frac{\sum y}{n} - \frac{b\sum x}{n}$$

$$= \frac{420}{7} - 6.79 \times \frac{28}{7} = 60 - 27.16$$

$$= 32.84$$

∴   the regression line for y on x is:

y   =   32.84 + 6.79x   (x in hundreds of kg per hectare
                                             y in tonnes per hectare)

(Always specify what x and y are very carefully.)

This line would be used to estimate the yield corresponding to a given amount of fertiliser. If, say, 250 kg/hectare of fertiliser is available, it is possible to predict the expected yield by using the regression line and replacing x with 2.5:

y   =   32.84 + 6.79 × 2.5

      =   32.84 + 16.975 = 49.815

∴ y = 50 tonnes/hectare (rounding to whole numbers in line with original data)

2.4   The regression line of x on y

If asked to find a line of best fit the calculations just shown are what is required. This second regression line is less likely to be needed in the exam, but it may be requested, and it gives some insight into correlation.

The method of finding the regression line is the same as for the regression line of y on x, but with x and y interchanged. Thus the equation is:

$$x = a' + b'y$$

where a' $= \bar{x} - b'\bar{y}$ $= \dfrac{\sum x}{n} - \dfrac{b'\sum y}{n}$

$$b' = \dfrac{n\sum xy - \sum x \sum y}{n\sum y^2 - (\sum y)^2}$$

To calculate the equation for the data of the previous section, $\sum y^2$ is required.

$$y^2$$

1,600
2,025
2,500
4,225
4,900
4,900
6,400
———
26,550
———

$$b' = \dfrac{n\sum xy - \sum x \sum y}{n\sum y^2 - (\sum y)^2}$$

$$= \dfrac{1,330}{7 \times 26,550 - (420)^2} \quad \text{(1,330 and 420 come from the previous calculation)}$$

$$= \dfrac{1,330}{9,450} = 0.141$$

$$a' = \dfrac{\sum x}{n} - \dfrac{b'\sum y}{n}$$

$$= \dfrac{28}{7} - \dfrac{0.141 \times 420}{7} = -4.46$$

$\therefore$ The regression line of *x* on *y* is:

$$x = -4.46 + 0.141y$$

This equation would be used to estimate the amount of fertiliser that had resulted in a given yield. Eg, if the yield was 60 tonnes/hectare, the estimated amount of fertiliser would be given by:

$$x = -4.46 + 0.141 \times 60$$

$$= 4.0 \quad \text{(hundreds of kg/hectare)}$$

$\therefore$ 400 kg/hectare of fertiliser would have been used to give a yield of 60 tonnes/hectare.

2.5   Activity

If $\Sigma x = 560$, $\Sigma y = 85$, $\Sigma x^2 = 62,500$, $\Sigma xy = 14,200$ and $n = 12$, find the regression line of y on x (the line of best fit).

2.6   Activity solution

Equation of line is: $y = a + bx$

$$b = \frac{12 \times 14,200 - 560 \times 85}{12 \times 62,500 - 560 \times 560} = \frac{122,800}{436,400} = 0.281$$

$$a = \frac{85}{12} - 0.281 \times \frac{560}{12} = -6.03$$

Regression line is: $y = -6.03 + 0.281x$

2.7   Regression and correlation

The angle between the two regression lines y on x and x on y decreases as the correlation between the variables increases.

In the case of perfect correlation the angle between the lines is zero ie, the two lines coincide and become one.

At the other extreme, the angle between the lines becomes 90^0 when there is no correlation between the variables. In this case one line is parallel to the x-axis and the other parallel to the y-axis.

Measures of correlation are discussed later in this text.

2.8   Interpolation and extrapolation

As has been shown, regression lines can be used to calculate intermediate values of variables ie, values within the known range. This is known as **interpolation** and it is one of the main uses of regression lines.

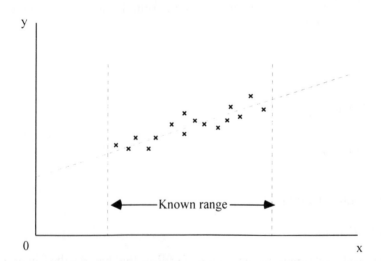

It is also possible to extend regression lines beyond the range of values used in their calculation. It is then possible to calculate values of the variables that are outside the limits of the original data, this is known as **extrapolation**.

The problem with extrapolation is that it assumes that the relationship already calculated is still valid. This may or may not be so.

For example, if the fertiliser was increased outside the given range there would come a point where it had an adverse effect on the yield. The seed might actually be damaged by too much fertiliser.

The resultant diagram could be of this form:

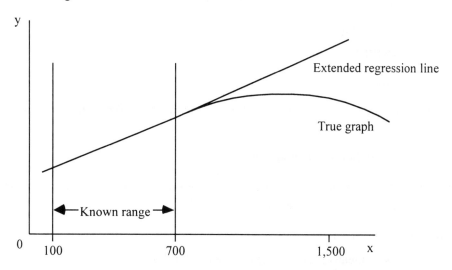

Therefore the yield from using 1,500 kg/hectare of fertiliser as estimated from the regression line may be very different from that actually achieved in practice.

Generally speaking, extrapolation must be treated with caution, since once outside the range of known values other factors may influence the situation, and the relationship which has been approximated as linear over a limited range may not be linear outside that range. Nevertheless, extrapolation of a time series is a valuable and widely used technique for forecasting.

3   CORRELATION

3.1   Introduction

Through regression analysis it is possible to derive a linear relationship between two variables and hence estimate unknown values. However, this does not measure the **degree of correlation** between the variables ie, how strong the connection is between the two variables. It is possible to find a line of best fit through any assortment of data points; this doesn't mean that we are justified in using the equation of that line.

3.2   Correlation coefficient

Pearson's correlation coefficient, r, is defined as:

$$r = \frac{n\sum xy - \sum x \sum y}{\sqrt{(n\sum x^2 - (\sum x)^2)(n\sum y^2 - (\sum y)^2)}}$$

Practice is needed at applying this formula to data and interpreting the result.

3.3   Example

Using the data of the example in 2.8 relating to fertiliser and crop yield calculate the correlation coefficient.

The totals required are:

$\sum x = 28$, $\sum y = 420$, $\sum xy = 1,870$, $\sum x^2 = 140$, $\sum y^2 = 26,550$, $n = 7$

3.4   Solution

$$\text{Thus}\quad r\ =\ \frac{(7\times 1{,}870)-(28\times 420)}{\sqrt{((7\times 140)-(28\times 28))((7\times 26{,}550)-(420\times 420))}}$$

$$=\ \frac{13{,}090-11{,}760}{\sqrt{(980-784)(185{,}850-176{,}400)}}$$

$$=\ \frac{1{,}330}{\sqrt{(196\times 9{,}450)}}$$

$$=\ 0.98$$

(If you look at your calculations for b and b' you will notice that you've already found the terms in this section.)

3.5   Interpretation of coefficient of correlation

Having calculated the value of r, it is necessary to interpret this result. Does   r = 0.98   mean that there is high correlation, low correlation or no correlation?

r varies between +1 and −1 where:

$r\ =\ +1$ means perfect positive linear correlation;

$r\ =\ 0$ means no correlation; and

$r\ =\ -1$ means perfect negative linear correlation

So in this case the value of 0.98 indicates a high degree of positive correlation between the variables.

In general, the closer that r is to +1 (or − 1) the higher the degree of correlation. This will usually be confirmed by the scatter diagram where the points will lie in a narrow band for such values.

It must be realised that r only measures the amount of linear correlation ie, the tendency to a straight line relationship. It is quite possible to have strong non-linear correlation and yet have a value of r close to zero. This is one reason why it is important in practice to draw the scatter graph first.

The more data points the farther r may be from 1 and still indicate good correlation. If there are few data points, as here, we would wish to see r very close to 1 (clearly if there were only 2 points they will lie exactly on the line of best fit.

3.6   Coefficient of determination

The coefficient of determination is the square of the coefficient of correlation, and so is denoted by r^2. The advantage of knowing the coefficient of determination is that it is a measure of how much of the variation in the dependent variable is 'explained' by the variation of the independent variable. The variation not accounted for by variations in the independent variable will be due to random fluctuations, or to other specific factors which have not been identified in considering the two-variable problem.

In the example on fertiliser and yield, r had a value of 0.98 and so $r^2 = 0.96$.

Thus, variations in the amount of fertiliser applied accounts for 96% of the variation in the yield obtained.

3.7   Spurious correlation

Students should be aware of the big danger involved in correlation analysis. Two variables, when compared, may show a high degree of correlation but they may still have no direct connection. Such correlation is termed **spurious** or **nonsense** correlation and unless two variables can reasonably be assumed to have some direct connection the correlation coefficient found will be meaningless, however high it may be.

The following are examples of variables between which there is high but spurious correlation:

(a)   Salaries of school teachers and consumption of alcohol.
(b)   Number of television licences and the number of admissions to mental hospitals.

Such examples clearly have no direct **causal** relationship. However, there may be some other variable which is a causal factor common to both of the original variables. For example, the general rise in living standards and real incomes is responsible both for the increase in teachers' salaries and for the increase in the consumption of alcohol.

3.8   Activity

If $r = 0.42$, how much of the variation in the dependent variable is explained by the variation of the independent variable?

3.9   Activity solution

If $r = 0.42$, then $r^2 = 0.1764$, so about 17.6% of the variation is explained by variations in the independent variable (poor correlation).

4   TIME SERIES

4.1   Introduction

A time series is the name given to a set of observations taken at equal intervals of time eg, daily, weekly, monthly, etc. The observations can be plotted against time to give an overall picture of what is happening. **The horizontal axis is always the time axis.**

Examples of time series are total annual exports, monthly unemployment figures, daily average temperatures, etc.

4.2   Example

The following data relates to the production (in tonnes) of floggels by the North West Engineering Co. These are the quarterly totals taken over four years from 19X2 to 19X5.

	1st Qtr	2nd Qtr	3rd Qtr	4th Qtr
19X2	91	90	94	93
19X3	98	99	97	95
19X4	107	102	106	110
19X5	123	131	128	130

This time series will now be graphed so that an overall picture can be gained of what is happening to the company's production figures.

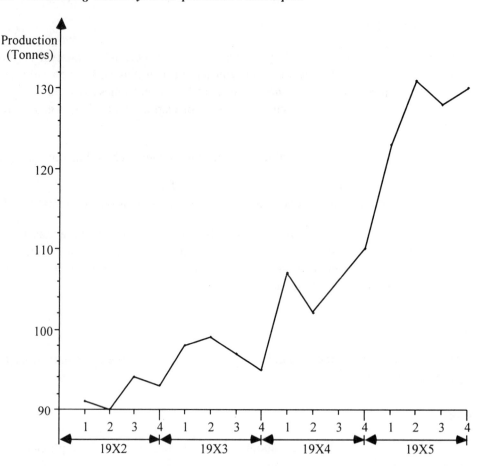

Note: that each point must be plotted at the **end** of the relevant quarter.

The graph shows clearly how the production of floggels has increased over the four-year time period. This is particularly true during the last year considered.

4.3   Variations in observations

A time series is influenced by a number of factors, the most important of these being:

(a)   **Long-term trends**

This is the way in which the graph of a time series appears to be moving over a long interval of time when the short-term fluctuations have been smoothed out. The rise or fall is due to factors which only change slowly eg,

(i)   increase or decrease in population;

(ii)   technological improvements;

(iii)   competition from abroad.

(b)   **Cyclical variations**

This is the wave-like appearance of a time series graph when taken over a number of years. Generally, it is due to the influence of booms and slumps in industry. The distance in time from one peak to the next is often approximately 5 to 7 years.

(c)   **Seasonal variation**

This is a regular rise and fall over specified intervals of time. The interval of time can be any length – hours, days, weeks, etc., and the variations are of a periodic type with a fairly definite period eg,:

(i)   rises in the number of goods sold before Christmas and at sale times;

(ii)   rises in the demand for gas and electricity at certain times during the day;

(iii)   rises in the number of customers using a restaurant at lunch-time and dinner time.

These are referred to under the general heading of 'seasonal' variations as a common example is the steady rise and fall of, for example, sales over the four seasons of the year.

However, as can be seen from the examples, the term is also used to cover regular variations over other short periods of time.

They should not be confused with cyclical variations (paragraph b) which are long-term fluctuations with an interval between successive peaks greater than one year.

(d)   **Residual or random variations**

This covers any other variation which cannot be ascribed to (a), (b) or (c) above. This is taken as happening entirely at random due to unpredictable causes eg:

(i)   strikes;
(ii)   fires;
(iii)   sudden changes in taxes.

Not all time series will contain all four elements. For example, not all sales figures show seasonal variations.

4.4   A time series graph

The graph in the example covered the quarterly production of floggels over a four-year time period.

The long-term trend (a) and seasonal (quarterly) (c) were obvious from the graph. However, in order to be able to observe any cyclical variations it is usually necessary to have data covering a much wider time-span, say 10 – 15 years minimum.

The following graph shows the production (in tonnes) of widgets for each quarter of the 18 years from 19X1 to 19Y8.

Production
(Tonnes)

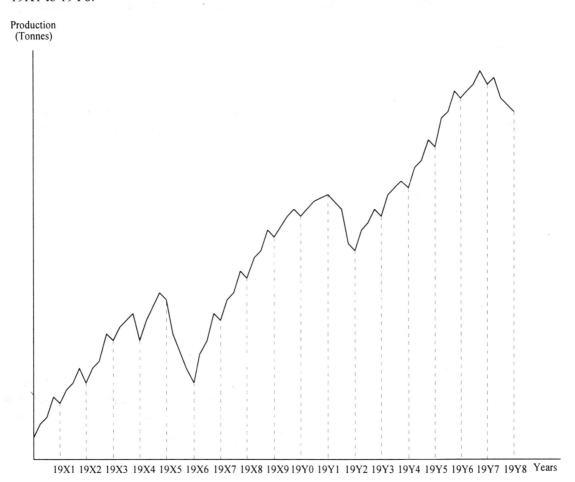

19X1 19X2 19X3 19X4 19X5 19X6 19X7 19X8 19X9 19Y0 19Y1 19Y2 19Y3 19Y4 19Y5 19Y6 19Y7 19Y8 Years

This time it is possible to detect:

(a)   The long-term trend – upwards in this case.

(b)   Cyclical variations – the wave like appearance of the graph shows that the cycle of production spans 6 years ie, the distance in time between successive peaks (and successive troughs) is 6 years.

(c)   Seasonal variation – since these are quarterly production figures this is sometimes called **quarterly variation**. These are the small steps in each year which are evident on the first graph. They occur because some parts of the year are busier than others and the actual pattern will depend very much on the type of industry eg, the building industry tends to be slack during the winter months because of the weather, whereas an engineering company may be quietest during the summer months due to holidays.

(d)   Residual variation – this is simply the difference between the actual figure and that predicted – taking into account trends, cyclical variations and seasonal variations. By its nature it cannot be fully explained.

4.5   Analysis of a time series

It is essential to be able to disentangle these various influences and measure each one separately. The main reasons for analysing a time series in this way are:

(a)   To be able to predict future values of the variable ie, to make forecasts.

(b)   To attempt to control future events.

(c)   To 'seasonally adjust' or 'deseasonalise' a set of data, that is to remove the seasonal effect. For example, seasonally adjusted unemployment values are more useful than actual unemployment values in studying the effects of the national economy and Government policies on unemployment.

5   ANALYSIS OF A TIME SERIES

5.1   Additive and multiplicative models

To analyse a time series, it is necessary to make an assumption about how the four components described combine to give the total effect. The simplest method is to assume that the components are added together ie, if:

$$A = \text{Actual value for the period}$$
$$T = \text{Trend component}$$
$$C = \text{Cyclical component}$$
$$S = \text{Seasonal component}$$
$$R = \text{Residual component}$$

Then $A = T + C + S + R$.   This is called an **additive model**.

Another method is to assume the components are multiplied together ie,:

$$A = T \times C \times S \times R$$

This is called a **multiplicative model**.

The additive model is the simplest, and is satisfactory when the fluctuations about the trend are within a constant band width. If, as is more usual, the fluctuations about the trend increase as the trend increases, the multiplicative model is used. Illustrated diagrammatically:

(a) y
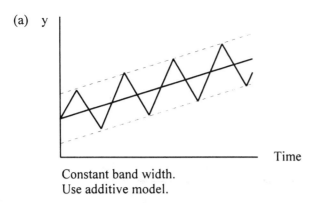

Constant band width.
Use additive model.

(b) y
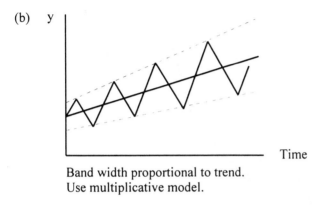

Band width proportional to trend.
Use multiplicative model.

5.2 Trend

The trend can be obtained by using regression to obtain the line of best fit through the points on the graph, taking x as the year numbers (1, 2, 3.... etc.) and y as the vertical variable. It is not necessary for the trend to be a straight line, as non-linear regression can be used, but for this method it is necessary to assume an appropriate mathematical form for the trend, such as parabola, hyperbola, exponential, etc. If the trend does not conform to any of these, the method cannot be used.

An alternative, which requires no assumption to be made about the nature of the curve, is to smooth out the fluctuations by moving averages.

The simplest way to explain the method is by means of an example.

5.3 Example

The following are the sales figures for Bloggs Brothers Engineering Ltd. for the fourteen years from 19X1 to 19Y4.

Year	Sales (£'000)
19X1	491
19X2	519
19X3	407
19X4	452
19X5	607
19X6	681
19X7	764
19X8	696
19X9	751
19Y0	802
19Y1	970
19Y2	1,026
19Y3	903
19Y4	998

Using the method of moving averages the general trend of sales will be established.

5.4 Solution

Step 1 First, it is advisable to draw a graph of the time series so that an overall picture can be gained and the cyclical movements seen.

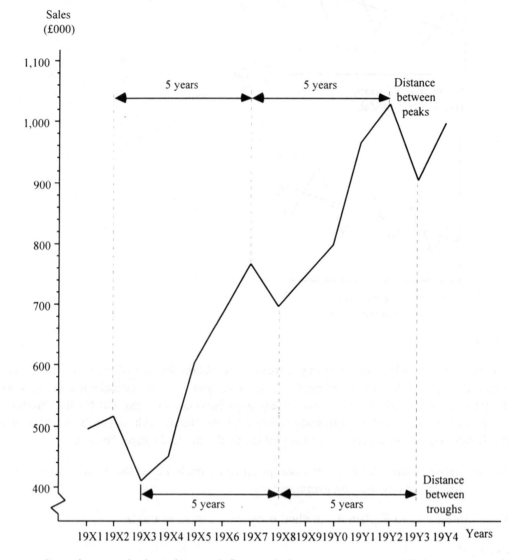

In order to calculate the trend figures it is necessary to establish the span of the cycle. From the graph it can easily be seen that the distance in time between successive peaks (and successive troughs) is 5 years; therefore a 5 point moving average must be calculated.

Step 2   A table of the following form is now drawn up:

Year	Sales (£'000)	5 yearly moving total	5 yearly moving average
19X1	491	-	-
19X2	519	-	-
19X3	407	2,476	495
19X4	452	2,666	533
19X5	607	2,911	582
19X6	681	3,200	640
19X7	764	3,499	700
19X8	696	3,694	739
19X9	751	3,983	797
19Y0	802	4,245	849
19Y1	970	4,452	890
19Y2	1,026	4,699	940
19Y3	903	-	-
19Y4	998	-	-

Notes on the calculation

(a)   As the name implies, the five yearly moving total is the sum of successive groups of 5 years' sales ie,

$$491 + 519 + 407 + 452 + 607 \ = \ 2,476$$

Then, advancing by one year:

$$519 + 407 + 452 + 607 + 681 \ = \ 2,666, \text{ etc.}$$

$$802 + 970 + 1,026 + 903 + 998 \ = \ 4,699$$

(b)   These moving totals are simply divided by 5 to give the moving averages ie,

$$2,476 \div 5 \ = \ 495$$

$$2,666 \div 5 \ = \ 533$$

$$4,699 \div 5 \ = \ 940$$

(c)   Averages are always plotted in the middle of the time period ie, 495 is the average of the figures for 19X1, 19X2, 19X3, 19X4 and 19X5 and so it is plotted at the end of 19X3, this being the mid-point of the time interval from the end of 19X1 to the end of 19X5. Similarly, 533 is plotted at the end of 19X4, and 940 is plotted at the end of 19Y2.

Step 2   A second graph is now drawn showing the original figures again and the trend figures ie, the five yearly moving averages.

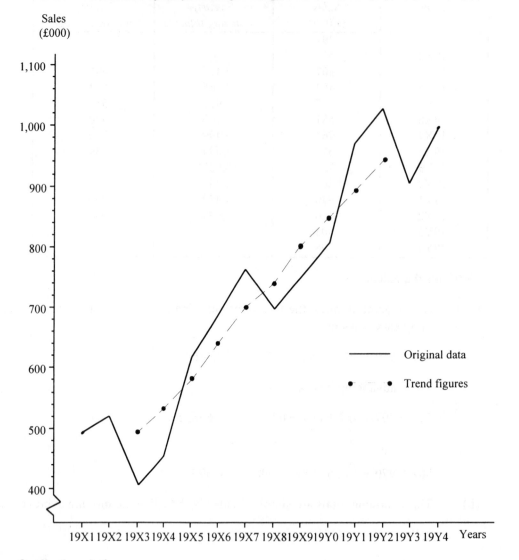

5.5   Cyclical variation

Having calculated the trend figures it is a simple matter to work out the cyclical variations.

For annual data, there cannot be a seasonal component. Hence, using the additive model,

$$A = T + C + R$$

Subtracting T from both sides,

$$A - T = C + R$$

So, by subtracting the trend values from the actual values, the combined cyclical and residual variation will be obtained.

If the multiplicative model is used, A must be divided by T,

$$A = T \times C \times R$$

$$\frac{A}{T} = C \times R$$

As before, this will be explained by way of an example.

5.6   Example

Using the same data, establish the cyclical variation, using the additive model.

5.7   Solution

Step 1   A table of the following type is drawn up:

Year	Period of moving averages	Sales (£'000) (A)	Trend figures (T)	Cyclical + Residual variation (A - T)
19X1	1	491	–	–
19X2	2	519	–	–
19X3	3	407	495	–88
19X4	4	452	533	–81
19X5	5	607	582	25
19X6	1	681	640	41
19X7	2	764	700	64
19X8	3	696	739	–43
19X9	4	751	797	–46
19Y0	5	802	849	–47
19Y1	1	970	890	80
19Y2	2	1,026	940	86
19Y3	3	903	–	–
19Y4	4	998	–	–

Notes on the calculation

The figures in the last column for the cyclical variation are just the differences between the actual sales and the trend figures ie,:

$$407 - 495 = -88$$
$$452 - 533 = -81$$
$$\vdots$$
$$1,026 - 940 = 86$$

The '+' and '–' signs are important since they show whether the actual figures are above or below the trend figures.

Step 2   To remove the residual component from C + R, another table must now be drawn up in order to establish the average cyclical variations.

	Period 1	Period 2	Period 3	Period 4	Period 5
Cyclical variation calculated above	– 41 80	– 64 86	–88 –43 –	–81 –46 –	25 –47 –
(i) Totals	121	150	–131	–127	–22
(ii) Average cyclical variation (= (i)/2)	60.5 61	75	–65.5 –66	–63.5 –64	–11

The individual variations have been averaged out for each year of the cycle ie,

$$\text{Year 1 of each cycle} = \frac{41+80}{2} = \frac{121}{2} = 60.5, \text{ rounded to } 61;$$

$$\text{Year 2 of each cycle} \quad = \quad \frac{64 + 86}{2} \quad = \quad \frac{150}{2} \quad = \quad 75$$

etc.

Step 3   One more step is necessary because the cyclical variation should total to zero, and 61 + 75 + (−66) + (−64) + (−11) = −5.

The adjustment is made by dividing the excess (− 5 in this case) by the number of years in the cycle (5 in this case) and subtracting the result from each of the cyclical variations.

Adjustment is −5 ÷ 5 = −1

Cyclical variations within each cycle are:

Year 1	61 − (−1)	=	61 + 1	=	62
Year 2	75 − (−1)	=	75 + 1	=	76
Year 3	−66 − (−1)	=	−66 + 1	=	−65
Year 4	−64 − (−1)	=	−64 + 1	=	−63
Year 5	−11 − (−1)	=	−11 + 1	=	−10

(and just as a check, the revised cyclical variations do total zero: 62 + 76 − 65 − 63 − 10 = 0)

5.8   Seasonal variations

When figures are available for a considerable number of years it is possible to establish the trend and the cyclical variations.

Usually, however, monthly or quarterly figures are only available for a few years, 3 or 4, say. In this case, it is possible to establish the trend by means of a moving average over an annual cycle by a method very similar to that used above. The span of the data is insufficient to find cyclical variations, but average seasonal variations can be found.

5.9   Example

The following table gives the takings (£000) of a shopkeeper in each quarter of 4 successive years.

Qtrs	1	2	3	4
19X1	13	22	58	23
19X2	16	28	61	25
19X3	17	29	61	26
19X4	18	30	65	29

Calculate the trend figures and quarterly variations, and draw a graph to show the overall trend and the original data.

5.10   Solution

Again the additive model will be used, but as the data is now over too short a time for any cyclical component to be apparent, the model becomes:

$$A \quad = \quad T + S + R$$

Step 1   It is necessary to draw up a table as follows:

1 Year & quarter	2 Takings (£'000) A	3 4 quarterly moving average	4 Centred value T	5 Quarterly + Residual variation S + R
1	13	-	-	-
2	22		-	-
3	58	29	30	28
4	23	30	31	-8
1	16	31	32	-16
2	28	32	33	-5
3	61	33	33	28
4	25	33	33	-8
1	17	33	33	-16
2	29	33	33	-4
3	61	33	34	27
4	26	34	34	-8
1	18	34	35	-17
2	30	35	36	-6
3	65	36	-	-
4	29	-	-	-

(19X1 covers quarters 1–4; 19X2 covers the next 1–4; 19X3 the next 1–4; 19X4 the final 1–4)

Notes on the calculation

Column 3

To smooth out quarterly fluctuations, it is necessary to calculate a 4-point moving average, since there are 4 quarters (or seasons) in a year.

ie, $\dfrac{13+22+58+23}{4} = \dfrac{116}{4} = 29$

then, advancing by one quarter:

$\dfrac{22+58+23+16}{4} = \dfrac{119}{4} = 30$ (rounding to nearest whole number)

$\dfrac{18+30+65+29}{4} = \dfrac{142}{4} = 36$ (rounding to nearest whole number)

Step 2   29 is the average of the figures for the four quarters of 19X1 and so if plotted, would be at the mid-point of the interval from the end of the first quarter to the end of the fourth quarter ie, half-way through the third quarter of 19X1.

Column 4

To find A – T, it is essential that A and T both relate to the same point in time. The four-quarterly moving averages do not correspond with any of the A values, the first coming between the second and third A values and so on down. To overcome this, the moving averages are 'centred' ie, averaged in twos. The first centred average will coincide with the third A value and so on.

Note: that this is necessary because the cycle has an even number of values (4) per cycle. Where there is an odd number of values per cycle, as in the previous example, the moving averages themselves correspond in time with A values, and centering should not be done.

The centering is as follows:

ie, $\dfrac{29+30}{2}$ =   30   (rounding up)

$\dfrac{30+31}{2}$ =   31   (rounding up)

$\dfrac{35+36}{2}$ =   36   (rounding up)

The first average now corresponds in time with the original value for the 3rd quarter, and so on.

These are the trend values.

Step 3   Column 5

A – T = S + R, hence the figures for the quarterly + residual variations are the differences between the actual figures and the centred values.

ie,   58 – 30   =   28
23 – 31   =   –8

30 – 36   =   –6

Step 4   In order to establish the quarterly variation another table must be drawn up to remove the residual variation *R*.

	Quarter 1	Quarter 2	Quarter 3	Quarter 4
	–	–	28	–8
	–16	–5	28	–8
	–16	–4	27	–8
	–17	–6	–	–
Totals	–49	–15	83	–24
Seasonal variation	–16	–5	28	–8

The individual variations have been averaged out for each quarter of the cycle:

ie,   Quarter 1 $\dfrac{-16+(-16)+(-17)}{3}$ = $\dfrac{-49}{3}$ =   –16

$$\text{Quarter 2} \quad \frac{-5+(-4)+(-6)}{3} \quad = \quad \frac{-15}{3} \quad = \quad -5$$

Step 5   The quarterly variations should total to zero again, but $-16 + (-5) + 28 + (-8) = -1$. However, the adjustment would only be $-1 \div 4$ ie, -0.25 which means using a spurious accuracy of two decimal places.   To avoid this one value only need be adjusted, choosing the greatest value as this will give the lowest relative adjustment error.

1st	Quarter	=		−16
2nd	Quarter	=		−5
3rd	Quarter	=	28 + 1	= 29
4th	Quarter	=		−8
				—
				0
				—

Step 6

Takings (£'000)

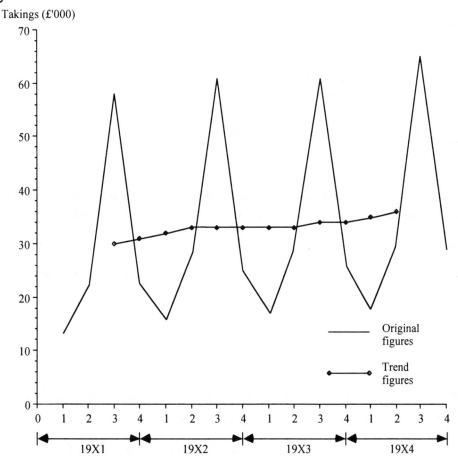

Step 7   **Comment**

As can be seen from the calculations and the graph, the takings show a slight upward trend and the seasonal (quarterly) variations are considerable.

5.11   Seasonally adjusted figures

A popular way of presenting a time series is to give the seasonally adjusted or deseasonalised figures.

This is a very simple process once the seasonal variations are known.

For the additive model:

Seasonally adjusted data		Original data		Seasonal variation		
	=		−		=	A − S

For the multiplicative model:

Seasonally adjusted data		Original data		Seasonal indices		
	=		÷		=	A ÷ S

The main purpose in calculating seasonally adjusted figures is to remove the seasonal influence from the original data so that non-seasonal influences can be seen more clearly.

5.12   Example

The same shopkeeper found his takings for the four quarters of 19X5 were   £19,000,   £32,000,   £65,000 and £30,000 respectively. Has the upward trend continued?

5.13   Solution

De-seasonalising the figures gives:

Seasonally adjusted
figures (£'000)

Quarter 1	19 − (−16)	=	35
Quarter 2	32 − (−5)	=	37
Quarter 3	65 − 29	=	36
Quarter 4	30 − (−8)	=	38

So, as can be seen from comparing the seasonally adjusted figures with the trend figures calculated earlier, the takings are indeed still increasing ie, there is an upward trend.

5.14   Example

Having mentioned a multiplication model (or proportional model) this now needs illustrating.

The following data will be seasonally adjusted using 'seasonal indices.'

	Quarter			
	1	2	3	4
Sales (£'000)	59	50	61	92
Seasonal variation	−2%	−21%	−9%	+30%

If $A = T \times S \times R$, the deseasonalised data is A/S.

A decrease of − 2% means a factor of 0.98. Similarly, an increase of 30% means a factor of 1.3. Hence the seasonal factors are   0.98,   0.79,   0.91,   1.30   respectively. The actual data, A, must be **divided** by these values to remove the seasonal effect. Hence:

A	*Seasonal factor (S)*	*Seasonally adjusted figure (= A/S)*
59	0.98	60
50	0.79	63
61	0.91	67
92	1.30	71

While actual sales are lowest in spring and highest in winter, the seasonally adjusted values show a fairly steady increase throughout the year.

5.15   Time series applied to forecasting models

It has been shown in the above sections how data can be de-seasonalised in order to identify the underlying trend. However, it is often the case that predictions are required to be made about the future, but taking into account seasonal factors.

This can be done in two ways:

(a)   by fitting a line of best fit (straight or curved) by eye (preferably through the trend found by moving averages); and

(b)   by using linear regression.

The line is then extended to the right in order to estimate future trend values. This 'trend' value is then adjusted in order to take account of the seasonal factors.

Hence, the forecast $= T_e + S$,   where T_e = extrapolated trend.

Residual variations are by nature random and therefore unforecastable.

5.16   Example

Using the data from the shopkeeper predict the takings of the shop for the first and second quarters of 19X5.

5.17   Solution

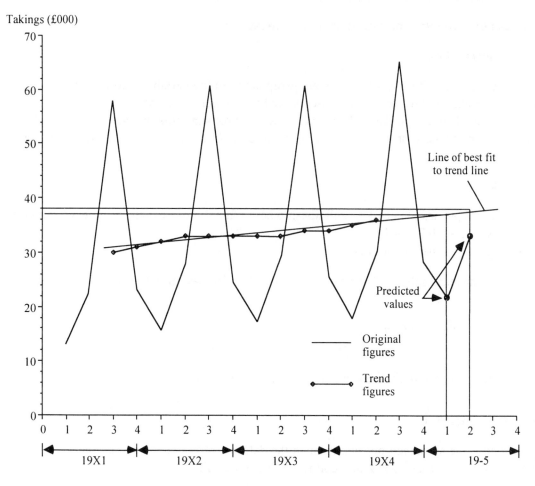

Takings (£000)

From the graph it can be seen that the trend line predicts values as follows:

Quarter in 19X5	(i) Trend value	(ii) Seasonal variation	(i) + (ii) Final prediction
1	37,000	−16,000	21,000
2	38,000	−5,000	33,000

The predicted values of £21,000 and £33,000 have been plotted on the graph.

For the multiplicative model, the extrapolated trend must be **multiplied** by the appropriate seasonal factor. Thus in the example in paragraph 5.14, if the predicted trend value for the first quarter of the following year was £65,000, the appropriate seasonal factor for this quarter being 0.98, the forecast of actual sales would be £65,000 × 0.98 = £64,000 (to the nearest £000).

5.18   Time series applied to forecasting models – alternative method

An alternative method for making predictions is to use linear regression in order to establish the trend line in the first place (rather than using the method of moving averages), and then on the basis of this regression line it is possible to predict the figures for the underlying trend. These are then used to estimate seasonal variations and the extrapolated trend values are calculated from the regression equation.

5.19   Conclusion

It is important to appreciate that although the various methods which have been used to identify seasonal (and cyclical) factors and hence predict future values of a particular variable will give different results, it is often not possible to say that any one answer is more valid than another. All methods essentially assume that whatever has caused fluctuations and trends to occur in the past will continue similarly into the future. Clearly this is often not the case and therefore any value forecast by any of the methods should be treated with due caution.

6   FORECASTING USING CORRELATION AND REGRESSION

6.1   The use of correlation and regression in forecasting

Causal forecasting

This is used where there is a causal relationship between the variable whose value is to be forecast and another variable whose value can be ascertained for the period for which the forecast is to be made. If, for example, there is correlation between the demand for sun roofs in a given year and the sales of new cars in the previous year, then this year's car sales could be used to predict sun roof demand for next year.

6.2   Example

Hi-Fi Videos plc has obtained the relationship between net profit (y) and number of sales outlets (x) as:
$$y = 0.25x - 1.9$$
where   y   =   net profit in £m.

It plans to increase sales outlets next year to 18. The forecast of net profit for next year will therefore be:

$$\text{Net profit} = 0.25 \times 18 - 1.9$$
$$= £2.6m$$

This is subject to the limitations of extrapolation already discussed.

6.3   Trend extrapolation

The trend is the smoothed-out line through the data when plotted against a time scale. The time scale is taken as the x-variable, and the trend is the line of best fit.

6.4   **Example**

Year	Sales (£'000)
19X3	12.0
19X4	11.5
19X5	15.8
19X6	15.0
19X7	18.5

To forecast sales for 19X8:

The sales in £000 units are taken as the y-values. Year 19X3 is taken as x = 1, 19X4 as x = 2, 19X5 as x = 3, etc., in which case the forecast for year 19X8 will be the value of y when x = 6.

The least squares regression line of y on x (the line of best fit) for this data is:

$$y \quad = \quad 9.61 + 1.65x$$

(Students should check this for themselves.)

Hence, the forecast of sales for year 19X8 is obtained by putting x = 6 in this equation, giving:

$$y \quad = \quad 9.61 + 1.65 \times 6$$
$$\quad = \quad 19.51 \ (\text{£000})$$
$$\quad = \quad \text{£19,510}$$

Notes:

(i)   Any consecutive numbers could be used for the year values; there are computational advantages in taking 19X3 as –2, 19X4 as –1, 19X5 as 0, etc. as this makes $\Sigma x = 0$. In this case the forecast for 19X8 would be obtained when x = 3; and the regression line would be y = 14.56 + 1.65x.

(ii) To forecast future demands, previous demands should be used, not previous sales. These are not the same as there may have been unfulfilled demand due to stock-outs.

7   **THE LEARNING CURVE PHENOMENON**

7.1   **Introduction**

Accountants are often said to assume that, within the relevant range of activity, costs display linear characteristics so that the variable cost per unit and the total fixed cost remain unchanged and can be depicted as lines (rather than curves) on a break-even chart. This section considers the learning curve phenomenon where the linear assumption is dropped.

7.2   **The phenomenon stated and illustrated**

It has been observed in some industries, particularly where skilled labour predominates, that as more of the same units are produced, there is a reduction in the time taken to manufacture them so that a learning process occurs when production on a new item is commenced; eventually the learning process will end and a steady state is reached.

The learning curve phenomenon states that each time the number of units produced is doubled, the cumulative average time per unit is reduced by a constant percentage.

If this constant reduction is 20%, this is referred to as an 80% learning curve, and a 10% reduction as a 90% learning curve.

This will be illustrated by assuming that it has taken 400 direct labour hours to manufacture the first unit of a new product. As in the past for this business it is anticipated that a 75% learning curve will be followed. A schedule can be drawn up with the following important headings and calculations:

(1) Cumulative number of units	(2) Cumulative average time per unit	(1) × (2) Cumulative total hours
1	400	400
2	300 (75% of 400)	600
4	225 (75% of 300)	900

The first two columns form the basis for the calculations as the cumulative total hours in the third column are obtained by multiplying together the figures in columns (1) and (2). As the output doubles the cumulative average time per unit is 75% of the previous figure.

Therefore, if one unit has been produced already taking 400 hours, the production of one more similar unit will only take (600 – 400) ie, 200 hours in the situation of a 75% learning curve. Once two units have been produced, and the learning process continues, the production of two more units will take only (900 – 600) ie, 300 hours. This represents 150 hours per unit.

7.3 Activity

Determine the cumulative total hours for 8 units and hence determine the total time to make the last four units.

7.4 Activity solution

Cumulative number of units	Cumulative average time per unit	Cumulative total hours
8	168.75 (75% of 225)	1,350

Therefore time for last 4 items = 1,350 – 900 = 450 hours.

7.5 Learning curve equation

The learning curve describing the cumulative average time per unit plotted against cumulative number of units can be represented by an equation of the form:

$$y = ax^{-b} \text{ or } y = \frac{a}{x^b}$$

where   y = cumulative average time
             a = time for producing the first unit
             x = cumulative number of units
             b = index of learning (0<b<1)

The index of learning, $b = \dfrac{\text{logarithm of the inverse of the learning rate (in decimal form)}}{\text{logarithm of 2}}$

Therefore, for a 75% learning curve the index of learning is given by:

$$b = \frac{\log \dfrac{1}{0.75}}{\log 2}$$

$$= \frac{\log 1.333}{\log 2}$$

$$= \frac{0.1249}{0.3010}$$

$$= 0.415 = \text{index of learning for a 75\% learning curve}$$

The following is a calculational check using the figures in the previous illustration, where one unit had taken 400 hours and a cumulative of four units of production is assumed:

$$y = ax^{-b}$$

where y = cumulative average time per unit
a = 400
x = 4
b = 0.415

$$y = 400 \times 4^{-0.415} = 225.01 \text{ hours}$$

This can be evaluated on a scientific calculator as follows:

(a)   Enter 4

(b)   Press $\boxed{x^y}$

(c)   Enter 0.415

(d)   Press $\boxed{\frac{+}{-}}$, $\boxed{=}$, $\boxed{\times}$

(e)   Enter 400

(f)   Press $\boxed{=}$

This gives y = 225.01 (2 dp)

(NB: on some calculators, the first $\boxed{=}$ may not be necessary.)

Therefore, the cumulative average time per unit when a total of four units is produced is 225 hours (as previously determined).

For a cumulative production of three units, one unit having been produced in 400 units, the calculations would be as follows:

$$y = 400 \times (3)^{-0.415}$$
$$= 253.5 \text{ (the cumulative average time per unit)}$$

The cumulative total time for three units would be 760.5 hours (3 × 253.5).

7.6   Activity

If the learning curve rate is 85%, what is the value of b in the learning curve model $y = ax^{-b}$?

7.7   Activity solution

$$b = \frac{\log(1/0.85)}{\log 2} = \frac{\log 1.1765}{\log 2}$$

$$b = \frac{0.0706}{0.3010} = 0.234$$

7.8   Pricing example

The following worked example illustrates that the benefit of the learning curve relates to labour *and* labour-related costs, but *not* to the cost of materials.

A company wishes to determine the minimum price it should charge a customer for a special order. The customer has requested a quotation for ten machines; he might subsequently place an order for a further ten. Material costs are £30 per machine. It is estimated that the first batch of ten machines will take 100 hours to manufacture and an 80% learning curve is expected to apply. Labour plus variable overhead costs amount to £3 per hour. Setting-up costs are £1,000 regardless of the number of machines made.

(a)   What is the minimum price the company should quote for the initial order, if there is no guarantee of further orders?

(b)   What is the minimum price for the follow-on order?

(c)   What would be the minimum price if both orders were placed together?

(d)   Having completed the initial orders for a total of twenty machines (price at the minimum levels recommended in (a) and (b)), the company thinks that there would be a ready market for this type of machine if it brought the unit selling price down to £45. At this price, what would be the profit on the first 140 'mass-production' models (ie, after the first twenty machines) assuming that marketing costs totalled £250?

Initial order

If there is no guarantee of a follow-up order, the setting-up costs must be recovered on the initial order. Costs are, therefore, as follows:

	£
Material (10 × £30)	300
Labour and variable overhead (100 × £3)	300
Setting-up cost	1,000
Total	£1,600
Minimum price each (£1,600 ÷ 10)	£160

Follow-on order

The setting-up costs have been recovered on the initial order. Output is doubled; therefore, average time for each group of ten machines is reduced to

100×0.8
$= 80$ hours

ie, cumulative time for twenty machines = 160 hours

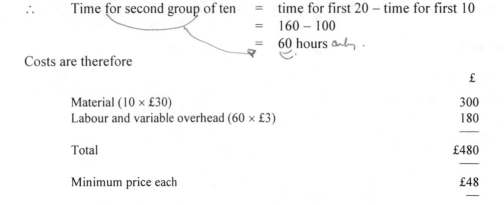

∴   Time for second group of ten   =   time for first 20 – time for first 10
=   160 – 100
=   60 hours only.

Costs are therefore

	£
Material (10 × £30)	300
Labour and variable overhead (60 × £3)	180
Total	£480
Minimum price each	£48

Both orders together

Total costs are:

		£
Material		600
Labour (160 hours)		480
Setting-up cost		1,000
		———
Total		£2,080
		———
Minimum price each		£104
		———

This is, of course, the mean of the two previous prices: cumulative costs are the same but they are recorded evenly over twenty units instead of most of the cost being 'loaded' onto the first ten units.

The time spent on the first 140 mass production models is calculated as follows:

Working in units of 10 machines, $y = ax^{-b}$ where $a = 100$

$$b = \frac{\log\left(\frac{1}{0.8}\right)}{\log 2}$$

$$= 0.3219$$

Average time/unit for first 2 units (ie, first 20 machines)

	=	$100 \times 2^{-0.3219}$
	=	80 hours
Total time for first 2 units	=	80×2
	=	160 hours (as before)

Average time per unit for first 16 units (ie, first 160 machines)

	=	$100 \times 16^{-0.3219}$
	=	40.96 hours
Total time for first 16 units	=	40.96×16
	=	655.36 hours

Hence total time for units 3 to 16 (ie, the 140 mass-produced units)

	=	$(655.36 - 160)$ hours
	=	495.36 hours

Cost of first 140 mass-production models

	£
Material $(140 \times £30)$	4,200
Labour and variable overhead $(495.36 \times £3)$	1,486
Marketing	250
	———
Total cost	5,936
Revenue	6,300
	———
Profit	£364
	———

8 EXPONENTIAL SMOOTHING

8.1 Introduction

This is a method of forecasting applicable to regular short-term forecasts, such as monthly forecasts of demand for stock control purposes. It is an adaptive forecasting method ie, the latest information is used to 'adapt' the previous forecast to provide a new forecast.

New forecast = old forecast + a proportion of the forecasting error;

ie: New forecast = old forecast + α (latest observation – old forecast);   (1)

or by re-arranging formula (1):

New forecast = α (latest observation) + $(1 - \alpha)$ (old forecast).   (2)

It can be seen from the simple formulae that only the most recent data is needed, since only the previous forecast and the value of α (the smoothing constant) are required, together with the latest observation, as it becomes available, to update the forecast. A low value for the smoothing constant, say $\alpha = 0.1$, is equivalent to a long period moving average, whilst a higher one, say $\alpha = 0.5$, is equivalent to a shorter number of periods. Hence, for time series which change only slightly, a small value of α is appropriate, whereas, if a more sensitive method is needed, then larger values of α are more suitable.

'Exponential smoothing' is a shortened term for 'exponentially weighted moving average', which indicates that various weights are given to different observations. We have already used moving averages earlier in the text when establishing a trend. Simple moving averages are a special case of exponential smoothing in so far as **equal** weight is given to each of the observations. As can be seen in equation (2) above, the latest observation has a weight of α, and the weights of the other observations decrease by a factor of $(1 - \alpha)$ as they become older. Clearly, the older the observations the less weight attached. Equations (1) and (2) are a convenient and simple form of a weighted average of all previous observations, viz:

$$F_O = a_1 D_1 + a_2 D_2 + a_3 D_3 + \ldots\ldots + a_k D_k + \ldots\ldots\ldots\ldots\ldots\ldots\ldots\ldots\ldots\ldots \quad (3)$$

where the subscript refers to the number of periods since the present:

F_O is the forecast made now

D_i is the observation i periods ago (ie, D_1 is the latest observation)

a_i is the weight for an observation i periods old.

8.2   Forecast example

Given a first period's forecast of 127, compare the effect of using different values of the smoothing constant for the following data:

133, 118, 150, 132, 157, 132, 130, 139, 170, 132.

8.3   Solution

The forecast for the first period's demand was 127 and it turned out to be 133. Hence, for $\alpha = 0.1$, the forecast of the second period's demand is given by equation (1):

$$F_O = F_1 + \alpha (D_1 - F_1)$$

So $F_O = 127 + 0.1 (133 - 127) = 127.6$

The forecast for the third period's demand is:

$$127.6 + 0.1 (118 - 127.6) = 126.6$$

A work table for $\alpha = 0.1$ can be set up as follows:

Demands D	Forecast F_1	Error $(D - F_1)$	x (Error)	New forecast F_0
133	127	6	0.6	127.6
118	127.6	-9.6	-0.96	126.6
150	126.6	23.4	2.34	128.9
132	128.9	3.1	0.31	129.2
157	129.2	27.8	2.8	132.0
132	132	0	0	132.0
130	132	-2.0	-0.2	131.8
139	131.8	7.2	0.72	132.5
170	132.5	37.5	3.75	136.3
132	136.3	-4.3	-0.43	135.9

8.4   Activity

Repeat the last example using alpha = 0.5 and compare the amount of smoothing that has been achieved.

8.5   Activity solution

Demands D	Forecast F_1	Error $(D - F_1)$	Alpha × error	New forecast F_0
133	127	6	3	130
118	130	-12	-6	124
150	124	26	13	137
132	137	-5	-2.5	134.5
157	134.5	22.5	11.25	145.75
132	145.75	-13.75	-6.88	138.87
130	138.87	-8.87	-4.44	134.43
139	134.43	4.57	2.28	136.71
170	136.71	33.29	16.64	153.35
132	153.35	-21.35	-10.68	142.67

The error terms are in general larger than using alpha equal to 0.10, hence the values have not been smoothed to the same extent.

8.6   Conclusion

It is important to appreciate that although the various methods which have been used to identify seasonal (and cyclical) factors and hence predict future values of a particular variable will give different results, it is often not possible to say that any one answer is more valid than another. All methods essentially assume that whatever has caused fluctuations and trends to occur in the past will continue similarly into the future. Clearly this is often not the case and therefore any value forecast by any of the methods should be treated with due caution.

9   UNCERTAINTY AND BUDGETING

9.1   Introduction

Since budgets are predictions and plans for the future non-controllable events will make the outcome of particular actions uncertain.

9.2   Factors affecting the budget process

There are a number of factors which contribute to the uncertainty surrounding the budget setting and budgetary control process.

Some of the factors may be internal to the organisation but not controllable in the short-term, these would include productivity and efficiency factors which may be controlled in the longer-term by re-training and investment.

However many of the factors are external to the organisation for example:

- sales may be lower due to recession;

- customers may be lost due to lack of goods due to lower productivity;

- inflation;

- government fiscal policy;

- natural disasters;

- changes in supplier costs and terms of supply

10   FLEXIBLE BUDGETS

10.1   Introduction

[Definition]   A flexible budget is one which, by recognising the distinction between fixed and variable costs, is designed to change in response to changes in output.

The concept of responsibility accounting requires the use of flexible budgets for control purposes. Many of the costs under a manager's control are variable and will therefore change if the level of activity is different from that in the budget. It would be unreasonable to criticise a manager for incurring higher costs if these were a result of a higher than planned volume of activity. Conversely, if the level of activity is low, costs can be expected to fall and the original budget must be amended to reflect this.

A variance report based on a flexible budget therefore compares actual costs with the costs budgeted for the level of activity actually achieved. It does not explain any change in budgeted volume, which should be reported on separately.

10.2   Flexible budgeting

The key points to note are:

(a)   A fixed budget is set at the beginning of the period, based on estimated production. This is the original budget.

(b)   This is then **flexed** to correspond with the actual level of activity.

(c)   The result is compared with actual costs, and differences (variances) are reported to the managers responsible.

10.3   Example

Bug Ltd manufactures one uniform product only, and activity levels in the assembly department vary widely from month to month. The following statement shows the departmental overhead budget based on an average level of activity of 20,000 units production per four-week period and the actual results for four weeks in October.

	Budget average for four-week period £	Actual for 1 to 28 October £
Indirect labour - variable	20,000	19,540
Consumables - variable	800	1,000
Other variable overheads	4,200	3,660
Depreciation - fixed	10,000	10,000
Other fixed overheads	5,000	5,000
	40,000	39,200
Production (units)	20,000	17,600

You are required:

(a)   to prepare a columnar flexible four-week budget at 16,000, 20,000 and 24,000 unit levels of production;

(b)   to prepare two performance reports based on production of 17,600 units by the department in October, comparing actual with:

(i)   average four-week budget; and
(ii)   flexible four-week budget for 17,600 units of production;

(c)   to state which comparison ((b) (i) or (b) (ii)) would be the more helpful in assessing the foreman's effectiveness and why; and

(d)   to sketch a graph of how the flexible budget total behaves over the 16,000 to 24,000 unit range of production.

10.4   Solution

(a)   Production level

	−20% 16,000 units £	20,000 units £	+20% 24,000 units £
Variable costs:			
Indirect labour	16,000	20,000	24,000
Consumables	640	800	960
Other overheads	3,360	4,200	5,040
	20,000	25,000	30,000
Fixed costs:			
Depreciation	10,000	10,000	10,000
Other overheads	5,000	5,000	5,000
	35,000	40,000	45,000

(b)   (i)

	Average four-week budget £	Actual results £	Variances fav./(adv.) £
Indirect labour	20,000	19,540	460
Consumables	800	1,000	(200)
Other variable overheads	4,200	3,660	540
Depreciation	10,000	10,000	-
Other fixed overheads	5,000	5,000	-
	40,000	39,200	800

(ii)

	Flexed four-week budget	Actual results	Variances fav./(adv.)
Sales (units)	17,600	17,600	-
	£	£	£
Indirect labour	17,600	19,540	(1,940)
Consumables	704	1,000	(296)
Other variable overheads	3,696	3,660	36
Depreciation	10,000	10,000	-
Other fixed overheads	5,000	5,000	-
	37,000	39,200	(2,200)

(c)   The flexed budget provides more useful data for comparison because:

  (i)   the fixed original budget makes no distinction between fixed and variable costs;

  (ii)   hence no data is available concerning the appropriate level of costs at the actual production level;

  (iii) this would lead to the conclusion that the foreman had done well, when in fact costs had not fallen nearly as much as anticipated for the actual production;

  (iv)   responsibility for the production shortfall is not known.

(d)   **Graph of costs in the production range 16,000 to 24,000 units**

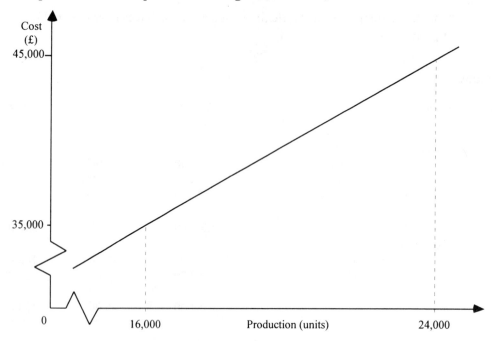

10.5   Flexible budgeting and management attitudes

The nature of cost behaviour patterns is not changed according to whether fixed or flexible budgets are used; what is changed is the way in which management view costs.

10.6   Example

The Alic Co Ltd has many small customers. Work measurement of the debtors' ledger shows that one clerk can handle 2,000 customer accounts. The company employs 30 clerks on the debtors' ledger at a salary of £3,600 each. The outlook for next year is of a decline in the number of customers from 59,900 to 56,300. However, management decides not to reduce the number of clerks.

Show the effect of this decision if debtors' ledger clerks' salaries are treated as:

(a)   variable expenses per customer per year;

(b)   fixed overhead.

10.7   Solution

		£
(a)	Allowed expense $56{,}300 \times \dfrac{£3{,}600}{2{,}000}$	101,340
	Actual expenditure $30 \times £3{,}600$	108,000
	Adverse variance	6,660 A

		£
(b)	Allowed expense	108,000
	Actual expenditure	108,000
		Nil

Neither approach says whether the management decision was right. Approach (a), however, does give the cost of that decision.

Consequently the way costs are classified can influence the way management views costs, and ultimately the decisions that are made.

10.8   Activity

A company's production overhead budget is based on the principle that each unit of production incurs variable overhead cost of £5.40 and that each month fixed production overhead of £6,750 is incurred.

During June the budgeted output was 460 units and actual output was 455 units.

Calculate the allowed expense for June.

10.9   Activity solution

(455 units × £5.40) + £6,750 = £9,207

11   PROBABILITIES

11.1   Introduction

We now turn to the use of probabilities to assist the budgeting process. This involves fairly straightforward applications of simple probabilities and the use of expected values.

11.2   Example

Consider the following example.

The following information and estimates were available for the management of Z Ltd.

For the year ahead the following cost and demand estimates have been made:

Unit variable costs:

Pessimistic	Probability	0.15	£7.00 per unit
Most likely	Probability	0.65	£6.50 per unit
Optimistic	Probability	0.20	£6.20 per unit

Demand estimates at various prices (units):

			Price per unit	
			£13.50	*£14.50*
Pessimistic	Probability	0.3	45,000	35,000
Most likely	Probability	0.5	60,000	55,000
Optimistic	Probability	0.2	70,000	68,000

(Unit variable costs and demand estimates are statistically independent.)

You are required to calculate the expected contribution at each selling price.

11.3   Solution

Expected contribution = expected demand × expected contribution per unit.

$$\text{Expected variable costs per unit} \quad = \quad £7 \times 0.15 + £6.50 \times 0.65 + £6.20 \times 0.20$$
$$= \quad £6.515 \text{ per unit}$$

Selling price = £13.50

Expected contribution per unit = £13.50 - £6.515 = £6.985

Expected demand = $45 \times 0.3 + 60 \times 0.5 + 70 \times 0.2$ = 57,500 units

∴ Expected contribution = £401,637.50

Selling price = £14.50

Expected contribution per unit = £14.50 - £6.515 = £7.985

Expected demand = $35 \times 0.3 + 55 \times 0.5 + 68 \times 0.2$ = 51,600 units

∴ Expected contribution = £412,026

11.4   Further example

E Ltd manufactures a hedge-trimming device which has been sold at £16 per unit for a number of years. The selling price is to be reviewed and the following information is available on costs and likely demand.

The standard variable cost of manufacture is £10 per unit and an analysis of the cost variances for the past 20 months shows the following pattern which the production manager expects to continue in the future.

Adverse variances of +10% of standard variable cost occurred in ten of the months.

Nil variances occurred in six of the months.

Favourable variances of –5% of standard variable cost occurred in four of the months.

Monthly data

Fixed costs have been £4 per unit on an average sales level of 20,000 units but these costs are expected to rise in the future and the following estimates have been made for the total fixed cost:

		£
Optimistic estimate	(Probability 0.3)	82,000
Most likely estimate	(Probability 0.5)	85,000
Pessimistic estimate	(Probability 0.2)	90,000

The demand estimates at the two new selling prices being considered are as follows:

If the selling price per unit is		£17	£18

demand would be:

			£17	£18
Optimistic estimate	(Probability 0.2)		21,000 units	19,000 units
Most likely estimate	(Probability 0.5)		19,000 units	17,500 units
Pessimistic estimate	(Probability 0.3)		16,500 units	15,500 units

It can be assumed that all estimates and probabilities are independent.

You are required

(a)   to advise management, based on the information given above, whether they should alter the selling price and, if so, the price you would recommend;

(b)   to calculate the expected profit at the price you recommend.

11.5   Solution

(a)

Step 1   Calculate the expected variable cost per unit.

		£	Probability	Expected VC £
10 + 10%	=	11.00	0.5	5.50
10	=	10.00	0.3	3.00
10 − 5%	=	9.50	0.2	1.90
				10.40

Step 2   Calculate the expected demand at £17 and £18

£17			£18		
Demand	Probability	Expected demand	Demand	Probability	Expected demand
21,000	0.2	4,200	19,000	0.2	3,800
19,000	0.5	9,500	17,500	0.5	8,750
16,500	0.3	4,950	15,500	0.3	4,650
		18,650			17,200

Step 3   Calculate the expected contribution at each of the selling prices.

*(**Note:** since **not** altering the selling price is an option to be considered, the contribution at the present selling price of £16 should be calculated.)*

	£	£	£
Selling price per unit	16.00	17.00	18.00
Variable cost per unit	10.40	10.40	10.40
Contribution per unit	5.60	6.60	7.60
Expected demand in units	20,000	18,650	17,200
Total contribution	112,000	123,090	130,720

Recommendation: increase selling price to £18 per unit.

(b)   **Expected profit**

	£
Contribution	130,720
Fixed costs (see below)	85,100
Profit	45,620

Fixed cost calculation:

Estimate £	Probability	Expected value £
82,000	0.3	24,600
85,000	0.5	42,500
90,000	0.2	18,000
		85,100

12   COMPUTERISED CASH FLOW MODELS

12.1   Introduction

Computer models provide an easy way of monitoring cash flows. The most suitable format is that of various **spreadsheet** packages now available on most micros - Supercalc, Multiplan, Lotus 1-2-3, Jazz and Excel are among the better known.

In the following example the cash flow data has been reduced to balance brought forward, receipts and payments:

	A	B	C	D	E
1		Jan	Feb	Mar	April
2					
3	Opening balance	1,000	1,100	1,000	550
4	Add: Receipts	700	800	500	850
5	Less: Payments	600	900	950	400
6					
7	Closing balance	1,100	1,000	550	1,000
8					

This table could equally well have been prepared manually, but in fact the columns containing balances consist of relationships, rather than numeric values:

	A	B	C	D	E
1		Jan	Feb	Mar	April
2					
3	Opening balance	1,000	=B7	=C7	=D7
4	Add: Receipts	700	800	500	850
5	Less: Payments	600	900	950	400
6					
7	Closing balance	=B3+B4−B5	=C3+C4−C5	=D3+D4−D5	=E3+E4−E5
8					

In order to understand the second table, it must be appreciated that the columns are labelled from left to right alphabetically, A, B, C, etc, and the rows numerically from the top down, 1, 2, 3, etc. Each cell is defined by the letter of the column and the number of the row, and calculations are by reference to cells rather than numbers.

Thus the opening balance for every month except January equals the previous month's closing balance. Similarly the closing balance is the Opening balance + Receipts – Payments.

The great advantage of this approach becomes apparent when applied to a large and complex flow projection:

(a)   a typical spreadsheet program can handle up to 8,192 rows and 234 columns, enough to accommodate a very complex model (though most micros would run out of memory if all the cells were used);

(b)   if any figure is amended, all the figures will be immediately recalculated;

(c)   the results can be printed out without going through an intermediate typing phase; and

(d)   most programs can also represent the results graphically eg, the above balances can be shown in a bar diagram:

Closing cash balances

In summary, spreadsheet cash flow models represent a very powerful tool for use by the accountant.

13   CHAPTER SUMMARY

This chapter has considered the use of quantitative techniques used in forecasting and budgeting.

Various techniques are available; cost estimation, the effects of the learning curve and probability to deal with uncertainty.

14   SELF TEST QUESTIONS

14.1   What is a 'line of best fit'? (1.7, 2.2)

14.2   What is the equation of a straight line? (2.4)

14.3   What is the difference between interpolation and extrapolation? (2.14)

14.4   What is Pearson's correlation coefficient? (3.2)

14.5   What is time series analysis? (4.1, 5.1)

14.6   What is a seasonal variation? (4.3)

14.7   What is the formula for an additive time series model? (5.1)

14.8   What is causal forecasting? (6.1)

14.9   How does the learning process affect production times? (7.2)

14.10   What is a flexible budget? (10.1)

15   EXAMINATION TYPE QUESTIONS

15.1   D & E Ltd

D & E Ltd produces brakes for the motor industry. Its management accountant is investigating the relationship between electricity costs and volume of production. The following data for the last ten quarters has been derived, the cost figures having been adjusted (ie, deflated) to take into account price changes.

Quarter	1	2	3	4	5	6	7	8	9	10
Production, X, ('000 units)	30	20	10	60	40	25	13	50	44	28
Electricity costs, Y, (£'000)	10	11	6	18	13	10	10	20	17	15

(Source: Internal company records of D & E Ltd.)

$$\sum X^2 = 12,614, \qquad \sum Y^2 = 1,864 \qquad \sum XY = 4,728$$

You are required

(a)   to draw a scatter diagram of the data on squared paper;   **(4 marks)**

(b)   to find the least squares regression line for electricity costs on production and explain this result;   **(8 marks)**

(c)   to predict the electricity costs of D & E Ltd for the next two quarters (time periods 11 and 12) in which production is planned to be 15,000 and 55,000 standard units respectively;   **(4 marks)**

(d)   to assess the likely reliability of these forecasts.   **(4 marks)**
(Total: 20 marks)

15.2   Daily visitors to a hotel

The number of daily visitors to a hotel, aggregated by quarter, is shown below for the last three years.

Year	Quarter 1	Quarter 2	Quarter 3	Quarter 4
19X6	-	-	-	88
19X7	90	120	200	28
19X8	22	60	164	16
19X9	10	80	192	-

The following additive model is assumed to apply:

Actual value = Trend + Seasonal variation + Residual (irregular) variation

You are required

(a)   to find the centred moving average trend;   **(5 marks)**

(b)   to find the average seasonal variation for each quarter;   **(5 marks)**

(c)   to plot the original data and the trend on the same time-series graph;   **(5 marks)**

(d)   to predict the number of daily visitors for the fourth quarter of 19X9, showing clearly how this is calculated, and state any assumptions underlying this answer.   **(5 marks)**
(Total: 20 marks)

16 ANSWERS TO EXAMINATION TYPE QUESTIONS

16.1 D & E Ltd

(a) **Scatter graph of electricity cost against production**

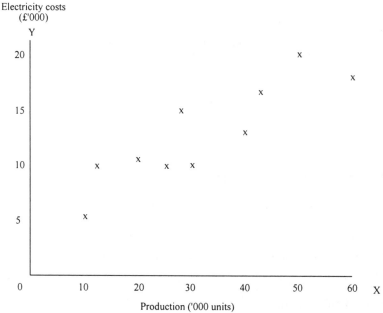

Notes:

(i) Choose the scales so that the graph fits the graph paper.

(ii) Do not attempt to draw a line through the scatter graph unless the question requires it.

(iii) Label the axes and state the units.

(b) The regression line of Y on X is Y = a + bX where

$$b = \frac{n\sum XY - \sum X \sum Y}{n\sum X^2 - (\sum X)^2} \quad \text{and } a = \frac{\sum Y - b\sum X}{n}$$

$$\sum X = 320$$

$$\sum Y = 130$$

$$n = 10$$

$$b = \frac{10 \times 4,728 - 320 \times 130}{10 \times 12,614 - (320)^2} = \frac{5,680}{23,740}$$

$$= 0.239$$

$$a = \frac{130 - 0.239 \times 320}{10}$$

$$= 5.34$$

The least squares regression line of electricity costs (Y) on production (X) is therefore

$$Y = 5.34 + 0.239X$$

where Y is in £'000 and X in '000 units.

Explanation

Assuming there is an approximately linear relationship between production and electricity costs, which is shown to be reasonable by the scatter graph, the electricity costs are made up of two parts, a fixed cost (independent of the volume of production) of £5,340 and a variable cost per unit of production of £239 per 1,000 units (or 23.9p per unit).

(c)   For quarter 11, X = 15, hence

$$Y = 5.34 + 0.239 \times 15$$

$$= 8.93$$

The predicted electricity cost for quarter 11 is therefore £8,930.

For quarter 12, X = 55, hence

$$Y = 5.34 + 0.239 \times 55$$

$$= 18.5$$

The predicted electricity cost for quarter 12 is therefore £18,500.

(d)   There are two main sources of error in the forecasts:

(i)   The assumed relationship between Y and X.

The scatter graph shows that there can be fairly wide variations in Y for a given X. Also the forecast assumes that the same conditions will prevail over the next two quarters as in the last ten quarters.

(ii)   The predicted production for quarters 11 and 12.

No indication is given as to how these planned production values were arrived at, so that it is not possible to assess how reliable they are. If they are based on extrapolation of a time series for production over the past ten quarters, they will be subject to the errors inherent in such extrapolations.

Provided conditions remain similar to the past ten quarters, it can be concluded that the forecasts would be fairly reliable but subject to some variation.

16.2   Daily visitors to a hotel

(a)   Trend using centred moving average

Note: you are given considerable help in finding the trend using moving averages, and you are told to find a centred moving average. Set out the original data on every other line, then the first 4 quarter moving average corresponds to a time period half way between the first two and the next two quarters. By finding an 8 quarter moving average a trend figure is found that can be compared with the original data. It is worth finding the seasonal variations for part (b) at the same time.

Year	Quarter	Visitors	4-quarter total	8-quarter total	Centred trend (8-quarter average)	Variations (visitors- trend)
19X6	4	88				
19X7	1	90				
			498			
	2	120		936	117	3
			438			
	3	200		808	101	99
			370			
	4	28		680	85	-57
			310			

19X8	1	22		584	73	-51
			274			
	2	60		536	67	-7
			262			
	3	164		512	64	100
			250			
	4	16		520	65	-49
			270			
19X9	1	10		568	71	-61
			298			
	2	80				
	3	192				

(b)   Average seasonal variations

Year/Quarter	1	2	3	4	Total
19X7		+3	+99	-57	
19X8	-51	-7	+100	-49	
19X9	-61				
Total	-112	-4	+199	-106	
Mean	-56	-2	+99.5	-53	-11.5
Adjusted mean	-53	+1	+102	-50	0.0

Note: the adjusted mean is the seasonal variations. The original mean variations add up to 11.5 so 3 is added to each of these figures, except Q3, to ensure that the total is zero.

(c)   Graph of time series

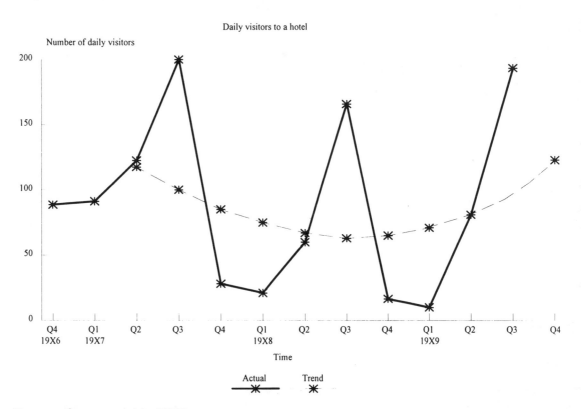

(d)   Forecast for quarter 4 in 19X9

The trend figure for quarter 4 in 19X9 is read from the graph as 120 visitors.

To this should be added the average seasonal variation for quarter 4 which, from (b), is −50.

This makes the best estimate for quarter 4 in 19X9.

$$120 - 50 = 70 \text{ visitors per day.}$$

The assumptions include:

- the additive model is more appropriate than the proportional model;
- the random variations for the quarter will not be material; and
- there are no unusual events that will make the quarter atypical.

19 ACCOUNTING CONTROL SYSTEMS: BEHAVIOURAL ASPECTS

INTRODUCTION & LEARNING OBJECTIVES

This third chapter on control systems considers the human aspects of budgeting.

When you have studied this chapter you should be able to do the following:

- Explain the effects of budgets on human behaviour.
- Contrast different management styles and their effect on the budgeting process.
- Explain the effects of change on budgets.
- Evaluate alternative budgeting methods.

1 BEHAVIOURAL ASPECTS OF BUDGETING

1.1 Introduction

If budgetary control is to be successful, attention must be paid to behavioural aspects ie, the effect of the system on people in the organisation and *vice versa*. Poor performance and results are more often due to the method of implementation and subsequent operation of a system, with a failure to allow properly for the human side of the enterprise, than to the system itself. The management needs to be fully committed to the budgeting system, and through leadership and education lower levels of management in the organisation should be similarly committed and motivated.

Budgets are one important way of influencing the behaviour of managers within an organisation. There are very few, if any, decisions and actions that a manager in an organisation can take which do not have some financial effect and which will not subsequently be reflected in a comparison between budgeted and actual results. This all-embracing nature of budgets is probably the most important advantage that a budgetary system has over most other systems in a typical organisation.

1.2 Roles of budgets

Budgets can take on a number of different roles in any organisation and each has important behavioural implications. The following main roles can be identified in many organisations:

(a) **Authorisation**

Once a budget has been agreed, it is not interpreted by many managers merely as an authorisation to 'spend up to the budget' but rather as an authorisation to 'spend the budget', otherwise there is a real fear that the following year's budget will be cut. Therefore, there is a tendency in an underspend situation, when approaching the end of the financial year, to spend money when it is not really necessary to do so.

(b) **Planning**

The budgeting system provides a formal, co-ordinated approach to short-term planning throughout the organisation. Each manager has a framework in which to plan for his own area of responsibility. Without budgeting it is difficult to imagine an alternative system, affecting all parts of an organisation, in which such planning could take place.

(c)   **Forecasting**

Short-term budgets covering the next one or two years may provide the basis for making forecasts beyond that period eg, in appraising a project with a five year life, data may be extracted from the budgets and used to make forecasts for another three years. The danger with this approach is that, if the budgets are incorrect, the extrapolations beyond the budget period are also likely to be wrong and the financial analysis of the project may be unsound. The budgets could be incorrect because 'slack' has been built into them. Budgetary slack is a common phenomenon in practice. It involves building 'padding' into a cost or expense budget to allow some leeway in actual performance; in a revenue budget it involves a deliberate understatement of budgeted sales or other revenue.

(d)   **Communicating and co-ordinating**

A budgeting system encourages good communications and co-ordination in an organisation. Information about objectives, strategies and policies has to be communicated down from top management and all the individual budgets in an organisation need to be co-ordinated in order to arrive at the master budget.

(e)   **Motivation**

Agreed budgets should motivate individual managers towards their achievement, which in turn should assist the organisation in attaining its longer-term objectives. Motivational effects and the concept of budget difficulty are dealt with later.

(f)   **Evaluation of performance**

A comparison between the predetermined budget and the actual results is the most common way in which an individual manager's performance is judged on a regular basis. The way this appraisal is made and how deviations are dealt with may influence how the individual manager behaves in the future. This role is also the subject of further discussion later.

The various roles identified for budgets may not all prevail at the same time, and some may assume greater importance than others. This will depend on each individual organisation and its operational environment. Some of the roles are indeed likely to conflict with others.

1.3   Problems associated with implementing budgetary control

(a)   There may be a general fear and misunderstanding about the purpose of budgetary control. It is often regarded as a penny-pinching exercise rather than recognised as a tool of management at all levels in an organisation structure. If this tends to be the attitude, a carefully planned campaign of education and understanding should be undertaken. Managers should be encouraged to discover what is in the budgetary control system for them.

(b)   Employees may become united against management and devote their energies to finding excuses for not meeting targets. Targets that are realistic, and are seen by the employees as being realistic, are what is required. Good communications involving consultation and participation should help to minimise this problem.

(c)   One of the key roles in any organisation is at the supervisor/foreman level where the continual interface between management and employees exists. The leadership and motivational function of a supervisor or foreman is very important if the work is to be done and targets are to be achieved.

(d)   The breaking down of an organisation into many sub-areas of managerial responsibility can lead to sub-optimisation problems as far as the whole company is concerned ie, the optimisation of an individual manager's department or section at the expense of the organisation overall. Such dysfunctional behaviour should be minimised. It reflects a lack of goal congruence.

(e)   If budgets are built up from the base of the organisation, with individual departmental budgets providing the input to the overall master budget, the tendency to incorporate slack into budgets needs to be carefully monitored.

(f)   Some desirable projects could be lost because they were not foreseen and therefore not budgeted for. The system needs to be flexible enough to avoid this problem.

All of these problems really relate to criticisms of the manner in which budgetary control systems tend to be operated, rather than of budgetary control *per se*.

1.4   Past exam question

The potential problems arising from inappropriate information employed within a management accounting control system were examined in June 1994, with particular reference to bias - this is covered in greater depth later in the chapter.

1.5   Motivating effect of budgets

Empirical evidence suggests that if a budget is set such that it does not contain a suitable element of targetry (ie, difficulty), then actual performance should be a little better than the budget but it will not be optimised. In other words, managers do not usually work to their full potential if they know that a lower level of performance will still meet the budget (and they are evaluated on the basis of a favourable result compared with the budget). On the other hand, if the budget is too difficult, because it is based on idealistic levels of performance, managers become discouraged at what they regard as an unattainable standard. The effect of such demotivation is that actual performance falls short of what might reasonably have been expected. The aim should be to agree a budget that falls between these two extremes and therefore incorporates just the right degree of difficulty which will lead to the optimal level of performance. At this level the budget should be challenging enough to motivate a manager to optimise on his performance without being too ambitious. The right level of difficulty is that element of targetry which is acceptable to that individual manager. This level of acceptability will differ from manager to manager, as each individual behaves and reacts in a different way in similar circumstances. This concept of budget difficulty can be demonstrated diagrammatically as follows:

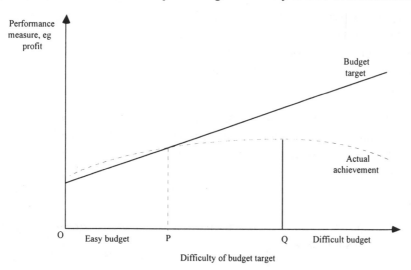

A budget set at the point where OP represents the degree of difficulty or targetry in it is referred to as an 'expectations budget' as budget and actual are likely to coincide. However, a relatively easy-to-achieve budget is likely to lead to a sub-optimal actual performance. In order to achieve a higher actual performance a more difficult budget needs to be set (an 'aspirations budget'). A budget set at the point where OQ represents the degree of difficulty or targetry in it should lead to optimal performance (highest point on the 'actual' performance curve). However, it should be noted that this would give rise to an adverse variance compared with budget. Senior management's interpretation of the reaction to such a variance needs to be carefully considered if the individual manager is not to react adversely in the future to not achieving the budgeted performance. It is in the overall company's best interest to optimise an individual manager's actual performance.

How the degree of difficulty, OQ, is determined is not at all easy in practice because it involves a knowledge of how each individual manager will react and behave. Attempts to quantify the degree of difficulty using work study assessments are a highly simplified approach to a very complex problem.

Furthermore, attempts to use the budget as a motivating tool in the manner described may in fact lead to the need for two budgets: one which is the summation of what all the individual managers have agreed to achieve (with the different degrees of budget difficulty incorporated into them); and a second which recognises that actual performance is likely to fall short of aspiration and is, therefore, a more realistic basis for planning purposes eg, placing capital expenditure contracts (budgets used for forecasting purposes).

1.6   Evaluation of managerial performance

In the previous section the motivating effect of budgets was considered, but it should be remembered that the budgets by themselves have a limited motivational effect. It is the reward structure that is linked to achieving the budget requirements, or lack of reward for non-achievement, which provides the real underlying motivational potential of budgets. The rewards need not be directly financial but could be in terms of future prospects of promotion.

A manager will need to regard the reward as being worthwhile if his behaviour is to be influenced so that he strives actively towards the achievement of the budget.

It has already been mentioned in an earlier section that it is a common practice to attempt to assess the performance of a manager by a comparison of budgeted and actual results for his area of responsibility in the organisation. The choice of which particular measures to use is important to ensure that the individual manager sees the attainment of his targets as worthwhile for himself and at the same time in the best interests of the organisation as a whole. In practice, conflicts can and often do arise between individual managers' personal objectives and those of the organisation as a whole.

The way in which the information in budget reports is used in the assessment of managerial performance has to be considered. Different degrees of emphasis on the results of budget versus actual comparisons can lead to different attitudes and feelings among managers. There is a need to achieve the correct balance between, on the one extreme, an over-emphasis on results leading to pressure and feelings of injustice from the system; and on the other, too little stress on results leading to a budget irrelevancy attitude and low morale.

AG Hopwood reported in 1973 on his research in this area. He studied the manufacturing division of a US steelworks involving a sample of more then two hundred managers with cost centre responsibility. He identified the following three distinct styles of using budget/actual cost information in the evaluation of managerial performance.

(a)   **Budget constrained style**

Here the primary emphasis is on the evaluation of a manager's performance in terms of meeting the budget in the short term.

(b)   **Profit conscious style**

The performance of a manager is measured in terms of his ability to increase the overall effectiveness of his area of responsibility in the context of meeting the longer term objectives of the organisation. At cost centre levels of responsibility the reduction of long-run average costs could be seen as achieving this. Short-term budgetary information needs to be used with care and in a flexible way to achieve this purpose.

(c)   **Non-accounting style**

A manager's evaluation is not based on budgetary information. Accounting information plays a relatively unimportant role in such a style. Other, non-accounting performance indicators are as important as the budget information.

A brief summary of the major effects that these three styles had on managers now follows.

The *budget constrained* style resulted in a great involvement in costs and cost information and a high degree of job-related pressure and tension. The latter often led to the manipulation of data for inclusion in accounting reports. Relations with both colleagues and the manager's superior were poor.

The *profit conscious* style showed good relations with colleagues and superiors. There was still a high involvement with costs but less job-related pressure. Consequently, the manipulation of accounting data was reduced.

The *non-accounting* style showed very similar effects to the profit conscious style except for the much lower impact of costs and cost information on the manager. Hopwood found some evidence that better managerial performance was being achieved where a profit conscious or non-accounting style was in use. Poor performance was often associated with a budget constrained style.

Subsequent studies involving profit centre managers in the UK coal mining industry undertaken by DT Otley (published 1978) did not always mirror Hopwood's earlier results. One particular area of difference was that the UK study showed a closer link between the budget constrained style and good performance.

The manager evaluated on a rather tight budget constrained basis tended to meet the budget more closely than if it was evaluated in a less rigid way.

The results of these studies by Hopwood and Otley can be reconciled in terms that each took place in a different organisational environment. The US study involved highly interdependent cost centres in a highly integrated production function; the UK study involved largely independent profit centres. Any generalisations about evaluation styles must take into account the contingent variables associated with differing organisational structures.

1.7   Participation in the setting of budgets

In some organisations budgets are set by higher levels of management and then communicated to the lower levels of management to whose areas of responsibility they relate. Thus, such budgets are seen by those lower-level managers as being imposed upon them by their superiors in the organisational hierarchy without their being allowed to participate in the budget-setting process and therefore without their being able directly to influence the budget figures. This approach to involvement in the budgetary system is consistent with Douglas McGregor's Theory X view of how people behave in organisations. The Theory X view is based on the assumptions that people in work environments are basically lazy and dislike work and any responsibility associated with it. They are motivated by money to meet their basic needs. Therefore, the Theory X style of management is authoritarian, based on direction and control down through the organisation and typified by a host of rules and regulations.

The other end of the spectrum is described by McGregor as Theory Y. This is a participative theory of management, assuming that people in a work environment do seek more responsibility and do not have to be so tightly controlled. Therefore, it is in organisations where a Theory Y style of management predominates that one is more likely to come across a fully participative approach to the setting of budgets.

The general argument is that the more individual managers are allowed to participate ie, to influence the budgets for which they are held responsible, the more likely it is that they will accept the targets in the budgets and strive actively towards the attainment of those targets. In this way actual performances should be increased by the motivational impact of budgets. An important point to recognise is the difference between *actual* and *perceived* participation. It is the extent to which an individual manager *perceives* that he has influenced the budget that is crucial in that manager's acceptance of it.

There are limitations on the extent of the effectiveness of participation in the budget-setting process. If budgets are used both in a motivational role and for the evaluation of managerial performance, then a serious conflict can arise. A manager through participation may be able to influence the very budget upon which he is subsequently evaluated. By lowering the standard in the budget he has biased the budget and he may then appear to attain a better actual performance in any comparison with it. There is evidence to show that this tends to occur where a manager is actively seeking progression up in an organisation. The effects of this sort of bias can be minimised by careful control, at the budget setting stage, over any changes in the budget from one year to the next which are not due to external factors.

Some people in organisations, by the very nature of the make-up of their personality, do not wish to participate in the wider aspects of their jobs. They prefer an authoritarian style of leadership and do not strive for independence. Participative approaches to budget-setting will be very limited in their effect in such circumstances.

Participation will be less effective in organisational situations where a manager or employee feels that he has little scope to influence the actual results for the budgeted area of responsibility. The lower down in the organisation structure the budget holder is, the more constrained is he by factors imposed from above. For example, objectives, strategies and policies, as well as the sales forecast and budget, limit the extent that a subordinate manager in the production function has for real participation in the setting of the budget for his area of responsibility.

1.8 Budget bias

Budget bias, or budget 'slack' as it is sometimes referred to, has been covered in earlier sections.

Briefly to recap, it is the common process of building room for manoeuvre when setting a budget by overstating the level of budgeted expenditure or by understating the level of budgeted sales. The following are possible reasons for the creation of the bias:

(a)   It should lead to the most favourable result when actual is compared with budget. Such a result should lead to the optimisation of personal gain for the individual manager.

(b)   Where reward structures are based on comparisons of actual with budgeted results, bias can help to influence the outcome.

(c)   In an uncertain business environment it is a way of relieving some of the pressures of a tight situation. The bias will allow some leeway if things do not go according to plan. An example at the factory floor level of this is where workers deliberately do not show how quickly a job can be completed when they are being closely studied by work study (time-and-motion) personnel. The standard time that results will leave the workers with room to manoeuvre in the case of non-standard or different work or where through more general dissatisfaction they do not want to work flat out.

(d)   Some people may see the creation of bias in a budget as a way of 'legally' beating the system. Human behaviour generally in other fields tends to follow such an approach eg, the legal avoidance of tax is a way of getting round the (tax) system. Therefore, a manager may regard the creation of bias as a desirable personal objective and success in achieving it as motivational towards the best actual performance.

Budget bias can sometimes be in the opposite direction to that which has been described already. A manager in the marketing function may bias his budget in an optimistic way by overstating budgeted sales. This could be due to a desire to please senior management by showing an optimistic forecasted sales trend. Alternatively, a manager whose performance has been weak previously may wish to show a promising situation in order to gain approval by his superiors. The short-term approval will usually be at the risk of future disapproval if the optimistic result is not reflected in the actual results.

Finally there is the question 'Is budget bias or slack good or bad?' It depends how the budget is used. If the bias has the effect of motivating a manager to his best actual performance, there would appear to be a good reason for its existence. However, if budgets are used to make forecasts and consequent major decisions then, to the extent that the budgets are biased , there will be errors in the forecasts being made beyond the budget period. Erroneous decisions may then be made. If budgets are to be made in this way the bias needs to be removed from any budgets before the forecasts are made.

1.9 Contingency theory of management accounting

There has generally been an approach over the years to identify one universally acceptable and ideal system of management accounting – not from a technical or mechanistic viewpoint but from an organisational/behavioural/political angle. First it was the development of the 'scientific management' approach in organisations. Then there was a move towards the behavioural/ organisational approach with its emphasis on participation.

The scientific management approach was based on the assumption that individuals in an organisation are mainly motivated by monetary rewards. Lines of authority in organisations should be well-defined in formalised systems. Many of the mechanistic management accounting systems (eg, process costing, standard costing, investment appraisal) fit such an approach where the maximisation of wealth is a prime objective.

The behavioural approach concentrates on the concept of an organisation being a grouping together of a number of individuals. It is the organisation and management of these people that is important because the success of a business depends on them. The organisation and its structure is really a facade and it is the formal and informal ways that people operate behind it that is of critical importance. Hence, the behaviourists are interested in people, the way they behave, their motivations, participation, consultation and so on.

More recently there has been some move towards what has come to be known as a contingency theory for management accounting generally and for budgeting more specifically. This approach assumes that there is no one optimal system of management accounting to meet the needs of all types of organisation in all circumstances. An appropriate model needs to be developed for each different situation rather than a general model (based on a scientific management or behavioural approach) being universally imposed on an organisation.

A basic, minimal contingency framework has been suggested by DT Otley ('The contingency theory of management accounting: achievement and prognosis' published in *Accounting Organisations and Society*, 1980). Briefly his open system identifies the following influences in organisations:

(a) **Contingent variables**

Some such variables are external to an organisation, others are internal.

Examples of exogenous (external) variables are the state of technology in the industry and the economic, social and political environments in which the organisation operates. The endogenous (internal) variables relate to factors such as the organisation's corporate objectives, its organisational structure and the behaviour of the individuals in it.

The apparent conflict between the results of the studies made by Hopwood in the US and Otley in the UK on the way in which budgetary information is used by management, can be explained by consideration of the contingent variables involved and particularly in terms of the different organisational structures.

(b)   **Organisational control networks**

The organisation will have to set up a number of control systems designed to evaluate the extent to which objectives are being achieved. Some will be accounting-based systems of control, others will not.

Control systems are usually more helpful to management where the organisation operates in a relatively stable environment in which decisions have to be made. The way in which the control systems are designed and operated to provide a feedback of information in a particular organisation is very important. Basic budgetary systems need to be adapted to the circumstances in which they are required to operate.

(c)   **Intervening variables**

People in organisations react in different ways to the same set of circumstances; they have different perceptions in terms of, for example, pressure and motivation in a budgetary situation. Some managers may see the budgets as pressures being placed upon them by superiors and react accordingly. This could lead to dysfunctional behaviour or falsification of information being communicated.

(d)   **End result variables**

These attempt to measure formally the achievements of the organisation. Traditionally, profitability measures have been widely used (ROCE, profit per employee, residual income). However, it is doubtful whether these are appropriate where it is the effectiveness of the organisation in achieving goals that is being assessed. A broader approach to assessment which measures a whole range of key performance indicators is suggested. The indicators chosen would need to be appropriate to the particular organisation involved. Concepts beyond profit need to be included so that factors such as employee satisfaction and welfare are assessed.

In summary, all these factors in (a) to (d) interrelate so that the important relationships start with the contingent variables and then operate through the organisational control networks and the intervening variables associated with the individuals who make up the organisation. The outcomes are measured as end result variables. The process is dynamic and operates in a loop system. These concepts are more complex attempts to relate the operation of management accounting systems to organisations than were envisaged by the scientific management theorists and the behaviourists.

1.10   Management by objectives

In a previous section it was argued that budgets should be agreed rather than imposed from above. At the same time it is necessary to achieve *goal congruence* ie, to ensure that individual managers are working towards the same or complementary targets and that their personal aims do not conflict with those of the organisation. Management by objectives (MBO), used in conjunction with systems of long-range planning and budgetary control, can help to achieve these aims and minimise the conflicts between individuals' and organisational goals.

Corporate objectives and other aspects of corporate planning relate to the whole organisation, and the budgeting process involves the setting of budgets for areas of responsibility in the organisation. Both these aspects of planning can be seen to relate to physical attributes of an organisation, whereas MBO is an attempt formally to relate plans and targets to individual managers in the structure and thereby to achieve goal congruence. The procedure is as follows:

(a)   Top management agree on long-term corporate objectives, strategy and goals for the organisation.

(b)   The existing organisation structure is revised as necessary and up-to-date organisation charts are produced which illustrate job titles, responsibilities and relative positions. Job descriptions would provide fuller details of these aspects.

(c)   Each senior manager is required to establish key tasks associated with the successful running of his own area of responsibility and agree quantifiable targets for the period under review (eg, the following twelve months) for each key task. These targets are established in a participative process involving consultation between the manager and his immediate superior. Just how far down through the levels of management the MBO system is operated will vary from organisation to organisation, but it is essentially a system which relates to the more senior management levels in all functions. If this approach is successful, MBO can be extended to the next subordinate level of management.

The targets which are set and agreed should be such that they provide a challenge to the individual manager, but they should not be so difficult or idealistic as to have a demotivating influence. The concept is the same as that already described in terms of 'budget difficulty'.

(d)   Periodically (eg, quarterly) actual results are compared with the agreed targets and some form of performance appraisal interview takes place. This is a formal interview, involving the manager and his immediate superior, when results and actions are fully discussed.

(e)   At the end of each period organisational goals are reviewed as a consequence of the actual results that have been achieved. This is essentially a stage that relates the MBO system back to the whole organisation.

If a system of MBO is to operate successfully, as with any system there must be commitment to it at all levels of management. It is usual to appoint an MBO co-ordinator – a senior manager whose role it is to receive copies of all targets that have been agreed and to provide the basic monitoring framework. At senior management levels the attainment of targets often depends not only on what happens in an individual manager's own department or function, but on other parts of the organisation. The MBO co-ordinator is responsible for ensuring that managers in the different departments and functions are aware of these overlaps, and tries to ensure that the required level of co-operation is attained.

As senior managers are involved, an MBO system is often directly (or more usually indirectly) related to a reward structure; such a reward structure encompasses promotion and career advancement as well as salary review.

One of the major problems associated with the operation of a system of MBO is that of sustaining the motivational impact on senior managers year after year. If each year a manager is expected to set targets which better those for the previous year, then there may be a tendency to hold 'a little in reserve' for next time. This is why a number of large organisations operating MBO do so for a limited number of years in order to obtain the maximum out of the system, then discontinue it and perhaps re-introduce it several years later when again there may be some benefits to be gained from its operation.

1.11   Important behaviourists and researchers and their ideas

In the last forty to fifty years a number of management writers have contributed significantly to the understanding of the behaviour of people within a business environment. This section deals in outline with some of these:

(a)   **Douglas McGregor** (*The Human Side of the Enterprise*, 1960) developed his well-known views on leadership styles that could be attributed to management. An outline of his Theory X and Theory Y styles appears above.

(b)   **Rensis Likert** (*The Human Organisation*, 1967) identified four management systems or different styles of management:

(i)   **System 1: exploitive-authoritative**

Rules and regulations are communicated down through the organisation from a powerful top management.

(ii)   **System 2: benevolent-authoritative**

This differs from System 1 in that there is more delegation to lower levels of management.

(iii)   **System 3: consultative**

There is some discussion between superior and subordinate before the rules and orders are set. Delegation is more pronounced.

(iv)   **System 4: participative**

A fully participative style, and where a high degree of goal congruence is likely.

This model tends to be consistent with that of McGregor, in the sense that Theory X and System 1 have similar characteristics and, at the other extreme, Theory Y and System 4 emphasise similar attitudes towards people.

(c)   **Abraham Maslow** (*Motivation and Personality*, 1960) is famous for his identification of a hierarchy of needs. Five such needs were identified as human motivators. These are illustrated in the following pyramid:

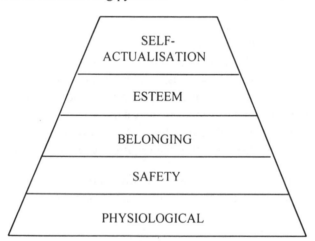

Maslow argued that basically physiological needs (food, clothing, housing, etc) need to be met as a prerequisite. The next level, that of safety needs, comprises more than physical security in its widest sense (including continued supply of food, clothing, housing, etc) and would include emotional aspects. Having met the personal needs of the lowest two levels of the hierarchy, the individual would want to satisfy belonging needs (ie, to the work or social group). Esteem needs are a desire to be recognised and valued by the group and oneself. When all four lower needs have been largely satisfied, the highest level is that of self-actualisation or self-fulfilment, perhaps best described as being able to 'do one's own thing'.

Money largely meets the needs at the lower levels of the hierarchy but not at the higher levels. As each need is largely satisfied, the individual moves up to the next level of needs and different motivators.

(d)   **Frederick Herzberg** (*The Motivation to Work*, 1959): his analysis identified job satisfiers or motivators and, on the other hand, 'hygiene factors'.

Satisfiers, such as achievement, recognition, interesting and challenging work, responsibility and advancement, are the true motivators because they are the vital ingredients of job satisfaction. The way to foster motivators is through schemes associated with job enlargement or job enrichment. It is the job satisfiers that meet the higher needs in Maslow's hierarchy.

Hygiene or environmental factors, such as supervision, pay and working conditions, are essentially ingredients but are not themselves motivators. If they do not exist, people are dissatisfied. Hygiene factors can be related to the needs recognised by Maslow towards the bottom of the hierarchy.

(e)   **R Blake and J Mouton** (*The Managerial Grid*, 1961) provided a basis on which to assess, in quantitative terms, managerial style. Using a two-dimensional grid, with a nine-point scale on each axis, they classify a manager. One axis relates to a manager's 'concern for people' and the other to his 'concern for the task (the job)'. Ideally a manager should have a (9,9) position on the grid with a high degree of concern for both people and the task.

(f)   **Anthony Hopwood** (*An Accounting System and Managerial Behaviour,* 1977) carried out research in the US on the way that budgetary information is used in a large organisation. He identified three styles of evaluation – 'budget constrained', 'profit conscious' and 'non-accounting'. These have been dealt with more fully above.

(g)   **David Otley** (*Budget Use and Managerial Performance,* 1978) repeated a similar study to Hopwood in the UK and obtained somewhat different results. Again, earlier sections have dealt with this in more detail.

The work of the behaviourists, like McGregor, Likert, Maslow and Herzberg, contrast strongly with that of the earlier management theorists who concentrated on the scientific management approach. Foremost among this group is FW Taylor who is generally accredited as being 'the father of work study'. Work measurement and method study are typical of the scientific approach to people in the work environment.

2   BUDGETING AS A BARGAINING PROCESS

2.1   Introduction

Whenever people are allowed to actively participate in the budget setting process there will always be negotiation and bargaining between those involved. There are two aspects to this in the budgeting arena:

(a)   allocation of resources; and
(b)   performance appraisal

although it is often difficult to separate them in practice.

2.2   Resource allocation

Every organisation has resource constraints. Indeed much of the planning and budgeting cycle is concerned with making the best use of limited resources. Individual resources may be limited in the short-term due to world economic situations, or it may be that there is a financial constraint which limits the organisation's ability to obtain resources which are available.

In both cases individual managers when preparing their individual budgets are competing with each other for the limited resources available. This can be seen most clearly in the context of capital budgets, where financial restrictions limit the investment projects to be undertaken. It can also be seen where zero based budgeting (ZBB) is being used and individual decision packages are evaluated on a cost/benefit analysis.

2.3   Performance appraisal

As will be explained later in this text, budgets may be used as a basis for appraising a manager's performance. For this purpose a manager will discuss their draft budget with their superior. The manager may be forced to amend this budget following such negotiations and the result of the amendment may make the achievement of the budget target harder. Since the manager will be appraised on the basis of their ability to achieve the target, the negotiations and bargaining between the manager and their superior are a serious matter.

3 ASPIRATION LEVELS AND BUDGETING

3.1 Introduction

An aspiration level is personal to an individual and represents a level of efficiency which the individual believes they are capable of achieving.

3.2 Goal congruence

In an ideal situation the goals of the organisation will equate to those of the individual responsible for their achievement. This it is argued will lead to motivational benefits with the likelihood that the targets will be achieved.

However, for the motivational effect to work, the target set must be achievable but not being too easy.

3.3 Aspiration levels

If the level of the budget is too easy to achieve the individual may see it as demeaning, and not make any effort to achieve it. This has a de-motivating effect and is worse than having no target at all.

Therefore it is necessary to identify the aspiration level of the individual before setting the budget. The budget should then take account of this aspiration level so as to ensure goal congruence and encourage motivational aspects.

4 BUDGETING AND CHANGE

4.1 Introduction

There are four aspects of change which may affect the budgeting process:

(a)   political change;
(b)   social change;
(c)   economic change; and
(d)   technological change.

4.2 Political change

A change in government policy, for example fiscal policy, may affect the demand for an organisation's products, and/or the costs incurred in providing them. Any such changes will affect both short-term and long-term planning. This is one reason why planning is a continuous process.

4.3 Social change

Changes in social responsibilities and people's attitude towards them affect every organisation. In recent years there has been much more concern about social responsibilities some of which are now recognised by law. All of these factors may impinge on the plans of the organisation.

4.4 Economic change

When there is a change in the economic climate from boom through to recession the demands upon people's income become more focused. Money tends to be spent on necessary goods with little left for 'luxury goods' and savings. The lack of savings deters investment with the result that plans have to be modified if they are to be realistic targets.

4.5 Technological change

When plans are made they are based upon the use of certain methods and equipment. As technology advances the older methods are proven to be inefficient with the result that decisions are taken to update the operation. As a consequence the aspects of the budgets and plans which related to the old method are no longer relevant. Revised plans must now be drawn up on the basis of the new technology.

5 QUALITY AS A STRATEGIC VARIABLE

5.1 The concept of quality

In recent times a great deal of attention has been devoted to quality issues. Although there has always been a general awareness of the need to ensure the satisfaction of the customer, it is the worldwide nature of competition that has focused attention on the need to act. Competitor pressure has often come from the Japanese, whose basic premise is that poor quality is unacceptable.

The term 'quality' is difficult to define because it has a wide range of meanings, covering a large and complex area of businesses and processes. Quality is also a matter of perception and relative measure. For example, if you asked a group of people to each nominate a 'quality sound system', it could be that you would get a different suggestion from each of them.

The Japanese have shown, with their highly competitive products, that high quality does not always mean high cost. The response in the West to improve quality is still really in its infancy.

Before we consider various approaches to improve quality, it is useful for us to consider the extent of **quality related costs**. Such costs exist because resources are wasted as a result of errors, poor workmanship, poor systems and poor communication. A recent statement from an executive from IBM stresses the importance of understanding the costs of quality. He suggests that '..measurement is the heart of any improvement process. If something can't be measured, it cannot be improved'.

5.2 Quality related costs

A report *'The effectiveness of the corporate overhead in British business'* Develin & Partners 1989, estimates that the average cost of waste and mistakes in the UK represents 20% of controllable corporate overhead.

(a) **Quality related costs**

> **Definition** Cost of ensuring and assuring quality, as well as loss incurred when quality is not achieved. Quality costs are classified as prevention cost, appraisal cost, internal failure cost and external failure cost.

(b) **Prevention costs**

> **Definition** The cost incurred to reduce appraisal cost to a minimum.

(c) **Appraisal costs**

> **Definition** The cost incurred, such as for inspection and testing, in initially ascertaining and ensuring conformance of the product to quality requirements.

(d) **Internal failure costs**

> **Definition** The cost arising from inadequate quality before the transfer of ownership from supplier to purchaser.

(e) **External failure costs**

> **Definition** The cost arising from inadequate quality discovered after the transfer of ownership from supplier to purchaser such as complaints, warranty claims and recall cost.

5.3   Quality equals profit

The evidence of the value that customers place on quality is all around us. For many years, both in the UK and the US, every survey of car quality showed Japanese producers way ahead. For ten years after establishing the PIMS database, the researchers argued that market share was the best way to achieve profits. But a re-analysis of the data showed that, while high market share does bring profit, sustainable market share comes from leadership in perceived product or service quality. The PIMS researchers now call relative quality ie, vis-a-vis competitors, the most important single factor affecting a business unit's long term performance.

5.4   Management role

Quality management suggests a concern that the organisation's products or services meet their planned level of quality and perform to specifications. Management has a duty to ensure that all tasks are completed consistently to a standard which meets the needs of the business. To achieve this they need to:

(a)   set clear standards;

(b)   plan how to meet those standards

(c)   track the quality achieved;

(d)   take action to improve quality where necessary.

(a)   **Setting standards**

To manage quality everyone in the organisation needs to have a clear and shared understanding of the standards required. These standards will be set after taking account of:

(i)   the quality expected by the customers;

(ii)   the costs and benefits of delivering different degrees of quality;

(iii)   the impact of different degrees of quality on:

- the customers and their needs;
- contribution to departmental objectives;
- employee attitude and motivation.

Having decided on the standards these must be communicated to everyone concerned to ensure that the right standards are achieved. Documentation of the standards must be clear, specific, measurable and comprehensive.

(b)   **Meeting the standards**

Having decided on appropriate quality standards management should then:

(i)   agree and document procedures and methods to meet the standards;

(ii)   agree and document controls to ensure that the standards will be met;

(iii)   agree and document responsibilities via job descriptions and terms of reference; and

(iv)   prepare and implement training plans for employees to ensure they are familiar with the standards, procedures, controls and their responsibilities.

(c)   **Tracking the quality**

After the process to achieve quality has been set up, an information system to monitor the quality should be set up. This is called quality control.

When a good system to track the quality has been achieved, it can be used constructively to improve quality and work on problem areas.

Employees within the organisation have a huge influence on the quality of their work and to gain their commitment and support the management should:

(i)   publish the quality being achieved;

(ii)   meet regularly with the staff involved to discuss the quality being achieved as well as the vulnerabilities and priorities as they see them and also agree specific issues and action points for them to work on to improve quality;

(iii)   encourage ideas from the staff about improvements and consider introducing short-term suggestion schemes.

6   BUDGETARY PLANNING AND CONTROL

6.1   Introduction

The subject of budgetary planning and control has been covered in detail earlier in this text. In this section we will critically review its use.

6.2   Budgetary planning

The planning process is a means of communicating objectives and co-ordinating organisational activities in such a way as to meet those objectives. To this extent budgetary planning is a useful device but there is a danger that budgets can constrain the organisation.

Often decisions have to be made which may alter the activities identified in the plan; provided such decisions consider all of the issues involved, the budget should not be allowed to constrain the decision maker.

6.3   Control

Control is the process of comparing the actual results with the target and investigating any differences to determine why they occurred.

This process is equally important as the process of setting the target. The comparison will identify areas of inefficiency which can be improved, but it will also identify areas where the target is unachievable.

Where the target cannot be achieved it will be necesary to review the long-term plans and objectives, and these may have to be modified.

7   FIXED AND FLEXIBLE BUDGETS

7.1   Introduction

You should be familiar with these types of budget from your earlier studies. In this section we shall identify their strengths and weaknesses.

7.2   Fixed budgets

Definition   A fixed budget is a budget which shows income/costs for a single level of activity.

A fixed budget makes no attempt to separate the costs into those which are fixed and those which are variable. It is therefore unsuitable for use as a basis of comparison with actual costs where such costs are known to vary with activity **and** the level of activity differs from that budgeted.

However a fixed budget is particularly suitable for controlling costs which are unrelated to activity. These are usually indirect costs and usually the aim is to limit expenditure on these items. An example would be Research and Development expenditure.

7.3   Activity

Identify another functional area where expenditure control is important.

7.4   Flexible budgets

[Definition]   A flexible budget is a budget which shows costs/revenues for different levels of activity by recognising the behaviour of each cost.

The flexible budget is suitable for use as a comparison with actual costs incurred when the activity level differs from that budgeted. Such budgets can therefore be used to measure efficiency but are not suitable as a means of capping expenditure.

8   ROLLING BUDGETS

8.1   Introduction

Budgets are deemed by many organisations to be unchangeable and sacrosanct. The reasons are twofold:

(a)   How committed would management be to the budget preparation process if they knew that senior management accepted that their budgets would need to be adjusted before the end of the budget term?

(b)   The comparison of the original master budget with annual revenues and costs is a useful one - even if the organisation operated under very changed conditions from that originally planned. Also the use of 'revision variances' can be used to bridge the gap and produce meaningful management performance reports.

However there are circumstances in which management may consider that the initial master budget is inadequate as a forecast of future outturn and/or as a control benchmark, and where alternative measures are required. For example, the environmental suppositions upon which strategic and budget planning are based may prove to be very unlike those conditions encountered during the budget term.

If change in the budget is required the options available to management are:

(a)   to continue with the original budget, making allowances as necessary;
(b)   to adapt the original budget to reflect the changed circumstances;
(c)   to adopt a 'rolling budget' or forecast revision approach; or
(d)   to re-budget from scratch.

The decision is liable to rely partly upon the degree of error from the budgeted assumptions, and partly upon the ways management use the budget, eg as authority to spend, or limits on spending.

If environmental states are not considerably different from those budgeted for, it may be pragmatic to retain the original budget and expect middle and junior managers to **adapt to the changed situation within the structure of the original budget**. This policy would maintain the integrity of the budgeting procedures and most likely be a practical and economic approach.

If the different states evolved around only one or two assumptions (such as interest rates and a certain material input inflation), it might be wise and feasible to **adapt the master budget to the new situation**, particularly if the budgetary data are held in a sophisticated computer financial model. As the revised budget would be based on the original budget it is more likely to be accepted by managers who would appreciate the need to reflect new conditions.

Rolling budgets (and forecast revisions) are more likely to be practised as a matter of routine managerial philosophy, rather than as a response to a particular or unexpected situation.

The bigger the divergence of actual conditions from those budgeted the more logical would be the decision to recognise the inadequacy of the original budget and the need to rebudget. Failure to do so might cause managers to waste limited resources or to use them inappropriately.

The many consequences of changing the annual budget can be reduced to a few major considerations:

(a)   a weakening of the importance placed on the budget system;

(b)   increased time spent by managers on budget preparation;

(c)   the problem of gaining budget acceptance;

(d)   the lack of clear financial objectives; and

(e)   the lack of meaningful management performance measures.

8.2   Preparation of rolling budgets

A rolling budget can be defined as "a budget continuously updated by adding a further period, say a month or quarter and deducting the earliest period. Beneficial where future costs and/or activities cannot be forecast reliably".

A typical rolling budget might be prepared as follows:

(a)   A budget is prepared for the coming year (say January - December) broken down into suitable, say quarterly, control periods.

(b)   At the end of the first control period (31 March) a comparison is made of that period's results against the budget. The conclusions drawn from this analysis are used to update the budgets for the remaining control periods and to add a budget for a further three months, so that the company once again has budgets available for the coming year (this time April - March).

(c)   The planning process is repeated at the end of each three-month control period.

The budgeting options available to management who face a dynamic business environment have been discussed above. The views outlined there suggest that rolling budgets are not essential if an organisation is undergoing rapid change, although there may be advantages for a company adopting this approach to budgeting. These include the following:

(a)   Budgets are more realistic and achievable since they are continuously revised to reflect changing circumstances.

(b)   The **annual** disruption associated with the preparation of an annual budget is removed.

(c)   The pressures (and stress) placed on managers to achieve unrealistic budget targets are eased.

(d)   Variance feedback is more meaningful.

(e)   It tends to reduce budgetary bias.

(f)   It reduces the rigidity of the budget system and builds contingency and innovation into the preparation/feedback stages of the control system.

(g)   The assessment of objectives and plans is continuous rather than being a one-off exercise.

(h)   Without some form of budget revision, operational management may continue to invest and recruit etc with the belief that management strategy holds firm.

(i)   It might help to increase management commitment to the budget.

(j)   The arbitrary and artificial distinction drawn between one financial year and the next is removed, since budgets always extend for a year ahead.

However the problems likely to be encountered with rolling budgets include the following:

(a)   If it is difficult to plan ahead accurately (and it always is!) when once a year managers spend a **lot** of time and effort on the task, how likely is it that managers can do the same forecasts more accurately every month or quarter when they are involved in other responsibilities?

(b)   There is a danger that the rolling budget will become the last budget 'plus or minus a bit' and will be representative of absolutely nothing in terms of corporate objectives and meaningless for performance control purposes.

(c)   Managers will be faced with a greater work load and additional staff may be required.

(d)   Managers may devote insufficient attention to preparing budgets which they know will shortly be revised.

(e)   The organisation might be required to operate annual budgets (such as enterprises operating in the public sector).

In conclusion it is worth noting that the relatively recent development of sophisticated computer budgeting models has increased the use of rolling budgets and similar concepts in organisations. Often figures are now revised by computers with minimal intervention by managers.

9   ACTIVITY BASED BUDGETS

9.1   Introduction

The preparation of activity based budgets was compared with traditional budgets earlier in this text.

9.2   Activity based budgets

The use of an activity based approach will assist in the comparison of costs with the activities which cause them. This should lead to a greater accuracy in the costs predicted and thus better management control. The disadvantage of the approach is that there are many more activities to co-ordinate thus increasing the time and cost of the planning process.

10   ZERO BASED BUDGETS v INCREMENTAL BUDGETS

10.1   Introduction

The techniques of zero-based and incremental budgeting were considered earlier in this text. This section compares them and identifies their strengths and weaknesses.

10.2   Zero-based budgeting

Zero-based budgeting requires that every activity be justified. It thus forces managers to examine the business and identify any unnecessary or inefficient activities. This form of budgeting is very costly in terms of management time, and can if care is not taken lead to short-term cost savings which are detrimental in the long-term. However, with care it can lead to improved efficiency.

10.3   Incremental budgeting

This system is based on the previous year's activity, which are then adjusted for volume and price effects. This system is used by many organisations on the grounds that it is a cheap method of budgeting.

The disadvantage of the incremental budgeting method is that inefficiencies are not identified, in fact they may be built-in to the following year's target, a feature which is often known as budgetary slack.

11   CHAPTER SUMMARY

This chapter has considered the behavioural aspects of budgeting, the effects of management styles on the budgeting process, and finally considered the strengths and weaknesses of different approaches to budgeting.

12   SELF TEST QUESTIONS

    12.1   Identify the roles of budgets (1.2)

    12.2   Explain the motivating effect of budgets (1.5)

    12.3   Explain why participation in the budget setting process is important (1.7)

    12.4   Explain budget bias (slack) (1.8)

    12.5   Explain how budgeting is a bargaining process (2)

    12.6   What is an aspiration level? (3.1)

    12.7   Distinguish between fixed and flexible budgets (7)

    12.8   What is a rolling budget? (8)

    12.9   Distinguish between zero based and incremental budgeting (10)

13   EXAMINATION TYPE QUESTION

13.1   Flexible budgeting

It is common practice to flex a budget linearly according to the volume of production, using labour or machine hours as a proxy, yet this often results in a budget which is inaccurate and is thus less useful for control purposes.

You are required

    (a)   to explain why inaccuracies may result from the procedures commonly used to flex a budget;

                                                      (7 marks)

    (b)   to explain how these inaccuracies detract from effective control;   **(4 marks)**

    (c)   to discuss alternative ways of budgeting which might improve both accuracy and control.

                                                            (6 marks)
                                                  (Total: 17 marks)

14   ANSWER TO EXAMINATION TYPE QUESTION

14.1   Flexible budgeting

    (a)   For the sake of convenience, it is common practice for all the variable elements in the budget to be flexed according to the **same** activity indicator. This technique assumes the same linear relationship between the activity indicator, and all the variable elements that are being flexed. This can result in inaccuracies in the flexed budget. In the case of raw materials, for example, this technique would assume that there were no economies of scale such as bulk discounts etc. Furthermore this technique ignores external factors, which can also have an effect on the actual costs.

           In flexible budgeting, we also assume that fixed costs remain unchanged. This assumption too has to be questioned, since fixed costs usually rise in steps as output increases and are rarely constant in the longer term.

           Due to the above inaccuracies, a flexible budget may not indicate the actual total costs.

    (b)   For reasons indicated in (a) above, since a flexed budget may not necessarily indicate the actual total costs, it would have limitations in its application as a control tool. For example, inaccurate figures in the flexed budget, which result in significant variances, could waste a lot of management time and expense in investigating what is in fact an incorrect figure. By the same token, variances which do not appear to be significant, may in fact be significant and management would be misled into not investigating such variances.

(c)   One way of overcoming some of the above inaccuracies is by the use of planning and operational budgets. In this technique, we compare the actual results with the revised budget results that takes into account the actual conditions. This technique groups the variances into two broad categories, which are planning variances and operational variances. To compute the operational variances, we compare the actual figures with the ex-post standard or budget figures, ie, the operational variance is simply the difference between the actual figures and the revised budget figures.

To compute the planning variances, we compare the ex-post standard or budget with the ex-ante standard or budget ie, the planning variance is simply the difference between the 'original budget' and the 'revised budget'.

Such a system would make budget comparisons more meaningful and direct management attention 'correctly', to those areas that require attention.

20 STANDARD COSTING

INTRODUCTION & LEARNING OBJECTIVES

When you have studied this chapter you should be able to do the following:

- Discuss the use of standard costing.
- Explain the installation of a standard costing system.
- Calculate variances to reconcile budget and actual profits.
- Interpret variances for management.

1 USES OF STANDARD COSTING

1.1 A few definitions

In order to put the subject of standard costing and variance analysis into context, and to provide a useful source of introductions to exam answers, we start with some definitions.

> **Definition** **Standard costing** - a control technique which compares standard costs and revenues with actual results to obtain variances which are used to stimulate improved performance.

This highlights the fact that variance analysis is one essential step in the operation of a standard costing system, the other two being the determining of standards and budgets and the recording of costs and transfers in cost ledger accounts. It also highlights the major purpose of operating a standard costing system: to provide a means of planning and controlling the day to day running of a business' activities - although there is also a subsidiary motivational function of operating such a system. This definition leads onto the second:

> **Definition** **Variance analysis** - the analysis of performance by means of variances. Used to promote management action at the earliest possible stages.

This purpose of variance analysis, trying to eliminate inefficiencies, is returned to later. Both these definitions refer to a third:

> **Definition** **Standard cost** - a predetermined measurable quantity set in defined conditions and expressed in money. It is built up from an assessment of the value of cost elements. Its main uses are providing bases for performance measurement, control by exception reporting, valuing stock and establishing selling prices.

This definition has provided another use of variance analysis namely to act as a basis for performance measurement. It also leads to the types of standard that may be set.

1.2 Types of standard

There is a whole range of bases upon which standards may be set within a standard costing system. This choice will be affected by the use to which the standards will be put.

Most commentators identify four:

- basic standard
- ideal standard

- attainable standard
- current standard.

The definitions are as follows:

Definition   **Basic standard** - a standard established for use over a long period from which a current standard can be developed.

Definition   **Ideal standard** - a standard which can be attained under the most favourable conditions, with no allowance for normal losses, waste and machine downtime. Also known as potential standard.

Users believe that the resulting unfavourable variances will remind management of the need for improvement in all phases of operations. Ideal standards are not widely used in practice because they may influence employee motivation adversely.

Definition   **Attainable standard** - a standard which can be attained if a standard unit of work is carried out efficiently, a machine properly operated or material properly used. Allowances are made for normal losses, waste and machine downtime.

The standard represents future performance and objectives which are reasonably attainable. Beside having a desirable motivational impact on employees, attainable standards serve other purposes eg, cash budgeting, inventory valuation and budgeting departmental performance.

Definition   **Current standard** - a standard established for use over a short period of time, related to current conditions.

Given the stated uses of standard costs, the first two types of standard will be rarely used unless a firm wants demotivated staff and information that provides little guidance for performance measurement or cost control. The third type of standard, attainable standards, will be used when operating a standard costing system and for two of the purposes previously mentioned, stock valuation and as a basis for pricing decisions. Whilst variance analysis will initially be carried out by reference to these attainable standards, more useful information comes by comparing with current standards as will be explained later.

1.3   Variance accounting

Definition   A method of accounting whereby cost variances are incorporated into ledger accounting records alongside the actual transactions.

1.4   Uses of standard costs

Standard costs may be used for stock valuation and as a basis for pricing decisions. They are implicit in the preparation of budgets and thus are part of the budgetary control/variance analysis activities of an organisation.

If standard costs are used they can minimise administration in the areas of stock valuation and promote the use of management by exception.

2   USING A STANDARD COSTING SYSTEM

2.1   Introduction

The operation of a standard costing system requires the accurate preparation of standard costs and their regular review.

2.2 Preparing standard costs

Standard costs are comprised of two estimates which are multiplied to produce the standard cost of the output unit. These two estimates are:

(a) a physical measure of the resources required for each unit of output; and

(b) the price expected to be paid for each unit of the resource.

The first step is to identify the resources required for each output unit. This includes:

- each type of different raw material or component;
- each grade and skill type of labour;
- each type of machine.

For each of these an estimate must then be made of the quantity of materials, number of components, number of hours etc, required for each output unit (allowing for normal losses, wastage, inefficiency).

For each of these resources an estimate must be made of the expected cost per unit of the resource (ie, per kg, per unit, per hour). When making these estimates regard must be given towards the likely level of inflation and price changes expected in the budget period.

2.3 Measuring actual performance

Standard costing is part of the cost control system. Control is achieved by comparing actual performance with the standard that has been set, and explaining the cause of the difference.

The difference may be caused by a difference in the quantity of resources used, the cost per unit of the resource or a combination of both. These differences are known as variances and are explained in detail later in this chapter.

2.4 Revising standard costs

The calculation of variances referred to above may identify that the standard is unachievable or that it is out of date. In such circumstances the standard is not providing a realistic target and it should be revised.

Similarly, changes in the method of operation will invalidate the standard previously set; it should be reviewed on a regular basis and where appropriate revised using the same principles as are used to set new standards.

3 CALCULATING VARIANCES

3.1 Introduction

The purpose of calculating variances is to show the effect of the variance on actual profit compared to the budget. This overall effect is known as the profit variance.

Variances which cause the actual profit to be greater than expected are known as FAVOURABLE variances (denoted (F)) and those causing the actual profit to be less than expected are known as ADVERSE (denoted (A)).

You should recall that profits can be measured on an absorption or marginal costing basis. The effect of this is that there are some differences in the calculation of variances relating to sales and fixed overheads. This difference is illustrated by comparing the variance pyramids below and is explained in more detail in the remainder of this chapter.

3.2   Pyramid of variances under absorption costing

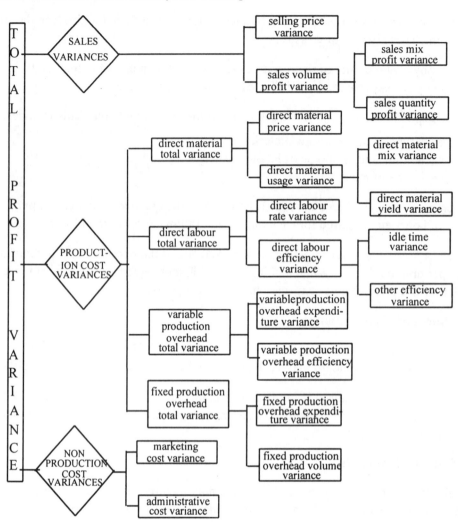

3.3   Pyramid of variances under marginal costing

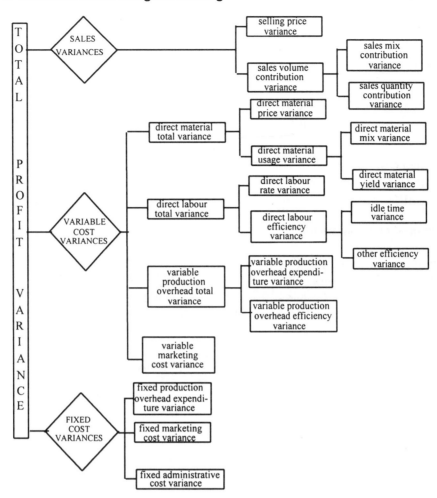

3.4   Variance calculations

The following sections (4-9) revise the calculations of conventional cost and sales variances. You should already be familiar with these from your studies of Paper 8; you should use the text to ensure that you are totally confident in this area.

3.5   Variances in examination questions

Past Paper 9 questions have tended to focus on one particular analysis area rather than asking for a complete profit variance analysis in the form of an operating statement.

In December 1994 a question was set requiring calculations of, and comments on, 'machine variances' - productivity, idle time and expenditure - which were analogous to conventional labour variances.

In June 1995, the sales volume variance was the subject of 23 marks worth of a question - including its split into mix and quantity.

In order to tackle these 'specialised' questions it is vital that you have the principles and mechanics of the conventional variances completely mastered.

Future exam questions are likely to focus more on the consideration of the relevance of standard costing and variance analysis in the modern manufacturing environment.

4   COST VARIANCES

4.1   Introduction

> **Definition**   A cost variance is a difference between planned, budgeted or standard cost and actual cost.

Cost variances occur when standard costs are compared to actual costs. There is one important feature of standard costing which must be remembered: standard costing carries out variance analysis using the normal, double entry ledger accounts. This is done by recording in the ledgers:

(a)   actual costs as inputs;

(b)   standard costs as outputs;

(c)   the difference as the variance.

4.2   Direct material cost variances

The purpose of calculating direct material cost variances is to quantify the effect on profit of actual direct material costs differing from standard direct material costs. This total effect is then analysed to quantify how much has been caused by a difference in the price paid for the material and how much by a difference in the quantity of material used.

4.3   Example

The following standard costs relate to a single unit of product X:

	£
Direct materials	10
Direct labour	8
Production overhead	5
	23

On the basis of the above standard costs if a unit of product X is sold for £30, the expected (or standard) profit would be £7 (£30 – £23).

However, if the **actual** direct material cost of making the unit of X were £12 then (assuming the other costs to be as per standard) the actual cost of product X would be:

	£
Direct materials	12
Direct labour	8
Production overhead	5
	25

Thus when the product is sold, the profit is only £5 (£30 – £25).

This reduction in profit is the effect of the difference between the actual and standard direct material cost of £2 (£12 – £10).

This simple example considered only one unit of product X, but it is the principle upon which variance calculations are made.

4.4   Direct material total cost variance

The purpose of this variance is to show the effect on profit for an accounting period of the actual direct material cost being different from the standard direct material cost.

4.5   **Example**

In July, 1,000 units of product X were manufactured, and sold for £30 each.

Using the data above,

(i)   the standard direct material cost of these 1,000 units of product X would be:

1,000 units × £10/unit = £10,000

(ii)   the actual direct material cost of these 1,000 units of product X would be:

1,000 units × £12/unit = £12,000

Assuming the other actual costs to be as expected in the standard, the actual profit and loss account would appear:

	£	£
Sales (1,000 × £30)		30,000
Direct materials (1,000 × £12)	12,000	
Direct labour (1,000 × £8)	8,000	
Production overhead (1,000 × £5)	5,000	
		25,000
Profit		5,000

The expected profit was £7 per unit (£30 – £23) so on sales of 1,000 units this would be:

1,000 units × £7/unit = £7,000.

Actual profit is £2,000 less than expected. Note that this is the same as the difference between the actual and standard direct material cost calculated earlier (£12,000 – £10,000).

This is known as the direct material total cost variance, and because it causes actual profits to be less than expected it is said to be an **adverse** variance.

Note that this total variance for the period can be shown to be equal to the difference of £2 per unit of X (calculated earlier) multiplied by 1,000 units.

4.6   **Activity**

The standard direct material cost of product A is £5. During August 600 units of product A were made, and the actual direct material cost was £3,200. Calculate the direct material total cost variance for the period.

4.7   **Activity solution**

	£
Standard direct material cost of 600 units: £5 × 600	3,000
Actual direct material cost	3,200
Direct material total cost variance - Adverse	200

4.8   **Analysing the direct material total cost variance**

When a standard material cost is determined for a unit of a product it is made up of two parts. These are estimates of:

(a)   the quantity of material to be used; and

(b)   the price to be paid per unit of material.

If we return to the earlier example concerning product X, the standard direct material cost per unit was stated to be £10. This was based on using 5 kg of a particular material to make each unit of product X and paying £2/kg for the material.

You should remember that the actual direct material cost incurred in making 1,000 units of product X was £12,000. The invoice for these costs shows:

4,800 kg @ £2.50/kg = £12,000.

It should be noted that this form of analysis corresponds to the two estimates which form the basis of the standard cost. It is this which allows the direct material total cost variance to be analysed.

4.9   Direct material price variance

The purpose of calculating this variance is to identify the extent to which profits will differ from those expected by reason of the actual price paid for direct materials being different from the standard price.

The standard price per kg of material was stated above to be £2/kg. This can be used to calculate the expected cost of the actual materials used to make 1,000 units of product X. On this basis the 4,800 kg of material should have cost:

4,800 kg × £2/kg = £9,600.

The actual cost of these materials was £12,000 which is £2,400 (£12,000 – £9,600) more than expected. Since the actual price was greater than expected this will cause the profit to be lower than expected. This variance, known as the direct material price variance, is adverse.

4.10   Activity

A raw material, used in the manufacture of product F has a standard price of £1.30 per litre. During May 2,300 litres were bought at a cost of £3,128. Calculate the direct material price variance for May.

4.11   Activity solution

	£
Standard cost of 2,300 litres: 2,300 litres × £1.30/litre	2,990
Actual cost of 2,300 litres	3,128
Direct material price variance - Adverse	138

4.12   Direct material usage variance

The purpose of this variance is to quantify the effect on profit of using a different quantity of raw material from that expected for the actual production achieved.

Returning to our example concerning product X, it was stated that each unit of product X had a standard direct material usage of 5 kgs. This can be used to calculate the amount of direct material (in kgs) which should be used for the actual production achieved.

1,000 units of X @ 5 kgs of direct material each = 5,000 kgs.

You should remember that the analysis of the actual cost showed that 4,800 kgs of direct material were actually used.

Thus a saving of 200 kgs (5,000 – 4,800) was achieved.

This saving of materials must be valued to show the effect on profit. If the original standard direct material cost were revised to reflect this saving of material it would become:

4.8 kgs (4,800/1,000) @ £2/kg = £9.60.

This is £0.40 per unit of product X less than the original standard and profit would therefore increase by this amount for every unit of product X produced. This has a total value of

  1,000 units × £0.40 = £400.

We achieve the same result by multiplying the saving in quantity by the standard price:

  200 kgs × £2/kg = £400.

In this case profits will be higher than expected because less material was used than expected in the standard. Therefore the variance is said to be favourable.

4.13 Activity

The standard direct material usage per unit of product K is 0.4 tonnes. The standard price of the material is £30/tonne.

During April 500 units of K were made using 223 tonnes of material costing £6,913. Calculate the direct material usage variance.

4.14 Activity solution

Standard usage of 500 units of K:	
500 × 0.4 tonnes	200 tonnes
Actual usage	223 tonnes
Excess usage	23 tonnes

Valued at standard price of £30/tonne:

Direct material usage variance is:

  23 tonnes × £30/tonne = <u>£690</u> Adverse

4.15 Raw material stocks

The earlier example has assumed that the quantity of materials purchased equalled the quantity of materials used by production. Whilst this is possible it is not always certain to occur. Where this does not occur profit will be affected by the change in the level of stock. The extent to which this affects the calculation of direct material variances depends on the methods chosen to value stock. Stocks may be valued either using:

(a)   the standard price for the material; or

(b)   the actual price (as applies from using FIFO, LIFO, etc).

4.16 Stocks valued at standard price

This is the most common method when using a standard costing system because it eliminates the need to record value based movements of stock on stores ledger cards (since all movements, both receipts and issues, will be valued at the standard price).

The effect of this valuation method is that price variances are calculated based on the quantity purchased rather than the quantity of materials used. This is illustrated by the following example.

4.17 Example

Product P requires 4 kg of material Z per unit. The standard price of material Z is £8/kg. During September 16,000 kgs of Z were bought for £134,400. There was no opening stock of material Z but at the end of September 1,400 kgs of Z remained in stock. Stocks of Z are valued at standard prices.

The price variance is based on the quantity purchased (ie, 16,000 kgs). The standard cost of these materials can be calculated:

	£
16,000 kgs × £8/kg	128,000
Actual cost of 16,000 kgs	134,400
Direct material price variance - Adverse	6,400

4.18   Stock account

Continuing the above example the issues of material Z of 14,600 kgs (16,000 – 1,400) would be valued at the standard price of £8/kg.

The value of the issues debited to work in progress would thus be:

14,600 kgs × £8/kg = £116,800.

The stock account would appear thus:

Raw material Z

	£		£
Creditor	134,400	Work in progress	116,800
		Price variance	6,400
		Bal c/d	11,200
	134,400		134,400

Note that the balance c/d comprises the closing stock of 1,400 kgs valued at the standard price of £8/kg.

1,400 kgs × £8/kg = £11,200.

The entry representing the price variance is shown as a credit in the raw material account because it is an adverse variance. The corresponding entry is made to a price variance account, the balance of which is transferred to profit and loss at the end of the year: The price variance account is as follows:

Raw material price variance

	£		£
Raw material Z	6,400		

4.19   Stocks valued at actual price

If this stock valuation method is used it means that any price variance is recognised not at the time of purchase but at the time of issue.

When using this method issues are made from stock at actual prices (using, FIFO, LIFO, etc) with the consequence that detailed stores ledger cards must be kept. The price variance is calculated based upon the quantity used.

4.20   Example

Using the data concerning material Z above, calculations of the value of issues and closing stock can be made as follows:

$$\text{Actual cost 1 kg} = \frac{£134,400}{16,000} = £8.40$$

Value of issues (at actual cost) = 14,600 kgs × £8.40
  = £122,640

Closing stock value (at actual cost)   =   1,400 kgs × £8.40
                                            =   £11,760.

The direct material price variance based on the issues quantity can be calculated:

	£
Standard cost of 14,600 kgs:	
14,600 kgs × £8/kg	116,800
Actual cost of 14,600 kgs (above)	122,640
Direct material price variance - Adverse	5,840

4.21   Stock account

If stock is valued using actual prices, the stock account will be as follows:

Raw material Z

	£		£
Creditor	134,400	Work in progress	122,640
		Balance c/d	11,760
	134,400		134,400

Note that the closing balance comprises:

	£
1,400 kgs × standard price of £8/kg	11,200
Adverse price variance not yet recognised:	
1,400 kgs × (£8.40 − £8.00)	560
	11,760

The price variance is shown in the work in progress account with the corresponding entry as before:

Work in progress

	£		£
Raw material Z	122,640	Direct material price variance	5,840

4.22   Direct labour cost variances

The purpose of calculating direct labour cost variances is to quantify the effect on profit of actual direct labour costs differing from standard direct labour costs.

This total effect is then analysed to quantify how much has been caused by a difference in the wage rate paid to employees and how much by a difference in the number of hours.

4.23   Example

The following standard costs relate to a single unit of product Q:

	£
Direct materials	8
Direct labour	12
Production overhead	6
	26

On the basis of these standard costs if a unit of product Q is sold for £35, the expected (or standard) profit would be £9 (£35 – £26).

However, if the actual direct labour cost of making the unit of Q were £10, then (assuming the other costs to be as per standard) the actual cost of product Q would be:

	£
Direct materials	8
Direct labour	10
Production overhead	6
	24

Thus when the product is sold the profit is £11 (£35 – £24).

This increase in profit is the effect of the difference between the actual and standard direct labour cost of £2 (£12 – £10).

This simple example considered only one unit of product Q, but it is the principle upon which variance calculations are made.

4.24   Direct labour total cost variance

The purpose of this variance is to show the effect on profit for an accounting period of the actual direct labour cost being different from the standard direct labour cost.

4.25   Example

In August, 800 units of product Q were manufactured, and sold for £35 each.

Using the data above,

(i)   the standard direct labour cost of these 800 units of product Q would be:

800 units × £12/unit = £9,600

(ii)   the actual direct labour cost of these 800 units of product Q would be:

800 units × £10/unit = £8,000.

Assuming the other actual costs to be as expected in the standard, the actual profit and loss account would appear:

	£	£
Sales (800 × £35)		28,000
Direct materials (800 × £8)	6,400	
Direct labour (800 × £10)	8,000	
Production overhead (800 × £6)	4,800	
	19,200	
		19,200
Profit		8,800

The expected profit was £9 per unit (£35 – £26) so on sales of 800 units this would be:

800 units × £9/unit = £7,200.

Actual profit is £1,600 more than expected. Note that this is the same as the difference between the actual and standard direct labour cost calculated earlier (£9,600 – £8,000).

This is known as the direct labour total cost variance, and because it causes actual profits to be more than expected it is said to be a favourable variance.

Note that this total variance for the period can be shown to be equal to the difference of £2 per unit of Q (calculated earlier) multiplied by 800 units.

4.26   Activity

The standard direct labour cost of product H is £7. During January 450 units of product H were made, and the actual direct labour cost was £3,450. Calculate the direct labour total cost variance of the period.

4.27   Activity solution

	£
Standard direct labour cost of 450 units:	
£7 × 450	3,150
Actual direct labour cost	3,450
Direct labour total cost variance - Adverse	300

4.28   Analysing the direct labour total cost variance

When a standard labour cost is determined for a unit of a product it is made up of two parts. These are estimates of:

(a)   the number of hours required per unit; and

(b)   the hourly wage rate.

If we return to the example concerning product Q, the standard direct labour cost per unit was stated to be £12. This was based on 4 direct labour hours being required per unit of Q and paying a wage rate of £3/hour.

You should remember that the actual direct labour cost incurred in making 800 units of product Q was £8,000. An analysis of the payroll records shows:

2,000 hours @ £4/hour = £8,000.

It should be noted that this corresponds to the two estimates which form the basis of the standard cost. It is this which allows the direct labour total cost variance to be analysed.

4.29   Direct labour rate variance

The purpose of calculating this variance is to identify the extent to which profits will differ from those expected by reason of the actual wage rate per hour being different from the standard.

The standard wage rate per hour was stated to be £3. This can be used to calculate the expected cost of the actual hours taken to make 800 units of product Q. On this basis the 2,000 hours should have cost:

2,000 hours × £3/hour = £6,000.

The actual labour cost was £8,000 which is £2,000 (£8,000 – £6,000) more than expected.

Since the actual rate was greater than expected, this will cause the profit to be lower than expected. This variance, known as the direct labour rate variance, is adverse.

4.30   Direct labour efficiency variance

The purpose of this variance is to quantify the effect on profit of using a different number of hours than expected for the actual production achieved.

Continuing with our example concerning product Q, it was stated that each unit of product Q would require 4 direct labour hours. This can be used to calculate the number of direct labour hours which should be required for the actual production achieved.

800 units of Q × 4 direct labour hours each = 3,200 direct labour hours

You should remember that the analysis of the actual cost showed that 2,000 hours were used.

Thus a saving of 1,200 direct labour hours (3,200 – 2,000) was achieved.

This saving of labour hours must be valued to show the effect on profit. We do this by multiplying the difference in hours by the standard hourly rate:

1,200 direct labour hours × £3/hr = £3,600.

In this case profit will be higher than expected because fewer hours were used. Therefore the variance is favourable.

4.31   Activity

The following data relates to product C

Actual production of C (units)	700
Standard wage rate/hour	£4.00
Standard time allowance per unit of C (hours)	1.50
Actual hours worked	1,000
Actual wage cost	£4,200

Calculate the direct labour rate and efficiency variances from the above data.

4.32   Activity solution

	£
Expected cost of actual hours worked:	
1,000 hours × £4/hr	4,000
Actual wage cost	4,200
Direct labour rate variance - Adverse	200
Expected hours for actual production:	
700 units × 1.50 hours/unit	1,050
Actual hours	1,000
A saving (in hours) of	50

These are valued at the standard wage rate/hour.

Direct labour efficiency variance is:

50 hours × £4/hour = £200 Favourable.

5   VARIABLE OVERHEAD VARIANCES

5.1   Introduction

These variances are very similar to those for material and labour because, like these direct costs, the variable overhead cost also changes when activity changes.

The most common examination question assumes that variable overhead costs vary with labour hours worked. This results in the calculation of two variable overhead variances which are illustrated by the following example.

5.2   Example

K Limited has a budgeted variable overhead cost for August of £84,000. Budgeted production is 20,000 units of its finished product and direct labour hours are expected to be 40,000 hours.

During August the actual production was 20,500 units. Actual hours worked were 41,600 hours and the variable overhead cost incurred amounted to £86,700.

5.3   Variable overhead total variance

In order to calculate the total variance it is necessary to calculate the standard variable overhead cost for the actual production achieved.

The budgeted variable overhead cost per hour is calculated by:

$$\frac{\text{Budgeted cost}}{\text{Budgeted hours}} = \frac{£84,000}{40,000} = £2.10 \text{ per hour}$$

Actual production was 20,500 units which is the equivalent of 41,000 standard hours. (According to the budget each unit should require 2 hours ie, 40,000 hours/20,000 units.)

	£
The standard cost of 41,000 hours at £2.10 per hour is	86,100
Actual cost	86,700
Variance	600 (A)

The variance is adverse because the actual cost exceeded the standard cost and therefore profits would be lower than expected.

5.4   Variable overhead expenditure variance

This variance measures the effect on profit of the actual variable overhead cost per hour differing from the standard hourly cost.

The actual hours worked were 41,600.

	£
If these had cost £2.10/hour as expected the cost would have been This is the standard cost of actual hours.	87,360
The actual cost was	86,700
Variance	660 (F)

This results in a favourable expenditure variance of £660.

5.5   Variable overhead efficiency variance

This variance measures the effect on profit of the actual hours worked differing from the standard hours produced.

Standard hours produced	41,000
Actual hours worked	41,600
Difference	600

This difference in hours is valued at the standard variable overhead cost/hour:

$$600 \times £2.10 = £1,260 \text{ (A)}.$$

The variance is adverse because actual hours exceeded standard hours.

5.6 Proof of total variance

Note that the sum of these sub-variances, representing expenditure and efficiency equals the total variance:

$$£660 \text{ (F)} + £1,260 \text{ (A)} = £600 \text{ (A)}.$$

5.7 When variable overhead cost varies with volume

If variable overhead cost changes not as a result of a change in direct labour hours, but as a result of a change in production volume it is not possible to calculate the sub-variances illustrated above.

Instead only the total variance can be calculated using the standard variable overhead cost/unit:

$$\frac{\text{Budgeted cost}}{\text{Budgeted units}} = \frac{£84,000}{20,000} = £4.20 \text{ per unit}$$

	£
Standard cost of actual production 20,500 units × £4.20/unit	86,100
Actual cost	86,700
Total variance (as before)	600 (A)

6 FIXED OVERHEAD VARIANCES

6.1 Introduction

These variances show the effect on profit of differences between actual and expected fixed overhead costs. By definition these costs do not change when there is a change in the level of activity, consequently many of the variances are calculated based upon budgets; however, the effect on profit depends upon whether a marginal or absorption costing system is being used. In the variance calculations which follow firstly an absorption costing system is assumed. These are then compared with the variances which would arise if a marginal costing system were used.

6.2 Marginal v absorption costing - a reminder

The difference between these costing methods lies in their treatment of fixed production overheads. Whereas absorption costing relates such costs to cost units using absorption rates, marginal costing treats the cost as a period cost and writes it off to profit and loss as it is incurred.

6.3 Fixed overhead total variance

Assuming an absorption costing system, this is the effect on profit of there being a difference between the actual cost incurred and the amount absorbed by the use of the absorption rate based on budgeted costs and activity. This is illustrated by the following example.

6.4 Example

Q Limited has completed its budget for October, the following data have been extracted:

Budgeted fixed overhead cost	£100,000
Budgeted production	20,000 units
Budgeted machine hours	25,000

A machine hour absorption rate is used.

The actual fixed overhead cost incurred was £98,500.   Actual production was 20,300 units using 25,700 machine hours.

6.5   Solution

The absorption rate per machine hour (based upon the budget) is given by:

$$\frac{\text{Budgeted fixed overhead cost}}{\text{Budgeted machine hours}}$$

$$= \frac{£100,000}{25,000} = £4 \text{ per machine hour}$$

This would be used to determine the fixed overhead cost absorbed (ie, attributed to the actual production achieved).

In a standard costing system the actual production achieved is measured in standard hours, in this case standard machine hours.

According to the budget 20,000 units should require 25,000 machine hours, this is the equivalent of 1.25 machine hours per unit (25,000/20,000).

Thus the actual production of 20,300 units is equivalent to

$20,300 \times 1.25 = 25,375$ standard machine hours.

The amount absorbed is therefore:

25,375 standard machine hours × £4/machine hour = £101,500

This is the standard cost of the actual production (using absorption costing). It is compared with the actual cost to find the total variance:

	£
Standard cost	101,500
Actual cost	98,500
Variance	3,000 (F)

Since the actual cost is less than the standard cost it is a favourable variance.

6.6   Over/under absorptions and the total variance

The comparison of actual fixed overhead cost incurred and the amount of fixed overhead cost absorbed is not new, it was used in your earlier studies to determine the extent of any under/over absorption. Often this is done using a fixed production overhead control account which is shown below based upon the above figures:

Fixed production overhead control a/c

	£		£
Creditors	98,500	Work in progress	101,500
P & L (over absorption)	3,000		
	101,500		101,500

You should note that the over absorption is equal to the total variance.

6.7   Activity

TP has the following data concerning its fixed production overheads:

Budget cost	£44,000
Budget production	8,000 units
Budget labour hours	16,000
Actual cost	£47,500
Actual production	8,450 units
Actual labour hours	16,600

Calculate the fixed overhead total variance assuming an absorption system based upon labour hours.

6.8   Activity solution

$$\text{Absorption rate} = \frac{\text{Budgeted cost}}{\text{Budgeted hours}} = \frac{£44,000}{16,000} = £2.75$$

$$\text{Actual output in standard hours} = 8,450 \times \frac{16,000}{8,000} = \qquad 16,900$$

Amount absorbed = 16,900 × £2.75 =	£46,475
Actual cost =	£47,500
	——
Variance	1,025 (A)
	——

6.9   Analysing the total variance

In the same way that any over/under absorption can be analysed into the causes known as expenditure and volume, the same analysis can be made of the total variance. The same terminology is used, and the method of calculation is the same as you learnt earlier in this text. The example we used earlier (reproduced below) will be used to show this.

6.10   Example

Q Limited has completed its budget for October, the following data have been extracted:

Budgeted fixed overhead cost	£100,000
Budgeted production	20,000 units
Budgeted machine hours	25,000

A machine hour absorption rate is used.

The actual fixed overhead cost incurred was £98,500. Actual production was 20,300 units using 25,700 machine hours.

6.11   Fixed overhead expenditure variance

This variance shows the effect on profit of the actual fixed overhead expenditure differing from the budgeted value:

	£
Budgeted expenditure	100,000
Actual expenditure	98,500
	——
Variance	1,500 (F)
	——

The variance is favourable because the actual expenditure is less than that budgeted.

6.12   Fixed overhead volume variance

This variance measures the difference between the amount actually absorbed based upon actual production (in standard hours) compared to the amount expected to be absorbed based upon budgeted production (in standard hours).

Budgeted production (standard machine hours)	25,000
Actual production (standard machine hours)	25,375
Difference	375

This difference of 375 standard machine hours is valued at the absorption rate of £4/hr:

$$375 \text{ hours} \times £4/\text{hr} = £1,500 \text{ (F)}.$$

This variance is favourable because the actual output exceeded the expected output. Since the cost is fixed, the actual cost/unit is lowered by making greater production and profits will therefore increase.

6.13   The total variance and the sub-variances

Note that the sum of the fixed overhead expenditure and volume variances equals the fixed overhead total variance:

$$£1,500 \text{ (F)} + £1,500 \text{ (F)} = £3,000 \text{ (F)}.$$

6.14   Activity

Analyse the total variance you calculated in the previous activity into the fixed overhead expenditure and volume variances. (The data is reproduced below for convenience.)

TP has the following data concerning its fixed production overheads:

Budget cost	£44,000
Budget production	8,000 units
Budget labour hours	16,000
Actual cost	£47,500
Actual production	8,450 units
Actual labour hours	16,600

6.15   Activity solution

Fixed overhead expenditure variance:

	£
Budget cost	44,000
Actual cost	47,500
	3,500 (A)

Fixed overhead volume variance:

Budget production (labour hours)	16,000
Actual production (standard hours)	16,900
	900

$$900 \text{ hours} \times £2.75 = £2,475 \text{ (F)}$$

Proof of total:

$$£3,500 \text{ (A)} + £2,475 \text{ (F)} = £1,025 \text{ (A)}$$

6.16   Fixed overhead variances and marginal costing

As was stated earlier, marginal costing does not relate fixed production overhead costs to cost units. The amount shown in the profit and loss account is the cost incurred. Since the cost is a fixed cost it is not expected to change when activity changes thus the expected cost of any level of production is always the budgeted cost.

The purpose of variance analysis is to calculate the effect on profit of actual performance differing from that expected, consequently, under marginal costing this will be the difference between the actual and budgeted expenditure.

Thus under marginal costing the total fixed production overhead variance will always equal the fixed production overhead expenditure variance which is calculated in the same way as for absorption costing systems (above).

7   NON-PRODUCTION OVERHEADS

7.1   Introduction

Since the purpose of variance analysis is to show the effect on profit of actual results differing from those expected, it is also necessary to compare the costs of non-production overheads such as selling, marketing and administration.

7.2   Non-production overhead variances

These costs are not related to the cost unit (even in an absorption costing system) so the calculation of variances for these items is exactly the same as that for fixed production overheads in a marginal costing system.

In other words the only variance is expenditure which is simply the difference between actual and budgeted expenditure. It is usual for separate variances to be calculated for each function (ie, selling, marketing, administration).

8   SALES VARIANCES

8.1   Introduction

The purpose of calculating sales variances is to show their effect when a comparison is made between budget and actual profit. There are two causes of sales variances, a difference in the selling price and a difference in the sales volume.

8.2   Sales price variance

This variance shows the effect on profit of selling at a different price from that expected. The following example is used to illustrate its calculation.

8.3   Example

TZ has the following data regarding its sales for March:

Budgeted sales	1,000 units
Budgeted selling price	£10/unit
Standard variable cost	£6/unit
Budgeted fixed cost	£2/unit*

* based upon annual fixed costs and activity levels

Actual sales	940 units
Actual selling price	£10.50/unit

If the actual sales volume had been sold at the budgeted selling price the sales revenue would have been

940 units × £10 =	£9,400
But actual sales revenue was	
940 units × £10.50 =	£9,870
	———
Variance	470 (F)

The variance is favourable because the higher actual selling price causes an increase in revenue and a consequent increase in profit.

8.4   Sales volume variance

The purpose of this variance is to calculate the effect on profit of the actual sales volume being difference from that budgeted. The effect on profit will differ depending upon whether a marginal or absorption costing system is being used.

Under absorption costing all production costs are attributed to the cost unit, and the fixed production overhead volume variance accounts for the effects of actual volumes differing from those expected. Whereas under marginal costing contribution is emphasised (ie, the difference between the selling price and the variable cost).

This affects the calculation of the sales volume variance, under absorption costing any difference in units is valued at the standard profit per unit, whereas under marginal costing such a difference in units is valued at the standard contribution per unit.

In neither case is the standard selling price used. This is because when volumes change so do production costs and the purpose of calculating the variance is to find the effect on profit.

8.5   Sales volume variance - absorption costing

Using the data from the example above:

Budgeted sales	1,000 units
Actual sales	940 units
	———
Difference	60 units

These 60 units are valued at the standard profit of £2/unit (£10-£6-£2)

60 units × £2 = £120 (A).

The variance is adverse because actual sales volume was less than expected.

8.6   Sales volume variance - marginal costing

The difference of 60 units (as above) is valued at the standard contribution of £4/unit (£10-£6):

60 units × £4 = £240 (A).

8.7   Reconciling the sales volume variances under absorption and marginal costing

Using the above example:

Variance under	- absorption costing	£120 (A)
	- marginal costing	£240 (A)

There is a difference between these variances of £120 (A).

Earlier in this chapter we learnt how to calculate fixed overhead variances. These too were affected by the choice of costing method. Absorption costing required the calculation of both an expenditure and a volume variance, whereas marginal costing only required an expenditure variance.

Continuing with the data from the above example there is a volume difference of 60 units. The fixed cost is absorbed at a rate equivalent to £2/unit.

Thus the fixed production overhead volume variance would be

60 units × £2/unit = £120 (A)

The variance would be adverse because actual volume was less than expected and, since the cost is fixed this would increase the cost per unit and so decrease profit.

Thus when reconciling the profits, the absorption and marginal systems would show:

	Absorption	*Marginal*
Variances:		
Sales volume	£120 (A)	£240 (A)
Fixed production overhead volume	£120 (A)	Not applicable
	£240 (A)	£240 (A)

All other cost variances and the sales price variance would be identical under both systems.

The reconciliation of profits is covered in more depth later in this chapter.

8.8   Activity

Budgeted sales	500 units
Actual sales	480 units
Budgeted selling price	£100
Actual selling price	£110
Standard variable cost	£50/unit
Budgeted fixed cost	£15/unit

Calculate:

(i)   the selling price variance;
(ii)   the sales volume variance assuming an absorption costing system;
(iii)   the sales volume variance assuming a marginal costing system.

8.9   Activity solution

(i)   480 units × (£110 − £100) = £4,800 (F)
(ii)   20 units × (£100 − 50 − 15) = £700 (A)
(iii)   20 units × (£100 − 50) = £1,000 (A)

9   RECONCILIATION OF BUDGET AND ACTUAL PROFITS - OPERATING STATEMENTS

9.1   Introduction

The purpose of calculating variances is to identify the different effects of each item of cost/income on profit compared to the expected profit. These variances are summarised in a reconciliation statement.

9.2   The reconciliation statement

The example which follows shows how such a statement reconciles the budget and actual profit of a period, based on absorption costing.

The statement commences with the budgeted profit which is based upon budgeted cost and activity levels.

This is then adjusted by the sales volume variance to reflect any difference in actual and budgeted activity. The result, which is referred to as the 'Standard profit on actual sales' represents the profit which would be achieved if:

(i)   the selling price was as budgeted; and
(ii)   all variable costs were as per the standard unit cost; and
(iii)   all fixed costs were as budgeted.

The selling price and cost variances are then included under the headings of adverse and favourable as appropriate. The total of these should reconcile the actual profit to the standard profit on actual sales.

9.3   Example

The following example illustrates the variances defined above.

Chapel Ltd manufactures a chemical protective called Rustnot. The following standard costs apply for the production of 100 cylinders:

		£
Materials	500 kgs @ 80p per kg	400
Labour	20 hours @ £1.50 per hour	30
Fixed overheads	20 hours @ £1.00 per hour	20
		450

The monthly production/sales budget is 10,000 cylinders. Selling price = £6 per cylinder.

For the month of November the following production and sales information is available:

Produced/sold	10,600 cylinders
Sales value	£63,000
Material purchased and used 53,200 kgs	£42,500
Labour 2,040 hours	£3,100
Fixed overheads	£2,200

You are required to prepare an operating statement for November detailing all the variances.

9.4   Solution

			£
Budgeted profit (10,000 cylinders) (W(a))			15,000
Add: Sales volume variance (W(f))			900
Standard profit on actual sales (10,600 cylinders) (W(c))			15,900
Less: Variances (W(f) – (i)):	*Adv.*	*Fav.*	
	£	£	
Sales price (f)	600		
Material price (g)		60	
Wages rate (h)	40		
Fixed overhead expenditure (i)	200		
Material usage (g)	160		
Labour efficiency (h)		120	
Fixed overhead volume (i)		120	
	1,000	300	
			700
Actual profit (W(b))			15,200

WORKINGS

		£	£
(a)	**Budgeted profit**		
	10,000 cylinders @ £1.50		15,000

(b)   **Actual profit**

		£	£
Sales			63,000
Less: Materials		42,500	
Labour		3,100	
Fixed overheads		2,200	
			47,800
			15,200

(c)   **Actual units/standard profit**

	£
Sales value 10,600 × £6	63,600
Less: Standard cost of sales 10,600 × £4.50	47,700
	15,900

(d)   **Standard hours**

10,600 cylinders × 0.2 hours = 2,120 hours

(e)   **Budgeted hours**

10,000 × 0.2 = 2,000 hours

Variances

(f)   **Sales**

The budgeted selling price is £6 per cylinder. Actual sales were 10,600 cylinders for £63,000. If the actual cylinders sold had been sold at the budgeted selling price of £6 then sales would have been

10,600 × £6 = £63,600.

Thus the difference in selling price resulted in a lower sales value by £600. This is an adverse selling price variance.

The budgeted volume was 10,000 cylinders costing £4.50 each. At the budgeted selling price of £6 each this is a budgeted profit of £1.50 per cylinder.

Actual sales volume was 10,600 cylinders, 600 more than budget. These extra 600 cylinders will increase profit by

600 × £1.50 = £900.

This is a favourable sales volume variance.

(g)   **Raw materials**

The standard price of the raw material is £0.80 per kg. If the actual quantity of 53,200 kg had been bought at the standard price this would have been

53,200 kg × £0.80/kg = £42,560.

The actual cost was £42,500. This is a saving caused by price, it is a favourable price variance of £60.

Each 100 cylinders should use 500 kgs of material. Therefore the 10,600 cylinders produced should use

$$10,600 \times 500 \text{ kg}/100 = 53,000 \text{ kgs}$$

The actual usage was 53,200 kgs. These additional 200 kgs of material have a value (using standard prices) of

$$200 \text{ kgs} \times £0.80 = £160.$$

This is an adverse material usage variance.

(h)   **Labour**

The standard labour rate is £1.50 per hour. The actual labour hours was 2,040 hours, so if they had been paid at the standard rate per hour, the wage cost would have been

$$2,040 \times £1.50 = £3,060.$$

The actual wage cost was £3,100. This extra £40 is the adverse wage rate variance.

Each 100 cylinders should take 20 hours to produce. The actual production was 10,600 cylinders so these should have taken

$$10,600 \times 20/100 = 2,120 \text{ hours}$$

Actual hours were 2,040 hours, a saving of 80 hours. These hours (valued at the standard rate) are worth

$$80 \times £1.50 = £120.$$

This is a favourable labour efficiency.

(i)   **Fixed overheads**

The standard fixed overhead cost is £20 per 100 cylinders. Monthly production is budgeted at 10,000 cylinders. Therefore the budgeted fixed overhead cost is

$$10,000 \times £20/100 = £2,000.$$

The actual cost was £2,200. The extra cost of £200 is an adverse fixed overhead expenditure variance.

But the actual production was 10,600 cylinders, 600 more than budgeted. This extra volume of 600 units (valued at the standard absorption rate of £20/100 units) is

$$600 \times £20/100 = £120$$

This is a favourable fixed overhead volume variance.

9.5   Marginal costing reconciliation

The above presentation was based on absorption costing; on a marginal costing basis it would appear as:

	£
Budgeted profit	15,000
Add: Sales volume variance (j)	1,020
Standard contribution on actual sales (Wj)	16,020

		Adv	Fav
Less: Variances (W(f)-(i)):		£	£
Sales price (f)		600	
Material price (g)			60
Wages rate (h)		40	
Fixed overhead expenditure (i)		200	
Material usage (g)		160	
Labour efficiency (h)			120
		1,000	180
			820
Actual profit (W(b))			15,200

WORKING

(a) to (i) are as in the previous example.

(j) $600 \times$ contribution of £1.70 each = £1,020 (F)

$$\text{Contribution/unit} = £6 - \left(\frac{£400 + £30}{100} \right) \quad = \quad £1.70/\text{unit}$$

10   CAUSES AND INTERDEPENDENCE OF VARIANCES

10.1   Causes of variances

The calculation of variances is only the first stage. Management wants information to plan and control operations. It is not sufficient to know that a variance has arisen: we must try to establish why. The figures themselves do not provide the answers, but they point to some of the questions that should be asked. Possible causes of the individual variances are now discussed.

Bromwich has proposed four general causes of variances:

*   bad budgeting;
*   bad measurement or recording;
*   random factors;
*   operational factors.

The following list concentrates on examples of the fourth of these causes.

(a)   **Material price variance**

This could be due to:

(i)   different source of supply;
(ii)   unexpected general price increase;
(iii)   alteration in quantity discounts;
(iv)   substitution of a different grade of material;
(v)   standard set at mid-year price so one would expect a favourable price variance in the early months and an adverse variance in the later months of the year.

(b)   **Material usage variance**

This could be due to:

(i)   higher/lower incidence of scrap;
(ii)   alteration to product design;
(iii)   substitution of a different grade of material.

(c) **Wages rate variance**

Possible causes:

(i) unexpected national wage award;
(ii) overtime or bonus payments different from plan;
(iii) substitution of a different grade of labour.

(d) **Labour efficiency variance**

(i) improvemer   f working conditions including better supervision;
(ii) consequen   effect;
(iii) introductio.   .heme or staff training;
(iv) substitution of a different grade of labour.

(e) **Variable overhead**

(i) unexpected price changes for overhead items;
(ii) incorrect split between fixed and variable overheads.

(f) **Fixed overhead expenditure**

(i) changes in prices relating to fixed overhead items eg, rent increase;
(ii) seasonal effect eg, heat/light in winter. (This arises where the annual budget is divided into four equal quarters or thirteen equal four-weekly periods without allowances for seasonal factors. Over a whole year the seasonal effects would cancel out.)

(g) **Fixed overhead volume**

(i) change in production volume due to change in demand or alterations to stockholding policy;
(ii) changes in productivity of labour or machinery;
(iii) production lost through strikes, etc.

(h) **Operating profit variance due to selling prices**

(i) unplanned price increase;
(ii) unplanned price reduction eg, to try and attract additional business.

(i) **Operating profit variance due to sales volume**

This is obviously caused by a change in sales volume, which may be due to:

(i) unexpected fall in demand due to recession;
(ii) additional demand attracted by reduced prices;
(iii) failure to satisfy demand due to production difficulties.

10.2 Interdependence of variances

The cause of a particular variance may affect another variance in a corresponding or opposite way, eg:

(a) If supplies of a specified material are not available, this may lead to a favourable price variance (cheaper material used), an adverse usage variance (cheaper material caused more wastage), an adverse fixed overhead volume variance (production delayed while material was unavailable) and an adverse sales volume variance (unable to meet demand due to production difficulties).

(b) A new improved machine becomes available which causes an adverse fixed overhead expenditure variance (because this machine is more expensive and depreciation is higher) offset by favourable wages efficiency and fixed overhead volume variances (higher productivity).

(c)   Workers trying to improve productivity (favourable labour efficiency variance) might become careless and waste more material (adverse material usage variance).

In each of these cases, if one variance has given rise to the other, there is an argument in favour of combining the two variances and ascribing them to the common cause. In view of these possible interdependencies, care has to be taken when implementing a bonus scheme. If the chief buyer is rewarded if he produces a favourable price variance, this may bring about trouble later as shoddy materials give rise to adverse usage variances.

10.3   Variances and their relevance to management

Variances may be used as part of a management by exception technique.

The variances represent the monetary measure of profits gained or lost as a result of the actual performance differing from the target set. However, the relevance of variances to management is not their value, though this can be used to identify an individual variance's significance, but their cause. If the cause of the variance can be determined, and it is found to be controllable by management, then action can be taken as appropriate.

Sometimes it is necessary to investigate a variance to establish its cause. This is covered in detail later in this text, but in principle it must be remembered that such an investigation:

(a)   will incur costs;

(b)   may not identify the cause; and

(c)   if it is identified the cause may not be controllable.

For these reasons management must establish a policy to determine which variances are sufficiently significant to warrant investigation.

10.4   Relevance of standard costing in the modern manufacturing environment

It is argued that the use of traditional standard costing and variance analysis is of decreasing relevance in the modern manufacturing environment, where JIT, TQM and other advanced manufacturing technologies (AMTs) and philosophies are becoming more prevalent.

The trend characteristics of such an environment that result in traditional costing methods becoming less useful include:

- an emphasis in the modern, globally competitive market, on continuous improvement. Setting standards can be said to create a climate whereby their achievement and maintenance is the ultimate goal, which is inconsistent with a philosophy of continuous improvement.

- an increasing trend away from mass production and towards customised, innovative products. This will lead to a greater variability in operating conditions, where constant standards are less useful.

- an increasing interest in the use of "benchmarking" as a means of establishing best practice and standards, by the use of both external and internal information. This will take account of the practices of other organisations in comparison with those of the company itself. The use of internally determined standards, based upon a company's own costs and procedures, may give too narrow a basis for measurement of the company's performance in a competitive environment.

- decreasing relevance of labour variances with increasingly automated production. Investment in AMTs has dramatically changed cost behaviour patterns; most of a firm's costs have become fixed in the short term and direct labour costs represent only a small proportion of total manufacturing cost.

- a move towards strictly monitored input systems, such as JIT, which decreases the variability in input costs.

In the modern environment, it has been questioned as to whether variance analysis will continue to provide useful information for cost control and performance appraisal.

Traditional cost control systems tend to place a great emphasis on direct labour expenditure and efficiency measures, with less attention paid to reporting and controlling direct material and overheads - the latter, in particular, being of much greater significance in the AMT factory. Absorption of overheads on a direct labour hour basis motivates managers to reduce direct labour, since this is the basis by which other costs are attributed to their cost centres and products. Direct labour is therefore given a prominence out of proportion to its contribution, and attention is distracted from control of overheads.

The use of standard costs and variance analysis as a central part of the control and performance measurement system inevitably focuses management's attention on costs. World class manufacturing companies follow a philosophy of continuous improvement, with strategic goals that require feedback on many other issues, such as quality, reliability, lead times and customer satisfaction.

However, surveys have indicated that standard costing is still extensively used in UK companies - including IBM - who have introduced JIT. Whilst standard costing systems may have a lesser role in cost control and performance appraisal, they continue to provide useful cost data for other purposes - budget setting, stock valuation, cost prediction for decision-making. Variance analysis can still provide useful feedback in highlighting the need for standards to be updated for these purposes.

11   MATERIALS MIX AND YIELD VARIANCES

11.1   Relationship to direct material price and usage variances

In many industrial situations, more than one material is used in the manufacturing cycle for a single product. If the various materials used cannot be substituted in any way for each other, the approach is to continue to look at each material quite separately. However, in many circumstances the materials used are to some extent substitutes for each other ie, the mix of materials used in the manufacturing can be altered without noticeably affecting the end product. It is in this situation that the calculation of a mix variance becomes appropriate.

11.2   Mix and yield variances as a sub-set of the usage variance

The following data will be used to show this approach:

Standard cost for 990 tonnes of production:

Material	Tonnes	Price per tonne	
		£	£
A	550	6.00	3,330
B	330	5.00	1,650
C	220	4.50	990
	1,100		5,940
Less: Normal process loss (10%)	110		-
Standard cost for	990	=	5,940

This represents a standard product cost per tonne of £6.00.

Actual material cost and usage to produce 990 tonnes:

Material	Tonnes	Price per tonne £	£
A	444	7.50	3,330
B	446	6.00	2,676
C	240	4.50	1,080
	1,130		7,086
Less: Process loss	140		-
Standard cost for	990		7,086

The following statements can be derived from the data:

Material	Actual quantity used at standard prices			Actual quantity used in standard proportions (mix) at standard prices		
	Tonnes	Standard price per tonne £	£	Tonnes	Standard price per tonne £	£
A	444	6.00	2,664	565	6.00	3,390
B	446	5.00	2,230	339	5.00	1,695
C	240	4.50	1,080	226	4.50	1,017
	1,130		5,974	1,130		6,102

The variance analysis is as follows:

	£	
Actual tonnes Actual mix Actual cost	7,086	Price variance £1,112A
Actual tonnes purchased (and used) Actual mix Standard cost	5,974	

Direct material mix variance

= (Total material input in a standard mix × standard prices) − (Actual material input × standard prices)

$$= \begin{matrix} A \\ B \\ C \end{matrix} \begin{pmatrix} 565 \times 6 \\ 339 \times 5 \\ 226 \times 4.50 \end{pmatrix} - \begin{pmatrix} 444 \times 6 \\ 446 \times 5 \\ 240 \times 4.50 \end{pmatrix}$$

= 6,102 − 5,974

= £128 (F)

Direct material yield variance

= (Standard quantity of materials specified for actual production × standard prices) − (Actual total material input in standard proportions × standard prices)

$$
= \quad
\begin{matrix}
A \\
\\
B \\
\\
C
\end{matrix}
\left(
\begin{matrix}
990 \times \dfrac{550}{990} \times 6 \\[2mm]
990 \times \dfrac{330}{990} \times 5 \\[2mm]
990 \times \dfrac{220}{990} \times 4.50
\end{matrix}
\right)
\quad - \quad
\left(
\begin{matrix}
565 \times 6 \\
339 \times 5 \\
226 \times 4.50
\end{matrix}
\right)
$$

= 5,940 − 6,102

= 162 (A)

∴ **Usage variance**   =   128 − 162   =   34 (A)

The mix and yield variances can be interpreted as follows:

(a)   the mix variance of £128F arises because, compared with the standard, less of the more expensive material (A) has been used and more of the cheaper materials (B and C);

(b)   the yield variance represents the fact that 1,130 tonnes of material in total were input into the process and, with a normal loss of 10%, the expected yield of good production was 1,017 tonnes (0.9 × 1,130). However, good production only amounted to 990 tonnes. The yield was lower than expected by 27 tonnes which, evaluated at the standard product cost of £6 per tonne, gives a yield effect of £162A.

These two variances are probably interrelated and should, therefore, be considered together. It is likely that the change to a cheaper mix of materials has resulted in the yield of good production being down compared with standard. The net effect of the two is an overall adverse usage variance for direct material of £34.

11.3   Mix variances related to individual material inputs

The worked example in the previous section produced a direct material mix variance of £128F in total. It is possible to show the build-up of this figure for materials A, B and C separately, as follows:

Material	Actual quantity used	Actual quantity used in standard mix	Mix variance	Standard price per tonne	Mix variance
	tonnes	tonnes	tonnes	£	£
A	444	565	121 F	6.00	726 F
B	446	339	107 A	5.00	535 A
C	240	226	14 A	4.50	63 A
	1,130	1,130	Nil		128 F

The same total favourable mix variance (£128) is made up of favourable and adverse sub-variances. A reduction in the proportion of the relatively expensive material A has given rise to a favourable variance and the increased usage of the relatively cheaper materials has given adverse variances for B and C.

The mechanics of the calculations are quite clear but how would a manager receiving such a breakdown of the total mix variance interpret the analysis? The manager might conclude that it was a good idea to reduce the proportion of A used as this produces a favourable variance, but a bad thing to increase the proportions of B and C with their resultant adverse effects. The two aspects are interrelated so perhaps the manager should concentrate on the net effect of the changes in the mix ie, the total direct material mix variance.

11.4   Mix and yield variances – a summary

The whole subject of direct material mix and yield variances can be confusing because there are several acceptable methods for their calculation. It is easy to concentrate too much attention on the mechanics of the various methods of calculation and to overlook the fact that variance analysis is a way of presenting information to management so that individual managers can take decisions on the most appropriate courses of action. In any organisation the method of variance analysis adopted should be the most meaningful in all the circumstances involved. It is important that the manager receiving the variance report should understand the meaning of any mix and yield variances in it.

11.5   Activity

The Acton company produces a product by mixing three chemicals X, Y, Z in the proportions 4, 3, 3 respectively. Minor variations on these proportions are acceptable. The standard prices for the chemicals are:

X	£3.20/litre
Y	£2.50/litre
Z	£3.60/litre

There is a 5% normal loss.

Last month's output was 210,000 litres.

The inputs were:

X	70,200 litres at £3.30
Y	69,800 litres at £2.45
Z	60,200 litres at £3.70

Calculate the material price, the material mix, the material yield and the material usage variances. Hence check the relationship between the mix, yield and usage variance.

11.6   Activity solution

Material price variance
= (Actual price – standard price) × Actual quantity

		£
X (3.30 – 3.20) × 70,200	=	7,020 A
Y (2.45 – 2.50) × 69,800	=	3,490 F
Z (3.70 – 3.60) × 60,200	=	6,020 A
Price variance		9,550 A

Material mix variance
(Actual mix – standard mix of actual) × Standard price

				£
.4	X	(70,200 – 80,080) × 3.20	=	31,616 F
.3	Y	(69,800 – 60,060) × 2.50	=	24,350 A
.3	Z	(60,200 – 60,060) × 3.60	=	504 A
		200,200 200,200		6,762 F = Mix variance

Material yield variance

= (Standard input for actual output – Actual mix in standard proportions) × Standard price

£

.4	X	(88,421 – 80,080) × 3.20	=	26,691 F
.3	Y	(66,316 – 60,060) × 2.50	=	15,640 F
.3	Z	(66,316 – 60,060) × 3.60	=	22,522 F

221,053   200,200   64,853 F = Yield variance

Standard input for actual output $= \dfrac{100}{95} \times 210,000 = 221,053$

Material usage variance

(Standard input for actual output – Actual mix) × Standard price

£

X (88,421 – 70,200) × 3.20	=	58,307 F
Y (66,316 – 69,800) × 2.50	=	8,710 A
Z (66,316 – 60,200) × 3.60	=	22,018 F

71,615 F   =   usage variance

| Check: | mix variance | + | yield variance | = | usage variance |
| | 6,762 F + | | 64,853 F | = | 71,615 F |

12   SALES MIX VARIANCE

12.1   Introduction

Where more than one product is sold, it is likely that each will have a different profit. If they are sold in a mix different from that budgeted, a sales mix profit variance will result. Even though the products are not substitutes, a change of sales mix may indicate a change in emphasis of selling effort by sales staff or marketing resources.

Example

Note: the profit figure used will be the standard profit (assuming an absorption costing system).

The Omega company sets the following sales budgets for three products:

			Budgeted profit £
A	400	units at a standard profit of £8	3,200
B	600	units at a standard profit of £6	3,600
C	1,000	units at a standard profit of £4	4,000
	2,000	units	£10,800

The company expects to sell A, B and C in the proportion of 4 : 6 : 10 respectively. Actual sales are achieved at the standard selling price:

				Actual profit £
A	300	units @ £8		2,400
B	700	units @ £6		4,200
C	1,200	units @ £4		4,800
	2,200	units		£11,400

There are many different ways of determining the effect of any change in the sales mix ie, the proportion of the total sales each product represents. The methods compared here rely on taking the actual total quantity sold and determining the quantity of each product that would have been sold had the standard mix been achieved.

12.2   Method

In this example any differences in selling price have been ignored. If products are sold for anything other than their standard selling price this variance should be calculated **separately** first. Thereafter the calculation of the sales volume variance can be done at a standard margin (profit, as here, or contribution) per unit. A tabular approach, analogous to that used for materials is strongly recommended, although other approaches can be shown. The column headings for the relevant tables are:

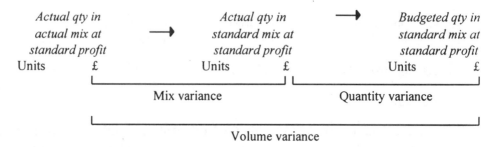

12.3   Solution

The previous figures show a favourable variance of £600 (£11,400 – £10,800) attributable to a change in sales volume which can be split into mix and quantity. A useful working is the average standard profit per unit

$$= \quad \frac{£10,800}{2,000} \quad = \quad £5.40$$

The table then shows:

	Actual qty in actual mix at standard profit		Actual qty in standard mix at standard profit		Budgeted qty in standard mix at standard profit	
	Units	£	Units	£	Units	£
A	300	2,400				
B	700	4,200		at £5.40		
C	1,200	4,800				
	2,200	£11,400	2,200	£11,880	2,000	£10,800

				£	
Sales mix variance	=	£11,400 – £11,880	=	480	(A)
Sales quantity variance	=	£11,880 – £10,800	=	1,080	(F)
Sales volume variance	=	£11,400 – £10,800	=	£600	(F)

Since the net effect of the quantity changes is always zero (ie, we are considering the mix with the total sales of 2,200 units) the overall mix variance will be favourable if more products with a higher profit per unit are sold in place of products with a lower profit per unit ie, in this case the proportion of B and C, which have a lower profit per unit has been increased whereas A, which yields a higher profit per unit, has been reduced. Hence an overall adverse mix variance.

12.4   Usefulness of the sales mix variance

Variances are calculated for the purpose of control. Managers are provided with a variance analysis of their areas of responsibility so that they can improve their decisions. The sales margin mix variance must be judged by this objective.

Two situations are possible:

(a)   The manager is responsible for two or more products which are to some extent substitutes for each other eg, ranges of cheap and expensive cosmetics. Since the mix variance represents shifts in demand between the product ranges, it has significance. As stated before, it is even relevant for non-substitutes.

(b)   The manager is responsible for one line of products; other managers are responsible for other totally different product lines. In this situation, to provide a product manager with a mix variance when he can control only one product is meaningless.

12.5   Activity

From the following information provide a comprehensive sales margin variance analysis:

		Product X	Product Y	Product Z
Budget:				
	Sales price	£20	£20	£10
	Cost	£10	£15	£8
	Units	100	700	200
	Total profit	£1,000	£3,500	£400
Actual:				
	Sales price	£21	£24	£7
	Units sold	200	700	100

12.6   Activity solution

Sales price variance

= (Actual price – Standard price) × Actual quantity sold

Product			£	
X	(£21 – £20) × 200	=	200	(F)
Y	(£24 – £20) × 700	=	2,800	(F)
Z	(£7 – £10) × 100	=	300	(A)
			£2,700	(F)

		Actual qty in actual mix at standard margin			Actual qty in standard mix at standard margin			Budgeted qty in standard mix at standard margin	
		Units	£	→	Units	£	→	Units	£
X		200	2,000						
Y		700	3,500			at £4.90			
Z		100	200						
		1,000	£5,700		1,000	£4,900		1,000	£4,900

Budgeted profits	=	£1,000 + £3,500 + £400	=	£4,900	
Average profit/unit	=	£4,900 ÷ 1,000	=	£4.90	
				£	
Sales mix variance	=	£5,700 − £4,900	=	800	(F)
Sales quantity variance	=	£4,900 − £4,900	=	-	
Sales volume variance	=	£5,700 − £4,900	=	£800	(F)

13   IDLE TIME VARIANCES

13.1   Introduction

Idle time variances may be related to labour hours or machine hours and consequently may arise in the context of both labour or overhead variances. Idle time may also be identified as a causal factor of the sales volume variance.

13.2   Planned idle time

When targets are set it may be anticipated that time will be lost as part of the normal working conditions. Such non-productive (or idle) time will incur costs which would normally be absorbed into the standard cost per unit by adjusting the hourly cost as the following example illustrates.

13.3   Example

PQ Ltd operates a 40-hour week and pays its employees £4.05 per hour. As part of its normal activity it is usual for there to be non-productive time equal to 10% of hours worked. Employee wages are paid at the same rate of £4.05 per hour for both productive and non productive time. Calculate the adjusted hourly rate to compensate for the idle time expected.

13.4   Solution

Cost of 40 hours attendance = 40 × £4.05	=	£162
Productive time 90% of 40 hours	=	36 hours
Adjusted hourly rate = £162/36 hours	=	£4.50

An alternative solution method is:

$$\frac{£4.05}{(1-\% \text{ idle time})} = \frac{£4.05}{0.90} \qquad = \qquad £4.50$$

13.5   Idle time labour variances

Idle time variances are a sub-variance of efficiency variances which arise when the actual idle time is separately measured and differs from that expected.

13.6   Example

ZS plc has a target time (standard time) of 0.5 hours per unit, and expects there to be non-productive time equal to 5% of hours paid. The following details relate to December 19X4:

Units produced	5,400
Hours paid	3,000
Non productive hours	165
Wage cost	£15,000
Wage rate variance	£NIL

Calculate the overall labour efficiency variance and analyse it between productive efficiency and idle time variances.

13.7   Solution

Standard productive hours for 5,400 units =	2,700 hours
Standard paid hours for 5,400 units = 2,700/0.95	2,842 hours
Actual paid hours	3,000 hours

Total efficiency variance (2,842 – 3,000 hours)
158 hours × £15,000/3,000 hours   £790 (A)

Actual productive hours (3,000 – 165)   2,835

Productive efficiency variance (2,700 – 2,835 hours)

$$135 \text{ hours} \times \frac{£15,000/3,000 \text{ hours}}{0.95} \qquad = £711 \text{ (A)}$$

Idle time variance:

Expected idle time 3,000 hours × 5%	= 150 hours
Actual idle time	= 165 hours
	——
	15 hours
	——

$$15 \text{ hours} \times \frac{£15,000/3,000}{0.95} \qquad = £79 \text{ (A)}$$

Note that:

(a)   variances and calculations of hours have been made to the nearest £1 and complete hour respectively; **and**

(b)   that the total efficiency variance is valued using the standard hourly rate; but the sub analysis into productive efficiency and idle time uses the adjusted hourly rate to value the differences in hours.

13.8   Activity

The following data relates to T plc for January 19X5:

Standard productive time per unit	2 hours
Standard wage rate per paid hour	£4.00
Actual production	1,200 units
Standard idle time as a percentage of hours paid	4%
Actual hours paid	2,600
Actual idle time hours	110

Calculate the labour efficiency variance and analyse it between productive efficiency and idle time.

13.9 Activity solution

Labour efficiency variance:

$$\text{Standard paid hours} = \frac{1,200 \times 2}{0.96} \qquad\qquad = \quad 2,500$$

Actual hours paid $\qquad\qquad\qquad\qquad\qquad\qquad = \quad 2,600$

Variance: 100 hours × £4.00/hour $\qquad\qquad\quad = \quad$ £400 (A)

Productive efficiency:

$$(2,400 \text{ hours} - 2,490 \text{ hours}) \times \frac{£4.00}{0.96} \qquad = \quad £375 \text{ (A)}$$

Idle time:

$$[(2,600 \times 4\%) - 110] \times \frac{£4.00}{0.96} \qquad\qquad = \quad £25 \text{ (A)}$$

13.10 Overhead variances and idle time

Where either labour or machine idle time exists and this is the basis of any variable overhead or fixed overhead efficiency variances, then the calculations illustrated above also apply to overhead variances.

13.11 Sales volume variances and idle time

Earlier in this chapter the calculation of sales volume variances was explained. You should remember that it is calculated by multiplying the difference in units between the budget and actual sales volume by the standard profit per unit (or standard contribution per unit if marginal costing is used).

The existence of idle time which is different from that expected is a cause of the sales volume variance as the following example illustrates.

13.12 Example

In this example above (ZS plc) it was shown that the actual idle time exceeded that expected by 15 hours.

You may also remember that the standard productive time per unit was 0.5 hours.

Thus if the unexpected idle time had been productive at the standard level of efficiency the 15 hours would have produced 30 units. This loss of production reduces the units available for sale and thus is one cause of the sales volume variance.

Assuming that ZS plc uses absorption costing the value attributed to the idle time causal factor of the sales volume variance would be:

30 units × Standard profit per unit.

(If a marginal costing system were in use the units would be valued using the standard contribution/unit).

14 CHAPTER SUMMARY

This chapter has considered in detail the use of standard costing and the calculation of variances using both marginal and absorption costing.

The interpretation of variances has also been explained, identifying the interdependence of variances and the relevance of variances to management.

15   SELF TEST QUESTIONS

15.1   What is the definition of standard costing? (1.1)

15.2   What are the four types of standard? (1.2)

15.3   How can a material cost variance be calculated? (4.5)

15.4   What are the various splits of a total fixed production overhead cost variance? (6.9)

15.5   What are the differences between operating statements based on standard absorption and standard marginal costing principles? (9.4, 9.5)

15.6   Give examples of possible causes of the labour efficiency variance. (10.1)

15.7   Give illustrations of likely variance interdependencies. (10.2)

15.8   Explain planned idle time. (13.2)

15.9   How are idle time variances calculated? (13.7)

15.10   Explain the effect of idle time on sales volume variances. (13.11, 13.12)

16   EXAMINATION TYPE QUESTIONS

16.1   Department X

The following statement has been produced for the general manager of Department X.

	Month ended 31 October 19X9		
	Original budget	*Actual result*	*Variance*
	£	*£*	*£*
Sales	600,000	550,000	(50,000)
Direct materials	150,000	130,000	20,000
Direct labour	200,000	189,000	11,000
Production overhead:			
Variable with direct labour	50,000	46,000	4,000
Fixed	25,000	29,000	(4,000)
Variable selling overhead	75,000	72,000	3,000
Fixed selling overhead	50,000	46,000	4,000
Total costs	550,000	512,000	38,000
Profit	50,000	38,000	(12,000)
Direct labour hours	50,000	47,500	
Sales and production units	5,000	4,500	

Note: there are no opening and closing stocks.

The general manager says that this type of statement does not provide much relevant information for him. He also thought that the profit for the month would be well up to budget and was surprised to see a large adverse profit variance.

You are required

(a)   to re-draft the above statement in a form which would be more relevant for the general manager;   **(6 marks)**

(b)   to calculate all sales, material, labour and overhead variances and reconcile these to the statement produced in (a);   **(9 marks)**

(c)   to produce a short report explaining the principles upon which your re-drafted statement is based and what information it provides.

(7 marks)

(Total: 22 marks)

16.2   Chemical company

A chemical company has the following standards for producing 9 gallons of a machine lubricant:

  5 gallons of material P @ £0.70 per gallon
  5 gallons of material Q @ £0.92 per gallon.

No stocks of raw materials are kept. Purchases are made as needed so that all price variances relate to materials used. Actual results showed that 100,000 gallons of material were used during a particular period as follows:

		£
45,000	gallons of material P at an actual cost per gallon used of £0.80	36,000
55,000	gallons of material Q at an actual cost per gallon used of £0.97	53,350
100,000		£89,350

During the period 92,070 gallons of the machine lubricant were produced.

You are required:

(a)   to calculate the total material variance and analyse it into its price, yield and mix components.

(11 marks)

(b)   to explain the circumstances under which a material mix variance is relevant to managerial control.

(4 marks)

(Total: 15 marks)

17   ANSWERS TO EXAMINATION TYPE QUESTIONS

17.1   Department X

(a)   **Revised statement**

A flexed budget corresponding with an output of 4,500 units is required.

	Budget			
	Original	Flexed	Actual	Variance
Units	5,000	4,500	4,500	
	£	£	£	£
Sales	600,000	540,000	550,000	10,000 F
Direct materials	150,000	135,000	130,000	5,000 F
Direct labour	200,000	180,000	189,000	9,000 A
Variable production overheads	50,000	45,000	46,000	1,000 A
Variable selling overheads	75,000	67,500	72,000	4,500 A
Total variable costs	475,000	427,500	437,000	9,500 A
Contribution	125,000	112,500	113,000	500 F

Fixed costs:

Production overhead	25,000	25,000	29,000	4,000 A
Selling overhead	50,000	50,000	46,000	4,000 F
Total costs	550,000	502,500	512,000	9,500 A
Profit	£50,000	£37,500	£38,000	£500 F

Variance of flexed budget against original budget: 37,500 – 50,000 =   12,500 A

Variance of actual against flexed budget: 500 F

Variance of actual against original budget: £12,000 A

(b)   **Variances**

(i)   Preliminary calculations

	Standard
Hours	50,000

Selling price $\dfrac{£540,000}{4,500} = £120$

Direct labour rate/hr. $\dfrac{£200,000}{50,000} = £4.00$

Standard hours per unit $\dfrac{50,000}{5,000} = 10$ hours

Var. prod. overhead cost/hour $\dfrac{£45,000}{45,000} = £1.00$

Var. selling overhead cost/unit $\dfrac{£67,500}{4,500} = £15$

Profit per unit $\dfrac{£50,000}{5,000} = £10$

Fixed production
overhead costs per hour $\dfrac{£25,000}{50,000} = £0.5$

Fixed selling overhead
cost per unit $\dfrac{£50,000}{5,000} = £10$

(ii)   Variances from flexible budget

	£	From (a)
Selling price = £550,000 – 4,500 × £120		10,000 F
Direct materials = £135,000 – £130,000		5,000 F

Direct labour:

Rate = £4.00 × 47,500 – £189,000	1,000 F	
Efficiency = (45,000 – 47,500) × £4	10,000 A	
Total		9,000 A

Variable production overhead:

Expenditure = £1 × 47,500 – £46,000	1,500 F
Efficiency = (45,000 – (1 × 47,500) × £1	2,500 A

Total	1,000 A
Variable selling overhead:	
£15 × 4,500 – £72,000	4,500 A
Fixed cost expenditure:	
Production overhead	
£25,000 – £29,000	4,000 A
Selling overhead	
£50,000 – £46,000	4,000 F
	£500 F

(iii)   Variance of flexible budget from original budget

Sales volume profit		
(4,500 – 5,000) × £10	5,000 A	
Fixed production overhead		
Capacity		
(47,500 – 50,000) × £0.50	1,250 A	
Efficiency		
(4,550 × 10 – 47,500) × £0.5	1,250 A	
Fixed selling overhead volume		
(4,500 – 5,000) × £10	5,000 A	
	£12,500 A	12,500 A

(c)   **Report**

To: The General Manager
From: The Management Accountant

Revised Budget Statement, month ending 31 October

The cause of the high adverse profit variance was the low volume of actual output. The budget statement has now been flexed to correspond with the actual volume produced so as to separate this effect. This has assumed that there is a linear relationship between volume of output, sales revenue and variable costs. Fixed costs, being independent of output volume, remain unchanged. A marginal costing approach has been used to show the contribution. The revised variances show a favourable profit variance of those variances controllable by the department; direct materials costs now have a favourable variance, direct labour and variable overheads have reduced adverse variances; although labour efficiency variances need investigating; the direct selling overheads variance is greater. The analysis does not show the causes of the variances nor of the failure to achieve the budget volume of output.

Note: various alternative presentations would be acceptable; in particular an absorption costing approach to part (a) could have been used.

17.2   Chemical company

(a)   **Variance calculations**

Standard cost card

Materials	*Gallons*	£/gallon	£
P	5	0.70	3.50
Q	5	0.92	4.60
Input	10 gallons	(at £0.81)	8.10
Normal loss	1 gallon		-
Output	9 gallons	(at £0.90)	£8.10

Standard cost of actual production

$$= \quad 92{,}070 \times £0.90 \quad = \quad £82{,}863$$

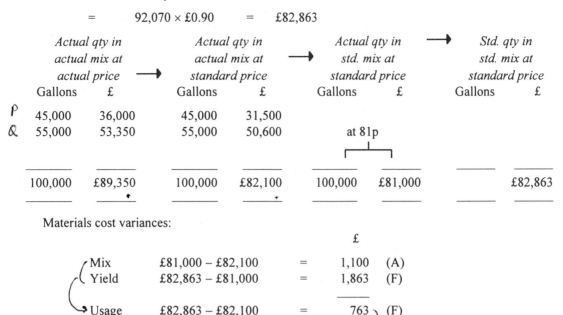

	Actual qty in actual mix at actual price		*Actual qty in actual mix at standard price*		*Actual qty in std. mix at standard price*		*Std. qty in std. mix at standard price*	
	Gallons	£	Gallons	£	Gallons	£	Gallons	£
P	45,000	36,000	45,000	31,500				
Q	55,000	53,350	55,000	50,600	at 81p			
	100,000	£89,350	100,000	£82,100	100,000	£81,000		£82,863

Materials cost variances:

				£	
Mix	£81,000 − £82,100	=	1,100		(A)
Yield	£82,863 − £81,000	=	1,863		(F)
Usage	£82,863 − £82,100	=	763		(F)
Price	£82,100 − £89,350	=	7,250		(A)
Total	£82,863 − £89,350	=	£6,487		(A)

(b)   **Usefulness of mix variances**

Manufacturing processes often entail the combination of a number of different materials to obtain one unit of finished product.   Examples of such processes are chemicals, paints, plastics, fabrics and metal alloys.

The basic ingredients can often be combined in a variety of proportions (or mixes), without perhaps affecting the specified quality characteristics or properties of the finished product.

The sub-analysis of variances into mix and yield components can provide a valuable aid to management decisions as these two variances are often interrelated.   The use of a different mixture of raw materials may reduce the cost of the mix but could produce an adverse yield effect.   However, a yield variance can arise for reasons other than a change in the mixture of raw materials, for example due to poor management supervision or deliberate wastage of materials by operatives.

A change in the mixture of raw materials may also affect other variances, in particular labour and variable overhead efficiency variances.

A study of mix variances (and of other related variances) may be particularly important when management is experimenting with the introduction of a material substitute.

21 ADVANCED VARIANCE ANALYSIS

INTRODUCTION & LEARNING OBJECTIVES

When you have studied this chapter you should be able to do the following:

- Explain planning and operational variances.
- Calculate planning and operational variances.
- Prepare operating statements using planning and operational variances.

1 PLANNING AND OPERATIONAL VARIANCES

1.1 Introduction

It has been suggested that a cause of variances is bad budgeting (an organisation is working to a reasonable level of efficiency but variances have been reported because its performance has been assessed by comparison with an unrealistic budget). More useful information can be obtained from variances if the original standards are examined at the end of an accounting period to determine whether or not they are realistic. It is found that the standards are unrealistic they can be revised, with hindsight, and performance compared with the revised standards.

Operational variances are those found by comparing actual performance with revised, more realistic, standards.

Planning variances are the differences between the original and revised standards.

These represent a split of the original total cost variance and can then be subdivided into price and usage or rate and efficiency. Rather than use easily understood terms such as 'original budget' and 'revised budget' it is customary to resort to Latin and use the terms:

Ex-ante budget   =   original budget

Ex-post budget   =   revised budget

The method of calculation is shown in the next few sections.

1.2 Past exam questions

Planning and operational variances were examined in June 1994, June 1995 and December 1995.

These questions required a sound working knowledge of the computations involved in determining these variances from narrative and numerical "hindsight" information given. It is essential that you master this topic.

The discursive elements of all the questions focused on the usefulness of planning and operational variance analysis in feedback and feedforward control. Ensure you understand the principles involved, as discussed in Section 3 of this chapter.

1.3 Example - materials price variance

Rhodes Ltd manufactures Stops which it is estimated require 2 kg of material XYZ at £10/kg. In week 21 only 250 Stops were produced although budgeted production was 300. 450 kg were purchased and used in the week at a total cost of £5,100. Later it was found that the standard had failed to allow for a 10% price increase throughout the material supplier's industry. Rhodes Ltd carries no stocks.

(a)   Provide a traditional variance analysis.

(b)   Reanalyse the variances along planning and operational lines.

1.4   Solution

(a)   **Traditional analysis**

			£	
Materials price:	$450 \times £10 - £5,100$	=	600	(A)
Materials usage:	$(250 \times 2 - 450) \times £10$	=	500	(F)
Total variance:	$(250 \times 2 \times £10) - £5,100$	=	£100	(A)

(b)   **Planning and operational analysis**

Step 1   The essential working is to produce three lines:

   1   Original flexed budget   (ex-ante)

   2   Revised flexed budget   (ex-post)

   3   Actual results

Step 2   Split the previous total variance into planning and operational variances.

   Total cost variance   =   (1) – (3)

   Planning variance   =   (1) – (2)

   Operational variance   =   (2) – (3)

Step 3   Analyse the operational variance in an appropriate way, here into price and usage. You may be asked to split the planning variance also, although in this case there is little information content in the split.

   Operational variances are analysed by using revised standards instead of the original standards.

   If planning variances have to be analysed then the approach is to treat the revised standards as 'actual figures'.

WORKINGS

(W1)   Original flexed budget (ex-ante)

   250 units at 2 kg per unit for £10/kg   =   £5,000

   Planning variance

(W2)   Revised flexed budget (ex-post)

   250 units at 2 kg per unit for £11/kg   =   £5,500

   Operational variance

(W3)   Actual results

   450 kg for   £5,100

Variances

				£	
Planning variance	=	£5,000 – £5,500	=	500	(A)
Operational variance	=	£5,500 – £5,100	=	400	(F)
Total variance (as before)	=	£5,000 – £5,100	=	£100	(A)

Further analysis

The planning variance is purely attributable to the change in price and therefore cannot be analysed further. The operational variance can be split into price and usage. The price variance can be calculated by reference to the new, more realistic standard; the usage variance is recalculated in terms of the ex-post standard.

Operational price variance

=   (Actual material used and bought × Revised standard price) – Actual cost of actual materials bought and used

=   450 × £11 – £5,100   =   **£150**   **(A)**

Operational usage variance

=   ((Revised) standard materials used for actual production – Actual materials used) × revised standard materials price.

=   (250 × 2 – 450) × £11   =   **£550**   **(F)**

Note: the total operational variance of £400 favourable has been split into price and usage.

1.5   Points to note from example

(a)   Under the traditional analysis whoever was responsible for purchasing would have been held responsible for incurring the £600 unfavourable price variance. In fact, analysis (b) shows that £500 of this, effectively, was uncontrollable, due to an *across-the-board* increase. The variance arose mainly as a result of poor forecasting.

(b)   Usage variance is more favourable under (b) because of the effect of the additional cost for the same saving in quantity.

(c)   The planning variance isolated under (b) is uncontrollable in terms of this report. No decision could have been made to avoid it. If, however, there existed a substitute for XYZ which under the *ex-ante* budget was more expensive, but turned out to be cheaper *ex-post*, the resulting variance would be controllable (see later).

(d)   The calculations are such that the two price variances will not add up to the previous traditional price variance. This must be the case since the usage variance has changed.

1.6   Further example - material price and usage

The previous example could be developed further if it were found at the end of the week that the materials usage standard was inappropriate following a change in production methods that brought the standard usage down from 2 kg per unit to 1.9 kg per unit.

Produce planning and operational variances under these new circumstances.

1.7   Solution

Once again the three line working provides the key to the new split of the £100 adverse total materials cost variance.

WORKING

Original flexed budget (ex-ante)

250 units at 2 kg per unit for £10/kg	=	£5,000	

Planning variance

Revised flexed budget (ex-post)

250 units at 1.9 kg per unit for £11/kg   =   £5,225

Operational variance

Actual results

450 kg for   £5,100

				£	
Planning variance	=	£5,000 − £5,225	=	225	(A)
Operational variance	=	£5,225 − £5,100	=	125	(F)
				___	
Total variance (again)	=	£5,000 − £5,100	=	£100	(A)
				___	

Analysis

The analysis of the operational variance, £125 (F), is straightforward; actual costs are compared with the new standard of 1.9 kg at £11 per kg as follows.

Operational variances:

				£	
Price	=	450 × £11 − £5,100	=	150	(A)
Usage	=	(250 × 1.9 − 450) × £11	=	275	(F)
				___	
Total operational variance				£125	(F)
				___	

Although little can be gained from splitting the planning variance in this instance, you may be asked to carry out the exercise. Price and usage variances are calculated as is conventional; the standards to use are the original standards, treat the revised (ex-post) standards as if they were actual costs.

Planning variances:

				£	
Price	=	(250 × 1.9) × £10 − £5,225	=	475	(A)
Usage	=	((250 × 2) − (250 × 1.9)) × £10	=	250	(F)
				___	
Total planning variance				£225	(A)
				___	

As has been said before, this split does not help management. The type of problem for which a split of the planning variance does help is if a firm has to make a decision such as over the choice of raw material used. This is illustrated in the next section.

1.8   Example - choice of materials

Cronje makes a produce which requires 5 kg of material. At the start of the current accounting period there was a choice of two materials X and Y. The original estimates of the cost of these two materials was:

Material X	£2.00 per kg
Material Y	£2.05 per kg

Based on these estimates the decision was made to use material X; contracts to supply the material were signed and the production process designed to suit the properties of material X.

Production in the period was 1,000 units which used 5,500 kg of material X at a total cost of £13,200. In view of the commitment to material X it was not possible to change to Y in a hurry when it was found, with hindsight, that typical average market prices for these materials bought in the sort of quantities that Cronje used were:

Material X	£2.25 per kg
Material Y	£2.10 per kg

(a)   Produce a traditional analysis of the materials variances.

(b)   Produce a full analysis using planning and operational principles.

1.9   Solution

(a)   **Traditional variances**

					£	
Materials:	price	=	5,500 × £2 – £13,200	=	2,200	(A)
	usage	=	(1,000 × 5 – 5,500) × £2	=	1,000	(A)
	total	=	(1,000 × 5 × £2) – £13,200	=	3,200	(A)

(b)   **Planning and operational variances**

Although the same three line working seen so far will provide a split of the £3,200 total cost variance into planning and operational variances, a fourth line can now be included to show what the materials cost might have been if the other material, Y, had been used.

The four lines are:

£

(1)   Ex-ante (original) flexed budget (X)

1,000 units at 5 kg/unit for £2/kg   10,000

(2)   Ex-post (revised) flexed budget (Y)

1,000 units at 5 kg/unit for £2.10/kg   10,500   P

(3)   Ex-post (revised) flexed budget (X)

1,000 units at 5 kg/unit for £2.25/kg   11,250

(4)   Actual results   O

1,000 units at 5,500 kg for   13,200

The planning variance is still the difference between the original and revised standard costs of actual production and the operational variance still the difference between the actual costs and the revised standards as follows.

£

Planning variance	=	£10,000 – £11,250	=	1,250	(A)
Operational variance	=	£11,250 – £13,200	=	1,950	(A)
Total (as before)				£3,200	(A)

(Note: Operational variances must compare like with like, actual results (using X) with a revised standard based on X.)

The operational variance can be split into price and usage as usual:

Operational variances:

£

Price:	=	5,500 × £2.25 − £13,200	=	825	(A)
Usage:	=	(1,000 × 5 − 5,500) × £2.25	=	1,125	(A)

Total operational variance (as above)   £1,950   (A)

The presence of an extra line in the original workings allows the planning variance to be split. The names given to the two variances are 'unavoidable' and 'possibly avoidable' as shown below.

Planning variances:

£

Unavoidable:	=	£10,000 − £10,500	=	500	(A)
Possibly avoidable:	=	£10,500 − £11,250	=	750	(A)

Total planning variance (as above)   £1,250   (A)

1.10   Comment on example

The *possibly avoidable* planning variance highlights to management the effect of the incorrect decision that was made when the budget was set. It is only 'incorrect' in that with hindsight it would have been a cheaper decision to use raw material Y and not X last period. Therefore, the variance is *possibly avoidable* in the sense that it would not have arisen if the alternative decision had been made at the outset, this would have only happened if better forecasts were available.

It was not possible to mix the use of materials X and Y so, once the decision to use X had been made, it was not practicable for Y to be substituted for X at short notice as the price moved. Clearly, if X or Y could have been mixed in one period's production, then the possibly avoidable planning variance should really be considered as part of the operational variances.

The identification of a possibly avoidable planning variance depends on the alternative raw materials being perfect substitutes for each other, so that the standard usage does not alter, as was the case with X and Y. It is possible to produce an analysis if quantities change as materials change, but it requires a little more thought.

It is important to remember the order of lines (1) to (4) in the initial workings. The easiest way of doing this is to remember that, when calculating operational variances, like must be compared with like.

The possibly avoidable planning variance, a cost that has been incurred as a result of making a wrong decision based on inaccurate estimates, was publicised by two authors Bromwich and Demski. When they produced a similar analysis under different circumstances, the name that they gave to their variance that resulted from an incorrect decision was an 'opportunity cost variance'; the term is sometimes applied in this context.

1.11   Variances and demand elasticity

Another decision that can be made on the basis of estimates which subsequently turn out to be incorrect is the pricing decision. As with the example of the choice of materials a variance can be calculated that represents the cost to a business of making the wrong pricing decision. Again this is referred to as an opportunity cost variance.

1.12   Activity

Hugh Ltd set a standard cost at £40 per unit. 10,000 units were produced with a total cost of £610,000. It is now felt that a more realistic standard cost would have been £68 per unit.

Calculate the total, operational and planning variances.

1.13   Activity solution

Total variance		£
Standard cost of 10,000 units at £40	=	400,000
Actual cost of 10,000 units	=	610,000
		————
Total variance	=	£210,000 A
		————

Operational variance		
10,000 units at £68 (ex-post)	=	680,000
Actual cost	=	610,000
		————
Operational variance	=	£70,000 F
		————

Planning variance		
Standard cost of 10,000 units at £40	=	400,000
10,000 units at £68 (ex-post)	=	680,000
		————
Planning variance	=	£280,000 A
		————

Note:

Total variance	=	Operational variance	+	Planning variance
£210,000 A	=	£70,000 F	+	£280,000 A

1.14   Market volume and market share variances

Another example of a planning and operational variance calculation becoming renamed arises when the exercise is carried out in the context of a sales volume variance. In these circumstances the new names given to the planning and operational variances are:

> planning   ⇒   market volume variance
>
> operational   ⇒   market share variance

The logic behind this is that the reason for the incorrect estimate of the budgeted sales was that the size of the total market (for all sellers) had been incorrectly estimated.

Example

Hudson Ltd has a sales budget of 400,000 units for the coming year based on 20% of the total market. On each unit, Hudson makes a profit of £3. Actual sales for the year were 450,000, but industry reports showed that the total market volume had been 2.2 million.

(a)   Find the traditional sales (margin) volume variance.

(b)   Split this into planning and operational variances (market volume and market share).

Solution

(a)   **Traditional sales volume variance**

=   (Actual units sold – Budgeted sales) × Standard profit per unit

=   (450,000 – 400,000) × £3 = £150,000 (favourable)

(b)   **Planning and operational variances**

Once again a three line working helps; the revised (ex-post) budget would show that Hudson Ltd should expect to sell 20% of 2.2 million units = 440,000.

Original budget (ex-ante)

400,000 units @ £3 per unit = £1,200,000   Planning
                                                        ('Market
Revised budget (ex-post)   volume')

440,000 units @ £3 per unit = £1,320,000

Actual results   Operational
                                                        ('Market
450,000 units @ £3 per unit = £1,350,000   share')

The analysis shows:

Planning (or market volume) variance

£

=   £1,320,000 – £1,200,000   =   120,000   (F)

Operational (or market share) variance

=   £1,350,000 – £1,320,000   =   £30,000   (F)
                                             _____
Total sales volume variance   =   £150,000
                                             _____

Most of the favourable sales volume variance can be attributed to the increase in the overall market volume; however some can be put down to effort by the sales force which has increased its share of the market a little from 20% to $\left(\dfrac{450,000}{2,200,000} \right)$ 20½%.

1.15   Advantages and disadvantages of the analysis

The analysis of the traditional variances into planning and operational categories has distinct advantages:

(a)   Variances are more relevant, especially in a turbulent environment.

(b)   The operational variances give a 'fair' reflection of the actual results achieved in the actual conditions that existed.

(c)   Managers are, theoretically, more likely to accept and be motivated by the variances reported which provide a better measure of their performance.

(d)   It emphasises the importance of planning and the relationship between planning and control and a better guide for cost control.

(e)   The analysis helps in the standard setting learning process, which will hopefully result in more useful standards in the future.

The use of planning and operational variances is not widespread. Therefore, there may be perceived disadvantages:

(a)   The establishment of *ex-post* budgets is very difficult. Managers whose performance is reported to be poor using such a budget are unlikely to accept them as performance measures because of the subjectivity in setting such budgets.

(b)   There is a considerable amount of administrative work involved first to analyse the traditional variances and then to decide on which are controllable and which are uncontrollable.

(c)   The analysis tends to exaggerate the inter-relationship of variances, providing managers with a 'pre-packed' list of excuses for below standard performance; poor performance is often excused as being the fault of a badly set budget.

2   OPERATING STATEMENTS USING PLANNING AND OPERATIONAL VARIANCES

2.1   Introduction

You should remember that operating statements are used to reconcile budget profits and actual profits by detailing the variances for the period. By calculating planning and operating variances it is being recognised that part of the profit difference is due to budget errors, inappropriate standards, or non-controllable external factors. By identifying these as planning variances management's attention is focused on the controllable items.

The following example illustrates how the use of planning and operational variances improves the relevance to management of the operating statement.

2.2   Example

POV Ltd uses a standard costing system to control and report upon the production of its single product.

An abstract from the original standard cost card of the product is as follows:

	£	£
Selling price per unit		200
Less: 4 kgs materials @ £20 per kg	80	
6 hours labour @ £7 per hour	42	
	—	122
Contribution per unit		78

For period 3, 2,500 units were budgeted to be produced and sold but the actual production and sales were 2,850 units.

The following information was also available:

(i)   At the commencement of period 3 the normal material became unobtainable and it was necessary to use an alternative. Unfortunately, 0.5 kg per unit extra was required and it was thought that the material would be more difficult to work with. The price of the alternative was expected to be £16.50 per kg. In the event, actual usage was 12,450 kgs at £18 per kg.

(ii)   Weather conditions unexpectedly improved for the period with the result that a 50p per hour bad weather bonus, which had been allowed for in the original standard, did not have to be paid. Because of the difficulties expected with the alternative material, management agreed to pay the workers £8 per hour for period 3 only. During the period 18,800 hours were paid for.

After using conventional variances for some time, POV Ltd is contemplating extending its system to include planning and operational variances.

You are required

(a)   to prepare a statement reconciling budgeted contribution for the period with actual contribution, using conventional material and labour variances;

(b)   to prepare a similar reconciliation statement using planning and operational variances;

(c)   to explain the meaning of the variances shown in statement (b).

2.3   Solution

(a)   **Reconciliation of budgeted and actual contribution using conventional variances**

		£
Budgeted contribution: 2,500 × £78		195,000

Variances			*Favourable*	*Adverse*	
Sales volume			27,300		
Direct material	–	Price	24,900		
	–	Usage		21,000	
Direct labour	–	Rate		18,800	
	–	Efficiency		11,900	
			52,200	51,700	
					500
		Actual contribution			195,500

Assumption: No sales price variance.

Workings

Conventional variances

(i)   **Direct material**

Price   =   (Actual material purchased × standard price) – (Actual cost of material purchased)

=   12,450 × £20 – 12,450 × £18

=   249,000 – 224,100

=   £24,900 (F)

Usage   =   (Standard quantity for actual production × standard price) – (Actual material used at standard price)

=   2,850 × 4 × £20 – 12,450 × £20

=   228,000 – 249,000

=   £21,000 (A)

(ii)   **Direct labour**

Rate   =   (Actual hours worked × standard direct labour rate) – (Actual hours worked × actual hourly rate)

=   18,800 × 7 – 18,800 × 8

=   131,600 – 150,400

=   £18,800 (A)

Efficiency = (Standard hours of actual production × standard rate) – (Actual hours worked × standard rate)

= 2,850 × 6 × £7 – 18,800 × £7

= 119,700 – 131,600

= £11,900 (A)

(iii) **Sales volume contribution**

= (Budgeted sales units × standard contribution per unit) – (Actual sales units × standard contribution per unit)

= 2,500 × £78 – 2,850 × £78

= 195,000 – 222,300

= £27,300 (F)

Reconciliation statement using planning and operational variances

				£
Budgeted contribution for actual sales:	2,850 × £78			222,300

		Favourable	*Adverse*	
Planning variances				
Direct material	– Price	44,887.5		
	– Usage		28,500	
Direct labour	– Rate: weather	8,550		
	– Rate: material		25,650	
		53,437.5	54,150	
				712.5

Revised budgeted contribution (77.75 × 2,850) 221,587.5

		Favourable	*Adverse*	
Operational variances				
Direct material	– Price		18,675	
	– Usage	6,187.5		
Direct labour	– Rate	0		
	– Efficiency		13,600	
		6,187.5	32,275	
				26,087.5
Actual contribution				195,500

WORKINGS

Planning variances

(i) **Direct material** = (Standard material cost) – (Revised standard material cost)

Price = 2,850 × (4 + 0.5) × £20 – 2,850 × (4 + 0.5) × £16.50

= 256,500 – 211,612.5

= £44,887.5 (F)

Usage $=$ $2,850 \times 4 \times £20 - 2,850 \times 4.5 \times £20$

$=$ $228,000 - 256,500$

$=$ £28,500   (A)

(ii)   Direct labour

Rate

(1)   Weather bonus

$=$ $2,850 \times 6 \times £7 - 2,850 \times 6 \times £6.50$

$=$ $119,700 - 111,150$

$=$ £8,550   (F)

(2)   Alternative material difficulties

$=$ $2,850 \times 6 \times £6.50 - 2,850 \times 6 \times £8$

$=$ $111,150 - 136,800$

$=$ £25,650   (A)

$\therefore$ revised unit contribution is:

				£	£
Selling price					200.00
Direct material:	$4.5 \times £16.50$	$=$		74.25	
Direct labour:	$6 \times £8$	$=$		48.00	
					122.25
			Contribution		77.75

Operational variances

(i)   Direct material

Price $=$ $12,450 \times £16.50 - 12,450 \times £18$

$=$ $205,425 - 224,100$

$=$ £18,675   (A)

Usage $=$ $2,850 \times 4.50 \times £16.50 - 12,450 \times £16.50$

$=$ $211,612.5 - 205,425$

$=$ £6,187.5   (F)

(ii)   **Direct labour**

Rate – nil.

Efficiency   = $2,850 \times 6 \times £8 - 18,800 \times £8$

= $136,800 - 150,400$

=   £13,600 (A)

(c)   The analysis of variances in part (b) makes it possible to separate those variances which are non-controllable (the planning variances) from the variances which are controllable by the individual managers (the operational variances).

In this case the change in type of material used was unavoidable.   Similarly, the change in weather conditions could not have been anticipated.   The cost implications of these changes are reflected in the planning variances.   Management's attention should be focused primarily on the operational variances.

In particular, why did the firm pay £18 per kg for material when this was expected to cost £16.50?

The operational material usage variance indicates that less material was used than expected – this could be due to the workers spending longer working with the material (as evidenced by the adverse efficiency variance).

3   PLANNING AND OPERATIONAL VARIANCES IN FEEDBACK AND FEEDFORWARD CONTROL

3.1   Introduction

The general role of budgetary control systems in feedback and feedforward control was discussed in Chapter 4. Here we shall consider the specific use of planning and operational variance analysis in these control areas - a frequently examined topic.

3.2   Feedback control

Feedback control involves the comparison of actual results with control (expected/standard/budgeted) results. Deviations are identified, investigated and corrected where possible and/or appropriate.

Planning and operational variance analysis provides feedback on two potential sets of deviations:

Planning variances identify deviations between the ex-ante (original) and the ex-post (revised) standards or budget. These are generally accepted as being permanent and non-controllable variances, and therefore should not be subject to further investigation.

Operational variances are deviations of actual results from the ex-post standards/budget. These are potentially controllable, and thus should be the focus of management attention. Further investigation/analysis of these variances will determine the extent to which they can be corrected, and cost benefit analysis can be used to decide whether this is worthwhile.

3.3   Feedforward control

Feedforward control involves the comparison of predicted results of the current plan at some point in the future with the desired results. Where deviations exist, corrective action may be taken to ensure achievement of the desired outcome.

The ex-post standards or budget identified in the planning and operational variance analysis process may be used as a base for the predicted results, adjusted for the proportion of operating variances that are not expected to be eliminated for the period under review (because it is not possible or worthwhile correcting them).

3.4   Example

Planop plc uses a marginal costing system, and has produced the following summary operating statement for the first quarter of the year, in which 18,500 units were produced and sold:

	£	£	£
Original budgeted contribution			
(20,000 × £15)			300,000
Planning variances			75,000 A
			————
Revised budgeted contribution			
(18,000 × £12.50)			225,000
Less: Fixed costs			
Original		180,000	
Planning expenditure variance		12,500 F	167,500
		————	————
Revised budgeted profit			57,500
Sales margin volume variance			
(500 × £12.50)			6,250 F

Other variances	*Variable*	*Fixed*	
Sales price	3,600 A		
Cost variances	2,400 F	1,800 A	
	————	————	
	1,200 A	1,800 A	3,000 A
			————
Actual net profit			60,750
			————

On investigation of the operating variances, it is estimated that all of the sales price variance and 25% of the fixed cost variances can be eliminated with immediate effect. 55.5% of the net favourable variable cost variances are expected to continue.

Revised budgeted sales for the next quarter are 19,000 units. The target profit for the first six months of the year is £150,000. Use the information given above to determine whether this will be achieved.

Solution

	£
Revised standard contribution per unit	12.50
Add: residual operational variable cost variances	
(55.5% × £2,400/18,500)	0.072
	————
Estimated actual contribution per unit	12.572
	————
Revised budgeted fixed costs per quarter	167,500
Add: residual operational fixed cost variances (75% × £1,800)	1,350
	————
Estimated actual fixed cost per quarter	168,850
	————

Estimated total contribution (£12.572 × 19,000)	238,868
Less: estimated actual fixed cost	168,850
Estimated actual profit for the next quarter	70,018

Estimated actual profit for the first six months = £60,750 + £70,018 = £130,768

Thus the target will not be achieved at a sales level of 19,000 units.

Assuming all other elements remain as above, the required sales level can be calculated:

	£
Net profit required for next quarter (£150,000 - £60,750)	89,250
Add: estimated actual fixed costs	168,850
Contribution required	258,100

Sales volume required = £258,100/£12.572 = 20,530 units.

Efforts must be made to increase expected sales by 1,530 units in order to meet the target. However, if this will incur extra costs (advertising/marketing) or involve a price reduction, the required volume will be increased.

4   CHAPTER SUMMARY

This chapter has built upon the knowledge of the previous chapter by analysing variances into planning and operational variances.

5   SELF TEST QUESTIONS

5.1   How are planning and operational variances calculated? (1.4)

5.2   What is meant by the term 'possibly avoidable planning variance' and by what other name may it be called? (1.9, 1.10)

5.3   What are market volume and market share variances? (1.14)

6   EXAMINATION TYPE QUESTION

6.1   Simplo Ltd

Simplo Ltd make and sell a single product. A standard marginal cost system is in operation. Feedback reporting takes planning and operational variances into consideration. It is implemented as follows:

(1)   Permanent non-controllable changes from the original standard are incorporated into a revised standard.

(2)   The budgeted effect of the standard revision is reported for each variance type.

(3)   The sales volume variance is valued at the revised standard contribution and is analysed to show the gain or loss in contribution arising from a range of contributory factors.

(4)   The remaining operational variances are then calculated.

Information relating to Period 6 is as follows:

(i)   A summary of the operating statement for Period 6 using the variance analysis approach detailed above shows:

	£
Original budgeted contribution	51,200
Budget revision variances (net)	13,120 (F)
	——
Revised budgeted contribution	64,320
Sales volume variance	16,080 (F)
	——
Revised standard contribution for sales achieved	80,400
Other variances (net)	8,200 (A)
	——
Actual contribution	72,200
	——

(F) = Favourable, (A) = Adverse.

(ii)   Original standard cost data per product unit:

	£	£
Selling price		100
Less: Direct material 5 kilos at £10	50	
Direct labour 3 hours at £6	18	
	—	68
		——
Contribution		32
		——

(iii)   The current market price is £110 per unit. Simplo Ltd sold at £106 per unit in an attempt to stimulate demand.

(iv)   Actual direct material used was 12,060 kilos at £10 per kilo. Any related variances are due to operational problems.

(v)   The original standard wage rate excluded an increase of £0.60 per hour subsequently agreed with the trade unions. Simplo Ltd made a short term operational decision to employ a slightly lower grade of labour, who were paid £6.20 per hour. The total hours paid were 7,600. These included 200 hours of idle time, of which 40% was due to a machine breakdown and the remainder to a power failure.

(vi)   Budgeted production and sales quantity   1,600 units
        Actual sales quantity   2,000 units
        Actual production quantity   2,400 units.

Required:

(a)   Prepare a single operating statement for Period 6 which expands the summary statement shown in (i) above.

        This single operating statement should clearly show:

        (i)   The basis of calculation of the contribution figures for original budget, revised budget and revised standard for sales achieved;

        (ii)   The analysis of the budget revision variance by variance type;

        (iii)   The analysis of the sales volume variance showing the quantity and value of the gain or loss arising from each of the following factors:

                Additional capacity available;
                Productivity reduction;

Idle time;

Stock increase not yet translated into sales;

(iv)   The analysis of the 'other variances' by variance type.   **(16 marks)**

(b)   Prepare a brief report to the management of Simplo on the performance in Period 6 making full use of the information contained in the operating statement prepared in (a). Your report should indicate the relevance of the analysis utilised in the operating statement.   **(6 marks)**

(Total: 22 marks)

7   ANSWER TO EXAMINATION TYPE QUESTION

7.1   Simplo Ltd

(a)

Operating statement - Period 6

	£	£
Original budgeted contribution (1,600 units @ £32)		51,200
Budget revision variances:		
Selling price (1,600 units @ £10)	16,000 (F)	
Labour rate (1,600 units × 3 hours × 60p)	2,880 (A)	13,120 (F)
Revised budgeted contribution (1,600 @ £40.20)		64,320
Sales volume variance:		
Additional capacity (W1)	37,520 (F)	
Productivity reduction (W2)	2,680 (A)	
Idle time (W3)	2,680 (A)	
Stock increase (W4)	16,080 (A)	16,080 (F)
Revised standard contribution for actual sales (2,000 @ £40.20)		80,400

Other variances:

	F	A	
Selling price (W5)		8,000	
Material usage (W6)		600	
Wage rate (W7)	'3,040		
Labour efficiency (W8)		1,320	
Labour idle time (W9)		1,320	
	3,040	11,240	8,200 (A)
Actual contribution			£72,200

(b)   The operating statement shows that the change in selling price and the effect of the wage rate increase combined so that the contribution from the budgeted sales was expected to be £64,320.

The actual sales achieved exceeded those expected because a greater number of units were produced albeit at a lower efficiency than expected and the incidence of lost time due to a machine breakdown and a power failure. Management needs to consider the costs/benefits of implementing planned maintenance to avoid future machine breakdowns and expenditure on a generator to be used in the event of power failure. Consideration should also be given to the policy of manufacturing items for stock; should production be restricted or demand stimulated?

Management should consider whether the payment of a lower wage rate than anticipated has caused the efficiency variance and the operational problems referred to in connection with the material usage variance.

WORKINGS

(W1) $[(7,600/3) - 1,600] \times £40.20$

(W2) $[(7,600 - 200) - (2,400 \times 3)]/3 \times £40.20$

(W3) $(200 \text{ hours}/3) \times £40.20$

(W4)   400 units @ £40.20

(W5) $2,000 \text{ units} \times (£110 - £106)$

(W6) $[(2,400 \times 5) - 12,060] \times £10$

(W7) $(£6.60 - £6.20) \times 7,600 \text{ hours}$

(W8) $[(7,600 - 200) - (2,400 \times 3)] \times £6.60$

(W9)   200 hours @ £6.60

22 INTERPRETATION AND INVESTIGATION OF VARIANCES

INTRODUCTION & LEARNING OBJECTIVES

When you have studied this chapter you should be able to do the following::

- Explain trend, materiality and controllability in the context of variances.
- Calculate variance trends.
- Explain the use of statistical charts.
- Explain when to investigate variances.
- Explain the impact of variance analysis on staff attitudes.
- Discuss the use of standard costing in the modern business environment.

1 TREND, MATERIALITY AND CONTROLLABILITY

1.1 Introduction

In the context of variance analysis trend, materiality and controllability are signficant factors in determining whether or not to investigate a variance.

1.2 Trend

When budgets and standards are set as targets they are averages for the budget period. It is therefore expected that there will be some differences between the actual results and the target set if a comparison is made on an individual period basis.

Trend indicates whether a variance is fluctuating around the target and is therefore under control, or consistently moving costs to a situation which is out of control.

1.3 Materiality

Materiality is an accounting term used to mean significance. In the context of variances such materiality can be measured in absolute terms (ie, £s) or as a percentage of the target set.

1.4 Controllability

Controllability relates to the ability of the organisation to take action to control the difference. If it cannot be controlled then it is argued that there is no benefit in reporting the variance.

2 CALCULATING VARIANCE TRENDS

2.1 Introduction

Variance trends may be calculated in absolute terms (ie, £s) or as a percentage of standard cost. By making such calculations over time, a trend may become apparent.

2.2 Example

The following details relate to a raw material used by Z Ltd in its production process:

Standard price/kg	£3.00
Standard usage per unit	5 kgs

Actual data:

	Production (units)	Materials used (kgs)
December	950	4,900
January	800	4,135
February	1,000	5,200

Calculate the material usage variance for each month

(a)   in absolute terms (ie, £s); and

(b)   as a percentage of standard cost.

2.3   Solution to example

December:

Standard usage = 950 × 5kg   =   4,750 kg

Standard cost = 4,750 kg × £3.00   =   £14,250

Usage variance = 150 kg × £3.00   =   £450 (A)

January:

Standard usage = 800 × 5kg   =   4,000 kg

Standard cost = 4,000 kg × £3.00   =   £12,000

Usage variance = 135 kg × £3.00   =   £405 (A)

February:

Standard usage = 1,000 × 5 kg   =   5,000 kg

Standard cost = 5,000 kg × £3.00   =   £15,000

Usage variance = 200 kg × £3.00   =   £600 (A)

Summary of variances

	£	%
December	450 (A)	3.16 (A)
January	405 (A)	3.38 (A)
February	600 (A)	4.00 (A)

Due to the changing production levels the absolute variance values suggest that the variance in January is less than that of December. Note though that as a percentage of standard cost, the variance is greater.

In such circumstances the percentage value of the variances is more meaningful than the absolute values. However both are recommended so that profits may be reconciled.

3   MANAGEMENT SIGNALS

3.1   Variances and management

Variances are merely a means of measuring the effect on profits of actual results being different from the target set.

Management must use variances to stimulate discussion with a view to identifying the cause of each variance. In this context management must be aware of the inter-dependence of variances.

Once the cause has been determined management may then make plans and take decisions which it hopes will improve future performance.

4   UNCERTAINTY IN VARIANCE ANALYSIS

4.1   Introduction

There are five possible areas in which uncertainty can affect the results of variance analysis. Each of these is considered in the following paragraphs.

4.2   Planning

If sufficient time and resources are not applied when setting the plan it is likely to be inaccurate or inappropriate in relation to the circumstances prevailing. This will cause the actual results to differ significantly from the target.

4.3   Measurement

Any inaccuracies in measuring actual results will have an obvious effect on the variances reported. In this respect there are three aspects to the measurement of actual results:

(a)   the measurement of activity achieved (including adjustments for work-in-progress);

(b)   the measurement of resources used (including adjustment for resources acquired by production but not yet used eg, materials held in the production department); and

(c)   the cost of those resources (adjusted by accurate accruals and prepayments where necessary).

4.4   The model

The predictive model upon which the targets are based may be inaccurate or no longer reflect the operating conditions. Such inaccuracy will affect the variances calculated.

4.5   Implementation

The implementation of a standard costing system and of senior management decisons is a human process. Sometimes humans do not follow instructions exactly as they were intended. In such circumstances this may cause variances to occur.

4.6   Random

It has been stated earlier that a target is an average for a period of time. It is therefore expected that actual results will fluctuate randomly about this target. Such fluctuations will be measured as variances, though they should not be of any significance.

5   TOLERANCE LIMITS

5.1   Introduction

A tolerance limit is an acceptable deviation from the target. This would be used to recognise that either the variance is a random fluctuation or is too insignificant to warrant management action.

5.2   Tolerance chart

The following chart shows how a variance may be illustrated graphically to show if it remains within acceptable tolerances over a period of time.

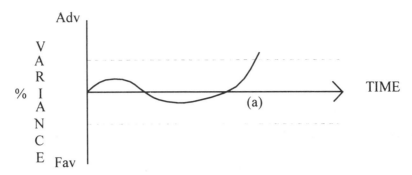

The dotted lines represent the upper and lower tolerance limits in relation to the target, denoted by the solid line.

The variance is plotted over time and whilst it remains within the tolerance limits it is said to be in control. However when it exceeds these limits (at time (a)) it is out of control and management action is required.

6   WHEN TO INVESTIGATE A VARIANCE

6.1   Factors to consider

When deciding whether or not to investigate a variance, various factors will be taken into account. The object of the investigation is to provide more useful information for performance assessment and cost control. In the first case the investigation will ascertain whether or not the variance was the result of bad budgeting and its controllability in general. In the case of cost control the major aim is to establish the specific cause of the variance and particularly if it is merely the result of some random variation in costs; it is then hoped that some significant cost saving can be made. The factors to consider when deciding whether or not to investigate a variance include the following.

1   **Size of variance** - it might be assumed that greater cost savings will result from investigating larger variances which also have a major effect on a manager's performance report.

2   **Favourable or adverse** - the general impression would be that only adverse variances should be investigated; although, by investigating favourable variances an organisation can:

-      remove the effect of budget padding when assessing performance;

-      produce more realistic budgets in the future;

-      establish ways in which performance might be improved still further in the future.

3   **Costs and benefits of correction** - if the likely cause of a variance is known but it is felt that it will cost too much to eliminate that cause, the variance may not be investigated; it may be that standards have to be revised.

4   **Ability to correct a variance** - this is related to the previous factor, but now the point at issue is whether a cause of a variance will stay corrected once money has been spent to rectify that cause.

5   **Past pattern of variances** - if a variance is merely the result of random variations in cost then no amount of remedial action will bring about a cost saving.

6   **Reliability of budgets** - whilst establishing the extent to which a variance is due to bad budgeting will have all the benefits set out for planning and operational variances, if a variance is purely the result of a badly set budget there will be no major cost savings following the investigation.

7   **Reliability of measurement and recording systems** - poor measurement and recording systems can give rise to a variance, for instance if closing stock is incorrectly recorded then an

incorrect figure for materials usage is assumed and a variance might result; the benefits of investigation are similar to those of investigating the consequences of bad budgeting.

Several of these considerations give rise to criteria or techniques for variance investigation. Point (5) is taken into account by constructing statistical control charts whilst points (3) and (4) can be assessed using decision trees. The matter of mere size gives rise to a number of investigation criteria.

6.2   How large a variance should be to be investigated

When an organisation has to decide whether or not a variance merits investigation one of several criteria can be adopted.

(1)   **Fixed size of variance** - a firm might investigate any variance over £x,000. Whilst this is easy to administer it ignores the fact that a variance of £5,000 in a total cost of £20,000 is more likely to indicate a fault than a variance of £5,000 in a total cost of £200,000. Hence (2).

(2)   **Fixed percentage rule** - a variance might be investigated if it is more than x% of the standard cost. Whilst this overcomes the weakness of method (1), it ignores the fact that some costs normally vary more than others. Hence (3).

(3)   **Statistical decision rule** - now a variance is only investigated if a study of past patterns of variances suggests that a variance of this size only occurs x% of the time that a process is under control. If there is only, say, a 5% chance that a cost can differ from standard by as much as the size of a particular variance it is much more likely that a problem has occurred that merits investigation. The problem comes with determining what the x% should be; the rule tends to be applied with ad hoc selections (5%, 1%, say) without taking into account the costs and benefits of correction or the ability to correct a variance.

A survey carried out in the USA reported that, of 100 large companies:

> 72% investigated variances based on managerial judgement
>
> 54% used a fixed absolute amount
>
> 43% used the fixed percentage rule
>
> 4% used statistical decision rules

It would seem likely that the 4% excluded all those firms that used the decision rule, which is about to be illustrated, as part of the regular statistical quality control checks carried out by most manufacturing organisations or firms concerned with packaging material.

6.3   Statistical control charts

Consider an operational process for which the mean time is 50 minutes with a standard deviation of 10 minutes. It is known from statistical theory that the pattern of actual times is likely to form a Normal distribution about the mean.

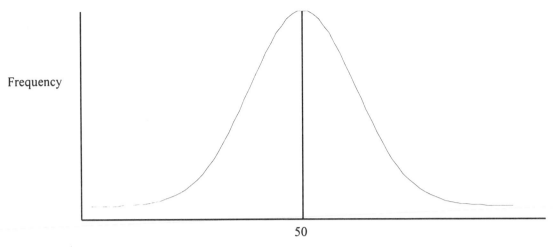

Time for operation (minutes)

Furthermore, it is known that specific proportions of the times will be within specified standard deviations of the mean.

The values are approximately:

1 standard deviation	68%	(68.26%)
2 standard deviations	95%	(95.44%)
3 standard deviations	99.7%	(99.73%)

This information can be used to create a statistical control chart. The mean time forms the standard; the control limits are set a given number of standard deviations from the mean.

Consider, as an example, a process for which the standard time is 50 minutes. The control limits might be set at 30 and 70 minutes, and actual times recorded as follows:

Time to complete operation

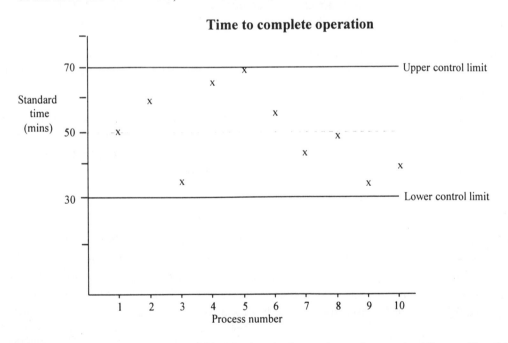

If the actual time taken falls within the bands the variance is not significant. For this reason the band limits are referred to as *control limits*. This poses two questions:

(a)   How are control limits set?

(b)   What action should be taken if results fall outside the control limits?

6.4   Setting control limits

Control limits should be set so that there is only a small chance of a random fluctuation falling outside them.

Distribution of time to complete

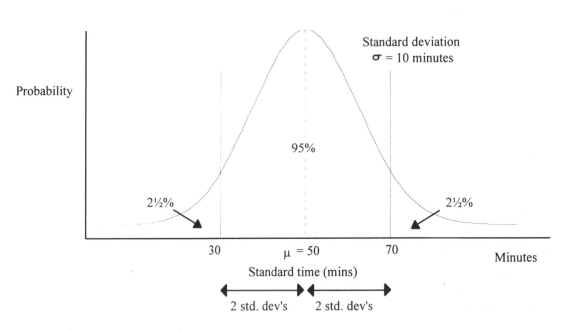

6.5   Using the control chart

In this example the control limits are set two standard deviations from the mean. Thus, 95% of the recorded process times should lie within the control limits.

The actual time is recorded on the chart after the completion of each process. It will soon be apparent if the mean time is shifting from 50 minutes, as the recorded times move outside the control limits.

If more than 5% of the observed results do lie outside the control limits, then the system may be referred to as being *statistically out of control*. At this stage management must decide what further action to take.

Merely determining initially whether variances represent random fluctuations or not does not tell us what to do about significant variances. The question is whether to investigate or not. In many cases the reason for a variance may be already known or easily ascertainable. In other cases, it must be a matter of weighing likely costs of investigation against likely benefits.

6.6   Activity

Donald Ltd has set the standard for a production process in such a way that small adverse variances would be expected to occur. Studies over several months have shown that, when no production difficulties arise, the average weekly variance is £150 adverse. They have also shown that the variances are normally distributed with a standard deviation of £100. Control limits are to be set such that the probability of a wasted investigation is 10% for adverse variances and 5% for favourable ones.

(a)   Suggest a reason why the standard has been set in this way.

(b)   Calculate the control limits.

(c)   What is the chance that the limits in (b) will fail to detect a detrimental change to the production process which increases the average size of the adverse variance to £400?

6.7   Activity solution

(a)   **Harshly set standards**

Whilst it is accepted that standards should not be set too toughly nor too loosely, it is thought that a standard slightly tougher than is actually expected to be achieved will motivate staff to work harder. This standard will have been set to get the best out of staff.

(b)   **Control limits**

When tackling questions to do with normal distributions it is useful to draw a diagram to represent the problem, as shown below.

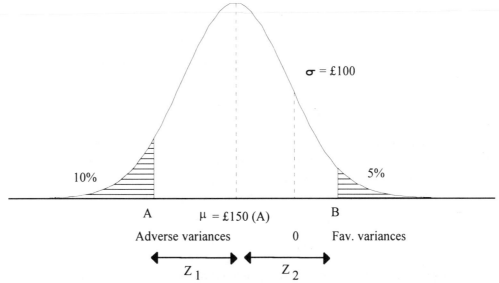

The tails of the distribution show the relevant 10% and 5% areas mentioned in the question. The values of Z_1 and Z_2 can be found from normal distribution tables.

$$Z_1 \quad = \quad 1.28 \text{ standard deviations}$$
$$Z_2 \quad = \quad 1.645 \text{ standard deviations}$$

Control limits:

A	=	£150 (Adverse) +1.28 × £100	=	**£278** (Adverse)
B	=	£150 (Adverse) – 1.645 × £100	=	**£15** (Favourable)

(c)   **Type II error**

The comparison is made with statistical sampling and statistical quality control; nevertheless, a diagram is again useful.

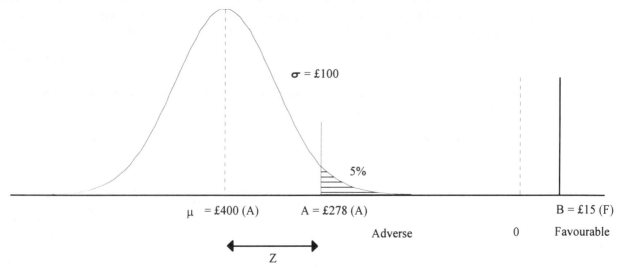

Variances will be investigated if they are bigger than £278 adverse or £15 favourable ie, they lie outside A or B. Variances between A and B will be ignored. With the process producing, on average, adverse variances of £400, the shaded area represents the chance of a single variance being produced that will not be investigated.

$$Z = \frac{A - \mu}{\sigma} = \frac{278 - 400}{100} = 1.22$$

From the tables, the probability of a variance not being investigated = 0.1112 (11.12%)

6.8   Effect of sampling

Some management text books take this analysis one stage further by talking about the average time taken to make a fixed number of units of production (or the average amount of material used). This is getting away from variance investigation and into the realm of sampling theory.

Although individual items (individual variances for single units) may be distributed with mean μ and standard deviation σ, once sample of a given size, n, are chosen and a sample mean, $\bar{x}$, found (average time, average weight, average variance) these sample means follow a different distribution. Since the distribution of individual items is deemed to be a Normal distribution then the sample means will also be Normally distributed. The mean of this distribution will be μ, but the standard deviation of the distribution (usually called the standard error) is given by $\sigma/\sqrt{n}$ (overall population standard deviation divided by the square root of the sample size).

It is not common to see this analysis extended still further to accommodate the practical problem of daily or weekly output levels varying making it difficult to talk about daily or weekly output representing samples of fixed sizes.

6.9   Variance investigation - costs v benefits and ability to correct

This approach to the investigation of a variance involves the application of decision-theory. The investigation is done if its cost is less than the expected net benefits involved.

The cost-benefit analysis can be depicted by a decision tree as follows:

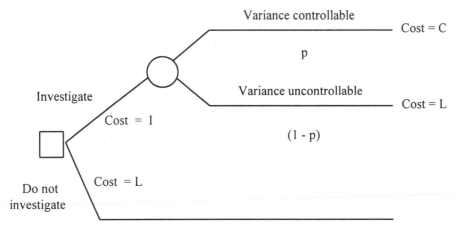

Key to symbols in decision tree

I	=	cost of investigating the variance
C	=	cost of correcting variance
L	=	cost incurred if variance not corrected
p	=	probability that the variance is controllable

The decision-making rule is that the variance should be investigated if the cost of doing so is less than the expected value of the net benefit ie, investigate if:

$$I + Cp + L(1 - p) < L$$

6.10   Example

Last month an adverse direct material usage variance of £1,000 arose.

On the basis of past experience, the cost of an investigation into the variance would be £400 and the cost of corrective action, if the situation is in fact controllable, is estimated to be £300. The net present value of the expected savings from taking the corrective action, assuming a controllable situation, is estimated to be £900. The probability that the variance is uncontrollable is estimated to be 0.3.

You are required to prepare a calculation to show whether the variance should be investigated.

Solution

Using the same tree and symbols as before:

I	=	£400
C	=	£300
L	=	£900
p	=	1 – 0.3
	=	0.7

Cost of investigating   =   £400 + 0.7 × £300 + 0.3 × £900 = £880

Cost of not investigating   =   £900

∴ It is just worth investigating.

Sensitivity

The illustration could be extended quite simply to determine the point of indifference between the 'investigate' or 'not to investigate' decision in terms of the value of:

(a)   p ie, the probability of the variance being controllable; and
(b)   the net present value of the expected savings (L).

The calculations which equate expected values of investigating and not are as follows:

(a)   £400 + p × £300 + (1 − p) × £900   =   £900

                        £1,300 − £600p   =   £900

                                    p   = $\dfrac{400}{600}$ or 0.67

Therefore, the estimate for the probability that the variance is uncontrollable could rise from 0.30 to 0.33 before the decision would change.

(b)   400 + 300 × 0.7 + L × 0.3   =   L

                        400 + 210 + 0.3L   =   L

                                    L   = $\dfrac{610}{0.7}$

                                          =   871.4

Therefore, with the probability estimate unchanged, the net present value of the expected savings could fall from £900 to about £871 before the decision would change.

6.11   Significance of variances in practice

Part of the difficulty of applying, for example, the formal decision-making associated with costs versus benefits analysis is in determining the probabilities and net present values involved with a meaningful degree of accuracy.

In practice, only a limited number of organisations *formally* use the statistical or decision-making criteria outlined in the previous sections. Instead, reliance may be placed on intuition, experience, managerial judgement or simple percentage rules (eg, variances below x% are regarded as insignificant and not subjected to investigation). Whilst such approaches appear to be cruder, nevertheless they implicitly use the same concepts and may well in practice lead to similar decisions.

It would be wrong to assume that all variances reported to a manager come as a surprise to him. They represent the monetary evaluation of the effect on profit of differences between budget or standard and actual. Decisions will have been made by managers during the period and they will be fully aware of these. The variances, when they are reported, possibly quite a while after the events to which they relate, only quantify in monetary values the effect of the decisions already made. Any corrective action should have been taken as soon as possible after the event – the manager would not wait to see the size of the variance before taking action. In such cases the investigation of perhaps a significant variance will be of little additional use in terms of information to the manager concerned. Clearly any formalised rules about the investigation and significance of variances need to be flexible enough to cope with the specific circumstances that arise. The investigation of variances is the process of increasing the information available to management and this must always be a prime objective.

7   WHY USE STANDARD COSTING AND VARIANCE ANALYSIS?

7.1   Advantages

There are three main advantages of using standard costing and variance analysis in management accounting:

(a)   the planning and communicating processes involved may improve efficiency;

(b)   the technique provides a target to be achieved; and

(c)   management by exception may be used.

7.2   Disadvantages

The main disadvantages are:

(a)   that it is difficult to set realistic standards and if this is not done, then any variances reported may be misleading; and

(b)   the targets may be seen as policing devices by managers and employees.

8   ALTERNATIVE APPROACHES TO VARIANCE ANALYSIS

8.1   Introduction

The most common approach to variance analysis is to identify the effect on profit but other approaches may be used. These are outlined below.

8.2   Revenue/expense reconciliation

Using this approach the comparison is made between actual and target revenue and expense items both in £s and as a percentage of the target.

Each item is then considered individually without relating it to overall profitability.

8.3   Quantity variances

Instead of measuring the variance in monetary terms, it is reported using resource quantities. There are circumstances when this information is more useful to a manager than the corresponding monetary values.

8.4   Composite analysis

This technique does not attempt to identify individual variances and report them to the single manager responsible. Instead the variance is reported jointly to both managers.

9   VARIANCE ANALYSIS AND STAFF ATTITUDES

9.1   Targets and motivation

The standard cost when set provides a target which it is hoped staff will be motivated to achieve. Such motivation is also derived from involvement, goal congruence and the recognition of common aspiration levels.

However there is a danger that the variances reported by the system may be seen by the staff as a policing device. It is essential that managers use the variance analysis to improve future performance without it being used as a stick to punish staff.

10   STANDARD COSTING AND THE MODERN ENVIRONMENT

10.1   Introduction

Standard costing was introduced as a costing method for manufacturing organisations which at that time tended to be labour intensive and companies acquired materials in bulk and used them as required.

Nowadays there is a lower proportion of manufacturing amongst organisations, and where it exists new manufacturing methods are used.

10.2   Standard costing and modern manufacturing

Modern manufacturing is highly mechanised and as a result traditional labour hour related variances are no longer appropriate. Instead it is more appropriate to use machine hours as the basis of efficiency measurement.

With regard to materials the use of Just-In-Time is more common and with it quality ordering procedures which eliminate material price variances.

The entire basis of accounting systems must be reconsidered to ensure that they are appropriate to the new environment. Much emphasis is placed on quality and quality costs.

Quality costs were not considered by traditional variance analysis. Nowadays quality is just another activity for which standard costs can be set and compared with actual costs.

10.3   Standard costs in non-manufacturing

The basic principle of standard costing is that it is used where there are common tasks which can be measured and targets set to compare with actual results.

Whilst it may be more difficult to apply standard costing in non-manufacturing environments, it may be used wherever tasks can be identified. A standard may then be set for each task. These targets may then be added together to the extent that the tasks are combined in order to provide the service to the customer.

11   CHAPTER SUMMARY

This chapter commenced by measuring trends in variances and considered the use of this analysis by management in the context of variance investigation. Variance analysis was then appraised and considered in terms of staff attitudes and its usefulness in modern business environments.

12   SELF TEST QUESTIONS

12.1   Explain 'trend' of variances. (1.2)

12.2   Explain 'materiality' of variances. (1.3)

12.3   Explain 'controllability' of variances. (1.4)

12.4   Explain how trends in variances may be calculated. (2.3)

12.5   What are the causes of uncertainty in variance analysis? (4)

12.6   Explain 'tolerance limits'. (5)

12.7   What factors should be considered when deciding whether or not to investigate a variance? (6.1)

12.8   What criteria or decision rules might a firm set up to establish how large a variance has to be before it merits investigatioh? (6.2)

12.9   What are the advantages and disadvantages of using standard costing? (7)

12.10   Explain how the use of variance analysis may affect staff motivation. (9)

12.11   Discuss the use of standard costing in the modern environment. (10)

13   EXAMINATION TYPE QUESTION

13.1   Trend

A company has an inspection department in which operatives examine fruit in order to extract blemished input before the fruit is transferred to a processing department.

The input to the inspection department comes from a preparation department where the fruit is washed and trimmed.

Stocks cannot be built up because of the perishable nature of the fruit. This means that the inspection department operations are likely to have some idle time during each working day.

A standard output rate in kilos per hour from the inspection process has been agreed as the target to be aimed for in return for wages paid at a fixed rate per hour irrespective of the actual level of idle time.

The standard data for the inspection department are as follows:

(i)   standard idle time: as a percentage of total hours **paid for:** 20%

(ii)   standard wage rate per hour: £3.00

(iii)   standard output efficiency is 100%, ie, one standard hour of work is expected in each hour excluding idle time hours.

(iv)   wages are charged to production at a rate per standard hour sufficient to absorb the standard level of idle time.

The labour variance analysis for November for the inspection department was as follows:

Variances	£	*Expressed in % terms*
Productivity	525 (F)	2.2 (F)
Excess idle time	150 (A)	2.5 (A)
Wage rate	800 (A)	3.3 (A)

The actual data for the inspection department for the three months December to February are as follows:

	Dec	*Jan*	*Feb*
Standard hours of output achieved	6,600	6,700	6,800
Labour hours paid for	8,600	8,400	8,900
Idle time hours incurred	1,700	1,200	1,400
Actual wages earned	£26,660	£27,300	£28,925

The labour variances to be calculated in the operation of a standard cost system are as follows:

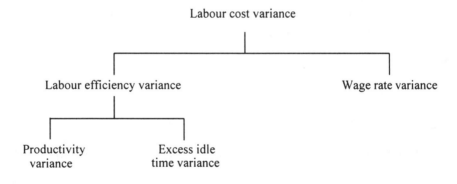

Required:

(a)   Calculate the labour variances for productivity, excess idle time and rate of pay for each of the months December to February.   **(9 marks)**

(b)   In order to highlight the trend and materiality of the variances calculated in (a) above, express them as percentages as follows:

Productivity variance: as a percentage of standard cost of production achieved;

Excess idle time variance: as a percentage of expected idle time;

Wage rate variance: as a percentage of hours paid for at standard rates of pay.   **(6 marks)**

(c)   Explain why variance trend and materiality data in percentage terms may provide useful additional control information for management. Comment on the data given for November and calculated for December to February, giving possible explanations for the figures produced.   **(7 marks)**

(Total: 22 marks)

14   ANSWER TO EXAMINATION TYPE QUESTION

14.1   Trend

(a)

	December £	January £	February £
Productivity (W1)	1,125 (A)	1,875 (A)	2,625 (A)
Excess idle time (W2)	75 (F)	1,800 (F)	1,425 (F)
Wage rate (W3)	860 (A)	2,100 (A)	2,225 (A)

(b)

	December	January	February
Productivity	4.5%	7.5%	10.3%
Excess idle time	1.2%	28.6%	21.3%
Wage rate	3.3%	8.3%	8.3%

(c)   The use of percentages allows each variance to be measured relative to the standard cost. This allows variances of different time periods to be compared even though the output achieved differs. The use of percentages also allows management to decide whether or not a variance lies within the tolerance limits which management finds acceptable.

There appears to have been a wage increase of approximately 5% in January. At the same time the peak of the excess idle time appears to have been reached as in February it is reducing again. This favourable idle time variance could be combined with the productivity variance to give the total efficiency effect. In January this is virtually nil. It could be suggested that the workforce did not work as quickly thus reducing idle time in order to obtain the pay award. However, once the award was received, the speed of working was increased, causing an increase in idle time. Management needs to consider the factors which cause stoppages in production in order to improve productivity.

WORKINGS

(W1)   Productivity

These variances are calculated:

[(Paid labour hours − idle time hours) − standard hours achieved] × (£3.00/0.80)

The standard rate of £3 is adjusted to compensate for the standard idle time of 20%.

(W2)   Excess idle time

These variances are calculated:

[(Paid labour hours × 20%) − Idle time hours] × (£3.00/0.80)

(W3)   Wage rate

These variances are calculated:

[(Paid labour hours × £3) − Actual wages]

23 PERFORMANCE MEASUREMENT - THE PRINCIPLES

INTRODUCTION & LEARNING OBJECTIVES

When you have studied this chapter you should be able to do the following:

- Describe the features of responsibility accounting.
- Describe the factors to be considered when designing a responsibility accounting system.
- Describe the features of an internal control system.
- Identify and explain different performance measures and how they may be used in different industries.
- Explain the conflict between profit and other objectives.
- Explain the use of measures to appraise managerial performance.

1 CONTROL OF ORGANISATIONS

1.1 Introduction

To control an organisation and ensure it attains its goals we must pose and answer the following questions.

- what do we intend to happen?
- what has happened?
- who is responsible for what has happened?
- how does what has happened compare with what we intended?
- what action is necessary?

to answer these questions each organisation needs

- a responsibility accounting system
- an internal control system
- a selection of performance measures.

2 RESPONSIBILITY ACCOUNTING

2.1 Introduction

The aim of responsibility accounting is to ensure that each manager has a well-defined area of responsibility and the authority to make decisions within that area, and that no parts of the organisation remain as 'grey' areas where it is uncertain who is responsible for them. This area of responsibility may be simply a **cost centre,** or it may be a **profit centre** (implying that the manager has control over sales revenues as well as costs) or an **investment centre** (implying that the manager is empowered to also take decisions about capital investment for his department). Once senior management have set up such a structure, with the degree of delegation implied, some form of responsibility accounting system is needed. Each centre will have its own budget, and the manager will receive control information relevant to that budget centre. Costs (and if relevant, revenue, assets and liabilities) must be traced to the person primarily responsible for taking the related decisions, and identified with the appropriate department.

3   THE FACTORS TO BE CONSIDERED WHEN DESIGNING A RESPONSIBILITY ACCOUNTING SYSTEM

3.1   Controllable and Uncontrollable costs

Performance reports should concentrate only on **controllable costs.** Controllable costs are those costs controllable by a particular manager in a given time period. Over a long enough time-span all costs are controllable by someone in the organisation eg, factory rental may be fixed for a number of years but there may eventually come an opportunity to move to other premises. Such a cost, therefore, is controllable in the long term by a manager fairly high in the organisation structure.

However, in the short term it is uncontrollable even by senior managers, and certainly uncontrollable by managers lower down the organisational hierarchy.

There is no clear-cut distinction between controllable and non-controllable costs for a given manager, who may in any case be exercising control jointly with another manager. The aim under a responsibility accounting system will be to assign and report on the cost to the person having **primary** responsibility. The most effective control is thereby achieved, since immediate action can be taken.

Some authorities would favour the alternative idea that reports should include all costs caused by a department, whether controllable or uncontrollable by the departmental manager. The idea here is that, even if he has no direct control, he might influence the manager who does have control. There is the danger of providing the manager with too much information and confusing him but, on the other hand, the uncontrollable element could be regarded as for 'information only', and in this way the manager obtains a fuller picture.

An illustration of the two different approaches is provided by raw materials. The production manager will have control over usage, but not over price, when buying is done by a separate department. For this reason the price and usage variances are separated and, under the first approach, the production manager would be told only about the usage variance, a separate report being made to the purchasing manager about the price variance. The alternative argument is that if the production manager is also told about the price variance, he may attempt to persuade the purchasing manager to try alternative sources of supply.

Some accountants would go as far as to advocate charging ie, actually debiting, departments with costs that arise strictly as a result of decisions made by the management of those departments. For example, if the marketing department insists on a special rush order which necessitates overtime working in production departments, then the marketing department and not the production departments should be charged with the overtime premiums incurred. However, there are practical problems with such an approach:

(a)   The rush order itself might actually be produced during normal time because, from a production scheduling angle, it might be more convenient to do it then (eg, because it would not involve a clean-down of the machines as it was compatible with some other orders currently in production) - meaning 'normal' orders are produced during the period of 'overtime'.

(b)   Re-charging costs to other departments can become a common occurrence because managers see it as a way of passing on not only the costs but also the associated responsibility eg, if the rush order is produced inefficiently in overtime, should the costs of the inefficiency also be charged to the marketing department?

| Conclusion | All managers work for the same organisation and, if the costs are shunted around, there is a nil effect on the overall profit of the organisation (except to the extent of any extra costs incurred in operating such a recharging system). Perhaps the effort expended on such a system could be more positively used to increase overall profit. |

3.2   Activity

What are the potential dangers of including uncontrollable costs in a performance report?

3.3   Activity solution

The dangers of including uncontrollable costs in a performance report are:

(a)   Managers might be demotivated if their performance is apparently affected by costs over which they have no influence.

(b)   Uncontrollable cost information can divert managers' attention away from what they actually are responsible for.

(c)   The manager who **is** responsible for the costs in question might feel that they are not his or her responsibility as they are reported elsewhere.

3.4   The problem of dual responsibility

A common problem is that the responsibility for a particular cost or item is shared between two (or more) managers. For example, the responsibility for payroll costs may be shared between the personnel and production departments; material costs between purchasing and production departments; and so on. The reporting system should be designed so that the responsibility for performance achievements (ie, better or worse than budget) is identified as that of a single manager.

The following guidelines may be applied:

(a)   If manager controls quantity **and** price - responsible for all expenditure variances.

(b)   If manager controls quantity but **not** price - only responsible for variances due to usage.

(c)   If manager controls price but **not** quantity - only responsible for variances due to input prices.

(d)   If manager controls **neither** quantity **nor** price - variances uncontrollable from the point of view of that manager.

3.5   Guidelines for reporting

There are several specific problems in relation to reporting which must be identified and dealt with:

(a)   **Levels of reporting**

The problem is how far down the management structure should responsibility centres be identified for reporting purposes? On the one hand, lower reporting levels encourage delegation and identify responsibility closer to the production process. On the other hand, more responsibility centres increase the number of reports and hence the cost of their production. One solution may be to combine small responsibility centres into groups (eg, departments) for reporting purposes.

(b)   **Frequency of reports and information to be reported**

The frequency of reports should be linked to the purposes for which they are required. This may well mean a variety of reports being produced to different time-scales for different purposes eg, some control information will be required weekly, or even daily. However, comprehensive budget reports are only likely to be required monthly.

The related problem is the content of such reports. It has been suggested that in computerised information systems the problem is often too much, rather than too little information. Generally, as reporting proceeds up the management pyramid, the breadth of the report should increase, and the detail should decrease.

4   INTERNAL CONTROL SYSTEMS

4.1   Control

Organisational control is:

> **Definition**   the process of ensuring that an organisation is pursuing actions and strategies which will enable it to achieve its goals.

One aspect of control is the assessment of actual performance against planned performance, and reacting to the results shown. To be effective, the internal control system must be designed to:

(a)   provide quick, accurate reports of deviations from planned performance;

(b)   produce reports which are phrased in the same terms as the plan;

(c)   report to the correct level within the organisation;

(d)   reflect the needs of the organisation.

4.2   Timing of information

One of the problems of control relates to the timing of information. If we have a negative feedback system (for example, a production control system where output was considerably less than planned), it would be necessary to alter some if not all of the inputs, such as materials and labour. However, it is likely that output varies from the plan each day and is said to 'oscillate' around the normal planned level of output.

Feed forward and feedback control

All performance measurements are part of a feedback/feed forward control model where progress against plans, budgets, targets and standards is monitored by the analysis of significant variances and the use of different performance measures across various dimensions.

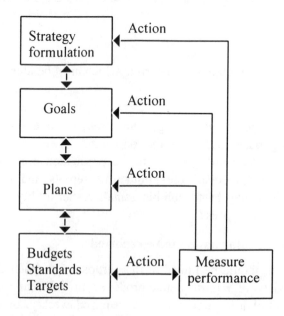

Feed forward/feedback control model

A feedback control measures the outputs of a process and then provides information regarding corrective action to the process or the inputs, after the outputs have been produced. In most management problems, because of time lags in implementing the corrective process, this is not good enough. For example if the chief accountant is informed in September that the administration department has overspent against budget due to a purchase in June, there is nothing that can be done.

Feed forward control will inform management of deviations from programme in time for them to take corrective action. This method is used to overcome the time lag problems often encountered by feedback systems, and also where future control is needed, for example in chemical and petrochemical process systems.

Feed forward systems monitor the inputs into the process to ascertain whether the inputs are as planned; if they are not, the inputs, or perhaps the process, are changed in order to ensure the desired results. In the above example, the administration department would have to submit an estimate for the item they wish to purchase. The organisation would then have to decide whether to refuse the request or change the budget in order to allow the purchase to be made without contriving budget restrictions.

4.3   Characteristics of operational planning and control

Operational plans are the short-term element of the company's overall plan. They are concerned with the day to day running of the company in the immediate future and usually cover a period of one year.

Operational planning and control can be defined as planning and controlling the effective and efficient performance of specific tasks. It therefore differs from management planning and control in focusing on one task at a time, whereas management planning and control focuses on resource requirements for the whole range of tasks.

A further difference is that management planning and control is essentially a matter of exercising management judgement, with some scientific forecasting and evaluation methods available to assist, while operational planning and control is in general far more scientific.

At the operational level, problems tend to be repetitive: general rules can often, therefore, be laid down as to how to respond to a given situation, though there are of course exceptions requiring management judgement. Anthony uses the terms 'programmable' and 'non-programmable' control: most management control is non-programmable while most operational control is of the programmable type.

Programmable control is applicable where the optimum relation between inputs and outputs can be established in advance and where rules can therefore be used to decide the action which will be most efficient in a given set of circumstances.

Examples are: inventory control, where stock levels can be decided when the storage cost, cost of losing an order etc, are known; the determination of the optimum mix under a set of constraints, which can be solved by linear programming techniques; production scheduling in automated plants. As new techniques are developed, more activities become susceptible to programmable control and the usefulness of computers is enhanced.

Because of the shorter time-scale involved, forecasting at the operational level can be more accurate than at the management or strategic planning levels, and actual data can be quickly obtained for comparison with the forecast or target. Continuous feedback is therefore possible as in the diagram below:

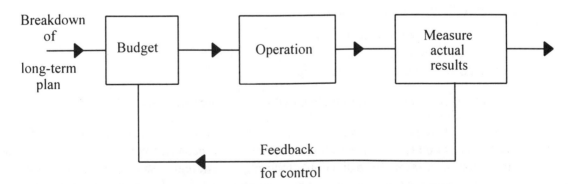

Contrast this with strategic or management control where, because plans are long-term, results may never be available for comparison with targets because plans may never be fully implemented. Only progress towards targets can be measured. Even if results could be measured they would come too late for effective corrective action to be taken. Because operational control does not suffer from such difficulties, it is considerably easier.

A good operational control system should require a minimum of management intervention. The principle of management by exception can be applied, the manager intervening only when deviations from the plan are revealed. Nevertheless, success is dependent on good management - a good information system alone will not solve all the problems. Intervention, when it is necessary, must be done promptly to prevent any further deviations, and it takes a good manager to recognise the warning signs early enough. In addition it is only the manager who can take account of human factors - morale, motivation etc. A computer can be used for comparing results with targets and analysing variances, but it cannot explain the variances.

4.4   Analysis and reporting of variances

The purpose of reporting variances to management is to enable them to take action which will improve future performance. Consequently it is very important to analyse variances by their cause and report them to the appropriate manager.

Such an analysis should also identify which variances are controllable and which are not. Controllable variances should be emphasised since it is in these areas that management action can benefit the organisation.

5   PERFORMANCE CRITERIA

5.1   Measurement and control systems

Perfromance criteria enable the measurement and evaluation of performance.

Tom Peters in his book *Thriving on Chaos*, states that our fixation with financial measurement leads us to downplay or ignore less tangible non-financial measures, such as product quality, customer satisfaction, order lead time, factory flexibility, the time it takes to launch a new product and the accumulation of skills by labour over time.

Drucker argued that the objectives set by the organisation should be supported by appropriate measures which could be used to continually monitor the organisation's performance against objectives. Since Drucker's work there have been many more authors identifying a range of performance areas which organisations have to control and measure. These cover areas such as profitability, cost control, competitiveness, product leadership, productivity, quality of service, quality of working life, delivery performance, innovation and flexibility.

5.2   Design of the system

The managers of every organisation will need to develop their own set of performance measures to help them gain and retain competitive advantage. The set of measures they adopt will be affected by the interaction of three contingent variables:

- the competitive environment they face;
- their chosen strategy; eg, cost leadership or product differentiation.
- the type of business they are running.

The design of the system is linked to these variables. The three steps are as follows.

(a)   The first stage is to determine the competitive environment that the organisation faces. If it is relatively turbulent and competitive (dynamic) the managers will need to build an interactive information system (by exception), focusing on strategic threats and uncertainties. Regular dialogue between top management and operating staff will facilitate organisational learning. If the conditions are stable, management can rely on delegated control of day-to-day operations to ensure sustained competitive success.

(b) What is measured depends on strategic intentions. Where an organisation decides to differentiate itself in the market on the basis of service quality, then it should design measures to monitor and control the quality of the service. If the strategy is based on technology and innovation, then it should be measuring its performance in these areas relative to its competitors.

(c) The third stage is to decide what type of business you are dealing with. Some measures may be feasible in one sector of the business, but not in others. Even when the strategy and what should be measured are known, it may not be that easy to see how to measure it.

The performance dimensions that are used also fall into distinct categories. Financial performance and competitiveness are set to measure the results of the organisation's strategy. All companies will wish to measure the results of their strategy. Innovation, quality measurements, resource utilisation and flexibility are measures of factors which determine competitive success and will vary between companies.

5.3 Activity

If an organisation is following a cost leadership strategy, what will their performance measurement focus on?

5.4 Activity solution

Cost leaders will tend to focus on measuring their resource utilisation and controlling costs along the value chain.

5.5 Performance measures

There are a large number of performance measures which may be used. These may be classified into various groups:

(a) **Quantitative and qualitative measures**

Quantitative measures are those which may be expressed in numerical terms; examples include profit and market share.

Qualitative measures are those which cannot be expressed in numerical terms, but which may be supported by numerical data. For example quality may be evidenced by the number of complaints.

(b) **Monetary and non-monetary measures**

Another classification distinguishes between monetary and non-monetary performance measures. Monetary measures are sometimes known as financial performance measures, and include turnover, profit, and return on capital employed.

Non-monetary performance measures include market share; capacity utilisation; labour turnover, etc.

Monetary and non-monetary performance measures may be expressed either in absolute terms or relative to other measures. Index numbers may also be used to show trends over a period of time.

The areas of performance criteria, as we have already discussed, will vary. Some of the criteria, and the control and measurement used, are as follows:

Financial performance	• cost • profitability • liquidity • budget variance analysis • capital structure • market ratios • level of bad debts • return on capital employed
Competitiveness	• sales growth by product or service • measures of customer base • relative market share and position

Activity	• sales units; • labour/machine hours; • number of passengers carried; • number of material requisitions serviced; • number of accounts reconciled. Whichever measurement is used it may be compared against a pre-set target.
Productivity	• efficiency measurements of resources planned against consumed • measurements of resources available against those used • productivity measurements such as production per person or per hour or per shift
Quality of service	• quality measures in every unit • evaluate suppliers on the basis of quality • number of customer complaints received • number of new accounts lost or gained • rejections as a percentage of production or sales
Customer satisfaction	• speed of response to customer needs • informal listening by calling a certain number of customers each week • number of customer visits to the factory or workplace • number of factory and non-factory manager visits to customers
Quality of working life	• days absence • labour turnover • overtime • measures of job satisfaction
Innovation	• proportion of new products and services to old ones • new product or service sales levels

Tom Peters argues that 'what gets measured gets done'. If something cannot be measured it cannot be improved. However, there are criteria which are more difficult to measure and control such as responsiveness, quality, flexibility, efficiency and effectiveness.

5.6 Responsiveness

Schonberger's World Class Manufacturing underscores the importance of measuring responsiveness, which he calls lead time: 'the number of believers in zero lead time as a primary target is still small but growing fast'. Many companies are coming to the conclusion that reducing lead time is a simple, powerful measurement of how well they are doing. Lead time is a sure and truthful measure, because a plant can only reduce it by addressing the problems that cause delays. If these problems are solved the lead times drop. They include:

- order entry delays and errors;
- wrong blueprints or specifications;
- long setup times and large lots;
- high defect counts;
- machines that break down;
- operators who are not well trained;
- supervisors who do not co-ordinate schedules;
- suppliers that are not dependable;
- long waits for inspectors or repair people;
- long transport distances;
- multiple handling steps;
- stock record inaccuracies.

5.7 Quality

Quality is difficult to measure and control. In most companies, poor quality cost includes such items as manufacturing (or any other function's) rework, warranty costs, cost of repair or return of goods from suppliers and inspection costs. In service industries the quality of service is measured by customers' letters of complaint. This is not a very good measurement as it only measures those customers prepared to write and many customers either remain silent or take their custom elsewhere.

Rewards based on quality are a good measurement of success as everyone becomes involved in the measurement and control process. One of IBM's cable suppliers paid a premium for 0.0 to 0.2 percent defects; for a 0.21 to 0.3 percent defect level they knocked $2 off the price of a cable; for 0.31 percent and over, there was a $4 reduction. With the system in place, a defect rate that had averaged 0.11 percent for years rapidly dropped to 0.04 in 60 days - and stayed there.

5.8 Flexibility

Flexibility concerns the organisation's ability to react quickly to changing customer demands and the external environment. Robert Reich, in his book *The Next American Frontier*, argues that rapid changes in the technology of products and production necessitate the development of 'flexible production systems' to sustain competitive advantage. Global market segmentation, better informed consumers, increasingly complex products and the rapid change in tastes and fashions mean that speed and flexibility of response are essential organisational characteristics. As international competition increases and companies are having to respond more quickly to market demands, they are seeking to increase their ability to re-deploy employees between different tasks (functional flexibility); to increase and decrease the number of their employees to match peaks and troughs of work (numerical flexibility); and to have the freedom to pay rates which reflect market conditions and not be constrained by pay differentials (financial flexibility).

Schonberger argues that 'world class manufacturing' status is not achieved merely by purchasing the latest equipment, and that the roles and skills of operators in equipment set up, maintenance and quality control, need to be re-combined. Companies want employees who are able to change jobs and develop skills as the products and production process develop. They want them to be able to deal with manufacturing problems on their own initiative, without management intervention and effectively operate expensive equipment and identify and fix expected faults.

Some ways of measuring and controlling flexibility as a criteria can include measuring:

- product/service introduction flexibility;
- product/service mix flexibility;
- volume flexibility;
- delivery flexibility.

Flexibility in a service industry such as a travel agency could include measures of the average time taken for one assistant to respond to a customer's service request.

Porter thinks that because flexibility means ensuring that every option is covered, as an objective it can lead to a misallocation of resources or insufficient resources being available to exploit new opportunities.

5.9   Efficiency and effectiveness

The essential principles of the classical management theory concerned the issue of how to allocate tasks, control the work being done and motivate and reward those doing it. The essence of the theory is the 'logic of efficiency', which stressed:

- bureaucratic forms of control;
- narrow supervisory span;
- closely prescribed roles;
- clear and formal definition of procedures, areas of specialisation and hierarchical relationships.

The management activities which are carried out in order to achieve this efficiency have generally been grouped in terms of planning, organising, motivating and controlling. However, this approach focuses on the **actions** (inputs) of managers rather than on **results** (outputs). One particularly influential writer on the subject of management effectiveness, Professor Bill Reddin, considers it essential for management to be judged on output, rather than input, and by achievements rather than by activities. In his book, he writes that there is a tendency to confuse efficiency with effectiveness.

(Definition)   Efficiency is the ratio of output to input.

However, this ratio allows for 100% efficiency to be achieved by high output in relation to high input but the same result can be obtained where both input and output are low. Effectiveness, according to Reddin, is:

(Definition)   'the extent to which a manager achieves the output requirements of his or her position'.

This assumes that the outputs have been identified and made measurable.

Examples of differences between 'effective' managers and 'efficient' managers, are that efficient managers seek to solve problems and reduce costs, whereas effective managers seek to produce creative alternatives and increase profits. On this basis, the management activities of planning, organising, motivating and controlling are more concerned with efficiency rather than effectiveness.

Because organisations are social arrangements in which people strive to achieve control over the use of resources to produce goods and services efficiently, some individuals (managers) hold positions from which they control and co-ordinate the activities of others. Members who have little or no influence must comply or leave. The concern with performance leads to work that is simple and monotonous and to strict rules and procedures which employees are expected to follow. These features may contribute to the efficiency with which collective activity can be carried out because they simplify the tasks of planning, organising, co-ordinating and controlling the efforts of large numbers of people. The need for efficiency, however, conflicts with human values such as individual freedom, creativity and development. It is difficult to design organisations that are efficient both in using resources and in developing human potential.

6   AREAS THAT REQUIRE PERFORMANCE MEASURES

6.1   Introduction

Each area of a business will have differing requirements for operational planning and control and thus will use different performance measurements. The following paragraphs illustrate these differences.

6.2   Sales/marketing

This department has to analyse sales statistics and salesforce returns in order to build up a file of customer characteristics for each type of customer, and for each product in each market. These statistics will be needed to analyse demand trends over time and to predict latent and incipient demand as an aid to strategic decisions.

The department will be responsible for conducting market research exercises to ascertain customer reaction to new products. Such exercises need to be carefully controlled in order to ensure that an unbiased sample is selected.

It will have to decide on advertising campaigns - which media to use, how long to run the campaign, etc. It will have to try and assess the effectiveness of different media to provide for planning future campaigns. For instance, if advertisements are placed in magazines with enquiry slips which the reader may complete, these should be coded so that the company can tell which magazine brings the best response.

In order to control selling activities, good communications are needed between head office, regional sales offices, and salespeople as they travel around. Data links connecting regional sales offices to a central computer can be very useful - by interrogating the central data bank, each regional office can obtain precise up-to-date information on availability of each product. Others can also be transmitted over such a link.

Example

In 1990 **Market Solutions** added the Distributed Database module to its SaleMaker Plus range of software. The module allows SaleMaker Plus client records to be distributed between corporate users in up to 999 remote locations. Any time a record on the user company's central database is added to, deleted or updated, the DDB changes the record in the remote locations. Two-way contact can be made by modem at night to take advantage of off-peak call rates, and special monitoring routines are said to guarantee error-free transmission during the process.

6.3   Credit control

The credit control department needs to analyse overall credit, on a year by year basis, to see if customers are beginning to take longer to pay and therefore whether credit arrangements need to be revised.

In addition, they will have to analyse credit on a product by product basis, on a customer type by customer type basis, and on a credit type basis, in order to see if there is any particular type of customer who is a bad risk, any type of credit which should be discontinued, or any products which should be sold only for cash. The statistics collected by the sales department will be useful in this analysis.

6.4   Production

The problem of the production department will depend on whether production is on a batch or continuous flow system. Production scheduling will be a particular problem if products are made to customers' specific order. The aim will be to minimise setting-up time and setting-up costs; to minimise machine idle time; to work as near as possible to economic batch quantities; to avoid production bottlenecks or hold-ups. Network analysis will help in scheduling.

When an order is placed, the production department will have to fit it into the production schedule in the optimum manner which allows the delivery date to be met; decide on the materials (type and quantity) to be used, and requisition the stores for same, decide on any overtime necessary to meet the delivery date; finally carry out the work in the most efficient manner possible. On all jobs, the department will have to ensure that material wastage is minimised, that overtime is kept to a reasonable level, and that optimum machine utilisation is obtained.

There will have to be some form of inspection to ensure the quality of the finished product - for instance Quality Control, which is a statistical method for sampling products for inspection and for deciding whether any deviations in quality are random only or are due to a defect in the process which should be investigated. This is a very cost-effective method of controlling quality: it provides the best assurance of quality possible short of inspecting every item, which is usually not feasible.

The production department also has to decide on maintenance methods - should maintenance be primarily on a preventive basis, or only when the machines actually break down? This will depend on the cost of maintenance, the cost of lost production if there is a machine breakdown, and the likelihood of machine breakdown. Again, this problem can be solved by statistical techniques. Indeed, the production department provides several very good examples of programmable control. Normally however companies opt for preventive maintenance.

The department should keep records which will form the basis of longer term decisions such as the need for capital investment. Records will be needed of the amount of overtime worked or the extent of idle time, machine utilisation (measured by capacity ratio), and deterioration in quality of output over time, wastage of materials, etc.

6.5   Personnel

This department will be responsible for specific industrial relations issues such as negotiating wage settlements. It is responsible for ensuring that the company complies with such legislation as the Health and Safety at Work Act, equal opportunities and race relations legislation, and other relevant labour legislation.

In addition the department plays an important part in helping to plan and operate the company's manpower plan, and is responsible for activities such as advertising vacancies, making arrangements for interviews (probably in conjunction with the relevant functional manager), arranging training, seeing that the staff appraisal exercise is properly conducted, etc.

This is not an area which is easily susceptible to programmable control.

6.6   Accounting

This department is of course responsible for seeing that accounts are prepared for audit in accordance with statutory requirements, for seeing that budgets are properly prepared and approved in accordance with the agreed timetable, and for seeing that management accounting information is extracted.

6.7   Purchasing and stores

This department will receive requisitions for stores from the production department and must ensure that the company receives the materials at the time required. Orders must be placed with suppliers in accordance with pre-determined re-order levels and economic order quantities which should be periodically reviewed. This department will be responsible for buying policy - whether to buy in large quantities to obtain discounts, whether to buy from several suppliers to retain flexibility, etc. They will have to decide, in conjunction with the production departments, which items to stock as standard and which to order only when required.

7   SERVICE INDUSTRIES

7.1   Introduction

A striking feature of the UK economy in recent years has been the growth in service industries in a highly competitive environment. Banks, airlines, transport companies, consultancy firms and service shops such as those that retail and/or rent consumer durables all function with an awareness of the need to demonstrate flexibility, competitive edge and quality.

Measurement of performance of a company within a service industry was examined in June 1995. The six dimensions of performance tabulated above were quoted, and you were required to comment on each of these using quantitative data given about a specific company. It is important that you can use your imagination and common sense, as well as the general principles discussed here, when devising such measures for a business about which you are not required to have specific technical knowledge. Chapter 24 considers further specific measures for different types of service businesses.

The importance of this topic is recognised by a research report written by Fitzgerald, Silvestro et al. As a result the designers of information systems are investing considerable effort in setting up systems for performance measurement and evaluation. The measurement and appreciation of service businesses covers both financial and non financial issues in seeking ways to inform management on how best to plan control and make decisions in order to achieve corporate goals.

Service industries are those included in Sections 6 to 9 of the Standard Industry Classification (SCI).

"In 1989 services accounted for 64 per cent of UK gross domestic product (CSO 89) and this proportion is growing. Since the mid-1970's services have grown at twice the rate of the rest of the UK economy, and this expansion has been mirrored elsewhere in the developed world. Some services such as tourism increasingly support the UK's declining visible balance of payments. In an interdependent economy the growth of the service sector underpins the health of the rest of the economy by providing a competent workforce to manufacturing industry and a demand for its products. 'It is an inescapable fact that services are a critical cost dimension to the nation's manufacturing competitiveness'." (Fitzgerald, Silvestro *et al*).

7.2   Key differences in measurement of services

In the literature of management accounting, performance measurement has been more extensively investigated in manufacturing businesses than in service businesses. There are four key differences between manufactured products and service products.

(a)   **Intangibility**

The purchase of a motor car is tangible; it is an object that can be touched. The outputs of a service provider may be performances rather than objects. When travelling by air one is influenced by many intangible factors, such as the helpfulness of the cabin crew, as well as more tangible and hence measurable aspects of the package: the arrival of your luggage with you. Customers are therefore buying a complex bundle of tangible goods and intangible services: this makes the service process difficult to control as it is hard to know what the customer values in the process.

Consider the use of a management consultant. The service is intangible; it can only be experienced when it is delivered.

(b)   **Heterogeneity**

Service outputs are heterogeneous. The standard of performance may vary, especially where there is a high labour content. It is hard to ensure consistent quality from the same employee from day to day, and harder still to get comparability between employees, yet this will crucially affect what the customer receives.

(c)   **Simultaneity of production and consumption**

The production and consumption of many services are simultaneous, for example, having a meal or taking advice from your solicitor. Most services therefore cannot be counted, measured, inspected, tested or verified in advance of sale for subsequent delivery to the customer. Unlike a motor car that delivers its potential over its useful life a service is immediate.

(d)   **Perishability**

Services are perishable; that is, they cannot be stored. Perishability thus removes the inventory buffer frequently used by manufacturing organisations to cope with fluctuations in demand. Therefore scheduling operations and controlling quality are key management problems in services, which are made more difficult by the presence of the customer in the service process. Although the simultaneity of production and consumption enables cross-selling and the collection of feedback from customers in real time, an unfavourable impression of the service process may erode a customer's satisfaction with the service product: which of us has not fumed at slow, thoughtless service in an otherwise excellent restaurant or despaired at the time spent queuing at a supermarket checkout?

7.3   Competitiveness

A suggested framework for building and routinely monitoring competitive advantage is that proposed by Day and Wensley. They argue that companies may build and maintain a competitive advantage in two ways: by focusing on the needs of customers, or by making comparisons with significant competitors. Ideally they should do both. A conclusion from Day and Wensley's work is that customers may be consulted when trying to measure the results of competitive success, but what determines those results largely depends on comparisons with competitors. Consequently, *relevant measures of competitive and financial performance will embrace both competitor-based and customer-focused approaches.*

The use of competitor comparisons is discussed further in 'benchmarking', section 8.

7.4   Measures of financial performance in service industries

Conventional financial analysis distinguishes four types of ratio: profitability, liquidity, capital structure and market ratios. Analysis of a company's performance using accounting ratios involves comparisons with past trends and/or competitors' ratios. As is well known, such time-series and cross-sectional analyses are problematical. Typical ratios for a service company could be:

Turnover per product group
Turnover per 'principal' in say a management consultancy
% staff costs to turnover
% space costs to turnover
% training costs to turnover
% net profit
Current ratio
Quick asset ratio
% market share
% market share increase year by year

The 'untraceability' of common costs to product outputs and the high level of stepped fixed costs will also make the use of financial ratios problematical.

7.5   Measures of quality of service in service industries - BAA plc

BAA uses regular customer surveys for measuring customer perceptions of a wide variety of service quality attributes, including, for example, the cleanliness of its facilities, the helpfulness of its staff and the ease of finding one's way around the airport. Public correspondence is also analysed in detail, and comment cards are available in the terminals so that passengers can comment voluntarily on service levels received. Duty terminal managers also sample the services and goods offered by outlets in the terminals, assessing them from a customer perspective. They check the cleanliness and condition of service facilities and complete detailed checklists which are submitted daily to senior terminal managers. The company has also a wealth of internal monitoring systems that record equipment faults and failures, and report equipment and staff availability. These systems are supported by the terminal managers who circulate the terminals on a full-time basis, helping customers as necessary, reporting any equipment faults observed and making routine assessments of the level of service provided by BAA and its concessionaires.

Examples of service quality measures and mechanisms at BAA plc are shown below:

QUALITY	MEASURES	MECHANISMS
Access	Walking distance/ease of finding way around	Surveys operational data
Aesthetics	Staff appearance/airport appearance quality of catering	surveys inspection
Availability	equipment availability	internal fault monitors
Cleanliness	environment and equipment	surveys/inspection
Comfort	crowdedness	surveys/inspection
Communication	information clarity/clarity of labelling and pricing	surveys/inspection
Competence	staff efficiency	management inspection
Courtesy	courtesy of staff	surveys/inspection
Friendliness	staff attitude	surveys/inspection
Reliability	equipment faults	surveys/inspection
Responsiveness	staff responsiveness	surveys/inspection
Security	efficiency of security checks/ number of urgent safety reports	survey/internal data

7.6 Internal quality measurement in service industries

Inspection and monitoring of the inputs to the service process is important for all organisations. The quality of the solicitors in a practice or the number and grades of staff available in a consultancy organisation are crucial to the provision of service quality. Multibroadcast measure the number of shop refits per month and BAA monitor the availability and condition of equipment and facilities.

Many service companies use internal mechanisms to measure service quality during the process of service delivery. Multibroadcasts use managers to formally inspect the premises, goods and service provided by the staff using detailed checklists covering, for example, the correct pricing of items, correct layout of displays and attitude of staff to the customers. BAA have advanced systems to monitor equipment faults and the terminal managers are expected to report any problems they see.

The quality of the service may be measured after the event, that is by measuring the results by outputs of the service. For example, Multibroadcasts measure the number of service calls they have to make for each of their products, in order to assess product reliability.

7.7   **Service quality measures - key points**

(a)   Providing high level of service quality may be a source of competitive advantage.

(b)   Achieving high service quality means ensuring all the factors of the service package meet customer requirements.

(c)   There are twelve factors of service quality; reliability, responsiveness, aesthetics/appearance, cleanliness/tidiness, comfort, friendliness, communication, courtesy, competence, access, availability and security.

(d)   The relative importance of the factors will vary from company to company and between customers.

(e)   Service quality can be measured using external customer satisfaction measures and internal organisational quality systems at different stages of the service process.

(f)   Both internal and external measures of the service quality factors are required to facilitate target setting, the tracking of the costs of changing quality targets and the linking of pay to quality performance.

(g)   Quality control systems vary between professional, service shop and mass service organisations.

8   **BENCHMARKING**

8.1   **Introduction**

As mentioned in the particular context of service companies above, comparison of an organisation's performance with that of others will be an important part of the overall performance measurement system. Benchmarking is the increasingly popular practice of identifying an appropriate organisation whose performance may be used as a comparator, or benchmark, for this purpose.

8.2   **Obtaining information for benchmarking**

Benchmarking against competitors involves the gathering of a range of information about them. Financial information will generally be reasonably easy to obtain, from published accounts, financial press etc. Some product information may be obtained by acquiring their products and examining them in detail to ascertain the components used and their construction ('reverse engineering'). Literature will also be available in the form of brochures, trade journals etc.

However, most non-financial information, concerning competitors' processes, customer and supplier relationships, customer satisfaction etc will not be so readily available.

To overcome this problem, benchmarking exercises are generally carried out with organisations taken from within the same group of companies (intra-group benchmarking) or from similar but non-competing industries (inter-industry benchmarking).

8.3   **Intra-group benchmarking**

This involves the co-operation between companies within a group. Divisions or other operating units within the group companies with similar products and practices pool information about their processes. A centrally appointed working party will analyse the information and identify the best aspects from each company. These will then be developed into a group policy.

8.4   **Inter-industry benchmarking**

This involves co-operation between non-competing businesses with similar processes, supplier and customer bases. For example, a book printer/publisher may liaise with an audio product manufacturer/distributor (CDs, tapes etc). Both will benefit from information obtained from a benchmarking relationship, without the danger of one gaining competitive advantage over the other, as may occur with intra-group benchmarking.

8.5   Specific benchmark measures

Particular measures that may be evaluated in a benchmarking exercise are discussed in Chapter 24.

9   CONFLICTS BETWEEN OBJECTIVES

9.1   Profit maximisation

Many of the theoretical models used for decision making assume an objective of profit maximisation; whilst this is a useful starting point such an objective is only one of the objectives pursued by organisations today.

Organisations are responsible for employee relations and have social responsibilities both of which incur costs which therefore reduce profits. Many of these responsibility areas are now considered extremely important if the business is to succeed. These are known as critical success factors.

9.2   Critical success factors (CSFs)

Critical success factors are defined as:

> **Definition**   The limited number of areas in which results, if they are satisfactory, will ensure successful competitive performance for the business. They are the vital areas where 'things must go right' for the business to flourish.

They were developed by John Rockart, at the Sloan School of Management at MIT, as an attempt to identify the real information needs of management, mainly chief executives.

The areas referred to in the definition include core activities, new markets and new products. For example, one of the critical success factors to run a mail order service is speedy delivery.

9.3   Past exam question

This topic was examined in December 1994; the discursive question required an explanation of the term CSFs, with examples, and an application of their measurement and control in the context of productivity.

9.4   Sources of CSF

Rockart claims that there are four sources for the CSF's:

(a)   **the industry that the business is in**; each has CSF's that are relevant to any company within it.

(b)   **the company itself and its situation within the industry**. Actions taken by a few large dominant companies in an industry will provide one or more CSF's for small companies in that industry.

(c)   **the environment** eg, the economy, the political factors and consumer trends in the country or countries that the organisation operates in. An example use by Rockart is that, before 1973, virtually no chief executive in the USA would have stated 'energy supply availability' as a critical success factor. However, following the oil embargo many executives monitored this factor closely.

(d)   **temporal organisational factors**, which are areas of company activity that are unusually causing concern because they are unacceptable and need attention. Cases of too little or too much inventory might classify as a CSF for a short time.

Examples of CSF's will include 'develop new products', 'market success' and 'support field sales representatives'.

Some CSF's are industry-specific, as we noted above. For example, one of the car industry's is 'Compliance with the Department of Transport's pollution requirements with respect to car exhaust gases'.

Rockart identified two types of CSF:

(a)   monitoring; keeping abreast of ongoing operations;

(b)   building; tracking progress of the 'programs for change' initiated by the executive.

CSF's vary between organisations, periods and managers. The higher an executive is in the organisation, the more building CSF's they have to deal with.

9.5   Critical success factors and performance indicators

The organisation will identify its CSF's by first determining its goals and objectives.

Definition   Goals are long-run, open-ended attributes or ends a person or organisation seeks and are sufficient for the satisfaction of the organisation's mission.

Definition   Objectives are time-assigned targets derived from the goals, and are set in advance of strategy.

Goals represent the aspiration of the organisation; the direction in which it will focus its effort. Objectives are measurable targets that an organisation sets to meet its goals. Each set of objectives will support one goal. There may be many or few objectives supporting one goal.

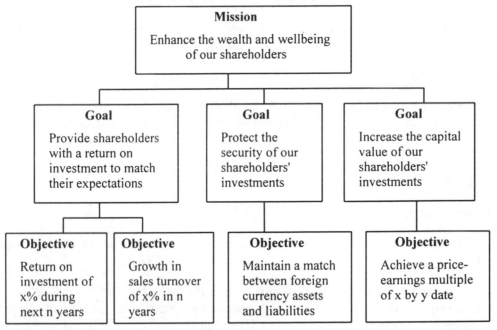

Once the objectives are identified, they can be used to determine which factors are critical for accomplishing the objective. The performance measure for the CSF is a characteristic of its associated objective. Knowing the units of measurement for each objective makes it easy to identify the information required. Once the critical factors have been determined, two or three prime measures for each factor are found. Some measures use hard, factual data and these are the easiest to identify. Other measures are 'softer', such as opinions, perceptions and hunches and take more analysis to uncover their appropriate source.

All CSF's should have a performance measure. It is this measure which is used to monitor the actual success of each factor and information will need to be supplied to managers in a form that they can use.

CSF's provide a way of achieving a clear definition of the information that is needed, limiting the costly collection of more data than is necessary. For example, where the CSF is to achieve market success, the information needs may be identified as the changes in market share over the last 12 months and the growth in the market over the same period.

10 MANAGEMENT PERFORMANCE MEASURES

10.1 Introduction

Earlier in this chapter various techniques of performance measurement were considered, often in relation to the accounting system and the measurement of actual results compared to targets.

Such targets are often set in the context of organisational objectives but many organisations use the same targets to appraise managers.

10.2 Management performance measures

The measures used to appraise a manager should be independent of the performance of the unit being managed. This is because not all units present the same degree of managerial problems and thus any manager comparisons based on unit performance are inappropriate.

Most management performance measures are qualitative though sometimes Residual Income is used.

10.3 What is residual income?

Residual income is the profit of the unit for which the manager is responsible less a notional interest charge based on the value of the assets used by the unit to generate its income. This is a quantitative measure, but it is based on the unit's performance.

10.4 Qualitative management performance measures

In small to medium sized organisations such measures will be in the form of internal judgement by senior managers of their subordinates and by staff of their manager.

The first of these requires a detailed knowledge of the problems faced by the subordinate manager and the techniques used to solve them. The appraisal by staff requires that there is a very good working relationship between the staff and their manager.

In large organisations it may be possible for such judgements to be made by outsiders, perhaps from other divisions or subsidiaries. Where this is possible the performance evaluation is likely to be impartial.

11 CHAPTER SUMMARY

This chapter has explained the features of responsibility accounting and the factors to be considered when designing a responsibility accounting system.

Performance measures were then considered.

12 SELF TEST QUESTIONS

12.1 What is responsibility accounting? (2.1)

12.2 Why is it important to distinguish controllable costs? (3.1)

12.3 Distinguish between feedforward and feedback control. (4.2)

12.4 Identify seven different areas of performance measures relevant to a business. (5.5)

12.5 Distinguish between quantitative and qualitative performance measures. (5.5)

12.6 What are critical success factors? (9.2)

24 PERFORMANCE MEASUREMENT: APPLICATIONS

INTRODUCTION & LEARNING OBJECTIVES

This chapter applies the principles of performance measurement to different business situations.

When you have studied this chapter you should be able to do the following:

- Describe different performance measures appropriate to different types of business and parts of those businesses.
- Discuss the behavioural implications of performance appraisal.
- Measure performance over time using indices.

1 INTRODUCTION

In chapter 23 we discussed the performance criteria that may be applied to any type of business:

- financial performance
- competitiveness
- resource utilisation
- quality of service
- customer satisfaction
- innovation
- flexibility

The types of measures that will be used under each of these headings were discussed in general terms. This chapter looks at some performance measures specific to different types of business:

- manufacturing (including specific order and process environments)
- service
- non-profit making

2 PERFORMANCE MEASURES IN MANUFACTURING

2.1 Introduction

The performance measures used in manufacturing may be either qualitative or quantitative and will be different for various parts of the business, and for differing manufacturing environments. Some specific measures for these areas are discussed in the following paragraphs.

2.2 Performance measures and sales

Sales may be measured in absolute terms and compared with targets, but other measures may also be used to identify the success of the selling activity. These include:

(a)   profitability by customer;
(b)   market share;
(c)   customer satisfaction;
(d)   orders as a % of quotations.

Each of these may be supported by numerical values which can be compared against targets and trends may be established from one period to another.

2.3 Performance measures and materials

In respect of performance there are three aspects to materials:

(i)   purchase;
(ii)   storage; and
(iii)   usage.

Each of these aspects must be monitored.

Purchasing performance may be measured using price variances, especially if planning and operating causes are separated.

Storage may be measured by considering:

(a)   average stock levels;
(b)   stock losses; and
(c)   number of stockouts.

Usage of materials may be monitored using:

(a)   usage variances, analysed into planning and operating causes;
(b)   wastage rates; and
(c)   rejection rates.

2.4 Performance measures and labour

Traditional variance analysis may be used to identify performance against a target in terms of rate and efficiency variances, especially if planning and operating causes are separated.

In addition idle time and absenteeism should be measured; these may be indicators of employee morale which could also be measured qualitatively by management.

Labour turnover is another performance measure which should be used. Comparisons can be made on a trend basis. Where possible the reasons for leaving should be identified and analysed.

2.5 Performance measures and overhead

Many of the overhead costs incurred are fixed in nature, so the use of variances merely places an accounting value on the underlying cause.

It is important to measure the utilisation of assets, relative to the available capacity and to identify the cause of any differences eg, machine breakdown.

2.6 Performance measurement in specific order environments

Specific order environments include job, batch, and contract situations where items are made to specific customer requirements using common skills. However each item/job is different in its finished form because it is customer specific.

The measures used may vary slightly between job/batch/contract environments but the general principles are the same.

Costs will be compared with estimates and any significant differences investigated to identify their cause. Where common tasks can be identified they may be the subject of standard times and costs which will allow traditional variance analysis to be used.

Time taken may also be compared with estimates and for more complex work (eg, contracts) the use of network analysis may be appropriate.

Suppliers' performances on delivery, quality of supply and price should also be monitored as failures by suppliers may be a cause of any differences in cost/time performance of the organisation.

2.7 Performance measures in process environments

Process environments are those where homogeneous items are made and later sold from stock to customers who may not be identifiable at the time of production. Typically there are a limited number of items which are made, often from a continuous process.

It is easy in such environments to set targets against which actual performance can be measured because the output may be clearly defined.

Cost may be controlled against a standard using traditional variance analysis.

Activity and the quality of output may be measured using:

(a)   output per input unit (yield);
(b)   output per shift;
(c)   wastage per good output unit.

3 PERFORMANCE MEASURES IN SERVICE ENVIRONMENTS

3.1 Introduction

Service environments exist to provide a service to a variety of customers. Some of such services (eg, accountancy/law) are specific to a particular client's needs and are therefore similar to the jobbing environment explained earlier. Other services (eg, retailing and transport) are not customer specific.

The four key differences between the products of service industries and those of manufacturing businesses were discussed in Chapter 23:

- Intangibility - the output being a performance rather than tangible goods

- Heterogeneity - the variability in standard of output performance due to the heavy reliance on human input

- Simultaneity of production and consumption - precluding advance verification of specification or quality

- Perishability - the inability to carry stocks of the product to cover unexpectedly high demand

These differences pose problems in measuring and controlling performance. A well-defined set of performance measures, both financial and non-financial, is essential, as set out in the matrix in paragraph 6.5 of Chapter 23.

The following paragraphs describe measures that may be used in some examples of service business, each of which will suffer to varying extents from problems caused by the four characteristics summarised above.

A comprehensive example for a particular service business, based upon a past exam question, then follows.

3.2 Performance measures in professional services

Accountancy and law are two examples of professional services. Such services tend to be specific to a client's needs, though the service provided is based on common skills and knowledge.

Whilst perishability may not be quite so relevant to professional services (work loads are generally reasonably well in advance and can be scheduled) the other three service characteristics will pose problems. The success of such a business can depend upon the performances of a few key personnel; the ultimate measurement of which will be customer satisfaction, which will directly impact upon financial performance. However, control systems should operate such that poor performance is identified prior to the point of losing important clients!

Performance may be measured in quantitative terms by considering chargeable time as a proportion of time available.

Qualitative measures centre around client satisfaction and the ability to adapt to clients' needs.

3.3   Performance measures in retail services

Retail services sell products to the general public. Their performance should therefore be measured in terms of profitability and customer satisfaction.

It is a business that could perhaps be said to be between manufacturing and pure service. It deals with tangible goods, the quality of which can be checked in advance and which can be stocked; however, the success of a retail business may also depend upon the service provided by the personnel involved (cashiers, shop assistants, store managers etc).

The balance of emphasis between goods and service related performance measures should be dictated by the relative importance placed upon these by the customer. For example, the quality of service provided by individual employees is unlikely to have the same impact on customer spending in large supermarkets as it would in the smaller, more personal shops.

Profitability can be measured in total, per product line, and per square metre of floor space. These may be compared with industry averages and as trends over time.

Customer satisfaction can be measured by monitoring the number of customer complaints and returns. Returns may be caused by poor stock control.

Stock control should be monitored by the rate of stock turnover, and the value and volume of stock losses. These losses should be analysed between perished and obsolete (out-of-date) stocks.

3.4   Performance measures in transport operations

Transport operations provide a service to convey goods or passengers from one place to another.

To some extent, the service output of a transport business is more easily standardised and tangibly measured than other service businesses. The objective is clear - to get the goods or passengers intact from A to B within a given time at minimum cost.

Cost measures will inevitably play a large part in the performance measure system, along with timing targets (particularly for public transport systems - the introduction of 'Passenger Charters' directly penalises operations that don't meet specified timetable criteria).

The service provided by personnel will probably be more important to passenger transport services than those relating to goods, although the customers may, in fact, have less choice between suppliers and thus be less able to reflect their satisfaction or otherwise in financial performance.

Costs may be analysed into standing (fixed) costs and running (variable) costs and those may be compared with pre-set targets. Costs per unit may also be calculated and trends established over time.

Other measures which may be used include the frequency of late arrival and the extent of the lateness involved. These factors will impact on customer satisfaction.

3.5   Example

This example is based upon an examination question set in June 1995.

FL Ltd provides training on financial subjects to staff of small and medium sized businesses. Training is at one of two levels - for clerical staff, instructing them on how to use simple financial accounting computer packages; and for management, on management accounting and financial management issues.

Training consists of tutorial assistance, in the form of workshops or lectures, and the provision of related material - software, texts and printed notes.

Tuition days may be of standard format and content, or designed to meet the client's particular specifications. All courses are run on client premises and, in the case of clerical training courses, are limited to 8 participants per course.

FL Ltd has recently introduced a 'helpline' service, which allows course participants to phone in with any problems or queries arising after course attendance. This is offered free of charge.

FL Ltd employs administrative and management staff; course lecturers are hired as required, although a small core of technical staff is employed on a part-time basis by FL Ltd to prepare customer specific course material and to man the helpline. Material for standard courses is bought in from a group company, who also print up the customer-specific course material.

Additional information for the year ended 31 March 19X6 is as follows:

(i)   Clients are charged at £400 per half day for tuition time and course set-up time (customer specific courses); course material is sold at standard cost (excluding set-up time) plus 120%.

(ii)   Extracts from management accounts:

Summary profit and loss account for the year ended 31 March 19X6

	Budget		Actual	
	½ days	£'000	½ days	£'000
Income				
Fees				
- Clerical tuition	360	144	520	208
- Management tuition	250	100	180	72
- Course set-up	80	32	110	44
	690	276	810	324
Material		185		240
		461		564
Costs				
Lecturer hire		171		204
Technical staff salaries		30		39
Material		84		136
Other operating costs		38		45
		323		424
Net profit		138		140

		Budget	*Actual*
Financial ratios			
Net profit margin on sales		29.9%	24.8%
Net profit on capital employed		42.7%	39.8%
Operating statistics			
Technical staff: non-chargeable time			
- help-line (days)		25	37
- other (days)		10	6
Tuition time analysis			
- standard		80%	68%
- customer specific		20%	32%
Client complaints received (prev yr =	10)		16
New course proposals			
- existing clients		6	5
- new clients		8	10
New courses undertaken			
- existing		3	2
- new clients		3	5

For each of the performance criteria measured below, comment on the perfromance of FL Ltd using the data given above to illustrate your answer:

- financial performance
- competitiveness
- quality of service
- flexibility
- resource utilisation
- innovation

Outline solution

The following summarises the computations and comments that could be made under each heading:

Financial performance

- Fees 17.4% up on budgeted, material sales up 29.7%, costs up 31.3%, net profit up 1.4%

- No fee increases, thus increase in fees all due to increase in chargeable time

- Outside lecturer cost up 19.3% - investigate why rates are higher than budget (or perhaps not all time invoiced by lecturers has been re-charged to clients)

- In-house technical time/cost analysis:

		% on budget
chargeable time:	course set-up	+37.5
non-chargeable:	help-line	+48
	other	-40
	total	+22.9
overall time		+33
cost		+30

The increase in set-up time ties in with the increased proportion of customer-specific tuition time.

Cost per day of technical staff appears to have fallen.

- Material costs are 61.9% higher than budgeted, against increased sales of 29.7% - the budgeted mark-out system is not being fully applied - check that stock is not being over-ordered and that clients are being re-charged properly.

- Overall, financial performance up on budget in absolute terms, but down in relative terms (net profit ratios): costs have increased out of line with income.

Competitiveness

- Usually measured in terms of market share or sales growth

- Limited information given here; sales up on budget - but need to look in terms of longer-term trend

- Success rate on proposals: budgeted to win 50% of new courses proposed for existing clients and 37.5% of those for new clients; actual success rates were 40% and 50%. In absolute terms, the number of new course proposals and wins were both down by 1.

  It would appear that FL are good at marketing to new clients, but not so good at expanding sales to existing clients. This may be tied in with quality.

Quality

- Lower than budgeted success rate in winning proposals for new business from existing clients may be indicative of a quality problem

- Help-line use was 48% higher than expected - this may tie into tuition quality, but will also be affected by standard of course participants, basis on which budget (for a new service) was prepared, problems with computers etc.

- Number of customer complaints up from 10 last year to 16 this.

Flexibility

- Relates to ability to cope with changes in volume and content of service

- Actual tuition time was 700 half days compared to a budget of 610; the use of freelance lecturers assists cost-effective flexibility here, although this will to some extent depend upon the amount of notice they need

- The level of course proportions moved from a budgeted ratio of 360 clerical to 250 management tuition half days to one of 520 to 180. Again, access to a bank of lecturers with varying skills will help to respond to such demand changes.

- The employment of some technical staff allows speedy response to additional demands for help and new course development, although the actual margin of "spare time" is now quite small and the trend in demands upon their time must be monitored to ensure sufficient room for flexibility in the future

- The mix of standard courses and customer-specific courses changed from a budgeted 80/20 ratio to an actual 68/32. This indicates the ability to be flexible in response to market demands - the design of the standard courses may be in the form of modules, that can be modified and combined to form the basis for customer-specific courses

Resource utilisation

- Use of freelance lecturers is an efficient use of resources, with 100% chargeable time

- There is a trade-off between resource utilisation, flexibility and innovation. Full resource utilisation restricts flexibility, and non-chargeable time invested in innovative schemes can impact on longer-term results

Innovation

- The introduction of the new help-line service must be assessed in terms of its impact on the previous five performance criteria, in both the long and short-term.

- Currently it is not having an obvious direct impact on immediate financial performance, as its resource needs can be met from technical staff availability, although alternative uses of this time need to be identified and evaluated in comparison.

- It is hoped that its longer term impact will be to increase the proportion of new proposals won, by increasing the competitiveness of the quality of the product offered and

- Use of technical staff time on this non-chargeable activity may limit the flexibility to respond to future new course development demand

- Consideration should perhaps be given to limitation of the amount of help-line time available for each course.

4 PERFORMANCE MEASURES IN NON-PROFIT MAKING ORGANISATIONS

4.1 Introduction

Non-profit making organisations often have as one of their objectives the concept of value for money. Thus it is important to measure cost and performance against targets to establish whether the objective is being met.

4.2 Performance measures in education

Education is an example of a non-profit making organisation whose objectives include the provision of a value for money service.

The costs of the service must be compared against budgets but other performance indicators may be used in total for the establishment and within each faculty/department. These measures include:

Overall:

Numbers of students

Amount of research funding received

Proportion of successful students (by grade)

Quality of teaching

Number of publications by staff

Faculty:

Cost per student

Staff : Student ratios

Availability of learning resources

Number of courses available

5 BEHAVIOURAL IMPLICATIONS OF PERFORMANCE MEASURES

5.1 Introduction

Both profit making and non-profit making organisations now use measures to evaluate performance. There are consequences of this which are outlined below.

5.2   Measuring staff performance

The purpose of providing targets and measuring performance is often intended to motivate staff to achieve those targets, but this will only be achieved through involvement and the development of goal congruence. Staff may well see the measurement of performance as a policing device particularly if it is used to assess their personal performance rather than that of the unit they manage.

It must be remembered that managerial performance depends on a number of factors; sometimes good results will occur despite poor management whereas in other areas average results will only occur due to very good management.

6   MEASURING PERFORMANCE DURING INFLATION

6.1   Introduction

Commonly used measures to evaluate performance, such as gross margin, return on sales and changes in market share all have a shortcoming: they do not take into account the financial resources committed to a particular product, customer, sales territory or market segment. This shortcoming can be corrected by using such measures of performance as return on investment, return on equity and return on assets employed.

Management must also be prepared to incorporate any known inflation-adjusted accounting information into these additional measures of performance. Costs must be redefined to take into account changes in prices of plant, equipment, raw materials, working capital, and the labour that have gone into inventories of finished goods and work in process. The effect will almost always be to reduce profit estimates below levels indicated by traditional accounting methods. Marketing units that look like real 'winners' on the basis of traditional accounting methods and measures such as gross margin and return on sales can quickly become 'losers' when inflation-adjusted costs and capital requirements are considered.

Marketing projects and activities, and marketing line managers such as field sales managers, sales promotion managers, product managers and market managers are characteristically evaluated by measures of sales volume, market share, and gross margin contribution.

Marketing personnel are under severe pressure to produce sales volume, to meet sales quotas, and to capture and hold market share. These are typical measures of operating performance, used to evaluate marketing personnel. There are now, however, more sophisticated measures of marketing performance, treating products, customers, market segments and sales territories as competing uses of scarce financial resources.

Inflation accounting adds yet another dimension to the increasingly sophisticated assessment of the financial implications of marketing decisions. The performance of marketing managers in the future is certain to be increasingly evaluated in terms of asset utilisation by measures of return on assets employed for product, market segments, sales territory, and other marketing control units, adjusted to reflect the current level of general or specific prices.

6.2   Simple price index

$$\text{Simple price index} = \frac{p_1}{p_0} \times 100$$

where p_0 is the price at time 0
        p_1 is the price at time 1

6.3   Example

If a commodity costs £2.60 in 19X4 and £3.68 in 19X5, calculate the simple price index for 19X5, using 19X4 as base year (ie, time 0).

6.4   Solution

Simple price index $= \dfrac{p_1}{p_0} \times 100$

$= \dfrac{3.68}{2.60} \times 100$

$= 141.5$

This means that the price has increased by 41.5% of its base year value, ie, its 19X4 value.

6.5   Weighted average indexes

An index number based on the prices of a number of items compares the price of each item in one year with the price of each item in the base year, expressing each as a percentage and then finds the weighted average of the percentages.

6.6   Example

From the following information, construct an index of the weighted average of the prices, with 19X5 as the base year:

Item	Price (pence)		Weights
	19X5	19X6	
A	10	20	100
B	25	26	182
C	35	33	132
D	12	13	13
			427

6.7   Solution

Index of the weighted average of prices

$$= \dfrac{\sum W \dfrac{p_1}{p_0} \times 100}{\sum W} = \dfrac{52{,}783.5}{427} = 123.6$$

where W = weight, p_1 = prices in 19X6, p_0 = prices in 19X5.

Workings

p_0	p_1	Price ratio $\dfrac{p_1}{p_0} \times 100$	W	$W \times (\dfrac{p_1}{p_0} \times 100)$
10	20	200.0	100	20,000.0
25	26	104.0	182	18,928.0
35	33	94.3	132	12,447.6
12	13	108.3	13	1,407.9
			427	52,783.5
			$\sum W$	$\sum W \times \dfrac{p_1}{p_0} \times 100$

6.8   Selecting weights

The weights applied to the price ratios should, in general, reflect the **amount spent** or total value of each item purchased, rather than simply the quantities purchased (however standardised). The reason is that this eliminates the effect of a relatively low-priced item having a very high price ratio from only a small price rise.

6.9   Example

The price of peas and bread, and the amount consumed in both years is as follows:

Item	19X5 price	19X6 price	Units consumed (both years)
Peas	2p	3p	2
Bread	15p	16p	5

You are required to construct a price-relative index using:

(i)   quantity weights;

(ii)   value weights.

6.10   Solution

(a)   (i)

Item	19X5 p_0	19X6 p_1	q (same consumption pattern for both years)	Quantity weight only $W_A(= q)$	Value weight $W_B(= p_0 \times q)$
Peas	pence 2	pence 3	2	2	$2 \times 2 = 4$
Bread	15	16	5	5	$15 \times 5 = 75$
				7	79
				ΣW_A	ΣW_B

Item	$\dfrac{p_1}{p_0} \times 100$	$W_A \times \dfrac{p_1}{p_0} \times 100$	$W_B \times \dfrac{p_1}{p_0} \times 100$
Peas	150.0	300.0	600.0
Bread	106.7	533.5	8,002.5
		833.5	8,602.5
		$\Sigma W_A \times \dfrac{p_1}{p_0} \times 100$	$\Sigma W_B \times \dfrac{p_1}{p_0} \times 100$

Therefore, using quantity weights only, the index is:

$$\frac{\Sigma W_A \dfrac{p_1}{p_0} \times 100}{\Sigma W_A} = \frac{833.5}{7} = 119.1$$

(This would imply an average increase in prices of 19.1%.)

(ii)   using value weights, the index is

$$\frac{\Sigma W_B \dfrac{p_1}{p_0} \times 100}{\Sigma W_B} = \frac{8,602.5}{79} = 108.9$$

(This implies an average increase of 8.9%.)

6.11   Laspeyre and Paasche indices

These are sometimes referred to as aggregative indices.

An aggregative price index compares the total expenditure in one year (ie, at that year's prices) on a particular collection of goods with the total expenditure in the base year, at base year prices, on the same collection of goods.

By using the term **total expenditure**, this statement assumes that the weights used are the quantities purchased (students should note that this is not invariably the case, and quite often the weights used will bear no relationship to either numbers, weights or volumes purchased).

Given this assumption, a choice of weights arises between the quantity purchased in the **base year** and the quantity purchased in the **current year** for which the index is being prepared. Both choices are acceptable and both have their respective merits and demerits. The resultant indices are named after their 'inventors'.

The **Laspeyre** price index uses base year quantities, the Paasche uses current year quantities. The Paasche index, for instance, compares the cost of buying current year quantities at current year prices with buying them at base year prices.

6.12   Formulae

(a)   Laspeyre price index $= \dfrac{\Sigma(p_1 \times q_0)}{\Sigma(p_0 \times q_0)} \times 100$

(using base year quantities as weights)

(b)   Paasche price index $= \dfrac{\Sigma(p_1 \times q_1)}{\Sigma(p_0 \times q_1)} \times 100$

(using current year quantities as weights)

6.13   Example

The Laspeyre and Paasche price indices will be calculated for the following data, using 19X4 as base year:

	19X4		19X5	
Item	*Price* (p_0)	*Quantity* (q_0)	*Price* (p_1)	*Quantity* (q_1)
Milk	19p a pint	50,000 pints	26p a pint	70,000 pints
Bread	39p a loaf	30,000 loaves	40p a loaf	40,000 loaves
Soap	42p a pack	20,000 packs	64p a pack	25,000 packs
Sugar	60p a kilo	10,000 kilos	68p a kilo	8,000 kilos
Eggs	84p a box	3,000 boxes	72p a box	2,500 boxes

6.14   Solution

(a)   **Laspeyre index**

Item	*Weight* (q_0)	*Price* (p_0)	$p_0 \times q_0$ £	*Price* (p_1)	$p_1 \times q_0$ £
Milk	50,000	19p	9,500	26p	13,000
Bread	30,000	39p	11,700	40p	12,000
Soap	20,000	42p	8,400	64p	12,800
Sugar	10,000	60p	6,000	68p	6,800
Eggs	3,000	84p	2,520	72p	2,160
			38,120		46,760

$\Sigma p_1 q_0 = 46,760 =$ last year's buying pattern at today's prices.

$\Sigma p_0 q_0 = 38,120 =$ last year's buying pattern at last year's prices.

$\therefore$ Index $= \dfrac{\Sigma p_1 q_0}{\Sigma p_0 q_0} \times 100$

$= \dfrac{46,760}{38,120} \times 100$

$= 122.7$

The cost of buying 19X4 quantities at 19X5 prices shows an increase of 22.7% over 19X4 costs.

(b)   **Paasche index**

Item	Weight (q_1)	Price (p_0)	$p_0 \times q_1$ £	Price (p_1)	$p_1 \times q_1$ £
Milk	70,000	19p	13,300	26p	18,200
Bread	40,000	39p	15,600	40p	16,000
Soap	25,000	42p	10,500	64p	16,000
Sugar	8,000	60p	4,800	68p	5,440
Eggs	2,500	84p	2,100	72p	1,800
			46,300		57,440

$\sum p_0 q_1$ = 46,300 = today's buying pattern at last year's prices.

$\sum p_1 q_1$ = 57,440 = today's buying pattern at today's prices.

$$\therefore \text{Index} = \frac{57,440}{46,300} \times 100$$

$$= 124.1$$

The 19X5 index shows an increase of 24.1% over 19X4 prices when buying 19X5 quantities.

Note: in calculating either type of index, a common mistake made by students is to add all the prices and all the quantities and multiply the two totals, ie, $\sum p \times \sum q$ is calculated instead of $\sum (p \times q)$. To do so is quite wrong and will be severely penalised in the marking of the examination.

7   INDICES USED IN TREND ANALYSIS

7.1   Chain base index numbers

Definition   If a series of index numbers are required for different years, such that the rate of change of the variable from one year to the next can be studied, the chain base method is used. This means the each index number is calculated using the previous year as base. If the rate of change is **increasing** then the index numbers will be rising; if it is **constant**, the numbers will remain the same and if it is **decreasing** the numbers will be falling.

7.2   Example

A shopkeeper received the following amounts from the sale of radios:

```
19X1 ———— £1,000
19X2 ———— £1,100
19X3 ———— £1,210
19X4 ———— £1,331
19X5 ———— £1,464
```

Is it correct to say that the annual rate of increase in revenue from sales of radios is getting larger?

7.3   Solution

Year	Sales	Chain base index
19X1	£1,000	$\dfrac{1,100}{1,000} \times 100 = 110$
19X2	£1,100	$\dfrac{1,210}{1,100} \times 100 = 110$
19X3	£1,210	$\dfrac{1,331}{1,210} \times 100 = 110$
19X4	£1,331	$\dfrac{1,464}{1,331} \times 100 = 110$
19X5	£1,464	

Although the sales revenue from radios has increased each year, the chain base index numbers have remained static at 110. Therefore, the annual rate of increase of sales revenue from radios is remaining constant rather than increasing.

The chain base is also a suitable index to calculate if the weights ascribed to the various items in the index are changing rapidly. Over a period of years, this index would have modified itself to take account of these changes whereas in a fixed-base method after a number of years the whole index would have to be revised to allow for the changed weighting.

8   INTER-FIRM COMPARISONS - BENCHMARKING MEASURES

8.1   Introduction

An inter-firm comparison helps to put the company's resources and performance into perspective and reflects the fact that it is the relative position of a company which matters in assessing its capabilities. The performance of different organisations, subsidiaries or investment centres can be compared ('benchmarked') by calculating suitable financial ratios for each of them to ascertain which are better or worse than the average. Comparative analysis can also be usefully applied to any value activity which underpins the competitive strategy of an organisation, an industry or a nation.

To find out the level of investment in fixed assets of competitors, the business can use physical observation, information from trade press or trade association announcements, supplier press releases as well as their externally published financial statements, to build a clear picture of the relative scale, capacity, age and cost for each competitor. The method of operating these assets, in terms of hours and shift patterns, can be established by observation, discussions with suppliers and customers or by asking existing or ex-employees of the particular competitor. If the method of operating can be ascertained it should enable a combination of internal personnel management and industrial engineering managers to work out the likely relative differences in labour costs. The rates of pay and conditions can generally be found with reference to nationally negotiated agreements, local and national press advertising for employees, trade and employment associations and recruitment consultants. When this cost is used alongside an intelligent assessment of how many employees would be needed by the competitor in each area, given their equipment etc, a good idea of the labour costs can be obtained.

Another difference which should be noted is the nature of the competitors' costs as well as their relative levels. Where a competitor has a lower level of committed fixed costs eg, lower fixed labour costs due to a larger proportion of temporary workers, it may be able to respond more quickly to a downturn in demand by rapidly laying off the temporary staff. Equally, in a tight labour market and with rising sales, it may have to increase its pay levels to attract new workers.

In some industries, one part of the competitor analysis is surprisingly direct. Each new competitive product is purchased on a regular basis and then systematically taken apart, so that each component can be identified as well as the processes used to put the parts together. The respective areas of the business will then assess the costs associated with each element so that a complete product cost can be found for the competitive product.

A comparison of similar value activities eg, cost structures, between organisations is useful when the strategic context is taken into consideration. For example, a straight comparison of resource deployment between two competitive organisations may reveal quite different situations in the labour cost as a percentage of the total cost. The conclusions drawn from this, however, depend upon circumstances. If the firms are competing largely on the basis of price, then differentials in these costs could be crucial. In contrast, the additional use of labour by one organisation may be an essential support for the special services provided which differentiate that organisation from its competitors.

One danger of inter-firm analysis is that the company may overlook the fact that the whole industry is performing badly, and is losing out competitively to other countries with better resources or even other industries which can satisfy customers' needs in different ways. Therefore, if an industry comparison is performed it should make some assessment of how the resources utilisation compares with other countries and industries. This can be done by obtaining a measurement of stock turnover or yield from raw materials.

8.2   Example of R&D indices

A typical analysis of the R&D expenditure of UK companies could take the following approach. Comparisons could be made with previous years, between industry sectors and also with international competitors. Some examples of the data that might result are as follows:

(a)   **Change on previous year**

	% increase in spend
All industry	12
Aerospace	27
Chemicals	7
Food	2
Leisure	46
Service industries	5

(b)   **Inter-industry comparisons**

	R&D per employee (£000s)	R&D / Sales (%)
Aerospace	2.32	3.33
Chemicals	2.72	3.29
Food	1.01	1.22
Leisure	0.22	0.37
Service industries	2.59	2.65

(c)   **International comparisons of R&D per employee (£000s)**

	UK	USA	Germany
All industry	1.53	3.73	4.32
Aerospace	2.34	2.42	17.48
Chemicals	3.02	4.96	5.57
Leisure	0.21	4.85	n/a
Service industries	5.82	n/a	1.89

(d)   **International comparisons of R&D/Sales (%)**

	UK	USA	Germany	Japan
All industry	1.69	3.80	5.09	3.71
Aerospace	3.34	4.20	23.78	n/a
Chemicals	3.56	4.50	5.79	3.88
Leisure	0.36	6.80	n/a	3.62
Service industries	4.51	n/a	2.75	n/a

The evidence seems to be that UK firms are not doing enough to match the efforts of their main competitors in other countries.

8.3   Other indices - an example

The financial results for two divisions for the years 19X1 - 19X3 are given below.

	Division X (£'000)			Division Y (£'000)		
	19X1	*19X2*	*19X3*	*19X1*	*19X2*	*19X3*
Estimated industry sales	10,000	15,000	17,000	31,000	34,000	42,000
Division sales	1,100	1,700	3,350	3,300	3,500	3,600
Direct labour	165	240	430	730	720	790
Direct materials	110	160	320	370	480	510
Plant, equipment depreciation	50	68	97	6	6	7
Plant leases	22	41	54	-	-	13
Factory rent	-	-	-	20	20	20
Maintenance and repairs	35	38	52	115	130	142
Energy costs	50	79	112	70	80	81
Indirect production overheads	100	142	205	377	369	372
Research and development	63	67	89	15	10	12
Advertising, sales promotion	78	81	147	193	211	215
Other committed costs	178	231	349	699	714	620
Other managed costs	104	113	315	330	310	298
Head office allocated costs	110	340	840	330	350	360
Total costs	1,065	1,600	3,010	3,255	3,400	3,440
Net profit	35	100	340	45	100	160

	Division X (£'000)			Division Y (£'000)		
	19X1	*19X2*	*19X3*	*19X1*	*19X2*	*19X3*
Assets employed:						
Fixed (net book value)	500	700	900	50	45	47
Current	500	500	800	450	465	433
	1,000	1,200	1,700	500	510	480
Liabilities:						
Long-term loans	90	460	560	-	-	-
Current	35	70	170	50	60	80
	125	530	730	50	60	80
Return on net investment	4%	15%	35%	10%	22%	40%

You are required to compare the performance of the two divisions.

8.4   Solution

Net profit percentage

	X	Y
19X1	$\dfrac{145}{1,100} \times 100 = 13.2\%$	$\dfrac{375}{3,300} \times 100 = 11.4\%$

19X2	$\dfrac{440}{1,700} \times 100 = 25.9\%$	$\dfrac{450}{3,500} \times 100 = 12.9\%$
19X3	$\dfrac{1,180}{3,350} \times 100 = 35.2\%$	$\dfrac{520}{3,600} \times 100 = 14.4\%$

Both divisions have been showing increased profits, although the growth of X is considerably greater than that of Y.

Sales growth

	X	Y
19X1/X2	$\left(\dfrac{1,700}{1,100} - 1\right) \times 100 = 54.5\%$	$\left(\dfrac{3,500}{3,300} - 1\right) \times 100 = 6.1\%$
19X2/X3	$\left(\dfrac{3,350}{1,700} - 1\right) \times 100 = 97.1\%$	$\left(\dfrac{3,600}{3,500} - 1\right) \times 100 = 2.9\%$

Again X is seen to perform well with significant growth in its new area. When this is matched with the increasing net profit percentage the eight-fold increase in profit is explained. The increase in the profit percentage may, in part, be attributable to this growth as fixed costs are more easily recovered at higher sales levels. Y is still growing but the falling growth rate should be investigated to see if it is due to the end of several product cycles, a fall in the overall market or inefficiency.

Market shares

	X	Y
19X1	$\dfrac{1,100}{10,000} \times 100 = 11.0\%$	$\dfrac{3,300}{31,000} \times 100 = 10.6\%$
19X2	$\dfrac{1,700}{15,000} \times 100 = 11.3\%$	$\dfrac{3,500}{34,000} \times 100 = 10.3\%$
19X3	$\dfrac{3,350}{17,000} \times 100 = 19.7\%$	$\dfrac{3,600}{42,000} \times 100 = 8.6\%$

This shows that X's market share is growing; Y's share on the other hand is falling.

Other useful ratios that could be found would be:

- Asset turnover   -   to see if assets are being utilised efficiently.
- Gross profit percentage   -   to compare margins from year to year.

9   CHAPTER SUMMARY

This chapter has described the various performance measures that may be used in different industries and organisations.

10   SELF TEST QUESTIONS

10.1   List the performance measures which may be used in sales. (2.2)

10.2   Explain the performance measures which may be used in specific order environments. (2.6)

10.3   Identify the performance measures which may be used in process environments. (2.7)

10.4   Explain the use of performance measures in service environments. (3)

10.5   Explain the behavioural implications of using performance measures. (5)

11   EXAMINATION TYPE QUESTION

11.1   A polytechnic

A polytechnic offers a range of degree courses. The polytechnic organisation structure consists of three faculties each with a number of teaching departments. In addition, there is a polytechnic administrative/management function and a central services function.

The following cost information is available for the year ended 30 June 19X7:

(i)   **Occupancy costs**

Total £1,500,000. Such costs are apportioned on the basis of area used which is:

	Square feet
Faculties	7,500
Teaching departments	20,000
Administration/management	7,000
Central services	3,000

(ii)   **Administration/management costs**

Direct costs: £1,775,000

Indirect costs: an apportionment of occupancy costs.

Direct and indirect costs are charged to degree courses on a percentage basis.

(iii)   **Faculty costs**

Direct costs: £700,000.

Indirect costs: an apportionment of occupancy costs and central service costs.

Direct and indirect costs are charged to teaching departments.

(iv)   **Teaching departments**

Direct costs: £5,525,000.

Indirect costs: an apportionment of occupancy costs and central service costs plus all faculty costs.

Direct and indirect costs are charged to degree courses on a percentage basis.

(v)   **Central services**

Direct costs: £1,000,000.

Indirect costs: an apportionment of occupancy costs.

Direct and indirect costs of central services have in previous years been charged to users on a percentage basis. A study has now been completed which has estimated what user areas would have paid external suppliers for the same services on an individual basis. For the year ended 30 June 19X7, the apportionment of the central services cost is to be recalculated in a manner which recognises the cost savings achieved by using the central services facilities instead of using external service companies. This is to be done by apportioning the overall savings to user areas in proportion to their share of the estimated external costs.

The estimated external costs of service provision are as follows:

	£'000
Faculties	240
Teaching departments	800
Degree courses:	
Business studies	32
Mechanical engineering	48
Catering studies	32
All other degrees	448
	1,600

(vi)   Additional data relating to the degree courses is as follows:

	Degree course		
	Business Studies	*Mechanical Engineering*	*Catering Studies*
Number of graduates	80	50	120
Apportioned costs (as % of totals)			
Teaching departments	3%	2.5%	7%
Administration/management	2.5%	5%	4%

Central services are to be apportioned as detailed in (v) above.

The total number of graduates from the polytechnic in the year to 30 June 19X7 was 2,500.

You are required:

(a)   to prepare a flow diagram which shows the apportionment of costs to user areas. No values need be shown;   **(3 marks)**

(b)   to calculate the average cost per graduate, for the year ended 30 June 19X7, for the polytechnic and for each of the degrees in business studies, mechanical engineering and catering studies, showing all relevant cost analysis;   **(14 marks)**

(c)   to suggest reasons for any differences in the average cost per graduate from one degree to another, and discuss briefly the relevance of such information to the polytechnic management.   **(5 marks)**

(Total: 22 marks)

(ACCA June 88)

12   ANSWER TO EXAMINATION TYPE QUESTION

12.1   A polytechnic

(Tutorial notes: the flow diagram is not difficult, but the time allowance for 3 marks does present problems. However, time spent on ensuring that a correct picture of the cost apportionments is depicted will not only gain these marks but help a great deal in answering part (b).

Part (b) is basically an arithmetic exercise. Good use of the flow diagram will help in breaking this down into a series of apportionments. The model answer uses a 'step' approach. Students should adopt this approach; any attempt to apportion all the costs in a single table is likely to fail.

There is no one answer for part (c). Use your common sense and make brief general statements.*)

(a)

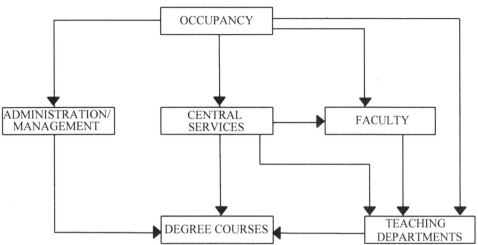

(b)   **Step 1**

Apportion occupancy costs: $\left(\dfrac{£1,500,000}{37,500 \text{ sq ft}} = £40 \text{ per sq ft} \right)$

	£'000
Administration/Management	280
Central Services	120
Faculty	300
Teaching Departments	800
	1,500

Step 2

Apportion central services costs:

$\left(\dfrac{£1,000,000 + £120,000}{\text{External Costs } £1,600,000} \right) = 70\text{p per £ of external cost}$

	£'000
Faculty	168
Teaching Departments	560
Degree Courses	392
	1,120

Step 3

Apportion teaching department costs (includes 100% of Faculty costs) and Administration/Management costs, to degree courses.

Teaching department: £800,000 + £560,000 + (£300,000 + £168,000 + £700,000) + £5,525,000 = £8,053,000

Administration/management: £280,000 + £1,775,000 = £2,055,000.

Total degree courses costs: £8,053,000 + £2,055,000 + £392,000 = £10,500,000.

Average polytechnic cost per student $= \dfrac{£10,500,000}{2,500 \text{ students}} = £4,200$

Step 4

Analyse £10,500,000 by degree course (in round £'000s).

	Business Studies £'000	Mechanical Engineering £'000	Catering Studies £'000
Teaching department	242	201	564
Administration/management	51	103	82
Central services (based on external costs)	22	34	22
	315	338	668
Average cost per graduate	£3,938	£6,760	£5,567

(c)   The average cost per graduate will differ from one degree course to another for several reasons, the most obvious of which is the very different nature of the courses.

The engineering and catering courses will require much greater use of expensive machinery and equipment, which in turn will need more room. In addition these courses will probably require much greater lecturer input than on the business studies courses. The much lower staff/student ratio will push up the teaching costs per student.

Another factor to be considered is the variability in the student numbers. This variable is unlikely to have an impact on many of the polytechnic costs, which are mainly fixed in nature. For example, if in the following year intake is up to sixty on the mechanical engineering degree, with a similar level of costs, the average cost per student would fall to nearly that being reported for a catering studies student.

These average cost figures must be interpreted with great care by the management. They give a 'rough' guide to the relative cost of degree courses but the arbitrary apportionments render them very nearly useless for decision-making. For decision-making, incremental costs are required.

25 TRANSFER PRICING: INTRODUCTION

INTRODUCTION & LEARNING OBJECTIVES

When you have studied this chapter you should be able to do the following:

- Explain the need for transfer pricing in a divisionalised organisation structure.
- Discuss the problems of setting an appropriate transfer pricing policy.

1 CREATING CENTRES AND DIVISIONS - DECENTRALISATION

1.1 Introduction

In order to approach the difficulties of managing a large organisation a structure based on several autonomous decision-making units is often created. 'Decentralisation' as this is called could be defined as:

> delegating authority to make decisions;

> or

> devolving responsibility for profit.

The second of these two definitions might be called divisionalisation rather than decentralisation, but the distinction is a fine one. Decentralisation can result in the creation of various types of unit for which definitions are set out below.

(a) **Cost centre**

> *Definition* A cost centre is a production or service location, function, activity or item of equipment whose costs may be attributed to cost units.

The manager of a segment of a business that is termed a cost centre has responsibility for certain costs and his performance and that of the business segment will be assessed by the extent to which those costs have been controlled. Typical cost centres might be the various central service departments such as maintenance, research and development or personnel; but the status of these departments can be changed using a transfer pricing policy.

(b) **Revenue centre**

> *Definition* A centre devoted to raising revenue with no responsibility for production eg, a sales centre. Often used in a not-for-profit organisation.

(c) **Profit centre**

> *Definition* A part of a business accountable for costs and revenues. It may be called a business centre, business unit or strategic business unit.

(d) **Investment centre**

> *Definition* A profit centre whose performance is measured by its return on capital employed.

When talking about a divisionalised or decentralised structure one thinks in terms of an organisation that has been split into investment centres. However, the degree of responsibility for and control over costs, revenues and investments may vary and therefore the validity of certain performance assessment measures may also vary.

1.2   Reasons for decentralising

The benefits of and reasons for decentralising are discussed further below.

Size - the process of decentralisation breaks an organisation up into more manageable units, this enables decision-making to proceed quickly and effectively and, in theory, a closer control to be maintained on the day to day running of a business's activities.

Need for specialists - as a business grows the nature of its activities often becomes more complex so that the entrepreneur/chief executive has to rely on experts to run particular segments of the business.

Motivation - if managers are made to feel responsible for a particular part of a business then it is generally found that their efforts within that part of the business are improved and, as a consequence the business prospers. Some form of incentive may be needed to reinforce this philosophy which has many advocates amongst 'behaviourists' of management accounting.

Uncertainty - with ever-changing market conditions, decisions cannot be pre-planned or centrally planned. It is important to have local managers who are closer in touch with each particular part of the business environment to be in a position to respond quickly as problems arise.

Geographical - decentralisation often refers to the delegation of responsibilities at a single location, an office or a factory; however, it is important for a business to get close to markets and to sources of supply and to have a responsible manager in those far-flung locations.

Fiscal - the chapter on transfer pricing stressed the efforts made by governments to prevent companies taking advantage of local favourable tax regimes. Nevertheless, this still remains a reason for decentralisation and even within the UK there are tax incentives for operating in areas such as Belfast, Scunthorpe or parts of Lanarkshire designated as Enterprise Zones.

Training - it is claimed that a divisional structure can provide a training ground for future members of top management enabling budding chief executives to acquire the required business skills in an environment that provides a stern, but not impossible, test. These managers are given a sense of independence which should allow them to flourish.

Releasing top management - in order to survive and expand time has to be found and efforts made by top management for strategic planning. Delegation of responsibility for mundane matters makes such time available and efforts possible.

1.3   Problems of decentralisation

Whilst it is generally agreed that some degree of decentralisation is essential for the efficient running of a large business there are some inherent difficulties.

Lack of goal congruence - having set up a number of autonomous divisions run by managers all keen to show themselves as potential main board members, the danger arises that divisional managers will make decisions which, whilst in the best interests of their divisions, are not in the best interest of the company as a whole. This lack of 'goal congruence' leads to 'sub-optimal' or 'dysfunctional' decisions which, in part, is a result of the inevitable interdependence of divisions. It is often suggested that a necessary condition for successful decentralisation is for:

- the business to have very separate activities;
- divisions to be independent of each other; and

- central management to be able to control divisions to avoid the problems of lack of goal congruence.

However, it is unlikely that these conditions will ever apply since a decentralised structure will either have arisen as a result of splitting up a business that formerly acted as one unit or else by a company taking over businesses with whom it traded.

Cost - the benefits of a large centralised structure result from the possibility of achieving economies of scale. One centralised buying department can achieve more favourable terms and requires fewer staff than if each division has its own buying function. Many examples such as this can be identified indicating that a decentralised organisation may be more costly to operate than a centralised one. Large companies overcome these problems by setting up centralised services, such as accounts departments, but there are problems of controllability and acceptability of these centralised services. One particular example of a cost of decentralisation that has been identified is a loss of 'managerial talent' who might be able to run a division without extending themselves to their full potential.

There is one company asset that is often put under central control whatever the incentive for decentralisation, and that is cash. Efficient cash management can be achieved much more effectively if all cash balances are centrally controlled. If 'head office' has one single bank account with a nil balance the company will incur no interest charges; but if one division has a balance of £50,000 in hand in one bank and another division has an overdraft of £50,000 in a different bank then there will be a net interest cost.

Loss of central control - with decentralisation top management loses some element of control to managers of independent, autonomous divisions. An effective system of divisional reporting should overcome this problem, but there is always likely to be some decisions made that main board directors feel are inappropriate. An additional problem is the attitudes of senior management and particularly chief executives who set up decentralised structures but then are unwilling to let loose the reins, still wishing to have complete day to day control of all aspects of the business.

Need for divisional reporting - whilst an efficient information system is important in any organisation, it is even more important in decentralised firms. In order for effective control of divisions a suitable reporting system producing the key figures that top management need must be installed, understood and operated conscientiously. The information is needed to help in decisions over divisions and to monitor divisional performance and motivate the staff.

2   BACKGROUND TO TRANSFER PRICING

2.1   Past exam questions

The principles to be applied when setting a transfer pricing policy were examined in discursive questions in December 1994 and December 1995. It is essential that you understand why such a policy is needed, the methods of arriving at an appropriate transfer price for a given set of circumstances, and the problems that can arise with inappropriate prices. These are all covered in this chapter, with numerical examples that are computationally straightforward, but are important illustrations of the principles involved.

Chapter 26 examines the more involved numerical approaches in a more theoretical context.

As well as being the subject of Section B discursive questions, transfer pricing may also be examined as part of a scenario question in Section A.

2.2   The need for a transfer pricing policy

One condition for successful decentralisation is that the various divisions should be more or less independent of each other. However, in practice, this is unlikely to be the case and a certain amount of inter-divisional trading will take place. A transfer pricing policy is needed if goods or services are passed between divisions.

It might appear that the credit to the supplying division is merely offset by an equal debit to the receiving division and that therefore, as far as the whole organisation is concerned, it has a net zero effect. This is true in terms of the physical application of a transfer pricing system once it has been decided upon and implemented. However, there are important behavioural and organisational elements associated with transfer pricing and the choice of which method to adopt. The transfer price does affect the profit of each division separately and, therefore, can affect the level of motivation of each divisional manager.

2.3   Criteria for judging a transfer pricing policy

Adopting a transfer pricing policy will result in:

- total corporate profit to be divided up between divisional profit centres, it may result in a cost centre being converted into a profit centre (eg, if centralised services charge other divisions for the work that they do);

- information becoming available for divisional decision-making (particularly over whether or not to accept an internal transfer and the level of activity required);

- information being made available to help assess the performance of divisions and divisional managers (for instance allowing the performance of former cost centres to be compared with outside, specialist, profit-making firms in the same field).

The rules for the operation of a transfer pricing policy are the same as for any policy in a decentralised organisation. A system should be reasonably easy to operate and understand as well as being flexible in terms of a changing organisational structure. In addition, there are four specific criteria which a good transfer pricing policy should meet:

- it should provide **motivation** for divisional managers;

- it should allow divisional **autonomy** and **independence** to be maintained;

- it should allow divisional performance to be **assessed objectively**;

- it should ensure that divisional managers make **decisions** that are **in the best interests** of the divisions and also of the company as a whole.

This final feature is usually referred to as **goal congruence** and is perhaps the most important of the four.

2.4   Divisional autonomy

[*Definition*]   Divisional autonomy is the term used to describe the power given to divisional managers to implement decisions for the benefit of their division.

2.5   Divisional performance measurement

In a divisionalised structure with inter-divisional trading, the use of transfer prices means that the division will be treated as either a profit centre or an investment centre.

The evaluation of a profit centre is achieved by comparing actual and target levels of profit, whereas in an investment centre performance is measured relative to the level of investment using either Return on Capital Employed (ROCE) or Residual Income (RI).

2.6   Goal congruence

This is the term used to describe the achievement of common goals. In the context of divisionalised structures goal congruence exists when the maximisation of divisional profits causes corporate profits to be maximised.

2.7   Transfer pricing policies

Ideally the transfer pricing policy used would encourage divisional autonomy, allow divisional performance to be measured fairly and would lead to goal congruence. In reality, however this is often unlikely to be achieved with conflict arising between these objectives.

If divisional autonomy is maintained it is likely that some decisions will be sub-optimal to the company as a whole. If corporate profit maximisation is achieved, this may only be possible by making some decisions centrally thus reducing divisional autonomy and invalidating divisional performance measurement.

3   SETTING TRANSFER PRICES

3.1   Introduction to different methods

There are three main types of transfer price:

- cost-based prices
- market-based prices
- negotiated prices.

The first of these uses a cost-plus approach to transfer pricing, the second uses intermediate market price and the third could be regarded as a particular form of bargaining. Each method will be discussed in turn. However, there are several variations on these that are of greater or lesser importance:

- **Using marginal cost and marginal revenue data** - much loved by academics and often tested in exams but rarely used in practice due to the lack of information;

- **Using dual prices** - the use of two prices to encourage or discourage a transfer, possibly by ensuring that each division makes a satisfactory profit from a desirable transfer (it can overcome some of the problems that may arise from the previous - MC & MR - method).

- **Incorporating opportunity costs** - this method, discussed briefly later, may simply provide support for cost-based or market-based methods under the relevant circumstances; however the term could also encompass the use of output from linear programming formulations to help arrive at transfer prices when divisions have limited production capacity.

3.2   Using opportunity costs

The general rule is that the transfer price should be equal to the opportunity cost of both the buyer and the seller.

Consequently both buyer and seller will be indifferent between trading internally or externally. Thus both should trade internally and this will maximise the use of organisational resources.

4   SIMPLE MARKET BASED METHODS

4.1   Introduction

Where the product (or service) that is subject to internal transfer could be sold to other outside organisations by the supplying division and, similarly, where the product could be purchased from other outside organisations by the receiving division, a competitive market exists and a market price will have been established under normal supply and demand conditions. Such a market price would be a very suitable basis on which to make inter-divisional transfers; it would be easy to operate provided the source of the market price was clearly stated.

It would allow each division to remain autonomous, so that the profit of the division would not be affected by any decision to buy/sell externally or to trade internally. The resultant profits would be determined in an objective way. In most situations the use of a market price as a transfer price will not lead to any divergence between divisional and company goals. However, there is a particular problem when there is spare capacity; this is dealt with in the next section.

Market prices are sometimes adjusted downwards for use as transfer prices, to recognise the benefits or savings from internal trading. Such a reduction might relate to:

- lower packaging and advertising costs for goods sold internally in comparison with outside sales;

- the benefits derived from purchases and sales in large volumes (where bulk discounts might be expected);

- the advantages of having an exclusive supplies contract.

An adjusted market price should encourage internal trading because it should lead to higher divisional profits than buying or selling in the open market.

4.2   Problems with market-based transfer prices

Before adopting a market-based transfer pricing policy, the inherent dangers must be recognised and, where possible, steps taken to overcome these problems.

- There may be **no intermediate market price**. The product or service might not be readily available on the open market (an example might be a partly completed car being transferred from one division to another).

- The market price might **not** be **independent**. This would occur if the transferring division was in the position of a monopolist both within the company and in the outside market.

- Difficulty in agreeing a **source of market prices**. Debates will occur over the size, quality, timing and location of internal transfers compared with a range of published prices.

- The need to adjust prices for **different volumes**. Prices quoted may well not relate to the levels of transfers that are likely to take place; in the same way, the extent of reductions due to saved selling costs will be difficult to estimate.

- Published **prices may be fictitious**. This is a variation on the previous problem but is typified by those products for which it is customary for a seller to publish a price then the buyer to negotiate a lower figure.

In a situation where there is spare capacity in the supplying division, the use of a market-based transfer price will not ensure that the divisional managers will be motivated individually to take independent action which is in the best interests of the whole company. This is because the manager of a receiving division may see his divisional profits fall as a result of a move to utilise spare capacity, even though it would benefit the overall profits of the company. A comprehensive example follows to illustrate this situation, and it will be referred to again in a later section.

4.3   Example

Kwaree Ltd, producing a range of minerals, is organised into two trading groups – one group handles wholesale business and the other deals with sales to retailers.

One of its products is a moulding clay. The wholesale group extracts the clay and sells it to external wholesale customers as well as to the retail group. The production capacity is 2,000 tonnes per month, but at present sales are limited to 1,000 tonnes wholesale and 600 tonnes retail.

The transfer price agreed is £180 per tonne, in line with the existing external wholesale trade price.

The retail group produces 100 bags of refined clay from each tonne of moulding clay which it sells at £4 per bag. It would sell a further 40,000 bags if the retail trade price were reduced to £3.20 per bag.

Other data relevant to the operation are:

	Wholesale group	Retail group
Variable cost per tonne	£70	£60
Fixed cost per month	£100,000	£40,000

You are required to prepare estimated profit statements for the current month for each group and for Kwaree Ltd as a whole when producing at:

(a)   80% capacity; and

(b)   100% capacity, utilising the extra sales to supply the retail trade.

4.4   Solution

(a)   **Wholesale group at 80% capacity**

Estimated profit statement for the current month

Transfer price: £180 per tonne

Wholesale group operating at 80% capacity.

	Wholesale group £'000	Retail group £'000	Kwaree Ltd £'000
Sales outside the company:			
1,000 tonnes @ £180/tonne	180		180
60,000 bags @ £4/bag		240	240
Internal transfer of 600 tonnes	108	(108)	Nil
Less: Costs:			
Variable:			
1,600 tonnes @ £70/tonne	(112)		(112)
600 tonnes @ £60/tonne		(36)	(36)
Fixed	(100)	(40)	(140)
Profit	76	56	132

(b)   **Wholesale group at 100% capacity**

Estimated profit statement for the current month

Transfer price: £180 per tonne

Wholesale group operating at 100% capacity.

	Wholesale group £'000	Retail group £'000	Kwaree Ltd £'000
Sales outside the company:			
1,000 tonnes @ £180/tonne	180		180
100,000 bags @ £3.20/bag		320	320
Internal transfer of 1,000 tonnes	180	(180)	Nil
Less: Costs:			
Variable:			
2,000 tonnes @ £70/tonne	(140)		(140)
1,000 tonnes @ £60/tonne		(60)	(60)
Fixed	(100)	(40)	(140)
Profit	120	40	160

If it is assumed that the group (divisional) managers of Kwaree Ltd are being measured in terms of the profitability of their divisions, then the effect on divisional profits of utilising the spare capacity in the wholesale group can be summarised as follows:

	Profits in Wholesale group £'000	Profits in Retail group £'000	Profits in Kwaree Ltd £'000
80% capacity	76	56	132
100% capacity	120	40	160
Increase/(decrease)	44	(16)	28

As a result of utilising spare capacity the profits of Kwaree would increase by £28,000. However, the wholesale group profits would increase by £44,000, whereas the manager of the retail group would see his division's profits fall by £16,000.

This fall is caused by the reduction in the selling price per bag of the moulding clay, affecting all the sales of the retail group and not only the additional sales. The manager of the retail group, acting independently, is unlikely to accept a decision to increase his production and sales if, as a result, the profit on which he is assessed is likely to decline. The action which he sees to be most beneficial for the retail group, for which he is responsible, is not the action which is in the best interests of the whole company. This is an example of sub-optimisation. Ideally the transfer price should be such that the profits of wholesale and retail groups and the company would all increase as a result of moving from the 80% to 100% capacity. Transfer price bases which would give rise to this situation are identified in the next section.

Where the goods produced by the supplying division are only transferred internally to the receiving division, so that there is no existing market price, it may be possible to establish the identity of a substitute product which is freely available and does have a market price which could be used as the basis for the transfer price. The problems are associated with determining whether the other product is a valid substitute and, if so, what is the appropriate market price.

4.5   Optimal transfer price - net marginal revenue

A transfer price must be adopted which will encourage the higher level of transfer to take place - since Kwaree Ltd then makes an additional £28,000 profit. At the moment it will not occur since the Retail Group can see its profits fall. The only way to encourage the Retail Group to increase its purchases from the Wholesale Group is to reduce the transfer price. Marginal cost and marginal revenue considerations will be used (strictly incremental costs and revenues).

As a result of increasing output:

	£'000
Retail Group's revenue increases by (320 – 240)	80
Retail Group's own variable costs rise by (60 – 36)	24
'Net marginal revenue' (£'000)	56

This must be compared with the cost which the Wholesale Group charges for these extra 400 tonnes. This cost is currently (400 × £180) = £72,000; hence the fall in Retail profit by £16,000.

The transfer cost of these 400 tonnes must fall to no more than £56,000 or (£56,000 ÷ 400) **£140 per tonne**.

Note: it is not sufficient to simply determine a new transfer price at which the retail group's profit at full capacity is higher than that at 80% **under the old transfer price**. Once a price is set, the manager of the retail group will pick the operating level that gives him **maximum** profit. Thus the new transfer price must ensure that the profits operating at 100% capacity exceed those when operating at 80% capacity **both under the new transfer price**.

If the Wholesale Group is considered the transfer price must be at least £70 per tonne (its own variable production cost per tonne). Although this range of £70 - £140 per tonne has been calculated by reference to the incremental sales (of 400 tonnes) the transfer price will apply to all transfers. As a consequence some care must be taken over where in the range (£70 - £140) the final price is set, since the two Groups must make enough contribution to cover their fixed costs. A transfer price at the top end of the range will prove more equitable, such as **£135 per tonne**.

4.6   Demonstration of goal congruence

If a transfer price of £135 per tonne is adopted both divisions will see their profits increased by increasing output, and this is in the best interests of the company as a whole. **Goal congruence** is achieved. The two profit statements, at 80% and 100% capacity, with a transfer price of £135 are shown below.

(a)   **80% capacity, transfer price £135**

	Wholesale group £'000	Retail group £'000	Kwaree Ltd £'000
Outside sales			
1,000 @ £180	180	-	180
60,000 @ £4	-	240	240
Internal transfer			
600 @ £135	81	(81)	-
Variable costs			
1,600 @ £70	(112)		(112)
600 @ £60		(36)	(36)
Fixed costs	(100)	(40)	(140)
Profit (£'000)	49	83	132

(b)   **100% capacity, transfer price £135**

	Wholesale group £'000	Retail group £'000	Kwaree Ltd £'000
Outside sales			
1,000 @ £180	180	-	180
100,000 @ £3.20	-	320	320
Internal transfer			
1,000 @ £135	135	(135)	-
Variable costs			
2,000 @ £70	(140)	-	(140)
1,000 @ £60	-	(60)	(60)
Fixed costs	(100)	(40)	(140)
Profit (£'000)	75	85	160

(c)   **Benefits from increasing output**

	Wholesale group £'000	Retail group £'000	Kwaree Ltd £'000
	26	2	28

Whilst noting the fact that this new transfer price 'works', a few points are worth making.

- If this problem was observed by top management and the transfer pricing policy changed as a result, the manager of the wholesale division would need to be reassured that his performance would be compared with earlier periods under the revised transfer price and he would not be penalised for the reduced profit that came from the change.

- The Wholesale Group can see two markets, external and internal, in which different prices prevail. The reason why the two prices are permitted is because wholesale sales cannot be increased at present. The manager of the Wholesale Group would wish to make initial sales outside then transfer the balance internally; however this makes no difference to overall sales and profit.

5   CHAPTER SUMMARY

This chapter has explained why organisations decentralise their activities into divisions, and has explained the principles of divisional management and performance appraisal in a transfer pricing environment.

6   SELF TEST QUESTIONS

6.1   For what reasons might an organisation decentralise? (1.1, 1.2)

6.2   If a firm uses a market-based transfer price, what justification would it have in reducing the price below market price? (4.1)

6.3   What are the problems of using market-based transfer prices? (4.2)

26 TRANSFER PRICING: FURTHER PRINCIPLES

INTRODUCTION & LEARNING OBJECTIVES

This chapter builds on the principles of transfer pricing explained in the previous chapter and illustrates different transfer pricing methods.

When you have studied this chapter you should be able to do the following:

- Explain when it is appropriate to use cost based transfer prices.
- Explain the use of opportunity costs in transfer pricing.

1 MARGINAL ANALYSIS

1.1 Introduction

As with pricing decisions for external sales, so for transfer pricing optimal policies can be reached using marginal cost and marginal revenue considerations. The prime objective is to maximise the profit of the company as a whole, therefore corporate marginal cost must equal corporate marginal revenue. The second objective is to achieve goal congruence, therefore the levels of activity and selling prices that achieve maximum corporate profit must also achieve maximum profit levels for each division. This maximisation of divisional profit is determined by, or usually determines, the transfer price - as seen in the earlier example Kwaree Ltd.

Throughout these calculations, which have their roots in simple micro-economics (or elementary calculus) it is important to look at problems practically - from the point of view of each of the divisional managers in turn. Remember that the transfer price represents additional costs to the buying division and additional revenue to the selling division. The precise approach depends upon the nature of the outside intermediate market for the product or service being transferred. Problems will be considered where there is:

- no intermediate market;
- a perfect intermediate market;
- an imperfect intermediate market.

The approach also depends upon the way in which information is presented. Questions in exams have been seen that require a tabular approach or an algebraic approach. In each case describing a problem graphically may help with the solution.

1.2 No intermediate market

Mention has already been made of the fact that market-based approaches to transfer pricing will not be possible if, for one reason or another, no intermediate market for the item being transferred exists. Care must still be taken in choosing an appropriate transfer price in order to achieve goal congruence. Essentially the approach to finding a suitable transfer price is to:

- find the level of activity at which the company's profit is maximised;
- pick a transfer price that ensures that each division's profit is maximised at that level.

Example

Pollock Ltd manufactures a machine in its Bedford factory, the engines for which are made in a separate factory at Alicedale. Because of the specialised nature of the equipment, there is no outside market for the engines. Set out below are figures for costs and revenues for a range of activity levels for the two factories.

Annual production	Total cost in Alicedale £'000	Total cost in Bedford £'000	Total revenue £'000
1,000	150	250	500
2,000	180	260	900
3,000	240	280	1,200
4,000	330	310	1,400
5,000	450	350	1,500

You are required to determine a suitable range for the transfer price. (Bedford's total cost figures exclude any transfer price from Alicedale.)

Solution

The level of activity that maximises the overall company profit can be seen by simply tabulating total costs and total revenue; alternatively by looking at the company's marginal costs and marginal revenues (once again 'incremental' would be more appropriate than 'marginal').

Annual production	Total cost £'000	Total revenue £'000	Profit £'000	Marginal cost (MC_C) £'000	Marginal Revenue (MR) £'000
1,000	400	500	100	400	500
2,000	440	900	460	40	400
3,000	520	1,200	680	80	300
4,000	640	1,400	760	120	200
5,000	800	1,500	700	160	100

The table shows that profit is maximised at an annual production level of 4,000 units. The final two columns show that as output increases up to 4,000 units marginal revenue always exceeds marginal cost. However, once a level of 4,000 units is reached, there is no point increasing output to 5,000 units since the additional costs (£160,000) exceed the additional revenue (£100,000). (With these discrete activity levels a point may not be reached where marginal cost and marginal revenue are equal, nor should attempts be made to interpolate such a point.) Although the optimal activity level has been found (4,000 units), it is not yet clear what transfer price will encourage each division to produce, transfer, accept and sell this quantity.

The optimal transfer price can be found by modifying the final two columns of the table above showing marginal costs and marginal revenues.

Annual production	Company's marginal cost (MC_C) £'000	Company's marginal revenue (MR) £'000	Alicedale's marginal cost (MC_A) £'000	Bedford's marginal cost (MC_B) £'000	Bedford's net marginal Revenue (NMR_B) £'000
1,000	400	500	150	250	250
2,000	40	400	30	10	390
3,000	80	300	60	20	280
4,000	120	200	90	30	170
5,000	160	100	120	40	60

This second table shows separate marginal (or incremental) costs for Alicedale and Bedford. The final column shows Bedford's net marginal revenue; this has been calculated as Bedford's (the company's) marginal revenue minus Bedford's marginal costs. The optimal activity level can be found by spotting the final point that Bedford's net marginal revenue exceeds Alicedale's marginal cost (once again it is at 4,000 units).

To find the transfer price that encourages both factories to adopt this level of activity remember the significance of the transfer price.

Transfer price   =   Alicedale's income ie, Alicedale's marginal revenue
Transfer price   =   Bedford's additional costs ie, Bedford's additional marginal cost

When this is linked to the idea that profit is maximised when marginal cost and marginal revenue are equal the result is reached that, for goal congruence:

Transfer price   =   Alicedale's marginal cost at 4,000 units

Transfer price   =   Bedford's net marginal revenue at 4,000 units

In the case of these discrete cost and revenue figures the transfer price must be sufficiently high to encourage Alicedale to produce up to 4,000 units (> £90,000 per 1,000 units) but not so high that the factory considers producing more than 4,000 (< £120,000). At the same time it must be sufficiently low to encourage Bedford to accept up to 4,000 units (< £170,000 per 1,000 units) but not so low that Bedford would wish to accept more than 4,000 (> £60,000). Looking at all four of these, the range of transfer prices that would encourage both divisions to adopt the output level that maximises total corporate profit, 4,000 units, is given by:

$$£90 \quad < \quad \frac{\text{transfer price}}{\text{per engine}} \quad < \quad £120$$

Precisely where the transfer price is set in this range depends upon how total corporate profit is to be divided between the two factories.

| Conclusion | If division A transfers an item to division B for which there is no intermediate market, the optimal activity level for the company as a whole, Q*, is found by:

either equating MC_C = MR

or equating MC_A = NMR_B
(where $MC_A + MC_B = MC_C$ and $MR - MC_B = NMR_B$)

The optimal transfer price is equal to MC_A at Q* and also equal to NMR_B at Q*.

The fact that in this case both divisions' profits are maximised at 4,000 units by a transfer price in the range £90 to £120 per unit can be seen by tabulating Alicedale's and Bedford's profits given a transfer price, say of £100.

Annual Production	Alicedale's cost £'000	Transfer price £'000	Bedford's net revenue £'000	Alicedale's profit £'000	Bedford's profit £'000
1,000	150	100	250	(50)	150
2,000	180	200	640	20	440
3,000	240	300	920	60	620
4,000	330	400	1,090	70	690
5,000	450	500	1,150	50	650

1.3   Perfect intermediate market

If the first situation was described with data in tabular form, this type of problem might be illustrated graphically with a comparison made with the previous problem. The optimal activity level was found where the companies' marginal cost and marginal revenue were equal, where:

$$MC_C = MC_A + MC_B = MR$$

This was seen in the previous table to correspond to the point where A's marginal cost and B's net marginal revenue were equal. This can be seen by rearranging the above equation (taking MC_B to the other side and changing the sign) to be where:

$$MC_A = MR - MC_B = NMR_B$$

These two could be shown graphically with the sort of increasing marginal cost functions and decreasing marginal revenue functions seen for Pollock Ltd.

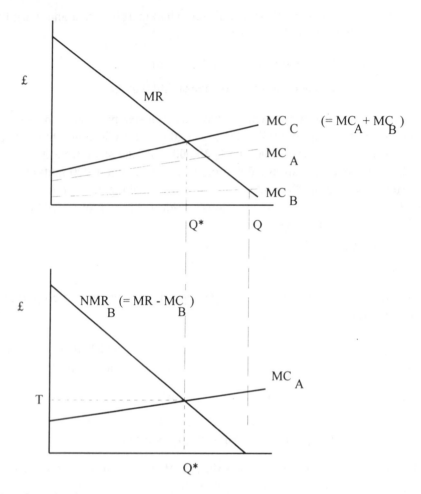

The transfer price is shown in the second graph.

It is this second graph that is used when a perfect intermediate market exists. If the item being transferred, say Pollock's engines - from Alicedale to Bedford, can be bought and sold easily outside the company at some fixed prevailing market price, then the intermediate market price must be used as the transfer price. If Pollock's engines could be bought or sold outside the company for, say, £160, the transfers between the two factories would not take place if anything else was used as the transfer price. If a price higher than £160 was quoted, the buying division (Bedford) would prefer to buy from outside; if a price lower than £160 was quoted, the selling division (Alicedale) would prefer to sell outside. The effect on activity levels is shown by the following graph.

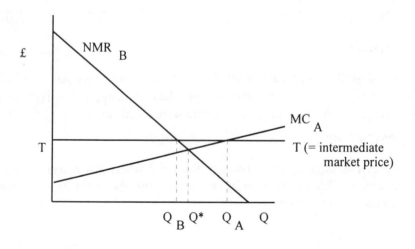

Once again each division's profit is maximised when marginal cost and marginal revenue are equal. The transfer price acts as marginal revenue to A and additional marginal cost to B.

Division A will produce a quantity Q_A

Division B will accept and produce a quantity Q_B

The extra production from A that is not transferred to B can be sold outside at the prevailing market price for the intermediate product. These activity levels could be derived by tabulation, as seen in the previous example, or algebraically, which is the method that will be used for the final example of this type.

1.4   Imperfect intermediate market

If the previous cost and revenue functions shown graphically could also be expressed as formulae, then optimal activity levels could be found algebraically; and it is an algebraic approach that will be adopted here. Now a product, such as Pollock's engines, can be transferred within the company or sold outside. The important difference now is the nature of the intermediate market; Alicedale can sell its engines outside at a price over which it has some control. The problem can be described diagrammatically.

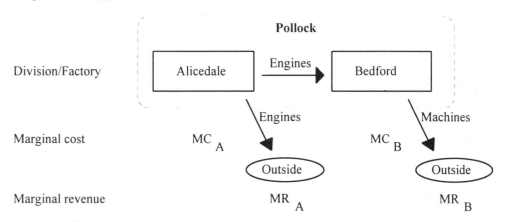

The decisions required are:

- how much should Alicedale produce;
- how much should Alicedale sell outside;
- how much should Alicedale transfer and Bedford accept;
- what should the transfer price be;
- what should the selling price be?

The problem is analogous to price discrimination; what should A produce and what should be sold in the two markets (intermediate and, via B, final).

The method of solution is the same; if sales of engines by A in the intermediate market are denoted by a and sales of machines in the final market by B (which require engines in them) are b, then total production of engines must be a + b.

The company's profit is maximised, as usual, when marginal cost and marginal revenue are equal. More specifically in this case when the marginal cost of making (a + b) engines is equal to the marginal revenue from sales of a engines and the **net marginal revenue** from sales of b machines, or:

Profit maximised when: $MC_A(a + b) = MR_A(a) = NMR_B(b)$

Example

Supposing that marginal cost functions and demand curves for Pollock's engines and motors were:

Marginal cost of Alicedale's engines, MC_A $=$ $20 + 0.03Q$

Marginal cost of Bedford's converting the
engines into machines, MC_B $\qquad = \qquad 30 \quad + \quad 0.01Q$

Demand curve for engines, P_A $\qquad = \qquad 400 \quad - \quad 0.04Q$

Demand curve for machines, P_B $\qquad = \qquad 600 \quad - \quad 0.05Q$

(where costs and prices are in £'s and Q is annual level of production or sales in units).

You are required to determine Pollock's optimal pricing and output policy and a suitable transfer price for engines to achieve goal congruence.

Solution

Step 1   Find expressions for (net) marginal revenue.

A's revenue	$R_A = P_A \times Q$	$=$	$400Q$	$-$	$0.04Q^2$
$\therefore$	$MR_A = \dfrac{dR_A}{dQ}$	$=$	400	$-$	$0.08Q$
B's revenue	$R_B = P_B \times Q$	$=$	$600Q$	$-$	$0.05Q^2$
$\therefore$	$MR_B = \dfrac{dR_B}{dQ}$	$=$	600	$-$	$0.1Q$
Finally $NMR_B = MR_B - MC_B$		$=$	$(600 - 0.1Q)$	$-$	$(30 + 0.01Q)$
		$=$	570	$-$	$0.11Q$

(Take care with the signs.)

Step 2   Redraft MC_A, MR_A and NMR_B, with A selling a units, B selling b units, A producing (a + b) units, rather than just Q.

$MC_A = 20 + 0.03(a + b);$ $MR_A = 400 - 0.08a;$ $NMR_B = 570 - 0.11b$

Step 3   Take (any) two pairs, equate and solve simultaneously.

MC_A & MR_A	$20 + 0.03a + 0.03b$	$= 400 - 0.08a$
MR_A & NMR_B	$400 - 0.08a$	$= 570 - 0.11b$

Rearranging:

(1)	$0.11a$	$+$	$0.03b$	$=$	380
(2)	$-0.08a$	$+$	$0.11b$	$=$	170
$8 \times (1)$	$0.88a$	$+$	$0.24b$	$=$	$3,040$
$11 \times (2)$	$-0.88a$	$+$	$1.21b$	$=$	$1,870$
Add			$1.45b$	$=$	$4,910$
			b	$=$	$4,910 \div 1.45 = 3,386.207$

Substitute in (1)	$0.11a$	$+$	$0.03 \times 3,386.207$	$=$	380
			$0.11a$	$=$	$380 - 101.586 = 278.41$
			a	$=$	$278.41 \div 0.11 = 2,531.03$

Step 4   Find the transfer price.

The transfer price to encourage A to make 5,917, sell 2,531, transfer 3,386 and for B to accept 3,386 will be:

MC_A (5,917) and also MR_A (2,531) and also NMR_B (3,386)

(It helps to find all three, they should be the same.

MC_A	=	$20 + 0.03Q$	=	$20 + 0.03 \times 5,917$	=	£197.51
MR_A	=	$400 - 0.08Q$	=	$400 - 0.08 \times 2,531$	=	£197.52
NMR_B	=	$570 - 0.11Q$	=	$570 - 0.11 \times 3,386$	=	£197.54

The slight difference is the result of having rounded the values of a and b. If unrounded figures are used £197.52 proves to be the most appropriate figure.

The transfer price for engines should be £197.52.

Step 5   Find the selling price for engines and machines. (Remember to go back to the original demand curves.)

Engines:	P_A	=	$400 - 0.04Q$	=	$400 - 0.04 \times 2,531$	=	**£298.76**
Machines:	P_B	=	$600 - 0.05Q$	=	$600 - 0.05 \times 3,386$	=	**£430.70**

2   COST-BASED TRANSFER PRICES

2.1   Introduction

The following cost-related transfer prices will be considered in this section:

(a)   total cost;
(b)   variable cost;
(c)   fixed charge plus a variable charge per unit;
(d)   apportionment of contribution.

In all cases the use of standard rather than actual cost ensures that the cost of inefficiency is reflected in the producing division's results, rather than being passed on via the transfer price to the receiving division.

2.2   Total cost plus

This approach involves the determination of the total cost per unit for the supplying division. This cost would include both fixed and variable elements. Such a total cost per unit would then be used to evaluate **each** unit of product internally transferred.

There is a fundamental problem with a transfer price based on an absorbed total cost, in that its use in a decision-making context by the manager of the receiving division can lead to action which is not optimal in terms of profit for the company. The reason for this is that, although the total cost is made up of fixed and variable cost elements relating to the supplying division, the one transfer price per unit is regarded by the receiving division manager as variable. This is understandable because the manager in the receiving division is always charged an amount equal to:

Number of units of product × Transfer price per unit

In other words, the receiving division manager recognises the cost behaviour of the transfer price he is charged as having the exact qualities of a truly variable cost ie, varying directly with the quantity (of units transferred).

The receiving division manager, making decisions for his own area of responsibility and thinking primarily of optimising the profits of his own division, is likely to treat the transfer price as a variable item in the analysis. The danger is that in situations where the receiving division has spare production capacity, the manager may make the decision not to accept business at a lower selling price than usual, because it would apparently not make a profit or even a contribution for that division. However, for the company as a whole the special price does exceed the variable costs and in the short term it would be worthwhile to accept the business.

The following example illustrates this situation.

Example

A company has two divisions – P and Q. Division P manufactures a product which it transfers to Division Q at a transfer price equal to the total cost of manufacture in Division P. Division Q incorporates each unit transferred from Division P into a product which it manufactures and sells.

Divisions P and Q currently have spare production capacity. Cost and selling price data are as follows:

	Division P £/unit	Division Q £/unit
Variable cost	3	
Fixed cost	2	
Total cost (= Transfer price)	£5	5
Variable cost	—	6
Fixed cost		3
Total cost		14
Profit		1
Selling price		£15

If an opportunity arose for Division Q to sell the same product for £12 per unit, without affecting its normal existing business and its selling price of £15 per unit on that business, the manager of Division Q would reject it, as the divisional profit would fall. The total cost per unit of £14 would exceed the selling price of £12. However, the manager may apply a contribution approach and argue that the additional business, to utilise spare capacity in the short term, is worthwhile because it would still make a divisional contribution. His calculations would be based on:

	£/unit	£/unit
Selling price		12
Less: 'Variable' costs to the division:		
Transfer price	5	
Variable cost	6	
	—	11
Contribution to Division Q		£1

Using the same set of data, but now assuming that the additional units could only be sold at a price of £10 each, the manager of Division Q would reject the business on both grounds ie, a reduction of divisional profit and the fact that the business apparently does not even produce a contribution for the division. However, it would be in the best interests of the overall company, in terms of short-term profit, if the additional business were accepted, even at a selling price of £10 per unit, as the following demonstrates:

	£/unit	£/unit
Selling price		10
Less: Variable costs in:		
Division P	3	
Division Q	6	
	—	9
Overall company contribution		£1

The foregoing illustrations are based on the following major assumptions:

(i)   the variable cost per unit and the total fixed costs of both divisions remain unchanged at all levels of activity under consideration;

(ii)   the additional business at the special selling price doesn't affect existing business at the existing selling price;

(iii)   the manager of the receiving division regards the total cost of the transfer price as a variable cost as far as his autonomous decision-making process is concerned;

(iv)   divisional managers are being assessed in terms of the profitability of their areas of responsibility.

As far as making optimal decisions is concerned, a transfer price based on total cost is to be avoided. In addition, if transfers are made on this basis, the manager of the producing division will not be making a profit on goods traded internally (but neither will he be making a loss), so it will be difficult for profitability to provide an objective measure of the performance of the producing division and its manager. It is for this reason that 'full cost plus' is sometimes used, adding some profit for the producing division but exacerbating the decision-making problems.

2.3   Variable cost plus

If the producing division transfers units at a price equal to its own variable cost of manufacture, the producing division manager is unlikely to show a profit on or even a contribution from that business. Again, an objective measure of performance based on profitability would not be achieved. Such a basis would not be motivational as far as the producing division manager is concerned.

The use of variable cost as a basis for setting the transfer price would mean that the receiving division manager would be provided with the most meaningful cost information as far as decision-making in his division is concerned. There should be no sub-optimisation, so that decisions made should be in the best interest of the division **and** the overall company.

Once again variable cost might just be the starting point for setting a transfer price and a contribution margin added for the producing division.

2.4   Fixed charge plus a variable charge per unit

In effect this represents a two-part transfer price – a fixed amount per period, which is charged irrespective of the number of units transferred, plus an amount which represents a fixed rate per unit. This concept is similar to the way in which domestic consumers are charged for electricity, gas and the use of the telephone; alternatively it could be viewed as a form of 'management charge'. An element of profit could be included in the two-part tariff to give the producing division manager the necessary motivation.

The advantage of this type of transfer pricing structure is that it will generally encourage the receiving division to accept more units from the producing division as long as the extra revenue is greater than the extra cost involved. It would be logical to base the fixed element in the charge on the fixed costs arising in the producing division, and to restrict it to any limit on the availability of capacity to supply the receiving division. The variable element would then approximate to the variable or marginal cost of manufacture (possibly plus a profit mark-up). The application of this type of transfer price would also avoid the problem that arose in the earlier example Kwaree Ltd.

If in Kwaree Ltd the transfer price were set as follows:

£50,000 fixed charge **plus** £96.66 per tonne transferred,

then the resultant profits for each division and the company as a whole when the wholesale group is working at:

(i)   80% capacity; and

(ii)   100% capacity

could be summarised as follows:

		Profit in Wholesale group £'000	*Profit in Retail group* £'000	*Profit in Kwaree Ltd* £'000
Wholesale group working at:				
(i)	80% capacity	76	56	132
(ii)	100% capacity	86.66	73.34	160

The following points should be observed:

(i)   The resultant profits for each group and the overall company are exactly the same, when working at 80% capacity, as those when the market price was applied in the original example. Therefore, the divisional managers would be indifferent, in terms of resultant profit, between the application of the market price or the two-part transfer price. The price of £96.66 is in the range £70 - £140; profit has been split more evenly.

(ii)   The fixed charge of £50,000 per period represents 50% of the total fixed costs of the wholesale group, on the argument that up to 50% of its capacity could be used to produce moulding clay for the wholesale group.

(iii)   The profits on both the wholesale **and** the retail group, as well as those for the company as a whole, would increase if the divisional managers decided to utilise the spare capacity and work at 100% capacity. They would be motivated to move to the optimal production levels automatically. It should be recalled that in the original application of the market price as a transfer price, moving from 80% to 100% capacity would have resulted in a fall in the profits of the retail group.

2.5   Apportionment of contribution

Another suggestion for establishing transfer prices is based on working out the total contribution made by the company on goods subject to internal transfer, and then applying some logical but arbitrary method of apportionment of this contribution between the two divisions involved. For example, it might be agreed that each division was to make the same contribution margin ratio (P/V ratio) on the goods subject to internal transfer.

This can be illustrated by again using the basic data from Kwaree Ltd. Assuming the 100% level of activity, a transfer price can be established such that each group makes the same contribution margin ratio on tonnes of moulding clay subject to internal transfer, as follows:

	Kwaree Ltd £'000	*Less: Outside sales by wholesale group* £'000	*Tonnes subject to internal transfer* £'000
Outside sales	500	180	320
Internal transfer less variable costs	200	70	130
Contribution	300	110	190
Contribution margin ratio (190 ÷ 320)			59.4%

The objective is then to set a transfer price such that each group makes a contribution margin ratio of 59.4% on the tonnes subject to internal transfer:

	Tonnes subject to internal transfer	*Internal transfer*	
		Wholesale group	*Retail group*
	£'000	*£'000*	*£'000*
Outside sales	320	-	320
Internal transfer		T	(T)
Less: Variable costs	130	70	60
Contribution	190	A	B

Contribution margin ratio   59.4%

Wholesale Group ratio   =   Retail Group ratio

$$\frac{T - 70}{T} = \frac{320 - T - 60}{320}$$

$$\therefore \quad 320T - 22,400 = 260T - T^2$$

$$\therefore \quad T^2 + 60T - 22,400 = 0$$

$$\therefore \quad T = 122.6 \text{ (or} - 182.6)$$

$$= £122.6/\text{tonne}$$

The application of this approach will involve determining a range of transfer prices at different levels of prices, as in Kwaree Ltd, because to sell more the retail group has to reduce its selling price. It is a cost-related basis because the variable costs arising in each division are critical figures in the determination of the transfer price.

The transfer price is still in the required range.

3   FURTHER CONSIDERATIONS

3.1   Negotiated prices

In any practical application of transfer pricing there is usually going to be some element of negotiation between the two divisional managers involved. Such negotiation may be loosely based on a market price or on costs, because it is difficult to negotiate in a complete vacuum. Empirical evidence has suggested that, where divisional managers are left to negotiate freely, market prices and costs do figure in the exercise. However, in addition the strengths and weaknesses of individual managers in a bargaining situation will play a role.

The problem with negotiated prices is when the two divisional managers cannot agree: they then have to seek a decision from higher central management on what transfer price to charge. This conflicts with one of the main criteria set out for transfer prices ie, that the divisions should remain as autonomous decision-making units. Management theory suggests that decisions should always be made at the lowest appropriate level in an organisation structure.

The following four principles have been recommended:

- Prices of all transfers in and out of a profit centre should be determined by negotiation between buyers and sellers.

- Negotiators should have access to full data on alternative sources and markets and to public and private information about market prices.

- Buyers and sellers should be completely free to deal outside the company.

- Negotiators should be fully informed on the significance of the transaction in relation to the profitability of the company as a whole.

If these principles are followed goal congruence should be achieved.

3.2 Dual prices (two prices)

Another approach to transfer pricing is the use of dual prices ie, one price for crediting the supplying division and another (usually lower) price for debiting the receiving division. The inter-divisional profit would have to be removed when combining the results of the two divisions. This is intended to represent a motivational approach to transfer pricing but the problem is that both divisions would appear favourably, in terms of profit, from the application of this approach. One then questions the objectivity of profit as a measure of performance in these circumstances.

3.3 A general rule for transfer pricing

The following general rule has been put forward for setting transfer prices.

Transfer price per unit = Standard variable cost in the producing division **plus** the opportunity cost to the company as a whole of supplying the unit internally

The opportunity cost will be either the contribution forgone by selling one unit internally rather than externally, or the contribution forgone by not using the same facilities in the producing division for their next best alternative use.

The application of this general rule means that the transfer price equals:

(a) the standard variable cost of the producing division, if there is no outside market for the units manufactured and no alternative use for the facilities in that division;

(b) the market price, if there is an outside market for the units manufactured in the producing division and no alternative more profitable use for the facilities in that division.

3.4 Taxation

It has not gone unnoticed by the Inland Revenue that companies can use transfer pricing policies to divert profits to subsidiaries based in countries with more favourable tax regimes. The first tax legislation to curb this practice was set up in 1951. The relevant provision became Section 485 in the 1970 Consolidation of the Taxes Act. The legislation now appears as section 770 of the Taxes Act 1988.

The anti-avoidance legislation provides that if a transaction exists such as the importing of goods from a foreign division or subsidiary at too high a price or the export at too low a price (thus transferring profits abroad), the Revenue can treat the transaction as having taken place at a fair 'arms length' price.

Similar legislation exists in the USA where the IRS appears to some observers to be trying to take matters one stage further by forcing companies to adopt transfer pricing policies that could be held to be based on unsound accounting principles in order to ensure that profits do not get diverted outside the USA.

3.5 Other factors

Other factors that might influence transfer pricing policies include the following.

Tariffs - If a country imposes tariffs on imports based on the 'value' of the item being imported, attempts might be made to place a low transfer price on that item. However, governments are aware of this practice and may adopt similar policies to that of the anti-avoidance tax legislation.

Currency fluctuations - The main problem of currency fluctuations arises when it comes to the settlement of debts. A common way of reducing the exchange risk is by paying early or late to take advantage of likely movements in exchange rates. However, attempts may be made to manipulate transfer prices to move funds out of a weak currency and into a stronger one.

4   CHAPTER SUMMARY

- A transfer pricing policy is needed if an organisation has decentralised and goods or services are transferred between divisions.

- An effective transfer pricing policy should achieve four aims:

    - motivation
    - independence
    - objective performance assessment
    - goal congruence

- Methods used include:

    - cost-based prices
    - market-based prices
    - negotiated prices

- Other methods that might be adopted use:

    - marginal cost and marginal revenue data
    - dual (two) prices
    - opportunity costs.

- A divisional manager would accept a product or service that is being transferred internally if it would result in divisional profit being increased (more than the purchase of that item externally).

- If no external intermediate market exists the company's profit is maximised at a level Q*, where:

$$MC_C \quad = \quad MC_A + MC_B \quad = \quad MR \text{ or}$$

$$MC_A \quad = \quad MR - MC_B \quad = \quad NMR_B$$

    The transfer price must be the value, at an activity level Q*, of MC_A or NMR_B.

- If a perfect intermediate market exists for the item being transferred, then that intermediate market price must be the transfer price; divisions may have different optimal activity levels with the difference being absorbed by the intermediate market.

- If an imperfect intermediate market exists then, if intermediate sales are a, final sales are b and total production is (a + b) then profit is maximised when:

$$MC_A (a + b) = MR_A(a) = NMR_B(b)$$

- Cost plus prices or full cost prices may encourage 'sub-optimal' decisions; transferring at variable cost does not motivate the seller.

- A general rule that can occasionally help determine transfer prices is:

Transfer price	=	Std Variable Cost in the producing division	+	Opportunity cost to the company of making the transfer

- Other factors to take into account are:

    - taxation
    - tariffs
    - currency fluctuations

5   SELF TEST QUESTIONS

    5.1   What are the two essential steps to finding a suitable transfer price when no external market exists for the intermediate product? (1.2)

    5.2   What is meant by net marginal revenue? (1.2)

    5.3   What is the only transfer price that would result in internal transfers being made of items that can also be bought and sold externally in a perfect intermediate market? (1.3)

    5.4   How are the optimal levels of activity found when an imperfect intermediate market exists? (1.4)

    5.5   State four recommended principles when setting transfer prices by negotiation. (3.1)

    5.6   State a general rule for fixing the correct value of transfer prices. (3.3)

    5.7   What does Section 770 of the Taxes Act 1988 allow the Revenue to do if transfers are not made at a fair 'arms length' price? (3.4)

6   EXAMINATION TYPE QUESTIONS

6.1   Quoin

    (a)   Quoin Ltd, an abrasives manufacturer, has two divisions. Division M manufactures abrasive grain, an intermediate product, which it can sell either to division D (where it is incorporated into coated-grain final products) or on the open market (where there is perfect competition). In order to maintain a sufficient element of divisional autonomy, division D is allowed to buy abrasive grain in the open market if it so wishes. There are no extra costs of buying or selling in the open market as compared with buying and selling between the divisions.

    You are required to demonstrate and explain the optimal transfer pricing policy which will maximise the profits of Quoin as a whole, showing how this profit would accrue to the two divisions.

    (b)   Son of Quoin Ltd has three divisions. Division S supplies grain to divisions X and Y (in lots of 100 tons) which each utilise in the preparation of their own final products. There is no other market for the special grain.

    Division S has the following cost structure:

Special grain

Tonnage produced	400	500	600	700	800	900	1,000
Total cost (£'000)	400	420	450	485	525	585	665

    Divisions X and Y can generate total net revenues (after meeting their own respective independent processing costs) as follows in relation to the tonnage of special grain processed:

Division X

Tonnage processed	100	200	300	400		
Total net revenue (£'000)	120	180	220	240		

Division Y

Tonnage processed	100	200	300	400	500	600
Total net revenue (£'000)	120	240	360	420	460	480

    You are required to show the price at which the special grain should be transferred from division S to divisions X and Y, stating your reasons.

6.2   Drums

    L Ltd and M Ltd are subsidiaries of the same group of companies.

L Ltd produces a branded product sold in drums at a price of £20 per drum.

Its direct product costs per drum are as follows:

- Raw material from M Ltd: at a transfer price of £9 for 25 litres.
- Other products and services from outside the group: at a cost of £3.

L Ltd's fixed costs are £40,000 per month. These costs include process labour whose costs will not alter until L Ltd's output reaches twice its present level.

A market research study has indicated that L Ltd's market could increase by 80% in volume if it were to reduce its price by 20%.

M Ltd produces a fairly basic product which can be converted into a wide range of end products. It sells one third of its output to L Ltd and the remainder to customers outside the group.

M Ltd's production capacity is 1,000 kilolitres per month, but competition is keen and it budgets to sell no more than 750 kilolitres per month for the year ending 31 December 19X0.

Its variable costs are £200 per kilolitre and its fixed costs are £60,000 per month.

The current policy of the group is to use market prices, where known, as the transfer price between its subsidiaries. This is the basis of the transfer price between M Ltd and L Ltd.

You are required

(a)   to calculate the monthly profit position for each of L Ltd and M Ltd if the sales of L Ltd are:

    (i)   at their present level; and

    (ii)   at the higher potential level indicated by the market research, subject to a cut in price of 20%;   **(10 marks)**

(b)   (i)   to explain why the use of a market price as the transfer price produces difficulties under the conditions outlined in (a) (ii) above;   **(3 marks)**

    (ii)   to explain briefly, as chief accountant of the group, what factors you would consider in arriving at a proposal to overcome these difficulties;   **(7 marks)**

(c)   to recommend, with supporting calculations, what transfer prices you would propose.

(5 marks)
(Total: 25 marks)

7   ANSWERS TO EXAMINATION TYPE QUESTIONS

7.1   Quoin

(a)   **Perfect intermediate market**

Under these conditions the transfer price has to be the intermediate market price (otherwise no transfers will take place). If the grain-manufacturing division, M, has increasing marginal cost and the final product division, D, has decreasing net marginal revenue (marginal revenue – marginal cost) then the problem can be shown graphically as follows.

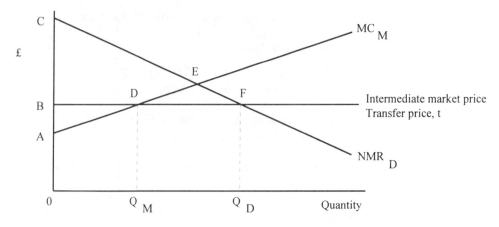

Division M should manufacture up to the point where its marginal cost and the intermediate market price are equal (Q_M). Division D should manufacture up to the point where its net marginal revenue and the intermediate market price are equal (Q_D). In this case D will have to purchase additional grain ($Q_D - Q_M$) from outside. Given its activity level (Q_D) division D can determine the selling price needed to generate that demand. Once the transfer price, output levels and sales prices have been found, profit can be calculated for each division, in this case being:

	D £	M £	Group £
Outside sales	S	-	S
Internal transfers	(T)	T	-
Outside purchases	(U)	-	(U)
Divisional production and selling costs	(V)	(W)	(X)
Profit	Y	Z	Y + Z

(Tutorial note

It is possible to see how contributions (but not profit) accrue to the divisions from the graph.

D's contribution can be found by comparing NMR_D and t; it is the area CBF.

M's contribution is seen from MC_M and t; it is the area ABD.

In the case of the diagram shown it is hoped that division M has considerably smaller fixed costs than division D or else a two part transfer pricing policy will be needed of a fixed cost per unit, t, plus a fixed cost per period.*)*

(b)   **Two selling divisions**

Although the question states that there is no intermediate market, the problem is identical to one in which one of the final markets (X's or Y's) is treated as an imperfect intermediate market for S.

The marginal cost of producing grain has to be compared with the net marginal revenue from sales as tabulated below.

Production Division S		Selling Division X		Selling Division Y	
Qty (tons)	MC_S £'000	Qty (tons)	NMR_X £'000	Qty (tons)	NMR_Y £'000
400	400 (1 - 4)	100	120 (1)	100	120 (2)
500	20 (5)	200	60 (5)	200	120 (3)
600	30 (6)	300	40 (7)	300	120 (4)
700	35 (7)	400	20	400	60 (6)
800	40 (8)*			500	40 (8)*
900	60			600	20
1,000	80				

The table shows incremental costs and revenues rather than strictly marginal costs and revenues. It is worth Son of Quoin increasing output provided the incremental net marginal revenue is greater than (not less than) marginal cost. Determining this requires a little care and makes use of the numbers in brackets.

(1 - 4) If S produces 400 tons its cost is £400,000 and they should be sold wherever net marginal revenue is highest. This is achieved by selling 100 tons in X and 300 in Y earning net incremental revenue of £480,000.

(5) The next 100 tons (up to 500) cost S an extra £20,000. If sold through X they would take X's sales up to 200 tons and revenue up by £60,000; if sold through Y they would take Y's sales up to 400 tons and also increase revenue by £60,000. The sales are shown going through X.

(6) The next 100 tons increases S's output to 600 tons at an additional cost of £30,000. If sold through X net revenue would now go up by £40,000; if sold through Y net revenue rises by £60,000. Therefore sales are made through Y and at this stage: S has produced 600 tones, X has sold 200 tons and Y sold 400 tons.

(7) S's additional costs are £35,000; sales could either be through X or Y, both earn an extra £40,000; X has again been chosen. Now S has produced 700, X sold 300, Y sold 400.

(8)* The final 100 tons produced by S costs an extra £40,000. If sold through X (X's sales rising to 400) they would only earn £20,000; if sold through Y (Y's sales rising to 500) they would earn £40,000. Son of Quoin would be indifferent over this last batch; it has been included for lovers of MC = MR.

The transfer price must encourage S to produce 800 tons, and no more; X to accept 300 tons, and no more; and Y to accept 500 tons, and no more.

To assure S's production level:	£40,000 $\leq$	transfer price per 100 tons	$\leq$ £60,000
To assure X's production level:	£20,000 $\leq$	transfer price per 100 tons	$\leq$ £40,000
To assure Y's production level:	£20,000 $\leq$	transfer price per 100 tons	$\leq$ £40,000

In this case, rather than there being a range of transfer prices, only one price satisfies all three conditions. The transfer price must be **£400 per ton**.

7.2   Drums

(Tutorial note:

This is a very typical transfer pricing question that has arisen in various very similar guises over the years. Part (a) asks for the profits of 2 divisions with the present transfer pricing policy at different levels of output. Part (b) requires a discussion of why dysfunctional decisions may arise and then asks you to explain how this could be solved. Part (c) asks you to follow your own advice and suggest an improved transfer price (at which point many different answers will be acceptable.)

(a) *Note:* many different layouts are possible. Shown below is one of the simpler ones.

(i)   **Current output level**

M Ltd's output 750 kl (∴ 500kl to external customers; 250kl to L)

M's contribution per kl   £

Price £$\frac{9}{25}$ × 1,000 =   360

Variable costs   200

             —

             £160

             —

L's contribution per drum   £

Price   20

Variable costs:

   External   3

   Internal   9   12

            —   —

             £8

             —

L's Current output 250kl ÷ 25l per drum = 10,000 drums

Profit statements (£'000) - current output

M Ltd   **L Ltd**

Contribution: external 500kl @ £160 =   80   Contribution 10,000 drums @ £8 =   80

    internal 250kl @ £160 =   40   Fixed costs   40

            —

            120

Fixed costs   60

            —

Profit   60   Profit   40

            —

(Note: Group profit = 60 + 40 =   100*)*

   (ii)   **Higher output level**

M Ltd's output = 750kl + (250 × 0.80) = 950kl

M's contribution per kl - as above £160

L Ltd's output 10,000 × 180% = 18,000 drums

L's contribution per drum   Price £20 × 80% =   £16

        Variable costs (as above)   £12

               —

               £4

               —

Profit statements (£'000)
Higher output

M Ltd   **L Ltd**

Contribution: external   80   Contribution 18,000 @ £4   72

    internal   72

    (450 @ £160)   —

           152   Fixed cost   40

Fixed cost   60

            —   —

Profit   92   Profit   32

            —   —

(Note: Group profit = 92 + 32 = 124*)*

(b)   (i)   The use of market price as a transfer price is likely to cause friction between the divisions because M Ltd make higher profit at the higher output whereas L Ltd's profit is greater at the lower output. Clearly, therefore, the market price does not represent the opportunity cost of the transferred units.

(ii)   There are three major stages in setting a transfer price, each requiring consideration of different factors:

Stage 1 - identify the output level that will maximise company profit. This will require consideration of all possible price v output combinations, and the effect of differing volumes on cost.

Stage 2 - identify the opportunity cost of the units demanded for internal transfer, when operating at the company's optimum output. Factors to consider might include: external demand; external market price; marginal production costs; and whether scarce resources are utilised.

This will establish the transfer price that is required in order to achieve goal congruence.

Stage 3 - consider whether the transfer price based on opportunity cost is likely to give a fair share of profit to both divisions. If not, possible solutions might be: 2 part tariff; full cost plus pricing; dual pricing.

(c)   From (a) company profit is greater at the higher output level (£124,000 against £100,000). We therefore need to establish the opportunity cost of the 450kl being demanded by L Ltd.

M Ltd has sufficient capacity to supply all 450kl to L, without affecting its supply of 500kl to its external customers. Therefore, since there is no mention of scarce resources, opportunity cost is M's variable cost of £200 per kl.

The next problem is whether a transfer price of £200 per kl will be fair to K Ltd and L Ltd. L Ltd will presumably be delighted in this reduction as it will significantly increase their profit. From K Ltd's view, however, it will be quite unacceptable to transfer at marginal cost - why should they do all that work and earn no contribution?

Solutions to consider might be:

(i)   2 part tariff (ie, MC +)
(ii)   full cost +
(iii)   dual pricing.

A fourth alternative in this case, would be to set the transfer price at a level so that both divisions benefit by operating at the higher output level.

Minimum acceptable to M Ltd

	£
Minimum contribution required on internal sales (as (a))	40,000
At higher output, variable costs on these sales will be 450 @ £200	90,000
∴ Minimum acceptable internal revenue	£130,000

÷ 450kl = £288.89 per kl

Maximum acceptable to L Ltd   £

Minimum contribution required (as (a))   (80,000)
Sales revenue will be 18,000 @ £16   288,000
Variable costs (excluding transfers) will
   be 18,000 @ £3   (54,000)
                                                          ─────────
∴ Maximum acceptable for transferred costs   £154,000
                                                          ─────────

154,000 ÷ 450kl = £342.22 per kl

∴ Recommend transfer price of say £315 per kl

27 DIVISIONAL PERFORMANCE EVALUATION

INTRODUCTION & LEARNING OBJECTIVES

When you have studied this chapter you should be able to do the following:

- Describe and calculate quantitative and qualitative performance measures.
- Discuss the uses and effects of different performance measures.

1 DIVISIONAL ASSESSMENT

1.1 Introduction

Having decentralised, it is essential that senior management monitors and controls the performance of the divisions and those with direct responsibility for those divisions. An accounting information system (a management control system) must be in place to allow for divisional assessment. The system used must have a close bearing on divisional goals and must recognise that some costs of a division will be controllable by its managers and some will not.

1.2 Methods

A range of methods are available for assessing divisional performance, the two most common being:

- Return on investment (ROI); and
- Residual income (RI).

These are discussed fully in the next two sections of this chapter. However other methods exist.

- **Variance analysis** - is a standard means of monitoring and controlling performance; care must be taken in identifying the controllability of and responsibility for each variance.

- **Ratio analysis** - there are several profitability and liquidity measures that can be applied to divisional performance reports.

- **Other management ratios** - under this heading would come contribution per key factor and sales per employee or square foot as well as industry specific ratios such as transport costs per mile, brewing costs per barrel, overheads per chargeable hour etc.

- **Other information** - such as staff turnover, market share, new customers gained, innovative products or services developed.

Whilst it is common to focus on one key measure of performance, it is important to keep an eye on, and stress the relevance of, a range of measures in order that performance in its widest sense is assessed.

1.3 Points on performance measures

The information system and reports that a company produces on divisional performance should follow three simple principles:

- **Timeliness** - any report should be produced sufficiently quickly after the end of an accounting period (week, month, quarter) to allow corrective action to be taken on any unsatisfactory performance. There is a balance to maintain here between the **speed** with which information is produced, the **accuracy** of that information and the **cost** of producing the figures.

- **Goal congruence** - the performance measures used, the assessment criteria, should not encourage divisional managers to make decisions which shows their divisions performing well against the criteria set, but adopting strategies which are against the well-being of the company as a whole. An example might be a sales department that is judged on total volume of sales made irrespective of the price charged or the credit worthiness of the customers.

- **Controllability** - the important measure of divisional performance will be linked to profit but care has to be taken in deciding how that profit is calculated. Much is written on this aspect of divisional assessment and five factors to consider are:

  - **Definition of controllable or managed cost** - a controllable cost is defined as a cost which can be influenced by its budget holder. It is not always possible to pre-determine responsibility, because the reason for deviation from expected performance may only become evident later.

  - **Division or manager** - the measure of profit will depend upon whether it is the performance of the division or its manager that is being assessed as discussed below.

  - **Short-term v long-term** - few costs are controllable in the short-term and it is only in the longer term that action can be taken to control most costs. For instance, if the rent on premises is deemed to be too high, moving an office or a factory cannot happen at a week's notice. This means that short-term performance reports should concentrate on those costs controllable in the short-term.

  - **Absorption v marginal format** - it is often suggested that a marginal costing format for profit statements and performance reports is more appropriate for management purposes. In divisional assessment there is an argument in favour of a marginal format to assess divisional managers since many fixed costs with which a division may be charged are unlikely to be under the control of the manager. However some fixed costs will be controllable at divisional level. It is suggested that a use of absorption costing information may, on the one hand, be demotivating (in view of uncontrollable costs it contains); on the other hand, it might encourage divisional managers (and therefore senior management) to question the wisdom of using certain central services whose costs are apportioned out to divisions.

  - **Interdependence** - whilst it is a desirable aim in a divisionalised organisation that the actions of one division cannot affect the performance of another, in most cases it is unrealistic. When assessing divisional performance, care has to be taken in deciding the true cause of any adverse performance by a division.

1.4   Divisional v managerial performance

The main board of a decentralised company will wish to assess two aspects of performance:

- the personal performance of the divisional **manager**;

- the economic performance of the manager's **divisions**.

The type of measures used and the way in which they are evaluated will vary according to who or what is being assessed.

It is quite possible that the best manager within an organisation produces the worst divisional profit; because that manager is operating in the toughest or newest market, but is still doing well under the circumstances. By the same token good divisional performance might not indicate a well-run division and a competent manager, but rather a controllable business environment. This raises the issue of performance targets. An organisation will compare the performance of divisions and set targets for managers, but this will have to be done with caution. Targets set should take into account:

- the difficulty of the economic environment in which a division is operating;

- the motivational value of tough or lenient targets for the divisional manager concerned.

Added to the difficulty or leniency of targets, the question must be asked of profit-based measures, 'which profit to use?' To answer this question the pro-forma below shows a profit and loss account (section of a performance report) for a division.

	£'000	£'000
Outside sales		X
Internal transfers		X
		X
Variable cost of goods sold and transferred	(X)	
Other variable divisional costs	(X)	
		(X)
Contribution		X
Depreciation on controllable fixed assets	(X)	
Other controllable fixed costs	(X)	
		(X)
Controllable operating profit (1)		X
Interest on controllable investment		(X)
Controllable residual income before tax (2)		X
Non controllable divisional fixed costs	(X)	
Apportioned head office costs	(X)	
Interest on non-controllable investment	(X)	
		(X)
Net residual income before tax (3)		X

The features of this statement are:

- **absence of tax charges** - it is generally felt that the tax charge of a company cannot be controlled at divisional level and therefore any profit-based measures should be pre-tax.

- **inclusion of interest charges** - this is a contentious issue and is discussed further when explaining the two main measures ROI and RI.

- **which profit?** - a divisional manager's performance should be assessed by reference to figures (1) or (2) whereas the division, which received the benefits from head-office costs and other non-controllable elements even if the manager cannot influence them, should be assessed by reference to figure (3).

2   RETURN ON INVESTMENT (ROI)

2.1   Introduction

Return on investment (ROI), or return on capital employed, is calculated for an investment centre for a particular period as follows:

$$\text{ROI} = \frac{\text{Earnings before interest and tax}}{\text{Capital employed}} \times 100$$

If assessing the performance of a manager the earnings figure should be controllable operating profit and capital employed should be controllable investment. When assessing a division's performance costs and assets that are not controllable at divisional level could be included, although all interest costs are usually excluded. This is very similar to the return on capital employed (ROCE) traditionally used to analyse capital investment projects; the only difference is that here the profits from all projects for a single year are compared to the book value of all investments, whereas in investment appraisal the profits of a single investment project over the several years of that investment's life are compared to the book value of that one single investment.

The return on investment is widely used by external analysts of company performance when the primary ratio is broken down into its two secondary ratios.

$$ \text{ROI} = \frac{\text{Earnings}}{\text{Capital employed}} \times 100 = \frac{\text{Sales}}{\text{Capital employed}} \times \frac{\text{Earnings}}{\text{Sales}} \times 100 $$

On the right, the first term is the asset turnover ratio and the second is the net profit percentage.

2.2 Advantages of ROI

Just as the IRR suffers from comparison with the NPV, so the return on investment is regarded as inferior to the residual income; nevertheless it is widely used and has several good features.

- As a **relative measure** it enables comparisons to be made with divisions or companies of different sizes. It could be argued that it is particularly appropriate for profit centres rather than investment centres since the former are not in a position to increase overall profit by undertaking further capital investments.

- It is **used externally** and is well understood by users of accounts.

- The primary ratio **splits down** into secondary ratios for more detailed analysis as mentioned above and discussed further later.

- ROI forces managers to **make good use** of existing capital resources and focuses attention on them, particularly when funds for further investment are limited.

- The nature of the measure is such that it can clearly be improved not just by increasing profit but by reducing capital employed; it therefore encourages **reduction in** the level of **assets** such as obsolete equipment and excessive working capital.

2.3 Disadvantages of ROI

The disadvantages fall into two categories: those that are problems common to **both** ROI and RI; and those that are **specific** to ROI.

Specific disadvantages

- **Disincentive to invest** - a divisional manager will not wish to make an investment which provides an adequate return as far as the overall company is concerned if it reduces the division's current ROI. By the same token existing assets may be sold if, by doing so, ROI is improved even though those assets are generating a reasonable profit.

- **ROI improves with age** - on the other side of the coin most conventional depreciation methods will result in ROI improving with the age of an asset, being unsatisfactory initially then improving as the net book value of assets improves. This might encourage divisions hanging on to old assets and again deter them from investing in new ones. Alternatively a division may try to improve its ROI still further by **leasing** its assets. It is suggested that gross book value or even replacement cost should be used when evaluating performance. Also complex depreciation calculations are recommended by academics to overcome some of these difficulties.

- **Corporate objectives** of maximising total shareholders' wealth or the total profit of the company are not achieved by making decisions on the basis of ROI. In this way, as a relative measure, it can be compared to the internal rate of return whose use is also dysfunctional.

General problems

Whether it be ROI or RI that are used, there are certain problems common to both measures.

- **Calculation of profit** - apart from issues such as its controllability mentioned earlier there is some scope, even within the strictures of a group accounting policy, for some variation in treatment of depreciation. Also the need to increase profit may lead to cutting down on discretionary costs such as training, advertising and maintenance which, whilst improving short-term profit figures, will jeopardise the long-term future of a business. Standards for these should be set and monitored.

- **Asset measurement** - again group policies should ensure a consistent treatment, but comparison is difficult when some divisions buy and some lease assets. Thought has to be given to the treatment of permanent bank overdrafts; are these current liabilities or a source of finance?

- **Conflict with investment decisions** - the performance of a division will be influenced by investment decisions that it makes; however those decisions should be made on the basis of NPV calculations, whereas the subsequent performance of the division is assessed by a different criterion. Clearly there is likely to be a problem when a long-term investment decision is accepted, but the short-term effect on profit is detrimental. Again academics recommend changing depreciation methods so that the ROI or RI calculation is consistent with DCF calculations. This is examined further in section 4.

  An alternative approach, where the actual cash flows associated with an investment that has been made can be identified, suggests that the performance of a division should be carried out by comparing those actual cash flows with the budgeted figures used when the initial investment decision was made.

2.4 Activity

The Arcadia division of Botten Ltd currently has an investment base of £2.4m and annual profits of £0.48m. It is considering the following three investments, funds for which will be supplied by the company.

Project	A	B	C
Initial outlay (£'000)	1,400	600	400
Annual earnings (£'000)	350	200	88

You are required to find the current ROI of the Arcadia division, the ROI of each investment and the ROI of Arcadia with each of the three additional investments added to current earnings in turn.

2.5 Activity solution

$$\text{Return on investment, ROI} = \frac{\text{Earnings}}{\text{Capital investment}} \times 100$$

(a) Current position

$$\text{ROI} = \frac{480}{2,400} \times 100 = 20\%$$

(b) Additional investments

$$\text{A:} \quad \text{ROI} = \frac{350}{1,400} \times 100 = 25\%$$

$$\text{B:} \quad \text{ROI} \quad = \quad \frac{200}{600} \times 100 \quad = \quad 33\tfrac{1}{3}\%$$

$$\text{C:} \quad \text{ROI} \quad = \quad \frac{88}{400} \times 100 \quad = \quad 22\%$$

(c)   Potential position

$$\text{Arcadia + A:} \quad \text{ROI} \quad = \quad \frac{830}{3,800} \times 100 \quad = \quad 21.8\%$$

$$\text{Arcadia + B:} \quad \text{ROI} \quad = \quad \frac{680}{3,000} \times 100 \quad = \quad 22.7\%$$

$$\text{Arcadia + C:} \quad \text{ROI} \quad = \quad \frac{568}{2,800} \times 100 \quad = \quad 20.3\%$$

Note that although all three projects have returns that are greater then the current 20%, once project B is accepted the ROI rises to 22.7% making C look less attractive. It would be worth Arcadia's while accepting projects A and B, if this were possible since this would raise its ROI to: 1,030 ÷ 4,400 = 23.4%.

2.6   Activity

McKinnon Ltd sets up a new division in Blair Atholl investing £800,000 in fixed assets with an anticipated useful life of 10 years and no scrap value. Annual profits before depreciation are expected to be a steady £200,000.

You are required to calculate the division's ROI for its first three years by expressing annual (post depreciation) profits as a percentage of the book value of assets at the start of each year.

2.7   Activity solution

$$\text{ROI} \quad = \quad \frac{\text{Earnings before interest and tax (but after depreciation)}}{\text{Capital employed (book value at start of year)}} \times 100$$

Year	Opening book value of assets £'000	Annual depreciation £'000	Closing book value of assets £'000	Pre-dep'n profits £'000	Post-dep'n profits £'000	ROI %
1	800	80	720	200	120	$\frac{120}{800} = 15\%$
2	720	80	640	200	120	$\frac{120}{720} = 17\%$
3	640	80	560	200	120	$\frac{120}{640} = 19\%$

Note that ROI increases, despite no increase in annual profits, merely as a result of the book value of assets falling. It would be more appropriate to use the average book value of assets, although the use of opening book values is common.

3   RESIDUAL INCOME (RI)

3.1   Introduction

In view of the disadvantages of ROI, particularly its tendency to induce under-investment, most management authors recommend that the performance of investment centres is assessed by calculating an absolute measure of profitability, residual income as follows:

$$\text{RI} = \frac{\text{Controllable}}{\text{profit}} - \frac{\text{Imputed interest charge}}{\text{on controllable divisional investment}}$$

The two figures shown in the earlier profit and loss account were residual income figures; one (with controllable profit and controllable investment) being used to assess a manager's performance, the other (with all costs included) being used to assess the performance of the division. The rate at which interest is charged on assets is open to debate; various possibilities exist:

- **Group cost of capital** - commonly used although it reflects the risk of the group as a whole and not the individual divisions.

- **Current group ROI** - again the specific circumstances of the division are overlooked.

- **Different rates** - either of the above might be starting points for an interest rate but it is then adjusted for the specific circumstances of the group: the business environment, the type of investments being made and the motivational requirements for the divisional manager. It may be necessary to use different interest rates for different types of asset.

3.2   Advantages of RI

Residual income overcomes many of the disadvantages of ROI, specifically:

- It **reduces the problem of under investing** or failing to accept projects with ROI's greater than the group target but less than the division's current ROI.

- As a consequence it is more consistent with the objective of **maximising** the **total profitability** of the group.

- It is possible to use **different rates** of interest for different types of asset.

- The **cost of financing** a division is brought home to divisional managers.

However, it will suffer from the same problems associated with profit and asset measurement, and potential conflict with NPV investment decisions, as the ROI.

Despite these advantages, and that there are few significant disadvantages that are specific to RI apart from the difficulty of comparison with different sized enterprises, it is not as widely used as ROI. In one of the more recent surveys on the subject, albeit with transatlantic origins, the methods used amongst a sample of 459 companies were:

	%
ROI only	65
Both ROI and RI	28
RI only	2
Other criteria	4
No response	1
	100

3.3   Activity

Division Z has the following financial performance:

Operating profit	£40,000
Operating assets	£150,000
Cost of borrowing	10%

Would the division wish to accept a new possible investment costing £10,000 which would earn profit of £2,000 pa if the evaluation was on the basis of

(a)   ROI;

(b)   Residual income?

3.4   Activity solution

(a)   Current ROI $= \dfrac{£40,000}{£150,000} = 26.7\%$

If the investment is accepted, revised ROI

$= \dfrac{£42,000}{£160,000} = 26.3\%$

ie, REJECT the project

(b)   Current RI = £40,000 − (10% × £150,000) = £25,000
Revised RI = £42,000 − (10% × £160,000) = £26,000

ie, ACCEPT the project

Note here is a classic example of ROI giving the wrong conclusion in that a project that was worthwhile as far as the company was concerned is rejected since it reduces the division's current ROI.

4   DIVISIONAL PROJECT EVALUATION - ROI, RI AND NPV

4.1   The potential for inappropriate investment decisions

It has already been identified that a potential problem with the use of ROI or RI as a short-term management performance measure is the possibility that this will encourage long-term investment decisions that are not in the company's best interest. Specifically, a project with a positive net present value (NPV) at the company's cost of capital may show poor ROI or RI results in early years, leading to its rejection by the divisional manager.

4.2   Past exam question

This potential conflict between project appraisal methods and divisional performance measures was examined in December 1995. The discursive question also incorporated a more general discussion of the problems of ROI/RI in terms of profit and asset measurement, as covered earlier in the chapter.

The topic could also be the focus of a computational question, and thus it is important that you can carry out the types of calculations shown in the following examples, as well as appreciating the general principles.

4.3   Example 1 - equal annual cash flows

Division X of ABC plc, currently generating an ROI of 12%, is considering a new project. This requires an investment of £1.4 million and is expected to yield net cash inflows of £460,000 per annum for the next four years. None of the initial investment will be recoverable at the end of the project.

ABC plc has a cost of capital of 8%; annual accounting profits are to be assumed to equal annual net cash inflows less depreciation, and tax is to be ignored.

NPV of project at 8%
This can be computed using the annuity discount factor for four years at 8%:
NPV = £460,000 × 3.312 - £1,400,000 = £123,520
The project is therefore worthwhile accepting from the company's point of view.

ROI and RI using straight line depreciation

Annual depreciation on a straight-line basis will be £1.4m/4 = £350,000 per annum.
ROI and RI computations will be as follows:

	Year 1 £'000	Year 2 £'000	Year 3 £'000	Year 4 £'000
NBV at start of year	1,400	1,050	700	350
Net cash inflow	460	460	460	460
Depreciation	350	350	350	350
Profit	110	110	110	110
Interest on capital @8%	112	84	56	28
RI	(2)	26	54	82
ROI on NBV	7.9%	10.5%	15.7%	31.4%

If the manager's performance is measured (and rewarded) on the basis of RI or ROI he is unlikely to accept the project. The first year's RI is negative, and the ROI does not exceed the company's cost of capital until year 2, or that currently being earned until year 3. Divisional managers will tend to take a short-term view; more immediate returns are more certain, and by year 3 he may have moved jobs.

ROI and RI using annuity depreciation at 8% (company's cost of capital)

A compatibility between RI and NPV may be achieved by using an alternative form of depreciation. This is calculated as follows:

- the equivalent annual cost (EAC) of the initial investment at the cost of capital is calculated:

$$\frac{\text{Initial investment}}{\text{cum. disc. factor at 8\%}} = \frac{£1.4m}{3.312} = £422,705$$

- annual depreciation is then computed such that [depreciation + imputed interest] on capital = EAC, ie Depreciation = EAC - interest on opening NBV

- So for the first year of Division X's project, depreciation = 422.7 - 112 = 310.7

The results for the project over its life will now be as follows:

	Year 1 £'000	Year 2 £'000	Year 3 £'000	Year 4 £'000
NBV at start of year	1,400	1,089.3	753.7	391.3
Net cash inflow	460	460	460	460
Depreciation	310.7	335.6	362.4	391.4
Profit	149.3	124.4	97.6	68.6

Interest on capital @8%	112	87.1	60.3	31.3
RI	37.3	37.3	37.3	37.3
ROI on NBV	10.7%	11.4%	12.9%	17.5%

The project now has an equal, positive, RI over its life, which will encourage the manager to invest, a decision compatible with that using NPV. This consistency will always be achieved because the method ensures that discounting RI for each year at the cost of capital gives the NPV - thus provided the first year's RI is positive, so will be the NPV, and vice versa.

However, there is still a problem if ROI is used as the performance measure, in that the short-term low rate of return may not encourage investment in what is, in fact, a worthwhile project. A way round this is to use annuity depreciation at a different rate that will ensure a level ROI over the project life. The rate to be used will be the IRR of the project.

ROI and RI using annuity depreciation at the project IRR

The IRR of the project, which has equal annual cash flows, is estimated from the IRR annuity factor:

$$\frac{\text{Initial investment}}{\text{Annual NCI}} = \frac{£1.4m}{£460,000} = 3.043 \longrightarrow 4\% = 12\%$$

Using annuity (cumulative) factor tables, the IRR is identified as approximately 12%.

12% is now used instead of 8% in computing both the EAC of the investment (which will simply revert to being the annual NCI), and the interest on capital, yielding the following results:

	Year 1 £'000	Year 2 £'000	Year 3 £'000	Year 4 £'000
NBV at start of year	1,400	1,108	781	414.7
Net cash inflow *constant.*	460	460	460	460
Depreciation	292	327	366.3	410.2
Profit	168	133	93.7	49.8
Interest on capital @12%	168	133	93.7	49.8
RI	-	-	-	-
ROI on NBV	12%	12%	12%	12%

The ROI (and the RI) is now level over the project life, ensuring a consistent decision whether the short or long term view is taken. Using 12% as an appraisal rate for the project yields consistent results under all three methods (NPV, ROI and RI) ie the project is at break-even.

This somewhat contrived approach is probably less useful than the one above - ie using RI with annuity depreciation at the company's cost of capital as a management performance measure, which will ensure compatibility with a DCF approach to project appraisal.

4.4   Example 2 - uneven cash flows

The use of annuity depreciation as illustrated above does not produce helpful results when cash flows are uneven.

Suppose Division X was considering an alternative project requiring an initial investment of £1m with annual cash flows of £380,000/£350,000/£320,000/£290,000 over the four years of its life respectively.

The NPV of this project at 8% = £119,063

The RI/ROI results, using annuity depreciation at 8%, are as follows:

- the equivalent annual cost (EAC) of the initial investment at the cost of capital is calculated:

$$\frac{\text{Initial investment}}{\text{Cum. disc. factor at 8\%}} = \frac{£1.0m}{3.312} = £301,932 \quad \longleftarrow A E C F \qquad \therefore \left[3 \cdot 1 9 3 2 - 8 0 (8 \cdot) = 2 2 1 9 3 2 \right]$$

$$\underline{Dep \cdot (8r1)}$$

- the results for the alternative project would be as follows:

	Year 1 £'000	Year 2 £'000	Year 3 £'000	Year 4 £'000
NBV at start of year *of Investment*	1,000	778.1	538.4	279.6
Net cash inflow *– uneven .*	380	350	320	290
Depreciation	221.9	239.7	258.8	279.5
Profit	158.1	110.3	61.2	10.5
Interest on capital @8%	80	62.2	43.1	22.4
RI	78.1	48.1	18.1	(11.9)
ROI on NBV	15.8%	14.2%	11.4%	3.8%

Consistency with the NPV using either ROI or RI is not guaranteed with uneven cash flows. If the pattern of cash flows had been increasing, it is easy to see that the RI in the first year could be negative, and the ROI low, discouraging investment in this worthwhile project.

Furthermore, comparing the results above with those for the original project in the early years (under the same depreciation method), early years RI and ROI measures look far superior, and thus, if a choice were to be made, the manager of Division X would be encouraged to accept the alternative project over the original. This is contrary to the DCF evaluation, which shows the alternative as having a lower NPV than the original.

There is an approach that can overcome this - the *adjusted RI approach* - which calculates annual depreciation by deducting interest on capital from the annual *net cash inflow* (rather than the EAC of the initial investment).

However, this results in depreciation charges that can increase and decrease according to the pattern of the cash flows, and although it makes comparisons between projects with uneven cash flows easier, it does not guarantee investment decisions compatible with NPV evaluations.

5   RATIO ANALYSIS

5.1   Introduction

One important means of assessing performance both of companies by outside observers and of divisions by senior management is by the use of assorted accounting ratios. The reason for this is the difficulty of getting a true picture of performance by just using one figure. The starting point for ratio analysis is the primary ratio ROI which then splits down into the asset turnover ratio and net profit percentage. The first of these, asset turnover, then leads on to various liquidity ratios whilst the net profit percentage can be investigated further by calculating additional profitability measures.

The whole process is best shown as a ratio pyramid or ratio tree.

5.2   Ratio pyramid

The initial split of ROI into secondary ratios has been mentioned before.

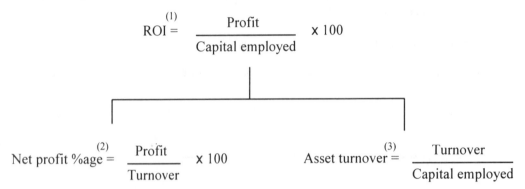

$$\overset{(1)}{\text{ROI}} = \frac{\text{Profit}}{\text{Capital employed}} \times 100$$

$$\text{Net profit \%age} \overset{(2)}{=} \frac{\text{Profit}}{\text{Turnover}} \times 100 \qquad \text{Asset turnover} \overset{(3)}{=} \frac{\text{Turnover}}{\text{Capital employed}}$$

They are linked since $(1) = (2) \times (3)$.

After this there is no clear relationship although:

Net profit percentage can be investigated by finding:

$$\text{Gross profit percentage} \quad = \quad \frac{\text{Gross profit}}{\text{Turnover}} \times 100$$

and $$\text{Operating ratios} \quad = \quad \frac{\text{Various expenses}}{\text{Turnover}} \times 100$$

Asset turnover can be investigated by finding:

$$\frac{\text{Turnover}}{\text{Fixed assets}} \quad \text{and} \quad \frac{\text{Turnover}}{\text{Net current assets}}$$

The first pair of ratios (or group of ratios) would require careful study if the net profit percentage indicated problems over profitability to determine whether this was due to an unduly low margin or poor control of overheads. The second pair of ratios would indicate whether sufficient sales were being generated and whether working capital was being sufficiently well controlled. If a problem was detected in this last area then various liquidity ratios would be found:

$$\text{Current ratio} \quad = \quad \frac{\text{current assets}}{\text{current liabilities}}$$

$$\text{Quick ratio} \quad = \quad \frac{\text{quick assets (CA's} - \text{stock)}}{\text{current liabilities}}$$
(Acid test ratio)

$$\text{Debtors period} \quad = \quad \frac{\text{debtors}}{\text{daily credit sales}}$$

$$\text{Stock period} \quad = \quad \frac{\text{stock}}{\text{daily cost of sales}}$$

$$\text{Creditors period} \quad = \quad \frac{\text{creditors}}{\text{daily credit purchases}}$$

These ratios could be found using year end figures or average figures. In some divisionalised companies some of these liquidity ratios are less important since the assets are managed centrally. Comparison would be made with group standards, other divisions, other periods and other firms in the same business.

5.3 Example

The example which follows shows an evaluation of the production, commercial and financial management of a company using key ratios.

The following information relates to a company manufacturing consumable goods.

	Actual 19X5/6 £'000	Actual 19X6/7 £'000	Budget 19X7/8 £'000
Sales	215	236	276
Less: Production costs:			
Material	79	82	96
Labour – direct	34	33	37
Labour – indirect	35	39	44
Other costs	26	29	36
	174	183	213
Administration	21	26	33
Selling	6	7	7
Distribution	3	3	4
	204	219	257
Net profit before tax	11	17	19

Balance sheet (at year end)

	Actual 19X5/6 £'000	Actual 19X6/7 £'000	Budget 19X7/8 £'000
Fixed assets at cost	120	155	175
Less: Depreciation	(65)	(65)	(80)
	55	90	95
Stocks and work-in-progress	55	62	68
Debtors	35	32	34
Bank	4	4	3
	94	98	105
Less: Current liabilities	(17)	(13)	(15)
	77	85	90
	132	175	185

	Actual		*Budget*
	19X5/6	*19X6/7*	*19X7/8*
Number of people employed:			
Average during year:			
Direct	43	41	47
Works indirect	31	35	40
Administration	30	37	36
Sales	6	7	7
	110	120	130
Floor space occupied (square feet)	30,000	30,000	32,000

Give your interpretation of the production, commercial and financial management of the company over the period shown illustrating your conclusion with selected key ratios through the period.

5.4   Solution

Evaluation of performance

			Budget
	19X5/6	*19X6/7*	*19X7/8*
Profitability			
Profit : Capital employed	8.3%	9.7%	10.3%
Profit : Sales	5.1%	7.2%	6.9%
Sales : Capital employed	1.63 times	1.35 times	1.49 times
Production costs			
% of works cost	%	%	%
Materials	45.4	44.9	45.0
Direct labour	19.5	18.0	17.4
Indirect labour	20.1	21.3	20.7
Other costs	15.0	15.8	16.9
	100.0	100.0	100.0
Labour			
Indirect/Direct			
Monetary values (£)	1.03	1.18	1.19
Numbers	0.72	0.85	0.85
£ per employee per annum:			
Direct	£791	£804	£787
Indirect	£1,129	£1,114	£1,100
Profit:			
Per direct worker	£256	£415	£404
Per indirect worker	£354	£485	£475

Sales

Selling costs/Sales	2.8%	3.0%	2.5%
Sales per sales employee	£35,833	£33,714	£39,429
Profit per sales employee	£1,833	£2,428	£2,714

			Budget
	19X5/6	*19X6/7*	*19X7/8*

Financial control

Stock period			
Stock and WIP : Production cost	115 days	124 days	117 days
Debtors period			
Debtors : Sales	59 days	49 days	45 days
Creditors period			
Current liabilities : Materials	78 days	58 days	57 days
Current ratio			
Current assets/Current liabilities	5.5	7.5	7.0
Acid test			
(Debtors + Bank)/Current liabilities	2.3	2.8	2.5

Interpretation

(a)   **Profitability**

The profit increase from £11,000 to £17,000 represented an increase of more than 50% from a sales volume increase of only 10%. The ROCE improved whilst sales as a percentage of capital employed declined, indicating increased efficiency but lower utilisation. This has been recognised in the higher sales to capital employed set for the next budget. Although budgeted sales are much higher for 19X7/8 the target profit to sales figures is reduced suggesting effort to increase volume at the expense of price.

(b)   **Production**

Material content as a proportion of total cost remains constant whilst direct labour is declining. Other costs have shown an increase in proportion suggesting a change in production methods. This is supported by the increased ratio and cost of indirect compared with direct employees. Profit per worker of both categories has risen whilst earnings have remained constant suggesting improved productivity as a result of plant and methods rather than labour. Selling costs to sales did not change significantly the addition to staff being represented by higher volume of turnover. Since no increase is planned in staff numbers to achieve the substantially higher sales budgeted for 19X7/8 there is still some capacity available in the existing sales force.

(c)   **Balance sheet**

Plant has increased this year and a further increase is planned for the coming year. The higher stock relates to the increased turnover budgeted but maintenance of the debtors figure suggests a quicker turnover confirmed by the debtors turnover rate. All working capital ratios are better than standard supporting interpretation of effective financial control. The current year indicates investment in new equipment reflected in higher productivity from labour. The budget forecasts the intention to continue this trend through the next period.

6   IMPACT OF INFLATION ON CURRENT AND FUTURE PERFORMANCE

6.1   Impact on consumers

A period of rapid inflation typically causes consumer incomes to start shrinking in real terms and leads to changes in consumer attitudes and behaviour. Consumers tend to adopt various forms of economising behaviour. The main consumer adjustments to inflation are the following:

(a)   Consumers postpone expensive discretionary purchases, such as new cars. They put their money into savings instruments that pay attractive interest rates.

(b)   Consumers engage in more comparison shopping to find the best prices on their preferred brands.

(c)   Consumers 'trade down' from preferred brands and products to acceptable brands and products. They buy private labels and generic labels in product categories that are not important to them. They do more bargain hunting and less impulse buying.

(d)   To save money, consumers move into more self-production.

Not all consumers change their behaviour in these directions. Those with high incomes and secure outlooks operate with 'business as usual'. Marketers must be aware that consumers will show different response patterns in the face of rapid inflation.

6.2   Strategies during inflation

Organisations need to adjust their marketing strategies during periods of high inflation. The amount and types of adjustment depend on the company's view of how steep the inflation will be, how long it will last, and how sensitive buyers will be.

During a period of rapid inflation, companies will have to pass on some price increases to customers. A likely consequence will be the loss of some accounts. The company should, therefore, review its major markets and customers to see which are central and which are peripheral. The organisation needs to be circumspect about its price increases to important markets and customers.

As far as the product or service and design are concerned, the company will need to review how inflation has affected the profitability of its different products. Products with a high content of the more cost-inflating inputs will fall in their profitability. If their prices cannot be raised sufficiently, and they are not essential to the product mix, the company might consider eliminating some of them.

Price adjustments are the most common response to inflation. Price adjustments can be instituted rapidly, and if successful, they will preserve the company's profit margin.

During inflation, customers will do more price-comparison shopping and buy more often from lower-cost outlets and suppliers. Companies therefore need to review their distribution channels and put more emphasis on lower-cost channels such as mass merchandising and discount operations.

Companies need to review their advertising budget, message, and media during a period of rapid inflation. Also, sales promotion as a marketing tool increases in importance during inflation. Consumers are much more responsive to price deals and premiums.

7   MEASURING THE RESULTS OF STRATEGIC DECISIONS IN INFLATIONARY CONDITIONS

7.1   Techniques

Strategic planning and marketing decisions need to be appraised so that control decisions can be made. Techniques of performance appraisal involve:

(a)   Comparison of budget and actual data.

(b)   Analysis of accounting data often by using ratios.

The effects of inflation need to be considered in any performance appraisal but are especially important for strategic planning and marketing decisions. The consequences of strategic planning and marketing decisions are often long term and thus the cumulative effects of inflation may be considerable.

The main approaches taken for the impact of inflation are:

(a)   Budget data is uplifted for expected inflation

Budgets are used for detailed short term operational control. The short run effects of inflation are best allowed for by uplifting costs and revenues by the expected inflation. Care should be taken when actual and budget data is compared that the actual inflation is at similar rates to expected inflation. If there are material differences, the price variances need to be considered in the light of the inflation experience.

(b)   Accounting data used for analysis is adjusted so that the data is 'inflation neutral'

Accounting data may be analysed over short and long periods of time. Long term trends will obviously be materially affected by inflation. For example, with a 7% inflation rate, prices over a 4 year period increase by 31% ($1.07^4 = 1.31$).

In addition however analysis of data at one point in time may be materially distorted by inflation as the numerator or denominator in a ratio may not be fairly stated. *Historic costs* suffer from this deficiency. Using *current values* is regarded by many as the best way to remedy the deficiency.

The analysis of data at one point in time is dealt with first as the solution to this problem may affect the means of solving the problem of the lack of comparability of data over time.

7.2   Use of accounting data at one point in time

Ratios are often used to measure the results of strategic and marketing decisions. For example a target rate for ROCE may have been set. Consideration must be given as to whether the return or the capital are distorted either because of current inflation or inflation in previous years.

If historic cost accounting data is used the capital figure is not inflation neutral if the assets of the organisation (or the part of the organisation being measured) are not stated at current values. Fixed assets are the main group of assets which create a distortion because:

(a)   for many organisations fixed assets are the major element of capital employed;

(b)   fixed assets still in use may have been purchased over a long period of time.

The principle should be that: *the assets stated in a balance sheet should be realistic up-to-date measures of the resources employed in an organisation.*

If historic cost accounting data is used the return figure is not inflation neutral as current revenues are matched with costs incurred at an earlier date. The main costs which are distorted are:

(a)   Depreciation. If the assets of the organisation are not stated at current values, the depreciation charged does not represent the current worth to the organisation of using those assets.

(b)   Other elements of cost of sales should be charged at their current value when an item is sold rather than at the historic costs of production.

The effect of depreciation and other elements of cost of sales being charged at current values is to remove *holding gains* from operating profits. Holding gains arise through holding stock in a period in which the buying price of the elements which make up the cost of a finished product increase and there is a gap in time between the costs elements being applied to the production of a finished product and its eventual sale. *If holding gains are left in profit, management's effectiveness in achieving operating results may be concealed.*

The dangers of using historic cost information as a performance measure are thus considerable. *Current cost accounting* provides a solution as it removes holding gains from profit and shows assets at current values. However there has been no success in establishing a mandatory accounting standard for financial accounting reporting, and this has not encouraged organisations to use current values for internal reporting. The practical problems of time and cost in preparing current value information means that many organisations do not take inflation into account in quantitative measures of strategic planning and marketing. Some comfort however can be taken from the practice by many organisations of revaluing fixed assets every three to five years. As a result values are not too far out of date.

7.3   Lack of comparability of data over time

In addition to the problems already detailed, historic cost accounting is very weak in providing information on the trends of an organisation's performance over time. This is because historic cost accounting uses a *monetary unit of measurement* eg, £s. Monetary measurements cannot show changes in real value over time. Thus if profits were £300,000 10 years ago and profits made this year are £350,000, it is pointless stating anything on the achievement by the organisation of its strategic plan until information is found on the rates of inflation over the last 10 years. If the rate of inflation has doubled prices in the 10 years, the organisation has suffered a fall in the real level of profits.

Current cost accounting does not remedy this defect as valuations of assets reflect prices ruling at a balance sheet date. Previous years' balance sheets only reflect valuations at previous years' prices. The same argument applies to the computation of profits. Continuing the example in the previous paragraph, profits on a current cost basis may have been £240,000 10 years ago and £310,000 this year. If prices have doubled the organisation has not achieved a real growth in earnings.

7.4   Methods of overcoming lack of comparability

(a)   **The use of ratios**

Ratios may be comparable from year to year as they are measuring performance based on common prices. Examples are:

- Return on capital employed

    This will be comparable provided both profit and capital employed have been adjusted to reflect current values relevant for *each year* ie, fixed assets in 19X3 have been adjusted to current values at prices ruling in 19X3, and fixed assets in 19X2 have been adjusted to current values at prices ruling in 19X2.

- Gearing ratio

    Liabilities will tend to be already stated at their current value ie, the amount repayable. Equity must however be computed to reflect the real value of the underlying assets at each balance sheet date.

(b)   **Restatement of comparative information in terms of a constant unit of measurement**

The restatement of comparative information in terms of a constant unit of measurement is a more comprehensive method of performance appraisal. The Accounting Standards Committee (ASC) issued 'Accounting for the effects of changing prices: a handbook' in 1986 following the demise of SSAP 16 as a mandatory standard. One of its central recommendations is: *for companies that publish five or ten year historical summaries to restate, in units of current purchasing power, certain figures which are either adjusted for the effects of specific changing prices (ie, current values) or require no adjustment (such as turnover and dividends).*

Companies that publish five or ten year historical summaries are mainly listed companies.

Although the recommendation appears a daunting prospect, the computations involved are straightforward and can be used to convert accounting information produced for internal purposes.

The restated figures can be calculated in two ways:

- by reference to the movement in the average RPI for each year (the average method); or

- by reference to the movement in the RPI from one year-end to the next (the year-end method).

The average method is the more appropriate method for restating profit and loss account information. The year-end method is more appropriate for the restatement of balance sheet information and is consistent with the objective of restating previously reported figures in pounds of the balance sheet date. Either method is acceptable as long as it is applied consistently.

7.5   Illustration

PLC historical summary

As reported *£ million*

	19X1	*19X2*	*19X3*	*19X4*	*19X5*
Turnover	25,737	29,314	32,381	37,933	40,986
Current cost operating profit	2,460	2,930	3,289	3,901	4,438
Earnings per ordinary share	63.9p	39.4p	47.5p	76.8p	87.4p
Dividends per ordinary share	20.25p	20.25p	24.0p	30.0p	34.0p
Net assets at current cost	32,564	38,799	47,021	52,564	56,163
Adjusted for the average UK retail price index of:	295.0	320.4	355.1	351.8	373.1

19X5 £ million

Turnover	32,551	34,136	36,053	40,230	40,986
Current cost operating profit	3,111	3,412	3,662	4,137	4,438
Earnings per ordinary share	80.8p	45.9p	52.9p	81.4p	87.4p
Dividends per ordinary share	25.61p	23.58p	26.72p	31.82p	34.0p
Net assets at current cost	41,185	45,181	52,353	55,747	56,163

The calculations have been made by adjusting the 'As reported' figures by:

$$\frac{\text{RPI for current year}}{\text{RPI for year in which figures were reported}}$$

Thus the turnover for 19X1 is restated in terms of 19X5 £m by:

$$25,737 \times \frac{373.1}{295.0} = 32,551$$

8   CHAPTER SUMMARY

- Decentralisation is the process of devolving the authority to make decisions; the divisions thus created are most likely to be investment centres or at least profit centres although they may only be cost centres.

- The most common methods of assessing divisional performance involve the use of return on investment (ROI) and/or residual income (RI); however, other methods include: variance analysis, ratio analysis and other management information and ratios.

- $$\text{ROI} = \frac{\text{Controllable divisional profit}}{\text{Controllable divisional investment}} \times 100$$

  $$\text{RI} = \underset{\text{profit}}{\text{Controllable divisional}} - \underset{\text{controllable divisional investment}}{\text{Imputed interest cost on}}$$

- Both measures suffer from: difficulty in defining which profit to use, asset measurement, conflict with investment decisions. ROI is often criticised for its disincentive to divisions to invest, the fact that it improves with the age of an asset and that corporate objectives are not achieved by acting on the basis of ROI information.

- The use of annuity depreciation can, in some cases, resolve the investment decision conflict between NPV and ROI/RI measures.

- The primary ratio, ROI, can be split into two secondary ratios: asset turnover and net profit percentage. The first leads on to various liquidity ratios, the second to other measures of profitability.

9   SELF TEST QUESTIONS

9.1   What are the advantages of ROI as a means of divisional appraisal? (2.2)

9.2   How do you calculate residual income? (3.1)

9.3   What are the advantages of RI as means of divisional appraisal? (3.2)

9.4   In what ways do consumers adjust their spending behaviour in times of inflation? (6.1)

9.5   What methods can be used to overcome the lack of comparability caused by inflation? (7.4)

10   EXAMINATION TYPE QUESTIONS

10.1   Theta Ltd

Theta Ltd compares the performance of its subsidiaries by return on investment (ROI) using the following formula:

Profit:	Depreciation is calculated on a straight-line basis.
	Losses on sale of assets are charged against profit in the year of the sale.
Capital employed:	Net current assets, at the average value throughout the year.
	Fixed assets, at original cost less accumulated depreciation as at the end of the year.

Theta Ltd, whose cost of capital is 14% per annum, is considering acquiring Alpha Ltd whose performance has been calculated on a similar basis to that shown above except that fixed assets are valued at original cost.

During the past year, apart from normal trading, Alpha Ltd was involved in the following separate transactions:

(A)   It bought equipment on 1 November 19X4 (the start of its financial year) at a cost of £120,000. Resulting savings were £35,000 for the year; these are expected to continue at that level throughout the six years' expected life of the asset after which it will have no scrap value.

(B)   On 1 November 19X4 it sold a piece of equipment that had cost £200,000 when bought exactly three years earlier. The expected life was four years, with no scrap value. This equipment had been making a contribution to profit of £30,000 per annum before depreciation and realised £20,000 on sale.

(C)   It negotiated a bank overdraft of £20,000 for the year to take advantage of quick payment discounts offered by creditors; this reduced costs by £4,000 per annum.

(D)   To improve liquidity, it reduced stocks by an average of £25,000 throughout the year. This resulted in reduced sales with a reduction of £6,000 per annum contribution.

The financial position of Alpha Ltd for the year from 1 November 19X4 to 31 October 19X5, **excluding the outcomes of transactions (A) to (D) above**, was:

	£'000
Profit for the year	225
Fixed assets:	
Original cost	1,000
Accumulated depreciation	475
Net current assets (average for the year)	250

You are required:

(a)   to calculate the ROI of Alpha Ltd using its present basis of calculation:

   (i)   if none of the transactions (A) to (D) had taken place;
   (ii)   if transaction (A) had taken place but not (B), (C) or (D);
   (iii)   if transaction (B) had taken place but not (A), (C) or (D);
   (iv)   if transaction (C) had taken place but not (A), (B) or (D);
   (v)   if transaction (D) had taken place but not (A), (B) or (C);

(b)   to calculate the ROI as in (a)(i) to (a)(v) above using Theta Ltd's basis of calculation; and

(c)   to explain briefly whether there would have been any lack of goal congruence as between Theta Ltd and the management of Alpha Ltd (assuming that Alpha Ltd had been acquired by Theta Ltd on 1 November 19X4 and that Theta Ltd's basis of calculation was used) in respect of :

   (i)   transaction (A); and
   (ii)   transaction (B).

Taxation is to be ignored.   **(25 marks)**

10.2   Hawlit Ltd

Hawlit Ltd, a transport company, is planning its future investment strategy. Hawlit's best projections of profit outcome are dependent upon the cost of diesel fuel.

	\multicolumn{5}{c}{*Annual net income at following costs per gallon:*}				
Annual investment level	£1.20	£1.25	£1.30	£1.40	£1.50
(£'000)	(£'000)	(£'000)	(£'000)	(£'000)	(£'000)
350	55	52	46	40	30
400	60	58	52	46	35
450	68	63	55	47	35
500	72	68	58	49	34
550	74	67	56	43	30
600	75	64	53	40	25
Estimated probability of outcome	0.1	0.1	0.4	0.3	0.1

The company's minimum required rate of return is 10% pa.

You are required:

(a)   to compute, for each level of investment, the return on investment (ROI) and the residual income.   **(10 marks)**

(b)   to calculate the optimal investment level, stating your reasons.   **(3 marks)**

(c)   to evaluate the merits of residual income and return on investment as measures of performance.   **(12 marks)**

    (Total: 25 marks)

11   ANSWERS TO EXAMINATION TYPE QUESTIONS

11.1   Theta Ltd

(a)   **ROI using Alpha's basis**

		£'000
(i)	Profit	225

Capital employed:

	£'000
Fixed assets (at cost)	1,000
Net current assets	250
	1,250

$$\text{ROI} = \frac{225}{1,250} \times 100 = 18.0\%$$

(ii)	Profit	225

Add: Savings less depreciation

$$\left(35,000 - \frac{120,000}{6}\right)$$ 15

    240

Capital employed:

	£'000
Fixed assets (at cost)	1,000
Add: Purchases (at cost)	120
	1,120
Net current assets	250
	1,370

$$\text{ROI} = \frac{240}{1,370} \times 100 = 17.52\%$$

(iii)	Profit as stated	225
	Less: Contribution lost	30
		195
	Add: Depreciation not charged	20
		215

Capital employed:		
	Fixed assets (at cost)	1,000
	Less: Disposals (at cost)	200
		800
	Net current assets	250
		1,050

$$\text{ROI} = \frac{215}{1,050} \times 100 = 20.48\%$$

Note: as the net current assets are average for the year the inflow of £20,000 realised for sale of asset has not been included. Similarly in (ii) above it is assumed that the machine was purchased out of additional funds and not from existing cash resources (a common assumption in this style of question).

		£'000
(iv)	Profit	225
	Add: Reduction in cost	4
		229
	Capital employed:	
	Fixed assets (at cost)	1,000
	Net current assets	250
		1,250

$$\text{ROI} = \frac{229}{1,250} \times 100 = 18.3\%$$

Note: the reduction in creditors is offset by bank overdraft therefore no change in 'net' current assets. Overdraft interest ignored.

		£'000
(v)	Profit	225
	Less: Lost contribution	6
		219
	Capital employed:	
	Fixed assets	1,000
	Net current assets	
	(£250,000 – £25,000)	225
		1,225

$$\text{ROI} = \frac{219}{1,225} \times 100 = 17.9\%$$

(b) **ROI using Theta's basis**

All profit figures are as computed in part (a). Capital employed must be recomputed on basis of original cost less depreciation for fixed assets.

			£'000
(i)	Profit		225

Capital employed:

		£'000
Fixed assets (£1,000,000 – £475,000)		525
Net current assets		250
		775

$$\text{ROI} = \frac{225}{775} \times 100 = 29.03\%$$

			£'000
(ii)	Profit		240

Capital employed:

		£'000
Existing fixed assets		525
Addition (£120,000 – £20,000)		100
		625
Net current assets		250
		875

$$\text{ROI} = \frac{240}{875} \times 100 = 27.42\%$$

			215
(iii)	Profit		215

Capital employed:

	£'000	£'000
Existing fixed assets		525
Net sales at book value		
Original cost	200	
Accumulated depreciation	200	-
		525
Net current assets		250
		775

$$\text{ROI} = \frac{215}{775} \times 100 = 27.74\%$$

			229
(iv)	Profit		229

Capital employed:

		£'000
Fixed assets		525
Net current assets		250
		775

$$\text{ROI} = \frac{229}{775} \times 100 = 29.54\%$$

(v)   Profit   219
                                                                                               ———

         Capital employed:
              Fixed assets   525
              Net current assets   225
                                                                                               ———
                                                                                               750
                                                                                               ———

$$\text{ROI} = \frac{219}{750} \times 100 = 29.2\%$$

Summary

	(a) %	(b) %
(i)	18.0	29.0
(ii)	17.5	27.4
(iii)	20.5	27.7
(iv)	18.3	29.5
(v)	17.9	29.2

(c)   **Goal congruence**

Goal congruence is the state that exists in a control system which leads individuals or groups to take actions which are both in their self-interest and also in the best interest of the entity.

(i)   **Transaction A**

Theta uses ROCE for assessing performance of subsidiaries. The implementation of transaction A reduced this ratio from 29.0% to 27.4% and from this point of view was incorrect.

Alpha uses the same ratio but a different base. Even here, however, there is a deterioration from 18.0% to 17.5%.

In answering parts (a) and (b) the cost of capital of 14% has not been utilised. From a decision-making point of view it may be informative to discount the annual cash flows of £35,000 in order to see how it relates to capital cost.

(ii)   **Transaction B**

The calculation for this transaction indicates that from the view of Theta there is a decline from 29.0% to 27.7%, whilst from the view of Alpha there is a rise from 18.0% to 20.5%. The movements are opposite, indicative of a lack of goal congruence. Without computation, it seems questionable whether selling for £20,000 a machine which is producing annual cash flows of £30,000 is good management.

11.2   Hawlit Ltd

(a)   ROI and Residual income

Price/ gallon £	Prob	£0.35m		£0.40m		£0.45m		£0.50m		£0.55m		£0.60m	
		£'000	EV £'000	£'000	EV £'000	£'000	EV £'000	£'000	EV £'000	£'000	EV £'000	£'000	EV £'000
1.20	0.1	55	5.5	60	6.0	68	6.8	72	7.2	74	7.4	75	7.5
1.25	0.1	52	5.2	58	5.8	63	6.3	68	6.8	67	6.7	64	6.4
1.30	0.4	46	18.4	52	20.8	55	22.0	58	23.2	56	22.4	53	21.2
1.40	0.3	40	12.0	46	13.8	47	14.1	49	14.7	43	12.9	40	12.0
1.50	0.1	30	3.0	35	3.5	35	3.5	34	3.4	30	3.0	25	2.5
	1.0		44.1		49.9		52.7		55.3		52.4		49.6

Annual and expected net income at the following annual investment levels

Annual investment level £'000	Expected annual net income £'000	Minimum required return on investment (10% pa) £'000	Residual income £'000	ROI %
350	44.1	35.0	9.1	12.6
400	49.9	40.0	9.9	12.5
450	52.7	45.0	7.7	11.7
500	55.3	50.0	5.3	11.1
550	52.4	55.0	(2.6)	9.5
600	49.6	60.0	(10.4)	8.3

Notes: (1)   Residual income = expected annual net income **less** minimum required return on investment.

(2)   ROI = expected annual net income as a percentage of investment.

(b)   Optimal investment level

On the basis of giving the highest level of residual income (£9,900) an investment level of £400,000 pa is the optimum.

The annual investment levels given are in steps of £50,000 and, in stating an optimum, any levels between these steps have not been considered. Further information would be required to determine a more 'precise' optimal level.

Residual income is chosen as the basis for determining the optimal level as it takes account of the **absolute** surplus of income after deducting the minimum required return on the investment. The maximisation of profit is assumed to be a major objective of the company, that is the maximisation of an absolute sum.

(c)   Residual income and return on investment (ROI) as measures of performance

Residual income and return on investment are just two approaches to the measurement of performance. The problem of measuring performance is considerably magnified in a company which has an organisation structure in which different segments or parts have been clearly defined. The management in each section should have clearly specified responsibilities and, therefore, there is a need to be able to assess segment performance.

Traditionally ROI has been considered the best measure of performance. It is an all-embracing ratio that relates net income to the level of investment. It is generally easily understood by all levels of management. It can be used as a basis for comparison with investment opportunities both inside and outside the company.

As the key ratio in a company it can be sub-divided into a series of secondary ratios as part of an analysis. The first stage in such a breakdown can be illustrated:

$$\text{ROI} = \frac{\text{Net income}}{\text{Investment}}$$

$$= \frac{\text{Net income}}{\text{Sales}} \times \frac{\text{Sales}}{\text{Investment}}$$

Such a sub-analysis assists management in making appropriate decisions and assessing their effect on ROI, which may well be the subject of a target or objective.

The use of ROI as a measure of performance focuses the attention of management on the key factors of net income and the level of investment. A profit maximisation objective for the company is assumed.

Briefly, the problems or limitations of ROI are very much associated with the measurement of net income and investment. The value that has to be placed on fixed assets is a particular problem; if valid comparisons are to be made, should it be based on historical cost, depreciated book value or on replacement cost? Furthermore, in a divisional organisation structure the apportionment of costs and assets between the different parts of the organisation has to be considered. This applies where there are shared facilities.

In a divisional structure, each segment will have a different ROI which will not necessarily tally with the overall company ROI. Where a division has a ROI in excess of the company's, the manager will not be motivated to accept a project which gives a lower ROI than his division currently attains although that return is above the company's ROI target. If the project was accepted the divisional manager would see his measure of performance fall, yet it would be in the best interests of the company as a whole to accept the project. (It was because of this type of conflict that the General Electric Company in the USA introduced the concept of residual income in the 1950s.)

ROI is a relative measure of performance (net income being related to investment), whereas residual income is an absolute measure, being the net income less the minimum required return on the investment. It is the return over and above the minimum required. A comparison can be made between the IRR and NPV approaches in capital budgeting, which are relative and absolute measures of projects respectively, and ROI and residual income in performance measurement.

The conflict, already mentioned, where the divisional and the overall company ROI do not tally can be overcome if a residual income approach is adopted rather than a ROI one. A project yielding at least the overall company's ROI will increase the division's residual income.

ROI, as a measure of performance, is widely used in practice. It relates net income and investment in an easily understood concept. The bases of measuring cost and investment need to be considered and consistently applied where ROI is used for comparison purposes. In a divisional organisation structure particularly, the residual income approach overcomes a lot of the conflict that can arise between divisional goals and overall company goals.

Student Questionnaire

Invoice number: . . . .

Because we believe in listening to our customers, this questionnaire has been designed to discover exactly what you think about us and our materials. We want to know how we can continue improving our customer support and how to make our top class books even better - how do you use our books, what do you like about them and what else would you like to see us do to make them better?

1 Where did you hear about AT Foulks Lynch ACCA Textbooks?

☐ Colleague or friend   ☐ Employer recommendation   ☐ Lecturer recommendation

☐ AT Foulks Lynch mailshot   ☐ Conference   ☐ ACCA literature

☐ Student Newsletter   ☐ Pass Magazine   ☐ Internet

☐ Other ....

2 Overall, do you think the AT Foulks Lynch ACCA Textbooks are:

☐ Excellent   ☐ Good   ☐ Average   ☐ Poor   ☐ No opinion

3 Please evaluate AT Foulks Lynch service using the following criteria:

	Excellent	Good	Average	Poor	No opinion
Professional	☐	☐	☐	☐	☐
Polite	☐	☐	☐	☐	☐
Informed	☐	☐	☐	☐	☐
Helpful	☐	☐	☐	☐	☐

4 How did you obtain this book?

☐ From a bookshop (name)   ☐ From your college (name)   ☐ From us by mail order

....

☐ From us by telephone   ☐ Internet   ☐ Other ....

5 How long did it take to receive your materials? .... days.

☐ Very fast   ☐ Fast   ☐ Satisfactory   ☐ Slow   ☐ No opinion

6 How do you rate the value of these features of this Textbook?

Paper No ....   Title ....

		Excellent	Good	Average	Poor	No opinion
1	Syllabus referenced to chapters	☐	☐	☐	☐	☐
2	Teaching Guide referenced to chapters	☐	☐	☐	☐	☐
3	Step by step approach and solutions	☐	☐	☐	☐	☐
4	Activities throughout the chapters	☐	☐	☐	☐	☐
5	Self test questions	☐	☐	☐	☐	☐
6	Examination type questions	☐	☐	☐	☐	☐
7	Index	☐	☐	☐	☐	☐

Continued/...

7 Have you purchased any other AT Foulks Lynch ACCA titles?
If so, please specify title(s) and your rating of each below:

Title	Excellent	Good	Average	Poor	No opinion
....	☐	☐	☐	☐	☐
....	☐	☐	☐	☐	☐
....	☐	☐	☐	☐	☐
....	☐	☐	☐	☐	☐

8 Have you used publications other than AT Foulks Lynch ACCA titles?
If so, please specify title(s) and your rating of each below:

Title and Publisher	Excellent	Good	Average	Poor	No opinion
....	☐	☐	☐	☐	☐
....	☐	☐	☐	☐	☐
....	☐	☐	☐	☐	☐
....	☐	☐	☐	☐	☐

9 Will you buy the AT Foulks Lynch ACCA Textbooks again?

☐ Yes   ☐ No   ☐ Not sure

Why? ....

10 Please write here any additional comments you might have on any of the above areas or tell us what you would like us to do to make the books even better:

....

....

....

....

11 Your details: these are for the internal use of AT Foulks Lynch Ltd only and will not be supplied to any outside organisations.

Name
....

Address
....

....

Telephone
....

Do you have your own e-mail address?	☐ Yes ☐ No	
Do you have access to the World Wide Web?	☐ Yes ☐ No	....
Do you have access to a CD Rom Drive?	☐ Yes ☐ No	

Please send to:

Quality Feedback Department
FREEPOST 2254
AT Foulks Lynch Ltd, 4 The Griffin Centre, Staines Road, Feltham, Middlesex, TW14 0BR.

Thank you for your time.

Examination Date: □ December 99 □ June 2000	**Publications**				**Distance Learning**	**Open Learning**
	Textbooks	**Revision Series**	**Lynchpins**	**Tracks**	**Include helpline & marking** (except for overseas Open Learning)	
Module A – Foundation Stage						
1 Accounting Framework	£18.95 [UK] [IAS]	£10.95 [UK] [IAS]	£5.95	£10.95	£85	£89
2 Legal Framework	£18.95	£10.95	£5.95	£10.95	£85	£89
Module B						
3 Management Information	£18.95	£10.95	£5.95	£10.95	£85	£89
4 Organisational Framework	£18.95	£10.95	£5.95	£10.95	£85	£89
Module C – Certificate Stage						
5 Information Analysis	£18.95	£10.95	£5.95	£10.95	£85	£89
6 Audit Framework	£18.95 [UK] [IAS]	£10.95 [UK] [IAS]	£5.95	£10.95	£85	£89
Module D						
7 Tax Framework FA98 - D99	£17.95	£10.95	£5.95	£10.95	£85	£89
FA99 - J2000	£18.95	£10.95 *	£5.95	£10.95 *		
8 Managerial Finance	£18.95	£10.95	£5.95	£10.95	£85	£89
Module E – Professional Stage						
9 ICDM	£18.95	£10.95	£5.95	£10.95	£85	£89
10 Accounting & Audit Practice	£22.95 [UK]	£10.95 [UK] [IAS]	£5.95	£10.95	£85	£89
10 Accounting & Audit Practice(IAS)	£23.95 [IAS]	£10.95				
11 Tax Planning FA98 - D99	£18.95	£10.95	£5.95	£10.95		
FA99 - J2000	£18.95	£10.95 *	£5.95	£10.95 *	£85	£89
Module F						
12 Management & Strategy	£18.95	£10.95	£5.95	£10.95	£85	£89
13 Financial Rep Environment	£20.95 [IAS]	£10.95 [IAS]	£5.95	£10.95	£85	£89
14 Financial Strategy	£19.95	£10.95	£5.95	£10.95	£85	£89
		*Available Feb 2000		*Available Feb 2000		
P & P + Delivery UK Mainland	£2.00/book	£1.00/book	£1.00/book	£1.00/tape	£5.00/subject	£5.00/subject
NI, ROI & EU Countries	£5.00/book	£3.00/book	£3.00/book	£1.00/tape	£15.00/subject	£15.00/subject
Rest of world standard air service†	£10.00/book	£8.00/book	£8.00/book	£2.00/tape	£25.00/subject	£25.00/subject
Rest of world courier service†	£22.00/book	£20.00/book	Not applicable	Not applicable	£47.00/subject	£47.00/subject

SINGLE ITEM SUPPLEMENT FOR TEXTBOOKS AND REVISION SERIES:

If you only order 1 item, INCREASE postage costs by £2.50 for UK, NI & EU Countries or by £15.00 for Rest of World Services

TOTAL	Sub Total £					
	Post & Packing £					
	Total £					

†*Telephone number essential for this service*   *Payments in Sterling in London* | Order Total £

DELIVERY DETAILS

□ Mr □ Miss □ Mrs □ Ms Other

Initials   Surname

Address

Postcode

Telephone   Deliver to home □

Company name

Address

Postcode

Telephone   Fax

Monthly report to go to employer □   Deliver to work □

PAYMENT

1 I enclose Cheque/PO/Bankers Draft for £_____
   Please make cheques payable to AT Foulks Lynch Ltd.

2 Charge Mastercard/Visa/Switch A/C No:

Valid from: └─┴─┴─┘   Expiry Date: └─┴─┴─┘
Issue No: (Switch only)   └─┴─┘

Signature   Date

DECLARATION

I agree to pay as indicated on this form and understand that
AT Foulks Lynch Terms and Conditions apply (available on
request). I understand that AT Foulks Lynch Ltd are not liable
for non-delivery if the rest of world standard air service is used.

Signature   Date

Please Allow:	UK mainland	- 5-10 w/days	***Notes:***	All delivery times subject to stock availability.
	NI, ROI & EU Countries	- 1-3 weeks		Signature required on receipt (except rest of world
	Rest of world standard air service	- 6 weeks		standard air service). Please give both addresses for
	Rest of world courier service	- 10 w/days		Distance Learning students where possible.